INTRODUCTION

As historian Geoffrey Blainey said of *Hawke: The Prime Minister*, the second volume of Blanche d'Alpuget's biography of the former prime minister, 'I admire the author's skill in painting that most elusive of portraits – a living politician. One doesn't need to agree with every page to relish the book's sweep and vivacity'. In *Bob Hawke: The Complete Biography*, d'Alpuget portrays Bob Hawke's political afterlife with the same flair and insight she displayed in her first two volumes. We now have the complete picture. Hawke had the advantage of an interpretation of his life being entrusted to a superb, award-winning writer. This latest edition is also written from the vantage point of a writer who knew her subject intimately, having shared the bulk of his life after politics as his wife. The result is a benchmark study on a man who has been described variously as Australia's greatest prime minister, greatest peacetime prime minister or greatest Labor prime minister.

The importance of the book still lies in the accounting of the Hawke Government. Much has been written since in biographies of other participants and broader analyses of its impact and significance. In the public outpouring of grief on his death, there was a sense of better politics at a tough time. There was a reflection on a desire to draw lessons from the way Bob Hawke governed, his policies and his principles. Among a younger generation with no personal memories of the time there was a sense we would do something better. That is a sentiment that makes updating this biography for a new generation eminently worthwhile.

The Honourable Kim Beazley
Governor of Western Australia
August 2019

PREFACE

In April 2019, Simon & Schuster contracted me to update *Hawke: The Prime Minister* for the nine years that had elapsed since it was first published, with the idea of one big volume covering his whole life. None of us imagined at the time that Hawke would be dead within three weeks. The short, final *Part III: At Large*, was begun just before he died, while I was his primary carer, and completed in the three months afterwards, as I struggled with an outpouring of grief from around the nation and the world, expressed in thousands of notes, cards, emails, texts, phone calls and speeches from the most humble admirers to the nobility, including an exquisitely sensitive letter from HRH, the Prince of Wales. The public sorrow was a piquant counterpoint to the happiest years of Hawke's adult life – even through the pain and sickness he endured, longing to embrace death; during this time he was able to return, unhindered by ambition, to his foundational value and inspiration: the sovereignty of love.

I have made a number of additions, deletions and corrections to *Hawke: The Prime Minister*, drawing on additional information that came to hand some months before and soon after his death, most especially re-shaping a warped depiction of the relationship between Hawke and Keating. I had been as guilty as other writers in accepting the conventional wisdom of the news media and other commentators, a Rorschach of unrelenting bile. The problem for journalists and others was that they faced the ineffable mysteries of the souls of two men, a topic too difficult to manifest to a mass audience. There was a titanic struggle for the prime ministership, but beneath it, not dead but in hibernation, a profound respect and admiration lived on between them. I've done my best in trying to present this delicate veil of feeling,

BOB
HAWKE

BOB HAWKE

The Complete Biography

BLANCHE D'ALPUGET

SIMON &
SCHUSTER

In traditional Aboriginal communities it is customary not to mention the name of, or reproduce images of, the recently deceased. Care and discretion should therefore be exercised in using this book within Arnhem Land, Central Australia and the Kimberley.

Author notes: In Parts I and II I have left Hawke's actions in the present tense for consistency and ease of reading.

A note on Cambodia/Kampuchea: I have consistently kept to Cambodia to avoid confusion from the name changes that occurred during the scope of the narrative.

First published in Australia in 2019 by
Simon & Schuster (Australia) Pty Limited
Suite 19A, Level 1, Building C, 450 Miller Street, Cammeray, NSW 2062

Part I was first published in Australia as *Robert J. Hawke: A Biography* by Schwartz Publishing Group, Melbourne, in conjunction with Lansdowne Press, 1982; and later as *Hawke: The Early Years* by Melbourne University Press, 2010

Part II is a revised and updated version of *Hawke: The Prime Minister* first published in Australia by Melbourne University Press, 2010

10 9 8 7 6 5 4 3 2 1

A CBS Company
Sydney New York London Toronto New Delhi
Visit our website at www.simonandschuster.com.au

 A catalogue record for this book is available from the National Library of Australia

Jacket design: Lisa White
Jacket and endpaper images: Front, endpapers: Courtesy of the office of the Hon R.J.L. Hawke; Back: Richard Freeman
Internal design and typesetting: Midland Typesetters Australia
Printed in Singapore by COS Printers Pte Ltd

The paper used to produce this book is a natural, recyclable product made from wood grown in sustainable plantation forests. The manufacturing processes conform to the environmental regulations in the country of origin.

To Craig Emerson, honorary son to Bob,
stalwart friend to both of us.

CONTENTS

PART II: The Prime Minister

PART III: At Large

enabled this time by the cooperation of Paul Keating himself, and others who observed them closely. Dr Craig Emerson was a crucial link between these men he loved, and succeeded in bringing together. I hope my small effort will correct a distortion of Australian political history, and uplift the hearts of readers who look for a Rorschach of the possibility of harmony in what has become our deeply troubled world.

Blanche d'Alpuget
Sydney, August 2019

PART I
The Early
Years

ONE

R.J. HAWKE WAS BORN, on the brink of the Great Depression, into a family and background that would seem rightly to have belonged not to the twentieth but to the early nineteenth century. People have come to see him as a worldly man, one who has built an international reputation for courage and who is now striving for the highest position of power in his country. What is forgotten, or has been grasped only fleetingly, is that he was reared in the narrowest of social enclaves: in small town, fundamentalist Christianity. The stresses set up in him by bursting free of that rigid mould, while retaining many of its values, have created an unusually complex personality.

The Hawkes accepted the popular meaning of the name Robert: 'Of shining fame'. His mother, who said she had moments of acute awareness resembling precognition – she would sometimes press her fingers to her temples and say, 'Oh! I've just had a flash!' – chose the name for him before he was born, sure that it would be suitable.

Ellie Hawke already had one son whom she loved passionately and she hoped that the second baby would be a girl. Her craving for a daughter was immoderate. But when she took out the Bible each day, keeping a vow she had made in childhood, she told friends and relations that she was astonished how often it fell open, as if by design, at the early chapters of Isaiah, and how her eye was drawn to the verses foretelling the birth of great sons – the sign of Immanuel and the Prince of Peace: 'For unto us a child is born, unto us a son is given: and the government shall be upon his shoulder ...'

Ellie had spent nearly a decade, since the birth of her first child, Neil, wishing to have another, a daughter. But in that time she had only a miscarriage. At last she consulted a doctor and took his advice to have an operation; by early 1929, soon after the family moved to Bordertown in South Australia, she was pregnant once more. At first she planned to call the new baby Elizabeth. However, when it seemed that the Bible kept leading her to Isaiah, Ellie began to feel that she was being given a sign, and told people, 'I think it's another boy'.

She and her husband, Clem, believed that events are planned by God. When, in the pre-dawn hours of 9 December 1929, in the darkness before a scorching summer day, she again gave birth to a son, they felt that the baby in some indefinable way was different from others, and that he was a destined instrument of the Lord.

Clem Hawke recalled:

> Even the matron in the hospital said, 'There is something special about this baby'. He was very beautiful. But there was something else, perhaps the configuration of his features or the way he moved in his crib. People felt it. When we had him christened a few months later by Dr Keik, my former theological teacher, Keik said, 'This is a *special* child'. Shakespeare summed it up: 'There is a divinity that shapes our ends, rough hew them though we may'. The same thing applies to destiny, I believe. We thought he was destined for a great future, even then.

The baby was christened Robert James Lee. James was the name of his paternal grandfather; Lee was his mother's maiden name.

Edith Emily Lee (as Ellie had been christened) was a woman who was outstanding in her community before she was thirty. Half a century later, when she was dead, there were people in the country towns of South Australia who recalled her as a force that had changed their lives for the better. Mostly they were women who, as girls, had come under the spell of Ellie's mission in life: to educate girls to be independent, forthright and teetotal. She encouraged these qualities in boys, too, but had a special tenderness for her own sex and its oppressions. She was not a feminine woman: by temperament she was impatient, aggressive and dogmatic. Physically she was plain-featured, although her smile was remarkably beautiful – 'She made you feel as if the world had lit up', a student recalled. She was of average height for a woman of those days, and slim, but strongly made: Ellie had splendid health for almost eighty years, and the energy of a racehorse. Those who loved Ellie remembered her with a mingling of affection and awe; beside her, other women appeared timid, enervated and dishonest. She would not tell or tolerate 'even a white lie, for the sake of making social relations easier'. Many found her frankness intolerable, as later others were to find the frankness of her son unacceptable. All her life Ellie lived in a rage of activity, even in childhood exhausting herself, collapsing temporarily, 'then jumping up and saying, "I'm right now!" and rushing off on some new project'. A brother-in-law said, 'Ellie was a woman who lived two years in every one'. She was the daemon, the driving force, in her son's life.

Clem Hawke was its star of navigation.

Many of the puzzling characteristics of Robert Hawke, much of his apparently paradoxical behaviour, can be traced to the fact that, in time, he rejected much of his early training, and to another fact – that from birth he was subjected to two strong, contrary forces: physically and temperamentally his parents were, in important aspects, opposites.

Clem was tall and slight, strikingly handsome, whimsical, diplomatic and flirtatious. His daughter-in-law recalled, 'Clem could make you feel as if you were the most interesting person he'd ever met in his life'.

He and Ellie were Celts, both with grandparents born in Cornwall who had immigrated to the copper fields of South Australia in the middle of the nineteenth century. Both had been reared as Methodists, both came from an age when worldly ambition and spiritual virtue existed in harmony and both, in their own ways, were agitators. They wanted to change the world by exhortation. Beyond that their social similarities went no further.

Clem left school at twelve and had worked on a milk run, then had been apprenticed to a blacksmith. His family was poor; his father, a Kapunda copper miner, was 'Labor from his toenails to his hair roots'.

Ellie had completed high school and teachers' college. Her family was prosperous and politically conservative. Her father, Will, who had begun life in poverty, became a wheat and barley farmer on the Yorke Peninsula and, in middle age, was able to afford the luxury of a trip 'home' to his ancestral village in Cornwall. He arrived there dressed in top hat and tails.

Methodist rectitude in the Lee household ruled the smallest details of daily life: Ellie, who could not tolerate idleness, was raised in the belief that it was wicked to knit on the Sabbath, for example. In her social milieu there were those who regarded playing-cards as toys of the Devil, and who would go without sauce for their Sunday lunch rather than break the Sabbath ruling against work, by drawing the cork from a sauce bottle.

In Will Lee's youth the fires of Methodist revivalism had swept the South Australian copper fields, arousing ancient passions:

> Unless one lived with [the miners] in those revival days it would be impossible to appreciate such scenes as occurred. Those were the days when preachers spoke of Hell with an absolute belief in it as the abode of damned souls. It can be imagined what an effect the denunciation of sinfulness would produce on the uneducated 'man with a past'. Swearers, blasphemers, drunkards, men with loud voices and boisterous in their excesses were caught up in the tide of revivals ... One evening [a preacher] became so overwhelmed with holy rage at those who had crucified Christ that he unconsciously turned and spat over in the western corner of the church.[1]

In Will's adulthood those fires still smouldered beneath his roof and in his talks as a lay preacher there was an echo of that old, sulphurous fury with the unrighteous.

James Hawke, in contrast, was an unemotional Methodist; the social properness, which was a strong characteristic of the Lee household and which never left Ellie, was less noticeable among the Hawkes. They were churchgoers, but nothing could quench the reckless gaiety and playfulness of the tribe of seven Hawke children. 'We Hawkes had a streak of devilry', one said. Others remember, 'You could not be in the door five minutes before Millie [one of Clem's sisters] would say, "Right! Now for a game of cards!"'

The Lee family had the Victorian passion for public duty, for helping others who, being less determined, less strong, less faithful to the Lord's commandments than they, had met misfortune. Will, a man of quick and fiery temper, had been 'a bigoted Methodist and a bigoted Tory', but he was also 'the most generous man in the world'. He had literally given itinerant men, whom he housed and fed when they called at his farm, the shirt from his back. Having retired comfortably from the land, Will Lee ended his days working in a cement factory and giving his wages to the needy. He dropped dead while helping a farmer plant a crop. Energetic determination was the mark of the Lees.

Optimism was the mark of the Hawkes: it flowed into them from the gospels and from the Labor movement. Of the five Hawke boys, two became ministers of religion, four attempted political careers, and one became premier of Western Australia. An uncle, Dick Hawke, was a Labor candidate in Kapunda 'but couldn't win against the farmers'. A Hawke cousin elsewhere in South Australia became a Country Party member of parliament. They had quick wits, the Celtic flair for oratory, and were born agitators, wanting to sculpt, from the public emotion they could arouse, the public will to reform society. 'The Hawkes had to use their voices – in politics or from the pulpit', Clem said. 'They had to spread the good news.'

Clem and Ellie both believed that the purpose of existence was a life of unity with God resulting in practical good works. Ellie, who like her father was a lay preacher, had struggled against convention for the right to have an education and a career as a teacher, so that she might educate others. Clem had been weighted down by poverty, unable to plot a course, and by eighteen had held half-a-dozen ill-paid, unskilled jobs. He was secretary of the Kapunda branch of the Australian Labor Party and began to dream of a career in Labor politics. He wrote to the premier of South Australia about the possibility of an urban seat if he moved to Adelaide, but before he had decided to act on the premier's advice (to contact the Trades Hall), Clem was drawn in a different direction.

By now he was working on a paper run and was always keen to arrive at the house of Kapunda's Baptist minister, the Reverend Mr John Murray, who had two pretty daughters. Clem spent a good deal of time chatting to them. At length, Mr Murray invited him inside for conversations of a more serious nature. Soon afterwards, on a wintry night, Clem was totally immersed in the cold font of Mr Murray's church to emerge a Baptist, ready to become a home missionary.

Two years later, by the time he met the schoolteacher Edith Emily Lee (and renamed her Ellie), Clem had left the Baptist church and returned to Methodism. He was now a Methodist home missionary, stationed at Forster on the River Murray in South Australia.

Ellie was in charge of her third school, at Forster. Her sisters had accepted the lot of farmers' daughters: they had left school at thirteen and stayed home to help their mother, but Edith Emily had been 'education mad' from early childhood.

Within days of meeting Clem Hawke, Ellie was much attracted to the charming young preacher, five months her junior, uneducated, unordained and with political views that for her were radical and for her father verged on treachery: the Hawkes were anti-conscriptionist.

For his part Clem was fascinated – as others were to be either fascinated or angered – by Ellie's strength of character, her forthright manner, her physical vitality and her sense of purpose.

Hawke said of his parents, 'Mum just loved Dad. He was the boss, but there beside him was this incredibly strong woman. And she would tend to take over. As a minister's wife Mum was unbelievably supportive – it was like having two ministers for the parish.'

In June 1920, a year after they met, Clem and Ellie were married, in Thebarton Methodist Church, Adelaide. In the meantime Clem, who was only twenty-two, had changed churches once more – this time, permanently. He had joined Congregationalism, the church that, as a radical puritan sect, had inspired Cromwell, the Pilgrim Fathers, Milton and Bunyan. It was committed to social equality (including the ordination of women) and the authority of the laity over the clergy. Of all Christian churches, it seemed to Clem, the Congregational was the most liberal, least dogmatic, least concerned with wickedness, most optimistic and the closest in its functioning to Labor's vision of the Brotherhood of Man.

In time, Clem converted Ellie to Congregationalism, but the old fire-and-brimstone pungency of outback South Australian Methodism, with its emphasis on sin and backsliding and its history of grim decorousness shot through with flares of revivalism, seems never completely to have left her. Ellie retained her Methodist indignation against the unrighteous, the slothful, the dishonest, the weak. Hawke was to learn from his mother that 'it would be sinful – she didn't use the word, but she conveyed the idea – sinful if I did not use my talents'. Clem took a gentler view of the world.

A few weeks after marriage Ellie became pregnant and her teaching career had to be abandoned. Her first child was born at Houghton in the Adelaide Hills where Clem, still unordained, had been invited by the congregation to become their minister. Ellie named the baby John (after her favourite brother) and Neil, a name whose popular meaning, accepted by the Hawkes, is 'champion'. He was known by his second name. From the beginning Ellie doted on him. Hawke said later, 'Neil was *her* son, her first-born, her favourite. He'd had nine years to be her son, before I came along.'

The family moved to New Zealand for a couple of years (where Clem was ordained) then back to South Australia, to Renmark. Here Ellie returned to teaching. 'Education is the key to the world', she told her pupils. 'Read, read, read. Learn, learn, learn. God gave you a brain – you're meant to use it. If you haven't got a book to read, get a dictionary and learn a page of it each day.' Although she was impatient with adults, she was patient and loving with children and, longing for a daughter of her own, she lavished affection upon parish girls, whom she treated as favourite nieces, and upon favourite nieces, whom she treated as daughters. Around 1926 she asked a sister to give her one of her daughters to rear. The sister refused.

When Ellie became pregnant again in 1929 she knew, from medical advice, that the second baby would be her last. Half a century later Hawke recalled, uneasily, 'My mother wanted me to be a girl. She used to say, "You were meant to be Elizabeth". That used to annoy me. I thought she was silly to say it, because I was me! Bob.'

From his early years his relationship with his mother was complex, even problematic, affected by his awareness that he had disappointed her in one area that he was incapable of changing – his sex – and also by the knowledge that, almost in recompense for his unwelcome gender, she had great expectations of him. In young adulthood he 'often shouted at Ellie', a relation said. The test of wills between them had a primal history and was perhaps the seed, developed later by Hawke's physical weakness and illnesses, of his striving to become powerful.

It took him half a century to make a sort of peace between the warring states within him, a confrontation that arose from his biological maleness on one side, and on the other, the phantom Elizabeth against whom he, Bob, had to fight from the beginnings of life. A defiant masculinity was a central aspect of Hawke's personality: its battles for ascendancy were to be played out through displays of swashbuckling virility – in language, sporting prowess, aggressive competitiveness, and through many invasions into enemy territory: in common speech, through womanising.

Ellie, for her part, quickly adjusted, at least superficially, to the disappointment of another son: to her it was God's will and she bowed to it. The boy, she decided, would be reared to social duty of a high order and his efforts would be recognised and honoured. When Hawke was in his early twenties she told his fiancée, 'We called him Robert because it would sound good later, when he became Sir Robert'.

Hawke was made a Companion of the Order of Australia, an honour superior to knighthood, in January 1979.

TWO

HEAVEN LAY AROUND Hawke in his infancy. He was reared in a country manse in a quiet way of life deeply rooted in tradition, the seasons accentuated by church festivals, the year divided according to divine significance. It was a world rounded and harmonious.

The community in Bordertown was still snug, not yet touched by the financial crash of the previous April. The Tatiara district, of which Bordertown is the centre, is one of the richest agricultural areas in Australia. In the late 1920s the town was booming: people there only read about the disasters in the cities. Scullin, who had been prime minister for two months, had, in the second week of December, just offered the state premiers £1 million for road work to provide employment. In the New South Wales coalfields the nation's greatest industrial dispute in the twentieth century, a lockout by employers, was dragging on and the miners and their dependants were half-starved. Police occupied the towns of the Hunter coalfields, scab labour was employed, a miner was shot dead, others were injured. But in Bordertown the only signs of depression were the scores of travel-soiled men jumping from trains then hanging around the railway yards, alert for a beckoning finger from one of the farmers loading his produce on the trains. 'It was a good year for hay, 1929. You could get any amount of labour', an old-timer remarked sardonically.

The Congregational parish was the largest in the district, exceeding the Methodists; Clem and Ellie were among the town's elite. Ellie was considered a snob by some parishioners, 'because she was educated – heddykated we used to say – and was a schoolteacher. It was something to be a schoolteacher in those days. I felt she looked down on people who weren't heddykated.' The 'Congs', as they called themselves, were in a mood as expansive as their district's in the late 1920s. When the horse selected for Clem's use on pastoral calls proved troublesome the laity decided, boldly, to buy him a motor car. It was a 1927 four-door, cloth-top Chevrolet and cost £150. With wheat selling at only a little less than its 1925 price and sheep still doing well, the parish could afford it. It could afford, too, to keep the minister's table supplied with mutton, butter and milk and his hearth with firewood. Ellie grew the best vegetables in town – 'lettuces, even in winter!' people remembered, fifty years later.

The manse was a four-roomed house of local limestone with high ceilings and a lean-to at the back for the kitchen, laundry and bathroom. A croquet green was across the road and a couple of minutes walk away was the church, also of limestone. Although it was built in the late nineteenth century it had the friendly, candid symmetry of Georgian architecture. It has been internally renovated in recent years but in those days its most striking feature was an arch painted on the wall at the head of the nave, lettered in blue, gold and black, with the motto 'He Who Watches Over Israel Slumbers Not Nor Sleeps'. Israel – sung about, spoken of, yearned for – glowed as a portentous presence at the heart of spiritual life. Israel was a distant, shining land, enigmatic and ageless, a link between the living and the dead, the present and the past, God and man. 'I vividly recall', a woman wrote to Hawke years later,

> watching your mother basking in pride when a piece of the Holy Land was named after her son for his great humanitarian efforts ... she had tears in her eyes listening to the sermon and speech given by your father on that glorious day in Israel ... one of the happiest that you could have provided for them in their lives.

Israel had entered Hawke's life before he could speak, for Ellie took him to church from birth.

It was in church that parishioners first noticed how he was being reared. 'The trouble was', a Bordertown man complained,

> his mother wouldn't smack him. He'd be up there in the front, wriggling and throwing things on the floor, or yelling. He was completely undisciplined. It wasn't fair to Clem, trying to give the sermon, when there was a baby disrupting things. I used to want to knock his block off.

In the twenty-five years Hawke lived with his parents he was never once struck by either of them. 'I was', he said, 'dreadfully spoiled'. The spoiling came from both parents, especially from Hawke's father.

Clem adored his second son. He said,

> From early on I felt special affinity, a drawing towards Bobbie. It's a mysterious thing – Ellie had it with Neil. It's something that just happens sometimes in families – you remember Joseph and the coat of many colours? His father felt it. You can't say it's right or wrong to have a favourite child … Bobbie had an outflowing magic about him.

He bathed and dressed this baby, things he had not done for Neil, and Hawke's earliest memories were all of 'love – an overwhelming love. I can't describe how passionately my father loved me; I was just Dad's boy.'

The relationship between father and son, which was so intense that Ellie worried about their dependence upon each other, equipped Hawke for life with the capacity to feel and, without embarrassment, to express love for his own sex. It also seems to have cast the emotional die that patterned his later relationships with other men: Hawke is intensely loyal and uncritical of his friends and in return evokes from them an unusual fondness, a paternal indulgence. All his closest men friends have been older than Hawke, either in years or in worldliness; all have had Clem's desire to give of themselves to him. Men have lent him their houses to entertain in, their motor cars to ride in, their yachts to holiday on; they have come to his kitchen to cook his meals; to sit at his bedside and amuse him when he was ill; they have taken him shopping and chosen his clothes. George Rockey, a co-builder of Australia's largest transport company, TNT, was a type of father to Hawke in the late 1970s. When Rockey was dying in 1981 and too weak to walk much, he worried about Hawke's health and his wardrobe: 'I send Bob to my tailor now, so his suits are good. But I'm not satisfied about his socks – I must take him to the proper place for underwear', he said. Sir Peter Abeles, Rockey's senior business partner, is another very close friend. A journalist recalled going to dinner one evening with Hawke and Abeles:

> Sir Peter gave Bob the keys to his Rolls Royce. Bob drove it, laughing his head off, like a kid with a fantastic toy ... I was in business by myself at the time, and in financial difficulties. A couple of days later I got a phone call from Abeles, whom I barely knew. He chatted for a while, then said, 'I think I could help you, if you would like'. I was staggered – he was offering me 25 grand at 5 per cent. Finally I asked, 'Why are you doing this?' He replied, 'Oh well, we both have a very close friend', and the penny dropped. He knew Bob and I had been mates for thirty years, so that made me somebody he would help, because of his affection for Bob.[1]

Throughout Hawke's life men have been drawn by 'the out-flowing magic' that Clem felt – and encouraged – and have responded to it by behaving like fathers or doting uncles. (Hawke called Rockey 'Uncle George', and Rockey signed himself by this name on letters to Hawke.)

It seems as if, in his earliest years, an emotional stage was set and roles allotted to actors, and that the play was performed again and again. While this welded psychological bonds of great

strength between Hawke and his friends, the son–parent config-
uration of relationships became, with Hawke's increasing age,
inappropriate – even undesirable – for it was holding part of his
personality in limbo. Men and women only a few years older
than Hawke called him 'The Boy' when he was in his late forties;
he was treated, by intimates, as a boy who needed adult care and
guidance. The role began to exasperate Hawke, and his friends.

Clem's special son, however, was also Ellie's special baby,
a gift to her from God. But the intensity of affection between
father and son tended to challenge her status with the child,
and later events in the family were to cause whatever incipient
competition there may have been between the parents to develop
into rivalry for the boy. A relation recalled, 'Bob could play his
family off against each other: he was the centre of attention and
the adults competed for him'. This was, perhaps, the origin of
Hawke's later extraordinary success in getting publicity: he had
learned, when very young, how agreeable it was to be a cyno-
sure, and in adulthood had an inner need to re-create – before a
bank of television cameras, or a roaring crowd – the emotional
landscape of earlier years. 'Publicity is one of the things that
keeps you going in politics', another politician remarked. 'The
days when Bob's been all over the newspapers and the television
I've seen him smiling. And sad, when he wasn't.'

Given the circumstances of his birth perhaps it was to be
expected that his parents would rear him more tenderly than his
elder brother. Certainly the difference in parental treatment of
the Hawke boys was profound: Neil had few of the indulgences
allowed to Bobbie. Before he was a teenager Neil was punished
for misdemeanours 'with a hiding from me once a fortnight –
and that's when he was good', Ellie said; sometimes Clem gave
him the strap. In his teenage years, in school holidays, Neil
worked as a farmhand. Hawke took his first holiday job when he
was at university.

Bordertown parishioners remembered Neil as a quiet,
well-mannered boy yet Clem and Ellie both fondly described
him as a young firebrand, physically reckless and deaf to caution,

while Hawke, they said, was a quiet, angelic child with whom they could reason. Perhaps both accounts are accurate, from different perspectives. But as Hawke grew older he developed some of the characteristics that his parents attributed to their elder son. Most people want their children to live for them the lives they cannot: it may be that at an unspoken level the Hawkes encouraged their sons to break free of the extreme decorousness of genteel, petit bourgeois parish life, while insisting that they maintain the essence of Christian values.

Clem took Bobbie on rounds of the parish and by the time the child was three he had begun to model himself actively on his father: a bleary box Brownie photograph of 1933 shows Hawke, hands raised, preaching to an old woman lying on a cane chaise longue in her garden. She was too ill to attend church; Hawke had announced, 'I'm going to cheer you up, like my Dad'.

Clem said,

> We taught him the whole time, not only by talking to him, but also by the practical life we lived … In the Congregational church we had no creeds as such – the only creed I'll accept is the Apostles – but we built religion around the human side of Christ's ministry. And, of course, the divine side. We built it around His example – giving counsel to the dejected and the despairing, healing the sick, putting out a social program for the betterment of the world. What's the use of preaching the gospel to a man with an empty stomach! It's all pie in the sky, when what he wants is pie now.

The crash came to Bordertown in 1931: wheat dropped to 2 shillings 7 pence a bushel (36.4 litres) and oats to 1 shilling 3 pence. A dozen eggs sold for three pennies. Hawke was too young to remember the boom years and knew only the period of struggle and misery for farmers. Childhood memories of his parents' friends talking about low prices, bad seasons and bankruptcies affected him strongly, instilling in him attitudes to rural life that were much more sympathetic than is normal among urban Labor movement officials. Country people noticed the difference: in 1979, in a national survey, farmers and cattlemen voted Hawke their first choice of leaders.

With the Depression, Clem and Ellie had to work much harder. On Sundays there was a special collection known as the Distress Fund. Ellie made meals from what she had to hand in the kitchen for the swagmen who came to her door, and would offer the manse's spare room to people in need of lodging for a night, or for weeks. The ethic of hospitality transmitted to Hawke: his own household, friends commented later, resembled a motel, with all sorts of people making themselves at home there. 'Bob's the easiest touch in the world', a man said of Hawke in middle age. 'I've seen real rogues, people you wouldn't look at, nudge him for a loan. He's gullible, like that.' It was a family characteristic: Clem and Ellie once lent most of their savings to a woman in distress, never to see the money again. Hawke recalled, 'I used to be angry with my mother sometimes, watching her give money to characters whom even I knew were telling lies'.

Clem was considered an outstanding minister because of his pastoral work: while other churches' congregations diminished in Bordertown during the Depression, the numbers in the Congregational parish grew. 'He had the gift of listening', a parishioner recalled. 'He would never reject anyone. One day he ate seven afternoon teas, rather than discourage people from telling him their troubles by turning down their food.' During these years when Hawke was his father's shadow, visiting with him the houses of the dejected, despairing and sick, he was absorbing attitudes that were to stay with him long after he had rejected the Congregational as his church and Christianity as his faith: he was learning to dream of a future career in which he would be able to benefit humanity directly and practically. He was also acquiring his father's habits – especially sympathetic listening, one of the most useful skills for a politician and a negotiator. Chris Crellin, Hawke's chauffeur–bodyguard during his latter years at the ACTU, recalled,

I used to watch Bob at social functions. The way he could listen to people was brilliant: he'd cock his head on one side, like he does, and would stand there letting them bash his ear for half an hour. Whether he was really listening or not, I don't know. But he always looked as if he were following every word they said. Getting him to leave a place was impossible. He'd say 'Goodbye' and two hours later would be only ten feet [3 m] closer to the door, listening to some story about a kid needing a job or somebody's aunty from India wanting a visa for Australia. When he'd finally get in the car he'd have a pocketful of bits of paper with people's names on them, people he was going to try to help. It was a never-ending thing. People would eat him up.

Hawke puts high value on what may be termed his pastoral skill. To a question about which of the thousands of newspaper articles about him he liked most, he replied, 'There was one in the mid-1960s, by Richard Hall. He said I was "a good listener". I was proud about that.'

While Clem's long suit was fellow-feeling, Ellie's was action. In Bordertown she was inaugural secretary–treasurer of the primary school welfare club; she gave lessons in handicrafts and divinity; she was an office bearer of the Girl Guides; she trained the children's choir; she worked for the Women's Christian Temperance Union. She was often in conflict with the parents of girls she was teaching because, with the crash, farmers were taking their daughters out of school and putting them to work as farmhands or housekeepers.

Before Ellie was married she had angered her sisters by resisting farm housekeeping; married, she maintained the view that housework should be shared by husband and wife, and so it was: Clem did half the chores. Ellie rescued several girls from manual drudgery by having them live in the manse. Parishioners had a respectful caution for what was known around town as 'the sharp edge of Mrs Hawke's tongue'.

There was never enough occupation for Ellie and in

Bordertown she took up croquet, becoming an office bearer of the club. She had been a keen tennis player but found croquet more mentally stimulating – 'tennis lacks skill', she declared – and in later life croquet became 'Ellie's second religion'. Hawke said, 'Croquet! The politics and rules of croquet that we used to get at home were enough to drive you bloody mad. It seemed to be the most important thing in the world.' He too plays croquet with enthusiasm; he once chased Margaret Whitlam across the green at the Lodge, waving his mallet at her when she beat him on a shot and whooping, 'I've got to win! You know I've got to win!' As a university friend remarked vividly, if not quite accurately, 'Bob was his mother – inside out'.

At the beginning of 1933 the family made an important decision. Neil, who was eleven, was sent to boarding school. Ellie was determined that he should have the best possible opportunities so he was enrolled at King's College, a Baptist and Congregational school in Adelaide. Neil's departure from home turned Hawke, in effect, into an only child. His 'spoiling' increased.

In 1935 Clem was called to his next post in the Yorke Peninsula town of Maitland. The congregation there knew nothing about their new minister and his wife, with the exception of a detail that had drifted across hundreds of miles of pasture, bush and desert: 'The Hawkes have a terrible kid'.

Hawke was not yet five. Already a motif in his life was emerging: people saw him as untamed, a disruptive element, an outsider who would have to prove himself before he would be accepted.

THREE

HAWKE WAS A HIGHLY strung child. Before the upheaval of moving to Maitland he had been robust but in the new environment, with a humid climate, he stopped growing at a normal rate and was often ill with respiratory tract infections.

He was sent to school in Maitland, where he was known as Little Bobbie, and was regularly bashed up – according to fellow pupils – because he started most of the fights himself. It seems he disliked school at first. 'I'd see him going off in the morning with his satchel on his back, bawling his head off all the way down the street', a townswoman said. His friends, after a time, were boys several years his senior, who acted as elder brothers, and his closest friend was one who was considered socially inappropriate for the minister's son. This was Reo Allen, one of the nine red-blooded offspring of the local truck-driver. The Allen boys were handy with their fists. Reo, who later worked in a factory in Adelaide, said, 'I was a kind of protector for Little Bobbie – anybody who punched him had to fight me. He was a real small kid, but a brainy bugger – if you'll excuse the expression.' Teasing girls, including a young woman teacher at whom they would shout insults in the street, was a favourite pastime.

Hawke was consistently top or next to top of his class, his rival being the headmaster's daughter. 'The fact was', he said, 'I had a head-start, because my parents read to me'.

What they read was significant. For both Clem and Ellie the Bible was the foundation of education. While Hawke was still too young to be introduced to the complex beauty of the King James translation, he was raised on a bowdlerised work, Hurlbut's *Story of the Bible*: 'The Complete Bible Story, running from Genesis to Revelations, Told in the Simple Language of To-day for Young and Old, Profusely Illustrated with Colour Plates and Half-tone Engravings'. In the charmed circle of family love, Clem, reading to Hawke at bedtime, introduced to his son's mind images of heroes that were to stay with him for life.

Hurlbut's is a handsome volume. The colourful frontispiece shows David, small and barefoot, barely more than a child, alone, facing a huge bearded man who has the advantage of standing on higher ground. Goliath is magnificently armoured in brass shining like gold: breast-plate, helmet, leggings. Behind him on a hill, registering amused disdain for David, lounge the bejew-elled princes of the Philistines. The caption reads, 'David's plan to fight the giant did not need any armour, but did need a quick eye, a clear head, a sure aim and a bold heart'. David was one of the many saviours who entered Hawke's imagination in childhood. Years later, describing his career as an industrial advocate, he said,

> I'd look up at the other end of the Bar table, crowded with silks and their juniors, able to buy the best economic advice in the country – they were *black* with money for research – and there I'd be, just me, and I used to think, 'Jesus Christ, it's David against Goliath!'

But the favourite character of Hawke's childhood was Samson, whose story is told in Hurlbut's as 'The Strong Man: How He Lived and How He Died', accompanied by black-and-white engravings of the young Samson slaying a lion; Samson beguiled by Delilah; Samson, aged and terrible, destroying the Philistines and himself in the temple of their fish-god, Dagon. Hawke knew the Samson story word for word and shared with him one circumstance: both were Nazarites. Like Samson, Hawke had been pledged by his mother to God as one who would never drink alcohol. In Bordertown Ellie had adopted as her consuming interest the work of the Women's Christian

Temperance Union (WCTU) and had enrolled Hawke in its children's branch, the Band of Hope.

The WCTU is a women's movement with a proud history. It was the cause around which nineteenth-century feminists gathered in the USA, the UK and the British colonies. Suffragettes wanted the vote so as to be able to bring in prohibition, for alcohol then, as now, was the single greatest catalyst for wife murder and assault, child bashing and other domestic brutality. The WCTU's motto is 'Agitate, Educate, Legislate' – a motto Hawke was to apply himself throughout his career.

Ellie had shouldered the cause of abstinence with indignation. A parishioner recalled that one afternoon he was taking tea in the manse when she gave him a lecture about the dangers of cigarettes (also disapproved of by the WCTU). After some time Clem, who was listening attentively, unbuttoned his jacket and discreetly held it open for the parishioner to see, in an inside pocket, a packet of Capstans. Clem gave the faintest smile, rebuttoned his jacket and returned his attention to Ellie's remarks. Twenty years later members of the Lee family at Christmas lunch found that Ellie had placed beneath each festive bonbon a WCTU pamphlet about the dire effects of drink.

She was an effective lay preacher – 'Ellie would always pluck at your heartstrings', a relation said – but whatever success she had in reforming outsiders, the response from those closest to her was rebelliousness. A niece upon whom she doted (the one she had wanted to adopt) put brandy in the Christmas trifle. A woman who lodged with the Hawkes and who, as a Methodist, disapproved of smoking herself, once smoked a cigarette in Ellie's presence, to defy her. Hawke became a heavy drinker.

In Maitland, parishioners who had heard that Hawke was 'a terrible kid' did not alter their opinion so much as expand it. He was terrible, but he was also lovable. Mothers, in particular, found him endearing – very friendly, full of wit, fun and daring. On Saturday night he would go off to the pictures by himself, while Ellie fretted, 'What's the use? I can't stop him.'

An honorary member of the household in Maitland, Gwen Geater, said:

> Bobbie was one of those kids that you had to make up your mind with, or he'd dominate you. I put him over my knee more times than I can count. It was the only way ... Clem had taught him to play cricket and on Sundays, when Clem was busy, if you wouldn't play cricket with Bobbie there was no peace. He'd drive you mad until you gave in. But he was so lovable – full of fun, and affectionate. I loved my Robert.

Miss Geater was fourteen years Ellie's junior, her closest friend and co-worker in the WCTU. She was a woman of feminine, dark-eyed good looks and was the dearest of Ellie's 'daughters'. Clem's predecessor in Maitland had been a bachelor; the manse was rundown and the church activities that fall to a minister's wife had not been performed. Ellie set out to revolutionise the parish – in short order she had organised the women into building a civic garden to celebrate South Australia's sesquicentenary, for example – but this extra work left her with less time than usual for running her household. Within a couple of weeks of arriving in Maitland she had said to Miss Geater's mother, 'You've got three daughters and I've got none. Give me one of yours', and Gwen had been given over to Ellie as a helpmate.

While many female parishioners, like Miss Geater, recalled Hawke with affection and often looked after him – Ellie worked a healthy 60- to 80-hour week – his mother was the single important female presence he remembered. He had no grandmother or aunt whom he saw often and doted upon; he could not recall a woman teacher influencing him.

Ellie filled the manse with women and girls; she was forever busy with them on parish or civic activities: women, it seems, entered Hawke's life as rivals for his mother's attention, probably compounding whatever hostility he already felt towards females, on account of 'Elizabeth'. For many years during adulthood there was a certain undertow of ruthlessness in Hawke's treatment of women, in marked contrast to his tolerance and affection for men.

His attachment to his father was still intense. Once, when Clem was called from Maitland to Melbourne to discuss the possibility of becoming a minister there, Hawke announced, 'I can't live without him. Send a telegram for him to come home. I'm going to die.' When Clem was not around and Hawke's contact with the world – even, as he experienced it, with life itself – was broken, the child retreated into nervous, almost hysterical demands and isolation. 'As a child I had few friends', he said. 'Dad was enough for me. I didn't want anyone else.'

Already one of the paradoxes of Hawke's life was beginning to reveal itself: he had an acute need to belong (to his parents, especially Clem) and an equally strong desire to avoid control (by Ellie and others). The shape of his later political career was beginning to show its outline: the man of the Left who refused to observe the Left's ideology, the labour leader who rejected the authority of the Labor leader. Speaking of his childhood friendships, Hawke observed: 'I was a loner. I wasn't interested in anyone else. I didn't depend on anyone else – I had no need for anyone else. I had my own views about life, I knew what was in my head.' Hawke's identity as a nonconformist was coming to life.

Meanwhile – perhaps because of the telegram episode – Ellie had begun to caution Clem about the pitch of emotion between him and Bobbie. Hawke recalled, 'My mother said Dad and I loved each other too much, in the sense that I expected too much of him, and he of me'.

When the family had moved to Maitland in 1935 it had been into a large manse set in a wilderness. Ellie was famous for her gardening and, without reticulated water, she transformed what Hawke called 'that desert of a manse' into an oasis of flowering shrubs, fruit trees and vegetables. There was a tennis court attached to the grounds, adding to the sense of spaciousness Ellie had created. They might have stayed in that town or others in South Australia for years, with Hawke in due course being sent to boarding school in Adelaide. But the summer of 1938–39 shattered the Hawkes' beneficent small world of weekdays spent in good works and Sundays in praise of God and the Holy Land.

That summer was a terrible one for the whole nation. There was the longest heatwave in living memory and bushfires consumed the countryside from Queensland to Tasmania. From Europe there rumbled rumours of war.

Seventy people died during the fires in Victoria; as well, babies died from dehydration and old people from heat prostration. The Adelaide Hills exploded in flames on Black Friday in January; factories had to close; the city ran out of soft drinks and ice, and food was scarce.

Neil Hawke – who had been dux of King's College and had recently landed a job in the state Treasury (at a time when unemployment for young people was running at 20 per cent) was one of those who tried to cool off at an Adelaide novelty, the indoor Unley Crystal Pool. He, like Hawke, loved swimming; he was a fine, manly lad, used to fending for himself and was already living up to the 'champion' of his name. Neil was swimming in competitions and had won prizes in bicycle racing.

The heatwave continued into February. On the 18th Ellie's mother, Matilda, died, aged seventy-seven. At her funeral in Adelaide Ellie and Clem noticed that Neil was pale and quiet. Two days after they had returned to Maitland a telephone call from Neil's landlady told Clem and Ellie that he had been taken to hospital with fever, headache and convulsions. Clem returned immediately to Adelaide. From there he rang Ellie to tell her to come urgently: Neil had meningitis. He had almost certainly contracted it from the Unley pool.

The progress of meningitis is horrific to witness. Headache and convulsions are followed by loss of normal motor functions, destruction of personality, and distortion of the face as purulent liquid from the meninges overflows the cranium and forces its way into the tissues of the face. The body wastes to bone as the head enlarges.

For forty-eight hours Clem and Ellie prayed by Neil's bedside. Next morning the drought broke in South Australia with one of the heaviest rains in living memory; it was also the coldest February day in Adelaide for more than thirty years. In the early hours of the following day hospital staff telephoned the Hawkes to come quickly. They set out into the cold, wet night, but by the time they arrived Neil had died.

FOUR

THEY WERE OPTIMISTIC people, trusting in God's mercy, and their response to Neil's death was a heroic manifestation of their faith.

Clem planted a wooden cross on the grave in the Mitcham cemetery, Adelaide, and placed a death notice in the *Adelaide Advertiser*:

> HAWKE, on 27 February at a private hospital. John Neil, dearly beloved elder son of Rev. A. C. and Mrs Hawke, Congregational Manse, Maitland ... 'The golden bowl is broken'.

They returned to Maitland. A parishioner said, 'We thought Clem was made of stone. He showed no emotion whatsoever but went on with his work as if nothing had happened.' For Ellie, sadness was 'too deep for tears ... [In sixty years] I don't think I ever saw the wife cry', Clem said.

People were astonished then, and afterwards, by how the Hawke family habitually eschewed any discussion of emotional pain, of anything that might be considered 'morbid'; how they and their surviving son denied the existence of personal distress. Hawke had been trained in contempt for wickedness. As the Hawkes rejected Satan, so they rejected the negative aspects of Neil's death and waited for the Lord to reveal to them why He had gathered in a young soul. Hawke never inquired into the nature of his brother's death, never visited his grave or even discovered where he was buried – although he had loved Neil who,

Clem said, 'hero-worshipped Bobbie and would rush to play ball with him as soon as he came home from school'.

For a man of emotional make-up, as Hawke is, the family taboo against dwelling on anything negative was a contradiction of nature. His later life was remarkable for moments when 'negative' emotions, kept at bay, would abruptly crowd upon him: Hawke would suddenly roar with anger, or begin to weep.

Hawke has no memory of his mother crying when she returned home, but he realised she was devastated:

> Totally devastated. I don't have a vision of wailing – she wasn't behaving irrationally or anything like that – but I just knew that she was deeply hurt, that she'd lost something that was irreplaceable ... I had these two problems in childhood: my mother wanted me to be a girl, and then her son died, and I had, somehow, to replace him.

The paradise of his early childhood had been broken: the life he had known as 'Dad's boy' was finished; his father had changed – Clem urged the child to turn his affections towards his mother, who awaited him with open arms, and acute anxiety. But as Hawke himself recognised, he could not really replace Neil as Ellie's son: he was a sort of impostor.

Relations said, 'When Neil died, Ellie turned all her attention on to Bob. She overindulged him. She was terrified she would lose him, too.' Indeed, within days of Neil's death Hawke became ill with fever and it was feared that he, too, had meningitis. But it was only one of his stress-related viral attacks.

As for Clem, the grief he had suppressed wore him out, and when parishioners noticed that his natural diplomacy had turned to melancholy aloofness they feared that he was on the path of a nervous breakdown. A fellow Congregational minister who visited Maitland in mid-1939 urged Clem to get away, to start a new life, and offered to arrange a transfer to Western Australia. Hawke remembered the move as 'Joy! As if it were yesterday, this enormous, enormous joy of going on a train across the centre of Australia.'

Clem's new church was in West Leederville, a lower-middle-class suburb of Perth, and within a few weeks the family had found a cottage on the rise of Tate Street, Leederville. Their new home had a meagre front garden, a generous back garden, five rooms, a screened-in back verandah, stained glass kookaburras set in glass panels in the front door and a porthole window in the hall. When Hawke became a householder he showed his affection for the landscape of childhood by choosing a house that carried echoes of the Maitland manse and the Tate Street house: it had a tennis court and a porthole window.

There were no fringe benefits in the West Leederville parish – no rent-free manse, no motor car, no firewood or food from the farms of parishioners. Clem's wage was the same as that for an unskilled labourer; suddenly life was frugal. For Hawke it was to become cut off from happiness as well, for in 1941 Clem enlisted in the AIF as a pastor. Within six months Hawke was in a second physical decline. He was still small for his age, with poor chest development and skinny limbs. He suffered repeatedly from attacks of sinusitis.

With Clem away, Ellie took in as boarders the wife of a Methodist minister who had also enlisted, and her son, but there was friction between the two women. The boarder recalled,

> In the evening she'd bring home from the WCTU a lot of pamphlets and over the tea-table she would give the boys lectures on drinking and smoking. I used to think, 'Oh, no. She'll drive them to it!' Ellie was still grieving over Neil – not openly, but there was an atmosphere in the house. She had kept some of his clothes and sometimes I'd see her open the wardrobe and bury her head in them.

To Hawke and others Ellie, who was a pacifist, remarked after the outbreak of war, 'God took Neil to spare him from shedding blood. Neil would have enlisted, if he'd lived.' The boarder felt that, 'She would be looking for Neil for the rest of her life'.

Ellie had flung herself into WCTU work in Perth and at night was often out at meetings or overseeing a hostel for homeless girls. At home, the other woman complained,

> She wouldn't discipline Bob, who used to be quiet for long periods then have outbreaks of deliberate naughtiness. Ellie would say to me, 'Oh, you speak to him'. She was out – it seemed sometimes every night of the week – and I'd have to put him to bed. He'd always want a bit of love at bedtime – he was a devil of a kid, he'd whinge and whinge until he got his own way, but he was very affectionate. The cat would be there in bed with him, hidden under the blankets. He wasn't allowed to sleep with the cat but every night, sure enough, there it would be. When I'd find it he'd roar with laughter.

In this early period in Perth Hawke developed a resentment for the WCTU, 'because I thought it took up too much of Mum's time, almost to my detriment'. He also began to manipulate his parents by throwing tantrums. On the weekends when Clem was due home on leave Hawke would stand at the front gate, staring up Tate Street for the first sight of his father walking down from the trolley bus. He had, he recalled, 'a tremendous tantrum, an unbelievable tantrum on my twelfth birthday, when Dad came home on leave and they wouldn't take me to a pirate movie, but went off to see *Pygmalion*'. Where once there had been 'overwhelming love', anger was now intruding more and more into Hawke's life. A sense of powerlessness had overtaken his existence, exaggerated by ill health.

During these years of severe upheaval for the family Hawke's health became so poor as to seem chronically afflicted. He had won a scholarship to Perth Modern School in 1942, but did not excel there. 'I was sickly in the first year at Mod. In my second year I seemed to be sick all the time.' There was a lot of physical fighting at the school and Hawke, smaller and weaker than other boys, got the worst of it. A fellow pupil remembered him as 'very thin, with a pinched look. He was sharp featured and had a hatchet face for a small boy.' Finally in 1944 Ellie, having exhausted other remedies, took him to a naturopath. The man recommended fasting, then a high-fibre diet with few dairy products, eggs or meat. To this day Hawke has thanked him for

> a total transformation. I became very strong. My body seemed to develop enormously quickly. I took great pride in my physical development – I could mix it with the other kids. I remember the feeling of joy in growing strong, of having a great feeling of confidence that no one physically worried me any more.

One unusual effect was that his hair, which had been straight, became thick and wavy. He had reached puberty, and was enveloped by an ecstatic sense of completeness, as if sexual definition as a male, as Bob, had brought a surge of power. Another pupil, Robin Morison, recalled Hawke after his 'total transformation':

> Bob was one of those often involved in punch-ups. He was very pugnacious. He didn't have a lot of girlfriends – he seemed more interested in sport and being tough than in chasing girls. Also, he did not suffer fools gladly, even then. He would abuse kids for asking silly questions and wasting the class time. He was a real tough-guy.

Hawke recalled,

> Adolescence was a *good* time ... The old masturbation syndrome hit me about the same age as everyone else. I felt guilty about it, I suppose – perhaps more than average guilt. But it didn't detract from the enjoyment. I found it a startlingly interesting new dimension to life. In an embarrassed sort of way Dad pushed a couple of books about sex at me.

I reckoned I knew as much about it as he did – and I was probably right! ... I was seventeen or eighteen before I learned about menstruation, and then it came as a terrible shock. I had a mixed-up, unreal, funny reaction. It convinced me that kids should have proper sex education when they're young.

With adolescence Hawke's yearning for Clem's physical presence abated: he no longer stood at the front gate waiting for his father. He said, 'I was a little boy when he enlisted, and a young man when he was demobbed'.

It was Ellie who had got Hawke into Perth Modern School. She had wanted Hawke, like Neil, to attend a private school,

because that would make a better person of one. There was an element of snobbery in Mum, an elitist thing. A private school was a proposition I resisted very stoutly and Dad was my ally in that, so we won the argument.

When Ellie discovered that Perth Modern School was academically elite, accepting each year only the top primary students in Western Australia, she coached Hawke to win a place there.

She sat down beside me every afternoon and would say, 'Come on. You've got to work and work and win that scholarship.' She taught me to work hard and she planted in me the idea that if I did work, I could do it. I enjoyed the lessons well enough, but I found the keeping-at-it tedious ... I have a hedonistic streak. To get things done I have to determine my priorities, or I spend too much time on things that aren't relevant ... After I won the scholarship, I didn't study. I treated school as a sleigh-ride. I had fun.

Having fun is a serious business for Hawke. His parents were keen bridge players and approached the card table with a gleam of purposefulness in their eyes. Ellie especially always strove to do well whatever she undertook – when she went to a film she would mentally grapple with the plot and characters afterwards – and she played to win. Hawke played bridge, tennis, table tennis and billiards and loved crossword puzzles. Fun took its most sublime form, at school, in cricket. He said,

> Somehow Dad had instilled in me, when I was about four, a love of cricket. When we'd gone on holidays back to his family home at Kapunda he had spent hours tossing me a ball to bat ... God invented cricket.

Hawke strove to excel as a cricketer; whenever Clem could, he would attend his matches. Hawke was a batsman and wicket-keeper, and, when he was chosen for the First XI, he fantasised about becoming a Test cricketer.

> There was a prize of a bat for anyone in the First XI who could make 100 runs in a final-year game. In the five years I'd been at Mod nobody had won the bat. The match came, and I'd made 93 runs and I thought, 'This is it! I'm going to crack the record!' I knew how proud Dad would be if I won it. Then Cyril Calcutt, who taught maths–science, bowled a ball that pitched outside the leg stump, and I went to hook the thing and was given lbw. There was no way in the world I was out! By God, I was so annoyed. I was enormously disappointed. It was, really, one of the biggest disappointments of my schooldays ... One of my only real regrets is that I didn't learn to bat well until I went to Oxford and had coaching. If only I could have learned when I was younger!

Perth Modern School has acquired a high reputation over the years because of its numbers of outstanding pupils, but while the school's intellectual material was first class the education it offered in Hawke's day was, in the opinion of an alumnus, 'limited'. Its atmosphere was authoritarian, its subjects career oriented: it was a showcase for the intellectually competitive.

'Mod was an exam factory', in the view of John Wheeldon, one of its former pupils, later a Labor senator and a minister in the Whitlam government.

> It was good for kids who were willing to knuckle down to the system, who were highly motivated. A lot of kids there were from very poor families. Doing well at Mod was their passport into the middle class. But for boys like Bob and me, who knew we would attend university and enter a profession, it was not an encouraging atmosphere in which to extend our minds.

The ornaments of education – drama, painting, music, literature – were not much regarded at the school. Wheeldon continued: 'We had few extracurricular activities, compared with the better private schools. Passing exams was all that mattered to the headmaster – he even disapproved of our attending ABC Youth Concerts, because in his opinion they were a waste of time.'

Hawke's cultural tastes remained undeveloped at high school; he acquired no interest in the arts, nor did he develop a love of reading for pleasure: reading was for self-improvement. The puritan attitude that fiction was basically a waste of time seems to have affected him. In adulthood Hawke's middle-class friends were often surprised that a man of his intellect and education read so few novels, and that when he did read one it was to pass the time while travelling, and therefore usually some light, racy yarn.

At school Latin became symbolic of high culture for Hawke, and Latinate English became his style – so much so that the satirist Barry Humphries, in a skit in the 1970s, announced that all trade union officials now used the word 'indicate' instead of 'said' because Bob Hawke had taught them to. Hawke said, 'If I were an educational dictator I would make Latin compulsory. It's a great aid to the development of logic.' He was already committed to 'useful' learning. Unsurprisingly, therefore, he did not feel the shortcomings of Mod keenly, as Wheeldon did. But like Wheeldon and many other pupils, he disliked, almost hated, the headmaster. With this man Hawke had his first major crisis with authority, and would have been expelled – for a prank during a chemistry lesson in third year – but for Clem's intervention. Wheeldon recalled,

> The headmaster was a Labor man. In my youth I was a dedicated Liberal, largely because of him. He left me with an abiding dislike of any sort of state control of anything, which I've found, even as a socialist, rather difficult to overcome.

Hawke was a Labor sympathiser at school and did not allow his dislike of the headmaster to influence his politics. He said,

> The best lesson I had from school was the development of scepticism about authority as such. I realised there wasn't such a thing as goodness in authority, that its goodness or badness depended upon the people who wielded it. That became very much part of my conscious belief and is still deeply ingrained in me.

Perth Modern School crystallised in Hawke's mind ideas that had a long history in his behaviour – rejection of control, 'the minister's son showing he was independent'.

Despite Ellie's protests he joined the school cadets but then found himself rejecting the commands of his senior officers and, after three years of training, was still a private. Only three boys, another being Wheeldon, managed to remain privates.

Wheeldon recalled that Hawke

> already had that larrikin streak. Since then I've seen him be abrasive with people, but he has never been with me. I've always had the impression that he is a warm-hearted fellow. As a boy he was already very interested in politics, as I was – the whole school had a high awareness of current affairs. Debating was one of the few extracurricular activities that the headmaster encouraged. Hawke took a leading role in

a debate on some current event, which was held before the
assembled school. He was a good debater, even then ...
I remember us one afternoon, when we were fourteen, talking for at least an hour about the American trade unions.
The Communists had tried to blow up the car of Walter
Reuther of the United Auto Workers, and we talked about
the problems of trade unions – how they had to deal with the
employers *and* the Communists. He was always very interested in events of that type.

The stimulus to Hawke's interest in politics was a change
in family circumstances: a new member had joined the Hawke
circle, with profound effect. Clem's favourite brother, Albert,
who at the age of sixteen had taken over Clem's job as secretary
of the Kapunda ALP, was reunited with him in Perth. Albert, also
known as Bert, was already a minister in the Western Australian
government and was being groomed for the premiership. He
was a professional politician of high calibre, combining skill in
administration with power and wit as an orator. He had a quick
mind and a charmingly suave manner. Ellie, who had been tepid
towards Labor, was converted. Clem, who had been obliged to
keep quiet about his political sympathies in the conservative
towns of South Australia, could now indulge his youthful enthusiasm. A Hawke household was once more Labor 'from toenails
to hair roots'.

Albert, who had no son of his own, came each week to dine
and play bridge with Clem and Ellie who, under Clem's influence, had years ago abandoned the idea that knitting on Sundays
was a sin and that playing cards was another. Albert made Hawke
his favourite nephew and became the boy's political mentor.
It was a piece of sweet fortune for Hawke: first, to have a mentor;
second, to have such a good one. Uncle Albert became a critical
figure in Hawke's development and later success. A schoolboy
friend of Hawke's said, 'His uncle showed Bob that there was a
wider world, that life was not all about God, and he introduced
Bob into that world'.

In 1945 when the prime minister, John Curtin, died Albert was asked to stand for Curtin's seat of Fremantle. His backers were confident that he could, after the departure of Chifley, become the next leader of the ALP. But Albert rejected the opportunity in favour of the certainty of becoming premier of Western Australia and lived afterwards with a lingering regret, shared by Clem and Ellie. In 1979, when Hawke was agonising about entering federal parliament, Uncle Bert took hold of him and said, 'Is another Hawke going to squib it?'

When Bert passed up his chance in 1945 he, Clem and Ellie turned their hopes on the boy. From the time the family had moved to Perth and Ellie had become a Labor enthusiast, she had begun to say she wished that Hawke would have a political career. She enrolled him when he was fourteen in classes for the Art of Speech, a subject not taught in state schools. It was the training ground for orators. The nineteenth-century canon that oratory was *the* political skill still prevailed – if not in the minds of politicians, certainly with large sections of the electorate, and particularly with Ellie Hawke. Her son was already showing the effects of a family background in which both parents were public speakers and where an insistence on fluency, in Clem's case, and accuracy in Ellie's, ruled daily life. (An exasperated niece once snapped at Ellie, 'We don't have to speak grammatically to get into the Kingdom of Heaven, Aunt!') From the time Hawke was twelve Ellie had been saying, only half jokingly, to relations, 'Bob will be prime minister one day – he has the gift of the gab'. Gradually the idea became family lore: Hawke *would be* prime minister. Robin Morison recalled that in his final years of high school,

> Hawke would often tell people he was going to be prime minister. Max Newton, who along with Hawke was the other most flamboyant boy at school, was very irritated by Hawke's saying this, and used to be sarcastic about it. He'd walk into class and say, 'The prime minister is coming' or 'He's just told me *again* that he's going to be prime minister ...'

Hazel Hawke said of the family in the 1940s, 'The idea [that Bob would be prime minister] was always around'.

Clem had been demobbed in 1945. During his four years in the AIF he had been in daily contact with men of a type he had seldom before encountered. They were swearers, blasphemers, womanisers, heavy drinkers, agnostics, atheists. Hawke said, 'The experience had a big effect on Dad. He was a liberated man.' Clem had begun to read psychological works to help him with counselling these wild, tough men; he had begun to drink alcohol with them; he had more liberal attitudes to social behaviour; the benign sophistication that was so noticeable in his later years began to settle upon him. But his occasional glasses of beer were anathema to Ellie and for the first time there were sharp arguments at home. Money was scarce. In the AIF Clem's pay had been better than it ever was in civilian life but now he was out of a job because his West Leederville church had gone to another minister, and it would be a year before a second church, at Subiaco, became available to him. In the meantime he worked in an insurance company. Ellie returned to teaching. Sometimes she upbraided Clem for 'weakness'. As had happened in thousands of other families during the war, she had become accustomed to being the head of the household, and readjustment was difficult.

Hawke looked back on the period from Neil's death to Clem's placement in a second Perth church as one of 'dislocation'. Contemporaries of his, who also had developed from children into young men under the guidance of their mothers, nevertheless found his family environment extraordinary. One said, referring to 1945 when he first met Hawke,

Ellie would talk of nothing but her marvellous son. It was always Bob Hawke, Bob Hawke – and God. And the necessary connection between them. Sometimes you would see a look of embarrassment on Clem's face when Ellie was going on and on about Bob's ability. When he came home from school he had to make an accounting to her of how he had done that day. She drove him. When there were exams there was a great discussion about why he had come sixth or seventh, not first. In Ellie's mind Bob was not God simply because he was not old enough to be God. She instilled in him the Inevitability Syndrome – that inevitably he would be the best. He had no idea that his upbringing was unusual ... For Ellie there was just Bob Hawke – the rest of the world was simply other people around him.

Hawke, however, did not respond to his mother's urgings to shine academically and to begin to fulfil his destiny. He matriculated at the end of 1946 with a good pass but one that, for Perth Modern students, was only average, and enrolled in law at the University of Western Australia. There had never been any doubt at home that he would attend university. Living in Perth made the process easier, for the University of Western Australia was, then, the only free university in the country. Hawke had no special reason for choosing law. It just seemed 'a useful sort of course'. He started at university with a vision of himself as a good–average student and a sportsman.

Six months later something happened that was to transform his life.

FIVE

ELONGING TO ORGANISED community groups was natural for people as highly socialised as the Hawkes. One of the first things Hawke did on entering university was to join the Labor Club. Another was to begin playing first-grade cricket. And a third was to join the Student Christian Movement. He was a deacon of the Subiaco church and was considered an outstanding chairman of meetings – years later his political enemies would acknowledge sourly his effectiveness as a chairman, their expressions brightening as they remarked, 'And that's something he can't do on television'.

At seventeen Hawke was still thin, almost skinny; his limbs were slender and he had small, well-shaped hands that he was in the process of disfiguring through playing cricket. His face was bony but agreeable, with a broad well-formed mouth and wide-set dark blue eyes that were both alert and candid. He had caught, from Ellie, the habit of moving them restlessly, and also had the trick of quizzically raising one eyebrow. His hair, which had been blond in childhood, had turned dark brown and was luxuriantly curly; it and his lustrous olive skin were his most attractive physical features. Then, and later, he lavished attention on both, keeping his hair groomed and his suntan in finest condition. A university friend said, 'One day he came to watch a cricket match, wearing shorts, and sat stroking his leg, looking at it as if he loved it. He was a narcissist.' Hawke said of himself, at the end of school days, 'I was proud of my good, strong body', and has never disguised his vanity about his hair and his skin. In later life he would ask women, 'What do you like best: my brains or my curly hair?' – or would say, 'Look at my beautiful suntan'. For all this, Hawke was not a handsome boy and good looks did not come to him until he was in his forties, when his hair turned into a magnificent grey wolf's ruff and his face was sculpted with experience. In youth his attractiveness to others, male and female, was his personality. With adults he was a friendly, conventionally well-mannered, strait-laced religious lad. He had not tried drinking or smoking, he disapproved of gambling – and continued to do so until he was almost forty – and he tried to uphold the virtues of social duty and reform that he had learned at home. With his peers he was high spirited, quick witted and a flirt. Few girls knew how to deal with his aggressive badinage. Meg Zanetti, a fellow pupil in Art of Speech, recalled, 'He was very cocky. I just couldn't cope with his teasing.'

The terrible kid was now the brash youth. Hawke said of himself as a teenager, 'I was obnoxious in many ways. I was self-confident, and that can come out as brashness.' Hawke did not confine his brashness to girls. Sectarian issues were important on the campus in the late 1940s and, as a Protestant, Hawke was sharp in his criticism of other streams of Christianity. John Toohey, a fellow law student, recalled that he spent much of Law I defending his Roman Catholicism against Hawke's jibes: 'All those stories about nuns and priests, and what happened behind the walls of the convent at the top of Tate Street – Bob brought them all out'.

Student politics were also of great importance at the university. Robert Menzies, six years out of office, was gradually evolving 'the Liberal philosophy', in opposition to the creeping authoritarianism that had come to infect Labor during its years as the wartime government and later as the instrument of post-war reconstruction. The international success of Communism during the 1930s and now, more dramatically, in the 1940s, was influencing politics everywhere, and at the University of Western Australia its strength was heightened by the numbers of ex-servicemen and women on campus. The year 1947 was the peak for ex-service enrolments and these older students brought to the campus a special worldliness and toughness. 'They were the stars, in class and on the playing fields', Toohey said. 'The university was more radical and adult at that time than it was for years later. Student politics were much influenced by events in Eastern Europe.'

When Hawke joined the Labor Club he was

> quickly disillusioned with the club as such. It clearly wasn't an ALP Club, it was more a Communist Club. At the time Russia seemed to embody a lot of good things: a better society, a fairer one, a more egalitarian one. None of us knew the evil that was being perpetrated there. I was never attracted to Communism, although I had much more sympathy towards it then than I have now. In the Labor Club I felt there was a subterfuge, that they were taking positions which were detrimental to the Labor Party. So I was forthright in expressing my views. I didn't have any feelings of reticence, as a freshman, about getting up in debates and being pretty forthright and critical. By the end of that year I'd left the Labor Club and set up the ALP Club, and was its first president[1] ... I had a capacity to get into arguments, and to influence people.

His style, developed through debating at Mod and attendances at state parliamentary debates, was already militantly rationalistic: he was beginning to learn to use logic as a weapon. Ellie, however, was not as impressed by it as some others were. When Hawke entered university he clashed with her over the logic of driving a motorbike.

Sweeping along the northern river foreshore of Perth there is a large reserve of bushland, King's Park, that separates the commercial centre and the university from the small, neat suburbs to the north and west. In the 1940s public transport from West Leederville to the university detoured around King's Park, involved several changes of trolley bus, and took at least half an hour. The alternative was to drive through the park, taking no more than ten minutes. Hawke said he needed a motorbike to get to university. Ellie argued that motorbikes were dangerous, and Clem agreed with her. It was a question of safety, not money.

From her salary Ellie paid for the family's modest luxuries. Throughout Hawke's childhood it had been a matter of honour for her that, although family finances were always straitened, Hawke was never to be allowed to feel disadvantaged.

> It was a big thing with Mum that I should not want for any-thing. It was part of that sense of security that I always had – I knew that if I had some reasonable request that I wouldn't be knocked back. When it was clear that I really wanted a new bicycle, there was a new bicycle. When I got into the First XI I wanted a bat. So I got a bat. At university, about the motor-bike, I had the logic of geography on my side. Of course it wasn't just that. A motorbike was – oh, big deal! I kept on and on about the logic of it. Finally, Dad came round.

Outvoted, Ellie capitulated.

Hawke was given a black Panther which, from the outset he rode, according to a contemporary, 'hunched forward, staring straight ahead, never looking to right or left, and convinced he was riding it well'. In the second-term holidays Hawke was riding the Panther through King's Park, returning from the university library. It was a stirring early spring day, but he felt off colour and had taken several analgesic powders. He was still suffering attacks of sinusitis and, more recently, tonsillitis. He remem-bers the bike going into a skid, being thrown from it and land-ing hooked through with agony. He lay on the side of the road, screaming with pain. After some time a passing motorist took him to hospital. Apart from bruising, Hawke had no sign of injury but was in unbearable pain: 'I was screaming and screaming, it was so unspeakable. I thought, death would be marvellous. I'd have deliverance from this.' Injections eased his agony down to a black labyrinth. Inside it he was left, entombed.

Medical staff began tests. Some internal injury had occurred when he had hit the ground and his abdomen had smashed against a metal stand (for the motorbike) that he had been carrying inside his windcheater. At eight o'clock that night Jack Knight, a boy Hawke played tennis with and a close friend, talked his way into the ward. Knight recalled,

> I'd seen the colour of death on my grandparents when they were dying. It's a deep grey. Bob was that same colour. He was conscious but in too much pain to talk and just lay there cursing and moaning. Ellie was fussing. She talked continuously when she was distressed, to cover up her emotions – it was as if emotions were too dangerous, you could keep them away by talking.

Twenty-four hours after he was injured Hawke was anaesthetised and woke up some hours later with an L-shaped wound, 18 centimetres by 18 centimetres alongside his navel, and no spleen. It, along with blood vessels, had been ruptured. He said,

> I can remember at one point my parents talking about the motorbike and how they cursed their decision to allow me to have it. When I came to after the operation next day I can dimly remember them talking to the surgeon and saying they blessed him for having saved me. I'd been on the critically ill list for several days. Time is vague – I have a vision of my mother weeping over me. I think it was after the operation that I realised what an enormous sense of tragedy Dad and Mum would feel, losing their only son. I was acutely aware of how close to death I had been, and I got this sense that the Lord had spared my life. I can't overstate how important that accident was. It was the total turning point of my life.

Emotionally, Hawke had had an experience of priceless value: he had faced death, and won.

At the same age Neil, in whose shadow Hawke had lived, had been defeated. There, in the anguish of his parents, was proof that he was no longer an impostor but the centre of both their lives. For all of them there was another level of meaning, one that transcended the ordinary world, for the Hawkes believed implicitly that God always acted with design. By threatening, then relenting over, Bob's life, they all felt that He had given them a sign. Hawke had forgotten or had never been told about the signs Ellie had read in the Bible before he was born: now he too believed he was an instrument chosen by the Lord.

> From very early Mum had told me I had great talents and that it was a duty to use them. It would be sinful – she didn't actually use the word, but she conveyed the idea – sinful, if I didn't use these talents. And there it was: The Parable of the Talents. Like the bad servant whom God had punished, I hadn't been using my talents. I hadn't taken school seriously; I hadn't taken university seriously. Lying there in hospital I decided I was going to live my life to my utmost ability, that I'd push myself to my limits.

And so, at seventeen, he was reborn. The sense of invulnerability, the prizes, the physical injuries, the soaring optimism, the last-minute timing, the grandiose schemes, the breathtaking stamina and equally astonishing bouts of idleness, the wild sober and drunken sprees, the fearless espousal of causes, the honours, the love affairs, the nobility of heart, the thousands of friends and the murderous enemies, were all to follow.

SIX

'He fascinated me. He fascinated everyone.' Jules Zanetti, a Sydney journalist, was talking about Hawke aged eighteen to twenty-four.

It was a foregone conclusion that Bob was going to be prime minister. I took it absolutely seriously – we had long conversations about it – he would be prime minister and I would be his press officer. There was magic in the way he could get you to believe in things. It was an ability to manipulate. He had it then.

Hawke had had it since early childhood; by his late teens the lovable devil-of-a-kid had the gift of creating in his friends an eagerness to please him while, tormentingly, he went his own way. There was a subtle imbalance in all his relationships: somehow, he was always the more important partner. Hawke's life as a captain with lieutenants to do his bidding was underway. Zanetti continued, 'With us, it was a love–hate relationship. Somehow, we've always kissed and made up ... The bastard!'

Zanetti, a returned serviceman almost two years Hawke's senior, met him at university. Other friends, who had known Hawke from schooldays, say they found no change in him after the motorbike accident, but what seems clear from his own testimony is that there had been an inner transformation. At school, when Hawke had talked of becoming prime minister, he was speaking a part created for him by Ellie. Now, he was writing the drama himself: he had taken over her dream for him as his

47

own. He spent the next five years, after his escape from death, in pursuit of the prizes that he now believed it was his duty and destiny to win. His confidence was boundless: any defeat he treated as a temporary, quirkish setback to be cast, after a period of sharp dejection, away from him. Then and later ebullient – even reckless – confidence became the Hawke style: he projected an image of the young man questing for glory and adventure, guided by the courage of high endeavour. A university tutor said, referring to Hawke aged about twenty, 'Bob had charisma at a time when most Australians didn't know the word existed'.

Hawke had not developed steady scholastic habits at school but had allowed himself to be forced to learning by Ellie who, in the very act of urging him to work, was also reinforcing the family belief that he was especially gifted. Even when most intensely mentally engaged Hawke's 'streak of hedonism' was present: he studied with his Persian cat draped around his neck. As he saw himself the gifted child, already an intellectual aristocrat, he had no need to apply himself to sensible, constant effort: he can succeed against the odds, with a burst of concentration. At Modern School Hawke had despised 'swots'. He still did. At university he set out to invent a way of becoming a top law student – the top law student – without diminishing his cherished status as extraordinary. His solution, arrived at, it seems, unconsciously, was alarming. 'He needed pressure', a friend said.

> He would let things slide until the examinations were upon him, then would study frantically. And he would almost always come down with sinusitis or tonsillitis just before exams, so that he would have to push himself even harder, to make up for the time lost while he was ill. Bob comes alive under pressure.

Many students study only at the last moment, but their aim is merely to pass. Hawke was different, in that his aim was, by daring failure, to leap to triumph. A certain air of 'You, dark forces, do your damnedest – and I'll beat you!' has clung to him ever since. Daring has recurred throughout his career. 'The mistake the Socialist Left made', an ALP official said, reflecting on the downfall of the Stop Hawke campaign of the late 1970s, 'was to triple-dare him, to threaten him with extinction. He took on the dare.'

Hawke had missed most of the third-term law lectures as a result of his accident but chose not to ask for posts. He sat for all but one of his examinations at the normal time, and passed. Although he would need to take honours in every subject in each successive year (to make up for the passes in first year) he believed he would graduate with first-class honours in law. John Toohey, later a distinguished judge, competed each year with him for top position and was, finally, the only student to graduate *cum laude*. Toohey said, 'Bob was very disappointed when he missed the First. He expected to get it – he always anticipated winning, and he wanted to carry off all the prizes.'

While Hawke wanted to be a top law student, many of the practices of lawyers and many of the traditions of the law disgusted him. Soon after beginning the course he had told Clem he would not enter the profession:

> I felt a lawyer was very much a hired hand who was prepared
> to argue the case whatever his view, and I found that offensive.
> I also thought there was a fair degree of pretension about the
> law, that it tried to invest itself with some intrinsically glorious
> majesty, as such, as The Law. And I could never be persuaded
> of that. I thought the law was an instrument of society and it
> could be and should be an instrument for a better society, but
> that it could be a very evil thing – it could be used to condone
> things that couldn't and shouldn't be condoned.

At twenty-one he had a second-class honours degree in law; he was a first-grade cricketer; a delegate to the ALP state conference (where Albert continued to coach him, and Hawke to show his independence of mind by referring loudly to the Labor Party state president as 'that baldy old bastard'). He was an active member of the Student Christian Movement; president of the Congregational Youth Fellowship; and president of the students' Societies Council. He had an urge to be involved, a rushing embrace of the world. A university friend said that Hawke, at twenty-one, showed 'an impatience, an eagerness to get to the point, whether it were of observation, principle or joke'. And, alongside that, he had a patient determination to equip himself for his long-term goal of leading the country. He decided to do a second – Arts – degree, majoring in economics, 'because if one were interested in government a knowledge of economics was sensible'. He also decided to earn some money. He took a job in the Vacuum Oil Company as a trainee executive and studied part time for a year. He disliked his job, which he found 'pointless' – that is, it had no social value – and he missed the expansiveness of university life. In 1951 he resigned from Vacuum Oil and returned to university full time, gathering his strength for a final effort to plant his flag at the summit of student life: he wanted to become president of the Guild of Undergraduates and to win the Rhodes scholarship for Western Australia. He said that, since his third year of law,

> it had become obvious that I was within that small range of students who would be relevant candidates for the Rhodes. A number of people mentioned it to me – student colleagues, and Dr Rossiter [the warden of Wesley College and a member of the University Senate] very strongly suggested it to me.

Zanetti by now was editor of the university newspaper, *Pelican*, and became Hawke's publicist in the campaign to make him president of the Guild:

> Bob wanted to be president because he wanted to bring in reforms. It wasn't a question of power for power's sake – he was totally sincere in wanting to use power for the public good. He was also totally determined about getting it. Presidency of the Guild was a huge step towards the Rhodes. Bob sat down and drew up a blueprint for action. He had two power bases,

the ALP Club and the Student Christian Movement. I used
to tell him he was a hypocrite, that he couldn't possibly still be
a believer, that he was just using the SCM for votes.

Zanetti himself was known as 'an operator'. His bargain
with Hawke for 'putting Bob's smiling face on the front page of
Pelican time after time' was that, once Hawke was president he
would get Zanetti a vote – as against just a seat – in the Guild.

In 1951 Hawke ran for president and won the position with
the support of both the ALP and the Liberal clubs. His old
friend Jack Knight was a Liberal activist and helped to carry
Liberal support for Hawke, who became, in Zanetti's view, 'the
best Guild president we ever had'. In the opinion of the vice-
chancellor, (Sir) George Currie, Hawke was

absolutely top-notch. He was almost the perfect president so
far as a vice-chancellor was concerned. He was gentlemanly,
co-operative and charming, and among the presidents was
outstanding for his sense of responsibility. He was a natural
leader. By tradition all the presidents of the Council had to be
of outstanding character, and all-rounders at the university.
Hawke was innovative and an excellent chairman of meetings. He was well spoken in those days. He had a distinctly
Australian voice, but it was not harsh ... It was hard to make
the connection between that man and the one we saw on television later, being rude and obviously having had too much
to drink. I suppose those things were there in him then, but
were never called forth.

As Guild president one of Hawke's first official duties was to
welcome the freshers of 1952. His speech (published by Zanetti
in *Pelican*) shows how strong, still, was his manse conditioning,
and his slight uneasiness about it:

You are coming from the somewhat restraining atmosphere
of the secondary school into an environment which gives you

every possible opportunity to develop your intellect, character and personality. You will find a comparative lack of discipline external to yourself – to a large extent you have become
your own disciplinarians. This, of course, involves distinct
responsibilities to yourself, to those by whose sacrifices it has
been made possible for you to attend the uni., to your fellow
students, and finally to the whole society of which we are all a
part ... I would ask that you keep an open mind on all things,
rid yourself of bias or preconceived prejudices and accept the
intellectual responsibility of thinking clearly. If you do this
you will find that at the end of your university career its main
purpose will have been achieved – you will be equipped for
worthwhile citizenship and to give a lead to those who may
be less fortunate than yourselves. I apologize for the fact that
the above sounds most sermon-like ... [1]

Hawke had been elevated, as the university's representative
student, into an unfamiliar social milieu of dignitaries, local and
foreign. The state governor, Sir Charles Gairdner, was guest
of honour at many university social events and it was Hawke's
duty to help to entertain him, to sit at the top table, dance with
Lady Gairdner, deliver speeches of welcome and of thanks. The
governor liked him enough to invite him to Government House
for weekend tennis. The vice-chancellor, 'a bloke I loved', and
his wife invited Hawke to afternoon teas. These social contacts
were important for Hawke's most ambitious scheme as Guild
president.

He had become friendly with some of the foreign students,
in particular a Singhalese boy, a Buddhist who was lonely and
missing his family, probably suffering what is now recognised
as culture shock. Hawke invited him home and encouraged him
to treat the Tate Street house as his own. In 1951 two Asian
students had hanged themselves, and in early 1952 a third was
taken to hospital with a nervous breakdown. The plight of foreign students stirred up Hawke's compassion: for him the next
logical step was to do something practical, to rescue them.

He first founded an Australian–Overseas Student Club, then on 9 April 1952 gave an afternoon tea for 'overseas students to exchange ideas and impressions and discuss a few of the problems associated with entering our university'. Slowly, the idea of building an International House emerged, and in August 1952 Hawke launched the concept with characteristic ebullience. The building would cost, he announced, £150 000, and 'the bulk of this sum will – we hope – come from Asian countries, grants from the Australian [federal and WA] governments and American foundations like the Rockefeller Institute'.[2] He flung himself into publicising and fund-raising. Sir Charles Gairdner agreed to become patron of the appeal; there was an impressive ceremonial opening; *Pelican* ran front-page stories about it; Hawke badgered the Western Australian news media for publicity; there were sporting competitions, a gala ball, male and female beauty contests, a huge fete . . . all in vain.

International House was the first of his doomed enterprises, a forerunner to the failures he would experience as president of the ACTU. The inner pressure of his optimism preserved in Hawke a naivety about the goodwill of others that was later to cause astonishing misjudgments. Only £2200 of the £150 000 was raised for International House. He said,

I had the feeling that if I could have gone into it earlier and been able to stay there longer we could have got it off the ground. I was disappointed that my concept of it came to me too late for me to have a chance to really get it going. There was some opposition to it, some on racist grounds, some feelings that it was a threat to new or existing colleges, but I think the problem was one of apathy and non-appreciation of the idea, rather than of opposition. I thought that the idea was so obviously good and sensible and right that it would get a momentum of its own. Well, it didn't.

Another student said, in the sour tone of envy that Hawke's contemporaries were increasingly beginning to use when they spoke of him, 'The trouble was, International House was all Bob's idea. He hogged the limelight.'

It was during the International House appeal that Clem and Ellie first had real cause for alarm about their son's behaviour. Hawke had been to the Guildford house of a businessman to ask for a donation; the man had offered him spirits and Hawke had arrived home drunk.

In 1949 he had been unable to withstand the pressure of his peers any longer and at a law faculty dinner had drunk a glass of beer. After about a week of illicit drinking he had come home one evening, told Ellie he wanted to talk seriously to her, and after the dishes were cleared away, sat at the table and confessed. He told her that not only had he begun to drink, but also that he was not going to stop. Their discussion was a long one and 'not very pleasant'. It ended with Ellie saying, 'I'm glad, at least, you had the honesty to tell me'.

It is a mark of the faith and strength of this extraordinary woman that she forced herself to endure her son's drinking. She prayed daily that he would stop, but she did not make scenes with him about it. Reflecting years later, when Ellie was dead, Hawke said with intense sadness for the anguish he had caused her, 'She learned to live with it. Better than I did.'

As a product of several generations of teetotallers it is possible that Hawke had no physiological resistance to alcohol and may even have been allergic to it at first. According to a student drinking companion,

> After two glasses of beer he would be whacked or throwing up in a way I've never seen before – it was an incredible cacophony, you'd think the whole world, including his feet, was coming up. But Bob was determined to improve as a drinker, as he was determined to improve at everything he did.

Hawke drank moderately for about two years but, as his tolerance improved, his intake increased: 'Mum could see that I was still working extremely hard; I hadn't become "a dissolute young man". There was never any drink in the home and I never drank at home. There was never any flaunting in front of her.' But he was beginning to get drunk often, and in 1952, in Melbourne for a National Union of Australian University Students meeting, went off for a boozy weekend, returned late and still drunk on Monday morning, and thereby missed the chance of the highest position for Australian university students, presidency of NUAUS. The right-wing lobby was able to convince the centre group, whose support Hawke needed, that he was too wild for the job. Twenty years later this opinion was to become a national refrain.

Jack Knight said:

> Bob had a terrific fear of Ellie catching him drunk. I used often to get him into bed – he was sleeping on the back verandah – and we'd creep around the side of the house. There was a watertank there where he could have a wash. Then I'd get him up the steps, through a flywire door and into bed. I was scared about Ellie catching us, too. She would have blamed me for leading Bob astray.

Gradually Hawke was able to hold his liquor better and in 1952 he won a university speed-drinking competition, organised by Zanetti, by downing three schooners of beer in 9.3 seconds. Within a few years the world was to know of Hawke's prowess with alcohol: at Oxford he drank 2.5 pints (1.42 litres) of beer in 12 seconds and was entered in the *Guinness Book of Records*. In competitions for long-distance drinking, however, he was a failure; Zanetti carried off the prizes. He, too, had come from a teetotal background and remarked wistfully in 1980, 'We worshipped the grog'.

Ellie's determination to endure and not to discuss Hawke's drinking became a cause of sometimes unbearable tension for her. One day when he was late returning home to meet a friend she became increasingly jittery. At last she fled into another room, flung herself on the floor and wailed. Almost thirty years later the household tension about alcohol and the family taboo on speaking about emotional distress had not lessened. In 1977 Kate Baillieu, a television journalist, was waiting at the Tate Street house to interview Hawke *en famille*. Baillieu had made the gaffe of bringing as a present to Clem and Ellie a bottle of whisky. They had laughed and explained they did not drink. Hawke was late. Everyone there knew that he had been drinking heavily the night before but, although the subject had been raised by Baillieu's inappropriate present, no mention was made of this. Ellie became more and more agitated, talking constantly, until she suddenly said to Baillieu, 'You know, he has blackouts'.

In this highly charged atmosphere it was inevitable that Hawke should begin leading a double life. On one side there was the gregarious student leader, already sexually experienced, a beer-garden king who when indignant would throw punches. On the other there was the minister's son who abhorred violence, who went to church on Sundays, was a deacon, taught Sunday school and helped to organise wholesome holiday camps and hymn-singing social evenings.

Because there was apartheid between the hymn-singers and the drinkers most people knew him only in one role. Because he could establish rapport so strongly with his companions of the hour, the whites, as it were, could not believe that he loved the blacks just as much. Those of his drinking contemporaries who did know about Hawke's religious life were baffled by the paradox they saw, and believed that his Christianity was bogus.

It was an older man, a tutor in the English department at the University of Western Australia, Bob Rogers, who recognised that Hawke, in public, dressed in camouflage. Rogers, who influenced Hawke strongly, wrote:

> It was the beer-garden Hawke only whom I knew, for a time – extrovert, bursting with boisterousness and vigour. For a time, but not for long. The passing show of Saturday afternoon football, of holding a charismatic court, was a sideline; his bar-room friends were just sidekicks. We began to

indulge, even on licensed premises, in serious inquiries, albeit seeing the comic dimension of so many academic issues. So I was surprised one morning to be severely reprimanded by the management of the hotel in which we frequently drank, for I am, generally speaking, inoffensive, certainly so in my cups. But I was upbraided as the friend of the bloke who had offered to change the publican's face. When I saw Hawke later I asked him why he had threatened to punch the publican. Bob replied that I ought to know.

The evasion intrigued me and in it lay, upon reflection, the key to an essential part of Bob. The publican represented an aspect of the Australian Way of Life which sends Hawkey up the wall. Wherever the type within a type occurs – used-car salesman, medical practitioner or PR consultant – Hawke senses someone *on the take*. And that he truly resents. Because Bob can so successfully perform as the voluble extrovert, the inner Hawke is underestimated and misunderstood. That is, the Hawke who sits and judges and loathes the operator – whatever his mask of bonhomie or of service – who is on the cheap grab.

Shortly, I was to graduate formally from knowing the barroom to meeting the carefully hidden private Hawke. Bob was uneasy. 'You are ... you aren't ... of course, you don't have to.' It was an invitation to meet his parents, to spend an evening playing bridge at their house.

Mr Hawke welcomed me – he was tall, lean, clean, not flowery and not to be trifled with. I met his strong handshake with deep misgivings. Our bridge party was all male: I was to partner Jack Knight. The booze Jack and I had organised for later was in the boot of my old-fashioned bomb. We sat down for our game: the tang of austerity dominated the card table and I had the feeling that Mr Hawke was observing me, rather than I, him. Yet he was completely self-contained and when the conversation touched on personalities in student politics, he showed something of disdain for those in the scrabble for power. Somehow, Clem Hawke intruded as a presence, gently, persuasively, intelligently, as, I suggest, he pervaded his son's life. Increasingly, I lost interest in the cards as they were dealt.

At supper, Mrs Hawke fussed over sandwiches, cakes and soft drinks. I was offered beer, presumably a concession to me as a practising Catholic. I felt as though I were accepting something unhygienic (and certainly unnecessary). I yielded, under pleasant, hospitable pressure and Bob, the unashamed hypocrite, condescended and accepted a small glass, too.

We had a bit of trouble starting my old bus and Bob was called out to give it a heave. He approached readily, suddenly remembered what was in the boot, then shunned my car as though it were a den of iniquity. I can still recall the look of distaste on his face as we left. Looking back, that perhaps was another key: the distaste of the party-goer who sees through the shallowness, the artificiality, the falsity, and despises those who take grog-ons seriously. Bob was tugged in two directions. He could see no reason for not joining the cultivated carefreeness of bonhomie and its amusing revelations and he had nothing but disgust for the emptiness behind it. He saw bonhomie as an aspect, a tool to be used.[3]

Already, apocryphal stories were circulating about Hawke on campus. One was that, when not selected for the first-grade cricket team, he had called a meeting, stacked it, had the selectors dismissed and installed new ones who promptly selected him. Within a few years the aura of success, the myths, the unspoken envy surrounding Hawke were so great that they combined to create an impenetrable disguise, and he became, increasingly, a puzzle. Rogers was the last man to see Hawke, as it were, alive.

In 1949 Hawke had defied a second major taboo of his background: he had lost his virginity. A university friend recalled, 'He could always line up girls, for himself and his friends. It was a case of "You provide the beer and I'll bring the girls", and we'd be off to the sand dunes with a couple of blankets.'

Another friend said, 'Bob was always on the lookout for love nests. He was a great key collector. If you found a door locked to which he had a key, you'd know Bob was in there with some girl.'

But while Hawke was, and continued to be, a womaniser, he had only one special love: his co-religionist, childhood acquaintance and fiancée, Hazel Masterson. Hazel was the girl Hawke trusted, the one who shared his dreams and would help him realise them. She was the younger daughter of a modestly well-to-do accountant, a man who was a staunch conservative and secret philanthropist. Unknown even to his family, Jim Masterson had for years made a habit of giving money to battlers. He had been a battler himself – his family was poor and he had come to the city and worked his way through night school. Hazel Masterson had grown up with the values of kindliness and social duty that had inspired the Lee household. She was five months older than Hawke, the same age difference between Ellie and Clem, and like them, she and Hawke met through the church. Hazel was a good musician and became a church organist at Subiaco and a focus for many of the Congregational youth activities, where she was always in demand as a pianist. In her later teenage years she was secretary of the Congregational Youth Fellowship while Hawke was its president. For both of them this was an ideal division of labour and one which became their settled modus operandi: Hawke the public figure; Hazel the administrator. In all their life together Hawke never paid household bills nor made a decision about its organisation.

Their courting began in the church community and continued in their parents' homes: 'The influence of home was very strong on us', Hazel said. Hawke recalled, 'Hazel was a vibrant person. She was interested in the church, music, tennis, and after a bit, me.' She was as emotional as Hawke, had a lively wit and among friends was full of irrepressible laughter. One recalled,

> I once travelled with Hazel in a small jet aeroplane and something would set her off – a remark, or a funny memory – and out would come this wonderful whoop of laughter. The other

passengers would start grinning, and after a while the whole plane was in fits, everyone laughing because Hazel had.

She was very good looking, with light brown hair and pale eyes and a fine, strong bone-structure in which could be seen the bloodlines of a Czechoslovakian Jewish grandmother. Among strangers, however, she was often shy and Hawke's university friends considered her 'withdrawn'. Some noted, later, 'sometimes a great sadness in her eyes'. Hazel was working as a stenographer and 'in the student community she felt at a disadvantage', Jules Zanetti said. He called her The Mouse, until he got to know her better when, like others, he realised she was 'a great girl, a lovely girl'.

She and Hawke had started going out together (on the Panther) in 1948. In the early summer of 1949 Hawke had made a formal call upon Jim Masterson to ask his permission to marry Hazel. Masterson had reservations: Hawke was only nineteen, he was a political radical – in Masterson's terms – and he had no apparent intention of settling down to earning a living and supporting a wife in the comfort that her father had provided. Masterson's doubts were similar to Will Lee's thirty years earlier, but greater, and in the end just as futile: 'We were madly in love. We were off our beans about each other', Hazel said. They were engaged. Ellie at last had a real daughter she could mother. A friend recalled,

> Ellie would bring them a cup of tea in bed on Saturday mornings and cluck about how sweet it was that Bob and Hazel were having a brotherly-and-sisterly cuddle. A cuddle! Ellie knew her son and she was determined he was not going to run off the rails with some girl she'd never met. She was delighted to have Hazel staying at Tate Street weekend after weekend, as a magnet to keep Bob at home. They were a terrific couple. People would talk about Bob-and-Hazel – 'We've invited Bob-and-Hazel, Bob-and-Hazel were there'.

As events turned out their engagement was to be almost of Biblical length: it lasted six years.

In 1951 Hawke was a candidate for the Rhodes scholarship, and failed. He was a candidate again in 1952, and in November that year was awarded the prize. A few weeks later he set out by P&O ship from Fremantle to represent the Congregational church at a world conference of Christian youth in south India. Clem and Ellie, Hazel, friends and parishioners farewelled him with pride, for he was the most distinguished student of his day in Western Australia, honoured by the church, the state and his peers.

He went off blithely, unaware that the summer sapphire of the Indian Ocean was carrying him towards a spiritual storm.

SEVEN

Hawke says of his childhood and youth,

> I accepted unquestioningly that God was the centre of
> everything. And it satisfied me. In later childhood I remember
> having uncomfortable thoughts about where did God actu-
> ally live? What was Heaven? What were its limits, shape and
> nature? What was involved after death – did people have their
> actual form in Heaven or Hell? But the substance of my faith
> wasn't in question. Subconsciously only I was beginning to
> feel uneasy about my total theocentric explanation of things.

In Perth in the 1940s church attendances were still high.
A pupil at Modern School estimated that at least half the pupils
attended church services and Sunday school. The difference
between Hawke and his contemporaries in religious matters
was the breadth of his knowledge of the Bible, hymns and rites
of the church, and the depth of his emotional commitment to
Christianity. It was part of the cluster of his imperial loyalties:
self, family and church were linked. At university he began to
encounter minds as vigorous as his own but with different ideas
about religion – specifically Roman Catholics. Hawke argued
with them vehemently. 'At university I became more conscious
of uneasiness. One of the great joys of student life was the long
theological arguments I used to have with Roman Catholics.
Catholics fascinated me. I sought them out.'

One was John Toohey; another a philosophy lecturer, Selwyn
Graves, who had been a Jesuit priest; and a third was Bob

Rogers, an upper-middle-class 'Evelyn Waugh type of Catholic', ten years Hawke's senior, the man Hawke had invited home to play bridge. The three were active members of the Newman Society. Hawke said,

> In our discussions certain questions would arise from propositions I put which challenged their dogma. They were able to say, and I was able to agree, that if you were astringent about some of those propositions you found a challenge to your own beliefs. I challenged papal infallibility. The Catholics argued back: How can you believe in the Virgin Birth, the raising from the dead and so forth? They asserted that the whole Protestant position was far too waffly and subject to the truth being what one wanted the truth to be, and that their dogmatism, far from being a weakness, was a strength. And, in a sense, I could see the logic in that: if there was going to be a Christian religion, then there had to be some parameters to what was the truth. The logic that followed from my questioning of Catholic dogma started to nibble, very slightly, around the edge of my own belief ... I felt some guilt, but not burdensome guilt, about defying some of the moral laws of the church, but really I regarded those laws as irrelevant to the realities of existence. I didn't want to burn the church on that account. In fact, I've never wanted to burn the church ... I didn't discuss these ideas with Dad because more than anything I didn't want to hurt him. I loved him so much, and I thought he might feel hurt.

At the age of twenty-three when Hawke embarked for India he was still a practising Christian who took the good government and welfare of the church seriously. The conference in India was to be a strategic exercise for Christian soldiers – or so he believed.

He knew nothing of India – that 'functioning anarchy', as Galbraith described it. He was an emotional young man, prone to moral indignation and the urge to give comfort to the depressed, the despairing and the sick. Like his parents he had a desire to rescue. His trust in the church was centred upon its succour. And he was travelling towards the most outrageously afflicted society on earth, where the very concept of effectively relieving distress was maddening. In India, skeletons walk about in the streets.

The ship berthed in Colombo 'which was a shock'; he then travelled by train and boat to Madras, 'a greater shock', and took a plane to Travincore Cochin and finally a bus to the conference centre, Cottyam. (Travincore Cochin became later Kerala state.) Three hundred Christians from different countries, including a large Indian contingent, were gathered in Cottyam. The conference complex was close to a bishop's residence that had spacious grounds shaded by large trees and maintained by a staff of sweepers. The local Christians financially dominated the country round about. Hawke noticed with gathering indignation that there was a sharp class distinction between them and the poor, disregarded multitude of Hindus. However, he was still cheerful, as usual: 'The experience of meeting people from all over the world was terribly exciting and stimulating to me'. Pastor Niemoller of Germany was the main speaker, and a good one; accommodation – in school dormitories – was comfortable and, most importantly, Hawke was not suffering the gut infections that were enfeebling scores of other visitors. He had decided not to take risks with his health and would eat nothing but cashew nuts and bananas.

As the conference continued, his moral indignation with his co-religionists increased:

> The culmination for me started to come towards the end of the conference. The Communist Party in the area was very strong, the strongest in India as a result – as I worked it out – of the activities of the Christian church. The church had created through their mission schools the highest level of literacy in India and the Communist Party had taken advantage of this to swamp the district with cheap literature. Communist proselytising was very much simplified by literacy. The Party

had organised an enormous rally and those in charge of our conference had issued an edict that none of us were to have anything to do with it. Of course, I took absolutely no notice of that, and went to the rally, and was taken up on the dais to meet the leaders. Their appeal to the people was so relevant! I forecast then that Kerala would be the first Communist state in the British Commonwealth, and I was right. Back at the conference centre there was some resentment that I'd gone to the rally. It was said I'd given comfort to the Communists by being present. A part of the whole unreality of the situation was the fact that the Communists had their propaganda on sale very cheaply, and even the Russian classics, beautifully bound, for unbelievably low prices. In contrast, a Bible cost twenty times as much.

A few days after the rally the Christmas celebrations began. There were two things that happened. The first was a great feast held in the grounds of the bishop's residence. Tables were groaning, groaning with food, and people were gorging themselves, while just a few yards away there were hundreds of the poor staring in through the bishop's fence, looking at us and our food. Then, on Christmas Eve there was an open-air service and afterwards Christmas parties in the homes of the Christians from Cottyam, to which we were invited. People were singing hymns and carols and the one that stuck in my mind was 'The World to Christ We Bring, Christ to the World We Bring', and it all seemed so bloody unreal and hypocritical. I wandered down to the village. It was hot during the day but became cool after sunset. The people who lived in the street had already settled down for the night; they were lying on the pavements with bits of rag pulled over themselves to try to keep warm. There was one little kid – he had a beautiful face with huge eyes – lying there with an older girl. He looked terribly miserable. It all suddenly jarred in my mind. There were those comfortable Christians up the road singing about bringing Christ to the world, and the world to Christ, and here *was* the world.

And to the Christians they seemed to be totally irrelevant as the Christians were irrelevant to them.

I went back to the dormitory and got a windcheater and took it down to the little girl for her baby brother. She put it on him. They thought it was the greatest thing that had ever happened – and it was nothing to me, in terms of material possessions. The whole conjunction of circumstances sickened me.

On Christmas Day there were more services and more irrelevancies and the conference broke up a couple of days later. I made my way from there with a young Anglican minister to Bangalore and Mysore, by bus and train, and back to Madras by train. We deliberately went third class. In Mysore and Bangalore the contrast between wealth and poverty, which I thought I'd seen, really hit me. We saw the palaces of princes and rajahs. In one, the stables had been converted to garages – there were twenty-five bloody motor cars and the place was lit up at night with light bulbs all over it, while all around there were people begging and half-starved ...

We arrived in Madras at dawn and were met by a local Christian, who owned a newspaper. People were just waking up, scores and scores of them lying in the shit and filth of the gutters. The newspaper owner took us off to lunch with a relation of his. He was driving a great flash car and on the way the relation asked how he liked his new car. Our host complained bitterly because there was something wrong with one of the doorhandles. Well, that jarred just a little with me.

I left India and returned to Colombo, where I was the guest of a Singhalese student I knew in Perth. They were Buddhists, their house was in the grounds of a temple, and the atmosphere of the household was very peaceful and unbelievably gentle. I talked a lot about Buddhism with them, and they took me up to a temple in the hills, in Kandy, where I met the monks and talked to a very old abbot, who explained more about Buddhism to me. I found Buddhism fascinating. Their concept that you progress towards the ineffable through a number of existences seemed to me much more intellectually satisfying than the Christian belief that you come just once and are cast into circumstances maybe of great wealth or of great moment, but that you come to God or don't come to God on the basis of that one life. The logical attraction of Buddhism after the devastating experience of India was a further part of my breaking down. I was never on the point of embracing Buddhism but I found, and still find, it infinitely more satisfying than the Judeo-Christian philosophy.

When I got back to Australia customs officials seized the Communist literature I'd bought in Cottyam, including pamphlets which purported to prove the use of germ warfare by the Americans in the Korean War. I was pretty savage about my rights to bring into the country Communist literature [the Menzies government had failed in 1951 to have the Australian Communist Party outlawed] and the next day a Commonwealth car arrived at Tate Street with some embarrassed-looking blokes who returned all the stuff to me.

Clem, with the Hawke characteristic of discounting the existence of distress, described his son as 'emotional' when he returned from India: 'I've only twice seen Bob emotional', he said. 'The first time was when he'd been to India. The second time was after the war in Israel.'

Hawke was experiencing a crisis of loyalty: he was disgusted with his church, but his church and his father were inextricably linked.

I talked about the politics, rather than the religious doubts, to Dad. Religion was his total life. I didn't want to say anything that might make him think it was all a charade or a joke or an unreality ... Looking back, I can see that time in India and Ceylon [Sri Lanka] was the turning point, but it was still a process which took a long time to work itself out. I continued going to church, with decreasing enthusiasm. It was years before I said to myself, 'I'm an agnostic'. I've never said 'I'm an atheist' – it's an illogical statement, I think.

Bob Rogers, who unwittingly had hastened the attrition of Hawke's faith, noticed how tense and defensive he was on return from India. Hawke rang Rogers and asked, in an urgent tone, to meet him at the students' pub, the Nedlands Hotel. When Rogers entered, 'Hawkey pretended not to notice that I had come in and talked energetically to people he could not stand and finally threw me an aside – "Let's go somewhere else."'[1]

Once they were alone together Hawke's furtiveness eased and he explained to Rogers how shaken he had been by his experience of India's appalling conditions. Again, Hawke expressed his political and humanitarian horror, not his religious doubts. But Rogers had an inkling that there was more involved, for he gently reminded Hawke that the existence of distress and oppression was not an argument against Christianity, that Christ himself had lived in such a society. Rogers wrote:

India seemed to spark off in Bob the role of a secular missionary, the Humanist who burns to reduce the store of so much socially induced human misery. 'It would be so simple if . . .' And I think that Bob does divide us into the Goodies and the Baddies. The Goodies are those who, either actively or as spectators, support reducing the level of human misery; the Baddies, those who, motivated by privilege or gain, do nothing to impede the war on human suffering.

That I have portrayed him as a missionary does not exclude the proposition that some missionaries can be ruthless and have flashes of irritation, in Bob's case, an irritation caused by those who, he considers, befog or arrest the campaign against human distress. Such irritation can cut across party or union affiliations and baffle those who try to pinpoint his position in the political spectrum.[2]

It was, however, to be another five years before Hawke would find an arena in which to express his secular missionary zeal, and that was in the Australian Conciliation and Arbitration Commission.

A few weeks after his return from India Hawke had to report on the Cottyam meeting to a Congregational conference in Adelaide. He went there *en famille*, with Clem, Ellie and Hazel, who was present in her own right, as a Western Australian delegate. There were a couple of hundred Congregationalists attending; Hawke was asked to address a plenary session.

> I wanted to be able to do it well, in a way which had a message, and not a destructive message, about my doubts. On the afternoon before I was to speak I went off into the bush by myself and thought and prayed. I had an intense desire to be helped. I prayed for help. What was going on inside me was a torment – those great doubts I had were doing something. I prayed again that night, in bed. I wanted to emphasise the things said at Cottyam about Christian concern, but I was in terrible doubt about the relevance of Christian belief, and in doubt about the concern that Christians *should* have for others. I was in a torment about the two aspects I had seen. When I began to speak something extraordinary happened. I felt something unknown – a capacity in myself which I had never suspected – it was as if it were not I speaking but someone else. My speech was brilliantly articulated – I had never been able to speak like that before – and it had enormous impact, people were moved in a way in which I've never been able to repeat – oh, just once it happened again, at an ALP meeting in late 1979. In Adelaide I had the feeling that something unique had happened, that there had been a response to my request for help.

A missionary jumped up and said, 'Thank God for Bob Hawke!'

That day in Adelaide was probably Hawke's last as a Christian; it was his first as a political agitator: he had swept the mood of the conference round from one of a condemnation of the expense involved in sending representatives to India to approval of the decision, and wild ovation.

He returned to Perth, to study and tutor in economics and to wait out the seven months until he was due to take up his Rhodes scholarship. He had lived five years convinced that the Lord had touched him with His hand; now this conviction seemed questionable. Hawke's next five years were unsettled. He was in the full flower of his youth and his life on the surface appeared joyous, full of novelty, madcap gaiety, intellectual challenge. However, an older man who got to know Hawke during this period remarked, 'I thought he was a soul in torment'.

EIGHT

O N THE DAY IN November 1951 when Hawke learned he had not been chosen as the Western Australian Rhodes Scholar for 1952 he went to the cinema with Hazel. Later he could not remember what film they had seen but Hazel recalled the evening vividly. The movie, chosen at random, had turned out to be about a Rhodes scholar; their outing was acutely painful. But within days Hawke had shaken off his disappointment and decided to reapply the following year.

As events unfolded, he was to be glad that he had at first failed to win the Rhodes. With hindsight he was able to see in the one-year delay to his ambition the origin of his career as a labour leader: the delay gave him a chance to complete his Arts degree, majoring in economics; this in turn determined the nature of his study at Oxford, which linked to his further research at the Australian National University, which led him to the attention of officials of the Australian Council of Trade Unions.

Rhodes had specified in his will the qualities he desired in scholars:

Literary and scholastic attainments; qualities of manhood, truth, courage, devotion to duty, sympathy for and protection of the weak, kindliness, unselfishness and fellowship; exhibition of moral force of character and of instincts to lead and to take an interest in his fellows, physical vigour, as shown by fondness for and success in manly outdoor sports.

They also had to be bachelors.

Hawke could not be credited with literary attainments but he possessed all the other attributes, plus another: a nose for pretension. Cecil Rhodes offended Hawke's deepest social beliefs. He regarded Rhodes as a colonial exploiter who, having amassed a great fortune from cheap black labour, had found it convenient to distribute his wealth posthumously to children of the upper middle class. Hawke's opinion of Rhodes scholars was not high, either. He wanted to win the Rhodes scholarship because it was there for the winning, and would enable him to study abroad. He had applied also for a scholarship to an American university and would have been equally happy with that, he said, but the Rhodes was decided first.

Hawke made no secret of his contempt for Rhodes (and Rhodes scholars in general) but did not explain his reasoning. He rarely does: for him, people are either trained to perceive social evil, as he is, in which case no explanation is necessary – or they are not, in which case explanation is futile. Furthermore, Hawke demands of his friends that they psychologically bond with him, spontaneously and without need for words – a demand that is often too great. Other students found his expressed disdain for Rhodes combined with his eagerness to win a Rhodes scholarship paradoxical and even improper. Repeatedly during his career Hawke's 'sort of terrific conceit, which won't allow him to share his mental processes' (as a close friend described it), was to cause misunderstandings and misjudgments.

The final interviews of the short-list candidates took place on Friday, 28 November 1952 at Government House. Six tense young men waited in an ante-room for the secretary, Josh Reynolds, to call them inside for the decisive meeting with the selection committee. It was made up of Sir Charles Gairdner; the acting vice-chancellor, Professor N. S. Bayliss; and five other men, most of them former Rhodes scholars. Hawke was friendly with the chairman (Gairdner) and the secretary. In the opinion of contemporaries he had cultivated the friendship of Reynolds, who was warden of St George's College, by taking holiday jobs at the university. It was an accurate assessment but to picture it – as some contemporaries did – as self-interested deviousness is too cynical.

From schooldays Hawke had worked at relating to others and had seen relating as work: the milkman, the corner-store shop-keeper and the dean of law were all subject to Hawke's self-aware desire to be liked. Clem operated in exactly the same way.

Hawke recalled,

I was second or third to be called in and was asked one question – I've forgotten what. Then this bloke, a lawyer, said to me: 'Mr Hawke, one of the important considerations in the mind of the Founder' – you were supposed to genuflect at the mention of the Founder – 'and one of our responsibilities, is to have a concern for what a Rhodes scholar will do. If we were to award you a scholarship, what would you do in later life?' I said, 'I don't know. I don't wish to practise law. The only answer I can give you is that it would be some sort of public service, by which I don't mean that I would necessarily go into *the* Public Service.' And he said, 'Come, come, Mr Hawke. You *must* have an idea.' And I said to him again, rather sharply, 'I'm sorry, but that is all I can honestly say. I just don't know. Perhaps within that definition of public service I would want to do some academic work, but I can't help you more than that.' And he then came back at me again and said that wasn't good enough. So I turned to the governor and said to him, 'I've answered the question honestly and to the best of my ability. And I resent the insinuation that I'm not being forthright about it. And I haven't come here to have my honesty impugned!' I really went off. I was then asked some other questions, by others, which I answered genially and then I was shown out, thinking, 'Oh, well. I've blown it.' The other blokes asked me how I'd done and I said, 'Aw, a bit of fun'.

Then the fateful moment came. Old Josh came out again and said, 'The committee would like to see Mr Hawke'. I went in and the governor walked round from behind his chair to greet me and said, 'Bob, we read all the references before we interview the candidates. I must tell you that my inclination was that you were the person for it.' Then he added quietly, 'If I had any doubts about it, your replies to that character confirmed my previous opinion'. And that was it. I'd won.

In the months between winning and embarking for England, Hawke had another serious injury. He was run down by a carthorse and had his thigh ripped open. Again he lost a lot of blood and when he was injected with penicillin in hospital suffered anaphylaxis, a violent allergic reaction that is often fatal. He had fallen off the motorbike a couple more times; he had been struck in the face by a cricket ball – a week after a young man, playing on the same pitch, had been killed by a ball – and brought home to Ellie covered in blood. Physical injuries were becoming a way of life. Pushing himself to his limits – even flinging away the idea of limits – Hawke suffered over the years broken wrists, sprained ankles, torn ligaments, smashed fingers, cuts, contusions and temporary paralysis from spinal injury.

There was, too, emotional hurt. He was deeply in love with Hazel but their marriage had been delayed and delayed and now he was leaving her. They wanted to have children. Their friends were already parents. A six-year engagement was cause for derision – as Hazel had accepted for some time and Hawke was accepting now, for the first time. In the days before his departure he was overcome with angry sadness, forced to realise that his career, his commitment to duty-and-destiny, would for years, or forever, override their private lives. Hazel welcomed her role as helpmate in Hawke's life, and along with Ellie had become his abiding champion and protector. But he was struck dumb, as he always is when distressed, gripped by a sense of horror and dishonour at delay. He had seen, for a moment, his selfishness and what burdens he was imposing upon both of them.[1]

He had already what Hazel later called 'a battery of defence mechanisms', and only those close to him had a vague uneasiness that something was disturbing him, as Bob Rogers revealed in this description of a party. It was the biggest of a round of farewells, the guests including everyone from the university

Young Liberals (the future Liberal leader, Billy Snedden, was a guest) to the Communists, and was held in Rogers' house. He wrote:

> The party was one of the merriest I have ever attended. We were disturbed by the police (who had received a complaint about noise) but that was the only jarring note in the saturnalia. Bob was gay, beaming: it seemed to be one of those moments in his life when he felt that jollity could go on forever. So I was surprised when, awakened by my bladder at about six in the morning, I found Bob on his knees in the kitchen scrubbing the floor. I told him to stop making a fool of himself and leave the floor as it was. He refused. I offered to help. He told me to get out. So I left him to enjoy his puritanical conscience in his own way. About ten, someone called in to take Hawkey for a swim. I checked the house. It had been meticulously tidied. About 2 o'clock there was a call from the pub. Remnants of the party were having lunch or breakfast there. Hawkey said he needed a shower and came back to my place.
>
> He reappeared sometime later dressed in a very conservative fashion and complaining of hunger. He refused to drink. I should have smelt a rat. Bob said he needed to get across to Subiaco in a hurry, so I drove him over. On the way we discussed some of the intellectual foibles of our guests and I asked him casually, but somewhat to the point, 'Where are we going?'
>
> 'Just drop me off in Rokeby Road', he said.
>
> I said, 'Yes, but where are *you* going?'
>
> As we were nearly at Rokeby Road he had to come clean: the Congregational Youth were giving him a grand farewell starting at 6 o'clock. I was entranced! I made a quick check and knew I was shaved and moderately well dressed. I then expressed my pleasure at going to a Congregational Youth dinner. I had never been to one and I looked forward to the occasion very much. I looked forward to the opportunity of

attempting to fathom ... We had reached the Congregational Hall.

'You are not coming in', Bob said.

'What!'

'You smell of *drink*.'[2]

On Saturday, 15 August 1953, Hawke was to set sail for England. He had, as usual, neglected his preparations until it seemed he would miss the boat. As usual, too, friends and relations rallied round and Hawke himself had an eleventh-hour burst of intense activity and somehow, amid alarums and confusion, he got on board the *Dominion Monarch* in time, with his papers in order and some money borrowed from a parishioner to help with small luxuries while abroad.

He was so broke that when he had won the Rhodes scholarship he had been able to afford only the cheapest passage, and had booked on a rustbucket called the *Mooltan*, known jocularly as the smallpox ship. But during 1953 one of the windfalls that were to become normal for him occurred: the Shaw Savill line reverted to a prewar policy of giving free return first-class berths to Rhodes scholars. Instead of travelling in a six-bunk cabin below the waterline next to the engine room of the smallpox ship he sailed in a stateroom of the well-found *Dominion Monarch*. He enjoyed himself inordinately and, having stayed up until three in the morning at a party following a call at the Canary Islands, caught a chill, had to be carried ashore in England and was taken by ambulance to Southampton Hospital, with pneumonia.

The college he had chosen at Oxford was University, one of the cheaper, smaller colleges. He had picked it for its price and because he was attracted by the work of a don there. Hawke said,

There had been earnest discussions back at the University of Western Australia about which was the oldest of Oxford's colleges – Merton or Univ. [An Oxford joke has it that King Arthur founded University.] When I first arrived and got shown to my rooms I was quite sure which was the oldest – University was, and I had the oldest rooms in it. In the bedroom there was a washstand with a bowl which my scout, Ernie, who was 180 years old, would fill each morning with warm water. The bathroom was downstairs. There was a coal fire, which Ernie used to light, and that left the room warm enough to freeze your balls. And there was some dreadful old furniture and a piece of bald carpet on the floor. My first impression was that it was all so bloody ancient and so unfunctional a place in which to live. But the sheer beauty of Oxford, the tradition as much as the beauty, hits you as soon as you arrive there – Magdalen and All Souls and Balliol.

On the whole, however, the mystique of Oxford, which in the 1950s was still considered the most significant university in the world, affected him little. 'I thought there was a fair degree of bullshit about Oxford. There was a lot of pretension and genuflecting to the glories of tradition. People called the terms Trinity, Michaelmas and so on. I called them First, Second and Third.'

He was quickly nicknamed 'Digger'. Graham Freudenberg wrote in *A Certain Grandeur*:

Robert James Lee Hawke may prove to be the first completely modern Australian politician. He was the only Australian to have left Oxford more convincedly Australian than before he went there. Oxford had much the effect on Hawke as Cambridge had on Lee Kuan Yew a decade before; both learnt that there was nobody better than them there, but that their destiny lay absolutely at home. Hawke, in his generation, was the most significant of those who learned in England to patronise the English, as the English had patronised the Australians for six generations.[3]

Because Hawke had failed to win the Rhodes on his first attempt he had completed all but one unit of a Bachelor of Arts degree while in Perth, and he took the examinations for this at the end of 1953 at Oxford. The normal course for Rhodes scholars with a background in Arts–Law is politics, philosophy and economics – PPE. But Hawke now had two undergraduate degrees and gaining a third seemed tiresome. He was bored by the work, older than other PPE students and homesick:

> I had a feeling of pointlessness. It was winter, cold, intensely lonely. I used to go back to my grim little monk's cell at night ... Not having something to which I felt strongly attached – to compensate for the security I'd known for the whole of my life – made it worse. Nothing in my work was exciting and challenging.

Again he was fretting himself into a decline.

After a month or so he wrote to Hazel and asked her to throw in her job and join him as soon as she could. She replied that she had booked to arrive at Tilbury in December 1953, and sent him money to buy a van in which they could tour England and Europe the following spring. Hawke was so elated at the prospect of seeing Hazel again that on the morning he set off to meet her at Tilbury his concentration lapsed, the van went into a spin ... Fortunately, there was no traffic.

With Hazel's arrival Hawke was renewed and Oxford became 'the happiest years of my life'. After a couple of weeks he had decided to cut his losses, abandon PPE and take up postgraduate work. He wanted to do a piece of original research but he had already lost too much time to write a doctoral thesis, so he opted for the lesser degree of Bachelor of Letters. He was mentally casting about for a topic that would marry his legal and economic work and that would be 'relevant to Australia', when one unusually bright winter morning he went to the library at Rhodes House and stood looking around at the shelves:

> It was fantastic! There was a full set of Commonwealth Arbitration Reports, a complete set of Hansards, a complete set of the Convention debates and a complete set of the newspapers of the 1890s – the period of the Great Strike that had

spawned arbitration. And there were all the relevant history books. It suddenly clicked! I'd study the Australian arbitration system – how wages were determined.

Afterwards he thought of that instant when something had pinched at him as another signpost of destiny.

Dr Colin Clark was then at Oxford directing the Institute of Agricultural Economics and agreed to become Hawke's supervisor. Their first contact was cordial and Hawke was excited (as he wrote to his financial benefactor, the parishioner who had lent him money and was to lend more) about having as supervisor 'certainly one of the foremost economists in the world today, and recently arrived from Australia, where during the past years he has been intimately acquainted with the economic situation and Government decisions at a high level'.[4]

With hindsight, Hawke's enthusiasm was ironic: Clark had been the economic adviser to E. J. Hanlon's Labor government in Queensland but in early 1952 his relationship with the premier had ruptured over the issue of a green revolution – a central concept of the National Catholic Rural Movement – in Queensland. Hawke was unaware that Clark had experienced the crisis of adult conversion to Roman Catholicism; that he had been deeply attracted by the spiritual qualities of the Rural Movement and, realising the impracticality of some of its program, had set about developing a workable economic scheme appropriate to its social concepts. Inflation in Australia was severe by 1952; Clark urged a brake on further industrialisation in favour of intensive settlement of the land; lower tariffs; and the abolition of automatic quarterly adjustments of the basic wage (to help combat inflation). He proposed that the adjustment-for-inflation system of wage fixation be replaced by productivity-geared wage increases. Clark was one of the few economists in the world who understood productivity gearing at the time. Unknown to Hawke, Clark's concepts, transmitted through the network of Catholic intellectuals in Australia, and applied without deep understanding of economics, had just caused a revolution in wage fixation.

In 1954 the name Santamaria meant nothing to Hawke. He was, however, a little uneasy about some facets of his supervisor's personality: 'He is an ardent R.C.', Hawke wrote, 'and in some respects this tends to colour his work. I am sure that during the course of my study under him there will be differences of opinion, but at all times I should be sure of stimulating supervision'.[5]

The stimulating supervision transmuted into an almighty row.

Clark believed he was to supervise an economics thesis that would be titled, as he recalled later, 'The Economics of Wage Arbitration'.[6] But Hawke wrote at the time, 'the topic for research is Wage Determination in Australia'.[7] Clark was expecting an economics thesis; Hawke was researching politics and history.

They continued to see each other for a couple of months until a day in second term when Clark, whose conversation is scintillating but whose manner can be cold and abrasive, lost patience with his student. Hawke said:

> I had just discussed with him my ideas on the development of the arbitration system with special reference to the concept of the basic wage. And then, Clark staggered me. He said, 'Mr Hawke, that is a matter that would be of no interest to me, but what is more important, it would be of no interest to the University of Oxford'. Me being me, I didn't accept that. I said, 'It may be of no interest to you, but there's no reason to believe it would not be of interest to the University of Oxford'. And I left.

Hawke had now had two false starts. His confidence was shaken by Clark's remark that his thesis would be of no interest to Oxford – for it suggested he would fail to get his degree – and he was indignant. 'I find it difficult', he wrote,

> to be at all unbiased when speaking of the man ... an individual who regards an interview with a student as an opportunity for a pedantic exercise in which he delivers himself of

certain pronouncements with an air of papal infallibility, and you have the feeling that if you attempt to push your own ideas you run the threat of excommunication.[8]

Clark's opinion of Hawke, as he expressed it to friends, was disdainful, particularly of Hawke's ability with economics. The units of economics in Hawke's Arts degree had not equipped him for the high-level economic research that Clark expected and he used later to refer to Hawke as 'that economic drongo'.

The wardens of University College and Rhodes House found a new supervisor for Hawke, the Professor of Government and Public Administration at All Souls, K. C. Wheare, an Australian and former Rhodes scholar. Wheare's field was constitutional law. He was considered one of the outstanding legal intellects of his time and was a kindly, diffident man, assuring Hawke he knew nothing of the development of the basic wage – perhaps Mr Hawke would teach him?

> It was well into second term before this was all sorted out. I was tremendously excited about doing major research for the first time in my academic life, and I had the added edge now that I wanted to demonstrate that Clark was wrong. I had thought the man must be mad, bonkers. *Later* I discovered what it was all about. Clark was the economic adviser to Santamaria. He was the evil genius behind the 1952–53 basic wage case decision – had just, in fact, been involved in butchering the basic wage, and here was a young man wanting to come in and research it!

Hawke never forgave Clark. In Oxford the stage had been set for his passionate assault upon the wage decisions of the Australian arbitration system.

Meanwhile, his decision to become a researcher had altered the way he looked at Oxford itself. He began to appreciate it as a sanctuary of freedom and tolerance. To the east, Europe was struggling out of the rubble of war, and across the Atlantic the

United States was deranged with McCarthyism. At home the ALP was boiling with sectarian hatreds, and Liberalism, in its 'first, fine careless rapture', was persecuting its political enemies. In the town of Oxford itself, in the tea shops, young men with crewcuts and sky-blue uniforms were a constant reminder that Europe and America now awaited nuclear war with the Soviet Union, for the airmen came from a base a few kilometres out of town, from which bombers armed with nuclear warheads flew on exercises twenty-four hours a day. But in the colleges Communists held professorships and walked the quadrangles with the springy step of free men. The University of Oxford seemed, Hawke said, 'an island in a mad world'. In the safety of isolation he had, for the first time ever, the opportunity to please himself entirely.

> I'd made a deliberate decision before I went there to put a moratorium on politics, student and party, because I knew that when I went back to Australia I'd be deeply involved in politics, probably for the rest of my working life. I decided to enjoy Oxford, but on my terms. I picked my friends in a way which had no care of the future. I had all kinds of relationships, just for relationship's sake – a pleasure I've never been able to have in any other two years of my life since.

His companions ranged from Sir Howard Florey (who developed penicillin) to a Dorset policeman. For no cost he indulged in a pleasure that he could not afford in Australia: he joined the Royal Air Force Reserve and learned to fly.

Hawke's friends (who had noted the way he piloted land transport) predicted that he would kill himself in an aeroplane. It was, however, his motor vehicle, the van known around Oxford as the fornicatorium, that led to trouble. In late 1954 he was at an Air Squadron dinner where one of the guests became paralytically drunk. With the help of another student, Jimmy Allan, Hawke drove the boy home and put him to bed. It was after midnight, pouring with rain, and Hawke himself had been drinking.

A police car followed the van back to the squadron party then, as Hawke got out, the police seized him and accused him of stealing the van. The ancient, once murderous, town-versus-gown feeling in Oxford was still strong and police harassment of students was common. Hawke was loud in his indignation. The commandant of the squadron had to be called out to vouch that the van was not stolen, and that seemed the end of the matter. But a few days later the police called on Hawke with a summons for dangerous driving.

Already he was something of a hero, a Wild Colonial Boy, to sections of the student community, particularly those in the sporting club, Vincent's. On the day his case was to be heard his friends packed the gallery of the magistrate's court. Hawke had not expected that the police would lie under oath, but they did. He was convicted, fined £40 and had his licence suspended for six months. His supporters heckled the police and the magistrate, and a number of them were arrested and charged with contempt. The case was reported locally, and in the West Australian press, under the headline 'Rhodes Scholar on Dangerous Driving Charge'. Hawke said, 'I felt terribly ashamed. I was also very angry – it was a cook! I decided to appeal, and if I lost the appeal to throw it in and go home.'

At the University of Western Australia Hawke had never joined in student pranks, and had given the impression to contemporaries that 'he thought such things were beneath him'. But at Oxford in November 1954 he was again caught by the police as he attempted to steal a street lamp. He was convicted and fined £5.

His second conviction complicated his appeal against the first. Hawke engaged a barrister, Oliver Popplewell, for the appeal. Popplewell wanted to bring up as evidence of Hawke's driving experience his previously clean driving record, but if he were to do this the police would bring forward Hawke's conviction for attempted theft. This had been such a footling matter that it had not attracted the attention of the press; Clem and Ellie were unaware of it. 'Bob was very anxious that his parents shouldn't get to hear about the street lamp', Popplewell said, and took instructions from Hawke to present the case in a different way. The police had said that Hawke had put his arm out the rolled-down driver's window and made a vulgar gesture at them. But the driver's window could not be rolled down, for it was made up of one fixed and one sideways sliding glass panel. Hawke told Popplewell to ask the police: how far was the van's window down when the defendant put his arm through it and made the gesture? As events turned out, the constable said the window was three-quarters to fully down; the sergeant that it was fully rolled down, and this time their perjury was revealed.

The appeal was heard in the Oxford Quarter Sessions in March 1955 before Mr A. C. Longford, the Deputy-Recorder. The main witness for Hawke was Jimmy Allan, a cricket Blue and also a member of the Worcester College rugby team, which on the day of the appeal was playing an intercollege final. To Popplewell's and Hawke's horror, when Allan was called he did not appear. The session was adjourned. Popplewell had not yet questioned the police.

A few minutes later Allan arrived breathless, covered in mud, and without a tie. An apocryphal story circulated later that he had come into court wearing a Hawk's tie – the Hawk's Club being the Cambridge rival of Vincent's. Popplewell 'washed him and brushed him up a bit and put a tie on him', and Allan entered the box.

The Deputy-Recorder was testy about the adjournment and demanded why Allan was late. When Allan admitted he had been playing rugby Longford became even more irritated and upbraided the young man for wasting the court's time. Allan had a Scots temper and replied it was important that he play, because it was the first time his college had been in Cupper's final. The case seemed lost. Longford glared, then abruptly asked, 'Which college?'

On hearing that it was Worcester, Longford's manner changed: 'That was my father's college', he said wistfully.

Popplewell recalled, 'And from that moment on everything Jimmy Allan said was accepted by the judge. The police's lie was exposed, their reliability was destroyed and we romped home, with costs, and had an enormous party that evening in Vincent's.'

After this troublesome period Hawke settled once more to 'enjoying my academic work beyond description and playing cricket to saturation point'. His working method was already established. It was a system of alternating intense pressure and détente. A don described it later:

> In summer he drank excessively, wenched excessively, played cricket excessively. We thought he was going to the dogs. When winter came, he stopped drinking, stopped wenching, and studied excessively. We thought he'd do himself an injury from over-work. But when summer came he forgot the library, returned to his girls and his beer. That was Digger for you.[9]

Hawke said, 'I had only three terms in which to prepare a 70 000 word thesis'. In fact, he had five, but his determination to play and his need for pressure made the other two a mental blank. As co-workers were to discover later, when Hawke has decided on a period of indolence it is impossible to cajole him out of it or to coax him into consideration of serious matters. Conversely, when he has marshalled his attention to a problem, he refuses to be distracted from it, and gives the impression that he has not only intellectually but physically entered into it.

Because it is a method that lacks administrative planning, to be effective it needs immense energy, a hit of inspiration and some luck. Many people agree with Hawke's own assessment that he is lucky, but half his luck is boldness.

As a cricketer at Oxford Hawke was unlucky. He was twelfth man in the Oxford team, and although he toured the counties for months he was never called upon to bat and so failed to win a full Blue. But academically he had good fortune. In 1955 he won a six-week scholarship to the Institute of American Studies in the Schloss Leopoldskron, Salzburg, for a residential course in American industrial law and relations. Leading American

academics and bureaucrats in the field of industrial relations conducted the lectures. Among them were the head of the Bureau
of Labour Statistics and the Director of Community Affairs
from the Jewish Labour Committee, Ben Seligman, who became
later Professor of Economics at the University of Massachusetts.
Seligman was attracted to Hawke and 'took me under his wing,
another father-figure thing, I suppose'. Like other men who felt
a desire to indulge Hawke, Seligman was tolerant of his protégé's harum-scarum behaviour and took it in his stride when,
as Hawke's host at a performance of *The Magic Flute*, his guest
fell asleep.

Hawke had his usual last-minute administrative chaos when
his thesis was due to be handed in. As usual, friends rallied around
and the work was finished in time. In December 1955 he presented himself in Schools for the viva voce on his topic, which was
titled, 'An appraisal of the role of the Australian Commonwealth
Court of Conciliation and Arbitration with special reference to
the development of the concept of the basic wage'. It broke new
ground and survived for a quarter of a century as an introductory
text for students of the history of industrial law. The Salzburg
work had enabled him to include a comparison between the
Australian system of wages arbitration and the American system
of collective bargaining. He had gained from Wheare an understanding of the Australian Constitution and its weaknesses, and
a desire to see it reformed.

> When I arrived for the viva the chairman said, 'Mr Hawke,
> you're in the fortunate position of knowing more about your
> subject than any of us'. They complimented me on the thesis.
> We had a genial yarn and that was it. I was a Bachelor of
> Letters.

Hawke's thesis is not so much the work of an intellectual, in
the sense of a theorist, as of a forceful intellect, a honed, logical
mind concerned with practicalities. The last paragraph reads:

At the time when it was becoming a nation Australia made a bold experiment [by establishing the arbitration system]. If the experiment … has become an inadequate instrument of self-realisation, Australia should recognise the fact and, equally boldly, seek to improve the instrument.[10]

These written thoughts of a postgraduate student are, at heart, a politician's speech. Aged twenty-six and unemployed, Hawke was addressing not his English examiners, but the Australian people.

His two insouciant years were over. When he arrived back in Perth in the summer of 1956 he discussed with Albert Hawke the possibility of a seat in parliament.

NINE

HAWKE'S YOUTHFUL FANTASY about becoming prime minister seemed, he said, when he cast a condescending backward glance at it in the summer of 1956, to be no more than that: a fantasy of youth. Examining the same idea again, with his Uncle Bert, he believed it *could* be realised: 'I talked to him in terms of a political career and obviously, if I had a political career, I would want to go to the top'. No seat was immediately available and anyway Hawke's formal education was incomplete: he had won a research scholarship to the Australian National University, which he was committed to take up in the early part of 1956. At the ANU he was to write a doctoral thesis on the basic wage; he would be the first PhD student in the Faculty of Law there. But before he began a new stretch as a student he had a different commitment: now that the enforced bachelorhood of the Rhodes scholarship was behind him he was free to marry Hazel.

Their wedding was in Trinity Church, Perth, on the afternoon of 3 March, a day with temperatures higher than 38°C and the air heavy with an approaching thunderstorm. A guest recalled:

> We were all dressed up and perspiring. Hawke's Uncle Bert gave the toast to the bride and groom and it felt like eight hours, though it probably only went on for forty minutes. It was a hot and long reception and there was only lemon cordial to drink.[1]

Hazel, whom the family described on ordinary days as 'bubbly', was laughing as she came out of the church on Hawke's arm; in their wedding photographs he is looking at her with a grin of rapt smugness. After a honeymoon on the coast at Yallingup they set out, broke and still owing the money borrowed for Oxford, for University House, Canberra.

In 1956 the national capital was an expanse of paddocks, bush and mountains surrounding a cluster of suburbs and government buildings. Kangaroos did not hop in the main street but they were a common sight on the edges of town; magnificent parrots – black and sulphur-crested cockatoos, galahs, rosellas and lorikeets – visited domestic and public gardens in noisy flocks. There was no lake then and few restaurants outside the modest hotels and clubs. For entertainment at night there were the pubs, a couple of cinemas and the Blue Moon Cafe in Civic, specialising in fried things. The Australian National University, almost at the centre of town, was a dozen buildings, some fibro huts, playing fields, lawns and bushland. 'We were used to small towns. We enjoyed Canberra', Hazel said.

University House was, by the standards of the city and the times, de luxe accommodation. It was new, attractively designed and centrally heated. Few of those who lived there liked it. There were no cooking facilities in its apartments and meals were taken in a communal dining room; its rules were strict and quirky: pregnant women were not allowed to be residents, for example. The Master of University House, Professor A. D. Trendall, was a man of extremely tidy habits who, on entering a scholar's apartment, would immediately begin to straighten up piles of books or other articles lying out of place. There were no undergraduates in residence but amorous liaisons on the premises were against the rules. 'It was run like a girls' boarding school', complained a senior academic. 'The rules *made* people break out.' In due course Hawke broke out in spectacular fashion.

The Hawkes' next-door neighbours were Peter Coleman and his wife, Verna. Coleman, who later had a distinguished career in journalism and a less distinguished one in New South Wales Liberal politics, was at the time uncertain of his future. He had attended the London School of Economics, had been a teacher in the Sudan, and had come to the ANU to read social philosophy. On his first day there he felt uneasy with the university's atmosphere, which he described as 'flab Lib-Lab', and with University House, and was already doubting his decision to live there when, after a few hours, he met Hawke.

> Bob was pleasantly atypical – he had an intense vitality. He was obviously a man from a wider world and was a most interesting and lively person. I thought, 'Oh, here's somebody to be friends with!' We chatted for a bit, then he turned round and shouted, 'Hizel' in that nasal, West Australian voice, and she came over. She seemed like a jolly, country girl – good humoured, with a very flat voice ... I envied Bob's sense of direction. His academic work had been of a piece, it all fitted together. He was a man following his star.

They had not long been residents in University House when, in the same week, Hazel and Verna Coleman discovered they were pregnant. Both couples had to move: from University House to the university-owned flats in Masson Street, Turner, where again, they were neighbours.

Hawke was delighted by the prospect of fatherhood and wanted his first child to be a son. 'He was so insistent about having a son that he gave the impression that Hazel's destiny in life was to be his wife and to have his son – something which I, then a bachelor, found extremely odd', a fellow scholar recalled. In January 1957 Hazel gave birth to a daughter, whom they christened Susan Edith, and called Susie. 'When we saw her we were overboard!' Hawke said. He was an extravagantly affectionate father and treated friends to descriptions of the undreamed of wonders of Susie – her first smile, the eruption of teeth, crawling. When she was about a year old he was in Melbourne and telephoned Hazel in Canberra; the person who overheard his conversation was astonished: 'He didn't even say hello to Hazel, but as soon as she answered the phone demanded, "Is Susie walking yet?"'

Hawke responded to the role of head of family with a burst of domesticity modelled on Ellie's example as a gardener. He set out to grow the best vegetables in Canberra, where the months of frosts and dry summers make the going hard. 'Supposedly it was to save money, but he treated it as a challenge and grew things that would have won prizes in a horticultural show', Coleman said.

> He used fish and vegetable compost and would go around the local fish and fruit shops collecting their detritus. It was like farming – squalid and hard work. We were fascinated to watch him spending days digging in fishheads and fishguts, out in the sun.

The Colemans were also intrigued by the periodic appearance of a local Congregational minister, who came to mow Hawke's lawn. Hazel remarked later, having observed for years the phenomenon of people eagerly offering themselves to Hawke's service, 'Bob's supporters do everything for him – except blow his nose'.

Coleman continued,

> Bob had charm, even charisma: the word was just coming into common use then. There was always a group of people around him, at the ANU usually younger students, who would do what he wanted. While I was very attracted to him I was also repelled – that is too strong a word – uneasy, about being with him when he was in his 'public figure' role, performing, being the hail-fellow-well-met centre of a fan club.

Hawke had been at the ANU only a few weeks when the position of scholar's representative, with a seat on the university council, came up for election. Coleman encouraged him to stand and 'he walked in'. Hawke was also involved in a political discussion club and played first-grade cricket. He had been a lusty, wild-hitting batsman before he left Australia; at Oxford he was described as overly confident and impatient, hooking too soon. He said, 'I had natural talent as a cricketer, but it was undeveloped until I had coaching at Oxford'. The ANU had only two first-grade cricketers playing for the Australian Capital Territory, one of them Hawke. Some observers thought that the effect of coaching had inhibited him so that now, in place of his full-blooded swipes at the ball, he was 'a bit of a prod and poke man', determined to avoid getting out but not yet master of the Zen-like cricket of England. 'In those days Australians played effective cricket; the English achieved grace', the ANU historian (and cricket buff), Manning Clark, said.

One day, however, playing for the ACT in Newcastle, Hawke had a second experience of what seemed supernatural grace:

> Something happened – I felt as if I were out of my body. I was hitting the ball and I suddenly knew that I couldn't miss it – every ball was coming straight to the bat. They changed bowlers and went through contortions to try to get me out but I just hit them and hit them – fours and sixes – until I was 78 not out. There was a New South Wales talent spotter there and he rushed over and talked about selection trials for me, said I should try out for a non-metropolitan team. I told him that wasn't me out there, it was somebody else playing. Next game I was out for a duck.

Within months of arrival in Canberra Hawke's ascendancy was established; he was, in the words of Ross Martin (later Professor of Political Science at La Trobe), 'the student star'. But in January the following year his high standing with the university establishment was swiftly and vigorously lowered.

A gathering of bishops was staying at University House on the night of a party there, at which Hawke was a guest. A professor who was host to the bishops got out of bed to complain that the noise was preventing his guests from sleeping; he ran into Hawke. There is an ornamental lily pond at University House that was known then, because of the pride Trendall took in it, as the Master's Pond. Hawke offered to throw the professor into the Master's Pond. Later that night, accompanied by a group of admirers, Hawke went swimming in it. Next day the professor lodged a complaint against Hawke with the vice-chancellor; Hawke resigned from the university council. Had he not done so he would have been dismissed.

This was only one of many escapades. 'We used to see Hazel crying', Coleman said.

> She was very supportive of Bob, you always knew that she felt he was a *special person*, that he had a great career ahead of him, and she would become upset when he was getting into scrapes that could damage his future. She used to say, 'It's Oxford all over again'. I often saw her take him to task, in a good-humoured way, about his behaviour. In those days Bob talked freely about the rows with the police he'd had at Oxford, and his great beer-drinking competition. Later he preferred not to mention those things and got angry with me for writing about them.

In Canberra Hawke became friends with two of the town's great characters: Max Newton and Dr Ron Hieser. Newton had been Hawke's verbal sparring partner at Perth Modern School and was considered along with another pupil, John Stone (who became secretary of the Treasury), to be an intellectual phenomenon. Newton had been to Cambridge and taken a First in economics and in Canberra was working as a journalist for the John Fairfax group. Hawke had not liked him at school, where Newton was known as 'a swot'; their friendship in Canberra was unstable and electric with challenge. Together with Ron Hieser, Hawke's closer friend, they drank in the back bar of the Canberra Hotel. Both Hieser and Newton had a touch of genius: Newton had a brilliant career as an economic journalist then became the publisher of a newspaper of vulgar titillation for several years before getting a new lease of life in his fifties, as one of the outstanding economic writers in the USA. Hieser worked on the development of econometrics in Australia, but became an alcoholic invalid in his fifties, and died before he turned sixty. Hieser had left school at fifteen, had various jobs, joined the Communist Party, spent five years in the AIF and was, by the late 1950s, a Left-wing member of the ALP. He already had a gargantuan appetite for liquor of all types and for argument; he was broken-hearted over the disarray within the ALP and had embraced the politics of despair – a subject over which he and Hawke constantly disagreed. He found Hawke 'completely uninterested in theory – he knew as much about Marx as the average journalist: Bob was a practical politician'. Hawke considered Hieser's despair useless and self-indulgent. Manning Clark recalled, 'They were an inseparable trio for a while. They came to play ping-pong at my house one day, rushing in together – it was like a huge snowball flying through the door – then rushed out together in a sort of ballet.' Hieser, who was eight years Hawke's senior and capable of bettering him in argument, was in the opinion of many a bad influence on Hawke.

John Knight, Hawke's old friend from Perth who had helped him win presidency of the Guild by bringing in Liberal Club votes, had also moved to Canberra and was working in the Treasury. He recalled:

I earned £28 a fortnight clear – we were all broke in those days and who ever had money spent it. One Friday in a non-pay week Bob rang me at two o'clock in the afternoon and invited me to join him and Ron Hieser in the pub. I told him I couldn't leave work. Hieser then came on the line and demanded that I come to the pub. Ron was much more aggressive than Bob – he was aggressive drunk or sober. When I told Ron I was broke he slammed the phone down. About an hour later I looked up to see Bob and Ron standing beside me, both of them in jolly spirits. 'Give us five quid', Bob said. I told him I was skint. Ron bellowed, 'Whaddya mean, you've got no money? They don't pay you enough! Where's Lennie?' *Lennie* was Lenox Hewitt [later Sir Lenox], a first assistant secretary of the Treasury. At that stage, as a base-grade clerk, I regarded class elevens as gods. My boss, Laurie Burgess [later president of the Superannuation Board] was an eleven. Burgess called me over and told me to make my friends leave the office. I pleaded with them, and after a while they disappeared. Then a bit later there was a commotion from the direction of the sanctum sanctorum, the first assistant secretary's office. Bob and Ron had gone to the men's lavatory, removed all the paper towels and rolls of lavatory paper and made a carpet with it, stretching from the lavatory, along the corridor and into the office of Hewitt's stenographer, up to Hewitt's door. They had stationed themselves there and were refusing to leave until they had spoken to Hewitt about his economic management in general and my low wages in particular. We tried threatening, then pleading, with them. It was no good. They finally left when Burgess handed over £5. It took me weeks to repay him.

Hieser was close to the Labor leader, Dr H. V. Evatt, and introduced Hawke to him, mentioning that Hawke was doing research work for the Australian Council of Trade Unions. Hawke said,

Evatt asked me, 'How can you work for the ACTU? They're the Groupers – there are Clerks [Union officials] and Ironworkers on its executive.' I replied, 'You don't avoid the ALP because there are some people in it with whom you disagree', and went on to have a violent argument. I told him I thought he was bloody mad.

Already Evatt's extraordinary memory was beginning to fail, but it was not realised then that a tragic mental decay was overtaking him. Hawke had been right: Evatt, always eccentric, was going mad.[2]

Some time after his first meeting with Evatt, Hawke and Hieser were in Melbourne together and attended a celebration in the Richmond Town Hall for the federal Member for Yarra,

Jim Cairns, who had just been awarded his doctorate. Evatt was presiding. He, Hawke, Hieser and some others moved on to the Windsor, which at that time was the leading hotel in Melbourne. Evatt, who had been a High Court judge, had another argument with Hawke, on this occasion about constitutional law. At some stage he left and Hawke and Hieser continued drinking until about 2 a.m. On the way out they came across a corridor of rooms outside the doors of which hotel guests had placed their shoes to be cleaned. 'Look how these rich bastards demean the workers!' Hawke said. He and Hieser rushed up and down the corridor rearranging all the pairs of shoes, placing brown ones with black ones, long ones with short ones, until there was not a matching pair in the corridor. When they discovered they had three odd shoes left over they threw them down the lift well.

Some months later Hawke and Hieser were again in Melbourne, drinking in a bar alongside some supporters of the National Civic Council, the body organised by B. A. Santamaria to maintain his anti-Communist campaign in the trade unions, and one closely associated with the Democratic Labor Party. The Split in the ALP was recent. Hieser and Hawke, ostensibly having a private conversation, talked loudly and provokingly about the NCC, until the other men wheeled around with their fists up. They ran out to a back lane, pursued by the NCC men, one of whom had marked down Hawke and was aiming to king-hit him. Hawke, who has never learned to box (and who abhors physical violence on principle, but when drink-taken would sometimes forget), leapt away, fell and crashed his forehead on the street, splitting open an eyebrow. The NCC men fled. Hieser took Hawke to Royal Melbourne Hospital, where the casualty doctor on duty was Chinese. Hieser said,

> Bob's presence of mind was beautiful. He was covered in blood and he looked up at the doctor and asked, 'Are you from Taiwan? Or Formosa?' The doctor murmured, 'Taiwan'. Bob cocked his good eyebrow at me and said, 'Hit by the NCC. Stitched by the Kuomintang!' Basically, Bob was strait-laced,

but he had an imp inside him which leavened the conventional lump . . . Oh, I *envied* his vitality.

Hawke's persona took on its mature form at the ANU. To male contemporaries – and the university was largely a male world – he presented the image of an excessively virile, vigorously intelligent, part-larrikin Australian mate. He was febrile in his boisterousness: indeed, a sort of fever seems to surround Hawke often when he is in company – even badinage on the telephone with friends will make him sweat. He was humorous and aggressive, and hectoring in debate. The ANU was self-consciously an intellectual meritocracy and Hawke's determination to be a winner further encouraged in him the style of an intellectual bully. Coleman said,

> He was a formidable opponent in his area of specialisation and he was very well informed on political matters, but in social philosophy he was a lightweight, and always regarded as one. Argument with Bob was not an intellectual excitement, for his intellect was limited, as were his interests – he had, for example, no interest in literature, the theatre or music, except for pop music. *Li'l Abner* and *Reedy River* were two popular musicals in those days; Bob had the records. I watched him one day play *Reedy River* about twenty times . . . It was his personality that was impressive. A strong, attractive personality.

Hawke was given to outbursts of sarcasm, or worse, when thwarted in argument. One night at a party he became so irritated by a scholar who was refusing to accept the logic of his case that he shoved her backwards into a wall, roaring, 'I'll bang some sense into you!' His friendship with Coleman was finally ruptured a few years after leaving the university when, during a night of political discussion, Hawke lost all patience with Coleman's now solid Liberal views and, according to Coleman, ordered his German shepherd dog to drive Coleman from the house. Hawke has no memory of this incident. Whatever did happen, Coleman was not bitten nor threatened by the German shepherd, with whom he was on good terms. He said,

> Hazel was almost in tears, and saying, 'Oh, Bob!' After that Bob put his arm on my shoulder and said, 'Well, Coley, we had a good barney, eh?' It was an attempt at the old winning mateyness. I don't mind a man who loses his temper. It was not his sooling the dog on to me that did it, but I realised I no longer knew the private man … [On the other hand] even at the ANU Bob had that soothing, mediator's ability that became famous later. Two of our neighbours at Masson Street, both of them academics, and one a philosopher, had a row over some domestic issue and by agreement they called Bob in to settle it for them.

Few people at the ANU glimpsed 'the carefully hidden, private Hawke' that Bob Rogers had discovered at the University of Western Australia. But older men sensed that beneath the public image there was a different personality. One such observer was a resident in University House, who often heard Hawke arriving late at night at the door of Emily Sadka, a Sephardic Jewess who had lived in Western Australia and had been to Oxford. She was about ten years Hawke's senior and was a woman of rare strength of character, visually enforced by exaggeratedly Semitic features. Conventionally ugly, her face had often, too, a sudden beauty. She died young. A friend of Sadka's recalled,

> Emily had a great sense of Biblical morality: This is Just, this is Unjust. She talked not like an orthodox Jewess but like an emancipated Jewess stepping out of the Bible. She was reticent, but at critical moments she would speak and when she did she spoke the Law of Moses. She was a retributionist: she wanted people to be punished for their sins, she demanded that they walk in the lee of Mount Sinai. Emily had an appeal to people who had a serious interest in life; she herself had a particular feeling for robust Anglo-Saxon men of intellectual quality.

Nobody imagined that Hawke and Sadka were having an affair: they were not. Her neighbour said,

> I would hear Bob whispering 'Let me in, Emily' late at night after he had spent the day boozing with his low-down friends – they could give you the low-down on anyone and were full of cynicism. Bob would come along, after that company, to Emily. It was touching how anxious he was to talk to her. I thought he was a soul in torment, looking for purification.

This observer had realised that beneath Hawke's gregarious machismo there was what Rogers had seen: a sterner character who sat in judgment and loathed the sharp operator – who was, sometimes, himself. What Hawke shared with Sadka was a system of values built upon the teachings of the Hebrew prophets: they could talk to each other in a private grammar.

One of Hawke's closest older friends – 'a bloke I loved' – was Sam Stoljar, then a Reader in Law at the ANU. Stoljar revelled in the excitement of ideas and had been on the lookout for Hawke from the time he arrived in Canberra because Professor Wheare had written from Oxford recommending Hawke to Stoljar as a man of great ability. Stoljar said,

> The flighty playboy would make fifty thousand circles around Emily's door before he would knock. Bob was not a playboy at heart. In spite of all his childishness, frivolities, pranks and drinking, and being a wild man – in spite of all these things he was sound at the core. There was a constancy to his convictions, he had a basic maturity. Along with the scandals he caused at the university – really, vastly innocent things – there was his concern for the public good. He was a man of energy, an improver of human life. To be a scholar in the ivory tower of your study required the kind of devotion that Bob does not have – all his interests led him away from the sleepier, less energetic, lazier if you like, academic's devotion. Bob had to

do things ... People recognised that he was not destined for our quiet world. One evening in a philosophy talk this question was set by the lecturer: 'On the day that Bob Hawke is Prime Minister of Australia can I say with certainty that I will still be a scholar?'

Uncertainty about the academic life had beset Hawke a few months after his arrival at the ANU, but he attacked his studies vigorously. His supervisor, Professor Geoffrey Sawer, said: 'I was very satisfied with my first PhD student – Bob was hard-working and although he would go on benders they never interfered with his academic progress'. Hawke's discontent was twofold: the unhurried pace of academic life frustrated him, and epistemologically his thesis topic was unattainable. Sawer explained:

> When Bob started his research he was sure he had a picture in his mind as to how to delineate the basic wage concept, but his great problem was that his topic was beyond the reach of anyone attempting to make a conceptual, as against a psychological, analysis of why the learned judges decided this or that. Matters he had set out to analyse simply defied analysis. The intellectual tool Bob had cultivated up till then – logic – would not serve his purposes. He simply *had* to change his topic, but it took him a long time to realise this and admit that his original vision was faulty.

Many scholars, economists in particular, have gone quietly mad with frustration or performed acrobatic leaps of sophistry in trying to apply to wage arbitration the rules of their discipline. The arbitration system is a social institution, like marriage, and can be just as wayward in rational terms. At the time Hawke was attempting, from a distance, to develop theories about its workings, the wage-fixing system was undergoing a particularly stormy and irrational period. When he finally became a part of the drama he did more than any other man, except the founder of wage fixing, Mr Justice Higgins, to force logic upon it.

A third cause of discontent with life as a student presented itself to Hawke in early 1957: he attended his first basic wage case.

At the University of Western Australia he had been inspired, he said, by an account of the career of Clarence Darrow, the great American lawyer and civil rights fighter, who had shown him 'what you could do, *against the odds*, if you were intelligent, articulate, and tough'. Rejecting the practice of law as personally offensive and morally indefensible yet moving towards a career as an academic lawyer, Hawke had suddenly, in the Arbitration Commission, come face to face with a branch of legal practice that roused his deep instincts to serve the community. Here was the real world, the practical forum where, for good or ill, human lives were affected. But he was held back on the sidelines, looking on, while barristers and Queen's Counsel argued the cases.

A roundabout path had led Hawke to the Arbitration Commission in 1957.

In mid-1956 the Australian Council of Trade Unions had called a special congress with two items on the agenda: atomic testing at Monte Bello Island and union policy on the basic wage and federal arbitration system that, under the chief judgeship of Sir Raymond Kelly, had been through a revolution.

The arbitration system had exercised three functions: it protected unionists against breadline wages; it periodically adjusted the income of unionists; it prevented and settled industrial disputes.

The protective function was fulfilled by the basic wage – the minimum that an unskilled man could be paid – that had been established in 1907 and since 1921 had been indexed for inflation. Every three months cost-of-living adjustments were made to it, automatically. The adjustments were a small, continuous check on the redistribution of income away from unionists, via price rises.

The large adjustment of income occurred at long, irregular intervals when it was widely believed that a new plane of prosperity had been reached in the nation. The primary large adjustment came through a basic wage inquiry; a secondary large adjustment occurred through a margins inquiry, the margin being that money paid for skill and added to the (unskilled) basic wage to make a single pay packet. Basic wage inquiries were marathon affairs lasting usually a year or more and occurring on average once a decade. During them arguments were made about 'the capacity of the economy to pay' and the 'needs' of a family of man, woman and 'about three children'. There was no precise way of measuring either capacity or needs; the unions on one side and the employers on the other argued for their measurements then the arbitration judges struck a compromise between them. During the Depression the arbitration system adjusted income by reducing unionists' wages by 10 per cent.

Dispute settlement, the system's third function and the only one required of it by the Constitution, took up most of its time. The prevention and settlement of industrial disputes formally occurred when 'paper' disputes over the basic wage and margins arose; very frequently real disputes arose, and these were settled by the judges and commissioners conciliating the parties or, if conciliation failed, arbitrating. If the disputants flouted arbitration they were punished. Depending upon the temperament of the federal government, arbitration judges were empowered by legislation to punish with fines, prison or banishment – that is, deregistration. Higher wage rates for a certain industry or group of workers nearly always resulted from the settlement of a dispute. Together, the system's three functions made up a fourth that, it can be argued, was its most important: it damped down the tendency to envy in the community. As the Australian Communist Party recognised more quickly than others, this softening effect of arbitration diminished the vehemence of socialism. Put crudely, the arbitration system has helped to keep radical and reform parties out of office in Australia.

The system had jogged along since 1904, always under attack from one vested interest group or another, and being respected for its activities – until 1950.

By a fluke that year a radical judge, Alf Foster, raised the basic wage from £7 to £8, an increase that by its magnitude staggered the employers and the government, and gave joy to the unions. Foster had led a mutiny on the Bench against the new chief judge, Sir Raymond Kelly. Kelly, too, was a radical, but a conservative one. Like Foster, who had been described by the press as 'the red judge', Kelly was a social engineer. He was a member of the South Australian Roman Catholic establishment, a man of gentle though authoritarian nature, eccentric and wholly well meaning. He was emotionally attracted, like Dr Colin Clark and thousands of others, to an idea that came into vogue in the late 1940s in Australia – although it was as old as the existence of cities. It was a vision of paradise regained: on a small farm, in a life of simplicity, voluntary frugality and communion with God. The mills of industry were to Kelly as dark and satanic now as they had ever been; he saw them as sucking the souls out of men's bodies.

Unlike other enthusiasts of the ideology of the National Catholic Rural Movement, however, Kelly was in a position to make changes to the lives of millions of workers. He believed that 'Foster's £1', as it was known, was a national disaster; a cause of inflation; and an encouragement for the industrial workforce to grow and, therefore, soullessness to increase. He determined to undo the damage he saw.

In 1953, in dramatic and secret circumstances, Kelly presided over a Bench of judges that revolutionised the role of the arbitration system, openly institutionalising it as manipulator of the Australian economy.[3] The coup was startlingly simple: like all coups, merely a matter of abolishing one set of rules, declaring another and establishing new managers. The Bench that year abolished automatic quarterly cost-of-living adjustments; it declared that henceforth wages – money wages not real wages, which were falling – would rise only when the economy had capacity to pay and *that* decision would be made by the managers of this new scheme for the distribution of cash, the judges in arbitration. This extraordinary power to decide upon the basic necessities of life for the workforce was vested in men who knew almost nothing about economics, not even how they could measure 'capacity to pay' in any sensible fashion or if, indeed, it was measurable. Nor were they familiar with poverty. Sociologically, the judgment was a stimulant to envy. One example: all the states except South Australia decided to maintain automatic adjustments; within three years workers under state awards were earning on average 19 shillings (just under £1) a week more than workers under federal awards, doing the same work, often in the same shop.

The 1953 decision convulsed the trade union movement. It had stripped workers of their protection against inflation – which had reached 22.5 per cent in 1951 – and had given nothing in return, except the demand for legal fees. If the unions wanted wage rises awarded in future they would have to employ a Queen's Counsel – Kelly did not care for mere barristers in his court – and hope that his arguments would persuade the judges that the economy had 'capacity to pay'. The tables had been turned for Foster's £1 and the employers gloated: they could not measure capacity to pay any more than the judges could, but the employers could scare the Bench by crying Bankrupt! And did.

As if all this were not unwelcome enough to the unions they then learned from their legal advisers that the 1953 judgment was written in such a way as to make it invulnerable to attrition. It was a monster of a document, knotted together with such ingenuity that the unions would have to persuade a future Bench to disown it *in toto*, for half measures were useless. After the unpredictable behaviour of the arbitration Bench in recent years another major swing of judicial minds would have raised the most serious questions; it was, therefore, most unlikely that the judges would have the nerve to disown the 1953 decision. The unions tried to persuade them to in 1956, and failed.

Meanwhile, the government had become alarmed by the bitterness in industrial life caused, in part, by the 1953 judgment, in part by the authoritarian and punitive atmosphere that the system breathed, under Sir Raymond Kelly. In early 1956 the government, using as its excuse the Boilermakers' Case,[4] split the Arbitration Court, removing the power to punish with fines and prison to a new body, the Industrial Court. It gave the economic functions and those for prevention and settlement of industrial disputes to another newly created institution, the Conciliation and Arbitration Commission. Mr Justice Foster, who was now seventy, believed that because of his seniority he should be made head of the Commission, but to his anger a younger judge, Richard Kirby, got the job. From the outset relations within the Arbitration Commission were strained.

Foster abhorred the 1953 judgment. Kirby, a man of more passive nature, had publicly associated himself with it, although privately the judgment embarrassed him. In 1956 Kirby presided on the Bench that refused the unions' application to overturn the 1953 decision; he presided and refused again in 1957, 1958, 1959 and 1960. Foster believed that Kirby was naive and had been tricked by Sir Raymond Kelly in 1953; that Kirby's continued support for Kelly's handiwork was caused by embarrassment and timidity. Kirby was certainly a very different chief judge[5] from his predecessor, Kelly; he described himself as 'an underdog's man' and by temperament was a peacemaker. Hawke was making his first live contact with the arbitration system in a promising new era.

The ACTU special congress of 1956 was to discuss trade union tactics on award wages in the wake of the revolution that had taken place. Hawke asked if he might attend, was welcomed, given a seat on the platform and introduced to the president, Albert Monk, and the secretary, Harold Souter. He said, 'It became clear to the executive of the ACTU that I knew more about the basic wage than anyone else in the country'. Souter, who had heard about Hawke through Horrie Brown, an ANU economist who had appeared for the ACTU in the 1950 basic wage case, invited him to assist by supplying historical and legal research for the first case to be argued, in early 1957, under the new annual system established by the Conciliation and Arbitration Commission.

Souter's invitation, however, was not the honour it might seem: then and later the stinginess of the trade union movement kept its peak council short of funds so that Souter was always on the alert for academics with a Labor movement bias who were willing to donate their expertise. He had been the ACTU research officer and advocate himself, but since moving into the secretary's job there had been no replacement. Instead the ACTU briefed a Queen's Counsel to present its cases, so that what was skimped on research was spent on fees for a silk, his junior and instructing solicitors. The ACTU advocate was Richard (later Sir Richard) Eggleston, a man whose arguments were faultless in logic and presented with exquisite lucidity of thought and whose knowledge of economics was unique in the legal profession. He was an acknowledged leader of the Melbourne Bar. For years he attempted to explain to the Bench that if 'capacity to pay' meant anything, it meant an increase in productivity. It seems strange now, when the concept is widely understood, but in the 1950s the legal profession in general greeted the terminology of economics with distrust and ridicule, inspired, one must suppose, largely by the intellectual snobbery that tends to attach to legal training. In 1950 and 1953 barristers had derided the work of Horrie Brown, who had developed an index for measuring productivity; in his 1950 judgment Kelly had dismissed Brown's work as fanciful.

Eggleston's instructing solicitor was Bob Brodney of Maurice Blackburn and Company, a firm that had advised the unions for more than thirty years and had its offices in the ACTU building, which was across the road from the Melbourne Trades Hall and next door to that other hub of trade union life, the Lygon (later the John Curtin) Hotel.

Eggleston opened the 1957 case but had to depart shortly afterwards for an employers' brief in the Privy Council, 'and that', in the words of Sir John Moore (the second president of the Conciliation and Arbitration Commission), 'was the beginning of the end of Dick Eggleston as far as the ACTU was concerned'. Eggleston left carriage of the unions' argument to his junior, who lacked Eggleston's flair and authority. Hawke sat in court during the case and recalled, 'My material was butchered by the junior! I suffered the tortures of the damned.'

Keith Hancock, another young academic whom Souter had asked to assist with economic research, said,

> Bob took a particularly severe view of the way the case was handled. In comparison, the employers' junior, Lindsay Williams, was continually feeding stuff to their silk, Drew Aird. Bob said the relationship between Eggleston and his instructing solicitor was irrelevant and totally inefficient.

In 1958 Hawke again assisted with legal and historical research for the unions' wage case and again suffered a ferment of indignation. Hancock (later professor, and vice-chancellor of Flinders University) had found Hawke:

> Well mannered and civilised. On one of his visits to Melbourne he stayed with my parents, who were most impressed by what a nice, quiet, refined boy he was. My mother was particularly charmed by him. He was obviously very intelligent and could grasp any type of argument quickly, including economic argument. I remember watching him do a very difficult crossword puzzle, full of historical and literary clues. Perhaps it's a comment on how naive I was, but Hawke seemed to me sophisticated and cultured. I later began to think he was a Jekyll and Hyde character, when I heard some of the stories about him at the ANU.

Hawke similarly puzzled the Bench of the Arbitration Commission. Kirby recalled that in 1957 and 1958 the judges had watched him and had been impressed by his enthusiasm and vitality:

> He was very fresh-faced and we thought he was only twenty-two or three. On occasions he was unable to sit still and we could see he was nearly going mad with frustration, wanting to jump up and have a say. We used to watch him with some curiosity and amusement, and wonder who this young

cove was. One day he suddenly stepped into my chambers, introduced himself as a research scholar and started asking questions as if he were entitled to, ignoring the fact that I was of judicial rank and deciding a matter that he was involved in. He had that academic's snobbery that he was entitled to badger anyone, and did so in a somewhat iconoclastic fashion, to knock you off your perch a bit. He asked what qualifications I thought each member of the Bench had for deciding very important questions of national economics. I told him we were chaps with trained minds, we picked up as much economics as we could, but I didn't go into any detail because he didn't make me feel I wanted to tell him. I went on to say that on a full Bench we did our best to work as a team, which amazed him and inclined him to ridicule. He said, 'How can you be a team, when you're talking about economics?' It was something like a confessional. Finally I told him it was no good discussing the matter any more. I thought him brash and almost rude, but the overwhelming impression was that I couldn't come to grips with him.

Besides ruffling the feathers of the chief judge, Hawke had unwittingly bumped into the internal politics of the Arbitration Commission: Kirby was *trying* to create a team, but he and Foster were not on speaking terms. The debacle of 1950 had arisen because Foster and Sir Raymond Kelly were not speaking. (A third silence between judges, in 1965, was to have the most far-reaching effect on Hawke's career – and the Australian economy.)

Meanwhile, Hawke had also prodded Kirby on that other vulnerable area – the lack of economic expertise on the Bench. It was an inauspicious first encounter for both men.

By early 1958 Hawke had collected a mass of material for his thesis, he was already a part-time lecturer in law at the Canberra University College, and he had been offered a senior lectureship at the University College, to divide his time between teaching industrial law in the Law Faculty and industrial relations in the Economics Faculty. He said, 'I had been going from one academic niche to another, it all had a logic about it, but I felt that somehow the academic life wasn't dragging out of me all that it could'. Increasingly he had been spending his time at the ACTU. Peter Coleman wrote of Hawke in this period:

> I met him in the Lygon Hotel, Melbourne, that unofficial Labor headquarters opposite Trades Hall and next to the ACTU. There, beneath faded framed pictures of old Labor leaders, present-day union officials and politicians gather to intrigue or get drunk. (The Groupers go to the Dover down the road.) Somehow we ended up at a party thrown, I think, by the Fuel and Fodder Workers' Union in Trades Hall, and after a few speeches about the old days, some songs about the Bush, the Wild West, and the Deep South, and a good deal of beer, Bob Hawke drove me home.
>
> As we shot along St Kilda Road, Hawke sat hunched grimly over the wheel peering through rimless glasses. At the Junction he swung, as it were, into orbit and without reducing speed spun around the circus about ten times looking for the right turn-off. Each time, as we sped past it, I called out, 'There it is! There!' – each time too late.[6] Then, apparently by a mixture of luck and intuition, he suddenly shot off at a tangent up the street leading to my flat. I last saw him disappearing ... at the maximum speed.
>
> Without straining things too much, the whole incident seems symbolic of Hawke at the time. Pugnacious, ambitious, full of confidence, in a hell of a hurry but not certain which way to turn and certainly not listening to anyone who wanted to advise him.[7]

One evening in mid-1958 Hawke was at an ACTU dinner in Usher's Hotel, Sydney, when late in the evening the president, Albert Monk, came over to him and put an arm around his shoulders. 'Albert was a man who erected big fences

around himself. He didn't want close friends, he didn't want intimacy – he was frightened of it', Hawke said.

> But when he'd had a fair bit to drink he would relax. And
> when he did make an intimate gesture, because it was so
> unusual, it had a strong impact. So, he put his arm around
> me and what he said came out of the blue:
> 'We'd like you to be our research officer. What about it?'
> It seemed as if suddenly everything was falling into place, as
> if it were a culmination of all that had gone before, so that,
> in an inexorable way, everything had been leading up to
> that moment: I knew more about the basic wage system than
> anybody else. I was uniquely well equipped to do the job.

He was to work for about two years at the ACTU, preparing
and arguing wage cases in the Arbitration Commission; Monk and
Souter presumed that after that he would return to academic life.
Their plan was that he should act as a bellwether for the unions
among other academic lawyers and economists. Souter said,

> We envisaged that we'd employ him for a couple of years,
> then replace him with someone else from the universities and
> in time would build up a group of academics who were inter-
> ested in and sympathetic to us, and that they would spread
> knowledge of wages arbitration throughout the university
> system.

Capturing Hawke, domesticating him and setting him to work
was to become the fierce obsession of many people; many of
them have been disappointed, at least in their original hopes.
Souter, who had persuaded Monk to hire Hawke, was soon to
discover that he eluded control.

Although Hawke was certain that the ACTU job was his destiny, he did not accept immediately. Instead he began a process
that, at other important times in his life, he was always to repeat:
he lobbied, he built up a power base of supporters, so that when

he left the ANU he did so on an indefinable but strength-giving cloud of others' hopes and good wishes. He succeeded, too, in persuading Sawer that he should be re-awarded a fellowship to complete his doctorate when the ACTU sojourn was over. Sawer said:

> He asked my advice about the ACTU job, saying it was the sort of work he would love doing and that, living in the atmosphere of unions, he could be even more effective than Eggleston. I believed that had Bob gone to the Bar he would have made a brilliant jury advocate, and in my opinion, the Arbitration Commission *needed* a jury advocate. I urged him to take it.

There were many other scholars whom Hawke infused with enthusiasm for the prospect of his new role; Sawer and they shared an opinion that working for the unions would be a ladder into politics for Hawke. 'It was exciting', Coleman said, 'to know somebody who was spoken of as a future prime minister'. The university community believed it was watching a drama unfold towards a denouement that they, the select, knew in advance.

For their part Monk and Souter had successfully lobbied the rest of the ACTU executive to accept Hawke. Their efforts were necessary because at the time the great influx of manual workers' children into universities – the 'gentrification', as it has been called, of the working class – had not begun and trade union circles were proudly anti-academic. Higher education was both frightening and cause for derision; the blue-collar ethos laid down that things working class and union were so unknown and unimaginable to an educated man from the middle class as to be beyond his comprehension or sympathy. The words 'intellectual' and 'academic' were often pejoratives for which 'pooftah' or 'pansy' could be synonyms. Hawke, aged twenty-eight, with education from three universities, never having earned his living – by union standards – in his life, was an astonishing employee for the ACTU. In his twenty-one years with that organisation he never completely overcame the class prejudice that first greeted him; initially, it was a prejudice of the Right.

When his appointment was announced the pubs buzzed with curiosity, scepticism and some loud ridicule about the outsider. Tom Dougherty, an old enemy of Monk and the mogul of the giant Australian Workers' Union (which was still not affiliated with the ACTU and had attempted to murder it at birth), scoffed in his union's journal 'From Eggleston to Egghead'. Doubts about Hawke's capacity to represent the tribe were such that the ACTU executive became nervous and established advisory panels of unionists to help him. Then Mr Justice Foster, who was to be one of the three judges Hawke would face in his first big case, sent word to Monk that he was much displeased about the change of advocates. Foster had not decided a basic wage case since 1950; he wanted, as he explained later, to overturn the 1953 decision but for that to happen he needed arguments to be presented to him with the utmost authority and persuasion. He wanted Eggleston, not some young man who was not even a barrister but had been plucked from a university course. Monk decided that, after all, Eggleston had better be the advocate. But Souter and some Left-wing members of the executive had become convinced that Hawke could and should present the case. After a couple of weeks of uncertainty, their view prevailed.

Hawke's test was to attempt what Eggleston had failed to achieve in three years of trying: to slay the monster of 1953.

For a boy raised on David and Goliath it was the perfect start to a career.

TEN

T HE LIVING REPRESENTATIVE of Hawke's enemy was the
chief judge in industry, Richard (later Sir Richard)
Kirby, president of the Conciliation and Arbitration
Commission. Kirby was the only judge sitting in 1959 who had
sat on the notorious Bench of 1953. He had chosen for this
year's basic wage case himself, Alf Foster and Frank Gallagher,
the latter a judge who had never before sat on a basic wage case,
and who did not share Foster's radical social views. Gallagher,
therefore, could be relied upon to side with Kirby. It followed
that Hawke's main task was to persuade Kirby to see the wrong-
headedness of the 1953 judgment and of his decisions to uphold
it in 1956, 1957 and 1958. But instead of persuasion Hawke
mounted an assault of unparalleled aggressiveness upon the
chief judge's actions.

'He is a man', Kirby said, 'of religious fervour'.

If the ranks of Gideon have to be slaughtered he will up and
into 'em, boots and all. He has a great religious strength inside:
there's something in Bob that makes him give everything he's
got, and he's just not a practical bloke ... He would not try to
persuade. He characterised me as a villain and a fool for the
1953 decision and for refusing to go back on it since then, and
he wanted confession and repentance. He hectored me. He
knew his case inside out – Gar Barwick is the only other cove
I've known who speaks from knowledge the way Bob Hawke
does. But Barwick was a great persuader. Bob just couldn't
bring himself to think, 'How can I persuade these judges to

go my way?' It was an underlying streak of puritanism in him: I had to change my mind and into the bargain admit I had been a bloody fool and a crook as well. He could have said, 'You can be pardoned for suspending the automatic adjustment system in 1953, but you should restore it as soon as you can, and it doesn't matter, Your Honour, about the subtle philosophy, just do the practical thing now, be pragmatic'. That's what a good advocate at the Bar would have come out with. Eggleston aside, I'd rank Bob Hawke above any of the silks who appeared before us, but he employed bad tactics. It's part of the honesty of the man, of course – he would not tell a lie, he would not pretend he thought I was a decent chap and those decisions of mine had been an aberration. He was determined to rub my nose in the dirt. If only he'd shown me a way that we could get out of that '53 decision, how we could rationalise it.

The Commission in those days was housed on the rising slope of Little Bourke Street, directly across the road from the High Court. It was a modern informal court: the building was new, the courtrooms appointed with nondescript pale timber furnishings, the judges and barristers wore neither wigs nor robes. Hawke made his first appearance, highly strung, restless in his gestures, continually pacing as he addressed the Bench above him, rolling on the sides of his shoes, gesticulating, swivelling his eyeballs to show impatience and flicking his eyebrows up and down as if they were attached to strings. 'He danced on his brief', a barrister said. Hawke was in the continuous motion of high nervous energy, his body language intensifying the message of his speech, all delivered in a rat-a-tat-tat of sentences bursting at up to 220 words a minute – too fast for all but the best shorthand writers – and in a very loud voice. It was said that union officials several blocks away in the Trades Hall could hear his submissions. But while there was an appearance of informality in the court, traditions died hard. The judges were used to, and expected, deference from advocates. Even Foster, the radical, had complained bitterly when the system was split in two in 1956 and powers of punishment were removed to the Industrial Court: 'They can throw inkwells at us and we'll be powerless to stop them!' Hawke's attacks upon Kirby and other judges of the cases from 1953 to 1958 would have, a few years earlier, had him put out of court, at the least; Kelly would have jailed him for contempt. Kirby and Gallagher were scandalised by Hawke; Foster, fighting with Kirby, abhorring the 1953 decision and regarding himself 'as the godfather of any union man who appeared before us', was delighted. Foster had a mane of white hair and eyebrows described as better than Menzies'; beneath them his dark eyes flashed with pleasure as he listened to Hawke attacking the chief judge.

On the first day of the case Foster had begun the morning by sniping at Hawke; before four o'clock that afternoon he was actively barracking for him from the Bench. The hostility between Foster and Kirby was obvious to all those in court and increased the pain that Hawke's arguments were causing the president of the Commission, but Hawke did not soften. He showed in that case a pattern of behaviour that was consistent throughout his career as an advocate and as a politician: he fought without mercy until he had won; as soon as defeat was conceded he became magnanimous; he would not humiliate a conquered enemy.

Throughout the 1950s the employers had used as a witness a businessman and company secretary, R. P. Truman, whose evidence had been the bane of the unions. Early in the case Hawke claimed he would in due course discredit Truman's evidence, to which Kirby remarked, 'Mr Truman . . . can always very ruggedly defend himself', to which Hawke replied, 'We'll see about that'. His attack on Truman was devastating, demonstrating that what he said now, and had said for years, was wrong. Truman's word was left supported by only one shred of evidence – figures that he said he had checked with the Commonwealth Bank. During a lunch adjournment Hawke rang the bank and discovered that Truman's claim was inaccurate. Kirby, now embarrassed, said the bank's statement ought to be authenticated. Hawke offered to do this by calling the bank official to whom he had spoken.

At this, the employers' advocate, Drew (later Mr Justice) Aird announced that Hawke's word was sufficient. Aird had realised that his witness's evidence was fallacious, as Hawke said it was, and was admitting defeat. Truman would never again be used as a witness. But Foster wanted the employers – and by extension, Kirby – publicly humiliated and demanded that Hawke go ahead and call the bank official. To Foster's anger, Hawke refused.

At the ANU Hawke had become friendly with the economist Horrie Brown, who had helped the ACTU for a decade and had spent a week in the witness box during the 1953 case under such strain that he had later suffered a heart attack. It was Brown who had recommended to Souter that the ACTU employ Hawke. Brown was an extremely gentle, softly spoken man, loved by all who knew him. 'He was my mentor', Hawke said. Before the case began Hawke spent hours with him, mastering the concepts of productivity measurements. Brown was not well enough to be a witness himself but he put Hawke in contact with another academic economist, Eric (later Professor) Russell of Adelaide University, who was. A third economic adviser for Hawke was Wilf Salter, an old friend from the University of Western Australia. Together the three men spent hundreds of hours with Hawke, teaching him economics. 'It was like having a university degree course in a matter of weeks. It is impossible to state adequately the assistance those blokes gave me – I just could not have done what I did without them', Hawke said.

Hawke probably knew no more economics than Eggleston, but Eggleston was a full member of the legal fraternity and a sort of mental huff had overtaken the arbitration judges at the idea that a legal brother could speak with authority on something that they did not understand. The Bench had consistently refused to allow Eggleston to put economic arguments to it. Suddenly, with Hawke – a legal outsider who, since he was not a barrister, was not entitled to and was never accorded the polite address of 'Learned Friend' – the reasons for objecting to economic arguments from the Bar table vanished. There was no discussion: Hawke simply stood in court and addressed the judges as both a legal and economic expert. And from him, they accepted it. It was an extraordinary change, and the first step to winning his case and to bringing logic to bear on wage fixation.

Besides demanding that automatic quarterly adjustments be reinstated, Hawke's brief also demanded that the basic wage be increased for gains in productivity. He hammered at the judges that productivity was a substitute for the nebulous term 'capacity to pay'; he produced evidence that since 1953 productivity had increased by 10 per cent and that therefore real wages ought to have increased 10 per cent. Instead, real wages had fallen by 5 per cent. Foster, who had little idea of what productivity was at the beginning of the case, was intrigued and continually interjected with questions. Kirby, for the first time understanding the enormity of the effect upon unionists of the 1953 decision, was appalled. He said,

> Bob did something that Eggleston was never able to do. He belted economic understanding into our heads. He stood there and lectured us for hours, like a schoolmaster, which I must say I did not like. Until then I'd shared the general view that productivity was a combination of efficiency and co-operation – an untidy sort of thing. He galvanised my interest in economics; I became determined to learn as much about it as I could. While I was seething with resentment against him, and spurred into hostility with Alf Foster at the time, Hawke had made me realise with his economic arguments that we had not only allowed wages to fall behind prices, but also that we had allowed them to fall behind capacity, which was the very basis of our decision.

Kirby could not bring himself to overturn the 1953 decision, but Hawke had persuaded him to take a critical step towards reform: he decided that the basic wage must be increased to at least the level it would have been had automatic adjustments not been cancelled. Foster wanted the reintroduction of automatic adjustments and an increase in the basic wage of £1 (20 shillings).

Gallagher, as expected, sided with Kirby in refusing automatic adjustments, and wanted to increase the basic wage by only 10 shillings. Kirby struck a deal: the judges increased the basic wage by 15 shillings, bringing it to 2 shillings more than if the old system had not been ruined.

It was a magnificent victory for Hawke, and instantly established him with the trade union rank and file as a brilliant advocate. He had arrived in the wage-fixing arena at the luckiest of moments: the Arbitration Commission was not yet three years old; the conceptual underpinnings of wage fixation were in need of reform; he had a chief judge open to rational argument and vulnerable to the plight of 'the underdog'; and, most importantly, the economy was surging ahead in the great wave that had swelled up at the end of the war and was rolling forward – to crash, in 1974.

Hawke had only a few weeks' respite before his next case began. This was the first margins case to be heard for five years. It was particularly challenging, because for the first time Hawke was 'getting right up to the work face', as he put it: learning what actually happened in shops. His brief had two strands: that the economy had 'capacity to pay' and that because the arbitration system had kept margin awards artificially low for several years (Kelly's influence, again), a parallel system of over-award payments had sprung up and spread, and that therefore the Commission ought to be realistic and award to unionists 'the going rate'.

For evidence about 'the going rate' Hawke produced more than a dozen union officials as witnesses; among them were John Ducker, then a lowly organiser for the Iron Workers, and Cliff Dolan, from the Electrical Trades Union. 'The long-haired intellectual', as Hawke was still characterised, impressed Dolan with his confidence in dealing with senior opposing counsel and his trade union witnesses. They became friendly. No friendship sprang up between Hawke and Ducker, although Ducker was one of Hawke's most effective witnesses. He said,

If there was an option open to John between drawing a long bow or a short one, he went for the long bow every time. He was a dedicated winner – tough and hard and aggressive, and he obviously had a future, though at the time he was a very minor figure.

Ducker, who was born in Yorkshire and spoke with a strong, expressive accent, had in due course the power to do more than most to nobble Hawke. If Ducker had had his way Hawke would not have become president of the ACTU. Later, Ducker helped to save Hawke's political life.

The employers' advocate in the 1959 margins case was Cliff (later Mr Justice) Menhennitt, a Queen's Counsel and an aggressive barrister. He and Hawke quickly established a dislike for each other and their submissions and cross-examinations became punctuated with snarling and snapping. Hawke won another major victory in the margins case, securing an increase in awards of 28 per cent.

His success in the two cases made him in the eyes of the trade union movement a phenomenon. Another employers' barrister, Jim (later Mr Justice) Robinson, said, 'He had the reputation of being a giant killer. The results he had put on the board in the two cases of '59 were unbelievable in terms of what had gone on since 1952–53.'

Hawke was treated as a celebrity in trade union circles. Officials now referred to 'the brilliant advocate'; his Rhodes scholarship became a matter of communal union pride, and Hawke tactfully stopped revealing his scorn for Cecil Rhodes and Rhodes scholars; his string of degrees was remarked upon with a certain puzzled favour instead of derision. Suddenly, employing 'an intellectual', as the trade union movement and industrial journalists insisted on describing Hawke, seemed an interesting idea. Jim Baird, the industrial officer of the Amalgamated Metal Workers and Shipwrights Union, who at the time was a research officer for the militant Boilermakers' Society, recalled,

Bob was the only person I knew in the trade unions at a national level who had any tertiary education at all. He set out to introduce into the trade union movement arguments about economics. Looking back, it was economics of a modest level, but I can understand why: few people knew what economics was in those days. We [the Left] saw him as a good thing ... There was a tradition in the trade union movement of making assertions and allegations, but we'd run into people who had tertiary education, who required us to *prove* our claims. And that was where the change in trade union thinking started to take place. It was one of the things Bob was able to do for the trade union movement: he made union arguments logical, reasonable and provable. He didn't always win, but he set in train that process. The days of wild assertions have gone.

Thanks to Hawke's successes, within a few years individual trade unions began to employ their own 'intellectuals' – either men and women with university training or tradesmen who were taken 'off the tools' and given time to read and think. This trend would probably have occurred anyway; it is certain that Hawke's example encouraged it, and that as advocate he gave to the Australian trade union movement something of as much value as money: a bold reinterpretation of ideas.

The employers were aghast at Hawke's success. He had persuaded the Commission to increase the national wages bill by £130 million – or £150 million, as the *Sydney Morning Herald* editorial writers said, or perhaps £165 million, as Peter Coleman claimed in the *Observer* – and was quickly dubbed Mr Inflation. The Commonwealth Treasury was known to be furious with the Commission. In the basic wage case of 1960, the Commonwealth, represented by Eggleston, departed from its practice of presenting neutral economic evidence and openly opposed the unions' case, saying that a wage increase would cause curtailment of plans for industrial expansion, weaken the confidence of overseas investors and cause a rapid spiralling of costs and prices. Hawke, who was asking for a 22-shilling increase in the basic wage, was so stunned by Eggleston's submission that he momentarily thought he had misunderstood it. When his former teacher replied that indeed the government stood against him, with the employers, Hawke snapped, 'This has never been done before'.

The Commission awarded an increase of only 5 shillings; it refused quarterly adjustments.

Hawke took the decision as a bitter defeat. He said,

In 1959 the judges had been malleable. Suddenly the dead hand of Menzies' conservatism descended. I was very crooked on the Commission for the 1960 decision, crooked on the system . . . I'd been in the centre of Labor politics. I think the 1960 decision was a factor in drawing me to the Left.

Left and Right, applied to the trade union movement, are terms which came into use from the late 1950s, to replace the earlier categories of Grouper and anti-Grouper. It is impossible to give a watertight definition of Right – people, and unions, could be Right on most issues but Left on others – but, in the broad, the Right was the child of the Groupers plus all those who so disapproved of the Communist Party (although they may have been anti-Grouper) that they supported the Menzies Government's strident anti-Communism. The Right of the trade union movement stretched from the NCC and the DLP to the centre of the ALP. The Left was everyone else. But in Victoria the Left was Lefter: radical and militant. Hawke's style fitted the Left (although the further Left disliked not only the workings of the Arbitration Commission, but also its very existence, and logically should have disapproved of Hawke as part of 'the system'). From the time he joined the ACTU, the Left treated him with interested curiosity, then support, then wild enthusiasm. He was for the Left a positive, progressive force. The Right, natural xenophobes – their political ancestors had invented the White Australia policy – thought of him as an outsider and therefore dangerous. After 1959 the Right treated

Hawke with grudging admiration. His defeat of 1960 brought them *schadenfreude*. On a personal level the Right found Hawke's lack of deference to the Bench improper and destabilising of a system that they supported though often disagreed with, but again on a personal level many Right-wing union leaders were vulnerable to Hawke's charm. However, once Hawke had been marked by the Left as *their* man he was fair game for the Right, for the two power blocs battled for territory continually. Hawke, always anxious to belong to a social group, was drawn into the embrace of the Left.

By the early 1960s there were widespread rumours that he was a Communist. Even Ellie got to hear of them and, on a trip to Melbourne, took her son aside to ask if he had become a Communist. Hawke was so irritated that he replied only, 'I'm not a card-carrying member'. In some of the employers' ranks a canard circulated that Hawke, a crypto-Communist, had as his real aim the shattering of the capitalist system – which he would accomplish by bankrupting it with wage increases. David McBride, who became a member of the Industries Assistance Commission after many years as industrial advocate for the Electrical Trades Union, recalled that an employers' represent-ative said to him, 'When I saw you and Bob Hawke kicking a football at lunchtime I realised he was just a human being. I'd thought he was a Com.' The man went on to make it clear he had considered Hawke a manifestation of evil. Throughout Hawke's career this theme of evil was to recur as people projected their fears on to him.

They were able to do this, in part, because of the intensity, 'the religious fervour', of Hawke's nature. When he had moved to the ACTU he had finally broken the psychological bonds of theism and Congregationalism; the spiritual struggle that had begun in adolescence was over. 'It was soon after I moved to Melbourne', he recalled, 'that I realised: "I am an agnostic".'

The trade union world has always been for the most committed of its members 'a religion'; Hawke entered it with the fervour of a convert. It was a slight change in emphasis only for the excessively combative Christian scholar to become the excessively combative rescuer of the workers – fired up, in 1960, by the indignation of defeat.

Increasingly, Hawke espoused the causes of the Left. In trade union circles he supported unity tickets – that is, Labor candidates and Communists standing together for election to union office. In ALP circles, which for historical reasons were more venomous and personal in Victoria than in other states, Hawke associated himself with the Left's position of anti-Americanism and a belief in a whole range of demons: the CIA, Santamaria, the Australian Security Intelligence Organisation (which he believed, as did others, had opened a file on him), class enemies, and, of course, Archbishop Mannix, who during the 1958 election campaign had achieved new heights for the rhetoric of guilt-by-association with his declaration: 'every Communist and every Communist sympathiser in Australia wants a victory for the Evatt Party'. Hieser recalled, 'When we drove past Raheen, Mannix's residence, Bob shook his fist and roared at it'.

Kirby, who already greatly admired Hawke's mind, recalled that he was acutely embarrassed by him around this period when, one night at a dinner party given by the United States consul general, Hawke and some trade unionists were openly contemptuous of their surroundings. The consul general's residence had a splendidly appointed dining room, with Aubusson carpets and other sumptuous fittings. Kirby said,

> The present Bob Hawke would be interested in them as civilised appurtenances, but then he and the other union fellows were contemptuous, almost swaggeringly rude, making snide remarks to each other in voices that were easily overheard. I'd been to numerous functions of that rather grand nature with trade union teams and they had always behaved properly. The next day the consul general rang me and in the course of conversation said, 'I hope I did not offend your young companions'. I apologised for them.

At another dinner Hawke shouted at Kirby's wife when she could not, momentarily, recall Hazel's name. He saw Kirby at the time, he said, 'as the big chief judge, the member of the Establishment', and once, when drunk, bailed up Lady Kirby to demand, 'Why does your husband hate me?'

Ralph Willis, who in late 1959 joined the ACTU as research assistant, recalled that Hawke was brusque and initially intimidating and that nothing in his behaviour suggested that he was the darling son of a devout household. But, as usual, older men knew intuitively that Hawke's gentle side could be evoked by a fatherly approach. In the trade union movement one such man was Jock Innes, who met Hawke in the Lygon Hotel just after he had begun work at the ACTU and 'took me under his wing'. Innes used to refer to Hawke as 'my other son'. His real son was Ted, one of Hawke's boon companions, then an official of the Electrical Trades Union, later a federal parliamentarian. In the Arbitration Commission Hawke attracted another father figure: Mr Justice Foster.

During the 1959 basic wage case Foster sent a note to Hawke asking for a meeting when the case was over. Foster lived three minutes walk away from Hawke, in Sandringham, and a regular Sunday morning visit from the advocate to the judge was established. While Innes, Terry Winter and other senior trade union men had taken it upon themselves to educate Hawke in union lore, explaining to him the complexity of alliances and rivalries, Foster performed the same function for Hawke about the arbitration system. Hawke said,

Alf had a very considerable affection towards me, and an enormous sense of gratitude. The first thing he said when I went to his house was how thrilled he was that I had understood the disastrousness of the 1953 judgment and had been so astringent in my analysis of it. He regarded it as his mission to change that judgment, and he had thought it was going to be a pretty lonely mission. Then I turned up.

When Foster learned from Hawke that Dr Colin Clark had rejected his thesis subject, the old man was gleeful. He told Hawke something of which he had been unaware during the 1959 case: 'That Clark was the economic guru to Santamaria. And that Santamaria had *worn the carpet thin* – Alf's exact phrase – going in and out of Sir Raymond Kelly's office before the 1953 case!'

When in 1961 Hawke returned to his assault upon the 1953 judgment he did so with the fire of avenging a personal injury. It was one of his greatest performances, in Australia, as an advocate.

Hawke's instant success in his career and his need to become one with the trade union brotherhood was achieved, predictably, at the expense of his family life.

He and Hazel, because of their small-town backgrounds, had felt nervous about living in a city as large as Melbourne. They decided it would be more enjoyable if they lived near the water, and if they had their own house. Hawke made it a condition of joining the ACTU that he be lent the deposit for buying a house. Harold Souter, the ACTU secretary, recalled, 'Bob was amazing for a lawyer. He just looked at the contract and said, OK. It was Hazel who did all the bargaining.' It was Hazel who did everything – she was the foundation of Hawke's support system. She said, 'He had a very difficult job ahead of him and I was determined there would be no chink in his armour'.

Within a few days they had bought a cottage in Keats Street, Sandringham, a pleasant but then unfashionable bayside suburb, half an hour's drive from the city. They were too much in debt to afford a refrigerator or furniture, even a bed, and slept on a mattress on the floor. Hazel made cupboards, bookshelves and a wardrobe out of appleboxes; she bought a second-hand stove for £7 from which she was still scrubbing grease in February 1959 when their second child, Stephen, was born. Ted Innes, an electrician by trade, rewired the house; Wally Curran, of the Meat Employees Union, laid concrete – an ironic fact, for by 1971 Hawke and Curran detested each other.

School aside, Hawke's childhood had been devoted to a life of games and religion and he never developed the practical skills of boyhood – carpentry, mechanical understanding, a basic knowledge of physics and management of finance. His only domestic skill was gardening and, when he was older, some cooking. Unless a piece of machinery fed the imagination – like an aeroplane, or a yacht (Hawke learned to sail) – it bored him, so much so that at the age of fifty he would stand squinting and puzzled at the printed instructions on the lid of an automatic washing-machine or some other electrical appliance, as if at a script written in Greek. He never paid household bills, or concerned himself about his overdraft or tried to administrate – even to getting his newspapers delivered – as long as there was someone around to do it for him. Jean Sinclair, his personal assistant in later years at the ACTU, became so used to Hawke's complaints that filing cabinets were stuck or electric kettles did not work or addresses were lost that she would wonder aloud sometimes how he managed to dial a telephone.

Hawke's major foray into the handyman field while at Keats Street was to build a carport: he cubed instead of squared the quantities of sand and cement he would need and for weeks afterwards the pavement was blocked by a sand dune. 'If he built a hen-house it would fall down!' Hieser exclaimed, not quite accurately for Hawke went on to assemble a splendid aviary for Susan (after Hazel had shown him how). But that was a labour of love, and for living things. Hieser's brother-in-law, Bill Mansfield, the CSIRO chemist famous for discovering a way to prevent evaporation from dams, built Hawke a fence.

From the day Hawke began work at the ACTU his family life became, he said, 'unusual'. He had to work extremely long hours; to overcome the prejudice against him and to make himself as effective as possible as an advocate he needed to rub shoulders with unionists. This meant spending hours yarning and joking in the smokey, smelly, red-linoed and cream-walled 'Trades Hall office' – the Lygon Hotel. He was rarely home. The running of the household and raising of the children fell almost entirely to

Hazel. She was a skilful manager and liked the traditional role of mother and chatelaine, although as she said later, 'No one will ever know how difficult it was'. It was to become more difficult. By the time his children were teenagers Hawke was so overcommitted to work and to his vast network of relationships that his family had to arrange appointments to be able to discuss problems with him. But in his early years at the ACTU part of Sunday, at least, was a family day and throughout the summer months Hawke, Innes, Mansfield, and David White (another research scientist) together with their spouses and children, played tennis and had barbecues.

White, later a professor at Melbourne University, recalled, 'Bob was out to win at tennis. You'd be walking back from the net towards the base line when his next ball would come whizzing past your head.'

At the time Hawke joined the ACTU its public image was at best sketchy. There were two full-time officials, Monk and Souter, and an executive that was elected at biennial congresses and made up of trade union leaders drawn from the state trades and labour councils and various industry groups. The trades and labour councils, which mesh with state Labor Party machines and are in some states the real centres of ALP power and patronage, operate as the state branches of the ACTU. Monk and Souter aside, the members of the executive owed allegiance first to their unions or trades and labour councils. The ACTU was a body for residual loyalty.

Against the bitter opposition of the huge, sprawling Australian Workers' Union, the trade union movement had created the ACTU in 1927 as a co-ordinating instrument; a negotiator during major strikes; and as a national representative of the movement to government, to overseas union groups, to the International Labour Organization, and so forth. Its single constitutional objective is: 'The socialisation of industry, i.e. production, distribution and exchange', an aim to which it has merely paid lip service. The union movement in Australia is highly fragmented; constantly distracted and enervated by Left–Right power struggles and intra-bloc rivalries; jealous; underfinanced; and used to an easy life – in the sense that in the twentieth century it was protected by the arbitration system from the protracted wars with employers that are waged in a collective bargaining system. Under collective bargaining a union must have the funds to pay its members to strike for three months at a stretch;[1] in Australia the majority of strikes last only a day. The ACTU was then and still is only of sporadic use to unions. They kept it broke by paying tiny fees for its upkeep, and in non-congress years often not paying at all. The ACTU is an inherently weak organisation, with no machinery for enforcing its decisions upon its affiliated unions. Its authority springs from the moral force of solidarity – with the occasional trip or plum job, arranged through a trades and labour council or the Conciliation and Arbitration Commission, to reward an especially helpful union official or to get rid of a mischievous one. But in the main it is powerless to give patronage or to punish, except with public shaming and isolation from the rest of the trade union movement.

Albert Monk, a great and very astute man in Australian industrial life, kept the organisation going and prevented an outright split in the movement in the 1950s – when the ALP split – by a combination of diplomacy, cunning and stubbornness. The Grouper unions, like the ironworkers, clerks and shop assistants, were not expelled nor encouraged to leave the ACTU voluntarily, because of Monk's determination to keep the movement whole.

He had the short rotund figure and round pudding face of a music-hall grocer; he wore pebble-lens spectacles, had a wall eye, and mumbled. Monk's manners were old fashioned and rather courtly, particularly with women whom, as a breed, he found intimidating. He disliked publicity and hated appearing on television.

Monk was committed body and soul to the trade union movement, to getting a fair deal for the working class. He had come to Australia from England at the age of eight, in 1908; at his roughneck school he had been abused and beaten up for his appearance and his accent. The unemployment of the 1930s burned an ineradicable fear into his mind – 'For Albert the Depression ended the day he died'[2] – and from then on he did all in his power to prevent its recurrence; this meant increasing the productive capacity of the Australian economy and, from 1949, co-operating with anti-Labor governments to achieve their economic goals. In 1956 the wharfies publicly denounced him as 'a scab' and 'Holt's Holiday Home Boarder' (Harold Holt being the Minister for Labour). Monk was highly strung, although this rarely showed in his enigmatically bland appearance. Before congresses his hands would tremble and his whole body seemed to shake with nervousness until the moment when he took the platform to give his presidential address, which he delivered in an inaudible mumble, to awed silence. Monk ran the congresses dictatorially: any motion of which his executive disapproved he ruled lost on the voices, and left it up to the floor to demand a division. By the 1960s he was an alcoholic and would make ten or more quick forays each day out of the back door of the ACTU and into the Lygon for a nip of whisky. He had a thousand acquaintances but few intimates, although many men who worked closely with him held Monk in loving admiration, and all respected him.

Monk left the administration of the ACTU entirely to Souter. The secretary, unlike Monk who had never been a blue-collar worker but had started his career as a shorthand writer, had been a fitter by trade and had risen through the ranks to become in the 1940s the industrial advocate of the militant Amalgamated Engineering Union, sire of the Amalgamated Metal Workers and Shipwrights Union. Souter came from a South Australian Seventh Day Adventist background and remained a teetotaller and non-smoker; he drank neither tea nor coffee. His wholesome regime showed in his appearance: he was small, lithe and energetic. Even in his sixties he had a bright-eyed, boyish air that went well with his salty, though decorous, turn of phrase. Souter's integrity was a byword in industrial life, as was his commitment to the movement. In the 1960s when the giant Australian Workers' Union was negotiating affiliation with the ACTU Souter drank two whiskies with the AWU bossman, Tom Dougherty – who regarded other liquids as fit only for bathwater or for babies – and the next day was blinded with headache. He had a thankless task in running an organisation that was always under-financed and understaffed, and that he had taken on without training in administration when the previous secretary, Reg Broadby, was dying. In the twenty years Souter was secretary of the ACTU employees and executive members complained frequently that he was secretive and refused to delegate. He was an administrator who finely constricted his own life and sought to constrict the lives of others. Being teetotal was an immense social disadvantage to him in the trade union world, with its obsession with the idea of 'a man's man', defined and revealed in the boozy, tactile fraternity of the pub. 'A sarsparilla drinker', (Sir) Jack Egerton said of Souter, his voice thick with disdain. Souter was all fastidiousness: alert, clear-eyed, clean and lean – an alien. His relationship with Hawke was, from the outset, uncomfortable.

Until 1952 the ACTU had been housed in a nook in the Melbourne Trades Hall, a Victorian elephant of a building with Doric columns, four-and-a-half-metre ceilings and a wholly impractical internal distribution of space. In 1952 it moved across the road into a two-storeyed red brick box of its own, with a flat roof and floors so badly laid that in the upper storey they rose and fell in waves. There was no furniture upstairs and Hawke at first had a cubby hole with a desk and telephone on the ground floor. His arrival brought the staff to six – Monk and Souter, their secretaries, and a junior, Jennie McAlpine – and upset their tiny, cosy nest. McAlpine recalled,

> The whole atmosphere changed when Bob arrived, and even before he arrived. We all worked at ordinary desks, but Harold said now that The Young Man was coming the women would have to have modesty boards on the fronts of their desks, so that The Young Man wouldn't look at our legs.

McAlpine was to work for Hawke, but when he moved upstairs, through lack of space on the ground floor, Souter 'would not allow me to move up, too, because we would be alone together'. McAlpine was a teenager and a devout Baptist; from the outset Hawke treated her like a kid sister and renamed her Susie, after his daughter. 'Susie' McAlpine had never tasted alcohol and when, towards Christmas in 1958, the other secretaries planned to introduce her to drink, Hawke wrote her an *Ode to a Plot*, which ran in part

> But even worse now comes to light
> They plan to get young Susie tight
> Who is to blame for this foul plot
> To turn young Sue into a sot?
> The temptress holder of the evil apple
> None other than our Tessy Chapple ...
> [who worked for Souter]
> But Susie now has been forewarned
> Before the evil day has dawned
> Now these females cannot harm her,
> Saved by her knight in shining armour.

He signed it, The Knight.[3]

Despite Hawke's chivalrous attitude to 'Susie', Souter remained suspicious, for Hawke's reputation for wenching was already known. A few months later Souter threatened them both with the sack for working alone together (on preparation of the 1959 basic wage case) on a Sunday. Bad feeling between Hawke and Souter was now firmly established, and was to grow. The atmosphere in the ACTU office, which had been good-natured, turned sour; by the time Ralph Willis joined the staff a year later there was 'a very unpleasant atmosphere in the place'.

'Susie' left the ACTU in 1962 to get married, but she continued to visit the office, to chat and show off her children. In the late 1960s she went to tell Hawke some terrible news. She said,

We'd been talking for a while when Bob said, 'What have you really come to tell me, Susie?' and I broke down and told him that I had been diagnosed as suffering multiple sclerosis. He came round to me and put his arms around me, then he got very angry. He said, '*Why you?* You've done nothing wrong in your life! You've been a churchgoer, you don't smoke, you don't drink ...!' I thought he was angry with God. That night he rang me to say he had arranged with a Professor of Medicine to do new tests on me. Two weeks later I got the results: they were negative. I went in to tell Bob and he saw the smile I was wearing as I came through the door, and he began to cry with relief. We both sat there blubbering.[4]

There was no properly organised library in the ACTU and throughout 1959 Hawke was without a research assistant. Because the basic wage cases began in February he was working most intensively during the humid Melbourne summer. He said,

The conditions were frightful. Because of the flat roof the temperature in my office used to reach about 120°F [47°C]. The way I had to discipline myself for work and sleep was remarkable. I'd leave home at four or four-thirty in the morning and work for five hours before going into court. I taught myself to lie on the floor and sleep during the lunch adjournment, then could return fresh to court. I'd have a nap again in the late afternoon, and work into the night. The pressure was unbelievable. In the peak periods it was seven days a week, eighteen hours a day, for several weeks. But that ability to catnap was a tremendous advantage. Ever since I've been able to sleep anywhere ... Eggleston had taught me that as long as I was prepared I need not be nervous in court. But I had to be right on top of it, because once I got on my feet I was totally vulnerable. I had to be on top of all the statistics, all the theories, and prepared to answer questions that were flung at me from the Bench, or that came from the Bar table – from employers or the Commonwealth – and they had all the resources in the world. The work had the beauty for me of a very concrete relevance to society. I think the joy of that carried me through.

It was obvious by the end of the year that Hawke had to have help. Ralph Willis (later the member for Gellibrand) was employed, and 'Susie' was allowed to move upstairs now there was a chaperon. Willis was another 'intellectual': he had an economics degree and had been working in the Department of Labour, but he had the advantage of being the son of a Boilermakers' Society official who was universally respected in the trade union movement. Willis recalled,

I had nicked out of work to a phone box in Bourke Street to ring Bob and ask him how I should apply for the job. He was brusque. He said, 'Do what you're doing now – organise a time to come and see us'. He gave the impression that he didn't give a damn whether I came or not. At the interview he made it clear that I would have to work bloody hard, and that was fully borne out. When cases were on they consumed our lives: we'd have a few beers in the evening, then return to the office for more hours of work. Bob used to write out his own notes, but he didn't read from them. His method was to prepare notes in a way which allowed him to expound upon them at great length. Once, in the 1964 case, he spoke for a whole day on only three lines of notes . . . It used to amaze me that he would walk out of the Arbitration Commision, having talked on one plane all day, step into the Lygon and swap yarns with blokes from the wharf, as easily as with barristers. His key attribute as a union official and a politician is probably that ability he has to relate to all levels. He really enjoyed mixing with unionists: he could spend hours listening to their stories. During his years as advocate he established a huge network of friendships through those pub contacts, and became known as 'a good guy' . . . Bob used to get drunk, but in those days he was a good drunk – he'd get into spirited arguments, and could always argue logically no matter how much he'd had to drink and he could still drive a car relatively safely.

An oddity of Hawke's drinking was that he did not have 'normal' hangovers: in his whole life he has never had a headache. Hieser, who stayed overnight with Hawke often, complained, 'He'd get up, after maybe an hour's sleep, bright eyed and bushy tailed and asking for his breakfast, when the rest of us were barely able to speak'.

After his defeat in the 1960 basic wage case Hawke partly recouped his dignity with a South Australian basic wage case later that year. The employers were presenting an ingenious and apparently logical argument that wages in the state should be reduced because of a lower cost of living there. Hawke had a flash of insight about the fault in his opponent's logic, which concerned 'the going rate', confirmed his guess, and won the case. The next national hearing was set for early 1961 before Kirby, Ashburner and Moore, the latter a new judge who had appeared as advocate for the Commonwealth during 1959. Ashburner was regarded by all sides as the most conservative member of the Bench. He had been an advocate for the meat industry employers and had held some briefs for shipping companies and BHP. He was a former Rhodes scholar. The employers, who had panicked after Hawke's successes in 1959 and dropped their usual counsel, Drew Aird, had hopes of sympathy from Ashburner. Moore was an unknown quantity. For the 1961 case the employers engaged a highly regarded common law Queen's Counsel from the Melbourne Bar, Dr E. G. Coppel. As they went into court photographs were taken: Coppel, white haired, wearing rimless half-moon spectacles and with a dignified demeanour, looked like a headmaster standing beside a bright senior boy. Hawke was grinning, as slim as a whippet, his pompadour of dark hair gleaming, and his eyes too – for he was about to eat Dr Coppel.

Hawke's brief was the same as before: that the cost-of-living adjustments should be restored so that real wages could keep pace with prices, and that gains in productivity be substituted for 'capacity to pay' and distributed to the community as an increase in the basic wage. This year he had extra psychological strength on his side: anger about the 1960 decision, and knowledge of Santamaria's role in the 1953 decision which, for the third time, he would be attempting to have overturned. He also had a trump card, a witness, Sir Douglas Copland, an economist who had been prominent in Australian public affairs in the 1930s and 1940s. During the war Copland had been adviser to Curtin and was known as the economic ruler of the nation. He had been ambassador to China and high commissioner in Ottawa; he was the first vice-chancellor of the Australian National University; he had nine doctorates; he had assisted the Victorian Employers' Federation in establishing an economic research project and was a director of it; he had coined the phrase 'milk-bar economy' for postwar Australia. He was a big, vigorous man with a large voice that in economic matters carried as if ringing down from Mount Olympus.

Under questioning from Hawke in the witness box Copland gave evidence that since 1953 productivity had risen by 19.5 per cent and wages by 18 per cent; he agreed with Hawke's suggestion that the lack of cost-of-living adjustments was an injustice to the lower level of wage earners; he also agreed that he could not see how the economy would be injured if automatic adjustments were resumed.

Dr Coppel had called as a witness a senior lecturer in economics at Melbourne University, Dr J. O. N. Perkins. In the economic fraternity, news had already spread that Hawke, because he understood economics, was much harsher than the ordinary barrister in cross-examination, and that his technique of taking a statement and tearing it into small, verbal shreds, and the sheer violence of the aura around him when he was battling with a witness caused embarrassment and intimidation. When Coppel announced his witness, Perkins, Hawke immediately requested the right of cross-examination on broad economic issues. Earlier in the case Hawke had cross-examined a leading agricultural economist, Keith Campbell, on broad economic issues and had overwhelmed him. Perkins considered for a few minutes outside the courtroom then announced that he would not be questioned on matters outside his field of expertise, and therefore would not appear. The practice of calling economic experts was over: Hawke had created a situation where his opposition would have, like him, to speak with authority.

Coppel knew little about wage fixing or economics. For the employers the case was, in the words of his junior, 'disastrous'.

Unexpectedly, Hawke had turned up a second trump card. His opening address lasted three days and was directed at the Bench in highly personal terms, a characteristic of his debating that, in later years, won him hundreds of arguments – and no friends. He told the Bench: 'You have perpetrated this situation ... You have inflicted hardship upon thousands of people ... Do not delude yourselves ...' Ashburner, a traditionalist, was offended by Hawke's hectoring and abusive tone and asked Kirby, as chief judge, to rebuke him publicly. Kirby refused. On the first day of the hearing a group of railway workers had marched on the Commission, made a row, then ranged themselves along the back of the court in such a way that letters pinned to their lapels had spelt out the message WE WANT MORE DOUGH. The chief judge's salary was almost ten times the basic wage. When Kirby announced, 'I am afraid we will have to adjourn' (because of the railway men) Hawke snapped at him, 'It's not something *you'd* know about'. Kirby was fearful that if he rebuked Hawke he would be so pugnacious in his response that the only option would be to put him out of court. That would inevitably lead to demonstrations, questions in parliament and so forth. With the chief judge sitting in furious silence, Ashburner decided to act. On his third day of non-stop talking Hawke burst out: 'It is indisputable that in real terms the output of goods and services has increased, but this Commission, particularly in that nonsense in the Annual Leave –' Ashburner interjected, 'I wish you would not distract me by using those adjectives, such as "absurd", words like "nonsense" and so on'.

HAWKE: I am using it in the strictly literal sense of 'non sense'.

ASHBURNER, J: It does distract my attention from the substance of your argument.

HAWKE: If it has that effect, Your Honour, there is certainly not much use in pursuing it because I do not want to distract Your Honour from what I was saying. I will contain my feelings.[5]

Hawke had abruptly realised his error, and an area for advantage: he had engaged Ashburner in personal debate – the judge had come forward and Hawke could now wrestle with him, one-to-one. Ashburner was the only member of the Bench unfamiliar with the arguments already enunciated in 1959 (Moore had heard them as counsel for the Commonwealth that year) and Hawke, having flushed him out, concentrated upon pursuing him. George Polites, who had recently been appointed as secretary of the Australian Council of Employers' Federation, said with a giggle, 'It was sick-making. Hawke talked to Ashburner like a Dutch uncle.' Hawke also wore his Oxford tie, an accessory that Ashburner, who liked to wear *his* Oxford tie, noted with approval.

The transcript of the case is full of questions from Hawke such as 'Does Your Honour appreciate my argument?' and 'Does Your Honour have any further reservations about this, because I can see that it is obviously a fundamental matter?' and 'I do not know whether Your Honour, Mr Justice Ashburner, has any reservations still to which you might like me to address myself?' Ashburner knew so little of economics that at one stage the whole Bar table had to suppress a convulsion of laughter when His Honour asked about 'the London funds', at that time a term synonymous for Australia's international reserves. The employers argued that the success of Australia's export earnings, reflected in the London funds, was fuelling inflation in Australia. 'How', asked the judge, 'can the money be in London and be used in Australia at the same time?' It took counsel almost an hour to explain the significance of high reserves. To his credit and to the credit of the system, Ashburner was prepared to reveal his ignorance.

Hawke's address in reply lasted twelve days. Sir John Moore recalled,

> He'd reached a stage where he physically couldn't stand, except by hanging on to the lectern. He was leaning over it, supporting his weight on it, and still talking to us. We were adjourning at regular intervals because his voice was giving out. I could see from where I was sitting on the Bench that he had kicked his shoes off and was standing there in his socks, just barely able to go on, but still arguing very forcefully. He was an extraordinarily strong debater.

Sheer will power and belief in his cause carried Hawke through and evoked his habitual lapses of tact – he referred to some of Kirby's judgments as 'pathetic', 'completely fallacious', 'objectionable', and accused the Commission of being cowardly. But it had been a magnificent performance: he had finally convinced the chief judge he must confess and repent for the 1953 decision, and he had won the minds of Ashburner and Moore. The reform of the system that Hawke had demanded so precociously, in Oxford, was about to take place.

The decision, which was unanimous, increased the basic wage by 12 shillings and decreed that in future it would be adjusted annually in line with the cost-of-living index, and triennially for increases in productivity. The onus would be on the employers to prove that this should not happen.

In the trade union movement, Hawke was a hero. The employers ground their teeth.

He spent some of his next year abroad, as a delegate to the Duke of Edinburgh's study conference in Canada, and later studying the effects of Britain's entry into the European Economic Community. In early 1963 he argued another margins case against yet another advocate the employers were trying out, and achieved a pleasing result. But while his career had reached a peak, Hawke was now in trouble with Monk and Souter and at home his family life was under strain. Both problems were due, in part, to his success.

From his first heady achievements in 1959 he had been in demand as a speaker at public functions. By May 1960 Monk, Souter and some Right-wing members of the ACTU executive were alarmed at the tendency for Hawke to be presented as a spokesman for the ACTU, and the question of the public statements of the ACTU's research officer became a matter for executive debate. Its discussion split, as ever, on Left–Right lines. Souter had forbidden Hawke to speak publicly about ACTU policy; there had been a row over an airfare; the ACTU junior vice-president, Bill Evans, of the Left, had asked Hawke for material to use in a speech but Souter had instructed Hawke not to supply it. Evans required Souter to defend himself, which he did, with the support of the Right-wing boss of the New South Wales Labour Council, Jim Kenny. The issue was settled, with bad tempers all round, to burst forth again a year later. In June 1961 Hawke attended the annual state Labor Party conference and in intemperate language attacked Sir Raymond Kelly (whom he once described, according to the *Financial Review*, as 'that Irish pig farmer'), the Democratic Labor Party and B. A. Santamaria for combining to defeat quarterly adjustments. Santamaria issued a denial of his involvement with Kelly; Senator McManus, the leader of the DLP, issued a demand for an apology. Monk was so angry with Hawke he issued a statement saying that Hawke had been attending the ALP conference as a representative of the Theatrical Employees' Association, not the ACTU. In ALP and Left-wing trade union circles the row increased Hawke's celebrity status and his opportunities for more agitating. He was asked to appear on television, a medium he was learning to master; newspapers pestered for interviews – and met him in different moods: the Melbourne *Sun* in 1963 described Hawke as, 'softly spoken, quiet'.

Life as a minor celebrity had an electric edge of excitement. There were more hours of jubilant exchange in the pub, more late nights with boon companions, more boon companions – for Hawke could be 'best mates' with thirty people at once – and his days see-sawed with the thrill of new friendships, new exquisite moments of fun and rapport. Repeatedly, when people attempt to describe why hours passed with Hawke seem magically charged with humour and play, they fall back to saying, 'He's just such *fun*'. But he was drinking too much and at home arguments were frequent.

Hazel had given birth to a third child, Rosslyn, in November 1960 and by July 1963 was 28 weeks pregnant with a fourth. Hawke used often to tell 'Susie', 'I'm going to have seven children – the Biblical number'. On 1 August Hazel was out shopping when she felt the pangs of premature labour. She was taken to the closest hospital where an emergency caesarian section was performed. The new baby was a fine-looking black-haired boy, but he had to be kept in a humidicrib while Hazel, who was very ill after losing blood, was too weak to see him. Hawke told her, 'He's a really strong baby – wait until you see his beautiful little chest!' To Hawke's delight she suggested that the new boy should be named Robert James. As events turned out, Hazel never saw her fourth child.

Within hours delight turned to anxiety, then despair. The baby, seven weeks premature, was dying. Hawke sat for twenty-four hours beside his crib watching him sink away from life. Hazel was too ill to leave hospital and Hawke, with one companion for support, saw Robert James buried, then arranged for Hazel to recover at the house of their tennis friends, David and Marjorie White. In the first days of shock he wept frequently and began to drink himself into oblivion. As always when deeply distressed, he became speechless and immobilised – he could not talk out his feelings, he would not return to the grave. Indeed, it was almost twenty years and Hawke was a different man before he could say, one day in 1981, 'I think I'll go and visit Robert'. On a Saturday afternoon about a fortnight after Hazel returned home he was to go to the football and insisted that she accompany him. They set out by taxi but had not gone far when Hawke had what Hazel described as 'a frightening attack: he was dis-oriented, felt paralysed and thought he was dying'. She took him straight to hospital. He was suffering alcoholic poisoning.

He was still ill from his self-punishment and Hazel was in the early stages of a long period of grief when, a few weeks later Hawke was pressed to begin his political career in earnest. He was attending an ALP dinner in a Melbourne hotel when Albert McNolty, secretary of the Victorian Labor Party, made a point of sitting next to him.

The prime minister, Robert Menzies, had won the 1961 election by only one seat and since then had been on the alert for an issue that would excuse him holding another, premature election. Since 1961 the economy had recovered; unemploy-ment, which had been 2.8 per cent, was once again negligible; and, most importantly, the ALP had recently committed one of its breathtaking public gaffes. Arthur Calwell, the leader, and Gough Whitlam, the deputy leader, had been photo-graphed late at night standing in the street under a lamppost, hunched in overcoats against the cold, waiting to be informed of a decision of the party's 36-member federal conference of which they, although the party's foremost public representatives, were not members. The photograph had been published under the heading '36 Faceless Men', a popular term for the confer-ence delegates, and had done the ALP immense damage, with its suggestion of sinister, unknown forces manipulating Labor's parliamentary politicians like puppets. Since 1951 when Menzies' legislation to ban the Communist Party had been defeated, due largely to the efforts of the former Labor leader, H. V. Evatt, Menzies had claimed that the ALP was ruled by 'outside forces'. Had he taken the photograph himself he could not have had a more dramatic illustration for his claims. Then, in early October 1963 the ALP, or rather the leader, Calwell, compounded the gaffe by asking the federal executive to give a ruling on state aid for non-government schools. State aid is Australia's most ancient and bitter political issue. Obligingly – for the prime minister – the ALP federal executive ruled against state aid.

Menzies called a snap election for 30 November 1963.

In addition to a domestic issue he had an external one: President Sukarno of Indonesia, the Great Leader of the Revolution, the Father of the Nation, the Champion of Islam, Field Marshal and Supreme Commander of the Armed Forces, President for Life, etc., had just launched Confrontation of Malaysia. A year earlier Sukarno's denouncement of Britain's manipulation of Asian affairs had been so enthusiastically received that the Jakarta mob had razed the British embassy. Effigies were burnt, cars thrown into canals. Sukarno was depicted in Australia as a dangerous lunatic, Joe Stalin in a black velvet fez. The electorate was encouraged to believe that at any moment a multitude of Indonesian soldiers would turn their attention to the south. The Australian government, having played a part in stimulating fear, promptly offered to assuage it. Menzies announced that Australia was buying a fleet of long-range, low-altitude bomber aircraft of the most contemporary design, then called the TFX, later famous as the F-111. With these, Australia could bomb Jakarta. The Defence Minister, Athol Townley, was despatched to Washington to lay a deposit on the table for these dashing war machines. It was not explained to the public that it would be at least eight years before they would be built and airworthy. Malaysia and Indonesia would be friends and Sukarno would be an invalid prisoner-of-state long before the first F-111 had a chance to crash. But meanwhile, Menzies had a cause.

Hawke said, 'I remember as though it were yesterday: Albert McNolty sat beside me and began to heavy me about standing'. McNolty had already done Hawke a favour: he was an official of the Sheet Metal Workers' Union, of which Hawke was a member of convenience, for as ACTU advocate he formally appeared for the metal trades unions. Hawke had asked McNolty to get him a 'good deal' on a refrigerator and one day a brand new refrigerator had been delivered to the house as a gift. Hawke continued:

His argument was simple. He said, 'Look, we can win government this election, we need only to hold the seats we've got and win a couple more. Corio is one we should win. You are a national figure now. You could win Corio. You've got a duty and an obligation to the whole Labor movement. You're a marvellous advocate, no one can do what you've been doing. *But*, winning government is more important. You can do it.' I was not very thrilled about the idea. Hazel and I talked it over. Next day I talked to Harold [Souter] and Albert [Monk] about it and said I felt I had an obligation to run, that it was a matter of duty. They were understanding, and gave me leave.

Within days Hawke had been formally selected as the candidate for Corio, a mixed rural and industrial seat south-west of Melbourne with its centre the city of Geelong. It was held by the Minister for Shipping, Hubert Opperman, an Olympic champion cyclist who was called Oppy by his constituents. Hawke would need a 3.4 per cent swing to unseat him.

Hazel said, 'We were both still very sick and sorry people. The election campaign was a necessary and practical commitment. It helped us, in some degree, to cope with the grieving.'

Once Hawke had overcome his reluctance he mentally changed gears; he shut the baby's death out of his mind and set out to become a parliamentarian.

ELEVEN

I<small>F I'D HAD ANOTHER WEEK</small> of campaigning, I would have won', Hawke said later. Time is always his enemy. But it is doubtful, given the events of October–November 1963, that an extra week on the hustings would have put Hawke in parliament as the member for Corio. The election campaign began with the assassination of President Diem of South Vietnam and ended with the assassination of President Kennedy of the United States; by 23 November not just the electors of Corio but the whole Western world was appalled and yearning for security. People, in those circumstances, do not dismiss conservative governments. The nation in 1963 clung to Menzies as a child to its father's leg.

Hawke polled 748 more primary votes than Opperman, creating a swing to Labor of 3 per cent in an election that brought a national 3 per cent swing away from the ALP and when its vote in Victoria as a whole dropped to 40.3 per cent, with 12.4 per cent of first preferences going to the DLP. His result was excellent, in the circumstances, but it was not good enough: after the distribution of DLP preferences he had only 22 456 votes to Opperman's 25 666. 'Who brought this Communist in here?' a member of the Corio Club had demanded when he saw Hawke being introduced around the clubhouse. Hawke's sponsor, a local businessman, strode forward and knocked the calumniator down. It was a nasty campaign.

It began badly for Hawke, with resentment of him among the local party faithful. The rulers of the Victorian ALP, the central executive, were dissatisfied with the two Corio men who had put themselves forward for the seat and on the eve of selection of candidates (having secured Hawke's promise to run), announced that nominations had been reopened. They gave the early election as their excuse for bending the rules. They then selected Hawke. An outsider. George Poyser, in 1963 the assistant secretary of the Victorian ALP, former secretary of the Geelong Trades Hall Council (and later a Labor senator), was appointed Hawke's campaign manager. He said, 'There was a lot of resentment that the executive had behaved in this way and a lot of resentment against Hawke who, party members felt, had been imposed upon them. I went down to Corio with a feeling of dread.'

Enthusiastic local members are essential in election campaigns: they do the chores – the letterbox drops, the handing out of advertisements, the lending of their motor cars, the cheering at meetings. There was only a month in which to campaign. Poyser said,

> Hawke had to be sold to the party faithful before we could sell him to the electorate at large. The key to it was that he was a Rhodes scholar and a working-class advocate. We pushed the Rhodes scholar line and within a week Bob had 100 per cent of the local organisation behind him.

But meanwhile, Opperman's machine had caught the scent of ALP discontent about the outsider and began to press hard on the 'local man' issue. A few weeks earlier the football team of the city of Geelong had played in the Victorian Football League grand final. Football is a matter of life and death to Victorians, who each winter become maddened, in their tens of thousands, as the grand final approaches. Opperman had made a highly publicised dash by air and road from Brisbane to arrive in time to see Geelong beat Hawthorn for the premiership. He still glowed, locally, from the heroes' reflected glory. Hawke gave an undertaking that if elected he would live in Corio, but a promise was not enough to quieten the clamour of criticism, so the party rented him a house in Portarlington. Hazel and the children moved down from Melbourne. She was still 'easily upset', as campaigners noticed, and not well enough to play a public role; 'I fed the troops', she said. Here again the Opperman machine had an edge: his wife was politically active and campaigned continually for her husband among local people she had known for years. Hawke's own health was a worry. While an inside group knew that he was recovering from alcoholic poisoning and grief, and described this to others as 'a bit of a chest problem', there was doubt whether he would be able to stand up to the campaigning. Poyser said,

> Every day there was a factory-gate meeting, each evening he went around the clubs and at weekends he met the football enthusiasts. We had to make him a byword in Geelong very quickly; he had to be given the maximum exposure to the electorate.

A sense of pathos is never far from the ALP and was expressed in the slogan Hawke's managers wrote: 'Bob's standing for you – give him a seat'. Opperman, in contrast, ran on the virile message, 'Performance not Promises! Your man is Opperman.'

On 5 November the press was forecasting the possibility of a Labor victory. On 6 November Calwell, in what he described as 'a red-blooded, face-to-face Australian political meeting open to all comers', launched Labor's campaign, promising a 5.5 per cent increase in economic growth, a revolution in education, a vigorous housing drive, tax concessions, improved social services, and a nuclear-free zone in the southern hemisphere. Menzies, who had perfected the appearance of lofty good temper with fools and such confidence in the job he was doing that he could afford a gentlemanly indolence, replied that the ALP was either promising 'roaring inflation' or intended to increase taxes. A nuclear-free zone was a 'suicidal proposal', he sighed. He had smacked at Calwell as if dislodging a gnat. He would open his own campaign a week later – on television.

The Corio campaign managers knew their candidate. Hawke was, above all, a debater and one suited to the unexpected and dashing. Poyser arranged to fill the Geelong West Town Hall with television sets; Menzies' speech would be screened to the audience gathered for Hawke, then he and Gough Whitlam would reply to it – as if they were both in debate with the prime minister. It was a clever piece of theatre that very few politicians would be capable of carrying off. While Menzies was speaking Hawke scribbled out only an opening paragraph:

> You have witnessed tonight in the speech of the P.M. the most amazing piece of hypocrisy in postwar Australian political history. This man *came to office on a hoax* – to put value into the £1 – and will now be thrown out of that office as a political burglar, a man completely lacking in integrity. The *millionaire* in words is starkly revealed as poverty-stricken in ideas ... By their deeds shall we know them ...[1]

Hawke had guessed, accurately, that Menzies would again, as he had in 1961, adopt as his own a number of Labor policies.

It was a night of strong assertions and superlatives: Whitlam told the audience of 750 Labor supporters that Hawke had 'greater industrial experience than any man in Australia'. With two fast-on-their-feet agitators on stage the evening went with zest.

But earlier that day, 12 November, the DLP candidate, J. J. Mahoney, had been reported at length in the *Geelong Advertiser* for a speech he had made to the local Polish community, during which he had dwelt upon the Indonesian peril. Mahoney had said that the election was the most vital ever to be held in Australia and that it was a question of 'safeguarding the nation's future'. It was necessary therefore that policies relating to defence and foreign affairs be placed above all else, otherwise coming generations might be forced to 'live in slavery'. He continued,

> Under the leadership of Dr Sukarno this threat is inspired by nationalistic tendencies, but Communism is helping to

ferment and incite Sukarno's lust for power. The children of Australia cannot vote in this election: their future rests upon the votes of older people.

Two days later the *Advertiser* reported him saying, 'Once the millions of Asia spill over into Australia this country cannot defend itself ...' The *Advertiser*, owned by the local Douglas family and managed by a former sea-captain who had married into the clan, was conservative. Poyser had been complaining to its management about bias since 1949. He said, 'It did no good. They would not give equal space, equally displayed, to Labor, but they raised no objections to running our advertisements, full-page, if we liked.' Hysteria in the electorate was building up and was thoroughly reported by the local paper. When Opperman opened his campaign a few days after Hawke he was continuously heckled for an hour and a half. He attacked Hawke as Left-wing and made repeated references to the sinister '36 faceless men'. The slurs about the ALP and Communism were everywhere, especially on local radio broadcasts aimed at housewives.

Hawke's health gave way and he had to spend three days in bed. Hazel recalled being enraged and mortified as she listened to gentle radio voices appealing to her, the mother in the home, to save her children's lives by refusing to vote for Labor. Hawke said,

> The Catholic Church was very very strong, and I remember one incident vividly: [Senator] Pat Kennelly, a devout Catholic, came down to campaign. There was an opening of a big new hall in one of the Catholic parishes on a Saturday and it was suggested he and I should go along there. The DLP had been putting out the most monstrous stuff about the party generally and about me – that the party was under the control of Communists and I was a disguised Communist. And this afternoon as we walked through the crowds little kids of eleven and twelve pointed at me and Pat,

Hawke's maternal great-grandfather, John Lee, 1834–1911.

Will Lee, Hawke's maternal grandfather, 1859–1922.

Will Lee's Bible class: Ellie is seated beside him, second from left; his youngest child, Lila, is seated on his other side.

Ellie, aged 20.

Clem Hawke, aged 20.

Bobbie, Bordertown, 1930.

Bobbie, Bordertown, 1933.

Clem, Bobbie, Ellie and Neil in Bordertown.

Bobbie selling hot cross buns.

Clem and Bobbie, 1941.

Ellie Hawke.

Hawke and Hazel on the Panther, about 1951.

At the University of Western Australia, about 1952.

Hawke and Ellie packing for his trip to Oxford, 1953.

Off the Cape of Good Hope en route to Oxford.

Receiving congratulations on winning a Rhodes Scholarship.

The University College, Oxford, Cricket XI, 1954. Back row: K. Baber, I. Morgan,
V. Lees, E. Thomson, J. Dunne, N. Corea, B. Jones; middle row: T. Horn,
P. Wilcox, R. Prentice, N. Colwell, R. Hawke; front row: J. Duncan and A. Monro.

As ACTU research officer and advocate in the 1960s.

Hawke and Hazel on the steps
of Parliament House, 1956.

Outside the Arbitration Commission, Melbourne, with David McBride, left, and
Ted Deverall, right, about 1960.

'Bob Hawke the Family Man': Corio election, 1963.

Labour leader and Labor leader: Hawke and Whitlam, 1970.

Hawke, Rachel Dayan, Moshe Dayan, Israel's Minister for Defence, and Clyde Holding.

Hawke and Susan returning from Israel (and Russia), 1971.

Father of the Year in 1971.

John Ducker comforting Hawke during the 1975 election campaign after news of a letter-bomb explosion, attributed to ALP supporters.

Sir John Moore, Harold Souter, Hawke, George Polites, Gough Whitlam and
Sir Richard Kirby, ACTU fiftieth anniversary celebrations, 1977.

The ACTU Executive of 1979. Standing: Edgar Williams, Ken Stone, Dick
Scott, John Morris, Peter Cook, Bob Watling, Barrie Unsworth, Fred Peterson,
Norm Gallagher, Keith Lawler, Ray Geitzelt, Ivan Hodgson, Bob Gregory,
Harry Hauenschild; sitting: Bill Richardson, Bill Kelty, Peter Nolan, Hawke,
Cliff Dolan, Jim Roulston, Phil Reilly.

Hawke receiving his Companion of the Order of Australia decoration from Governor-General Sir Zelman Cowen in January 1979.

Hawke and Speaker of the House Sir Bill Snedden, 1981.

Addressing a rally while Shadow Minister for Industrial Relations, Canberra, 1981.

The uranium debate, ACTU Congress,
September 1979.

Bill Hayden, Hawke, David Combe and
Bob McMullan, the successor to Combe
as federal secretary of the ALP, 1981.

Hawke after the sacking of the Whitlam Government in 1975. His stance says it all.

saying 'Communists, Communists, Communists'. Pat nearly wept. He couldn't believe the church was doing that.

However, Hawke had already established a swing, and was holding it. He had also had a stroke of luck: the shipping, coal and hotel magnate, R. W. Miller, held a grudge against Opperman and wanted him sacked as Minister for Shipping. Opperman had refused to grant permits to Miller's ships to operate on the Australian coastal trade, while granting permits to ships flying flags of convenience and owned, mostly, by the major oil companies. Miller saw his chance in Hawke and offered to support his campaign financially. Poyser said,

> We kept the Miller money separate from the official Labor accounts, so that it did not appear in any of the books. We were frightened that the Liberals would accuse us of overspending. We worked through a Mr Taylor in Miller's office. We would ring him up, tell him how much a full-page advertisement or a radio ad. would cost, and the cheque for the exact amount would arrive next day.

Huge advertisements about Hawke began to appear in the *Advertiser*, and Hawke, who is always at home with debate on specifics, began to castigate Opperman for his handling of the shipping portfolio. The minister was piqued into reply, saying Australia could not afford to establish its own shipping line for carrying import and export cargoes.

On 20 November Hawke addressed a lunchtime meeting of factory workers at Alcoa, telling them, 'Australia must move positively and quickly to establish an overseas shipping line', and that the country was being held to ransom by the Overseas Shipping Conference, which decided the freight charges to be imposed on Australian exporters. On the same day the Miller *Canopus* sailed into the port of Geelong. The crew lowered a huge piece of cloth, which covered almost one side of the ship, with an advertisement painted on it urging a vote for Hawke. The next day there was a half-page advertisement in the *Advertiser* saying, 'The Labor Movement Welcomes R. W. Miller's *Canopus* to Geelong, The First Australian Owned Tanker To Enter Corio Bay With An Australian Crew'. There was a picture of Hawke and one of the tanker. Hawke repeatedly challenged Opperman to debate with him face to face, but the minister wisely declined and instead rode around Corio on his bicycle. He had said in one speech that there were six Communists among Labor's '36 faceless men'; the Labor machine was demanding stridently and futilely that he retract the statement. Opperman was so hard pressed by Hawke that he left the electorate only once during the campaign and had ministerial documents sent by car to Geelong for signing.

By the morning of 23 November, a week before polling day, Hawke was running away with the seat. His handbills announced:

His outstanding academic career ... He has conducted all recent major cases before the Arbitration Commission which have resulted in INCREASES in the BASIC WAGE and MARGINS and THREE WEEKS ANNUAL LEAVE. His recent international experience. His armed services experience. Bob Hawke flew as a pilot with the Oxford University Air Squadron of the ROYAL AIR FORCE VOLUNTEER RESERVE.

Sport: An all-round sportsman ... played 1st grade cricket ... toured with the Oxford University side. He has YOUTH – EDUCATION – EXPERIENCE – VIGOUR – INTEGRITY.[2]

The electorate had been lavishly papered with these bills. Once Hawke had been accepted by the party, he had stirred such enthusiasm that scores of volunteers had joined his campaign and five times had filled the letterboxes of Corio with campaign leaflets. When Harold Holt, the federal Treasurer, had challenged anyone to name a country more prosperous than Australia Hawke had challenged Holt to debate the government's economic management. Holt had declined. Hawke said, 'None of them would debate. I talked about defence and international affairs, but basically I talked about economics. I tried to tell the story about the attack on living standards via wages and wages policy that was involved in the Menzies government approach. I had the authority of my position as ACTU advocate.'

Then, in the late morning of Saturday, 23 November, the forward rush of enthusiasm hit a wall: President Kennedy had been shot dead. It was as if the planet had lurched in its orbit.

Poyser heard the news over the radio in the Geelong Trades Hall and thought, 'Nationally, we can't win'. Hawke, who'd been told early that morning, was stunned, but remained optimistic. The old campaigners, however, knew that a different message was necessary now that people were frightened. New, full-page advertisements of Hawke were made, picturing, for the first time, Hazel and the children all seated together on a settee and announcing, 'Bob Hawke the Family Man'.[3]

Labor was in retreat. By 25 November the party's defence policy had been swept away. In Brisbane Calwell announced that Labor's nuclear-free southern hemisphere idea had been misunderstood; that in a war the USA would 'give Australia nuclear arms'; and that 'we, the ALP, would use any weapon to defend Australia if attacked'. Menzies smiled and pointed out that he had already ordered TFX aircraft, which 'rounded off the largest and most ambitious re-equipment program in the peace-time history of Australia'. Hawke said,

> The atmosphere the Libs created in that post-Kennedy assassination period was unbelievable. They had B-47 bombers flying over Australia; there was constant talk about 'the Asian hordes', as some people chose to refer to the Indonesians, and about the F-111s. Menzies was brought down to Corio on the day before the election to speak at the Ford factory. There had never been so many police in the area – police were wandering around with rifles, on the roofs of buildings, and they went through the lockers in the factory – there was supposed to be an assassination threat to Menzies. The atmosphere was electric. At the Ford meeting people were expecting to see Menzies shot. And they had conjured up the whole bloody thing!

Poyser recalled Menzies' address to the Ford workers: 'He had turned up surrounded by police. In the crowd some joker ignited a cracker he had in a cigarette packet. When the thing went bang people's faces turned white.'

By election day the polls showed that Labor would lose. In Corio there were police stationed at the booths. The *Geelong Advertiser* that morning ran an editorial spurning Labor's 'gaudy bait' and noting, 'Mr Opperman in his younger days was idolised by Geelong and district people as a world famous figure in sport ... The electorate is not likely to forsake him now.'

By ten o'clock that night television commentators announced that Menzies was back in government, while in a maverick result Bob Hawke had beaten the minister for shipping. Hawke said,

> People around me were saying, 'Hey, you've won it!' I found George Poyser, who knew how every booth in the electorate had to vote for us to win. He used the East Geelong High School booth as his litmus test: if my vote was of a certain percentage there, I would be in. I told him everyone thought I'd won and he replied, 'Well, you haven't. The figures from East Geelong High School are not good enough.'

It was a week before the result was officially known. Opperman, in accepting victory, commented with spleen on the ALP expenditure and Miller's generosity to Hawke's campaign: 'Never has so much been spent in so short a time by so varied interests to effect a defeat'.

Hawke said, 'It was a disappointment – I don't like losing anything I do – but I knew I had achieved an enormous result. And I had something to go back to that I was very much involved in and deeply committed to.'

The basic wage case for 1964 was due to open in ten weeks, with a new young advocate representing the employers. In the Conciliation and Arbitration Commission the dawn was breaking for what was later called 'the heroic age of advocacy'.

The wage fixation changes of 1961 had been, in the words of the chief judge, Sir Richard Kirby, 'a great reformative step'. They had worked in relation to prices in 1962 and 1963 and now it was time for the triennial review of productivity. If that went smoothly, the unions could begin to relax: they would have a whole package of wages adjusted to prices and productivity: their decade-long fight against the decision of 1953 would have succeeded; and they would have a planned, stable system for the allotment of money logically intermeshed with the Australian economy. At least, in theory.[4]

Hawke approached the 1964 case with confidence. The economy was booming, with international reserves of £840 million – higher than ever before; there had been a 40 per cent increase of exports of manufactured goods compared with the same period twelve months earlier, and it followed upon the increase in margins and annual leave that Hawke had won in 1963. The employers could not cry Bankrupt! A new mood of buoyancy was sweeping the nation, summed up in the title of a recently published book, *The Lucky Country*. Unemployment was negligible. People swollen with abundance went on diets of grilled rump steak. We had never had it so good and we were going to have it better, for the drumbeats of the mining boom were already audible in the distance. London was swinging. Western Europe (and Japan) danced and shrieked with Beatlemania. In America, Kennedy's Camelot was changing into Lyndon Johnson's Great Society, which would see an end to poverty, inequality, ignorance. The heady, golden '60s were underway.

The wage case for that year reflected the confidence and good temper of the times. It was a friendly, humorous case, with the Bar table and the Bench swapping jokes and passing notes about the cricket scores. It ended in Sydney with the chief judge and the two leading advocates boozing together, and later Hawke and the employers' new man, Jim Robinson, dancing pas de deux in the foyer of the Menzies Hotel at four o'clock in the morning.

A few weeks later the full Bench gave its decision: the basic

wage would be increased by £1 to take account of price and productivity increases.

The unions were jubilant. The employers' counterpart to
Albert Monk, George Polites, invented a judges' jingle that did
the rounds of all the industrial relations pubs: 'The economy
in the round is sound – we'll give a pound!'

The night before the decision was given the defence minister,
Senator Paltridge, had told parliament that the United States
had been pressing Australia to join more actively in supporting
the sagging anti-Communist front in South Vietnam, and that
Australia would therefore be sending military instructors to help
out the American military instructors already in the country. His
statement was the proverbial cloud no bigger than a man's hand.
In the wage case, too, there had been a little cloud: it was called
the total wage. The employers wanted it; the unions rejected it,
and so did the Bench. But it kept on growing. 'The heroic age of
advocacy' between Hawke and Jim Robinson was the battle for
the total wage, which opened in 1964. The economic nightmare
of Australian wage fixation, which came to a climax in 1974 and
again in 1981, began then.

Wage fixation and its economic consequences is a highly complicated – and controversial – area that only a full-length book
could adequately cover. For brevity, one can give this equation: under the system of basic wage and margin an annual pay
packet was made up of, say, £1000 basic wage and £1000 margin,
increased one part at a time, with a lag of several years for margins'
increases. With a total wage the annual pay packet is still £2000,
but it is increased at one blow. If a flat-rate increase is awarded, the
lesser-paid worker tends to catch up with the better paid. Better-
paid workers want percentage increases, for it takes no talent in
mathematics to realise that, say, 10 per cent of £2000 is greater
than 10 per cent of £1000. The most militant unions are the craft
unions, and they are better paid; therefore, over a period of time,
they will tend to get their own way and have percentage increases
awarded. This means that the highly paid workers will be even
more highly paid in relation to the poorly paid. Relativities are

badly disturbed; envy arises – the fitter earns more so the labourer demands more and the brain surgeon puts up his fees. Taxation swallows most of the gain, but more of the brain surgeon's, so he hires a lawyer/accountant to figure out how to pay less tax. Governments discover they needed the extra tax wealth all along and spend it on causes appropriate to their political priorities; this creates resentment in half the electorate. The result is bad temper, high wages, cheating, and huge tax returns to the government. Prices increase – for whatever reason (drought in the wheat belt, a consumer fad) – and the fitter demands a wage rise.

The employers had designed their total wage argument with a different scenario in mind. They wanted the total wage increased only for gains in productivity. But for the unions productivity increases are mere gravy. Their meat is prices and their measuring stick is the consumer price index, which is expressed in percentage terms. Australia ended up with a total wage increased for prices at a time of low productivity movements.

George Polites, the executive director of the Australian Council of Employers' Federation (ACEF), has the credit for designing the case for the total wage but had no hand in the botched-up way it was applied in law. Polites had come to the Employers' Federation in 1959, having worked his way up from industrial advocate for the Victorian employers to the job of personnel director of the then small but ambitious transnational company, Utah, before becoming the dynamo of organised employers. He was short, energetic, full of nervous energy and shrewdness, his speech terse and humorous, prickling with shafts of epigrammatic wit. He had been dissatisfied with the advocacy of Drew Aird but the internal politics of the ACEF had prevented him from making real reforms until the annual leave case of 1963. That year he had persuaded his colleagues that a young barrister he had spotted in the South Australian basic wage case of 1960, a case known as 'The South Australian Employers versus The World', was the man to establish against Hawke. Polites' protégé was Jim Robinson, a barrister four years Hawke's senior, who had not, as was customary for the employers' counsel, taken silk. He was, like Hawke, a son of the manse.

Polites had a stroke of genius in promoting Robinson, for he was an opponent whom Hawke could not dislike, could not regard as a personal enemy – as he had, so notably, Cliff Menhennitt. (A few months earlier, in the 1963 margins and annual leave case, clashes between Hawke and Menhennitt had filled the courtroom with emotional lightning, causing pain to observers and judges.) As well, Robinson was malleable: Polites, as his mentor, was to be the phantom general directing his young warrior's fight.

Robinson was slim, blue eyed, with delicate, almost fawn-like features and, although aggressive in court, was a man of instantly recognisable good nature and good humour. Like Hawke he had the faculty of becoming, in a few seconds, a boy again – Kirby used to call him Peter Pan – and his boyishness, which was whimsical, complemented the naughty innocence of Hawke's sudden reversions to childhood play. His manner was languid; his speech finely modulated and slow, touched, as was Hawke's, by Biblical allusions. Robinson's mother had alarmed her wealthy family by marrying a missionary and going off to China. Robinson was born there. His childhood was characterised by the external chaos of the warlord period and the internal control of a stern, anaemic Christianity. He had grown up with evening prayers and daily Bible readings, church four times on Sundays and caveats against the sin of worldliness. His father was formidable – 'a headmaster in another form'. Robinson said, 'There was no smoking, no drinking, no lipstick for girls, no movies – Hollywood was the workplace of the Devil – no radio on Sundays. Even the *Women's Weekly* was a bit risqué.' At the age of twelve he had come to Australia, and rebelled – by breaking Sabbath observance and, in secret, playing sport. Hawke was fascinated that Robinson had defied the church so young. Having discovered the similarities of their childhoods they were charmed by each other and spent hours discussing how they should rear their own children with greater liberty than they had known. Robinson was particularly attracted to Hawke's relationship with Clem and Hawke's openly expressed affection for men he admired. By 1964 they were already warm friends. Hawke had loathed some advocates on ideological grounds: Robinson was non-political. 'Jim didn't believe he was going to save the nation, like Cliff Menhennitt. I often thought he wouldn't mind taking a case for our side', Hawke remarked. Robinson was already in Hawke's debt: in the 1960 case one of the employers' witnesses had gone to Hawke and suggested that Hawke cross-examine his evidence in a certain way, which would discredit it. Hawke had dismissed the man and so as not to distress Robinson – who was on trial for his future career – had waited until the case was over before telling him about the perfidy. Robinson said, 'That remains with me twenty years later as being what typified Bob's integrity'. From that case on they had bonds of trust: to save time and work they exchanged the names of witnesses, and witness statements, and later gave warning of procedural changes although, as Robinson said later,

> Bob played the game straighter than we did. He would as a matter of course give us as much notice as possible of procedural points. We would consider the length of notice we'd give him as part of our tactics. Perhaps it made no practical difference, because Bob thrived on surprises, but it was an article of faith with him that he never sought to take advantage of trust. And he never complained about not receiving identical treatment from me and George.

Since he had taken over as head of the employers' body Polites had become determined that its traditional argument to the Commission, a brief he described as 'no increase, no time, no how', must be changed. He thought the employers' refusal to concede any award wage increase, in a time of full employment and strong economic growth, was sterile and unreal – and ultimately damaging. While employers asserted fiercely in court that they could afford not a penny more in wages, outside court they were already paying large over-award rates as they competed among themselves for labour. The unions, therefore, regarded the employers' submissions as exercises in hypocrisy.

The employers had come to behave like hapless virgins in court – and wantons outside – and regarded the unions as bent upon rape, in court and out. Polites recognised how bad for industrial relations this situation was and determined that there must be some rapprochement between desire and its rebuff, that some award wage permissiveness was in order. He fought hard in the employers' councils to persuade his colleagues that it was in their best interest to give something – and to ask for something in return – instead of having the process of exchange accomplished by *force majeure*. His solution, unveiled by Robinson in the 1964 case, was the New Look Wages Plan. With it, the employers were offering to increase wages in line with productivity increases; they asked in return for the abolition of the basic wage and margin system and its replacement by a total wage. Welding the two-part system into one would prevent the unions having 'two bites of the cherry', as it was commonly described – that is, winning an increase in the basic wage then topping this up with an increase in margins, using as a major reason the disturbance of relativities.

The unions could never agree to the New Look Wages Plan, for it ruled out cost-of-living adjustments and without them any inflation would shrivel the value of wages. It would be back to the days of Sir Raymond Kelly. At the time neither side imagined that over a period of years the Arbitration Commission would mediate the issue by giving the employers part of what they wanted and the unions part of what they wanted, and that the final result would be a hybrid, a total wage adjusted for inflation, not productivity. Productivity could drop to zero, but if inflation were 10 per cent wages would be increased by 10 per cent, or almost that amount – and that is what happened, and what institutionalised the wage crises of the 1970s and early 1980s. In 1964 the word 'stagflation' did not exist.

The day after Robinson revealed the New Look Wages Plan there was a big union rally in Melbourne, addressed by many officials, including Albert Monk. It passed a resolution: 'This meeting is emphatic that the move to abolish the basic wage is no more than an attempt to satisfy further the selfish demands of employers and from which no benefit can possibly result to any member of the work force'. The meeting called on workers to 'support the basic wage struggle'. In court Hawke poured scorn on the total wage and productivity gearing of it, summoning to his aid the work of the attorney-general, Garfield Barwick. In 1961 Barwick had prepared a White Paper on restrictive trade practices in Australia that showed that a system of monopolies and inhibitions upon free trade existed. Hawke argued that these practices, long outlawed in other countries, rendered invalid the employers' theory that wages be increased only in line with productivity increases, for the theory depended upon the free working of the market. He was, during these years, already developing the idea that was to sweep him to national prominence later, when he set out to break retail price maintenance.

Hawke had a receptive audience for his case. The Bench for 1964 was Kirby, Gallagher, Moore and John (later Sir John) Nimmo, the last a new judge who had come to the jurisdiction only a month before. Hawke knew he could rely upon Kirby and Moore to uphold the 1961 judgment, and probably Gallagher. Even if the decision were split 2–2, the chief judge would have a casting vote, so whatever Gallagher and Nimmo decided, Hawke could not lose. He was at his most relaxed and agreeable in court that year, confident of a victory and not required to engage in the verbal brutality of cross-examination. After 1961, when Dr Perkins had decided he would not face cross-examination from Hawke, the employers had abandoned the habit of calling witnesses. The transcript is scattered with flashes of humour and some unexplained adjournments, when in fact proceedings were halted so that Hawke and Robinson could go to Kirby's chambers to listen to the cricket. At the end of the day Hawke and Robinson would have a beer in the Beaufort Hotel on the corner of Queen and Little Bourke Streets, where they burlesqued their performances in court, acting out imagined conversations between the judges about how each advocate had behaved. Robinson recalled,

> The thing I remember most about Bob in those days was his enthusiasm for debate, on any topic. Whether in court or out, he always had a view – a strong, well-articulated view, on all subjects. And he thrived on debate ... His style of advocacy sought to force a response from the Bench so that the members would become involved, rather than just listen. Once the response came he switched from formal advocate to informal debater. You could almost hear him say, 'Now I've gotcha!' It was the tactic he had used so successfully with Ashburner, in 1961. Kirby was difficult to corner, and when cornered would wax wrathful, but Moore could be drawn into a discussion. We both used a variation of the technique with a commissioner, Terry Winter [who for technical reasons was part of a second Bench simultaneously hearing the 1964 case]. Winter would ask a question when Bob or I was addressing and the one of us concerned would straight-faced say something like, 'I'm glad you asked that question, Mr Commissioner, it shows a shrewd appreciation of the argument I was putting and with the benefit of that observation I can move now directly to the development of a related issue'. And then without answering the question we'd simply resume our submissions. Bob and I used to joke about this in the Beaufort and picture Winter going home that night, wondering, 'What was it that I asked that was so brilliant?'

Another aspect of Bob's advocacy was its apparent credibility. In the 1963 margins case I sarcastically referred to him as 'the golden prophet of economic analysis'. This was, of course, to suggest that he really had feet of clay. Bob presented to the Bench his more difficult economic propositions like a big game fisherman showing off his personal trophies. How then could one doubt the authenticity of such a presentation! If a judge were bold enough to question Hawke's reasoning Bob would take his argument step by step, stopping to ask, 'Does Your Honour follow me so far?' I could never bring myself to do that, but it was sickeningly effective. You see, unless the judge said, 'No. I'm not satisfied – what about XYZ?', Bob felt he'd won him over. It worked more often than not. Even today there's no other advocate who does that in the same way as he can. Every question is an absolute plus to him; he uses a question as a catalyst to embellish his arguments, and the embellishments fit – they sound arguable. That is a very complete forensic skill.

Predictably, for a man who aimed at the brilliant coup and had little patience for detailed planning, Hawke was not so outstanding as a tactician. He was more generous – or naive – than his opponents in the exchange of information. He had a fixed hatred of Kelly and returned repeatedly to Kelly's wickedness, lecturing the Bench about old cases until 'Hawke's historical exercise' became a standing joke and Robinson would suggest languidly that there could be nothing of any moment in the rest of what Mr Hawke had to say, since he had spent two days giving a history lesson. This was a technique that Hawke had learned from Eggleston and did not abandon, presumably, because he so loved to be right – as Sir John Moore described it later, 'banging my head against a wall and saying, "You're a bloody nong!"' The judges were often noticeably bored by Hawke's long harangues on times past and wrong decisions. In the employers' camp George Polites was a born tactician. He planned for Robinson not only the preliminary points, the order of addresses, the nature of the case, its length and how to counter Hawke's arguments, but also such details as whether to avoid splitting Robinson's case over a weekend. Robinson said, 'Bob was less concerned with the peripheral matters surrounding a case: he went for the jugular'.

By 1964 the president of the Commission, Sir Richard Kirby, had overcome his initial hostility to Hawke and treated him and Robinson as favourite nephews. He had come to expect cheekiness and intemperate language from Hawke in court and out. When the case ended in May, in Sydney, Hawke, Robinson and

Kirby were invited to an employers' function held at a golf club, and happened to be sitting together in an alcove. Robinson said,

> Bob was calling Kirby 'Dick This' and 'Dick That'. I never called him anything but Your Honour, or Judge or Sir Richard and Bob got irritated by this. He said, 'For Christ's sake, Jim, be a man. Call him Dick.' And I said – we'd been drinking since eleven o'clock that morning, and it was now about eight at night – 'Now, look here, Bob, that is my choice. I will call him what I want. I might even call him "ya old bastard", but I won't call him Dick.' Kirby sat there, listening to us arguing and highly amused by the pair of us.

Within less than a year Kirby's avuncular tolerance for Hawke was to become a major factor in an industrial relations scandal, the national wage case of 1965. This case, Hawke's worst defeat, led directly to his decision to run for the presidency of the ACTU.

The seeds of the 1965 judgment, which equalled in notoriety the decision of 1953, were planted in 1964. Although Hawke won a victory in gaining an extra £1 for unionists, its award was made on a decision split between Kirby and Moore on one side, and Gallagher and Nimmo on the other, and to make it law Kirby had to exercise his right of the casting vote. On the question of *how* wages should be determined, Kirby, Moore and Gallagher upheld the principles of the 1961 decision; Nimmo rejected them. Since Nimmo was new to the jurisdiction his action was discounted. It should not have been. It was the first public sign that inside the Conciliation and Arbitration Commission a challenge to the authority of the president was evolving. There was a complex of reasons for it; one major one was anger about Kirby's failure to restrain Hawke. Three judges at least – Gallagher, Nimmo and Sweeney – all deplored Hawke's lack of respect, his 'dyslogistic' mode of address, as they called it; his contempt for 'the majesty of the law'.

The whole system had been shaken by his style. Even when most polite, Hawke talked man to man or even teacher to man – 'like a Dutch uncle' – to the Bench. Kirby said,

> While he wouldn't persuade, he was totally honest. Other coves would try to mislead you, but Bob would never, either to strengthen his case or to preserve it from weakness, lie or mislead us. He was like the good little boy who would always own up.

Among the employers and the more conservative union officials there was grave concern about Hawke's style, for he had set a fashion in tough talking that other young union advocates were copying, and they were not always as honest, or logical, as Hawke. In 1963 the Electrical Trades Union called an officers' meeting at which one of the agenda items was: Should an industrial advocate be aggressive? The question was decided in the affirmative only after long debate. There were many less formal arguments. George Polites said,

> We took a conscious decision not to embrace Bob's style of advocacy. We thought it was bad in itself, and bad for the system ... There was a double standard, anyway. Robinson could never have got away with the violent language accepted from Hawke. In his opening submission in 1964 I instructed Jim to needle the Bench, accusing it of having 'a bet both ways'. Kirby became enraged. He called Jim 'a disgrace to your principals' and demanded an apology. I refused to let Jim apologise in the way Kirby had asked. What he had said was nothing compared to the extravagance of Hawke, of his personalised attacks. Bob had the Bench *in terrorem*.

The question of 'Hawke's style' was spreading.

The 1964 decision was given in June; in July Hawke went to Western Australia to argue for a £3 1 shilling increase in the state basic wage. In the opinion of observers he angered the arbitrator by his forcefulness. The awarded increase was only 3 shillings.

While in Perth Hawke appeared on television and, asked about Labor's failure in the 1963 election, replied that the party had been 'inefficient in enunciating its principles in terms of the needs of present-day society'. Within a decade members of the ALP would be able to point to a hundred similar statements from Hawke, his supporters quoting them as examples of honesty and clear thinking, his enemies as instances of contempt for the rules of solidarity.

There were already small signs that Hawke, while a man of the Left, did not fit snugly into its mould. One was his house. In 1964 he and Hazel had sold the Keats Street cottage and bought a two-storeyed orange brick house in Royal Avenue, Sandringham, a street of large and expensive residences owned by business and professional people. There was nothing working class about the place, from its price – £17 250 – to its tennis court. It was well beyond Hawke's means, for he was earning only a little more than £2000 annually. The house had been on the market for eighteen months without attracting a buyer and, although imposing outside was, according to Hazel, 'a soulless place inside, painted battleship grey'. Hawke had fallen in love with its tennis court: it was a piece of his childhood recreated to have a house with a tennis court attached. The owner agreed to sell the house for £12 250 and allow Hawke a year's option to buy the tennis court for £5000. 'My bank manager took a tremendous gamble and agreed to give me a huge overdraft', Hawke said. As a financial proposition for the bank Hawke had one advantage: in 1963 the Sydney *Sun* had published a story referring to, 'R. J. Hawke, the Communist industrial officer of the Waterside Workers' Federation'. (The name should have been Norm Docker.) Hawke sued for libel. One week before his option on the tennis court was due to expire the settlement, for £1000, came through. It was the first of many. Hawke continued to spend his libel settlements on improvements to the house, or in reducing his debts. In later years he would lead guests to 'the Frank Packer swimming pool' and 'the Maxwell Newton sauna bath', but he did not know how much over the years he has won in libel cases, for his lack of interest in handling financial matters was total. He said, 'I had no qualms about libel settlements. The people gathered at the other end of the Bar table to oppose me were earning in *one day* what I earned in a year. I reckoned I deserved the extra cash.' In the 1960s the grandness of the Royal Avenue house excited comment among trade union friends, even though it was half-furnished. 'Most people said it looked as if we couldn't afford to live in it – the curtains were rotting and all the furniture was second-hand', Hazel recalled. In those days the adverse comments were mere ribbing.

Besides the house, another sign that Hawke felt free of the bonds that were willingly, even exultantly, worn by other people of the Left was his choice of friends. From his first years out of school Hawke had enjoyed friendships across the political and social spectrum: Jules Zanetti had been intrigued that Hawke, after tea with the governor, would go to the pub to yarn with men in blue singlets – or vice versa. There had always been some version of hymn-singers and boozers, thesis and antithesis, with *his* life as the synthesis. But it was years before the trade union movement realised that Hawke had many friendships, and a second life, among 'the ruling class'.

In the 1960s one of these friends was Rod (later Sir Roderick) Carnegie, known from Oxford, where he had been a famous oar. Carnegie was a young man on his way to the top in business, already the Australian principal of the American consulting firm McKinsey & Co. They met for lunch every three months or so. Carnegie said,

I found his views on the overall society interesting. I think we shared a common belief that Australia was a country that had to find its own independent identity. The issues that concerned him were: What does it mean to be an Australian? What does Australia stand for? Should Australia depend upon the tradition of great and powerful allies? Whether totally owned foreign companies were good for Australia, or not? Were we developing the country in a way that was most appropriate? He was concerned about the way in which society tried to work together on issues.

These were all matters to which Carnegie, over the years, has also addressed himself. He continued,

> I remember at one lunch we got into disagreement about Menzies. Bob took the line that Menzies would be ultimately assessed as a very bad prime minister, and while I could agree with part of what he was saying, I thought he was not providing a balanced point of view. Among the older members of the community, who were just coping with the shock of England entering the Common Market, and other changes in relationships – the Suez Canal, for instance – I can see how Bob would have come across as a radical person.

By the late 1970s Hawke's friendship with Carnegie and other captains of industry was public knowledge, and the cause of fury in trade union and Left-wing circles. It was thought to demonstrate a change of personality in Hawke, a corruption. In fact, while his attitudes have changed over the years, his behaviour has remained consistent. The boy who did not accept the authority of his headmaster, or the intrinsic majesty of the law, or the church's bans on alcohol and sex, or the drinker's bans on the church, or the judiciary's demands for respectful language, rejected too the authority of his political colleagues to define how he should live.

As an advocate Hawke was about to face his biggest crisis with authority, in the national wage case of 1965. The result was a personal disaster, sweeping away six years of his work. Nationally, it was disastrous also, for the 1965 decision crumpled the trust that both the trade union movement and the employers had vested in the wage-fixing system.

Authority was at the heart of the 1965 case: the authority of legal traditions; the authority of the chief judge; the authority of employers of labour. Industrially, the challenge to authority had already begun. After more than a decade of quietude when there had been a minimum of industrial unrest, and most of that on the wharves, in the boom year of 1964 men and women members of blue- and white-collar unions began to demand their share of increased prosperity, by going on strike. Railwaymen and wharfies, mannequins and public servants struck work and the year had drawn to a close on a note of rising industrial discord.

The employers did not wait, as was usual, for the unions to go through the legal process necessary to create a national wage case but took the initiative and brought on the case themselves. They had decided to apply again in 1965 for the total wage. As a tactic, they were going to carp at the Bench about the increasing turbulence of industrial life – which, they were to submit, the total wage would calm. The idea was a piece of Polites' wizardry.

The Bench for 1965 was Kirby, Moore, Gallagher, Sweeney and Nimmo. Kirby and Moore, Polites knew, viewed strikes as a fact of life in a buoyant economy; the other judges believed strikes were preventable.

The hearing opened in late January but did not get properly under way until 2 March, with Robinson instead of Hawke appearing first. He tendered fifty-seven exhibits, many of them leaflets and articles from union journals that urged demonstrations by members to influence the Commission's decision. One exhibit, the 'militant's blueprint', was an outline for a strike campaign for higher wages. Robinson said,

> We culled the unions' own publications, because they had the ring of their own free minds, and were absolutely delighted to find an editorial, the 'militant's blueprint'. We were using it to scold the Bench for granting £1 in 1964 and were using it, even more importantly long term, to achieve the total wage. In early cases we had produced dozens of examples of nastiness from the trade union movement. But the reaction on a

new mind [that is, Mr Justice Sweeney] to national wage proceedings was quite dramatic – greater than we had expected.
I don't think anybody really *in* the industrial relations jurisdiction would have taken any of the material as gospel without discounting it. What unions say and what they do is
different. There was an unworldly reaction from the Bench.

It was obvious early in the hearing that some judges viewed
militant behaviour with disfavour. For Sweeney and Nimmo this
reaction was understandable, for they were new to industrial relations and unused to the belligerent coloratura of union rhetoric.
Gallagher, however, was one of the most experienced industrial
lawyers in the country. But he held strong views on law and order
and had a reputation for being the most outspoken member of
the Commission on the subject of strikes. Robinson added, 'It's
fair to say that Gallagher was always capable of responding to
that sort of material – an emotive response'. Robinson was offering a 6-shilling increase in wages, for productivity increases, to
be made to a total, not a basic, wage.

He was followed by John Kerr, QC, representing the
Commonwealth. Hawke disliked Kerr, who had an impressive
head of prematurely white hair, and a falsetto voice. When he
swept into court Hawke would remark loudly, 'Here comes
Goldilocks', or, 'The Liberace of the Law ...' Kerr's submission
stated that any wage increase in 1965 'would be fraught with
danger' but was silent on the Commonwealth's attitude to the
total wage – to Hawke's considerable irritation. Hawke's brief
was to apply for an increase of between 12 and 15 shillings in
the basic wage for an increase in prices and productivity, and
to object to the request for a total wage. For the first time since
1953 the unions were *not* demanding reinstatement of automatic
adjustments, such was their faith in the Commission.

Polites, who said later, 'Hawke never understood Gallagher,
and neither did Kirby', had shrewdly assessed the psychology of
all the actors: Robinson was totally prepared and confident. The
minefield had been laid and Hawke strode manfully into it.

Hawke said,

> There clearly was a determination on the part of three
> members of the Bench not to do me, but to do Kirby and
> Moore, and that meant having me as an object of consider-
> able dislike. It was an incredible performance. They behaved
> totally unjudicially.

Polites added, 'Bob made up his mind he had lost the case right
at the start'.

Before the hearing began the Melbourne Trades Hall
Council had circulated a pamphlet reading: 'We ask workers
in all factories, shops, offices, depots, etc. to elect and send
representatives in a continuous stream to fill the Conciliation
and Arbitration Commission's chamber during the hearing of
claims. DO IT NOW!'

Hawke's opening address was smothered by the shouts of his
supporters, proceedings had to be adjourned and Hawke had to
give an undertaking that there would be no more rumpus. On his
first day he clashed with Gallagher; Kirby rebuked him; then he
clashed with Sweeney when he referred to the 1953 judgment as
'infamous'; then with Gallagher again over the question of strike
campaigns. Gallagher, a warm-hearted and emotional man, was
losing his temper with Hawke, who had already affronted him
and Nimmo by attacking them for their dissent from the prevailing decision of 1964. Hawke accused the Commonwealth of
'flagrant and blatant dishonesty' for not stating plainly that it
neither supported nor opposed the total wage. Kerr, when he
had a chance to reply, was scathing about Hawke's 'extravagant
language'.

Early in the case there were lively, amicable exchanges
between Hawke and Sweeney, who arrived each day with an
index of transcripts of earlier cases and was taking an acute interest in Hawke's submissions. Sweeney was known as 'a lawyer's
lawyer'; increasingly, he began to debate with Hawke, to raise
queries, to demand further proof. The hearing had moved to

Sydney on 16 March, to Temple Court where, across the corridor, a royal commission was in progress. Hawke was speaking so loudly that he disrupted its proceedings and a note was sent in asking that he lower his voice; he was also speaking so fast that the shorthand writers could record him for only ten minutes at a time. His voice had broken down in earlier cases; on Hawke's fifth day of talking, to an increasingly irascible Bench, George Polites nudged Robinson and said, 'They're after him. He'll lose his voice in a minute.' Hawke needed a week to recover his voice. He returned full of fight. On 6 April there was another rumpus when 200 wharf labourers picketed Temple Court and stood in the street shouting, 'We want wage justice!' so loudly that their voices penetrated to the hearing, on the building's third floor. After an hour Kirby announced the case was adjourned and police were summoned. The next morning there was a police guard, for the wharfies as they had prepared to move off under orders had shouted, 'You wait! The women are coming tomorrow.' The atmosphere was jittery in expectation of a female demonstration. Hawke assured the Bench there would not be another onslaught, male or female, but Kirby decided that the police guard should remain. Hawke launched back into an attack upon Gallagher and Nimmo, and an attempt to defend to Sweeney the principles of the 1961 judgment that, for days, the judge had been disparaging. The exchanges between Hawke and Sweeney were becoming increasingly splenetic and at the lunch adjournment a group of union officials, including David McBride and Cliff Dolan, took Hawke aside and said, 'Look mate, go easy. He's getting under your guard.' After lunch Hawke had been speaking for only a few minutes, directly to Sweeney, when this exchange took place:

> HAWKE: I think Your Honour will see that there is a classic illustration of the sort of stupidity, if I may say so with respect to the tribunal at the time, that they were getting themselves into.

SWEENEY, J: It is a very different thing to say 'with respect'. If you want to be consistent, you should delete the 'stupidity' reference or the 'respect'.

HAWKE: In that case, I would prefer to delete the 'with respect'.

SWEENEY, J: You please yourself, as far as I am concerned.

HAWKE: Yes, I will please myself, Your Honour.[5]

The atmosphere was electric. Along the Bench faces were pale with anger. Kirby sat in silence and, after what seemed a lifetime, Hawke began speaking again.

Sweeney had clearly rejected the 1961 wage-fixing principles that Hawke had fought for over years; Nimmo had rejected them in 1964 and would do so again. That left Gallagher.

At 10 a.m. on 28 June in the Conciliation and Arbitration Commission Building in Melbourne, the Number 1 courtroom was packed with union and employer officials and journalists waiting to hear the decision. The judges trooped in, sat, then Kirby, his voice shaking with distress, announced that their decision was split, and to the disbelief of his audience continued, 'The majority view will be given by Mr Justice Gallagher on behalf of other members of the Bench'.

It was fifteen years since a chief judge had been rolled.

As Gallagher read the judgment on behalf of himself, Sweeney and Nimmo the shock in the courtroom turned to dismay. The majority decision did not do the one thing that by law a wage case is required to do: settle an industrial dispute. Hawke had lost shatteringly: the 1961 principles, which the unions had so deeply trusted that they had not even asked for automatic adjustments, were gone.

The judgment rejected the unions' formula of prices and productivity. It adopted 'capacity to pay' but rejected the employers' formula for measuring capacity – productivity. It refused to increase the basic wage at all, but awarded an additional 6 shillings to margins, calculated, strangely enough, on the productivity formula. It rejected a total wage, but decided that in future basic wage and margins cases be heard simultaneously, which was tantamount to making the acceptance of a total wage inevitable. It adopted the view that wage increases should be compatible with price stability. It condemned a strike in Mount Isa and the waterside workers' campaign against involvement in the Vietnam War. It pointed out that strikes reduced the capacity of the economy to pay higher wages, inflicted hardship on the general body of employees and asserted that a policy of strike action was diametrically opposed to arbitration, and that strikes were a calamity for the whole community.

Within minutes of the court adjourning, militant union officials were demanding that the ACTU demonstrate the anger of the movement by calling a national strike. An emergency executive meeting was arranged for the following week.

Cliff Dolan recalled,

> Bob was absolutely furious. I sat through the whole case and right from the word Go it had been obvious that Sweeney and Nimmo had a prejudice against him. There was no doubt, if you were in that courtroom, that they were out to get him. His submissions were as good as ever, but he'd lost the case before it started. However, we all still expected a certain amount of justice. There was no justice in the decision ... A big group of us had discussions, going on until the early hours of next morning, about what he could do. Bob was looking for some way to appeal the decision.

There is no appeal against decisions of a full Bench. Nevertheless Hawke called on Kirby in chambers and asked him to overturn the decision. Kirby refused.

In some shops workers had downed tools immediately on 29 June; there were scores of wildcat strikes and the large Communist-led Amalgamated Engineering Union began churning out pamphlets titled, 'Arbitration Be Damned'.

When the ACTU executive met, Hawke addressed it for an hour about the legal possibilities. After another five hours of discussion the executive decided not to call a national strike and directed Hawke to apply for a review of the 1965 decision. Kirby rejected his application, mentioning in passing that judgments need not be 'treated as dogma which cannot be departed from in the future. Indeed the contrary is the case.' It was as good as a promise that, one way or another, the 1965 decision could be reversed but that legal niceties would have to be observed. Meanwhile, Hawke's detractors on the Right-wing of the union movement and among the employers were laughing up their sleeves. In those circles it was held that Hawke had mismanaged the 1965 case and brought calamity on his own head.

Hawke's commitment to a career in the trade union movement had waxed and waned for six years. He had begun work as ACTU advocate with a determination to force reforms in wage fixation, and with his eye on parliament. When he had been rebuffed in 1960 his commitment had taken a further vigorous leap. By 1963 it had relaxed once more. Abruptly in 1965 defeat converted ambivalence to a consuming passion to achieve reform. Within weeks of Kirby's refusal to overturn the decision Hawke had made two resolutions: 'I got hold of that judgment, which was both incompetent and devious, and I determined I would go through it, paragraph by paragraph, sentence by sentence, word by bloody word – and destroy it!' He had also decided to become the next president of the ACTU.

When the news got round industrial relations circles, which it did quickly, for Hawke confides his plans in many, including journalists, some people laughed out loud. The ACTU was a blue-collar organisation; Monk aside, its executive was made up of men who had worked their way up from 'the tools' to jobs within their unions and finally to the top of the union tree. Conventional wisdom of the Right, which controlled the ACTU, had it that *only* a union official could aspire to replace Monk. For an employee and former academic, like Hawke, the ambition seemed as risible as a donkey in the Melbourne Cup. Hawke said, 'Albert and Harold never let me forget that I was only an employee'. Eighteen months earlier when a member of the ACTU executive had suggested the presidency idea to Hawke he had laughed himself and replied, 'I wouldn't have a feather to fly with'. What he needed was a machine.

In the spring of 1965 Hawke began assembling a machine that would drive him forward into the president's job.

TWELVE

Hawke had two recognised, potent skills to counterbalance his handicap as a trade union outsider: one was his capacity to establish rapport – the vast network of friends, the 'good guy' of the pub – the other was his ability as a debater, which at this stage of his career he was restricted to using, in the main, as a wages advocate. Heated and welded together by the fire of moral conviction these skills made Hawke a political agitator, a man who could emotionally bond with an audience and shape the response of huge numbers of people. But only success would give him the chance to address huge numbers of people; meanwhile, he had to rely upon stretching the range of his rapport with trade union officials, whom he could meet face to face, and upon establishing himself as a champion in the minds of the rank and file through his skill as a wages advocate. The authority of his position as ACTU advocate had been important in the Corio election; it would be critical in the ACTU presidential election because Hawke had nothing else that was concrete to point to – no trade, no time as a shop steward or as an organiser, no experience as a union negotiator, no proof that he was authentically of the trade unions and should be their leader.

He turned his attention to advocacy with determination in late 1965. He had two great challenges: one was the wage case of 1966. It was a matter of personal vindication and was vital to his aspirations for the presidency. The other was the 'Local Officers Case', the first major wage case to be held in Papua New Guinea. This was for Hawke a fight against racism – and as such, an issue of Good against Evil. He lost the New Guinea case, but he had a galvanising effect upon political awareness in the territory, and when he left it was amid shouts from white colonialists that he was a rabble-rouser, and from black indigenes that he had given them courage and shown them skills to use in the quest for independence.

In the spring and early summer of 1965, before either of these cases began, Hawke was already busy, with a beer glass in his hand, lobbying people to support him as the next president of the ACTU. Ray Geitzelt, a formidable Left-wing numbers man in New South Wales, remembered that it was close to Christmas time, in the Lygon, when Hawke first talked to him about his ambition, using the exhortation-cum-threat, 'If blokes like you won't support me, I might as well go back to the ANU!'

David Combe, a young but already influential figure in the South Australian Labor Party, who in late 1965 was working on the staff of the state attorney-general, Don Dunstan, recalled,

> I was looking forward to meeting Bob, but having heard that he was the son of a Congregational minister and knowing what the Congregational church is like in South Australia, I assumed he didn't drink. It was 100° [38°C] on the day I went to the airport to pick him up and I was determined to have a beer.

Combe is a tall, friendly man, a Prince Alfred College boy whose speech has a distinctive South Australian plumminess; he was federal secretary of the ALP from 1973 to 1981. He continued,

> I thought I'd say to him, 'Look, you can have a lemon squash, but I must have a beer'. Then this rough little diamond came along and said, 'Bob 'awk. You lookin' for me?' and I said, 'Oh, yes. David Combe. Delighted to meet you, Mr Hawke.' And he said, 'Listen, I don't bloody well know about you, but I gotta have a beer!' So we went to the nearest pub, then to my place and had another, then we stopped at a couple

of pubs on the way to his hotel. And we seemed to strike a tremendous rapport, straight off. He was very open to me about his ambition to be president of the ACTU, and asked me to sound people out, to try to find support. And I did that for him ... It was an idea that was totally offensive to a lot of trade union blokes at that stage. I would talk to union officials, saying how outstandingly competent he was – on that first night I met him a group of us ended up drinking all night and Bob didn't have more than half an hour's sleep, but the next morning he delivered the speech he'd come to make, without a note, and it was brilliant. We brought him back to Adelaide to speak again, and made sure there were heaps of trade unionists in the audience, so they could judge themselves how impressive he was. It was a case of breaking down barriers among people whom he would not have a chance to get to know personally, people who would be participating within the forums of their own unions, as to how they'd vote as ACTU Congress delegates.

Some weeks before either of these direct approaches Hawke had already, obliquely, begun his campaign: in late August 1965 he had attacked the federal Budget on television, speaking as ACTU advocate, and had so inspired some of his friends who were industrial journalists that they had written articles speculating that he was being groomed for the presidency. While the whole Hawke family spontaneously felt the need to 'use their voices, to spread the good news', Hawke himself also had a highly developed sense of the usefulness of the news media. His success in using the press and television was so great largely because publicity – being the centre of attention – corresponded perfectly with a major element in his personality, laid in infancy and childhood. Hawke had mesmerised his parents: he relished and had the knack of mesmerising. As his personal assistant, Jean Sinclair, commented later, 'It was cruel to watch Bob with journalists. They were lambs to be slaughtered. He's so complex, and so defensive, that there was never one who got close to understanding him.'

A few weeks after the president-to-be stories had appeared Albert Monk, flanked by George Polites and another senior employers' representative, Doug Fowler, arrived in the chambers of Sir Richard Kirby. They were there to lodge a formal complaint, on behalf of organised labour and organised capital, about the ACTU advocate. Kirby recalled,

> I couldn't understand what Albert was getting at, initially. He shifted from foot to foot and mumbled behind his hand. I can still see the smirk on George Polites' face – he'd taken a step or two back and was standing behind Albert. Albert finally said, 'Look here, young Hawke is getting too big for his boots. We want you, as President of the Commission ...' It was some footling thing about an adjournment I'd granted Bob, which he had not first cleared with the ACTU. George's eyes were shining – he was almost bursting with suppressed laughter.

Monk was sixty-five, but he had given no sign about when he might retire, and Harold Souter was his obvious successor as president. The war of nerves had begun, and was to last another four years. In the meantime, Hawke had to recoup his losses of 1965 in the 1966 wage case.

At the ACTU biennial Congress of August 1965 the militant Left of the trade union movement had demanded a new wages policy: the Left wanted to abandon the prices and productivity argument and to replace it with a submission for a 'living basic wage'. The 'living basic wage' was new only in name; it was the old 'needs' concept which Mr Justice Higgins, the philosopher-king of wages arbitration, had made famous in the Harvester Judgment of 1907 when he had referred to the needs of 'a man, wife and about three children ... living in frugal comfort in a civilised community', and had thus begun the whole process of centralised wage fixation in Australia. In the image of that family group of little battlers there is something peculiarly appealing – there is pathos, courage and solidarity. Higgins himself had decreed that such a basic wage should be 'sacrosanct, beyond the reach of bargaining'. His words were engraved on the hearts of the trade union movement and on those of the electorate at large. During the Depression, a judge who was required to reduce the basic wage publicly described his job as 'disgusting'. The Harvester Judgment was a great piece of law; it was also a grand piece of nonsense, for it supposed the male worker was married and sire of three children – which was pure fiction. By 1920, as a commission of inquiry discovered, all these notional marriage beds had produced 2 100 000 phantom children;[1] by 1965 Australia's population, if one went on the Harvester Judgment, would have rivalled Indonesia's. However, the official of a male-membership trade union who will publicly acknowledge this little curiosity of wage-fixation has not yet been born. One practical effect of the Great Law was that women could not, while the basic wage existed, get equal pay – *logically*, because working women were not – or had no right to be – supporting spouses and three children. Another effect, obviously, was that the single man was very much 'overpaid'.

While the definition of the basic wage created a gross injustice to working women (the influence of which is still evident, in the 1980s), and has been a factor in youth unemployment, it has had another egregious effect, for it mixed together the concept of employee and of citizen. Trade unions were established for a specific purpose: to get the best possible conditions for the working man, through bargaining with employers. There have always been paternalistic employers who have, like kindly feudal lords, cared for their employees' security throughout life. But the Harvester Judgment, the very foundation of wage fixation, institutionalised feudal thinking: by it, the employer was required to bargain with the whole man – the worker producing goods, the citizen raising a family. This system can work very well – for example, in Japan, where the roots of feudalism have never been severed and are the support structure for a mighty industrial tree. But in Australia, matters that in a democracy *should* be dealt with in regard to the whole nation – for example, accident compensation and superannuation – have been made the responsibility of employers. As for the unions, they are mentally and emotionally so accustomed to mixing up the concept of worker and citizen that it seems to them as proper as a law of nature. The corollary is that there is little reason for this vast number of working people to elect governments that will diminish the relationship between labour and capital, sever the feudal bonds, and take responsibility for the welfare of the whole citizenry. The very effectiveness of trade union bargaining makes federal Labor governments unnecessary for the trade union movement. Liberal–Country Party (and later Nationals) governments have known this for a long while, and have known, too, that the responsibility for reform can be carried lightly.

Meanwhile, particularly for the Left of the trade union movement, it is now unacceptable *not* to mix up worker-and-citizen.

At the ACTU Congress of 1965 the Left demanded that a 'living wage' of £22 a week, some £7 higher than the existing basic wage, become the new ACTU policy. Hawke, already beginning to build upon the support of the Left-wing for his presidency campaign, gave an impassioned speech of opposition. He said, 'I was told beforehand that I would prejudice my position with the Left, but I thought, too bad – they are wrong and I am going to say so'. Sir John Moore commented later,

> I think he personally very deeply believed in trying to improve wages and conditions, but that is overlain by his understanding of economics. He understands that if wages go too far, other economic results happen, which may not be good for the country, and he has to balance those two things. Inherent in everything he does is a strong sense of trying to look after the ordinary person.

Hawke defended the 'prices and productivity' formula at Congress while personalising his address in such a way as to make a vote against 'prices and productivity' a vote against his competence as an advocate. It was a ploy he was to use time and again: at heart, an unconscious emotional manipulation. The Left's proposal was defeated. A decade later Left-wing union officials were to recall the arguments they had had with Hawke – in the public forum of the 1965 Congress and privately, in bars – about ACTU wages policy and to think that they had misjudged him all along: at the very moment when he was gathering them to his cause, when they were falling in love with him, he was, in disguise, 'just a pragmatist'. The danger is always there for the man who, even unwittingly, sculpts from the emotion of his supporters a response that, without emotion, they would not give: when the love affair is over, when they reflect in solitude, they believe themselves robbed. The passionate hatred the Left came to feel for Hawke should be seen in the context of the see-saw's crash from the heights of rapport – infatuation – and the use that Hawke made of it, thudding down to resentment.

The 1966 case, which because of the complicated nature of the competing union and employer claims was called the Basic Wage, Margins and Total Wage Cases, began in February 1966 before Judges Wright, Gallagher and Moore, and Commissioner Winter. Kirby had put Sweeney and Nimmo off the Bench and, diplomatically, himself.

The new presiding judge, Syd Wright, had been in the 1930s and 1940s the employers' greatest advocate and when he had been elevated to the Bench in 1951 there had been rejoicing in their ranks. But Syd, a man of mischievous wit that was enhanced by a deep, melodious voice, had, on becoming Mr Justice Wright, abruptly appalled his former patrons. He declared he was a child of the working class himself and was for the employers what John Kerr became for Gough Whitlam – in the words of one of Wright's former clients, 'the worst appointment we ever had'.

The case got properly underway on 8 March, when Hawke – appearing for the Electrical Trades Union, the Amalgamated Engineering Union, the Blacksmiths' Society, the Boilermakers' Society, the Federated Moulders' Union, the Sheet Metal Workers, Agricultural Implement and Stovemaking Industrial

Union, and the Miscellaneous Workers' Union – began his
opening address. He had been sitting in the sun in his back
garden, watching his children playing, when he had made the
decision that he would go through the 1965 judgment 'word by
bloody word – and destroy it!' The hour was now approaching.

His opening address lasted for three weeks, a display of stamina that, in itself, was extraordinary. For the first week Hawke
concentrated on the function of the Conciliation and Arbitration
Commission as defined by law, which, he submitted, it had not
been properly exercising:

> the overwhelmingly important issue which you must decide
> in these proceedings: what is the function and charter of this
> Commission ... ? Is it to be a tribunal for the prevention and
> settlement of interstate industrial disputes ... Or are [you]
> going to abandon and substantially submerge that function
> in an attempt to assume and discharge primarily the role of
> an economic sub-legislature ... trying to create and sustain a
> favourable economic climate ... ?

He was gingerly in his criticisms of Gallagher: '... we do not
necessarily identify with that [1965] judgment a representation
of Your Honour's complete position on these basic issues ...'
Again he performed 'Hawke's historical exercise', to the considerable interest of the presiding judge, Wright, who had not
heard it all before. Gallagher grew restive when Hawke gave
quick jabs at the 1965 judgment; however, Hawke remained cir-
cumspect in his replies to the judge, sprinkling 'with respects'
through every answer to him. But on 15 March, the first day
of the second week, Hawke got into his stride, and the fight
between him and Gallagher was on, for Hawke had begun his
destruction of the 1965 judgment and in terms of the 'fools and
crooks' who had written it. After the lunch adjournment, Wright
exercised the responsibility of the presiding judge by saying:
'Mr Hawke, you have been invited to criticise quite freely; you
realise that. But I would suggest to you that words like "blithely"

and "outrageous" do not help your case at all.'[2] Hawke withdrew the words and five minutes later used 'blithely' again. By 16 March the transcript was studded with Hawke's sarcasms: 'now this remarkable statement', 'what sense can one make of a judgment which does this?', 'the Commission has come to a hopeless position', 'what meaning can this sort of language have?', 'literally non sense', 'in my unceasing search in trying to make sense of these things, I went to my dictionary', 'now this is a completely objectionable sentence', 'one is certainly indebted for the increase in the fund of knowledge which is involved in this next sentence', 'but the next paragraph is equally objectionable'. By lunchtime the following day Hawke had goaded Gallagher into a rage and the judge burst out:

> I place on record that this is a wanton, reckless statement which should never have come from a senior advocate before this Commission. It is the sort of statement you expect from the lips of some Domain Demosthenes or a Hyde Park Cicero. It is absolutely unworthy of you and it is absolutely untrue.
>
> HAWKE: Then it will probably be necessary to pursue that after lunch, Your Honour.
>
> GALLAGHER, J: You please yourself about that.
>
> HAWKE: Yes, I shall.[3]

The court adjourned. After lunch Hawke returned, still determined to overwhelm Gallagher with shame for the 1965 decision, but taking a different tack, and one that, if anything, was more intimidating.

> HAWKE: I have a job to do, not for Hawke ... it is not Hawke speaking, but the representative of all those people ... 80 per cent of the Australian population.[4]

Already he had begun the political leader's practice of referring to himself in the third person, as an instrument through
which the voice of the people is heard.

On 18 March the court adjourned because Hawke had again
infuriated Gallagher by referring to the 1965 judgment as a
'diatribe' and 'absolute humbug'. When the judges returned
to their Bench Hawke was required to assure them that he was
not imputing personalities. On 22 March, when Hawke was still
continuing his attack on the 1965 judgment, Wright was moved
to say: 'Mr Hawke, there will have to be some limit as to which
we can conduct a post-mortem on last year's proceedings, you
know ... I would ask you to spare us everything you can as regards
the past.'[5]

Hawke continued his opening address on 23, 25, 29, 30 and
31 March, and then the Commission, punch-drunk, adjourned
for a couple of weeks. Perhaps the attention of Jim Robinson and
George Polites had wandered during Hawke's marathon forensic
autopsy (which Polites described as 'the hypnotic approach – if
you say it often enough, people will believe it'). At some stage
before Hawke had begun his third week of talking, he had been
at Melbourne airport and had bumped into his old friend Keith
Hancock, who was now Professor of Economics at Flinders
University. Before going to different flights, they had a quick chat
during which Hancock, who had been an adviser to the Vernon
committee, told Hawke that he had, since writing a chapter on
wages for the Vernon report, changed his mind, and that he had
made a speech to the Victorian Chamber of Manufactures about
his revised ideas on wages. He gave Hawke a copy of his speech
and, on 23 March, Hawke referred to it in the Commission and
offered to make copies of Hancock's speech available to the
Bench. Somehow, Robinson and Polites overlooked the warning
sign. Robinson began his opening address on 21 April, compli-
menting the Commission for its 'courageous' 1965 decision –
and the next day made the first of many references to the Vernon
report, for its chapter on wages had numerous points in common
with the 1965 decision, and substantiated the employers' claims.

The Vernon report was one of the great controversies of the mid-1960s. To counter criticism of government actions that were said to have led to the economic recession of 1961, Menzies had in 1963 established a Committee of Economic Inquiry, under the chairmanship of Sir James Vernon, chairman of the Colonial Sugar Refinery, and including Sir John Crawford, director of the Research School of Pacific Studies at the ANU, Professor Peter Karmel, Dr D. G. Molesworth and K. B. Myer – a distinguished selection of leaders from the fields of business and academia. Their report, which had inquired into Australia's demography, employment, basic resources, savings, imports, exports and likely growth patterns, was one million words long. It had been tabled in parliament in September 1965 and had embarrassed the government – and angered the Treasury. There was heated argument for and against its recommendations, with comments being sought from overseas economists and with every newspaper editorialist in Australia dashing into print about which of its one million words should be considered sacred, which profane. Inside the hubbub there was a still, quiet centre; the Prime Minister, Sir Robert Menzies, was exercising a prerogative of power: inertia. In the long run, Menzies ignored the Vernon report.

On the next day of sitting Robinson talked at length about the Vernon committee and tendered, as his ninth exhibit, a report on its chapter that dealt with wages. It looked like an ace for the employers. But Robinson and Polites had just made an egregious tactical mistake with Exhibit R 9. They had cornered Hawke, and in that position, he dares.

Hawke recalled,

It was a backs-to-the-wall job. Jim was carrying on about the Vernon report, which endorsed everything the employers had been saying, and ruined us – knocked off our conceptual approach. Finally I thought, 'God, we've got to do something, or we're going to be battered to death'. We were still getting our ears belted off when the court rose for lunch [on 3 May]. So I went back to the office and I put it to Harold

Souter that what we had to do was to call the Vernon committee and examine them. Albert Monk rejected the idea out of hand, but Harold, to his credit, was positive; he was superb, and finally Albert accepted Harold's arguments. So when the court resumed after lunch I announced that we wanted the Vernon committee called for cross-examination. Well, Jim and George Polites had kittens, on the spot!

Hawke had asked that the Commission itself call the Vernon committee; the Bench refused to do so. The next morning Hawke announced his second step: he had prepared subpoenas for the men to be summoned to court. Robinson argued desperately that the Bench should not allow the Vernon committee to be subpoenaed and questioned by Hawke but as Polites, at least, knew intuitively, there was no chance that Mr Justice Wright would pass up such an opportunity for amusing diversion. The prospect of a rough and tumble union gladiator taking out his net and sword against the lions of the Establishment was too great a temptation for His Honour to resist. Robinson argued on; Wright observed with a note of wicked amusement, 'Sir James ... may be straining at the bit to get here!' The employers and the Commonwealth, represented by Kerr, continued their objections, for hours, until the Bench announced it would adjourn to consider the matter, but before rising Wright had interjected, 'Mr Robinson, what is so obnoxious about our witness box? You speak of it as though it were in the category of a jail', and Gallagher had added, 'Or at least a dock'. Again, the decision would hinge upon Gallagher; everyone knew that Moore would not allow Hawke's subpoena because, as he explained later,

> If you had the Vernon committee subjected to cross-examination the government might well find it very difficult to get people in public life ever to undertake these tasks. Hawke was a ruthless cross-examiner; there were no holds barred. I thought the Vernon committee shouldn't be exposed to that kind of thing – for they may well have submerged

some of their own views in order to get unanimity. That's what happens with unanimous decisions – you have to learn to yield, but you wouldn't want to be cross-examined on every aspect of it, because you might not agree with every aspect of it. And yet, you've put your name to it.

At 12.20 p.m. on 6 May the judges returned, sat, and two minutes later Mr Justice Wright announced to a packed court-room that he and Mr Justice Gallagher were in favour of the Vernon committee being subpoenaed, and that summonses for them were to be issued. The court then adjourned until 17 May, with journalists running for telephones, Hawke and the union people jigging with excitement and the employers' men cursing. Hawke recalled,

I'd been able to say that here were the employers relying upon this document, this revelation of divine economic truth, and now, Your Honours, they don't want it examined. It was a pretty nice position to be in. When the Bench agreed that the committee could be called the government went mad, everyone went mad. There was an enormous kerfuffle. The government was pleased with the Vernon committee's line on wages – the process of disowning the report had not begun at that stage. When the hearing resumed and Vernon arrived it was unbelievable how many lawyers came in with him: there was Jim Smythe and Hal Wootten – *two* Queen's Counsel to protect him – plus all their juniors. And Kerr. At the Bar table you just couldn't move for silk!

The David-and-Goliath atmosphere was, for Hawke, a pure delight. Kerr was particularly active, supporting Smythe's objections about Hawke's questions to Vernon, objections that came with a leaping to the feet every minute or so. For Hawke there was an added pleasure: Clem and Ellie were in Melbourne on holiday and spent much of each day in the court, which was packed solid. Ellie, aged 67, could not tolerate idleness any better than she could at twelve, and sat in the courtroom knitting like a machine, until a tipstaff ordered her to stop. She was attending adult education lectures and was contemplating travelling abroad, since, officially, she was too old to work. Although her hair was grey, she looked a good fifteen years younger than her age and could still run everyone, except Hawke, to a standstill.

On 27 May, the first morning that Sir James Vernon spent in the witness box, his lawyers were so assiduous in his protection that proceedings became farcical. They jumped up to object to every question of Hawke's that even nudged towards economic matters, claiming that he was cross-examining his own witness. Hawke was unusually polite. He said,

> My blokes were really frustrated; they thought we would be unable to get to Vernon. I told them, 'I think you'll find it's different after lunch': at one point Vernon's counsel had objected, 'That is like asking a plumber a question about medicine', which I had thought would appal Vernon.

At the luncheon adjournment Sir James joined his counsel at the Windsor Hotel and told them he was prepared to answer Hawke's economic questions. That afternoon Hawke's real examination of the Vernon committee's wisdom got underway and, as Sir John Moore recalled, 'the people who were worried that Bob would tear Sir James to pieces were left gasping'. Hawke was as gentle as if he had been talking to Clem.

Hawke said,

> Essentially, the statistical point upon which the committee had hung its theoretical argument was that there had been a stability of wages' share of national income over a period of years. Our argument was that because of wrong policies of the Commission, wages' share of national income had declined. Now the committee, using its figures showing a stability of wages' share, had gone on to argue that the Commission should base its judgments upon economic capacity – in other

words, the employers' productivity approach – and that it should not consider productivity *and* prices. Well, if you consider only economic capacity there is always *something* the employers can produce to show that economic capacity will not allow an increase on wages – either farm income is too low or too high, or exports are down or up, or investments are too low, or retail trade is going bad, or secondary industry is wobbly – there is always some bloody thing the employers can pull out of the hat, and say, 'This proves any increase in wages will be a disaster, Your Honours'. Well, we were sure that we could show that the Vernon committee's basic premise about the share of wages was wrong, and that therefore, the committee's argument fell apart. And the beautiful thing was that Sir James Vernon was a very honest witness. I took him through the report's statistics and our statistics, step by step, and he said, 'I'll have to agree that we were wrong'.

By the end of Hawke's questioning of Vernon on Tuesday, 31 May, Robinson's case was in serious disarray. Hawke recalled,

The employers were saying, 'Vernon is not a professional economist; wait until Hawke has to deal with Professor Karmel'. Karmel was put in the box and agreed with everything I'd put to Vernon; Myer was next and was almost embarrassingly willing to confirm what had been said by the others.

It was all over for Robinson.

The hearing ended on 16 June and he and Hawke went off for a jubilant spree. During hearings neither of them drank more than a couple of glasses of beer each day and the tradition was now established that when the court finally rose they should set out to get drunk. The party following the 1966 case was famous. Robinson recalled,

We finished early – about 11 a.m. – and decided we would drink nothing but champagne. In those days a lot of people

would come down to the Beaufort for after-case celebrations – unionists, Commissioners, people from ICI and
TAA – and would want to drink with us. So we made this
condition: they were welcome to join us but they had to buy
a bottle of champagne – and having done that, they would
have the privilege of trying to shoot the champagne cork into
a brass pisspot which was up on a ledge in the Beaufort, above
the bottles of spirits. The barmaid, Vi, said that if anybody
could do it the pub would donate another bottle of champagne. There were scores of people shooting at the po, and
on the other side, in the public bar, people were staring at
us – in the mid-1960s drinking champagne in a pub was a
peculiarity.

By five in the afternoon nobody had succeeded in shooting the
po, then, as Hawke recalled, 'A secretary from the Commission
walked in, a kid about twenty, and said, "Give me a go" and
bang!, she did it in one'. Festivities continued.

On 8 July, amid a tumult of publicity, the Bench gave its decision. A photograph of Hawke that took up almost all the front
page of the Melbourne *Herald* shows him reading the judgment
with such intense pleasure that the tip of his tongue is pressed
against the corner of his mouth and he looks ready to eat the
document. The basic wage had been increased by $2, a disap-
pointingly small amount, but the principle of fixing wages according to prices and productivity had been reinstated. Hawke had
burnt down the 1965 judgment. However, he had not destroyed
the employers' arguments for a total wage. A minimum wage had
been instituted (paving the way for equal pay); the Bench had
decided to inquire into the margins system and when its inquiry
was completed it would, with certainty, bring in the total wage.

As nobody then realised, the Commission had set in train a
fateful process with its decision, in 1966, to inquire into the metal
trades (margins) award. There are some things, the *arcana arcanis-
sima* of life, that are very ancient, queer and untidy – like the
relativities within the metal trades, the origins of which stretch

back to the Middle Ages or perhaps further – and that are safest left alone. To a tidy legal mind, however, the desire to impose logic and order can overwhelm common sense. This happened. The Commission, after its inquiry, tampered with the metal trades and brought not order, but chaos. As Polites remarked, 'When you alter the fitter's margin you start a landslide'. The landslide resulted in the great industrial battle of 1968 that the unions very convincingly won and that sealed the fate, as far as major Australian employers were concerned, of the new prime minister, John Gorton. He had not supported them. The victory for militants was followed by the Clarrie O'Shea case of 1969,[6] and another victory: the penal powers of the Industrial Court, hated by the Left, were transformed into meaningless pieces of paper. Union militancy had won vindication and encouragement in a time of economic boom, when employers were willing to pay higher rates, on a base that was already enhanced (by the total wage) and in a world that was economically overheating, thanks mostly to that monstrous dollar-making machine, the Vietnam War. Hawke's campaign for the leadership of the trade union movement was to coincide with the greatest surge of industrial militancy for twenty years, and he would be swept into the office of president on a wave of excitement and apparently endless prosperity. The Hawke style – of aggression and optimism – was beautifully matched to the looming hour.

Within a couple of days of the Beaufort celebration Hawke was in Papua New Guinea for the case he considers the most interesting and important of his career. It was called, mildly enough, the Local Officers Case, and was about the pay rates of black members of the Papua New Guinea Public Service Association (PSA). But at heart it was a question of colonialism, independence and racism – above all, racism. 'We truly believed we were part of a crusade. Spontaneously, at parties, we would begin singing that song, "We Shall Overcome"', a former PSA official, Rod Madgwick, recalled. 'It was an amazingly emotional case.'

Albert Maori Kiki (later Sir Albert) wrote of Papua New Guinea in the mid-1960s:

> ... we used to have district officers in the Gulf district who brought local girls into their compound, stripped them naked in the garden, hosed them for twenty minutes, then slept with them and kicked them out immediately afterwards ... What I find most offensive is the way Europeans have native women and despise them at the same time. Even today, in 1967, a former district officer, W. Kennedy, can write in all seriousness: '... Few Melanesian women are attractive. On our accepted standards most men would actually find them repugnant.' And he can get this published in a serious magazine like *New Guinea*.[7]

In the small, stifling, white community of Port Moresby, with its neat fibro bungalows and its men servants referred to as Boy to their faces and Rock Ape behind their backs; in the slatternly sprawl of native dwellings, built without kitchens or bathrooms, where only the rich owned a pair of shoes, where a man wearing a suit was regarded with fear – there, in that atmosphere of distrust, racism was the very air people breathed, even in their dreams. Hawke arrived like a wind from the sea on a dead summer afternoon. 'He came into our lives with a great whoosh!' the wife of an Australian journalist said. Madgwick recalled,

> He was bubbly and charmed everyone; he seemed to have no sense of race. He brought a feeling of creativity, of original thought and encouragement. For example, there was something called the Papua New Guinea Society. The atmosphere in Moresby was so conservative that the very word 'union' was embarrassing and unions made sure they never called themselves unions. Bob gave a talk to the Papua New Guinea Society, which was multiracial, about the Australian trade union movement and people couldn't believe their ears. Their eyes were bulging. Blacks and whites. He was frank and assertive.

He dared to talk about things [like the rights of labour] which were unimaginable ... Bob is a great encourager.

The people whom Hawke encouraged are a who's who list of the independence leaders of Papua New Guinea, in politics and the civil service. 'He was a hero there', Madgwick continued. 'I think Bob's work in New Guinea was his finest hour.'

Hawke first went to New Guinea in late 1965 for the opening manoeuvres of the case. As usual, he was initially distrusted by some as 'an outsider', and worse: a man brought in to abort the plans already laid to improve the wages of blacks. Paul Munro, then the industrial advocate of the PSA, said,

I distrusted Hawke. The PSA was run by whites. Among the local officers there was total disenchantment with it, and splinter groups had formed, outside the PSA. A case had been dragging on about expatriates' territorial allowances and the arbitrator was delaying finishing it. Meanwhile, we were planning the case for the local officers. The Administration [the government in PNG] made an offer on territorial allowances which was unacceptable. Suddenly Bob Hawke arrived to argue the second case and I thought, 'Well, hell, here's the sell-out. It will all be done by reference to the superior expertise of an Australian lawyer. The whites will get a good deal and the blacks will get nothing. And Hawke has been brought in to fix it – to tell everyone that it's got to be like that.' So we went into negotiations with the Administration and Hawke, to the great horror of a couple of us – almost disbelief – threatened the arbitrator [L. G. Mathews] that if he did not finalise the territorial allowances issues the PSA would *withdraw* the local officers' case. You could have knocked the Administration side over with a feather. I still remember the pause in which people caught their breaths, and the look on Hal Wootten's face [Wootten was the Administration's legal adviser for the wage cases] as he tried to work that one out. But whatever was the shock of our opponents, it was only matched by the shock on our side. What if the Administration said, 'OK, withdraw'? We'd be lost. I was totally convinced, as was everyone else in the room, that Hawke was serious. And it was a bluff. But it was a bluff made possible by his aggression. You see, he dropped it suddenly, unexpectedly and with extraordinary aggression – shouting something like, 'If you don't settle we'll bloody well withdraw the local officers' claim!' – and it was the aggression that carried, people responded to his anger and were unable to think rationally. After a couple of minutes the Administration buckled and said, 'All right, we'll deal with the territorial allowances'.

If Hawke had any doubts that his opponents in Papua New Guinea – that is, the government and its representatives – were fools and crooks who required intimidation to bring them to reason and goodness he showed no sign of indecision. Soon after he took over the case, which was part-heard by mid-1966, he established what he called, 'the Pavlovian treatment' for the arbitrator, Mathews. As with Kirby and later Gallagher, Hawke set out, in part, to browbeat Mathews into accepting the PSA claim. 'It was a professional tactic', Munro recalled.

Bob's theory was that he would put Mathews on the spot. If he didn't respond in the right way, Bob would have a public altercation with him. If he did respond nicely, Bob would be soft. Mathews used to get discomfited. He'd twist and show obvious physical embarrassment whenever an uncompromising request was put to him. Another tactic was to have our witnesses present their evidence with aggression, to stand up in court and say how angry they were about their rates of pay. This aggression was not directed at Mathews but at the whole Administration – and, of course, the press. Bob believed that the decision was going to be taken not in Port Moresby, but in Australia. It wasn't a matter of influencing the local Administration so much as of influencing Barnes, the Minister for Territories, and the Australian population.

We [in the PSA] were utterly oblivious to the significance of the press. Bob flattered, coerced and seduced the local press-men into covering the case, and he was always extremely alert to discover in a statement – or to have someone else discover in a statement – the newsworthy lines. And he got tremend-ous publicity that way.

One night Rod Madgwick chipped Hawke about the press coverage he was getting, implying that Hawke was mostly seeking publicity for himself. Hawke was drunk. 'He tore me to shreds', Madgwick recalled. Paul Munro had realised that Hawke was working for a cause larger than (although concentric with) his own ego:

> The publicity affected the courage of our witnesses. By the two things – encouraging them to be assertive and state their grievances in public (and proving to them that they could do that without the sky falling on their heads) and, second, by showing them how to get the news media on side – Bob was training Papuans and New Guineans in basic political tactics. He worked by example, but awarely. And a big group began to pattern around him.

Pangu Pati, the political party that formed the first independ-ent government of Papua New Guinea, had not yet come into being in 1966. But when Pangu did form in mid-1967 every member of it had taken part in the Local Officers Case, either as a witness or as a researcher or as a participant in the subculture that the case generated.

An early problem was the local officers' disenchantment with the PSA: they had to be convinced that the union was sincerely concerned about them before they would agree to help. Hawke was taken along to address the most radical and sophisticated group of disillusioned blacks – teachers – and won their trust. 'I loved them and they loved me', he said. Once the teachers were on side, the others followed.

The case itself had come about due to an extraordinarily insensitive Administration decision: in September 1964 the Administration had imposed salary cuts on black employees; as a result a black doing the same job as a white received about half the pay; in addition, blacks had to pay going prices for house rental, while whites had their rents subsidised. Added up, a white public service employee had at his or her disposal about two to three times as much money as a black colleague of the same sex doing the same work.

The Administration justified its decision on two grounds: the economy could not afford more (for a variety of reasons, including the danger of rural workers leaving plantations to seek higher wages in towns); it was necessary to pay whites higher salaries for without financial inducement they would be unwilling to work in the Territory.

The least skilled public service employees – all blacks – were reduced to penury, unable even to afford a weekly tin of the ubiquitous and loathsome (but nourishing) bully beef. The case that the PSA decided to mount in defence was monumental, based on 'needs' and 'capacity' and embracing in its sweep a mountain of evidence about nutrition, social customs, the state of the economy and regional differences in it, and the danger inherent in allowing resentment to fester in a colony – one that was so central to Australia's defence. There were more than a hundred witnesses for the PSA side and their evidence has provided a transcript that is a goldmine for historians, sociologists and economists. Hawke said,

> It was *immensely* challenging. I arrived cold and had immediately to absorb an enormous quantity of information in areas about which I knew nothing. I had to get on top of a mountain of material about New Guinea's economy, and about sociology and nutrition. I loved that challenge. I worked harder in that case, I think, than I have ever worked in my life. Paul Munro and Rod Madgwick had done the leg-work of finding witnesses and preparing them and for the first few months

I was operating as a real barrister, not knowing the witnesses before I had to examine them in the box. For me the exercise idealised the concept of a barrister, mastering a huge mass of material, for a case in which he deeply believed.

The transcript, read fifteen years later, sounds like an account of life in some province of economic disaster, yet the Australian economy and the international commodity market, upon which the Territory's trading income depended, were buoyant in 1966, and the witnesses were all employed. From transcript:

Nearly all of us trainee information officers have to go without breakfast in the second week after we are paid. Sometimes we have to go without food at lunchtime, because we do not have enough money . . .

I had no sheets or blankets until Mr Newly bought me some, on the condition that I repay him . . .

I am Thomas Vincent To Bun Bun, a teacher . . . I cannot afford to buy a second-hand VW . . . I am embarrassed by my house . . . I cannot afford to dress my sons properly . . . Australians ask me to their houses, but I cannot reciprocate their hospitality . . .

I am a medical officer . . . we begin to hate our colleagues, the overseas officers, who get much higher salaries than we get . . .

I am Michael Somare, an announcer with Radio Wewak . . . my income is $37.38 a week; my family expenses are $33.80 a week . . . we need decent, neat clothes . . . I have been to Australia and seen houses like the Administration is building for [black] Local Officers, used for cattle sheds or hay stacks on farms . . . In most of the Administration-type houses in Wewak – I am occupying one – there is nothing like stove, sink or proper bathroom and laundry facilities provided. Bathrooms are placed next to the lounge room or entrance to the room, and water has to be carried in buckets to the room: if there were visitors it would be an embarrassing thing or sight to see wife carrying water in it – just walking into the lounge room where you are sitting and getting the bucket into the shower room ... if wife wants to do washing she has to wash outside and empty dishes just on the grass ... our toilet stinks. I had some officers from Canberra. I asked them to come in ... They said, What is smelling? I said, That is toilet ... I am ashamed to invite [whites] to my home ... I now have an opinion that many Australian clerks are employed here so that what the Australian taxpayers contribute goes back to their people's own pocket ... As my friend Albert Maori Kiki puts it, New Guinea is 'whiteman's paradise' ...

I am Dr Reuben Taureka, District Medical Officer for Madang ... I earn $3810 ... I have 386 people working under me, including 45 overseas officers ... my highest-paid subordinate, a surgeon, earns $10 200 ... I cannot afford a car, but most of my subordinates own cars ...

The theme of shame recurs throughout the witnesses' evidence for throughout Melanesian society male self-esteem depends upon ability to give and to repay hospitality, measure for measure, or better. The pay rates and the slum housing of blacks meant that they felt not mere embarrassment, in the Western sense, but unmanned, eunuchs, vis-à-vis white males. It's no surprise that rape was a problem in the Territory and that white women lived in fear of it.

Munro said,

Just a few years earlier a deputy administrator, Gunther, had scandalised the white community by inviting Reuben Taureka and his wife to a cocktail party. Drinking at the time was prohibited for blacks and only became legal in 1962–63. It was a totally paternalistic society. White officers wanted and expected the blacks to behave like orderly sons and children, not to swear back or resent white authority. So when a Papuan stood up in court and made these statements of resentment and anger white officers felt terribly wounded and confused.

The Administration was alarmed by the publicity and aggression that had surrounded the case since Hawke had taken over in June 1966 and on 13 July the arbitrator, Mathews, had rebuked Hawke and the PSA for using the press. On 30 August the Territory's Treasurer, A. P. J. Newman, announced that if blacks' salaries were increased there would have to be budget cuts: roads and hospitals, for example, would not be built. The case had been adjourned; when it resumed on 12 September Hawke applied his 'Pavlovian treatment' to the arbitrator, saying,

> As far as we are concerned in these proceedings we are fighting the Administration, and as far as I am concerned the Administration was having its budget presented through its spokesman, Mr Newman. We ask that … you should take the first available opportunity to rebuke the Administration for offending the canons of common courtesy, responsible behaviour and, in fact, your clear observations of 13 July … The Treasurer's statement in the House [of Assembly] must be seen, and is seen, as pointing a gun at your head, Mr Arbitrator.

Hawke referred to other statements made by Administration representatives in the House of Assembly and went on to ask Mathews to declare his independence, 'to protect the integrity of the office you hold'. He called the Treasurer's remarks 'contemptuous of this tribunal', 'political dishonesty' and 'intimdatory of the arbitrator'. Mathews refused the request. The emotional temperature of the case heightened: Hawke's next witnesses were policemen and Hawke demanded that the tribunal hear them in camera, for the men were fearful of speaking out publicly. There had already been acts of insubordination by blacks to whites in the police force, thanks to resentment about pay. Mathews agreed to a closed session. The Administration had not yet made an offer to the PSA on what it would be willing to pay the least skilled black workers; Hawke's tactic was to keep up the heat while the Administration was considering the matter. After the police, he requested permission to include in evidence a document that revealed that district officers (whites) were alarmed by and condemned the blacks' wages. The Administration claimed privilege and Mathews upheld their claim, refusing to accept the document as an exhibit. Hawke demanded higher authority, and the question had to be argued in the Supreme Court. It upheld Mathews' ruling. At this point the Administration made its offer: the lowest paid workers had their salaries increased – from about $7 to about $15 a week. (A chicken in the Rabaul market cost $1.50, and in the Kerowagi market $2.70.)

As Hawke began his summing up of the evidence of the 112 PSA witnesses, he argued fiercely the issues of morality and common sense: that the existing salary structure was improper and immoral and 'positively dangerous'. For this last claim Hawke drew on the police evidence and the work of Dr T. B. Millar, a defence expert, who had written in his book, *Australia's Defence*, that PNG was 'essential', and that the attitude of the local population was a factor in handling any threats to the Territory. Hawke argued that the dissatisfaction created among black public servants opened the possibility of subversion; that the advantages of defence spending in the Territory, which had increased by 10 000 per cent in the past seven years and, in 1966 stood at $20 million, could be negated. His submissions recognised that to attract Australians to work in the Territory, high salaries had to be paid; he sought for the blacks 55 per cent of the white rate, and a single man's rate – thus avoiding the great pitfall in the Harvester Judgment. And then, in repetition of his daring a few months earlier with the Vernon committee, Hawke dropped a bombshell: he demanded from Mathews permission to put Hal Wootten, QC, the counsel for the Administration, in the witness box. What happened next is still remembered by old New Guinea hands as one of the most passionately debated issues of the 1960s; in New South Wales legal circles, from which Wootten came, Hawke was regarded as a scoundrel. Even Munro, who was as committed to the case as Hawke, 'felt uncomfortable. I had a lawyer's distaste for calling the opposing advocate.'

Wootten [later Mr Justice Wootten] was a liberal and a friend to PNG; he had been concerned about the salary cuts of September 1964 and had written an article, which was published in the *Bulletin* of 27 February 1965, pointing out that there were 'serious implications for race relations' because of the salary cuts. He had then accepted the Administration's brief to argue against significant pay increases for blacks. For Hawke, this was a perfect example of what he had despised since Law I: the advocate as hired hand, arguing for a cause in which he did not believe. Wootten's later career revealed a man of considerable social conscience, and already he was a member of the Association for Cultural Freedom, had done much to develop the Law School in PNG and had many black friends in the Territory – the distinctive mark there of the liberal. Because of Wootten's sympathy the Administration's case was 'probably presented with a little bit more compassion', in Munro's view. Indeed, when Michael Somare was in the box (as Hawke's witness) he had become carried away by his own rhetoric and had added flourishes to what he was saying, under oath. Wootten could have demonstrated that Somare was not a totally reliable witness, but he stopped short in his cross-examination and allowed the issue to slide away. Munro continued,

> None of those things about Hal rated with Bob. Bob was very judgmental: he wasn't a cab-off-the-rank sort of a lawyer, and Hal was. Bob caught Hal between his conscience and his professional obligations, and embarrassed him ... It was a *political* as well as an industrial case, but I was tremendously naive. I didn't understand that, in such a context, you might call a witness just for effect, or for the *political* argument. Calling Wootten had great significance for it dramatised, it kept the story hot, it demonstrated that even the opponents of the case had misgivings about the propriety and long-term validity of what they were espousing. And that should have an influence on the arbitrator, but above all it should have an influence on the political system that the arbitrator represented.

Mathews spent four days considering Hawke's request to put Wootten in the box, during which Wootten's junior, the Sydney barrister R. J. Marr, argued vigorously, claiming that Hawke and the PSA had lied about their purpose and that their real aim was not to elicit evidence from Wootten, but to force him to withdraw from the case. Hawke is enraged whenever he is accused of lying, and indeed throughout his life his only lies have been to women (about other women). His exchanges with Marr were acrimonious; he accused Marr of 'the most vicious personal attack you could conceivably imagine'. Mathews adjourned for a day. On 14 October he announced that Wootten could be sworn.

Wootten's article had said, referring to earlier times: 'Natives felt that "white men" regarded them not as fellow human beings, but as tools or domestic animals, well cared for and courteously addressed by the enlightened, abused and insulted by the ignorant or neurotic, but accepted as an equal by none', and that these prewar attitudes were returning.

> Before the recent Public Service salary cuts there was a growing body of natives who could afford homes and meals to which they could invite Europeans without embarrassment, although if present policy continues this advantage will be confined to native politicians, businessmen and private practitioners in the professions. Until these cuts ... native Public Servants received the same basic salaries as Europeans ... the general expectation amongst natives was that by hard work and the acquisition of Western skills they could hope to attain something approaching the envied standard of living of the white man. Now they are to receive a markedly lower salary (e.g. a fully qualified native medical practitioner will start on about £9 12s. a week), which they are told is related to the economic capacity of their country ... a round of drinks costs the same for [black and white].

Hawke questioned Wootten with all the power of his own, outraged conscience; Wootten fought back, with dignity:

The role of barrister is not to assist those with whom they [*sic*] happen to agree, but to provide a service to the community ... That entails, sir, a duty on a barrister to accept any brief offered to him, unless he has a good reason for refusing and his personal views on the issues involved are not such a reason.

After a morning of high drama, during which Port Moresby talked of nothing else, it was over: Mathews announced, 'I will now adjourn. I look forward to easier times for all concerned.' Hawke spent the next three days summing up his evidence, then the court went into recess until January 1967, when the Administration was to present its case. While the PSA witnesses, with a few exceptions, had been blacks, the Administration witnesses, without exception, were whites.

For the PSA side one of the most useful occasions for encouragement and display of solidarity had been mixed race parties. Munro recalled,

Even until 1965 there was still an awkwardness in multi-racial parties. Most of the PSA officials, other than me and Madgwick, were not at all sure about how to go about inviting blacks, or how to serve local people when they came to parties.

As the case progressed blacks and whites overcame their uneasiness and their socialising became euphoric occasions, with laughter and rousing songs. Hawke has always enjoyed singing – he knows scores of hymns and in his drinking days would bellow renditions of 'Abide with Me' or 'Onward Christian Soldiers', champagne or beer bottle in hand. The songs in New Guinea were 'We Shall Overcome' and 'Whose Side Are You On?' Munro recalled the atmosphere of the parties,

We were all mounted on our white chargers, pursuing truth and justice, and Bob was the hero, the champion of a cause in which we all believed. What people were seeing and experiencing was unique: here was an Australian, an extremely gifted one, fiercely presenting everything we believed in, in a totally uncompromising way, completely committed. There was warmth; there was adulation; there was a collective sense of belonging to a crusade. We were a subculture in the community, members of a political-movement cult.

On the eve of one of Hawke's departures for Australia during a recess, there was a grand celebration that was interrupted by a dog fight. The blacks and wiser whites stood back but Hawke and two other men rushed in to separate the animals. A minute later they retreated: two pairs of spectacles had been smashed, one human leg ripped open and Hawke had a broken wrist. The dogs, looking puzzled, trotted outside to the street to fight in peace. Hawke had involved himself even more recklessly a few months earlier when, walking from his hotel at night, he had come across a large crowd watching two blacks fight; he had broken through the crowd and separated the combatants. As both blacks and whites told him later, it was sheer luck that he had not been set upon by either the fighters or the crowd and beaten to a pulp, for payback is central to honour throughout Melanesia and for all he knew, the fight may have been a matter of high principle.

At thirty-six Hawke carried within him still some of the prejudices of his upbringing: one night in PNG he saw a blue movie, an experience he found 'awful' and never repeated. It confirmed his disapproval of pornography. He also scorned gambling. There was little public entertainment in Port Moresby and Saturday afternoons were particularly empty. Munro and the foreign correspondents of the Australian newspapers, with whom Hawke spent much of his leisure time, were keen on punting, and Don Hogg, of the *Australian*, ran a book. The journalists also played one of the favourite card games of South East Asia, variously known as 'Oh, Hell', 'Bum' and, in the more vulgar argot of the Australians in Port Moresby, as 'Fuck Me'. Hawke and Hogg's wife, Gail, were rival champions. On one of his visits to Perth in this period Hawke said excitedly to Ellie, 'I know a tremendous new card game; it's called "F... Goodness Gracious Me"' (which is what journalists later called 'Oh, Hell' in Port Moresby).

When Hawke first saw his friends crouched around the radio on Saturday afternoon listening to the Australian races, he took a step back and repeated the phrase, famous in the Lygon Hotel, of an old Communist trade union man, 'Hush, the workers are at prayer'. At first he refused to take any interest in punting. But one day Munro asked Hawke, who was going to visit Hogg, to place a bet for him there. Hawke asked Hogg for a form guide, picked a horse, and laid a bet himself. With typical bravado he returned to Munro, announcing, 'I've picked the winner!' He had. Soon afterwards he had a strange experience: he dreamed a race that had not yet been run. 'I saw every detail, and a horse called Pirate Bird winning.' When the race came up it was as he had seen: he won at 16 to 1 on Pirate Bird. Hawke was hooked. Punting became for him what croquet had been to Ellie, a second religion. In 1967, when he returned to Australia and began to keep office diaries, their pages were filled with two categories of name: those of trade unionists he was lobbying in the ACTU presidency campaign, and those of potential race winners.

When he returned for the easier section of the case, during which the Administration would put its arguments, Hazel and the children came too. He had been missing the family, talking frequently to Munro, who was a bachelor and had a bachelor's uninterest in children, about his wonderful offspring. Hazel by now had recovered from her long grief over the death of Robert and was as warm-hearted and jolly as she had been in her twenties; she enrolled the children in a mixed-race school and took them swimming in the afternoons at what was considered 'the black' beach. Years later, when Stephen had refused to attend university, despite his outstanding academic potential, and instead committed himself to working for Indigenous Australians, Hazel suddenly remembered him frolicking in the sea with Melanesian children and caught her breath as she was describing their life in Port Moresby, to say, 'Oh! ... I've just seen another connection'.

Moresby friends recalled, 'Hazel thought Bob was wonderful. She was terrifically proud of what he was doing.'

The key witness for the Administration was Sir Leslie Melville, a distinguished economist, who had made a study of the PNG economy for the case. His evidence embraced three major economic themes: urban drift theory, projections about the gross national product in the Territory, and the type of wage structure suitable for the Territorial workers, urban and plantation. Hawke cross-examined him for three days. Munro said, 'I think it was probably Bob's best cross-examination: an absolutely searching analysis with a very guarded, cautious witness, traversing a huge area. People, including all the resident practical and academic economists, were fascinated by it, for it was a very complex debate.' Hawke considers his handling of Melville the high point of his career as an economist-advocate, yet it went virtually unreported in Australia, as complicated matters tend to do. A much more dramatic, newsworthy exchange occurred towards the end of the Administration's case when Dr Roy Scragg, the director of public health in the Territory, appeared. Scragg had been a medical officer in PNG since 1947; he gave evidence that 'a person can physically adapt himself to an intake of 2000 calories [8400 kJ] and when this is all the body will receive he can remain a healthy person'. Much PSA evidence had been concerned with the poor nutrition, due to low pay, of blacks. Scragg said that only one in 1636 native men grew to six feet (1.83 m), and therefore it was wrong to set a calorific allowance, for the food intake suggested by the PSA was only necessary for the exceptional person, and unnecessary for the normal, small one. He said that if blacks' salaries were increased the money would not be spent on food, but 'for other purposes'. (He meant alcohol.) Scragg also said that shoes were not necessary in the Territory – sandals or scuffs were good enough – and that most local officers were 'overpaid'. He added that a salary increase contented only for a short while, then the local officers wanted another increase. Hawke was in a cold rage as he questioned Scragg, so alarming the arbitrator, Mathews, that he broke in, 'Can you take it quietly, Mr Hawke?'

Hawke's cross-examination went on for three days until, at last, Scragg's word was left supported by one thread: assertions about the prevalence of Vitamin A deficiency, as revealed by clinical cases of eye disease in Port Moresby. Hawke cut that thread then abruptly, as he had done before, with Truman, he allowed Scragg to escape. Munro recalled,

> Bob would not go in for the *coup de grâce*. He was very gentle. He just stopped. It's such a rare thing for barristers to be able to destroy an important witness, and the most natural self-indulgence is to go for the kill, to ram his lies down his throat and do an exultant dance around him, so that when he steps down he is a totally humiliated person, without self-respect. Now, lesser people – and, in fact, I – would have done that with Scragg. Bob went as far as he had to, then gave quarter. I can still remember the silence in the courtroom as Scragg shuffled his papers together and stepped down.

On 11 May 1967 Mathews gave his decision in an 88 foolscap-page document: while middle-ranking black public servants had some gains, the lowest paid officers had got only an extra $40 a year, leaving their salaries a quarter of the effective base rates for whites. Hawke had been in Australia since the end of the case and had returned for the decision. A party had been arranged for that evening, in anticipation of great news. From the outset the atmosphere was tense.

The party was held in a block of flats and among the blacks were Henry ToRobert, an economist (and later, Sir Henry, governor of the Bank of Papua New Guinea), a Tolai educated at St John's College, Sydney University; and a Tolai friend, Robin Koemina. Munro said,

> There was acute bitterness about disappointed expectations. About ten o'clock Robin Koemina came in and complained that a white, who'd somehow come to the party, had propositioned his wife as if she were a prostitute. Henry ToRobert,

who was in his twenties then, about 6 feet tall [1.83 m] and very fit, went for the bloke.

What happened next was terrifying: David White, the *Sydney Morning Herald* correspondent, said,

> It took four, maybe five, men to hold Henry down – you can't believe how strong he was. I will never forget the look in Henry's eyes. I grabbed hold of the Australian and said, 'You must leave!' but he was so drunk he didn't understand what was happening, so to save him I pushed him over the balcony and he fell about ten feet [3 m] to the ground.

Munro and Hawke had not moved. Munro said,

> Robin Koemina, one of my long-time friends, and very friendly with Bob, walked up and stood about a foot in front of us and screamed into our faces, 'That's integration for you!' The racial hatred in the whole room … it was horrifying. At that moment, if Bob or I had said or done anything – well, we would have been blasted across the floor. Then somebody, Reuben Taureka, I think, said, 'I think you had better go home'. What made the hatred more unbearable was that it came from and was expressed through people who'd been educated in Australia.

Hawke said of the decision, 'In terms of destroying their witnesses and establishing our witnesses, we won the case *overwhelmingly*. But the tribunal was predisposed to the Administration's case.' He was angry and now his sense of the dire had been aroused by the passion he had witnessed. He returned to Australia and immediately began publicising the injustices and dangers of the pay scales. He wrote a resumé of the case then persuaded Senator Sam Cohen (Labor), Edward St John (Liberal, MHR) and – such was his commitment – Senator Frank McManus (DLP) to take the matter up in parliament.

Meanwhile, there was a storm of debate in the Territory's House of Assembly. On 3 June, a Saturday, 1500 black public servants and a few whites had marched on Government House to present a petition to the Administrator, David Hay. Many carried placards, one of which was a drawing of Mathews holding two blacks down by their necks. Such a demonstration had never happened in the Territory before. The *South Pacific Post* reported the event as 'wildly dangerous' and warned of 'bloodshed', although there had been no violence. When the House of Assembly sat again on 6 June a coffee planter, Ian Downs, Member for the New Guinea Highlands, said that Hawke had fomented and organised the march, referred to him as 'a rabble-rouser' and 'this demagogue' and went on to claim, 'This arrogant advocate was much more concerned that the arbitrator did not kiss his feet in submissive adulation by meekly succumbing to a racist approach before the Arbitration Court than he was really and genuinely concerned with the result'. Downs also referred to the lack of 'gratitude' shown by New Guineans. He spoke for many white planters and other expatriates, who saw Hawke as close enough to the devil to make no difference. Back in Australia, Hawke issued a statement to the press saying he had no supernatural powers and therefore could not organise a march at a distance of 5000 kilometres, and invited Downs to repeat his remarks outside the House, so he could sue him. He continued his campaign to swing Australian public opinion behind the local officers. On 7 July the *Australian* ran a story by John Hurst, headlined, 'It's not just a question of salaries, says Mr Hawke ...' that told of the threat to security from a discontented public service. Hawke appeared on television and radio; he spoke to ALP branch meetings. On 30 September the *Age* had a headline: 'NG Pay Policy a "Tragic Blunder": Hawke Warns of Bloodshed'. In November he returned to Port Moresby to argue before Mathews for a review, saying, 'a massive section of significant Australian opinion demands that the judgment be reviewed', adverting to the speeches of St John, Cohen and McManus, and adding, 'throughout the political spectrum

there is support for a review'. The application was refused. But
the Territory would never be the same again. When the case
had begun the idea of self-government was discussed, if at all, in
terms of something which might be possible in the twenty-first
century. By November 1967 self-government, followed by independence, was inevitable. Pangu Pati had been formed. Michael
Somare became chief minister in 1975 and seven months later,
prime minister.

The new government left the public service pay scales virtually unchanged. Munro, reflecting on the PSA case later, said,
'We were wrong'. He and Madgwick both made the point that
Hawke was unwilling, afterwards, to re-examine the wisdom of
the PSA case, in the light of what would be best, economically,
for an independent PNG. Hawke commented: 'At the time independence was an unreality, a Sometime-Never discussion. It was
futile to discuss the appropriate wage structure for an independent country when the country was, and would be for the foreseeable future, dependent.'

Somare's private secretary, Tony Voutas, said later, 'Hawke had
a great influence on Michael'. Hawke had influenced others,
too, for he had talked constantly, while in the Territory, of
Australian political and trade union events, with such zest
and optimism that he inspired enthusiasm where none or
little had existed before. One of his close associates in PNG
was Ian Macphee, eleven years his junior, a barrister who had
presented the early sections of the Local Officers Case while
Hawke was in Australia arguing the 1966 basic wage. Hawke
talked to Macphee about his ambition eventually to enter –
and lead – the Australian parliament. Munro said, 'Ian told me
that if Bob could have those ambitions, so could he'. A decade
later Macphee was one of the Fraser government's most successful and progressive young ministers, and at Hawke's direct
urging both Munro and Madgwick had become activists in the
Australian labour movement; by the late 1970s Munro was
federal secretary of the Administrative and Clerical Officers'

Association, and one of the most powerful union leaders in the country.

Meanwhile, Hawke's own parliamentary dreams were once more in abeyance. In 1966 Whitlam had called on Hawke at the ACTU and asked him to run for Corio. Hawke had refused and in the 1966 elections Opperman held the seat. When Opperman resigned the following year Whitlam, who by now had replaced Calwell as leader, again called on Hawke, who recalled, 'Gough was all over me. "You've got to! You've got to run for Corio!"'

By this time, however, Hawke's campaign for the ACTU presidency was gathering momentum; Labor had been out of office for eighteen years and the trade union movement was, as it has always been except during World War II, a far greater force in the community than its legislative sprig, the federal Australian Labor Party. The state Labor parties had more power, but Hawke had no ambition to be a premier. He told Whitlam that if he failed to win the presidency of the ACTU he would want to go into federal parliament immediately; if he did become president of the ACTU he would need about six years in the job, and added that presidency of the ACTU appealed to him more than parliament, 'because in that job you're making decisions all the time. In parliament, at best, half the time.' Years later, while recalling the meeting, Whitlam in his tone of voice showed irritation with Hawke for raising such an objection – but by then, they were estranged. At the time they admired each other's talents and had a warm friendship, based on solidarity in a common cause. It was a friendship that concealed, for years, the undercurrent of rivalry and disapproval on both sides. Whitlam, a puritan himself, condemned Hawke's boozing and womanising; Hawke thought Whitlam lacked emotional depth and that his compassion was merely intellectual and, ultimately, jejune. They disliked each other's arrogance. Each assumed himself the star around which dimmer constellations moved. Fortunately, both had a sense of the ridiculous. In moments of extreme exasperation with the leader Hawke would inhale deeply, frown, then burst into a breathy, trochaic Whitlamesque speech – like,

'Why, have you given me this written in Látin? You know I only read Gréek.'

Whitlam was of the upper middle class and his formal educa-tion, though shorter than Hawke's, was superior in breadth and ornament. While the foundation of Hawke's education had been the Bible, the foundation of Whitlam's had been the encyclopae-dia. Whitlam loved the elegant – in the arts, in clothes, in food. His mother was a sublime cook, and in adulthood Whitlam's love of elaborate cakes was famous. Hawke has no eye for ele-gance (he discovered only in his mid-twenties that he is colour blind) and little interest in it. Within his own world, in which the red spectrum does not register, Hawke's taste may be exqui-site but to people with normal colour vision he dresses loudly, or did, before he began to take advice from friends. Hawke, whose appetite is small, thinks about food only when he is hungry, and if the ambience is right will relish a takeaway hamburger or a tub of chips. His vice is sweets: Violet Crumble, Mars Bars, chocolate almonds, ice cream and strawberries. (As a young child he was seriously rebuked only once, and that was for stealing a sweet from the corner store.) Round the dinner table in Hawke's child-hood conversation had been about distress in the parish and the appropriate verses of inspired writing that could offer guidance; in Whitlam's household the discussion had been of literature, classic and contemporary, of national and international issues, with members of the family rearing to their feet to consult refer-ence books to check precisely what Clemenceau or Pericles had said. Whitlam had a vision of Australia as the new Hellas, socially enlightened, flourishing in the arts, an example to the world of intellectual vigour and creativity. Hawke's vision was far more austere and laconic: Sparta, to Whitlam's Greece. He knew the spartan world of pinched finances, hard work and inferiority. It was the common man, not the grandiloquent spirit, at whom Hawke looked and whom, through the trade union movement and, after that, the parliament, he yearned to rally and uplift.

When he returned from New Guinea in May 1967 he had a national wage case to present, which inevitably he would lose, for his brief was to object to the total wage and, obviously, the Bench was going to introduce it.

(When the Bench did, the ACTU, on Hawke's advice, appealed to the High Court. The appeal was rejected; Hawke then set himself to discover how the trade union movement could use the total wage to its advantage. Apart from Kirby, who thought the total wage was dangerously double-edged, Hawke was the first to recognise that the trade union movement could transform what it believed was a straitjacket on wages into an area of freedom. He was condemned for this insight at first by some union leaders, later by the employers. When Hawke entered parliament, conservative politicians accused him of responsibility for the high level of wages in Australia. They ignored or were ignorant of two facts: that it is the Arbitration Commission that determines wages, and that it was they and theirs who had insisted upon the total wage in the first place. By 1981 Hawke was again arguing that the total wage should be rejected for a return to the basic wage and margins system, or a similar system, under new names. He argued for the cause that was always uppermost in his mind: the well-being of the ordinary worker. The craft unions, highly skilled, highly paid and Left-wing, were furious with him: from them there was much talk about 'a new Billy Hughes' and 'Labor rat'. Indeed, such a system as Hawke proposed would be repulsive to, for example, an AMWSU member earning, as the best-paid did in 1981, $35 000 indexed for inflation.)

By 1967 Hawke was becoming jaded with the wage cases. He had accomplished far more than had seemed possible nine years earlier: the employers now espoused, as their own, half of his argument (productivity increases); the judges acknowledged the importance of prices and were studying economics; and scattered throughout the trade unions there were other, younger advocates who had learned from him and would be able to carry on when he stepped out of the arena. Jim Robinson was so disconsolate at the thought of losing his sparring partner that he decided to abandon advocacy and become a judge. Moore said nostalgically, 'When Bob went, the sting was gone from wage cases'. The heroic age of advocacy was ending. Hawke had agitated and educated. But his focus had been narrow; he wanted now to widen his lens, to take in all the concerns of the union movement.

Albert Monk was in his sixty-seventh year and in poor health but he had as yet given no sign as to when he might retire, held back because the ACTU was without a provident fund for its president. He would certainly not step down before the biennial Congress, to be held in August 1967, but it was unlikely that he would stay on past 1969 for it was a trade union canon that a man *should* retire at sixty-five. If Monk were to retire between congresses the executive would appoint an acting president; the danger for Hawke's ambitions was that the executive, elected in 1965, was weighted to the Right and would, if unchanged in 1967, appoint a Right-winger. Souter was the Right-wing favourite to succeed Monk – ironically, because in the 1950s he had won the secretaryship thanks to Left-wing support, for in those days he was a radical from whom the Left hoped for great changes in the ACTU. By the mid-1960s he was spurned by the Left. In the words of Sir Jack Egerton (another man in whom political change was later to be observed) Souter had become 'the complete bureaucrat. A big disappointment to us.' Hawke's task of unseating an Acting President Souter would be almost impossible.

As soon as he had returned from New Guinea he launched an offensive to shake the Right's grip on the executive at the 1967 Congress.

That Congress became what Right-wingers called later, in rankling voices, 'the boilover year'.

THIRTEEN

T HE ORGANISATIONAL WORK that achieved the 'boilover' of 1967 owes most to the General Secretary of the Miscellaneous Workers' Union (MWU), Ray Geitzelt, of the Left.

Geitzelt, who had trained as a chemist, had, after serving in the AIF, joined his father's chemical company as an employee and become active in the MWU, which, in the early 1950s, was under Right-wing control. In 1954 he set out to defeat the union's leadership; he took legal action to have MWU elections declared invalid. Geitzelt's instructing solicitor was Neville Wran and his junior counsel was Lionel Murphy. The action succeeded and Geitzelt became one of the most formidable numbers men in New South Wales; nationally, his union was active throughout the state structures of the ALP. It was on the say-so of the MWU that Wran (later premier of New South Wales) was appointed to the Legislative Council in that state and Murphy (later attorney-general and self-appointed to the High Court) was selected for a winnable place on the New South Wales Senate ticket. By the mid-1960s Geitzelt was on the central executive of the New South Wales ALP, where moderate and Left-wing colleagues of his were Charlie Fitzgibbon of the Waterside Workers' Federation; Fred Hall, of the Meat Industry Employees' Union; and Joe Anderson of the Painters' Union. That other most important part of New South Wales machine politics, the Trades and Labour Council (TLC), was controlled by a confederacy of Right-wingers: Jim Kenny, the secretary; Ralph Marsh, the assistant secretary; John Ducker, the organiser and Freddie Brown, the president. Already the Left–Right fight within the New South Wales machine which, in 1970, led to federal intervention, was being waged and a spirited feud established: Geitzelt and Ducker were learning to dislike each other to the point of detestation.

Geitzelt had, until the mid-1960s, committed his talents to state politics and to building up his union – which he did with notable success, raising it from 19 000 members in 1955 to more than 60 000 a decade later. In 1965 he had backed a move to have one of the New South Wales Right's most intelligent and articulate spokesmen, Joe Riordan (later Minister for Housing in the Whitlam government and vice-chairman of the New South Wales Electricity Commission) unseated from the ACTU, but had failed on a tied vote. He had held no ambition to be a member of the ACTU executive himself – until the Left's defeats at the 1965 Congress.

In that year the 16-member executive slewed to the Right. The economy was booming; Australia was about to send conscripted, unenfranchised youths to fight in a foreign war; and there were many trade union leaders, Left and centre, who had grown tired of waiting for a federal Labor government to take up causes and who believed that the time had come for the unions to wage major industrial and social campaigns. However, they were held back by a cautious ACTU, and cautious trades and labour councils: the Right had effective control of the trade union movement in New South Wales, Victoria, Tasmania and South Australia, and in Queensland the flabby giant, the Australian Workers' Union, acted as counter-force to the more energetic, Left-wing TLC.

When, soon after the 1965 Congress, Hawke asked Geitzelt to support him in a campaign for the presidency, Geitzelt telephoned his union's federal president, got his blessing, and pledged to run against Joe Riordan in 1967. He worked quietly and efficiently: Hall, Anderson and Fitzgibbon all joined the Geitzelt–Hawke team. Of these, Fitzgibbon was crucial, for the transport group of unions (which he could influence) had a large block of Congress votes and, personally, Fitzgibbon was a man of notable ability, especially in administration and in framing resolutions that would outwit or sidestep ambushes from the Right. His rather frosty manner, his command of language and his capacity for sarcasm caused many to fear him. The AWU hierarchy, with sly Queensland humour, referred to Fitzgibbon as 'The Educated Waterside Worker'. The AWU was another reason why Left and moderate union leaders were prepared to join in the early sparring that would precede the real fighting for the ACTU presidency. After 1965 the AWU began negotiating in earnest to affiliate with the ACTU, a move that for forty years it had resisted. The AWU would bring a large batch of Right-wing votes into the 1967 Congress; it had bargained, as the price of its affiliation, to have its own permanent seat on the ACTU executive. The executive membership would increase to seventeen. (Needless to say, all seventeen would be white males born in Australia or the UK and, with the exception of Geitzelt, not a 'foreign' name among them.) The AWU's decision to affiliate was an irony for Hawke, because the union would stand against his presidential ambitions, yet it was joining the ACTU in part because its boss, Tom Dougherty, had been so impressed by Hawke's ability as an advocate.

As the Congress approached, the Right felt no frisson of alarm; Souter, although he continued to place restrictions upon Hawke's activities as an employee, had not yet begun manoeuvres to ensure his own succession. As usual, the executive had allotted Hawke time on the agenda to deliver a major economic policy speech. Like every other Congress there would be Left–Right skirmishing and the Right would end up firmly in control. Or so it was thought.

But to this basic plot a fine machiavellian twist was added. In February 1967 Whitlam replaced Calwell as leader of the ALP and from that moment a new type of Labor Party began to reveal itself. Whitlam appealed to large numbers of Australians who had been ignored by both major parties. He appealed to women; Indigenous Australians; immigrants; artists of all types – and to

the arrivistes of Australian society, the sons and daughters of the
working class who had recently climbed in to the middle class.
In realising their dreams they had shucked off their parents' class
ideologies, but still had a nostalgia for Labor, and were eager
for someone to give expression, in modern, materialist terms, to
their old family loyalties. The new Labor Party that Whitlam
was shaping with such verve and urbanity relegated the rhetoric
about Communists and anti-Communists, the very foundation
of the DLP, to the level of a barnyard cackle. Riordan said,

> There were those in the DLP who foresaw that with a
> moderate ALP, under Whitlam, the DLP would disintegrate;
> it was, therefore, to the DLP's advantage if the ACTU execu-
> tive could be pushed to the Left, for then the Right could
> scream, 'Look what's happened! The trade union movement
> has fallen to the Left!' On the eve of the Congress I knew
> that something was going on; two very senior officers of the
> ACTU shared my concern that the extreme-Right had done a
> deal with the Left for its own, undisclosed political purposes.
> The size of the vote for Geitzelt confirmed my worst fears . . .
> It also illustrated that there were forces against Souter being
> very effectively organised.

In a landslide victory, Geitzelt defeated Riordan for a seat on
the ACTU executive by 83 to 56. When all the balloting was
over there were six new faces on the ACTU executive, five of
them Hawke candidates. The *News Weekly*, organ of the National
Civic Council, announced: 'Left-wing march to power', a cry
that had already been uttered by sections of the mass media.
It was malarkey. The slewing to the Right had simply been
adjusted; the victory had been for moderates, and could have
been greater if Laurie Short, a Right-winger, had not suddenly
contested a seat that he had no chance of winning, split the contest between a Left-winger and the moderate Cliff Dolan, and
thereby given another executive place to the Left. At the end of
the Congress the numbers on the executive were 9–8 in favour

of Souter. Hawke had taken the opportunity offered to him to give a rousing campaign speech to the 'Workers' Parliament', as Congress is called. The federal Budget had been brought down a few days before Congress opened and followed upon a survey that showed that one person in sixteen in Melbourne was living in poverty. The Budget had paid scant attention to the poor, as Hawke pointed out.

It is, in many senses, the most objectionable and grotesquely inequitable budget of the whole postwar period. It is a budget of the privileged, by the privileged, for the privileged. It is contemptuous of the plight of the needy and warrants the utter condemnation of this Congress ... For the tremendous effort of picking up his telephone and saying one word – 'sell' – to his broker [a speculator] would make a completely tax-free capital gain of $37 000. Compare this with the worker in BHP from whom the government demands an increasing proportion of his income by way of tax. In one day alone earlier this month ... the face value of BHP shares rose by $44 million ... But this government refuses to tax any part of this unearned income. This sacred right of profit-taking must be protected at all costs for the privileged minority.[1]

Having roused passions on this subject Hawke moved to the next stage of a leader's speech – an exhortation for constructive activity to counter the challenge:

There may be a number of issues which divide us. But let us remember that we are a powerful movement. The substance of economic and wages policies being put before you provides the opportunity, I suggest, for wielding our power unitedly, progressively and without friction ... Let us unite so as to achieve a rejection of the powers of privilege and, positively, establish that which we are all concerned to establish – a society whose resources will be utilised to the maximum and wherein the reward for labour shall be fair and equitable and the needs of the weak and those unable to fend for themselves shall be our overriding concern.[2]

His had been a star turn: aggressive, logical, compassionate and responsible, a speech structured on the classic formula of 'agitate, educate, legislate' and appealing to the deepest emotions of the trade union movement – envy, sense of pathos, altruism. After two years of very quiet planning – Riordan said later he had no idea that Geitzelt was Hawke's numbers man in New South Wales – Hawke's challenge for the leadership was now in the open.

Immediately a 'Hawke cell' formed on the ACTU executive, meeting in private and with Hawke present, to plan manoeuvres. Hawke, as an employee, was allowed into executive meetings only if invited to speak on a specific issue, while Souter, by right, was present at all meetings. But Hawke was to have two years' training for running the executive through these private meetings (of which the Right, for some months, remained unaware). During this time he drafted many of the recommendations that his supporters then presented, as their own, to executive meetings. However, before the first gathering of the new executive was held, something happened which polarised the ACTU into bitter factions. Jim Kenny, the senior vice-president of the ACTU (and secretary of the New South Wales Trades Hall) died. Hawke's supporters proposed that he should be replaced by the moderate Cliff Dolan. The AWU's representative on the executive, Edgar Williams, arriving at his first meeting and expecting that things would continue as they had in the past, with the odd far-Left dissent from a majority view, recalled:

Now, there must have been an understanding of some importance, some deep appreciation of each other, because a group arrived at the first executive meeting and announced that Cliff Dolan was ready, with his bag packed, to take Jim Kenny's seat. As soon as they proposed that, the meeting deadlocked eight-all.

Ducker, who had been busy in New South Wales, said with relish, 'We chopped off Cliff Dolan's head'. They certainly had: Dolan was never allowed into an official position in the New South Wales Trades Hall and it was four years before he could enter the ACTU executive. From the moment the Hawke cell had shown its nerve in proposing that a non-Rightist step into a Right's seat, the forces lined up and the ACTU executive was in total deadlock. Every issue, except the most trifling, went to a vote of eight-all. Executive meetings became increasingly acrimonious and irrational, and a cause for hilarity in the press.

In Hawke, the struggle produced a change, a new seriousness. Ralph Willis recalled,

> I had spent an enormous amount of time with Bob at work and after work, but then, from before the 1967 Congress and onwards, our relationship changed, because he had moved on to a new plane of power-seeking. He was on the telephone all the time, steeling the backbones of people to stand at Congress, and then organising them into a united group against Monk and company. One of Bob's fellows, who was not too brave, worked just around the corner and whenever Bob would see him passing he'd run out and pounce on him. He was doing less and less as research officer because so much of his time was taken up in organising. The phone never stopped ringing, people were popping in and out of our office, distracting me, and Bob had become less fraternal with me. I was intolerant of what he was doing – not because I was doing more of the work – but because I thought he should be concentrating on the area in which he was so outstanding, and which in my view was more important than being president. I guess I was a bit immature.

Willis had five months leave due, took it and went abroad. The option of simply moving away until Hawke had achieved his mission was closed to Hawke's family. As events turned out, the months they had all passed together in Port Moresby were the last spent in a normal, carefree family manner. Hawke had his job as advocate to continue, his habitual fraternising in the pub, and now the constant need to massage the spirits of his supporters and, increasingly, the press. He was travelling even more than usual, snatching at every opportunity to talk to meetings of rank-and-file unionists. The Right-wing state machines would not allow him in to talk to their members, the officials of unions, so he was forced into the more time-consuming exercise of addressing individual groups of men. When he was home he was exhausted and stressed, for his skill in public speaking did not alter – and was, perhaps, heightened by – the fact that he was highly strung. He had the *trac*, the 'nerves', that most good musicians and actors have before a performance and that afterwards the body can only slowly quieten.

He said afterwards, 'In that period when I was constantly politicking for the presidency of the ACTU the family suffered dreadfully – Hazel and the kids ...' At that stage none of them realised how much greater a price they would pay when he became president.

In late 1968 Hawke was to go to Geneva to attend an International Labour Organization meeting. Before he left, he and Geitzelt discussed the progress they had made and Hawke gave Geitzelt his phone number in Switzerland in case trouble arose. After months of pressure the Hawke cell had succeeded in forcing Bill Brown, secretary of the South Australian United Trades and Labour Council, a Souter supporter, to change sides on the issue of replacing Kenny. Hawke had just arrived in Geneva and was having a shower when Geitzelt telephoned him with the news that Brown had died, and that they now had the chance to replace him with a Left-wing candidate. David Combe's efforts on Hawke's behalf, begun three years earlier, were paying off: the South Australian trade union movement, whipped along by Geitzelt and other federal secretaries of unions from outside the state, elected Jim Shannon of the Amalgamated Engineering Union as the new South Australian secretary. There had been a technical reason for the Right to refuse to fill the ACTU's vacant vice-presidency (created by Kenny's death) but there was no such technicality to debar Shannon from entering the ACTU executive. He did so in February 1969, the ridiculous 8–8 tie was broken, and from then on the Hawke cell had a 9–7 majority. However, this did not assure Hawke of the presidency; it merely prevented Souter's appointment as acting president should Monk retire suddenly, and, as yet, Monk had not revealed his plans.

He did so within days of Shannon's entry into the executive. At a Labour Day dinner in Melbourne on 8 March 1969 he announced that he would step down later that year. (A little earlier the executive, in one of its few unanimous decisions, had adopted a decent superannuation scheme for ACTU officers and staff, and had shown Monk that the trade union movement really did love him – although, during rows in the 1950s, it had called him 'Scab!' – by commissioning a portrait of him for the boardroom.)

Hawke said, 'From the moment of Albert's announcement all the stops were out'.

The next five months were ones of loud and frantic activity in the trade unions, which were already highly stimulated by a different issue: the penal powers of the Industrial Court.

A year earlier, because of a naive decision by the Conciliation and Arbitration Commission following its inquiry into the metal trades award, there had been a huge row between the metal trades unions and their employers, which became known as the Absorption Battle. The employers, with a good deal of vindictiveness, had applied for penal sanctions against their striking employees and had even managed to have unions fined if their members worked normally but refused to work overtime. In the end, after thousands upon thousands of dollars in fines and millions of dollars lost in production, the Commission stepped in, altered its original decision (which had caused the fracas) and thereby awarded victory in the Absorption Battle to the unions. However, this did not solve the problem of the huge costs that victory had incurred; throughout the rest of 1968 and into 1969 the unions were rankling: if they were to obey the law – which the employers had announced they were using as a tool to bankrupt them – they faced fines of more than a quarter of a million dollars, plus towering legal fees.

And there were other, less obvious, discontents. The drums of the mining boom were pounding by 1969. People who would not have known a blue chip from a Smith's chip a few months earlier were holding forth on buses, in trams, wherever two or three gathered together, about portfolios of shares and the fortunes they had happened to make that afternoon. The middle classes were wallowing in paper money. But award wages were being kept down (to guard against further overheating the economy) so the working class was again locked out of the party. And everywhere, everyone talked of the war – read of it in the newspapers; heard its explosions over the radio; watched on their TV sets as it consumed screaming children with napalm; saw the boys going off, jaunty, grinning, ready for killing that was, under international law, murder – since there had been no declaration of war. What was known of the ancient conflicts of Indo-China was written by historians, in French. A plague of impassioned ignorance, a virus of unknowing, swept the nation. Conservative governments and the Right of the trade union movement were, by definition, eager crusaders against 'the march of Communism'; the extreme Left of the union movement was, by definition, prepared for counter-crusade. The rest agonised. Government and its institutions of enforcement became increasingly tyrannical. Young men were jailed for refusing the draft; when war protestors blocked the roadway in front of the New South Wales premier's car, he ordered his chauffeur to 'run the bastards over'.

The Right has always rejected 'political' strikes; it was holding the line against Left-wingers who wanted the unions to swing behind a gathering revulsion for the Indo-Chinese conflict that, in America, was already cleaving the nation. The Right was also only tepid in its objections to the penal powers of the Industrial Court, and secretly liked them. Nevertheless, Left and Right had suffered together during the Absorption Battle and throughout the country trades halls were arranging meetings and discussions with industrial lawyers to try to clarify the issue of the penal sanctions. That the same people who most hated 'the war against Communism' also most hated the penal sanctions was an immense confusion for the thinking of the Right, and this discord revealed itself in gathering paranoia.

Then at 11.40 a.m. on 15 May 1969, John Kerr, QC, now Mr Justice Kerr of the Industrial Court, jailed Clarence Lyell O'Shea, an official of the Tramways Union, for one year for contempt of court. It was eighteen years since a union official had been jailed in connection with his work – and that man, like O'Shea, had been a Communist. When unionists in the courtroom shouted 'Shame!' Kerr threatened to jail them, too. The union movement was outraged: here was the ultimate tyranny of the penal powers. In fact, O'Shea's jailing had nothing to do with the penal powers and strikes. The unions either misunderstood – or misrepresented – the truth; the press from ignorance or mischief misinformed the public; Mr Justice Kerr bumbled the public relations aspect of his job, and a thunder of anger burst. Within hours thousands of Victorian workers were striking and demonstrating and within days the trades halls of Queensland, Western Australia and South Australia had announced 24-hour strikes. The Right was severely embarrassed. In Victoria, where O'Shea was remembered as the man whose defiance of the Cain (snr) government over penal powers had precipitated the Split in the Victorian branch of the ALP in 1954, the secretary of the Trades Hall, Mick Jordan, tried to convince people that the whole affair was a Communist plot. About a million unionists struck work over a period of five days – until a friend of Albert Monk paid O'Shea's fine and Kerr, discomfited, released him.

At any trade union demonstration the chant, like a sudden choiring of cicadas in high summer, can suddenly swell out: 'The worKERS uNITED will NEVer be deFEATED!' It is one of the great truths in democracies – but the workers are, so rarely, united. Over the O'Shea case there had been enough unity to drown the voices, like Jordan's, of the Right. The government did not dare to try to collect fines and the employers did not dare to seek their imposition again. But despite months of talks with the ACTU the government refused to remove the penal powers from industrial legislation: there was stalemate. Hawke had been among those who, months before the O'Shea jailing, had spoken out against the penal sanctions, arguing, 'We are prepared to acknowledge that the trade union movement has to justify its wages before a tribunal, *provided* others do too'. He gave instances of employers (manufacturers) increasing their prices, without hindrance or need for public justification beyond the assertion that a price rise was necessary. 'Give us the same freedom as BHP – or demand that BHP justify its price increases. Give us equality before the law', he had said repeatedly. (The argument that market forces controlled manufacturers was invalid in Australia, for by the 1960s there was a system of monopolies and cartels operating: while free enterprise flourished, free competition was a figment.) Hawke's supporters included those who objected most fiercely to the penal powers; they had no particular interest in achieving a balance in the law; their overriding concern was to do away with restrictions on the right to strike – and devil take the hindmost. Hawke was moving towards power in an age of unreason manifest from London (giggling with Indian messiahs) to Paris (having a 'revolution') to New York (where liberals sang the praises of a Stalinist regime in North Vietnam) to China (where children put dunces' caps on their professors and set them to work in the fields) to South Vietnam (where GIs smoked dope on patrols and were blown away). And nearer home, in Hobart, there was unreason to Hawke, in the form of Brian Harradine of the Trades Hall Council. Harradine was convinced that Hawke was an incarnation of evil. His attacks upon Hawke set the tone of the Right's campaign against him, a campaign that imposed a terrible cost on the trade union movement, for its bitterness ensured that the movement would lack unity, that the president of the ACTU – whoever he was – would be ineffectual. Years later John Ducker, who had fought shoulder-to-shoulder against Hawke, said wistfully, 'I wonder what good the Left–Right fight has done us? When someone comes to write a history of the Australian trade union movement, I wonder if they won't find it's done us no good at all.'

Even before Monk announced his retirement, Harradine in November 1968 had reported to the Tasmanian Trades and Labour Council that an article Hawke had written for the *Federal Law Review* about the total wage was contrary to ACTU policy, and undermined the trade unions. (Monk had read and approved publication of the article.) In December 1968 Harradine had laid a complaint about Hawke to Monk; involved the press in the issue and instructed an industrial advocate to raise Hawke's article unfavourably in a Tasmanian Wages Board case. The upshot had been a story in the Hobart *Mercury* of 25 January 1969: 'ACTU Man Employers' "Weapon": Arguments of Advocate Used Against Unions', its headline said. The national news media picked up this juicy morsel. At the ACTU meeting of March 1969 the executive, by nine votes to seven, censured Harradine for using the press to attack Hawke, noting, 'The basis for the attack on Mr Hawke is so unfounded that the only conclusion to be drawn is that Mr Harradine deliberately chose to manufacture a public controversy to further his own purposes within the Labor Movement'. Then on 26 March *News Weekly* ran a headline: 'As deadly as the Mafia', over an assertion from Harradine that 'pressures exerted by certain Left-wing and Communist opponents of Souter contributed to the deaths of two trade union secretaries – Jim Kenny's and Bill Brown's'. Two days later the *Mercury* ran an almost identical story and, the following day, so did the *Age*. Harradine appeared on television and spoke of the 'psychological murder' of Kenny and Brown. Charlie Fitzgibbon, Jim Shannon, and Ray Geitzelt[3] demanded that Harradine publicly name them as the men whom he was calling 'psychological murderers', so they could sue him. Harradine declined. The *Catholic Worker* of April 1969 wrote of 'the lengths to which Mr Brian Harradine ... and those associated with him in the extreme Right-wing of the Labor Movement are pre-pared to go in their desperate attempts to disparage Mr Hawke' and referred to Harradine's 'despicable' assertions about mafias and murderers. Hawke circularised friendly unions with copies of the *Catholic Worker* story, together with a handwritten note that said, 'This is the best possible source as far as we are concerned to combat the Right-wing hysteria about a pro-Communist alliance front. If you can do with more copies please let me know and I will get them to you immediately.' He signed it 'Bob'. His note was soon leaked to the press and there was further scandal, with headlines asking who had written the note (anybody who had ever seen Hawke's handwriting could recognise it), who was 'Bob', what was going on, and other mysterious foolishness.

Then on 5 June Mick Jordan, the secretary of the Victorian Trades and Labour Council, died. Jordan had declared that Hawke would become president of the ACTU 'over my dead body'. The claim was not made in writing, or on television, but the implication that the Hawke forces had now psychologically murdered Jordan – who happened to weigh twenty stone (127 kilograms), and was a medical miracle in terms of delaying a heart attack – was everywhere.

When Monk had made his Labour Day retirement speech he had referred to 'disruptive elements in the trade union movement'. The Souter camp, which had already decided upon a fear campaign, seized upon this reference and the following day, 10 March, Souter issued a 'Declaratory statement ... on behalf of the non-alliance members of the ACTU executive supporting President Monk's warning to combat disruptive elements ...' Souter wrote of 'the inherent dangers of the opportunist "alliance front" of the so-called "New Left Movement", which seeks to control the Trade Union Movement to the exclusion of the fundamental inherent rights of trade unionists'. He continued:

> This opportunist front is seeking to gain control through dictatorial pressure tactics by dissident groups rebelling against democratic decisions and self-imposed discipline of the Trade Union Movement and attempting to impose conditions to obtain minority control. Therefore, the situation has reached such proportions that we would be failing in our duty ...

not to alert the unions ... to take effective counter-action ... Anything done to destroy or assist to destroy the Trade Union Movement ... is ... the enemy of the Trade Union Movement ... Our great Movement cannot be allowed to be fragmented by this senseless thrust for power for individual or sectional gain ... We therefore call on individual members and union officials to take a more direct and responsible part in union affairs to achieve the objectives of the Trade Union Movement along planned and organised lines determined by the ACTU and its State branches.[4]

It was hardly a frank statement by Souter, for in the full text of 400-odd words he did not mention anywhere that he happened to be fighting for the presidency of the ACTU and that references he made to 'considerable personal sacrifice and hardship over years' and 'planned and organised lines' were covert advertisements for his qualifications for the job. The next day Hawke issued a statement that said:

The [question] has now publicly arisen of who will succeed Albert Monk as President of the ACTU. It seems the main contenders will be Mr Souter and myself. My opponent has seen fit in these circumstances to issue a statment to the Press, and he refers to a 'pro-Communist alliance front' which seeks to take over the trade union movement. I expect I will receive the support of the Left wing of the movement. I know I will receive the support of many unions not normally classified as being on the Left. I expect Mr Souter will receive the support of unions, or branches of unions, under the control of the extreme Right-wing, including the DLP. I don't expect he will reject that support. Nor do I think the fact of that support says anything about his capacities or incapacities relative to my own for the position of President of the ACTU. I hope that the trade union movement will make its decisions on the basis of assessing our respective capacities. I have always regarded the technique of guilt by association and the tactic of the smear as abhorrent, and I refuse to resort to it myself.[5]

He did refuse. His campaign was straightforward, expressed in a press release he wrote:

> Father was a Congregational minister. Hawke is a Socialist by belief, by intellect and because he believes that equality of opportunity should be more than a political slogan. 'If the Australian worker doesn't fairly partake of what he produces then hard work doesn't make any sense to him.' He sees the future of the ACTU as 'unlimited', with closer working-relations between the traditional 'white-and-blue-collar unionists', with scope widened to include all the real needs of the worker. 'There should be no dividing line in the trade unions. We are there to help the worker, so – anything that constitutes discrimination or hardship and in we go.' Hawke holds strong feelings about: Educational opportunity, the Penal provisions of the Arbitration System, Equal Pay for women, shorter working week and the obvious penalties imposed on a low-income family by the exorbitant hire-purchase interest rates on homes and consumer durable goods. Once we broaden into the areas of environmental development, the quality of urban development and town planning, the combined forces of the white-collar movement and the ACTU will have a social significance. We will be better able to make an impact with our combined resources.[6]

He expanded on these themes in public addresses: while socialisation of the means of production, distribution and exchange was the ideal of the labour movement (and the single objective of the ACTU Constitution),

> we have to concentrate on the here and now. We must try to achieve the highest possible living standards for the Australian population ... The trade union movement has

an immense reserve of power. If we are to use that power to improve living standards, we must expand our horizon, broaden our thoughts. We have a responsibility in the here and now to improve things in the society we have.

He called for no campaign against the Vietnam War, nor for the nationalisation of industry. He talked only of improving the lot of the ordinary worker and his/her dependants. However, his opponents could not be persuaded that he meant what he said. Above all, they feared a loss of their own power – which, in theory and in fact, they used, if in a blinkered way, for the same causes he espoused. Ducker, who by now was assistant secretary of the New South Wales Trades and Labour Council, recalled:

> You see, the Communist Party thought it could use Bob. Felt at the very least he was going to smash the Right-wing control of the ACTU. And they were using Bob as an instrument. So it was a fight against Communist Party influence, and against its being increased. And, at that time, it was a legitimate fear. There was a sincerely held belief that a Hawke victory would mean an increase in Communist–Left-wing influence. You couldn't really say that Bob was a Communist, or anywhere near it – although one night I'd got drunk with Hawkey, around the time of the Chinese invasion of Tibet. And he and I had a slanging match about that. He said it was a CIA plot to suggest that the Chinese had done what they did. I said he was just a bloody front-man for the Communist Party. So there was that bit of history between Bob and me. But, looking back, Bob stood on a policy of reform and modernisation. And there's nothing particularly Left-wing about that.

As the 1969 Congress approached the cries of 'Communist takeover' and 'Red dupe' – that is, Hawke – became more frequent and shrill. The abuse edged perilously close to breaking the male code of honour and self-defence that tabooed public references to a man's sexual life, when an epithet for Hawke,

'Communist lover-boy' – with its neat double entendre – was reported in the press.

While Hawke and, after his initial faux pas, Souter, behaved with dignity and sense, both camps engaged in what Ducker later described, with a sigh, as 'gutter fighting' – for the question of who would be the better man to lead the ACTU had been lost in the shouting and it was now a Left–Right brawl, such as had not occurred for twenty years. It may seem senseless to outsiders, but it should be remembered that trade union officials are politicians and therefore a warrior caste: they love fighting.

There were many small unions that had never bothered to affiliate with the ACTU; they were encouraged – through cajoling and threats – to join it and thereby add their votes to one side or the other at the 1969 Congress election. Unions habitually understated their membership so they could reduce their affiliation fees to the ACTU. But the more members, the more Congress votes: suddenly unions discovered they had hundreds more members than they had thought. Workers who had been retired for years, it was realised, were technically still members if they had taken out life tickets. (In the Hawke camp Fitzgibbon was the first to discover the benefits of this technicality, his attention drawn to it by a circular that Souter had issued.) Intra-union rows that had seethed for years abruptly stilled on the promise of a vote – and, when promises were broken at the Congress, new feuds began. In 1981 there was still resentment in the AWU against two groups of its delegates who had 'ratted' and given Hawke twelve votes. Ducker said: 'There was standing over people. Threatening them with dismissal. Threatening them with being defeated [as union officials]. A bit of persuasion that life could be better for them.' (For example: preselection for a seat in federal or state parliament, or membership of 'Australia's best club', the Legislative Council, part-time parliament with a gold pass for travel. A Hawke man who switched allegiance later entered the New South Wales Legislative Council. In Victoria, there were jobs in the Melbourne Harbour Trust to be awarded to the helpful.) Ducker continued,

It was said that it might be possible to organise a trip abroad . . . Ray Geitzelt was determined to win and whatever it took, whatever way, that was legit. To some degree it was a fight between me and Ray Geitzelt, and that was an inducement for me: I had the blood in my nostrils.

Geitzelt's opinions of Ducker's tactics are, under Australia's libel laws, unprintable, but along the same lines. Ducker said, 'Ray would say, "John's a twister, a turner, devious – don't trust him!" It was no afternoon-tea party.'

Ducker is a man of dextrous intelligence and notable charm which, combined, were to make him the colossus of the New South Wales ALP machine for a decade. He could perform small miracles of persuasion: once, for example, he convinced the New South Wales ALP Left to waive its claim to a Senate seat, for reasons that seemed lucid when he explained them but which later nobody could quite understand. He created the Labor government of Neville Wran in New South Wales, when he realised that Wran, although close to and promoted by Geitzelt, was a winner. Geitzelt tried to chop off Ducker's head – as Ducker had 'chopped off' Dolan's and was later, in his own words, to 'do everything, and I mean *everything*' to smash the political career of Geitzelt's brother, Arthur. Geitzelt moved for federal intervention into the New South Wales ALP and Ducker, with breathtaking nerve, immediately seconded his motion. And survived. Only Ducker's Yorkshire accent debarred him from playing a far more public role in Australian politics. At the ACTU Congress of 1969 he was to use 'every bit of influence and persuasion I could' in pressuring waverers to vote for Souter. The Hawke camp received 51 fewer votes than it had been promised, in part thanks to John Patrick Ducker.

His and other Right-winger's fears about Communist influence on Hawke were not without foundation, for many of Hawke's most active organisers were Communists. One was George Seelaf, then secretary of the Victorian branch of the meat workers' union and among Hawke's warmest friends.

Seelaf was a man of boisterous high spirits – 'Look! A butcher's canary!' he shouted when a blowfly rumbled past – and shone with the boyish optimism that is so often a characteristic of old-guard Communists. He had been instrumental in arranging the publication of *Power without Glory* and was a friend of its author, Frank Hardy, whom he introduced to Hawke. Seelaf and Hawke were working closely during 1969 on the Equal Pay Case. At one of their celebrations the proprietor of Jimmy Watson's, a popular Melbourne wine bar, locked them and a meat industry employer in a back room because of their loud singing of revolutionary songs. Years later, when Hawke had come to detest Communism, he would insist, '*George* isn't a Communist. I never thought of him as a Communist. He just calls himself one.' Seelaf said of his part in the presidency campaign:

> We got the list of delegates for the 1967 Congress and analysed their politics. The committed Right and committed Left we put aside. What remained was a list of eighty or ninety people. We then got to work to lobby them: found out all we could about their political attitudes, who their best friends were, if they were Catholics or Masons. We then chose the most appropriate people to do the lobbying. I don't like to raise the sectarian issue, but if we were dealing with a Catholic, we got a Left-wing Catholic to do the lobbying; if a Mason, we got a Hawke-committed Mason. I burnt the files, afterwards.

Another Communist Hawke-man was Alec Macdonald, secretary of the Queensland Trades and Labour Council. Macdonald was a man of extreme gentleness, beloved in the union movement. The AWU aside, he delivered the Queensland vote to Hawke, but died a week before the Congress and Hawke, in the midst of victory, was also in mourning for him. He had loved Macdonald with the extravagant affection he feels for all close friends and years later said that the high edge of excitement in triumph had hurt, because Macdonald was not there to share it.

While Hawke's agents were eliciting votes, his job was to do that at which he excelled: establish rapport with great numbers of people, to project himself as the corporeal form of their hopes. For while the Left would support him, willy-nilly, and sincerely if mistakenly believed that he was their captive – Pat Clancy of the Building Workers' Industrial Union described Hawke as 'a very strong, positive Left force ... he made many fiery and inspiring speeches ... and at that stage he was very amenable or susceptible to collective consideration of matters' – it was the large centre ground that would decide the issue. To the centre and, most importantly, to industrial journalists, Hawke had an unacknowledgeable appeal to snobbery: a Rhodes scholar, a middleclass white-collar man proposing a New Deal for the working class. By 1969 the rush of manual workers' children to the universities was in train. It was still forbidden in trade union circles to admit that middle-class status and values were attractive, but all the behaviour of the working class revealed its yearning. 'Bob had been a Rhodes scholar – and there's snobbery in everyone', Egerton remarked later, when he had been expelled from the ALP for his own vulnerability to the glitter of status. 'The Rhodes had a big effect on trade unionists.' This was especially relevant, because a decline in blue-collar unionism had already occurred (and was growing) since, with technological change, the workforce had moved away from manufacturing into service industries. Blue was fading into white, and the white-collar sector was little unionised. Union officials knew this, and recognised that Hawke had the social appeal to create regrowth in unionism, among white-collar workers. He talked constantly of the need for the ACTU's 1.5 million affiliated members to be joined by the half million public service unionists – a proposition to which both Monk and Souter, and the Left, were opposed. To them, the white-collar public service employees spelt corruption of working-class values. Hawke's committed supporters, when they actually listened to what he was saying, discounted his ideas as the rhetoric of campaigning. And the Right, which had many white-collar members, did not listen at all. From the outset, Hawke was to be at cross-purposes with many of his most ardent admirers, while appealing, increasingly, to the centre ground. And again, it was a problem of style: Hawke was fiery: when speaking from a platform he used the gestures, the body language, that in Australia, at that time, announced 'Left', and it was necessary to stand at a distance and pay attention to his long, Latinate sentences to understand their meaning. Many did. On 27 June the *Age*, in an editorial headlined, 'The New Unionists', wrote:

> Mr Hawke is articulating, in concrete terms, the problems which will face the trade union movement in the 1970s. He is also proposing solutions to them. Many of Australia's more conservative trade union leaders may be suspicious of his proposals because they call into question all the traditional assumptions about the role of trade unions in society. But the time has come when assumptions must be questioned, when new directions must be sought, if unions are to have an effective future. For this reason alone, Mr Hawke is doing the trade union movement an invaluable service.

Hawke himself knew his appeal was more practical:

> I'd been the wages advocate for ten years and had helped change a situation whereby the basic wage had declined in real value by 5 per cent, to one where, by 1967, it had increased in real value by more than 6 per cent. For that, I had the overwhelming support of the rank and file.

By the eve of the Congress, which opened on 8 September in the grey, echoing Paddington Town Hall, Sydney – a larger than usual assembly hall was necessary, for, such was the increase in membership and affiliation that there were 101 more delegates than in 1967 – the Hawke camp was confident of victory. Again, the support of Geitzelt was critical, because the services group of unions had the largest Congress vote and Geitzelt had them counted to the last one. Meanwhile, the Souter camp knew they would be hard pressed but believed, from promises made to *them*, that they still had a 50–50 chance. Until a week beforehand George Polites – and all the employers – had been convinced that Hawke could not succeed. In the Conciliation and Arbitration Commission, which was watching events with professional interest, only Sir Richard Kirby had long believed that Hawke would win, 'and my own reason for belief was that Bob was so insistent to me that he would'. Hawke told the press he would win by 100 votes and, obligingly they reported this. He stood in the doorway of the Paddington Town Hall, hugging his supporters, smiling at and handshaking the uncommitted. To his old mentor, Jock Innes, he murmured, 'You've stood by me for twelve years. Stand by me now.' The voting was still three days away. Whips had been appointed to organise the factions on every issue that might, before the election, divide the Congress. The uncommitted would be watching every division on the floor, to calculate in which direction power was flowing. The big unions had marshals for the elections, for they did not allow their delegates to vote according to individual preference, but forced them to vote in accordance with instructions, and the marshals were present to ensure that instructions were followed. Any delegate defying policy could expect to lose his union job. 'We had no slippage', Geitzelt remarked with satisfaction, afterwards; Fitzgibbon said, 'When you asked them later, everybody had voted for the winner'.

On the afternoon before the next morning's election Monk announced that Hawke would speak, as research officer, reporting on economic policy, and would be followed by Souter, who would move the adoption of the executive's official economic policy statement. Both candidates were therefore to have a chance for a last appeal to the electorate. Hawke's address was rousing and fluent (he attacked the latest federal Budget), and lasted exactly thirty minutes. He returned to his seat, Souter took over the microphone – and what happened next was extraordinary. Souter gave up.

As if bored, he stood at the microphone and read out the policy statement, a copy of which every delegate already had, then, although he still had minutes left to rally support, he made a perfunctory gesture – and sat down. The Hawke camp was incredulous. The hall had been silent when Souter began, but after about ten minutes a hum of conversation arose that became so loud that twice Monk had to call the delegates to order. One thing that everyone was talking about was that Hawke had written the economic policy statement, which Souter, instead of speaking to, was reciting. The four-year campaign was over.

Next day Hawke was elected president of the ACTU by 399 to 350.

Over in Washington George Meany, the boss of American labour, heard the wire-service news, 'and nearly had a heart-attack. "The Aussies have gone Communist!" he said.'[7]

It is doubtful that any of the delegates gathered in the Paddington Town Hall and shouting with joy fully understood what they had done: they had created the Australian hero of the 1970s.

When Hawke bounded to his feet to accept victory he moved towards the conclusion of his speech with the declaration:

> Let me make it abundantly clear that I will not be the president merely of those who worked for and voted for me. I will be the president of the whole of the ACTU – equally of those who exercised their democratic right to work for another result. My door will be as open to you, Ralph Marsh, as to you, Jim Shannon. I will seek genuinely to work in harmony with all sections of this movement.[8]

The Right thought he was lying; the Left that he was giving a victor's magnanimous flourish. Their disillusion was to be intense. They spoke later with the sadness of suppressed anger, or made excuses: Hawke was gregarious, he socialised with capitalists and was led astray; he was prepared to be kind, when he should not have been; he was naive and did not understand how vicious the Right was; John Ducker was the complete political animal, and had seduced him; Hawke became bewitched by politics and abandoned the workers – this from the spokesman of the workers of the world, Joe Morris, a Canadian, who had groomed Hawke to succeed him. The Communists said he was a middle-class opportunist all along, who took some time to reveal his true colours. And the National Civic Council, which had thought Hawke a 'Red dupe', said the same thing. Or it was said that he was a Jew. Or that his wife was a Jewess . . . The explanations were as various as the people who gave them. Unionists have always been agreed on one thing; that Hawke is unusually truthful, but they chose to believe that he was not *really* telling the truth about himself.

The fact was, as Hawke had repeatedly said, he wanted to exercise power and to do so in a way that he defined as being in the public good. It was all he had ever wanted and if, to achieve that, he had to do deals with the Right or with millionaires or with conservative politicians, or Communists, he would. He had been a fundamentalist Christian ideologue at nineteen; he had been fed on ideology with his mother's milk; he had lived and breathed the beliefs of the Second Coming, when the righteous dead would rise from their graves to walk in glory with the Lord. And twenty years later, when he became president of the ACTU, he by then believed that a socialist Australia was as distant as the millennium; that what mattered was the justice of the here and now. He had no inner need for the direction to life that ideology gives. He was free. He thought he had been grandiosely enabled to realise his dreams.

As they gathered their papers and prepared to leave the Paddington Town Hall, Cliff Dolan said to Hawke, 'Don't rush things, mate. The trade union movement is really very conservative, you know.'

It was years before Hawke would acknowledge the defeats foreshadowed by that acute observation.

FOURTEEN

AWKE HAD WON THE presidency narrowly. Twenty-five votes would have given the prize to Souter – and in that case one can only speculate on what disruption the disappointed Left would have caused, for 1968–69 marked the beginning of years of industrial unrest. It would be Hawke's job to attempt to harness restlessness, while himself remaining a central figure in the upheaval of change that was altering the old relationships within society. Every generation has its radical alternatives: the difference now was in their extent. Men wore pony-tails; women didn't wear corsets; merchant bankers smoked marijuana; cocaine was the millionaire's snuff; millionaires were cloning, as the property and stock markets soared; their children ate and dressed in earnest counterfeit of Javanese peasants, or terrorised their professors; or copulated on the university lawn, or dug it up, or sat on it – practically anything, so long as it was forbidden. Psyches were psychedelic. Policemen were pigs; men were soon to become male chauvinist pigs. And vegetarians would inherit the earth – for, underneath the libertine surface, a new puritanism was already assembling its symbolic behaviour. The conservative federal coalition government was falling to pieces. The boom babies who had been born in the almost forgotten years of war and postwar Labor governments had grown up, were voters, and in terms of numbers of votes had, in December 1969, voted in Gough Whitlam. The necessary number of seats had eluded him, however. But Whitlam was approaching the height of his powers – and the next election would be his. Hawke had come to lead a trade union movement

240

that, like the wider society it reflected, was excited and unstable. People were looking for leaders to express and channel the huge energies that demographic and technological change had released. His first fan letters began to arrive in late 1969. A man who described himself as non-political wrote: 'I am confident of your personal future and consider your experience will be vital for one day I foresee you worthily filling the office of Prime Minister of Australia. Keep this in mind. Australia needs you, you would be the man for the job.' And another, 'We now have a visionary at the helm!'

Meanwhile, almost half Hawke's crew was sullen, ready for mutiny. The bitterness of the election campaign had bequeathed him an executive that was divided 9–8 in his favour and a secretary with whom he was barely able to speak. He had gone through a period of hatred for Souter and before the election had told his supporters that he could never again work with him. But when the results were announced Souter had immediately lent forward to shake Hawke's hand and since then there had been an icy civility between them (which Hawke, characteristically flinching from the unpleasant, called later, 'Some tension. But we soon got over it.') It was more than a year before their mutual hostility abated enough for them to speak naturally to each other. On the executive, too, uneasiness was acute for more than a year. Ducker recalled, 'Everybody was extremely suspicious, and bitter'. At Hawke's first experience of chairing the executive, in 1970 (Souter's forces had outwitted his at the Congress on the timing of succession, and delayed Hawke's presidency by four months) Hawke announced that he wanted the trade union movement to join in a huge anti-Vietnam rally that was being organised by the Left of the ALP. He had the numbers. His resolution passed on the mechanical majority. Then Ducker, representing the New South Wales TLC, announced that, this being an important decision, it would need ratification from a majority of the state branches. Hawke said, 'John left me in no doubt about the outcome of a state branch vote. I'd been rolled.'

The Right feared that Hawke was biding his time, until he could ambush them. It had been widely advertised that Geitzelt was urging Hawke to move in on the Tasmanian Trades Hall and demolish Harradine. There was fear that New South Wales would be next. Ducker said,

> When Hawke was elected it had been open to him to do what some of his supporters wanted, and that was to lead a thrust head-on against the Right-wing of the trade union movement. He could have elected to try to knock over the leadership of the New South Wales Labour Council; he could have elected to *actively* organise in unions against Right-wing incumbents. He could have made life very bloody hard – he could have pushed us in New South Wales a long way. If he'd demanded his right to speak to a Labour Council and said, 'These men here are enemies of the working class' – well, that's the sort of thing that has some impact. And it's the sort of thing we could certainly do without. Because Hawke had such ascendancy, such charisma.

It is an article of faith in the labour movement that the capitalist press is its enduring enemy, committed to leading hapless readers astray, and that the wise course is to avoid it (except when one can employ it to frighten adversaries in a faction fight). During the penal powers debate, Hawke had often referred in speeches to unionists to the way the federal government and the press were attempting to instil the idea that strikes were illegal; he had complained of public misrepresentation of the activities of the Arbitration Commission, and had always gone on to point out that the trade union movement had taken no action to counter misinformation:

> We as a trade union movement have failed signally to publicise ... we took it in our stride ... I don't think a word was said ... We should be shouting from the rooftops ...

Monk and Souter had repeatedly warned him against adopting the role of ACTU spokesman: when television channels began, in 1965, to ask him to comment on the federal Budget there was, annually, a row in the office about it. Even before Hawke had formally taken over the presidency in January 1970, he set out to make use of the news media 'to put the message of the trade union movement across'. Hawke said,

> I had the feeling that the big gap in Albert [Monk] in the 1960s was in the area of communications. He didn't get to the people, or even to his own constituents, in a way which explained issues and defended positions. He tended to be very much afraid of the media and I think time after time opportunities were lost to establish positions in the minds of the people and of the government. It didn't matter what the issue was, Albert wanted to avoid the media. For instance, Budget time: there were clear positions about what the ACTU thought; we [research staff] would prepare stuff for Albert and he'd say a couple of things, but it was under pressure that he would communicate our position. And I used to feel frustrated. We had a lot to say, and could say it effectively, and would prepare material but Albert would perfunctorily – even diffidently – talk to the media and make a point. And then he wouldn't follow that up. He'd done his duty. But there was no *depth* of communication or *persistence* of communication. And there was nobody else who could speak for the ACTU. The ACTU was Albert Monk.

Hawke set out to improve the image of the unions in Australian society.

For a complex of reasons this is extraordinarily difficult. Australia is one of the most unionised countries in the world; because collective bargaining is embryonic (growing in the 1980s) there are numerous short strikes; because of the number of unions demarcation strikes are frequent – and are impossible to justify in terms of social principle; because of the very high level of government and semi-government ownership of utilities – transport, telephone services, postal services, electricity, gas, garbage collection, water supply and so forth – strikes in these areas incur a challenge to legitimate, elected authority and to employers who have a vast supply of money to tough-out strikes and to wage a propaganda war against strikers. In many Western countries strikes in government-owned utilities are illegal. In Australia, they are not. (Fraser government legislation of the late 1970s restricts them.) Until Hawke became president of the ACTU the unions had never emerged from a strike against the employer-government without being covered in calumny – for no matter how just their cause, their officials had been unable to explain it to an inconvenienced public above the shouting of the politicians. And if workers were forced back without the change they had demanded by drastic action, that seemed to prove that their claim and actions had been unjustified and irresponsible. Anything that fails seems stupid, and it is only in the long term that many strikes – for example, against shipping pig-iron to Japan just prior to World War II; against supplying material and food to the Dutch counter-revolutionaries in Indonesia – are seen in perspective, and that a new generation can acknowledge that the unions had a stronger grasp of reality than the government. When Hawke became president the 'political' strike – that is, one not concerned with wages and conditions, or demarcation – was popularly presented as a type of trade union terrorism. Eleven years later, when he stepped down, the term had vanished. The unions were no better loved than they had been, but they had learned, from Hawke's example, publicly to present and logically to debate their actions. By the end of the 1970s it was commonplace – almost automatic – for trade union officials to appear on radio and television news to explain why strike action had been taken, something that a decade earlier had been unimaginable. Society at large benefited. In a decade of social upheaval, had the trade union movement continued its tradition of ignoring public relations, the way would have been open for governments – of whatever persuasion – to transform their propaganda superiority into a weapon of repression against the unions. Repression, once begun, has a life of its own.

Hawke was armed with the skills necessary to begin the Herculean task of clearing away the debris of a century of trade union neglect of public relations: he was, as he had dreamed of becoming while still at university, 'articulate, logical and tough' – and an exotic. His Rhodes scholarship and his swash-buckling personality dazzled the press. From the moment of his election the news media was mesmerised by Hawke. Within a couple of years his face and brazen voice were among the best known in the nation; within five they were recorded in the brain cells of the whole society. An image of him had physically entered the Australian people and he could not walk down a street or enter a shop without being besieged by the curious, anxious to verify that part of themselves that he represented. He was constantly handled – Ducker noted the 'mystical touch-ing of Hawke's clothes' – and after a day in public would show the signs of extreme nervous stress: his eyes bright and hard, his movements quick and tense, sweating, hyperactive, flitting from topic to topic in conversation, argumentative, craving the anaesthesia of more alcohol. The distinction between work and leisure blurred, then vanished. He had become an object of dis-play and was at work at the races, at work while having a haircut. His close friends all knew the physical change that overcame Hawke, in a moment, when he was introduced to a stranger or was in a public place: a sudden tenseness and unnatural vivacity would envelop him. Friends hated to be present and feel the change but would accompany Hawke to protect him from the clamorousness of crowds. At home, the telephone never stopped ringing, for he had set out to make himself available to the news media and would talk to journalists at any hour of the day or night, drunk or sober, clothed or undressed. And in this lay a key to his phenomenal media attention. From early on many news-paper editors were aware that Hawke was able to 'snow' their reporters and had inchoate suspicion that he was, in some way they could not quite determine, manipulating them. There was much that was known about Hawke – his drunken bad temper; his womanising, including outrageously public propositioning of women when he was drunk – that was never reported and that journalists, the world's most avid gossips, were unwilling to discuss. The editors were half-right: Hawke unconsciously inhibited the journalist's inclination to detract by trusting her or him. He is an unusually trusting man – frequently naively so, and was to suffer rages of disillusion when people betrayed him or turned out to be, as others had already recognised intuitively, rogues. The honesty and honourableness of his upbringing had ill equipped him for dealing with the dishonest and devious; it had the benefit that his own trustfulness inspired trustworthy behaviour: there were only two major occasions when journalists broke faith and wrote stories about things Hawke had said when they knew he was talking to them off the record. One of the most effective ways of arousing journalists' hostility is to flatter them by treating them as powerful: insisting upon questions in advance and on knowing the content of a story before publication; by trying to control them. Many public figures make this error: the immediate – and justified – assumption is that they have something to hide. Hawke worked with the news media in the opposite way: he *refused* to be told questions in advance; he did not require reporters to check back with him; he was boldly open in conversation with them. And he always had something to say. For most of Hawke's first two years as president, Bill McMahon was the Prime Minister and was disastrously mishandling the press, by flattery: he repeatedly telephoned journalists to give them tips for stories, and among themselves they treated his eagerness to please with contempt. Newspaper cartoonists expressed their colleagues' attitudes to the Prime Minister in drawings of merciless disparagement.[1]

Ducker said of the result of news media attention to Hawke:

> You weren't dealing with flesh and blood. You were fighting a supreme being, and you always expected that you'd

come off second best. We'd arrive sometimes at an executive meeting to discuss something, and find that the newspapers were reporting that we'd decided in a particular way – and we bloody well hadn't. Bob had just had a few beers with the press and told them what he thought should happen, and they'd taken that as gospel. Standing up to the ascendancy he'd established through the press wasn't easy and you'd be inclined to roll with the punches.

Since the days of the Groupers, the Left and Right wings of the executive have held separate caucuses before and during executive meetings, stayed in separate hotels and drunk in separate pubs. Monk had caucused with the Right and had used various go-betweens to the Left, including George Seelaf for the Communists. Hawke naturally caucused with the Left but he set out to try to calm the fears of the Right on a personal level and to lessen the tension that existed between the factions. The Left was uneasy. Geitzelt said, 'On the question of overseas trips, for example, Bob would say, "We'll give the Right a berth, eh?" If there were five people to go, there would be three places for our blokes and two for theirs. We accommodated the Right. Perhaps too much. The Right never shares – it keeps all the spoils for itself.' And Ducker recalled,

Bob tried to create a bit of goodwill. One of his constant irritations was that the Right would not drink with the Left. At lunchtime and in the evening Bob repeatedly asked the Right to come and have a drink. I would occasionally break off from my mates and go over and drink with Geitzelt and Fitzgibbon. And I think Bob had more than some problems about that, and would have to kid to his blokes: 'Look, suffer him, won't you?' He kept trying to work at it and would come to the Dover and drink with Edgar Williams and Ralph Marsh and others. And it was funny, because when Bob sets out to be charming and interesting and pleasant there are few who can do it better. So they used to enjoy it, although a bit sheepishly. But as soon as he'd gone they'd want to talk about what a bastard he was.

Hawke never stopped hoping that he would be able to heal the ill feeling between Ducker and Geitzelt. He said, 'Ray is a man of tremendous ability and so, obviously, is John. It just seemed so *sensible* to try to get them together.'

The Right's suspicion of Hawke continued through 1970 and 1971. At the Congress of that year there was another dramatic Left–Right clash, and then a sudden ganging up against Hawke. The Right was furious about the leadership he had given to 'political' strikes, most notably, the Springbok tour, and both Left and Right were frightened by the power he had established, through the news media, and outside their control. He had one spot of complete vulnerability: money. Without money his schemes would be difficult to realise, his power limited. Already he had established one enterprise, Bourkes–ACTU, and had been treated to an orgy of publicity and acclaim. At the 1971 Congress the executive was requesting an increase in affiliation fees, necessary, it argued, to carry through the reforms promised in Hawke's election campaign. Delegates voted for no increase. Hawke refused to admit defeat for years, but from that moment his vision of the role the trade union movement could play in Australian society was, effectively, futile. The independence from employers that he sought for it, the loosening of the feudal bonds, would be long delayed, for without money the ACTU could not establish the insurance-superannuation and hire-purchase schemes that would give unionists the freedom to move from one employer to another or to abandon work temporarily for retraining or even to be sick for long. They would have to remain wage slaves, prisoners of the cost of their possessions. The big unions were immensely rich; a few had insurance schemes, a few had credit facilities, but there was nothing coherent; and unions chose to invest their funds conservatively, mostly in real estate. Those who had supported Hawke had paid, as events were to show, only lip service to his ideas for reform for the whole trade union movement. They preferred the old, familiar ways – the hardship, but also the comforting warmth and solidarity of being victims of capitalism. From the 1971 Congress, Hawke's presidency could only be disappointment after disappointment for him. He had envisaged himself calling forth and directing the blossoming of a newly awakened force in society. Instead, his job would be what it had been for Monk: bargaining, settling strikes, doing deals with the government, bullying and cajoling the irrational, being abused as a 'class traitor' – in short, choosing between the unpalatable and the disastrous, and putting a brave face on things. He would clench his fists sometimes and say, 'If *only* we had the sinews of war ... Money!'

By the time Hawke became president of the ACTU he had been studying and analysing the Australian economy and its institutions for more than a decade and had evolved an elaborate critique of the soggy patches, areas of corruption and injustice. Annually he and Willis had written submissions to Cabinet on the federal Budget. The taxation system was one area Hawke deplored. Trading monopolies and cartels, which maintained artificially high retail prices, was another. Hawke felt passionately affronted on behalf of the ordinary worker that, while she or he sold labour according to market forces (with only some protection and much restriction from the arbitration system), manufacturers and shopkeepers, banded together, defeated the laws of free trading and sold their goods at any price that suited them. In the UK and USA this practice had been illegal for years, but in Australia, despite the efforts of the Attorney-General, Garfield Barwick, Menzies had refused to outlaw it. ACTU Budget submissions to the succeeding Holt and Gorton governments on the issue had been ignored. Then in 1970 Hawke met a retailer who was interested in breaking cartel power in retail trade.

This man was Lionel Revelman, of Lithuanian descent, the youngest of ten children of a widowed mother, who with scholarships and by driving taxis at night had worked his way through law school and been articled to the trade union legal firm, Maurice

Blackburn. At twenty-one Revelman became a barrister and at thirty-three had taken silk. He had voted Liberal throughout the Menzies reign and had switched to Labor when Menzies and Calwell departed from public life. By the time Hawke met him, in the house of Sam Goldbloom – a leading figure in the ALP Left – Revelman was a director, with his brother George, of an electrical store called Bourkes. He was prosperous: he owned a 17-room house in Balwyn, Melbourne, which had a tennis court in nearly half a hectare of garden. Tall and fit, with rugged good looks, Revelman was a taciturn, determined individualist. He was prudish and had never been heard to swear; aloof, courtly, and so loathed social gatherings that he once went abroad to avoid an engagement party. He was a perfectionist, by nature fascinated by detail (Hawke, by nature, is bored with detail) and was so averse to personal emotionalism that he would refuse to watch anything 'emotional' on television. He was eight years older than Hawke. When they met it was as if two half-souls had clicked together. Of all the men Hawke loved in his adulthood, he loved Revelman most: 'He was a father to me', Hawke said. Revelman told his family, 'Bob is the only man I've met to whom I can talk'.

A decade earlier, during the television boom, when Bourkes had been 'selling TV sets day and night', the Revelman brothers had sued every major supplier of television receivers for inhibition of their trade. The big traders, among them Myers, had so pressured manufacturers that they had refused to supply Bourkes, which was undercutting agreed retail prices. The Revelmans lost the case but had won a two-year breathing space; in this interregnum other discount stores had sprung up in Melbourne. The Revelmans continued to skirmish with big stores and suppliers, and bore particular resentment for Myers. There was an old grudge held by the Revelmans against the Myers; the Revelmans' grandfather had started the first cash-order business in Melbourne with Sidney Myer and, according to Revelman family lore, had advised Myer to open a bargain basement. 'People will steal the stock!' Myer, it is said, objected.

He split with Revelman and went on to found the greatest retailing empire in Australia.

In 1970, before he met Hawke, Revelman had involved Bourkes with a group of Left-wing unions that was in revolt against the Victorian Trades Hall Council and which had espoused many fashionable causes. Inflation was already stirring by 1970. The rebel unions had allied themselves with housewives' associations to boycott companies considered to be overcharging. Boycott lists were published in union journals; activists stationed themselves in shopping centres to distribute leaflets advising which brands to avoid – for reasons of price or because they were environmentally damaging. There were big rallies in the Melbourne Town Hall to complain about price racketeering. Revelman thought that high profit and small turnover was both inefficient and socially objectionable. He saw a useful ally in the rebel unions, but a joint advertising campaign had barely begun when the Trades Hall stepped in and aborted it.

Hawke, at the time he met Revelman, had already widely advertised his dreams of expanding the scope of the ACTU and the horizons of the whole trade union movement. A flood of requests for interviews and to make speeches had swept into the ACTU from soon after the 1969 Congress, and the tide of publicity, instead of abating, continued to swell. Small companies had written to him suggesting joint-venture schemes, many of them hare-brained, some sensible, all of them needing investigation that the ACTU could not afford. It had no money. There were six people on the staff: Hawke; Souter; Willis; an assistant research officer, Jan White; a press officer–personal assistant to Hawke, Geoff Gleghorn; and an education officer, Peter Mathews; plus stenographers. All but the stenographers were underpaid for the hours they worked: Hawke's salary, at $11 000, was a fraction of that of his counterpart, George Polites. There was too little space in the Lygon Street building and too few telephones to meet the demand during the week-long executive meetings there, when the executive members would often be called outside from the boardroom to negotiate in strikes that were on in Queensland or Western Australia and would have to do so standing up at somebody's desk. Souter managed the accounting by a method of his own, 'shuffling money backwards and forwards from the International Fund', in the words of Cliff Dolan. 'I never once understood an ACTU balance sheet.' Neither did others, for Souter was given to secrecy and would become testy when the executive asked for more details. Hawke, with a combination of delicacy and uninterest, never sought to involve himself in the secretary's domain.

While Hawke had stirred up enthusiasm for the idea of ACTU enterprises he had nothing with which to start them: no capital, no staff and no supply of cash to hire consultants. The most the ACTU could afford was legal opinions. As the central body of the Australian trade union movement the ACTU was already far behind the organised employers in research facilities, even for the basic issue of economics. Research on industrial health was an impossible luxury for it. It had formal ties with trade union groups throughout the world, but when their represent- atives made fraternal visits or requested information there was only one person available for the job: Hawke. When the head of the West German trade union movement visited Australia in the early 1970s and inquired, bewildered, 'But where is your International Department?' Hawke, who had visited their International Department, with its large staff, spacious offices, library and translation facilities, replied bitterly, 'You're looking at it'. The Australian trade union movement, to the disadvantage of its members, was simply too faction- and envy-ridden to pay its peak council to operate effectively. Of the advanced Western countries – and, one might add, of the Communist countries, where trade unionism is a black joke – the ACTU was the most under-financed peak council. The New Zealand Federation of Labour put it to shame.

Enter Lionel Revelman.

Whether he or Hawke first thought of the scheme, together they developed a plan that swept them both to imaginative heights: the ACTU and Bourkes would establish a joint venture that would have two primary functions – to break retail price maintenance in Melbourne, and to give the ACTU 'the sinews of war'. The former goal anticipated by more than two years *the* problem of political economics of the Whitlam government: how to reduce prices without reducing the income of workers? Bourkes–ACTU broke retail price maintenance, but the ACTU was not to get the sinews of war.

According to Revelman's calculations, for no capital outlay the ACTU could expect a profit of $750 000 after eighteen months of joint trading and $3.5 million annually after five years. The money would be kept as internal savings until 1976, when the ACTU could elect to buy out the Revelman family, or to continue in joint venture. Either way, the staff Hawke needed for trade union education, the scholarships he wanted to give to unionists' children, the economic research he wanted done, even office space – all would be provided. The office space would come early, because Revelman had already planned to expand the store, and would now do so in a way to house the ACTU, rent free. Hawke believed, and his infectious enthusiasm was shared by Revelman, that unionists would flock to 'their' shop, that the 'brand loyalty' known, for example, among cigarette smokers, would become Bourkes–ACTU loyalty for the ordinary working person. This idea was, for both of them, an astonishing misjudgment. In Hawke it arose from his vast inner optimism, self-confidence and his faith in the workers' loyalty; in Revelman, from rapport with Hawke. Bourkes was situated on the corner of Elizabeth and La Trobe Streets, an ugly, rundown part of town – and as any real estate agent will advise, there are three rules for real estate: locality, locality, locality. Also, shoppers in the early 1970s were housewives; men shopped only for very expensive goods, and working women were notoriously quick, price-careless shoppers for their major concern was time. This pattern did not augur well for trade union loyalty to the store. But more importantly, many unions already had agreements with shops to give discounts to their members. In due course, these unions actively campaigned against Bourkes–ACTU; union journals ran advertisements telling their members *not* to patronise the store. And, overlying all this was the fact that Victoria, as a state, was in an economic decline. Signs of the state's underlying economic weaknesses were disguised, for a time, by the general prosperity that had arisen in Australia from the Johnson administration's misfinancing of the Vietnam War. President Nixon had already created a mild recession to try to suppress the excess-demand inflation of the war, but inflation had not shrunk in America and unemployment there was growing towards 6 per cent. We felt a shiver in Australia, but it seemed just a cool breeze while we basked on in the sun.

Hawke engaged solicitors and chartered accountants to examine a draft contract for the ACTU. While making no comment on Revelman's projected trading figures, they advised that the ACTU's option to withdraw from the venture after five years and without liability was a 'major safeguard'. The executive invited Revelman to explain his plans at its November 1970 meeting.

There was suspicion in the room. A capitalist had never entered the ACTU boardroom; Revelman was a Jew and the trade union movement, heavily Catholic and of a generation raised on the vile disingenuity 'the Jews killed Christ', had the undercurrent of uneasiness that has marked the history of relationships between Gentiles and Jews. (Years later, trade unionists complained of the ACTU enterprises: 'Why were we always asked by Bob to deal with Jews?') The trade union ethos makes it difficult to think that any capitalists are full members of the human race, have sensibilities, bleed like other men – just as, one must say, middle-class conservatives seem to think that trade unionists are somehow separate from the Australian community, and pernicious. Years of Cold War, business affluence and conservative government had enforced such views. Even Hawke's very close supporters did not realise the strength of the bond between him and Revelman, that for both there was an intermixture of emotion and pragmatism – that, as another of Hawke's father figures, Sir Peter Abeles, said later of a failed ACTU joint venture, 'There was so much emotion. Bob and I dreamed dreams

together.' Revelman had told Hazel that if he could persuade
the ACTU to join the scheme and move into Bourkes' premises, he could help to combat Hawke's drinking problem, for
Hawke would be nearly a kilometre away from the Lygon. It
is Hazel's belief that a major motivation for Revelman was to
get Hawke to moderate his drinking, a subject he discussed only
with her. There has usually been a hidden life, a second soul, in
Hawke's most intense friendships, as if his animal warmth, boisterousness, indignation, confidence or courage expressed, for
the other, a part that lay suppressed.

The ACTU executive quickly grasped the unspoken tech-
nicalities of Revelman's proposition: Hawke, using the power
of his position in the trade unions and the press, would out-
bully the big retailers should they refuse to supply Bourkes.
Manufacturers and distributors would be more frightened of him
than, for example, of Myers – and the entire structure of retail
price maintenance in Melbourne would come tumbling down.
That was straightforward bargaining, the coin of which is units
of anger and determination. All the executive members were
experts themselves in the bargaining game. Revelman told the
executive that Bourkes' policy was 'to sell the best possible article for the least possible price, coupled with the best possible service', and that 'all the ACTU is putting in is its good name'.
But the executive was still uneasy: intuitively some knew there
was something unspoken. They feared that Revelman was offering them a Trojan horse – as Fitzgibbon said, 'I don't believe in
Santa Claus'. At last Fitzgibbon voiced their fears: 'Why are you
doing this? Why are you offering us such a good deal?' Revelman
replied, 'If I'm to go broke because of Myers I want to do it roaring like a lion, not squeaking like a mouse'. In such company it
was the perfect answer, for it was the businessman's equivalent
of deciding to go on strike. However, the extreme Right was
most unhappy, for the whole bargaining exercise to be launched
by Hawke would be 'political', not 'industrial'. B. A. Santamaria,
a theorist of great acuity, had already warned that Hawke was
forming the trade union movement into a political movement of

a nature as yet unknown. The extreme Left, represented by Pat
Clancy of the Building Workers' Industrial Union, was wildly
enthusiastic. Clancy said,

> Hawke made a stunning impact on the thinking of trade
> unionists. He opened his presidency with a big burst and
> carried through the positive progressive ideas for which he
> had campaigned. Bourkes' store was an idea which at that
> time many people found very new and outgoing – although
> it was not a new concept, for over the centuries the labour
> movement has tried similar things, for instance, the Miners'
> Co-operative Movement. [In the 1950s and 1960s, at Souter's
> encouragement, the ACTU had also considered joint ven-
> tures to try to stimulate a flow of needed cash, but they had
> amounted to nothing.] I was in favour of Bourkes. It's essen-
> tial to bring forward ideas, to broaden the activities of the
> trade union movement, and Bob Hawke approached this
> problem with honesty and with great vigour.

The Left and the centre were similarly enthusiastic and John
Ducker, who thought ACTU enterprises were 'tinsel', decided
not to fight over a popular cause. All of them welcomed the
prospect of decent office space: as Ducker said, 'You get bloody
sick of living on top of each other for a week, and not being able
to have a private phone conversation'.

A month later Bourkes–ACTU opened its doors. The excitement that had surrounded Hawke in his first year of office turned
into hysteria. Hawke appeared on one television channel after
another, on every radio station – hourly, it seemed – was reported
by the metre in the press, constantly talking of the iniquities
of retail price maintenance, the need for legislation against it,
the determination of the trade union movement to smash it.
In six weeks the store's turnover increased by 100 per cent. But
twenty major manufacturers refused to supply more stock; Myers
ran full-page advertisements asking customers to inform it if it
was being 'undersold' and promising 'to correct the situation

immediately'. Repeatedly, during 1970, conservative politicians had accused Hawke and the unions of causing inflation – Hawke had been a negotiator in some significantly successful wage disputes that year – and suddenly he was turning their argument (which was, at best, only a fraction of the truth) against them and theirs. Retail price maintenance, which was more widespread in Melbourne than in Sydney, was, Hawke argued, the culprit and so was the federal government for tolerating it: the action of the manufacturers in refusing to supply the public with cheaper goods, via Bourkes–ACTU, was proof. Some of these manufacturers enjoyed tariff protection; Hawke announced that unions that supported tariff protection would reconsider their attitudes. He made it nationally known that there were 13 000 price-fixing agreements currently registered with the Trade Practices Tribunal.

There was a massive swell of public support. However, the Prime Minister, Bill McMahon, took the unwise step of presenting the issue as a trial of strength between himself and Hawke, whom he accused of 'lawlessness', 'ruining the country' and other fancies. McMahon's brother, Sam, who ran a Sydney bond-store, and had a mischievous sense of fun, promptly offered capital for expansion of Bourkes. The New South Wales Premier, Bob Askin, was loud in his condemnation of Hawke; the Sydney tabloid newspapers referred to 'the power-mad Mr Hawke' and 'this puffed-up Napoleon', and one remarked, 'He is very clearly a socialist who believes in the concept of "class war" '. In Melbourne a Collins Street clubman told the journalist Maximilian Walsh, 'I haven't seen the boys in such a state since Jack Lang's day, forty years ago. They talk about this fellow Hawke now much as their fathers spoke of Lang.' People were confused and exhilarated. Old-timers, whose opinions were sought by the news media, said, 'The big money boys will get Hawkey'. Throughout early March, Hawke held private talks with the executives of the major manufacturers who were refusing supplies. Then on 17 March he made telephone calls to twenty companies, among them Singer, Julius Marlow, Crestknit, Sheraton, Bata, Tosca

Leather, Marathon Footwear, Parker Pens, Onkaparinga ... his diary records to the minute the hour of conversations. It was time for a showdown. That afternoon Hawke announced that the ACTU was advising its affiliates to stop the movement of all goods to and from the Dunlop group of companies in Victoria. Dunlop had been the most intransigent. It appealed to the federal government for help against the unions. The government, after so much threatening talk, refused to guarantee Dunlop that it would fight and twenty-seven hours later it was all over: Eric Dunshea, the chairman of Dunlop, telephoned Hawke to tell him that his London directors had instructed him, failing government support, to surrender. Bourkes–ACTU would have supplies. Melbourne talked of nothing else. Many people were now thoroughly frightened of Hawke, among them Dunshea. He had agreed to hold a joint press conference at which they would announce the news of surrender. Dunshea told his friend, Isi Magid, with whom he lunched every month at their club,

> I was dreading the press conference. I'm not used to public speaking and press conferences and that chap Hawke could handle the press so well, he was so forceful and articulate. I thought he was going to humiliate me and I'd have to sit there while he rubbed salt in my wounds. But he was like a son protecting his own father. He answered most of the questions for me, before the press could get stuck into me. And he avoided the use of the term 'surrender'. He'd conducted all our negotiations as if we were in a boxing ring – everything was in the open, there were no behind-door deals. Then, in the hour I dreaded most, he was like that – he made it as gentle, easy and honourable as any person could.

Hawke's statement to the news media was: 'The practice of retail price maintenance in Australia has been abolished'. It had been – at least in the eyes of the law.[2] It meant that Bourkes–ACTU, no longer unique, would now have to battle with the disadvantage of its location, and the ill will of the unions that had their own discount arrangements with other stores. Revelman, however, was an ingenious retailer. When the first flush of excitement about the store abated later in 1971 he organised advertising campaigns in which Hawke was the central spokesman.

They spent much time together, especially from the beginning of 1972, when the ACTU moved from the Lygon Street office into its newly constructed and spacious accommodation above Bourkes. After work and at weekends they played snooker and tennis together. Revelman was a tennis fanatic and, when dissatisfied with an aspect of his play, took coaching to correct it. He had suffered two mild heart attacks, but treated such signs of infirmity with disdain; during one of them he pretended he was not in pain at all but had simply bent down to retie a shoelace. After recovering from his second heart attack, in February 1972, he announced he was fitter than ever before; indeed, his tennis was at its peak. One evening in May 1972 Hawke asked Revelman to accompany him on a harrowing excursion:

> I'd had some letters from a woman whose husband had cancer and who wanted to meet me before he died. Then I got a message from her saying it was urgent, he had only days to live. His house was near Lionel's place and I asked him to come along. It was a helluva experience: the woman was overcome with emotion ... So I sat on the bed and talked, and Lionel sat on the end of the bed. Lionel didn't say much, but it was comforting having him there. Then we went back to Lionel's place and had something to eat and he said, 'Let's have a game'. And I said, 'Would you rather play snooker?' And he said, 'No! Tennis!' I won the first set 6–3. I said to Lionel, 'Would you rather go in?' and he said, 'No. It's my serve.' I was walking away from the net, I had my back to him, and I heard a thud.

Hawke rushed to his friend, tried to pick him up, but Revelman died in his arms. Tup, Revelman's widow, recalled,

Bob came tearing into the house and said, 'I think something's wrong with Lionel', then he sat down and burst into
tears ... He couldn't stop crying and he didn't have a hand-
kerchief. I had to find him one – he was weeping like a child.

The funeral service was held in Revelman's house. It was a
very large funeral and Hawke had agreed to give the eulogy. He
started to speak but after a few minutes covered his face with
his hands and began to sob and Geoff Gleghorn, his personal
assistant–press officer at the ACTU, stepped forward, took him
by the elbow and led him outside.

While the death was a horrifying personal blow to Hawke,
who agonised that he had caused Revelman's final heart attack
by playing tennis too vigorously with him, it was also a blow to
Bourkes. George Revelman was heartbroken over his younger
brother's death; he did not have Lionel Revelman's flair for
retailing. The store began to slide. Hawke consistently refused to
tell the ACTU executive what the financial position of Bourkes
was, on the grounds that it was a family-owned company and
such information was private. Hawke has never mentioned the
issue, but it seems that the information may have been difficult
for him to obtain. In 1980 when George Revelman was asked
for an interview about his brother and Hawke, he replied he had
no comment to make, and rang off. Failing information from
Hawke, the ACTU executive became increasingly ill humoured
and suspicious about Bourkes. From the latter part of 1980
and through 1981 signs in titanic black letters were painted
on the whitewashed windows of Bourkes, announcing baldly:
'BOURKES–ACTU IS FINISHED'. They could be seen two
city blocks away, almost from Myers. After a while some wit
changed one of the signs to read: 'HAWKE IS FINISHED'.
Nobody bothered to erase it. Anyone entering the ACTU or
walking down La Trobe Street had to see it.

While Bourkes had not generated for the ACTU the funds
Hawke had hoped for, it had provided a substantial financial
benefit: in the winding-up of the enterprise it was agreed that the

ACTU would continue to have rent-free accommodation until 1988. A general estimate was that sixteen years rent would have cost the ACTU $1 million. Ironically, just as the store was closing down and Hawke preparing to leave the ACTU, construction had begun on a new train terminal opposite Bourkes and its problem of unfavourable location appeared ready for solution.

From all over the country letters and telegrams had arrived by the bagful to congratulate Hawke for defeating retail price maintenance, many of them from unions, many from pensioners' associations, many from ALP branches. Those from individual citizens are most revealing of the image that Hawke was establishing in the community:

> At last we have a man of courage, champion of the poor and helpless. God will guide you all the way to a successful end to tyranny.

> You are the Billy Graham of the workers.

> I wish you could be our Prime Minister

> You are like Ben Chifley and John Curtin.

> Strength to your arm, then, Mr Hawke. There are thousands like me who are looking to you for a better Australia in which to live and bringing to their knees all the powerful business monopolies who would prostitute this country in order to assuage their own gluttonous ends.

> May I say how wonderful it is to see you on television bringing the financial moguls to their knees.

> Congratulations on Dunlops. I wonder if you would be interested in sheep drenches, dips, fly dressing and jetting material. Sheep drench is $20 to $27 a gallon [4.5 litres] ...

> Champion for justice and for a better country ... you are a leader of courage and principle and hope for a brighter

future. To help save Australia the people are grateful to you and proclaim you President of Australia.

Do not work too hard and look after yourself as the little man cannot afford to lose a man like you.

I am an old woman. I am glad I have lived long enough to see this happen.

Permit me, Sir, to say that your obvious sincerity and dog-gedness of purpose leaves me drained and inadequate . . . May you remain in good health.

We love you.

A couple of years ago I listened to you make a speech at the offices of the Insurance Staff Federation . . . I got the idea you were a somewhat devious gentleman with political ambitions and would promise anything to gain publicity and personal admiration. I used to think, 'Here he goes again on another publicity-seeking self-promotion campaign – what does he care for the worker? As long as he gets to the top, we can go to the Devil.' How completely and utterly wrong I have been. I trust you will accept my apology for being so wrong.

Due to an old injury I have to use Dr Scholls supports in my shoes. The price . . . Could you do something?

Have you ever considered the poor deal the average man receives when he enters the usual superannuation scheme run by a Life Office? Or an ordinary life assurance policy?

I am going to ask you to do something re the abolition of the Means Test. Please, Mr Hawke, try!

I have to wear dentures. Isn't there anything you can do to stop this scandalous dental bill from being introduced?

We bless you.

. . . the unassuming manner in which you extended mercy to a fallen foe. The charitable way in which you relieved a squirming adversary from his embarrassment will, I doubt not, remain as an inspiration in the minds of many who were privileged to view the programme.

You have stirred me into new hope.

From the hundreds of letters there were only a couple expressing opposition. One said:

Our Australian king of the unions, Hawke by name and nature, the blackmailing, mafia-type, stand-over boss of the workers … The workers … go on strike at his commands … like a lot of sheep. The industries and business houses are frightened of him and the Government is frightened of him … Hawke's definition of democracy is: 'I do what I like, and everyone else does what I tell them'. [The letter was from a false address.][3]

Before Hawke had assumed the ACTU presidency he had, in vehement terms, condemned the 1969–70 national wage decision of the Conciliation and Arbitration Commission and had asserted that such decisions would lead to an increase in collective bargaining in Australia. Since 1907, whenever the unions have been angry with arbitrated wages they have threatened to reject arbitration and embrace collective bargaining – which, of course, they then ask the arbitration system to approve, as a 'consent award'. Arbitration judges, conciliation commissioners, union and employer officials all know the rules of this game and play it with gusto. There are solemn statements, warnings, questions in parliament – it is all part of the bargaining process to determine who has the largest pile of chips; that is, which party is really most angry and must be assuaged. Unfortunately, it is only the cognoscenti of industrial relations who do understand the process, for both the news media and the universities have failed to explain to the public what is really going on behind the rhetoric, and it is in the interests of politicians of all persuasions not to clarify. Only some of them understand it themselves: Sir Richard Kirby said of the years after Harold Holt ceased to be Minister for Labour,

> It was as useful as having Billy the Cat as minister. The government put coves in the job who didn't have a clue. I'd see their eyes glazing as I tried to explain things – they literally could not understand what industrial relations was about.

In desperation Kirby would sometimes use the analogy of marriage, in which tension builds up until there is an argument: 'I'd tell them, "That is a strike. It's letting off steam" … However, they still couldn't grasp the idea that industrial relations operate on the same principles as family relations …'

It is the job of union leaders to bargain as hard as they can. That is, to express anger. Hawke's unusually developed capacity for the expression of anger in logical terms was to make him the greatest union negotiator there has been in Australia, and, in the opinion of the international trade union community (represented at the ILO), one of the greatest in the world. Meanwhile the public at large, innocent of the processes of industrial relations and seeing only a very angry man, started to become frightened of Hawke. An early letter to him from a correspondent self-described as 'ex-serviceman, non-striker', said 'Heil Hitler. Why don't you go to Russia, you power-hungry bastard, and take all your stinking Left-wing fascist parasites with you. Australia will be better served by your absence.'

After the showers of congratulations that greeted the Dunlop drama in early 1971 – and which were, notably, less concerned with the economic principle for which Hawke had fought than, in a majority of cases, with revenge – his popularity took an abrupt downturn when he adopted, and in the trade union movement became the leader of, the anti-apartheid cause.

As early as March 1971 students had begun protests against a tour in Australia of a South African rugby union team, due to arrive in June. In early April the South African government banned the inclusion of two non-white players in the team, the Springboks. A few days later Hawke announced that the ACTU 'had a strong policy against apartheid' and implied that there would be union bans against the Springboks. The ACTU's policy against apartheid had first been stated in 1963, the year in which the Organisation of African Unity was established, and that marked the real beginning of the Third World's struggle against the domination of the First and Second Worlds. On 16 April 1971 Hawke said publicly that South Africa should be isolated from international sport. Labor politicians made similar statements. The Prime Minister, McMahon, said that the ACTU and the ALP were 'ganging up' and that their actions were discreditable. Hawke said the unions would impose bans. The *Rand Daily Mail* ran an editorial headlined, 'An Appeal to Mr Hawke' asking that there be no union action. The Australian news media reported it. The government and press editorialists took out their violins and played, fortissimo, what by now was a national refrain: 'Who runs the country? The government or the unions?'

By late April the parliamentary Labor Party was alarmed that a campaign against the Springboks by the trade unions would damage Labor's electoral chances. The Commonwealth Labor Advisory Council (the formal meeting ground between the ALP and the trade union movement, a body later named the Australian Labor Advisory Council, called ALAC, pronounced 'Alac') recommended on 27 April that the government should be pressed to ban the tour on 'moral' grounds and that the unions should not take independent action. Hawke said:

> We were very strong in the position, both in discussions within the ACTU and in all my public statements, that we, the unions, didn't want to be forced into a situation where we had to take action. We wanted the government to act. And that was not just a tactical decision – it was what we really believed. But it was 1971 and they were simply slow learners. The standard argument trotted out was that politics should

be kept out of sport; that it wasn't appropriate for either governments or trade unions to intrude into sport – which was a pretty funny argument, considering that the exclusion of blacks from sporting teams was a political act, it was the policy of the South African government. Well, we weren't prepared to accept that argument, either vis-à-vis the government or vis-à-vis the Labor Party. There were two aspects to our position vis-à-vis the ALP. One, on pragmatic grounds, was that we did not accept that trade union action would damage the party, come election time – which was more than eighteen months away. Indeed, I believed, as did others in the ACTU, that there were certain issues where, if we were ahead of public opinion and totally convinced of our position, we had an obligation to *act* ahead of public opinion, to act as leaders, in the hope that the public would come to understand. The second aspect was: opposition to apartheid was not merely ACTU policy. The ACTU was part of the international trade union movement and the unequivocal policy of the ICFTU [International Confederation of Free Trade Unions], of which we were part, was opposition to apartheid, and the ICFTU had called upon the ACTU to take action. Therefore we should.

On 5 May Hawke had talks with Charles Blunt, head of the Australian Rugby Union. Hawke recalled:

It was a civilised meeting. He wasn't one of the troglodytes who said we were totally wrong to have an interest in this area, he was a reasonable bloke, but it was quite clear from our conversations that nothing looked like coming out of them to change the head-on situation that was looming in Australia.

On 13 May the ACTU executive met and decided (only the extreme Right objecting):

to request the government to inform the government of
South Africa that no team from that country will be received
in Australia unless that team has been chosen or has been
free to be chosen on a non-discriminatory racial basis ...
to indicate that should positive steps be taken by the South
African government to ensure that [no racial discrimination]
is applied to the Rugby Union and cricket teams proposed
to be sent to Australia, then the teams would accordingly be
welcome. Should these representations prove to be unsuccessful we advise our affiliated unions to take whatever action
is necessary as an act of conscience on their part to with-
hold their services from any activities directly associated with
these proposed tours ...[4]

The executive also instructed Hawke to write directly to the South
African Prime Minister, Vorster, stating the ACTU's decision and
requesting a non-discriminatory team be sent to Australia. His
letter was conveyed by the South African ambassador and within
a few days Hawke had received a rejection. Hawke announced
that union action was now inevitable. There was immense publicity; student and civil liberty groups were vociferous. Newspaper
editorialists wrang their hands, complained the unions were
running the country, apartheid was wrong – *but* politics should
not enter sport. The nation was deeply divided, the trade union
movement as much as the rest. The Springboks were due to
begin their tour in Perth, on 24 June. On 25 May the Western
Australian branch of the Transport Workers' Union (TWU)
announced that it would not take action; airport refuellers would
service the South African Airways plane bringing the team;
porters would handle their luggage. The TWU's decision was in
part the result of brawling within the union's Western Australian
branch, and brawling between the branch and its federal body.
The branch was refusing to take orders from the TWU head
office. The government saw a vulnerable spot. It announced
that if other TWU branches prevented aircraft from flying
the Springboks around Australia, the RAAF would be used. It

commended the Western Australian TWU for being 'responsible'. Then the Western Australian Barmaids' and Barmen's Union announced that it would serve the Springboks. Hawke was due to leave Australia on the day the Springboks were due to arrive, and from Perth. The TWU announced it would blackban his flight out of Perth; at Melbourne airport two men burnt their union cards in front of Hawke. Hawke said that South African Airlines would lose its Australian market if it flew the team into Australia. He telephoned SAA and Qantas to tell their executives that their planes would be black banned indefinitely – something that never happened. Commenting on this, he revealed the gamesmanship involved:

> Well, you expressed a view as to what you hoped would happen, and certainly put it in terms that it, in fact, would happen. Then you worked in terms of what the unions involved would, in fact, be prepared to do. And, you had to judge how far you could push that.

In Perth people telephoned Ellie to abuse her. One said, 'Why didn't you strangle him at birth?' Another, 'You gave birth to a monster'. There were repeated claims that Hawke was a Communist.

Hawke was taking his daughter Susan abroad with him. For the first time he was to visit Israel, then would fly on to a conference in Europe, while Susan stayed in Israel on a kibbutz. He was acutely aware that Hazel was rearing the children single-handed, for already his job required him to be overseas or interstate for six months of the year, and when he was in Melbourne he was hardly a normal father: the phone began ringing at 7 a.m. There were press interviews while they were trying to eat breakfast. Hawke had arranged at the last minute that Susan should accompany him abroad. He said:

> There were a group of young fellows, musicians I think, on the flight with us over to Perth. I had some apprehension

about what would happen when we landed in Perth and these musicians said, 'We'll walk off with you'. I said to Susan, 'There might be some unpleasantness'. And, indeed, it was a never-to-be-forgotten experience, one of the most unpleasant of the whole time I was president of the ACTU. We got off the plane and there were hundreds and hundreds of people there. Masses of them. And they were screaming abuse and spitting and shouting all sorts of epithets. Susan was frightened, but she was good, she kept cool. We walked through it. The people were there to meet the Springboks. Exquisite timing. We went home to Mum and Dad's place. We were due to fly out the following night. And there was a lot of talk about that plane being bombed, so there was a very thorough search of baggage. [There was a phalanx of police to escort Hawke and Susan on to the plane.] I said to Susan before we boarded, 'Look, we shouldn't be surprised if once we take off something happens and we have to return to Perth'. It seemed to be sensible to say that to her. Well, we took off and had been flying for about an hour and I said, 'Well, love, it looks as though it's all right'. And the words were hardly out of my mouth when I noticed a change in the altitude of the plane and in the sound of the engines. Then a few minutes later the captain said, 'We are returning to Perth'. He made the usual reassuring noises. So, zoom! We returned to Perth. As we landed and were disembarking some bastard walking past turned to me and said, 'I might have known – you Commie swine', something like that, and I was pretty annoyed, and made a comment back. There was another search, and of course there was no bomb on the plane. It had been a hoax. But it had taken about two hours and I was worried about whether we'd be able to take off again, because of the question of hours for the aircrew. Anyway, off we went again. And after a while the captain came down to talk to me, and not in the friendliest of terms, somewhat cold. He made the point about the aircrew. And I had the distinct impression that he was less than enthusiastic about me. As he turned to go he said, 'By the way, Mr Hawke, it may interest you to know that I am Rhodesian'.

The Springbok riots of 1971 are now a part of Australian history. No apartheid sporting team has visited Australia since, but the principle was established at horrible cost to protestors, and police. The Victorian police force, which bore the brunt of protestor fury, reacted with savagery. Someone threw black paint on Hazel's car. At Sandringham she read letters addressed to Hawke that were filled with vilification. She said, 'Sometimes I'd retch, just reading them'. Twice, inside parcels, there was excrement. At school, the Hawke children were tormented. Rosslyn, the youngest, an affectionate child who adored her father, was made to watch while a group of children symbolically killed Hawke by grinding his photographs into a paste. Hawke had always striven to keep what might be called his woman problem separate from his family life; people, often wearing a mask of sympathy, now took the opportunity to tell Hazel and the children all they knew of Hawke's peccadillos, with flourishes. Hazel said, 'Kids at school and even *adults* said things to the children about their father with a criminal disregard for what effect they would have'. Years of harassment, at first from racists and sadists, later from anti-Zionists and sadists, had begun for the Hawke family.

Peter Coleman, who met Hazel in late 1972 for the first time in a decade, was shocked by the change in her: 'I remembered her as so friendly and open, and here seemed a cold, tough woman. I guessed she must have had a rough spin.' Of necessity, with all but those whom she knew she could trust, Hazel had turned into a tigress. Ducker, who took his family on the same cruise ship as the Hawkes after the 1972 election, said: 'It was a bit difficult for me to get friendly with Hazel. I was the bloke who had tried to knock off her husband – and the iron had entered her soul, as far as I was concerned.' There are scores of stories from journalists and others about tongue-lashings they received from Hazel for criticism of Hawke or for impositions upon the children. She had always been fiercely protective of him; she was now in constant battle for the four of them against what seemed, at times, the entire nation.

Although Hawke's trip to the International Labour Conference was an annual obligation, for he was the workers' spokesman there for Australia and Asia, Brian Harradine publicly accused him of 'skipping out of the country when the going got tough'.

In May 1971 Hawke's popularity had first been tested by a Gallup poll: 42 per cent approved, 30 per cent disapproved of him. By August 1971 the balance had changed: 28 per cent approved, 55 per cent disapproved of him. In the white-collar trade unions only 24 per cent approved, 61 per cent disapproved; in the blue-collar unions 51 per cent approved, 32 per cent disapproved; and in the trade unions as a whole 48 per cent were dissatisfied with him. While Hawke was abroad there were two by-elections in Queensland registering massive swings against the ALP – 18 per cent in Maryborough – and it was generally accepted that Hawke's unpopularity was a major factor. The *Australian* of 22 August announced: 'Hawke is clearly a vote-winner for the coalition parties ... one of the most unpopular men in the country ... does not even have the support of a majority of trade unionists'. Hours later Gough Whitlam used the opportunity of his Budget speech-in-reply to defend Hawke (and the ALP's electoral prospects), saying the president of the ACTU had saved the country millions of dollars through strike settlement and the breaking of retail price maintenance. Whitlam pointed out that Hawke had been 'subjected by ministers and the media to a campaign of abuse and denigration unparalleled in Australia's history, except, possibly, for the late Dr Evatt'. A couple of days later a Liberal backbencher described Hawke as 'the arch-enemy of Australia'. On the following Monday, 30 August, the ACTU's 1971 Congress opened – Hawke's first as president.

The Right had its strategy: it would attack Hawke for leading the ACTU to exceed its legitimate functions by authorising industrial action for 'political' ends, and for neglecting to act on other matters of proper concern to the trade unions. The Left had its plans, too. In Victoria, where the state ALP had been a militant industrial party, different, from all other Labor machines, Hawke had been transformed from hero (of sorts) to 'traitor', 'Judas' and the like, because of his role in federal intervention in the affairs of the Victorian branch. At the height of excitement over this issue, in late 1970–early 1971, passions had run so high that it had required physical courage to walk into the Lygon Hotel. Many of Hawke's old Left-wing friends in Victoria would never speak to him again, among them Wally Curran, who in earlier days had helped Hawke build a carport and had been assistant to George Seelaf during the ACTU presidency campaign. Hawke had compounded Left-wing anger by settling a strike in the oil industry in 1970. Officials considered that Hawke's intervention had prevented their achievement of a bigger wage increase. By late 1971, although the public was unaware of it, the extreme Left was extremely cross with Hawke. The Left's Congress strategy was to support his candidates for the executive elections, while attempting to have Congress bind the ACTU to militant action on key issues, specifically wage campaigns and fights against the penal powers.

From this confluence of pressures Hawke and the moderate Left emerged victors: he was voted an executive that divided 10–7 in his favour and a two-year policy platform that rejected 'massive industrial action' in favour of pragmatism. 'It is not any part of our policy to abandon arbitration', Hawke announced at the opening of Congress, and this attitude was formally accepted by delegates later, as was a resolution on the penal powers that stated that the ACTU was to continue its negotiations with government about them and 'to work out ways and means of ensuring that industrial agreements are honoured by the Trade Union Movement'. This latter statement was significant, for it was an acknowledgement by the unions that relations with employers were a two-way deal – that if the unions demanded to be free of penal sanctions while employers were forced, by the arbitration system, to pay certain wages, the unions would have to give some undertaking that would accept the limitations upon employers as responsibilities upon themselves.

Hawke's Congress success had, however, one fateful setback: the affiliation fees. Hawke had taken the exceptional step of leaving the chair to second the executive's recommendation for a fee increase of 100 per cent, and had done so angrily. He described the ACTU's staffing position as 'ludicrous' and derided objections to the increase: 'To suggest that 24 cents a member is unreasonable is in itself inexcusable'. He already knew that a compromise between a 100 per cent increase and no increase had been framed, recommending that the extra money be paid over two years; the night before the issue arose numbers men told him they thought this 50–50 amendment could get the votes. Hawke's tactic was to bully the Congress into adopting at least a half-measure. He has an ability to switch on rage: sometimes, before he is to make a telephone call during which he intends to browbeat somebody for being in his opinion a fool or a crook, he will throw an aside, 'This might be a bit rough', then will spend a couple of seconds of intense stillness, like a gymnast collecting his energy for a leap. He then lets fly. The harangue that follows can go on for an hour. (In 1980, over Aboriginal land rights, Hawke was so savage during a telephone conversation with a senior businessman who had not been honest in the matter that the man had a blackout that night and took three months leave. Hawke, who liked and otherwise admired him, was mortified.) A verbal Hercules, Hawke often breaks things unintentionally – people, like china ornaments, bewilderingly come apart in his hands. And cut him. Don Dunstan, himself an adept at sudden anger, noted, 'Bob does not have the sensitivity to an audience that, for example, a good actor has'. A group of half-a-dozen people can be intimidated by Hawke's anger and collapse. At the Congress he was facing 764 men. The delegates voted for no increase.

Perhaps they would have anyway, for there is no end to the wheeling and dealing and last-minute reversals of an ACTU Congress. But Hawke had provided his already choleric

Left-wing critics with another grudge against him, of the 'Who does he think he is?' variety.

Within hours, however, Congress had endorsed the ACTU's association with Bourkes and the executive's decision to investigate the feasibility of entering consumer credit, insurance and housing finance. Hawke had left the chair to speak on these matters also, and his speech had been moderate. As a chairman, Hawke was both more efficient and fairer than Monk, who would declare votes against executive recommendations lost on the voices, as a matter of course. Hawke actually listened to the voices and declared that the executive had lost, on the voices, seven times. In the old days Congress sessions had never started on time; Hawke managed to open all but two sessions within five minutes of the advertised time and, to the shock of delegates, enforced an extra hour's sitting one day. With individual speakers he was, as Monk had been, impartial and courteous – not an easy matter for anyone, for Congress is *the* arena for unionists to perform, and the executive and the president take their share of abuse. During debates at the 1971 Congress, Joe Riordan, Hawke's old adversary, was subjected to some harsh personal attacks by Hawke supporters. Hawke, with great gentleness, called Riordan's attention to the fact that his speaking time had run out. It was a tiny matter, but the Right noticed compassion in a man they had thought too wild for it. Slowly, he was bringing them round. After 1971 the ACTU executive began, for the first time in four years, to vote unanimously, and Hawke began his long reign as a consensus leader.

The Right had realised that Hawke would not, after all, assault them. Ducker said,

> Now that must have been a vast disappointment for, particularly, the Communist Party and the active Left, because it meant that their success was limited. Bob wasn't prepared to factionalise the ACTU to the position where it was split. He was prepared to respect and uphold the constitutional authority of the trade union movement, he was careful to

try to work through the structures, the proper procedures. He stood up to the madmen of the Left ... A lot of it was Bob's gentleness, an ease of manner, being kind to people. Gradually, he and I were getting to know each other and to see in each other something more than we had previously perceived. Fortifying this was our relationship in the Labor Party federal executive. That was neutral ground, and an opportunity for socialising – and we had to get on in the Labor Party because, by late 1971, we were looking at a federal Labor government. We both wanted to assist that. It's difficult to be cordial and friendly in the Labor Party and, often about the same issue, to be at loggerheads in the ACTU ... I'd seen that the ascendance *was* with Hawke and with the policies and philosophies he was espousing, and I was concerned that the Right could become isolated. That was what the National Civic Council grouping [in the trade union movement] wanted; they wanted total split, in the belief that they would win on that basis. I thought they were bloody mad. So I played my cards carefully. I didn't take the Springbok tour head on. I didn't object to the first 24-hour strike [in 1970] on the Budget, I went with it, and was often able to take a step in advance. And would delight in the fact that I could take a Left position, with Geitzelt following up behind. And I'd tell the Labour Council that, 'despite some reservations by delegate Geitzelt we were able to take a firm, strong, militant position ...'

On 1 September 1971 Hawke was named Victorian Father of the Year. A photograph of Rosslyn, plaits flying, rushing into his arms, was widely published. It marked the turning point of Hawke's unpopularity. He had been embarrassed by the honour, which he told the news media should properly have gone to Hazel for she was, he said, mother and father – and gardener. Later that month he gave interviews acknowledging that his abrasiveness had alarmed people, implying regret for this. The September Gallup poll showed his public approval had increased by 4 per cent and his disapproval had fallen to 43 per cent. Only 26 per cent of women approved of Hawke.

He had caused serious affront to the burgeoning feminist movement earlier in the year when, appearing on television with Zelda D'Aprano, a leader of the cause, he had felt her shoulder to find out, as he explained, if she were wearing a bra. D'Aprano was a postal worker; Hawke asked her, 'You do mean M-A-I-L Exchange, don't you?' The feminist magazine *MeJane* named him Male Chauvinist of the Month, and feminists never forgave him. At the time women were just learning to bargain: in Hawke they had encountered an expert, who could have taken up their cause but did not. Back in the early 1960s, when it was unfashionable, he had accepted that women should have equality and had publicly argued for it. His commitment, however, as for many of his generation, lacked a broad conceptual base. He had read Greer's *Female Eunuch* – and in early 1972, when he was working hard on his image, had a lively, genial discussion on television with her – but Greer's work had little effect on those who were not already converted or were psychologically ready to be converted. And Hawke was not. He was in his fiftieth year before he read the seminal text of feminism, de Beauvoir's *Second Sex*, and was appalled by her description of the female condition and by what he had failed to understand. 'It's a disaster! A disaster!' he said. 'I'd not realised ...' In the meantime, he had showed much hostility to women: his language, his excessively virile swagger, the way he stood – legs straight, calves pushed back, hips forward – his every public gesture revealed dominance, including sexual dominance. Feminists had only to look at Hawke to see The Enemy. Many women found him magnetically attractive. Some daring – and silly – ones pursued him, the more so as his fame grew, and he became their prey rather than the reverse. He would often leave public gatherings in a temper, saying, 'There was a woman there – Christ Almighty! – all over me like a rash'. A certain smugness was always mixed with annoyance. By the late 1970s, when Hawke's womanising had been, at last, publicised, women and girls he had not met would telephone him or write notes suggesting dalliance. Hawke behaved as if he were irresistible to all women and, when drunk, would proposition anyone who caught his eye. He always thought of himself as a man who liked women – as womanisers invariably do; it took him years to acknowledge that his 'liking' was possibly not what it seemed on the surface.

As Ducker noted, by late 1971 a major concern for leaders of the trade union movement was the election of a federal Labor government. Following intervention in Victoria, Hawke had become a member of the ALP federal executive, which had been reformed since the days of the '36 faceless men'. Hawke had his seat as one of two Victorian representatives; Ducker was a New South Wales representative and Egerton a Queensland one. A major danger for the party was that the McMahon government and conservative state premiers were pressing hard on the 'law and order' issue and that strikes, no matter what the political complexion of the unions who staged them, would be blamed on the ALP. In his first year of office Hawke had given leadership to union opposition to what was deemed unreasonable government action: one celebrated example was a union ban against the export of merino rams that became such a cause célèbre that many members of the public revealed, in letters to the newspapers and to Hawke, that they believed the export of rams was illegal, similar to gunrunning. Others, of course, saw Hawke as 'dictator', a term applied to him constantly. (All that had happened in the merino rams issue was that the ACTU had responded to requests from farmers' groups to prevent export.) Meanwhile, trade union demonstrations against the Budgets of 1970 and 1971, co-ordinated by the ACTU, had raised an outcry from conservatives. There were many press assertions that the trade union movement, under Hawke, was the true Opposition, and Hawke the real leader of the Opposition, dictating to Whitlam – a curious idea, indeed.

By the beginning of the election year, 1972, it was essential for the party's well-being that such imagery be changed.

The industrial horse, as it were, had already bolted – and had done so before Hawke became president of the ACTU – but it was his job to try to catch it and put it back in the stable. From the beginning of 1972 Hawke was engaged in strike settlement and in dampening down the pent-up frustrations of a trade union movement that had learned how to live without a federal Labor government. Many union leaders were difficult to convince that it was worth delaying militant action now in the interests of the longer-term goal of 'their' government coming to power. Communist union leaders had even greater reservations: they looked with a jaundiced eye upon Labor and reform. From the beginning of 1972 Hawke, Ducker and Egerton – a former boilermaker and a man who had a lifetime's experience of the labour movement and 'knew his way in all the little nooks and crannies, better than anyone else', in Ducker's description – began to operate as a triumvirate. All three were wary of each other, but they managed to co-operate quietly and efficiently. Ducker and Egerton (president of the Queensland TLC and president of the Queensland ALP) had real power. Hawke had the illusion of power, through the news media, but ultimately he had only the weapon of oratory, and the fragile 'authority' of the ACTU, while the other two could make threats and promises of substantial nature. 'There were a lot of strikes we stopped', Ducker said; Egerton remarked, 'It always suited me to have Bob up there in front, while I was down shooting the bullets'.

One serious dispute that could not be averted was in the Victorian State Electricity Commission. It had been smouldering for months and the Arbitration Commission had been trying to contain it when, in February 1972, it broke out. The unions rejected arbitration; the SEC, under pressure from the Victorian Bolte government, reacted with provocation and intransigence; the unions replied by changing their bans into a strike and chaos was created. Strikes in power generation are the most damaging of all, for they can gallop wildly, stopping industry and throwing hundreds of thousands out of work within days. This happened. The McMahon and Bolte governments blamed the ALP and Communists. A quarter of a million people were without work; the federal Minister for Social Security, Bill Wentworth, announced that people put out of work by the strike would not receive dole money. When Hawke announced, after days of private talks with the unions and arbitration judges, that he was formally intervening to try to settle the dispute, someone telephoned the ACTU to say that he would be murdered. Police were put on guard at the Sandringham house and moved around with Hawke.

The strike by now was so critical that Hawke hired an aeroplane to fly to the south coast of New South Wales to hold discussions with Kirby, who had been ill and was convalescing there. The two men had wanted their meeting to be secret, but the press had picked up Hawke's movements through car radios, which monitor police radios, and his meeting with Kirby took place in a glare of publicity. As events turned out, the appearance of a breakthrough that their meeting suggested was the only lever Hawke had when he returned to Melbourne and had to argue to officials of the unions involved that they must recommend a return to arbitration. During strikes there are three internal levels of authority: there are the union officials; the shop stewards; and the rank and file. Frequently, one or two of the groups is in conflict with the third. The most unnerving situation occurs when the shop stewards and the rank and file gang up against the officials. When Hawke returned from his stay with Kirby and entered the Melbourne Trades Hall for talks with officials they told him their fears about the shop stewards: that they would refuse to accept a return to arbitration. Hawke said,

> The officials told me that if I went down to Yallourn the men were going to throw me in the duckpond there. Anyway, I went. There was a police escort. I had to talk to the shop stewards first and really, I barely had a feather to fly with. Dick [Kirby] and I hadn't been able to think of anything much; the whole situation was just a bloody-awful schemozzle, with thousands of people out of work and people going hungry,

and the conservatives belting it for all it was worth politically. So I went in to see the shop stewards, and the atmosphere was not exactly warm, and I just told them straight: I could not promise them anything *but* if they would recommend a return to work I would argue the case before the Arbitration Commission. And they accepted that. Then I went out to address the men and there was – oh, you know, some shouting, 'Throw him in the duckpond', 'Sell-out', that sort of thing, but I gave them the same message and they listened, and listened to the shop stewards. And that was it.

The strike had cost an estimated $79 million in lost production. Meanwhile Hawke's action cost him what support he still had in the Left of Victorian Labor politics. There had been a growing estrangement between him and the Left of the party since about 1966, when the Victorian central executive and its supporters had a renewed seizure of sectarian hatred, directed against Roman Catholics. As Dr Bob Smith, a member of the Victorian branch of those days, recalled, 'The way to prove you were ideologically pure was to be anti-Mick'. The central executive was already authoritarian; there were many in the party who wanted change, some democracy in the party. Among them was one of Hawke's closest friends, Barney Williams, who had founded the Australian Council of Salaried and Professional Associations (ACSPA) and who was the secretary of the Sandringham branch of the ALP, to which Hawke belonged. Hawke said,

He was the most devoted man I have ever met in the Labor movement. There was not an ounce of selfishness in him. The hard Left vilified Barney as a Santamaria stooge because he was a Catholic and wanted change. It sickened me. There was an atmosphere of starry-eyed radical socialism in the early 1960s. I began to think it wasn't radical and wasn't socialism, but something else.

Hawke had tried to prevent federal intervention in the Victorian branch but, like others of the centre and Left, had finally agreed to it, and had co-operated with the interveners. The party was split into three factions: Socialist Left, the Centre Unity, and the Participants (the Right). Hawke became the leader of Centre Unity, which caused the Socialist Left to regard him as a political rat. Following the SEC dispute, they regarded him as an industrial one as well. However, it took several years for the Socialist Left's hatred of Hawke to become public; they needed an issue.

Within weeks of the electricity dispute Hawke was involved in an even more complicated strike, in the oil industry. It began, on paper, in March and dragged on, through negotiations, breakdowns in negotiations, renewed negotiations, slowly increasing in acrimony. The argument was over a 35-hour week in the oil industry. The claim for a shorter week had a long history, for twenty years earlier an ACTU Congress had endorsed a recommendation that 35 hours should become the normal working week for the entire trade union movement. In the interim, little had been done to turn the policy into reality. When the unions presented their claim for a shorter week, in 1972, the oil companies refused to negotiate on the question. The McMahon government encouraged the companies to stand firm.

By June there were 24-hour strikes. The companies applied for bans clauses that would mean, if flouted, the penal powers would be applied. There were compulsory conferences in the Arbitration Commission; more strikes; when officials recommended a return to work the rank and file refused. By the end of June there were strikes in Queensland, Victoria and New South Wales refineries. Only about a thousand men were involved, but in a high-technology industry massive strikes are unnecessary. The unions made an offer: the companies refused to talk to them. The news carried stories of a national fuel shortage, which were not denied but instead were encouraged by the government and the companies, although both knew there were vast, untouched reserves of petroleum. Tanker drivers were thrown out of work; there was panic buying, rationing, bad tempers.

Hawke was in a delicate position: not only were the employers intransigent, the officials themselves were refusing to allow him to enter the dispute. He had been ill during its early stages, stricken with a back injury. Hazel had bought a wig and Hawke had been playing with her and the wig one evening at home, putting it on and parading around the living room; he took it off, threw it down, bent to pick it up and suddenly could not stand. He said,

Anyone who's had a back injury knows what the pain is like. It's terrible. I was totally incapacitated for three weeks, flat on my back, in traction. When I was able to walk it was awful: I had to hobble along, crouched over. Getting out of the car at the office would take me – well, it seemed like half an hour. I was in pain most of the time and would have to lie on the floor in the office . . . Laurie Carmichael was handling the oil industry dispute for the AMWSU. By this time there was a standard pattern about disputes; union officials had done all the originating work, drawn up the log of claims, and they wanted to handle disputes themselves, without interference from the ACTU. That was valid, in terms of the ACTU Constitution. But there came a point where we had to say, we *are* going to be involved. This was the first really dramatic case and we had to be quite tough about it, because while some of the other unions – the Ironworkers and the Australasian Society of Engineers, for example – did not object too strongly, Laurie Carmichael felt very paternalistic. This was his baby, and he was not going to have any paternity suits about it. It was *his*. While I've never been able to agree with Carmichael's political philosophy [Communism], Laurie is straight to deal with. You know where you stand with him and if he gives his word he keeps it. He's tough but reliable. One of the problems on the other side was that the oil companies' industrial officers did not have authority to make decisions. There were two elements to this: in the general scheme of things industrial officers are rarely in the limelight. Suddenly, they are, and they have an almost vested interest in seeing the dispute continue. So one wanted to get to the actual bosses of the companies, to make them face up to their responsibilities. This problem is particularly egregious in the oil industry – the companies' priorities are wrong, and they get themselves in knots. And there was another problem: there was a collusive position between the oil companies and the government. McMahon was threatening to recall parliament on the issue, and then to go to the people on it. There was a vested interest in trying to precipitate a position of chaos and suffering for the community, and using guilt by association, to blame the ALP and advantage the McMahon government.

Hawke decided to play his news media card: he appeared on radio, television and in the press, announcing collusion. Behind the scenes, he was attempting to split the companies, to persuade one to hive off, and bargain. He was in contact with government, the companies, the Arbitration Commission and the various unions, flying interstate frequently, making hundreds of telephone calls each day. Grudgingly, on 19 July, the men returned to work, on the premise that the companies would resume negotiations. The next day, when they discovered the companies were still intransigent, the men went out again. Hawke had been working for twenty-hour stretches. That night, accompanied by Hazel, he was to launch an art exhibition in Melbourne. He rose, said, 'I'm relieved to see this is not an opening in oils. I couldn't stand it', spoke for a minute then murmured, 'I can't go on', and collapsed.

The Hawke children were at home watching *Hogan's Heroes* on television when a message flashed on the screen: 'HAWKE HAS HEART ATTACK'. By the time a family friend arrived at the house the telephone was ringing incessantly with calls from journalists wanting to know if Hawke were still alive, a question the children could not answer, because Hazel had been unable to contact them by telephone. She had taken Hawke to a nearby hotel and put him to bed, and later told the press that Hawke had not had a heart attack, adding,

It seems to me that not enough people work hard enough in this world to understand what it's like to be so completely exhausted. He's propped himself up for so long – he keeps propping himself up because he's a man of good faith.

Telegrams and telephone calls streamed into the ACTU. Some read: 'Sincere wishes speedy recovery from 27 fork-lift drivers Kent Brewery', 'Darwin Telegraph Staff very sorry ... Welcome to recuperate in sunny Darwin', 'Seamen's Union, Melbourne, wishes speedy recovery ... take a rest'.

Hotel and motel owners in holiday resorts rang urging Hawke to be their guest; other people offered the relaxation of their sauna baths. Charlie Fitzgibbon, who was familiar with Hawke's overwork–collapse syndrome, and his wildness, sent him a card of a man praying, 'Forgive me now ... Tomorrow I may not be sorry'.[5]

The next day Hawke had recovered, but his doctor insisted that he take a week's rest. He continued to negotiate from home. The dispute was dragging on; there were queues for petrol; TAA and Ansett were progressively limiting their flights. But Hawke was having some success in splitting the companies and by the last week of July announced an ACTU plan whereby the refineries of certain companies would be exempted from strike action so that essential services, at least, could be maintained. The crisis was near: on 26 July McMahon called an emergency Cabinet meeting, which was to decide if parliament should be recalled – an extraordinary action for this had occurred before only for the abdication of Edward VIII, the declaration of war against Japan, and the commitment of troops to Korea. If parliament were recalled, it would be to announce a 'law and order' election.

Hawke said,

Lynch [the Minister for Labour] had been pleading with me to go to talk to him. I told him, 'Everything that you've done in this dispute has been pro-company. You haven't been in any sense objective about it, all your pronouncements have come from ignorance of the facts – or, if you've got knowledge, of putting knowledge aside. And you've tried to precipitate a situation so bad that you can go to the country on it. Well, you're not going to bash us into submission. So I won't talk to you.' Things got grimmer and Lynch contacted me again and said, 'Let's talk'. I said, 'Sure'. And he said, 'Come to my office'. I said, 'No bloody way in the world'. He said, 'Let's meet in an independent place – a hotel or something'. I said, 'No way, Phil. You want to talk – you come to the ACTU.' I was still in a lot of pain with my back and couldn't stand up properly. Well, McMahon had his Cabinet meeting which was going to frighten us all to death, and what did they decide? That Lynch, Nixon [Minister for Shipping] and Greenwood [the Attorney-General] would come to the ACTU. You've never seen such embarrassed people as those three as they walked into the old ACTU building, past the media. But they faced up to it. And we just belted at them that what they were doing was totally unacceptable, and that was the beginning of the end, in the sense that the government had collapsed. The oil companies were unbelievably apprehensive about a Labor victory, which, as we moved into 1972, became increasingly likely. There is no doubt in my mind that at an early stage there were a lot of discussions between the oil companies and the government as to whether the two-year agreement between the oil industry unions and the companies could not be used to take on the labour movement, get sympathy, and divert the thrust towards Labor … Later John Gorton, with whom I've always got on well, said to me, 'If I'd still been prime minister I would not have allowed my ministers to call on you!'

At mass meetings on 3 August workers decided to return to work while Mr Justice Moore, acting president of the Arbitration Commission, resumed what he had been forced to abandon a month earlier, chairmanship of discussions. By 21 August a settlement had been reached, and the oil industry was peaceful – for another two years.

There were many telegrams of congratulations to Hawke, among them several from people who signed themselves 'usual Liberals'. They indicated that the flow towards a Labor government was gathering pace, but also something else: Hawke himself had some appeal for the middle ground of Australian politics. Every time he appeared in a television discussion the channel's switchboard would receive a score of calls demanding to know why 'that Communist' had been allowed air-time. But gradually anti-Labor people were beginning to realise that Hawke did not have horns and cloven hooves, that he actually had the good of the community at heart. Newspaper cartoonists began to draw him as a knight in armour. On 18 October the *Australian* ran a full-page feature, headlined 'HAWKE – THE MAN ON THE WHITE HORSE', and noting 'his towering intellect' said, 'He is, if it is possible, perhaps too big a man for the job [of ACTU president]'. It also described him as 'the X-factor in Australian politics ... Many people, quite simply, will vote for or against Bob Hawke [in the federal elections].'

In October Hawke began campaigning. He said:

I travelled all over the country. I enjoy campaigning. It's unbelievably tiring and for me in those days it was more tiring than for the leading pollies, because I had no support staff, so all the mechanical things that aides can do, I had to do for myself. I think I was good at it – because I really do enjoy meeting people and getting involved with them, and I enjoy the inter-reaction with crowds – and I think I got better at it. I got a technique of reading all the newspapers in the morning and would pick out statements around which I could develop the basic themes of the campaign. One of the problems in campaigning is that you've got to repeat the same stuff, over and over. The audiences don't mind, because they're new audiences every day, but *you* get bored and so does the press ... I remember at the official opening, Clyde Cameron [later Minister for Labour] and I were driving out together to the Blacktown Town Hall [in Sydney] and we had a discussion about the head of the Department of Labour. Clyde and I were in agreement that the man had exceeded the role of a public servant, and instead of being a detached expositor had adopted the role of advocate when the ACTU had been in discussions with Lynch about the penal clauses. I'd laid down the law and said to the departmental head that if he were going to behave like that, the ACTU would walk out. Clyde had no time for the man; we were in consensus. And I remember the look on Clyde's face: he's got a special smile he wears when he's holding a knife in his hand, and I thought, Well, that's one decision that has already been taken.

The campaign had barely begun when Hawke was contacted by a stranger who told him that he could supply material about the private life of a senior Liberal minister, for whom the man worked, which was of a scandalous nature and could well cost the minister his seat. Hawke said,

> I don't go in for that stuff. So I said, 'Thank you very much, friend. Put it in writing', and I rang the Liberal bloke and told him ...
>
> The party arranged that if Gough was in one city, I'd be in another, but there were a few occasions when we appeared on the same platform, and I think we were a great combination, we enjoyed one another with the natural element of competitiveness – I suppose we were watching one another, listening to all the decibel counts. Without any question the most memorable meeting was the last one, in the St Kilda Town Hall [Melbourne] on the Thursday night before *the* night. By that stage the certainty of victory was there, we knew we were the first Labor government after twenty-three years and the crowds – it was just unbelievable – the Town Hall was packed and there were thousands outside. And I remember we'd arrived and were being prepared in one of the ante-rooms, there was Gough and me and Margaret [Whitlam] and Hazel,

and the atmosphere was just electric. Then we moved out to go through the corridors and into the hall, and from the corridors – oh, it was deafening. Almost frightening. I remember thinking that there had been these sorts of meeting throughout the campaign, that there was hysteria, and while that was marvellous for one's ego and flow of adrenalin, I had this sense of – oh, I'm unsure of the word – apprehensiveness. You know, the explosiveness of the hysteria. Walking through that is a very strange experience, an enormously moving experience. The next day, the last day, we had a barbecue on the banks of the Yarra, for supporters and campaign workers, and there was a beautiful feeling of relief that it was all over, and that the next day we would win. It was an emotional feeling I'll never forget.

On 2 December 1972 Labor won government by seven seats, with a swing of 2.6 per cent. Since Whitlam had become leader of the Labor Party in 1967 he had achieved a total swing of 9.6 per cent. The euphoria among Labor supporters was mind-splitting; they had returned from exile, led by a king. In the trade union movement it was as if the millennium had been announced: everything that was bad would be swept away. And indeed, within days, without waiting for a Cabinet, Whitlam had begun his reforms, performing coup after coup against his stunned opponents. Draft resisters were freed from jail, troops ordered to withdraw immediately from Vietnam, Australia's ambassador to the United Nations was instructed to cease his support for South Africa and to vote with the Third World. Schools would be reformed; there would be changes in social welfare and the arts. For fourteen days edicts poured from the Prime Minister's office. But Whitlam had not won the Senate.

Perhaps Ozymandias had such an Upper House.

Later, David Combe, the federal secretary of the ALP, said, 'If only Whitlam had listened to Hawke, we would have survived'.

FIFTEEN

THE YEARS SINCE 1965 had been a banquet for Hawke. There had been plenty of buffeting in public and in private, but the round of his life, once he had focused upon the presidency of the ACTU, had been a succession of delights. His victory in the leadership of the trade union movement, then three years later the shared victory of a Labor government elected to office, had turned Hawke's world into an Olympus in which he was, unarguably, a senior god. 'Next to Whitlam', he said, 'I'd done more than any other member of the party to have the government elected'.

Aged forty-three, his early portrait was complete: he had a mane of glossy dark hair, now touched with grey at the temples, his face had filled out, his neck and torso were powerful, his chest a barrel from the years of exercising, in court and on the hustings, the muscles around his lungs. His eyebrows were thick and expressive, the look in his eyes was friendly but sharp. That aura of vitality that had surrounded Hawke since youth had by this time become something more, a furnace blast of energy and a self-conscious awareness of power. He had often a feline expression of secret triumph. In private he frequently dressed in nothing but a pair of shorts; he would swim naked in the pool at home and once scandalised a group of male trade union officials by doing so, then sitting down and chatting to them, still unclothed, while Hazel poured drinks. Room-service hotel waiters became accustomed, over the years, to seeing Hawke without any clothes and journalists to his giving interviews in a swimming costume. In public

Hawke dressed with extreme neatness, in off-the-peg suits that verged on flashiness.

When he was drunk, as he was more often now without the pressure of wage cases – he twitched his eyebrows and had a dangerous, slightly demonic look, like an angry cat. He was as lithe as a cat: the gallons of beer he drank had not produced the usual beer-gut, perhaps because his appetite, which had always been small, was diminished by alcohol, and he took plenty of exercise. He could do twenty-five push-ups without puffing and when in high spirits would issue challenges to other boastful men to stretch out on the floor and try to match him. He weighed 76 kilograms and stood 1.80 metres, a good five centimetres of that accounted for by his hair. He was both smaller and stronger-looking than people who had seen him on television expected – 'like a bantam fighting cock', as a journalist exclaimed. Indeed, Hawke was, as ever, ready for a fight. He was a man who had succeeded dramatically, and yet ... He had not kept all his promises to himself.

His old dream seemed closer by early 1973; it looked like sunlight standing tiptoe on the horizon, just waiting for dawn. It was a false dawn.

In the middle of 1973 Hawke was offered, and seized, another great prize: he became president of the ALP. 'I'd earned it. I was ambitious for it. I cherished it', he said. And so he did: too well, perhaps.

Hawke said, when he took on the second presidency, that he would hold the job for two years. He held it for five, in the teeth of advice from his political supporters who saw the long-term damage he was doing, within the ALP, to his ambitions. Don Dunstan told him, 'If you want to be prime minister, for God's sake give up the party presidency. It's a millstone round your neck.' Years later, asked if he had made a great mistake in taking on the job, Hawke's instant reply was, 'No. I enjoyed it.'

Within days of his becoming president of the ALP, troubles began. They multiplied. In retrospect the whole period from 1966 to 1980 is cleft in equal parts: seven years feast, seven years famine, with mid-1973 as the point of separation. At the conclusion of the time span Hawke looked, when tired, an old man. His hair had turned grey and by 1980 was white in parts; his shoulders hunched; he was shorter for he no longer stood straight; his face, which in profile had become a nutcracker, was marked with lines chiselled by pain and alcohol; his lips had disappeared and what had once been an attractive mouth had become a thin line. The expression in his eyes had changed from sharp curiosity to a baleful suspicion and had that suggestion of emotional damage one sees sometimes in the eyes of intelligent and sensitive men who have been through a war. For Hawke, 1973 opened with joyous enthusiasm and closed with a despair that seemed endless.

He had been in office at the ACTU three years when Labor won the election. In that time he had learned some hard lessons about the limits to power.

Among themselves trade union leaders of the Right had discussed a contingency plan if it should happen that Hawke pressed them too far: they would have him sacked. A president of the ACTU can only be sacked for gross misdemeanour; however, once a powerful group is determined upon removing an enemy there is always something that it can find and exaggerate wildly: an expense account does not add up, an office car has been misused. Nobody who spends the money of others and who is busy is ever safe. Ducker said with a grin, 'Y'know, if we'd really wanted to . . .' then added, 'Hawkey had a law degree – he could have become a judge', and gave a broad, whimsical smile. In the event it was unnecessary for Hawke's enemies to do more than play with the idea of deposing him. He respected the position of the Right; he was given freedom to pursue the goals of his campaign platform. At least, in theory.

In practice, the ACTU's lack of money, the under-financing of the trade union movement as a whole and its many rivalries were to make his task almost impossible. The unions wanted Hawke to carry through the reforms he had promised but only if somebody else would pay.

The problem in Australia was that, except for crises, the idea of consistency in the trade union movement was an ideal rather than a reality; the movement was, and is, as various and conflicting in its parts as the nations of Europe. Outside Europe one may speak of 'the Europeans': in Europe, they do not exist – there are only Spaniards and Dutch, Greeks and Germans. The Clerks Union is as different from, say, the Transport Workers as Poles are from Portuguese.

Besides the frequent reminders Hawke had been given during ACTU executive meetings, the 1971 Congress had made him acutely aware of the difficulties of exercising power, of persuading people to pay for what they said they wanted. He had seen the potential danger for a Labor government: like him, it had a broad program of reforms; like him, it could be handicapped in implementing them.

In September 1972, at an ALP federal executive meeting in Sydney, Hawke and Clyde Cameron argued that during the forthcoming election campaign there should be no promise that a Whitlam Labor government would not increase taxes. For years Hawke had been advocating that tax loopholes must be closed, that the rich must be made to pay their share of taxes. He recalled,

> By that stage [September 1972] we all believed that we were going to win, so what we were talking about was Labor in government. I was casting my mind ahead and I was quite certain that the Whitlam Labor government would be judged on its handling of the economy, and that it would be a total tragedy if all that happened was that we came to office and were a one-term government, because we would not be able to do things of a lasting nature in one term. I said this at the federal executive meeting, and privately. I can remember almost my exact words: Whatever great social changes and foreign policy changes were made, we would live or die on our handling of the economy, and that I didn't want to see us unnecessarily constricting ourselves by promising no increase in

taxation. Because, if we were to be able to achieve the things we wanted to regarding redistribution of wealth and positive change, and to do that in the least inflationary way, we *needed to have the revenue available.* The tax system in Australia by 1972 represented twenty-odd years of conservatism, and had been structured in a way which the conservatives regarded as appropriate to their philosophy. I didn't object to that, because they'd been democratically elected, so were entitled to do what they wanted – for example, to make, through the child deduction system, kids worth more to a bloke on $50 000 a year than to a poor person. But that did not mean that we should say, 'Oh, just elect us and we won't change the tax structure and make any greater imposts'. I certainly wasn't arguing that we hit the poor – on the contrary – but I was arguing that the wealthy and upper-income groups should not regard themselves as sacrosanct, and be allowed to think that a generation of conservatism in regard to imposts would continue with a Labor government. My view was that the Australian community was ready for change, and that we should be direct with the community, that we should not get into a position of saying, 'Things won't change regarding imposts'.

What I was saying at the executive meeting was very much related to my concern about the economy, because I believed that the signs were already evident that the economic situation was beginning to change, that we weren't in the situation of limitless vistas of expansion that had characterised, or had seemed to characterise, the 1950s and 1960s. And my concern was related to wages: that in this coming period one of the issues would be wage justice and wages policy. For us to be able, as a labour movement, to get a situation of wage earners accepting restraint the sine qua non would be a belief on the part of the trade union movement that Australia had an equitable tax structure. In 1972 there was a belief within the Labor Caucus that growth was still continuing. There wasn't a general perception that the bubble had burst. I didn't realise that myself. But there was, by the latter part of 1972, evidence around that things were getting tougher – overseas, inflation was starting to roar ahead. And it was quite clear that the electorate would be much more astringent in its judgment about the economic performance of Labor than it would be about the conservatives. Even if one's perception of the economy was that we would continue to zoom forward, that there would be low inflation, continued full employment, no international problems – whatever the context – I still would have held the view that we must not tie one hand behind our backs by committing ourselves to an *unnecessary* restriction.

Now, throughout the 1972 campaign, while Whitlam did not promise 'We won't raise taxes', the view was projected to the electorate that we would not. The campaign speeches were carefully written to avoid saying, We Will or We Won't. But the electorate got the message: We Won't. And I thought that was wrong.

Labor's policies on taxation were to be the cause of one of the many rows between Whitlam and Hawke.

During 1972 Hawke had irritated Whitlam by suggesting to him that he should study economics. He said,

My view was that Gough was such an extraordinarily intelligent man, he had a barrister's ability to get on top of a huge mass of material very quickly, that he could acquaint himself with economics in a couple of months. I offered to arrange for him to have private tuition from economists I knew, who would have made themselves available to him at whatever times suited him. But he wasn't interested. He made the point, 'I have economic advisers'. He just would not accept the points I was making: that economics was going to be central, that it is no use having economic advisers if one could not determine the value of their advice, that the man at the top must be involved.

Perhaps the very suggestion was counter-productive. Someone close to both Whitlam and Hawke observed, 'Bob tried to give Gough advice – and that's fatal'. And Egerton, reflecting on the ALP federal executive years from 1971 to 1976, remarked, 'With Whitlam and Hawke, it was the old bull trying to keep the young bull out of his paddock'. The rivalry between them was to become intense.

From early on relations between the new government and the ACTU, representative of the government's largest constituent, were strained. Things had started well: the new Minister for Labour, Clyde Cameron, had attended the first ACTU executive meeting to be held after the election and announced that he intended to make changes to the *Conciliation and Arbitration Act*. But within weeks, a row blew up between Cameron and the ACTU.

The president of the Conciliation and Arbitration Commission, Sir Richard Kirby, had decided to retire. His obvious successor was Mr Justice Moore, a man whom Kirby had groomed for the job for years and who had proved his ability through his handling of scores of wage cases and dispute negotiations. Moore was trusted by the unions and the employers, and was, after Kirby, the most senior member of the Arbitration Bench. Cameron, however, had promised the job to a barrister, John Sweeney, who had devised the legal means that had allowed federal intervention in the Victorian branch of the ALP. There was outrage in the Commission when Cameron's plan became known. Kirby telephoned Hawke requesting him to persuade Whitlam to tell Cameron to reverse his decision. Moore was appointed. Cameron, however, was so angry that, in the words of Harold Souter,

> for a couple of weeks he stopped talking to me. Relations between the ACTU and the Whitlam government set off on the wrong foot because of the row over Sweeney, and they worsened because of the failure of ALAC [the Australian Labor Advisory Council] to hold meetings.

ALAC[1] was the meeting ground between the Labor Party and the trade union movement and leading up to the 1972 election it had convened regularly. It was made up of the four parliamentary Labor leaders; four ALP federal executive members; the president, secretary and two vice-presidents of the ACTU. In the pre-election period ALAC meetings had been the critical area for discussions about how union leaders could defuse potential strikes and how they could defuse the McMahon government's attempts to explode the 'law and order' issue. It was the forum in which, when Labor was in office, wages policy should have been discussed.

Souter continued,

> When Whitlam came to office there was one punctual meeting of ALAC, but successive meetings went astray. Once we waited an hour and a half for Gough to turn up and he only arrived when Bob threatened to walk out. We [the ACTU] wrote a letter of protest about the falling away of ALAC. Gough was apologetic and he called another meeting, turned up, then left after about fifteen minutes. It was hopeless. We *couldn't talk to the government*, and eventually ALAC just disappeared.[2] For the ALP and the ACTU the lack of communication was a disaster. We did have contact through Clyde Cameron but he was an old AWU man and he was always set against the ACTU. In his early days as minister, Clyde would telephone me every Sunday morning and would talk for an hour or more, often not restricting himself to industrial matters, but going on about his political problems. It got to the stage where I dreaded Sunday mornings. So it was a relief when he was in a temper with us, over Sweeney, and left me alone for a fortnight.

When Clyde Cameron was embarrassed over the non-appointment of Sweeney to head the Commission, he appointed him, again without prior consultation with the ACTU, to inquire into industrial relations in Australia. That is rather like inquiring into the sanctity of marriage. Both the ACTU and the organised employers were irritated, and suspicious. Souter recalled,

> Clyde introduced a Bill to amend the *Arbitration Act* in 1973 and we learned of it only when the Bill had its first reading in the House. Clyde's office then sent us a copy. Frankly, we were better off under the Liberals as far as communications were concerned. If they were going to amend the Act they would show us the draft legislation and, while they would not introduce changes that the ACTU requested, they would not introduce changes of their own if the ACTU raised strong objections. From very early on the ACTU felt a disillusionment with the Whitlam government. Our relations reached a nadir over the tariffs cut, and a terrible disillusion spread, not only through the ACTU, but through the whole trade union movement.

George Polites recalled,

> Clyde was a great hater. It was as simple as that. He hated the AWU hierarchy and, hell and high water, he was determined to get them. So he introduced a lot of amendments to the Act which were designed to hurt the AWU, but they hurt as well a whole range of other unions. We tried to tell him – I tried, Bob tried, Harold tried. Clyde would not listen. He had his own views about everything, he lived in the past, he pursued old scores and maintained retribution against old enemies. He thought that because he was labour minister in a Labor government and came from a trade union background he knew everything and nobody had a right to question anything he did. I made a public statement early on that this was 'a know-all government', that it just doesn't want to talk to you, and if that's the way it's to go on it will commit bloody suicide. And it did. Personally I got on with Clyde – he's a most likeable bloke. He would cuddle up to unions whom he thought were politically useful to

him – they could see him any hour of the day or night – but everyone else was Out.

By late 1974 wages were running madly out of control; Cameron (and other ministers) appealed to the trade union movement to restrain itself. The government had not reformed taxation; its policies had created unemployment. The unions co-operated to restrain wages on terms that suited the highest paid: they agreed to indexation of the total wage. This was a formula for the well paid to be even better paid in relation to the less well-paid; for tax to eat up a larger slice of the increase; therefore, an encouragement for tax avoidance. And, of course, for a massive wages bill to employers, for unemployment and, in due course, for falling government revenues as the world and his wife learned the tricks, once the sport of the upper middle class, of tax evasion. At the time it was the best deal Cameron could strike with the trade union movement and the arbitration system, and there is no doubt that indexation was preferable to the hysterical scramble for higher wages that was going on: unions were badgering the Arbitration Commission with ambit claims as high as $1000 a week. The treatment, however, while bringing the disease to stability, made it chronic. The problem was, and is, not that unionists are wickedly greedy or that arbitration judges are lunatically extravagant but that the Australian wage fixation system, designed in 1907, had become an inappropriate tool of social and economic policy. Hundreds of people – politicians, unionists, employers and the wage arbitrators themselves – will have to agree before it can be reformed, for it is they themselves who make up the system. However, virtually all members of the system choose to believe differently: 'I am a bird, look at my wings', said the bat. 'I am a mouse, look at my coat', said the other bat.

Cameron, in an article that was published in *Labor Essays 1981* and that when read in full richly confirms the opinions of Polites and Souter, blamed Hawke and the ACTU for the chronic wages mess of the late 1970s. He wrote:

The reforms I made to the *Conciliation and Arbitration Act* to ensure that elected union officials properly represented their membership ... were the finishing touches to a struggle I had waged over many years, first as a member, and later as an elected official, of the large and powerful Australian Workers' Union ... Some union officials opposed my proposition to outlaw the collegiate system of electing executive officers and for making the embezzlement of union funds an offence against the *Crimes Act* ... many union officials disagreed with me. But all of these differences were with union officials over issues on which they, not I, were out of touch with the real trade union movement, ie. its rank and file ... Tom Dougherty [boss of the AWU] spoke for many of his fellow bureaucrats in the AWU when he used to refer to the rank and file as the 'crank and vile'. He and some of his yes-men literally despised their union's membership ... [When it came to an agreement about wage indexation] I was unaware of Hawke's plan to bring about an amalgamation between the Australian Council of Salaried and Professional Associations (ACSPA) and the ACTU.[3] ACSPA was committed to full indexation of total wages irrespective of how high those wages might be. Hawke was anxious that the amalgamation between the two large organisations should take effect. And for this to happen the ACTU would have to tailor its wage indexation policy to accommodate ACSPA demands ... I believe that the record of the ACTU, in respect of wage indexation, will be viewed by historians as one of the most shameful chapters in the whole history of labour relations in this country.[4]

Hawke commented,

It's just a nasty perversion to explain the ACTU wage index-ation decision in terms of Hawke's plans about amalgamation with ACSPA. We had fought for years for a two-tiered wage system, and we'd lost: the trade union movement was con-fronted by the fact that the system had been turned on its head, against us. And we then had to face up to that reality, and also to the reality that our constituency was a very broad one. The ACTU executive debated at length the possible applications to be put to the Commission – for flat increases; for plateaus; for percentages. We decided to argue strongly for protection of the minimum wage, and for the value of tradesmen's incomes to be protected. Cameron suggests that it did not matter at all if tradesmen's wages were allowed to be eroded. That was not the view of the majority of ACTU executive members. It had nothing to do with ACSPA. Our submissions and theirs were entirely separate and we often had sharp disagreements with them. A reading of ACTU submissions shows that we qualified some of our demands for percentage increases.

Whitlam finally sacked Cameron as Minister for Labour and earned his undying enmity. Unions made polite growls in defence of a fellow trade unionist, while sighing with deepest relief. By then relations between the government and its largest organised constituent, the unions, were in a shambles. Egerton said later, 'If Whitlam had not been sacked he would have had no option but to have taken the unions on. And I tell you, he would have won, and Hawke would have been finished.'

In early 1973 the public became aware that a Labor government and a trade union movement, while in broad agreement upon ends, do not necessarily agree upon means. The issue was French atmospheric testing of nuclear weapons in the Pacific. The government, Whitlam in particular, wanted the fight against France's behaviour to be conducted through diplomatic and legal channels; the trade union movement, Hawke in particular, wanted to confront France head on, through a campaign of strikes that would isolate metropolitan France from the rest of the world. Whitlam feared that strike action against France's communications would put Australia in breach of international law and jeopardise the Australian case that had been argued by the Attorney-General, Lionel Murphy, in the International Court.

He sent Hawke a long, friendly, admonishing telegram saying, in part, 'Having invoked international law against France ... it would never do if Australia were herself in breach of obligations ... under international law', and going on to request the strike action against French communications be halted. Already, without consulting the ACTU, many unions had black-banned French aircraft, shipping, goods and communications, and for once the public was in support of a 'political' strike.

Whitlam had first announced Australia's objection to the tests in January 1973; the ACTU had decided six months earlier to ban French vessels and aircraft, including a planned flight by the new high-speed aeroplane, the Concorde. Public outrage had been gathering. Since the 1960s, when France had begun atmospheric testing in the Pacific, ACTU congresses had called for strike action against France, but in those days the electorate would not tolerate the trade unions assuming a role that was considered properly to be government's. But in Hawke's time as president his repeated challenge, 'Anything that affects our people – and in we go!' had won, at least in this case, public acceptance. Telegrams and letters poured into the ACTU from June 1972. Some read:

> Keep it up, and, as soon as possible, Hawke for Prime Minister!

> You are clearly the only one that Australia has with enough guts and determination to ... stop the French.

> Please stop the French.

> Australia needs you.

> Our Government [McMahon's] has been gutless. You must act. (signed) Staunch Liberal.

And one:

> *You are destroying the Labor Party* because you want to run this country, (signed) Labor Supporter.

By May 1973 concerned citizens were producing pamphlets that said:

> Do you WANT
> To have deformed children!
> To have leukemia!
> To be sterile!
> To have cancer!
> To risk destroying the earth!

In February 1973 Hawke held talks in Geneva with the International Confederation of Free Trade Unions (ICFTU) about the possibility of international action against the French. The ICFTU represents 92 million trade unionists, all from non-Communist countries. Its secretary was Otto Kersten of West Germany, who had been a senior official in the DGB, the Deutscher Gewerkschaftsbund, the largest free trade union organisation in the world. When the DGB speaks, the governments of Western Europe listen.

Hawke and Kersten were friends. Kersten told Hawke that the Finance and General Purposes Committee, the highest executive organ (after the Executive Board, which appoints it) of the ICFTU would be meeting in Mexico in late April. He suggested that if, by April, the French still seemed determined, Hawke could approach the ICFTU hierarchy in Mexico – although the French tests were, superficially at least, of no concern to the majority of ICFTU members, since radioactive particles would not fall on *them*.

By 21 April Murphy's mission to the International Court had, in effect, failed for the French announced that they did not recognise the authority of the Court. Hawke talked to Whitlam, but they were unable to reach agreement upon the proper role of the trade unions. He said to the Prime Minister, 'We [the unions] are not tools of government. And the obverse is true.' The Australian trade union movement planned to boycott

French cargoes, planes, ships and communications. By itself, such action would be futile: France could hardly be bullied into changing its defence program because of loss of Australian trade and communications. Hawke, however, had devised a grand strategy, an action unique in the history of the trade union movement, not just in Australia, but in the world: through the ICFTU he planned to involve the workers of the world in action against France. He flew to Cuernavaca:

> I'd been inundated with requests from people to do something, and had had a lot of heart-rending letters from people saying they'd lost contact with their families in France and less heart-rending ones from people complaining that their goods from France were being held up on the wharves and requesting that they be released. It's a problem that always arises – somebody gets hurt. You know, they've bought a Citroën and can't see that waiting for the Citroën might be less important than saving somebody's life. But, overwhelmingly, the public wanted action. A number of scientists had approached me, blokes from Melbourne University and elsewhere, and had offered to tutor me in the scientific and biological questions, so by the time I left for Mexico I had the scientific evidence about dangers to the living and the unborn, and the technical terms pretty well in my head. I've got a limited capacity with science, but I'd been able to master the ideas. The structure of my argument in Mexico was this: the tests were dangerous; it was futile to say, as the French were, that there was no danger, because if this were so why weren't they testing in France? From that base, I went on to argue for international trade union solidarity and demanded that we be given support. It was well received; there was no opposition. But some of the Europeans pointed out that there were legal constraints upon action of the type we talked about. Then others said that, in addition to the ICFTU, we should get the ITS [the international trade secretariats] to make their own decisions to join: for example, the International Transport

Workers' Federation, the International Metal Workers' Federation, the International Postal and Telecommunications Union. And the ICFTU decided to contact the ITS and ask them formally to support the decision. And that happened. The ICFTU resolved 'to make preparations to take full and appropriate action against French interests throughout the world' to try to stop the tests. Then, I went to Geneva, to the International Labour Organization. And there was a tremendous response in the ILO.

The International Labour Organization was established in 1919 as an autonomous institution associated with the League of Nations, its original constitution having been adopted as Part XIII of the Treaty of Versailles. With certain amendments this constitution remains the charter of the ILO today, bringing governments, employers and trade unions together to discuss international labour and social problems. A new declaration of the aims and purposes of the ILO, known as the Declaration of Philadelphia, was added to the constitution at the 1944 session of the International Labour Conference (the ILO's annual meeting) and this asserted the responsibility of the ILO to combat poverty and insecurity. In 1946 the ILO became the first of the specialised agencies of the United Nations Organization. Over the years the ILO has built up an immense list of recommendations and resolutions about the treatment of workers that its members are required to observe within their own countries. However, unlike the UN, it has no army so it cannot enforce obedience, but it can publicly humiliate disobedient members. If a government withdraws, its workers and employers need not withdraw, for the ILO's unique tripartite structure gives equal authority to each part of a national delegation: that is, the government, the employers, and the workers. If a government wants to rejoin the organisation it must promise to observe the rules before it will be readmitted. Not to belong to the ILO or to be condemned by it is to declare oneself before the international community to be uncivilised and to weaken one's potential for bargaining and lobbying in the United Nations and its other agencies, for example, the World Health Organization. The game at the ILO is national pride and avoiding injuries to it. Trade union leaders who cannot, in their own countries, criticise their governments for fear of harassment, can do so in the ILO. The Workers' Group, of which Hawke had been a member since he became president of the ACTU, is the cutting edge of ILO debate.

Of its very nature, the ILO is volatile and highly political. The people who run it, the members of the secretariat, must be politicians, diplomats and administrators – skills that are reflected in their wages: currently the director-general's salary plus allowances is approximately $90 000, after tax. The ILO was founded by white Christians and its rules were inspired by Judeo-Christian ethics; the feasibility of persuading the rest of the world to abide by those ethics and the laws they have formulated is problematic.

When the USSR was expelled from the League of Nations in 1939 it ceased to attend the ILO, but on Stalin's death in 1953 the USSR applied for readmission, which was granted the following year. Then in 1970 the ILO director-general, David Morse, decided that it was unrealistic to be without a Communist in the secretariat. He appointed a Soviet diplomat as an assistant director-general. Morse's action, just before his retirement, precipitated for his successor, Wilfred Jenks, what became known as 'The Crisis of 1970'.

Like some other international organisations, the ILO is heavily dependent upon the USA for finance. It was unfortunate, therefore, that George Meany, the boss of American labour and a man noted for his fanatical anti-Communism, had flown into a rage over the appointment of a Russian – for Meany had much influence with the US State Department. The American government drastically cut its financial contributions to the organisation. Hundreds of employees had to be sacked; much of its research work curtailed or abandoned.

Hawke, in 1970, was attending the ILO as a workers' delegate for the first time. The organisation's legal adviser, Francis Wolf,

said, 'Bob took a systematically courageous line in defending the
director-general and in working behind the scenes to soften the
anger of the USA. He helped to overcome the Crisis of 1970.'
It was particularly difficult for Hawke to work behind the scenes,
for George Meany, who was instructing the American workers'
delegation, was still convinced that the new president of the
ACTU was no better than a Communist. A further problem
was Hawke's style – especially for Meany, a devout, moralis-
tic Roman Catholic, whose prejudices were all confirmed by
Hawke's swearing, boozing and womanising. There are many
cocktail parties for ILO delegates and these were potentially
disastrous occasions for the wild colonial boy in those days.
Australian diplomats posted in Geneva have anecdotes about
muscling a roaring drunk Hawke outside and into a limousine.
The story ran like fire that, on being introduced to the director-
general of the ILO, whom others addressed as Mr Jenks, Hawke
had said, 'G'day, Wilf', and later in the evening had caused his
host, an ambassador, to turn pale, by saying 'That's bullshit,
Wilf! And you ought to know it!' The Europeans considered his
accent outlandish, while some of the more formal ones, especially the French – and nobody is quite as formal as a genuine
French mandarin – referred to him as 'the barbarian'.

However, even the most formal acknowledged, 'He was
something extraordinary'. In the words of Francis Wolf, 'One
was struck by his energy, frankness, dynamic approach, his quick
understanding and spontaneous friendliness. He was one of the
highest elements, intellectually. And then we saw he had courage.' For his defence of the director-general, Hawke had won
respect and gratitude in the secretariat. The following year he
won the admiration and affection of the African delegates for his
efforts in Australia to prevent the Springbok tour. Hawke's status
with the black African delegations – not only of workers, but of
governments and employers – was to be important in later ILO
dramas. By 1973 he was an identity in the ILO, still a newcomer,
but a man who had aroused the interest of those who had met
him. However, he had not yet addressed the conference, where

governments, employers and workers all attend, and it was only in the Workers' Group that he was well known.

The International Labour Conference is held annually, in the Palais des Nations on the shores of Lake Geneva. Bold hearts had constructed the Palais des Nations as the meeting place for men whose discussions would save the world. However, the imagination and humanistic optimism of those who founded the League of Nations and had the Palais built somehow escaped its architects. It is a huge, austere building, entirely lacking in charm, the cream and green marble columns of its halls soaring ten metres to unadorned ceilings. There are some vast, ugly murals of 'Mankind', executed in socialist realist style. On a clear day you can stand on the terrace and look across the lake to Mont Blanc, curved like a giant meringue, riding in the sky. The main conference hall seats 2000; architecturally chilling as it is, its sheer austerity is awe inspiring.

The most daunting of those who regularly spoke in the conference hall of the Palais des Nations was a Frenchman, Alexandre Parodi, leader of the French government delegation. Parodi was a septuagenarian by 1973, and a hero. He had been a leader of the French resistance during World War II; when Germany surrendered, France had been handed to Parodi, who became president of the transitional government until de Gaulle could arrive back from exile. Parodi had been close to de Gaulle, who made him Minister for Labour. He had presided over the ILO at its first postwar session in 1945, and was a man of intimidating formality and dignity. At casual weekend gatherings, when others wore sports clothes, Monsieur Parodi dressed in a dark suit and tie. Respect for him was such that nobody in the ILO could remember an occasion when someone had publicly argued with Parodi. Then in 1973, to the thrilled disbelief of the delegates, Hawke leapt to his feet and accused Parodi of hypocrisy in the matter of the French nuclear tests. Hawke did not use that word – his language was suitably tactful – but he conveyed his meaning clearly.

A Spanish delegate, Jose Aguiriano, recalled,

It was electric. Nobody had ever spoken like that to
M. Parodi. People were stunned … Hawke was the soul,
the engine and the spirit of the international trade union
action against the French tests. The French had been using
delaying tactics, so that the nuclear testing issue could not be
raised in conference. But Hawke brought on this very high-
level controversy.

For several minutes there were sharp exchanges between Hawke
and Parodi. Then, as Hawke had already arranged, when the
French Minister for Labour rose to speak, 200 workers, with
a noisy shuffling of papers and stamping of feet but not a word
said, walked out.

Aguiriano, who was a director of the Geneva office of the
ICFTU, said,

It was the first time ever that a world trade union boycott
had been planned. Our boycott failed, because the French
exploded their bombs. But for the first time the trade union
movement had brought to public awareness, particularly in
France, the danger of nuclear testing. And that was all Hawke.

On 21 July 1973 the French exploded a nuclear device, a
second on 29 July and a third on 19 August. On 31 August the
French Minister for Defence hinted that future tests would be
underground. They were. Two senior French officials – one
from the Quai d'Orsay, another the French consul in Noumea –
later told Hawke that the world trade union reaction had accel-
erated the change in French policy.

Meanwhile Parodi and Hawke, predictably, had become
friends. Hawke said, 'I had a great affection for the old bloke.
He was a most elegant opponent and we came to respect each
other and to have a very very warm friendship.' Parodi, who had
referred icily to Hawke in 1973 as 'an interesting man', was soon
afterwards calling him, 'my most honourable opponent'. An ILO
bureaucrat remarked, 'The French stopped saying, "Monsieur

Addressing the crowd outside Parliament House after the dismissal of the Whitlam Labor Government in 1975.

HERALD

WEDNESDAY

MY BOY FOR PM: HAWKE'S DAD TELLS

Hawke with his father, Clem.

Hawke and Bill Hayden at a press conference after the unsuccessful leadership challenge in Canberra, July 1982.

Hawke and wife Hazel in the tally room on election night, Canberra, March 1983.

Victorian State Secretary, Bob Hogg, in the ALP office during the successful 1983 election, March 1983.

Mick Young and Paul Keating in the tally room on election night, March 1983.

Hawke and Hazel celebrate Labor's victory on election night, 5 March 1983.

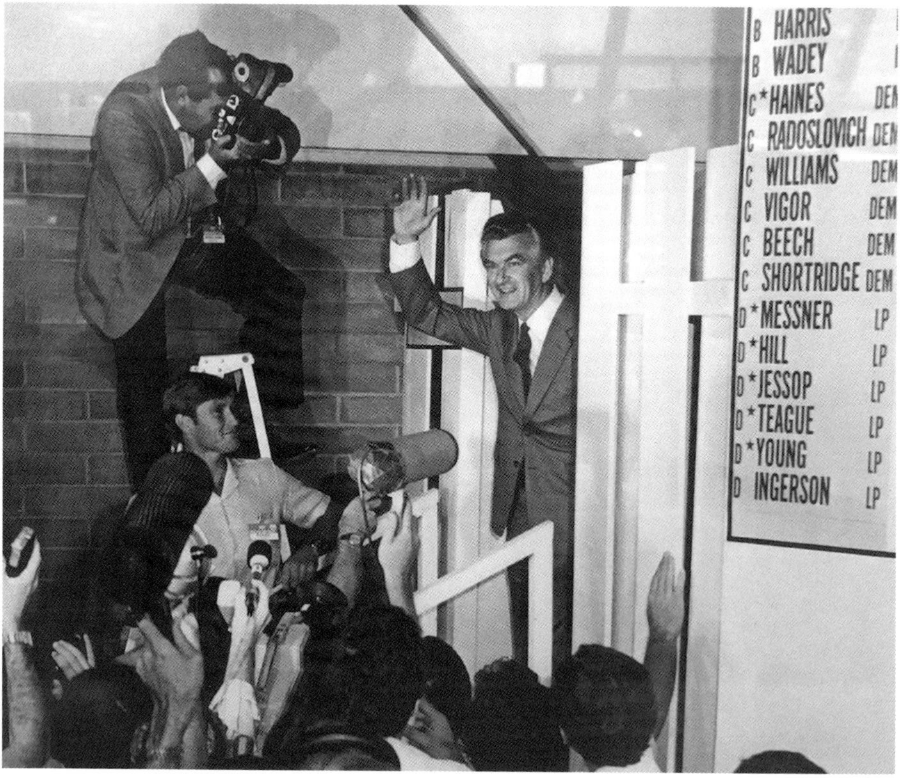

After Labor's historic victory on 5 March 1983, Hawke acknowledges supporters and the waiting media.

Hawke celebrates election victory, July 1987. From left: Craig Emerson, Jackie (nanny to Rosslyn's children), Sue, Hawke, Rosslyn, Hazel and Roger Martindale (head of security).

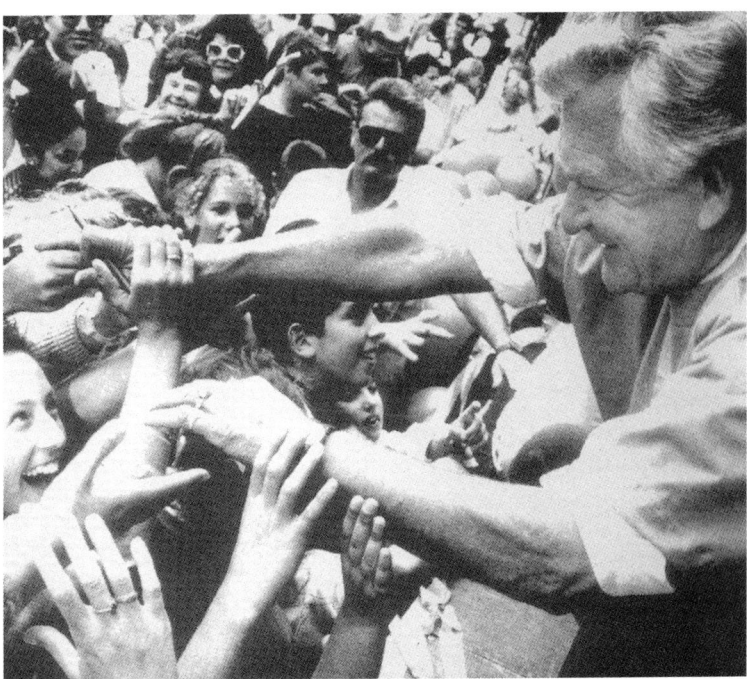

Hawke's relationship with the Australian people was a source of great joy for him.

The first Hawke ministry, Canberra, March 1983. Front row (left to right): Peter Morris, Mick Young, Paul Keating, Don Grimes, Sir Ninian Stephen (Governor General), Hawke, John Button, Lionel Bowen, Ralph Willis. Second row (left to right): John Brown, Michael Duffy, Arthur Gietzelt, Stewart West, Neal Blewett, John Kerin, John Dawkins, Tom Uren, Gareth Evans, Brian Howe. Back row (left to right): Susan Ryan, Peter Walsh, Clyde Holding, Gordon Scholes, Barry Jones, Chris Hurford, Kim Beazley, Barry Cohen, Bill Hayden.

The first caucus meeting, March 1983.

Francis Blanchard, Director General of the International Labour Organization, with Geoff Walsh, Hawke and John Bowan, Geneva, June 1983.

Sir Peter Abeles, Hawke's close friend and the chairman of Ansett, February 1990.

Paul Keating and Graham Richardson, Canberra, July 1984.

Hawke arrives at Richmond RAAF base to thank airforce pilots for their help during the pilots' industrial dispute, August 1989.

Hawke with speechwriter Graham Freudenberg, Parliament House, Canberra, November 1991.

Hawke and Keating enjoy a lighter moment during the Tax Summit debate, July 1985.

Hawke playing golf with George Schultz, San Francisco, October 1987.

Playing golf with Greg Norman in 1988.

With Allan Border, Australian Cricket captain, at Lords in 1989.

Celebrating the America's Cup victory, Perth, September 1983.

Sir Geoffrey Yeend, Hawke and General Secretary of the Communist Party
Hu Yaobang, Beijing, February 1984.

Hawke celebrates his birthday, Old Parliament House, Canberra, with Michael Lavarch, Allan Griffiths, Peter Walsh, Kim Beazley, Paul Keating, Ted Lindsay and Barry Jones.

Hawke on Christmas Day with his four-year-old grandson, Paul Dillon, at Kirribilli House, Sydney, December 1988.

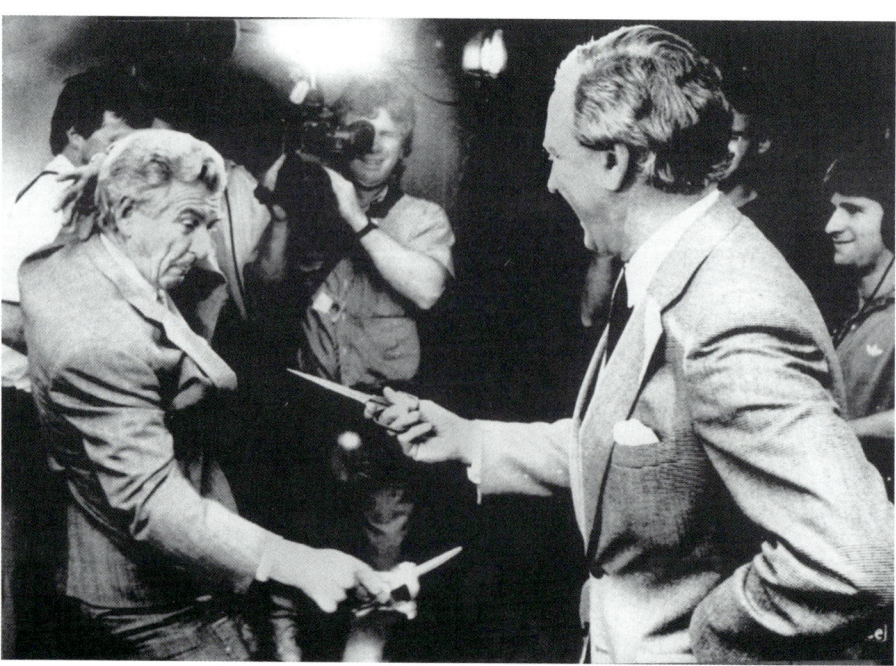

Hawke with Soviet leader Mikhail Gorbachev, Moscow, December 1987.

Hawke and deputy Opposition leader Andrew Peacock at the opening of the radio alley in the new press gallery at Parliament House, Canberra, November 1988.

Awk is a barbarian". They said, "Well, he is a strange fellow, but he is a brave fellow".'

Hawke loved attending the ILO. He is strongly attracted to the cosmopolitan and the ILO provided a marketplace for ideas. In later years he loved, too, the anonymity he had in the streets of Geneva and would say, 'It's a beautiful feeling to be able to go into a shop or a restaurant and not have people staring at you'. In 1972 Hawke had been appointed to the governing body of the ILO and had to go to Geneva three times a year for meetings.

He also had to attend regional meetings of international union organisations and he travelled interstate frequently, often at short notice. He was absent from the ACTU office for a total of six months each year. In early 1973 the executive complained that the president's office was running poorly. One man, Geoff Gleghorn, had been doing the job of two people, working as the ACTU press officer and as Hawke's personal assistant. The press office work in itself was nightmarish because Hawke's policy of being available to the news media at all times meant that 'every journalist in Australia knew his private phone number' and Hawke would make statements or give interviews whenever requested, without first checking what other arrangements might have been made. Gleghorn had put in his resignation; the executive decided that two people would be needed to replace him – another journalist and somebody to be personal assistant to Hawke and Souter. The new press officer was Graham Hardy, a young man who had worked on country newspapers. The personal assistant chosen was Jean Sinclair.

Sinclair was as exotic an employee for the ACTU as Hawke had been himself. She was English-born, the eldest daughter of a comfortable Melbourne family, had attended Merton Hall, one of Australia's best private girls' schools, had an economics degree from Melbourne University and was a director of her family company. She had earlier worked for an investment counsellor, Jim Cowan, analysing the stock market for investors, and later in Australia and the USA, for Rod Carnegie of McKinsey & Co. Her manner is that of a woman not to be trifled with:

firm, pleasant, well organised and very quick witted. She and Hawke came to dote upon each other. When Sinclair was on leave Hawke would complain constantly, 'Where's Jean? Where are things? I don't know where anything is. We'll have to wait for Jeanie.' Sinclair became a sort of devil's advocate, scolding him roundly, for example, for appearing on television drunk or giving ill-prepared press interviews. She would sometimes emerge from his office with her lips pursed, saying, 'We have had words'.

Everyone who has ever been close to Hawke has felt the necessity to give him advice or to criticise him – Hazel said, 'All Bob's life people have been telling him what to do'. It is as if the 'constant teaching' of his childhood has made Hawke an eternal pupil, and yet one who is selectively stubborn. At times, Hawke is deaf; at others, as impressionable as a boy. Since he will not reveal the details of his inner thoughts and what system they follow, even his closest friends do not know in advance how he will react to advice.

Souter interviewed Sinclair for the job, which had appeared as 'a tiny advertisement in the *Age*, saying, "Assistant to President and Secretary of the ACTU"'. At one point Hawke came in and asked, 'Do you know anything about trade unions?' Sinclair replied, 'No'.

I thought that would be the end of my chances. I'd given them in writing the details of my background, thinking, 'They'll accept that or they won't'. During the interview Harold had not explained what I was meant to do, so I asked the president, 'What is the job?' And he said, 'Well, I'm away half the year, so you're sort of to look after things'. I didn't see him for the next six weeks ... A couple of days later I reported for work. Harold took me to a room where there was a Clifton Pugh painting of a naked woman on the wall. He waved at the picture and said, 'Don't worry about that, we'll have it removed'. Then he left. What I found was incredible! It was beyond description. There were boxes all over the floor, papers and letters piled up, files which had no indexes and when I opened them there might be inside a letter and a shorthand book with two pages of notes, or just an unused shorthand book. Mail was arriving for the president literally by the bagful each day and there was no system for filing it, or answering it ... There was no airmail paper; the secretaries had typewriters with different typefaces, so that it was impossible to divide, for example, the typing of a report between them. The telephone system, which was new, was useless – I couldn't switch a call through to the president's office.

About 5000 people knew the president's private phone number, and would ring him direct, so if he were away I'd have to run into his office to answer the phone and half the time it would be some racing friend who had a hot tip, or someone who had met Bob at a party last Thursday and wanted help from him ... In McKinsey all senior staff were Masters of Business Administration. There were office managers. Efficiency ruled, naturally, because the motive was profit. The ACTU was not stimulated by the profit motive, so nobody had given any thought to efficiency. To get airmail paper, and save on the postage bills, an official request had to be written to Harold. The secretary of the ACTU was in charge of the stationery! And he had a separate filing system; in seven years I never did discover what was in it. Letters from unions about disputes would arrive and I'd file them, then weeks later discover that the rest of the correspondence was in Harold's files. If we'd had four or five more secretaries we might have been able to answer the correspondence which arrived each day.

There was an incident, very early on, which on reflection, best illustrated what working for Bob was like. He had to address a lawyers' dinner in Geelong, something which Peter Redlich [a president of the Victorian branch of the ALP] had arranged. I looked at the invitation in the morning and noticed that the dinner was black tie. There was going to be no time for Bob to go home and change, so I said, 'Shall I send a taxi to Sandringham to collect your dress clothes?' I was rather taken aback when he said, 'I haven't got any'. He frowned and added, 'I'll look a bit funny – can you fix that up?' I presumed he meant would I hire him a dinner suit. So at lunchtime I went to a bridal wear shop and picked out a jacket, trousers, shirt, studs and so forth. Bob is an odd size – his chest is much larger than normal for his height. I had a guess at what might fit, thinking that he could try it all on in the afternoon, and I'd have time to change it before the evening. I was young and foolish in those days. Some union discussions went over time, then without warning Bob decided to hold a press conference, so by the time that was over it was past five o'clock and too late to change the clothes. Peter Redlich arrived looking magnificent; Bob saw him and said, 'Gee, you look great! Where are my clothes?' and went off to have a shower. [Hawke's new office, above Bourkes, had a private bathroom.] He reappeared in the trousers, which fitted perfectly and the shirt, which fitted perfectly, and said to me, 'Tie the tie thing, will you?' So I did, then he put on the jacket, and it was extraordinary – the whole outfit could have been made to measure. He said to Peter Redlich, 'Now I'm as pretty as you', and off they went. The next morning I said to him, 'Weren't you surprised about the dinner suit?' He said, 'No'. I said, 'Well, I picked it out without any idea about the sizes, and it all fitted – weren't you surprised?' Bob stared at me for a minute, then replied, 'I asked you to fix it, and you fixed it. Why should I be surprised?' . . . It was all like that. You were expected to *know* intuitively what to do. And somehow it worked.

Sinclair became Hawke's fourth arm, in constant battle with what she called 'Bob's third arm – the telephone'. When he was abroad once she had his private number changed, and gave the new number out to about thirty people with whom he needed to be in contact. But within a month he had given the new number to most of the Australian population, not to mention people over-seas, and I realised it was no use arguing: when he needed to have a conference in his room, uninterrupted, I would simply unplug the phone. But it was marvellous fun. I'd set out for work in the morning wondering, 'What crisis will we have today?' A lot of the time we used to get through on laughter.

Hawke returned from the ILO drama about French nuclear tests and had to leave within days for the ALP biennial confer-ence at Surfers Paradise. Just before he left for Queensland he met George Seelaf, who said, 'Don't you take on the presidency of the ALP. The trade union movement has no class conflict, but the ALP does. It's a two-class party. You'll have nothing but con-flict if you become president of the Labor Party.' Seelaf parted from Hawke in the belief that he had taken this advice.

There was already some underlying strain in the relationship between the government and the trade union movement, but the conference heard none of this. It was the happiest ALP confer-ence anyone could remember, rather too happy for some, who expressed their joy at Labor's return from exile by celebrating in the Pink Elephant Bar. Part of the get-together was a crying-and-singing Irish wake for Arthur Calwell, who had died while the meeting was in progress. Ministers gave speeches about their magnificent achievements during a mere few months in office, and the wonders that were to come. There was altogether too much sunshine, too much thirst-quenching, too many loud shirts and ringing hurrahs. 'We were like kids let loose in the lolly shop', John Ducker said.

Hawke was giddy with euphoria over his election, unopposed, as president of the party. Sinclair, who had barely seen him since she had begun working for him, recalled the mood when Hawke returned from Surfers Paradise and came into the ACTU office with Hazel. 'They were on a cloud. They were drinking cham-pagne in Bob's office and telephoning people, calling everyone darling. Hazel was laughing, Bob was laughing. They phoned darling Jack Egerton and darling this and darling that.' Ellie, having heard the news, exclaimed, 'The prophecy of Isaiah has been fulfilled!'

Hawke saw his job as president of the ALP as a powerful symbol to the trade union movement of bonding between it and the Whitlam government. In a radio interview he said

> I was prompted to accept the post by the untidiness of relations between the political members of the socialist movement and the trade union movement ... Lack of communication, gaps, helped defeat the Wilson government in the UK. I want to bridge those gaps.

This desire to bridge the gaps, to reconcile opposites, has been a major shaping force throughout Hawke's life: hymn-singer and boozer; family man and philanderer; mate of the manual worker and the millionaire. Sinning saint. But in view of Hawke's longer term ambition – to be prime minister himself – it is difficult not to agree with George Polites: that taking on, while president of the ACTU, the presidency of the ALP, was 'Bob's greatest mistake. He attempted to straddle two things which simply could not be straddled.'

Within days it became obvious just how difficult life was going to be for him. One morning a couple of weeks after his triumphal return from Queensland, Sinclair entered Hawke's office to find him glaring. He roared at her, 'Get me fucking Whitlam!' Without any warning to the president of the ACTU, Whitlam had announced a 25 per cent tariff cut, which would, the Prime Minister asserted, combat the inflation that had been troubling Australia since the days of the McMahon government. Hawke was outraged: as he knew, the tariff cuts would cause unemployment. He suspected, too, that they would not reduce inflation. He and Whitlam had a heated discussion on the telephone.

That afternoon Hawke, wearing both presidential hats at once, released a tortured press statement:

... any unemployment effects of the tariff cut will be offset by such factors as the upsurge in consumer demand and export demand, increased government expenditure, the existence of unused tariff and the fact that there is ample room to squeeze the profit-competing producers in Australia.[5]

Of course, a good barrister can assemble arguments to justify anything. But Hawke, while he could produce a defence of the government's action, could not conceal his bad conscience in arguing for something in which he did not believe. The *Bulletin* reported: 'Hawke was nervous, made simple mistakes and gave the impression of somebody trying to sell an unroadworthy used car'.[6] He admitted to the news conference that he had been 'stunned' by Whitlam's announcement. He added that he had spoken to the Prime Minister, who had promised him that anyone put out of work would not be obliged to seek alternative employment at a lower rate. This undertaking in due course was to cause further trouble.

When importers and retailers learned of the tariff cuts they immediately telexed and telephoned exporters and manufacturers in South-East Asia and South America, bought cheap and sold dear in Australia. So prices did not fall; Australian manufacturers went broke; their employees were sacked; there was anguish in the trade union movement and much merriment among those over whom the government had inadvertently poured gold. By 1 August Hawke, again wearing both presidential hats at once, was warning that importers and retailers who did not pass on the tariff cuts to consumers would face industrial action. Meanwhile, an income-maintenance scheme of $25 million had been hastily devised for those who would suffer on account of the tariff cuts. The government decided that people thrown out of work would be paid at their rate of average weekly earnings. But these were swollen with overtime money, so, unemployed, they earned more than others whose jobs had been saved but who had lost the potential for overtime earnings. Result: the employed resented both their unemployed former workmates and the government.

The unemployed resented the government. Manufacturers resented the government. Trade union officials were furious with Hawke for publicly defending the tariff cuts.

And there was more disillusion about 'their' government in store for the trade union movement. The August Budget increased indirect taxes, which hurt the poor, but not direct taxes, which affect the rich. Hawke wore his ACTU hat and publicly condemned the Budget. Result: anger in the Caucus and hilarity in the Opposition parties, the news media and among other wicked people who had a sense of humour. Meanwhile, row number three between the Hawke–union camp and the Whitlam–Caucus camp was brewing. The ACTU executive had asked the government to take the measure that would have made the tariff cuts work. It had requested that the government gain power, through a referendum, to control prices. But the Caucus, without consulting the ACTU or discussing the matter in ALAC (which by now was dead anyway, except in name), decided to hold two referenda: one to gain control of prices and one to gain control of incomes. In the trade union movement control of incomes has one meaning: a wage freeze. If the government had set out to insult and unnerve its largest single constituent it could hardly have done a better job. The ACTU executive decided to campaign against the income referendum, so again the nation was treated to the ironic spectacle of the president of the ALP opposing the policy of the ALP government. Campaigning went on over several months and in December 1973 the electorate overwhelmingly rejected both referenda. By then relations between Whitlam and Hawke were at their nadir.

The trade union movement never forgave Whitlam for the tariff cuts and Hawke and others on the ACTU executive had to argue vehemently soon afterwards to secure an invitation for the Labor Prime Minister to address the Congress that year.

Meanwhile, Hawke's second presidential hat had caused other problems. It had increased his workload but he had not been given extra staff with which to cope with the extra responsibilities. There were more demands from the news media for interviews; more requests for Hawke to be a guest speaker; more letters from a public already used to treating Hawke as national ombudsman; more lobbying from business and other groups; more meetings to chair, more travelling. More worries. More attacks to field, for Hawke's wearing of the two hats was disliked not only within the ALP Caucus, but also within the trade union movement. Sinclair said,

> At first there was euphoria. Then this began to change to frenzy. Things became more and more frenzied. It was as if a car had been parked on a hill and the brakes had gone – it began running downhill, slowly at first, then faster and faster ... We didn't even have the paper for Bob to answer letters to him as ALP president. I had to demand ALP stationery from the federal secretariat, in the end. I was paid by the ACTU, so I could not do ALP work in ACTU time. I would do it after hours, and think of it as a donation to the party. You could criticise the way Bob chose to play the role of ALP president, that he was very high-profile, but you couldn't criticise him for being half the time in a blur. The workload was intolerable.

Within weeks of the row over the Budget, the 1973 ACTU Congress opened, on Monday, 3 September, in Sydney. Just beforehand the Communist Party ran a banner headline in its weekly *Tribune* asking, 'Can Hawke's Wings Be Clipped?', for now the rupture between Hawke and his erstwhile far-Left supporters was out in the open. After fifteen years of accusations about being a Communist or a crypto-Communist, and all the weary mischief that had caused, he was at last free of that particular problem. But he faced a new one because the extreme Left of the union movement and the extreme Right had formed an alliance against him: smiling hard and, no doubt, holding their ideological noses, the Clerks and the AMWSU hopped into bed together. The 1973 Congress was to see another major challenge to Hawke's personal position in the ACTU.

Things could have been worse for him if the alliance had been more disciplined but the strength of the extreme Left was undermined by external events. Within Communist ranks there had been fraternal strife waged quietly, for more than a decade, when in 1972 China had emerged from its long period of weakness to reissue that challenge to Moscow that dates back to Ghengis Khan. Australian Communists reacted immediately and at the ACTU Congress of 1973 the supporters of the Middle Kingdom and those of Mother Russia fell to spirited fighting with each other. The result was that Pat Clancy, a Moscow-line Communist, was deposed from his ACTU executive seat by a Mao sympathiser, Norm Gallagher. Gallagher's first act was to refuse to attend the traditional dinner of welcome for new executive members.

Thanks in part to the disarray and misalliances among Hawke's enemies at the Congress, he won handsomely on the personal issue of the ACTU economic enterprises. But he lost disastrously on the personal issue of an executive vice-president for the ACTU.

Hawke had barely managed to convince his faction on the executive that such a position should be created and that Charlie Fitzgibbon was the man to fill it. He saw a Fitzgibbon vice-presidency as having two functions: to bring administrative order to the chaos of the ACTU office; publicly, to promote Fitzgibbon as the next president. He said,

> Charlie was the man who would stand up to me and argue. It was, well, easy for me to establish dominance over a lot of people and I valued Charlie's refusal just to go along with my ideas. And he was immensely capable. My concern was for the good of the ACTU, at the time and in the future.

Fitzgibbon commented,

> I thought it would be good for the ACTU: Bob has no application for administration. And Harold Souter is not a good

administrator – although he is almost incomparable in certain areas: dealing with government employment; knowledge of the various Acts; negotiations. I thought I'd end up with a good relationship with Harold. I'd have taken over the pure administrative work and would have provided a link to industrial areas where we could have taken a tougher line – for example, in campaigns and demarcation disputes. Bob would have had more time for the publicity functions … All the signs were there that he would eventually want to move from the ACTU to parliament, but that was not something he and I discussed in relation to the vice-presidential idea. He didn't need to talk openly about parliament: it was obvious. There was a wide spectrum of trade union movement people who didn't realise that Bob had a desire to enter the parliamentary arena. My colleagues weren't very perceptive.

With Fitzgibbon established as dauphin, Hawke would have been able to abdicate from the ACTU with a minimum of fuss, at a time of his own choosing.

It was not to be.

There was no question that the trade union movement could bear another Left–Right brawl for the presidency like that of 1967–69, so Hawke's failure to secure the succession for Fitzgibbon meant that he would be unable to leave the ACTU for years.

That things turned out this way was in part Hawke's fault, for he failed to try to persuade. Pat Clancy of the Building Workers' Industrial Union, one of Hawke's champions throughout the presidency campaign and later, on the executive, said, 'Bob began to show a lack of understanding for the trade union movement. Increasingly, his approach was a top-level one.' Clancy is a classic-style trade union leader, and is a man of impressive personal dignity and decency. By 1981, when this interview with Clancy took place, he had come to feel betrayed by Hawke, because of Hawke's support for what Clancy termed, 'that rapacious, bandit government of Israel'. He talked with regret rather than bitterness:

Bob seemed to have developed a concept that if he proposed something, it would be instantly clear to everyone that what he was saying was quite right. And if there were misunderstanding, and debate revealed that misunderstanding and opposition, in reply he would clear it all up. He's a brilliant debater and certainly a brilliant replier to a debate. In the tactics of the trade union atmosphere, if you can give a good, powerful reply you've got a lot on your side, especially if you hold the position of leader. I think that Bob became deceived by this, thinking that he was all powerful.

By 1973 Hawke was already severely overstretched and it was years since he had known solitude or contemplation. He had no time to reflect, no time to consider problems. He was becoming a human pressure-pack: push the button, and Hawke would give a statement or rush into action. Everyone who worked in the ACTU knew what a maelstrom it was.

A few weeks before the Congress, Hawke had his inspiration about Fitzgibbon, who recalled,

> I was unwilling, but Bob got me at a weak moment. We sat down over a bottle of Greek brandy – I had the most terrible hangover next day – and at some stage during the night I agreed that I'd do it. I did not want to move from Sydney, I knew my wife would be unhappy, but … well, Bob talked me into it.

Hawke then went into an ACTU executive meeting, rode down opposition – Souter, for one, was sharply against the proposal – and secured from the executive a recommendation to the Congress that Fitzgibbon be elected. Union officials heard of the plan only days before Congress opened. Grumbling began immediately. Hawke had been high-handed, in the opinion of executive members, and they passed on this view to other union leaders. There were also objections to Fitzgibbon himself – industrial and personal. Fitzgibbon has an acute intelligence and a cold manner, and says of himself, 'I can be a very rude man'. Many had felt the lash of Fitzgibbon's sarcasm over the years, and resented him. There was, too, envy of his ability. And complicating everything there was a network of industrial grudges. Fitzgibbon was a moderate. More than a decade earlier he had won the leadership of the Waterside Workers' Federation (WWF), once one of the biggest unions in the country, from a Communist. Some of the big Right-wing unions had supported Fitzgibbon's campaign to become federal secretary of the WWF, and when he had been travelling around the country to gather votes, at certain places AWU employees, for example, would be waiting to meet him, ready with a car to drive him about. Edgar Williams, the national president of the AWU said, 'We felt, after he was elected, that Charlie didn't show the gratitude he might have for the fraternal help we gave him'. Fitzgibbon had become the leader of the waterside workers in 1962, during a period of rapid technological change on the waterfront, an upheaval that, in 1982, is still working itself out. The introduction of mechanisation for bulk-loading had been diminishing waterfront work since the 1940s; the trend increased in the 1950s and by the 1960s the WWF was faced with a disastrous novelty: containerisation. Unions, like businesses, thrive or decay according to their adaptability to new products and new processes. Containerisation had fearsome effects upon the WWF: overnight it wiped out the jobs of thousands of wharfies. Before the war there had been 80 000 members of the WWF; by 1956, 27 000. By 1973, five years after the introduction of containers, there were officially 16 000, although other union leaders put the figure at 12 000. Fitzgibbon had adapted the federation to this dramatic assault upon it: the WWF was very lean, but very tough. He had won for his shrunken membership excellent rates of pay, and job security – something that had not existed in the old days, when wharf labourers had been treated like cattle for auction and overseers would pinch men's biceps before saying, 'OK. You', and giving a day's work. Fitzgibbon stayed on the alert for recruits to the WWF and the union's award made his invitations enticing. Edgar Williams said,

Charlie was not the *beau ideal* of everybody at the 1973 Congress. He had just gone through an exercise of accepting a reduction in the WWF workforce all round Australia and a helluva lot of his people were getting the golden handshake. The membership was right down. Now, in Western Australia, we [the AWU] used to have all the northern ports. And Charlie tried to thieve them off us. When he couldn't do it, he got Clyde Cameron, the Minister for Labour, to refuse to pay the AWU members appearance money. But if they became WWF members, Cameron would have their appearance money paid. So, in their own interests, we had to let them go. Then, on top of that, Charlie commenced his drive to take members not just from the AWU all around the ports in Australia, but to body snatch from every other union he could. He took 160 off his mates in Melbourne. Even the AMWSU. He hooked in and took their members. So, he wasn't exactly a pin-up boy with everybody, he was unpopular even with his so-called friends. And he got knocked over.

When the issue of Fitzgibbon's vice-presidency came before Congress on its second day, Souter spoke strongly against it and was joined in his opposition by the Left's best orator, John Halfpenny of the AMWSU. Hawke, whom observers noticed had been on edge throughout his opening address to Congress, intervened in the debate and 'seemed uncharacteristically nervous'. In response to charges of undue haste about the proposal, Hawke snapped at the 700-odd delegates: 'Aren't you sufficiently mature and intelligent and in touch with your members to make up your minds?' They voted 432 to 352 against him.

On the final day of the Congress, however, Hawke had his victory. The ACTU enterprises were at stake. Throughout 1973 Hawke had made frequent announcements about planned joint ventures: cheap housing, a holiday village, an insurance company. There had been immense publicity. The enterprises were glamorous in a period when glamour was more than usually attractive, and they seemed to be just around the corner. However, the far

Left had turned sour on the idea of enterprises; the far Right had never liked it. Fortunately for Hawke the moderate Right and Left were still enthusiastic. On Friday morning he reported to Congress about the progress of the enterprises. He was confident, but low-key. The numbers men had done their work and despite the alliance of far Left and far Right, Hawke knew he had the votes. During the debate that followed, John Maynes of the Clerks (far Right) and John Halfpenny (Communist) spoke in opposition. Then Hawke exercised his right of reply, and in his first sentence – 'Comrades, don't some debates throw up some strange bedfellows?' – launched into assault upon his enemies. Professor Ross Martin of La Trobe University, whose field is the trade unions, wrote:

> All the stops were out as he soared into a savagely personal attack upon Mr Maynes and Mr Halfpenny, in turn. Delegates were rapturous. The applause was deafening. Yet it is doubtful that many, or any, votes were swung as a result. The big delegations at least were already committed ... This is not to say that the speech with which Mr Hawke wound up the economic enterprises debate was pointless. It was in fact highly important because it ensured, beyond all doubt, that Congress's favourable decision on the issue would be widely interpreted as a highly personal triumph ... But, resounding as the triumph was, it could not in the end obliterate memories of the vote three days earlier [about Fitzgibbon] when the President suffered his greatest, though not his first, Congress defeat. Nor was his prestige helped by the confused outcome of the executive elections. On balance, it would seem that Mr Hawke personally lost rather more than he gained ...[7]

The press reported that the 1973 Congress was 'cynical, even by the standards of the trade union movement'. The far-Right–far-Left alliance was clearly cynical, but there was more to it than insincerity. From the moment that Hawke opened the week-long meeting, reading his speech, trying to pull applause,

nervous – he had been threatened with death by a man pur-
porting to represent the Black September movement a few days
earlier – there was a tense undercurrent of disappointment in
his audience. It was exactly nine months since Labor had been
elected and, strangely, the millennium was not turning out in the
way the trade union movement had imagined it would. Indeed
the government, taking its lead from the leader, had a style that
appeared unnervingly middle class. Ministers all had advisers
and press officers; the press officers and advisers were party
faithful who, in their new jobs, were earning unfamiliarly high
salaries. They lunched not in pubs or from brown paper bags but
in restaurants where they drank champagne. There were many
opinions and many loose tongues. Increasingly Canberra was
resembling a nouveau expense-account School for Scandal.

Hawke devoted much more than half of his presidential
address to the 'implications for the trade union movement' of
the Whitlam government. He spoke of the policy areas in which
he saw benefits in line with trade union wishes, placing particular emphasis on the abandonment of the penal clauses; the
government's intervention on the side of the unions in a recent
national wage case; the 're-creation of full employment'; and the
government's intention to provide 'advanced facilities' for trade
union education. He then turned to the central problem, saying:

> One thing must be made perfectly clear at the outset and what-
> ever may be said by the – of course – dispassionate observ-
> ers about my various head-gear, I have no difficulty making
> it. However large the part played by our individual affiliates
> and by the ACTU itself in the election of the federal Labor
> government, that does not put us in permanent political check
> to our colleagues in government. The price we were paying
> for the occupancy of the Treasury benches by an anti-Labor
> government was extraordinarily high – but no higher price
> could be paid than the absolute loss of integrity involved
> for the industrial movement in its becoming the automatic
> guarantors and endorsers of every action and policy decision

of Labor in government. Such a position should be degrading for us, and dangerous for them.[8]

Hawke then elaborated on the differences of opinion over the Budget; the tariffs; and the amendments to the *Conciliation and Arbitration Act*. Later in the Congress he was able to take a more positive stance, telling delegates of promised government help for the ACTU enterprises and the possibility of government help with research costs incurred by the ACTU in connection with hearings on tariff bodies and the Prices Justification Tribunal. But on the whole Congress tended to harp upon the dangers and difficulties in the relationship between the unions and the government. One man, a timber worker, was fierce in his attack upon the lack of consultation and the tariff decision, shouting bitterly about the loss of jobs in the timber industry – 'and this from a Labor Government I worked my guts out for!'[9]

A few hours later Whitlam strode into the hall, to a standing ovation. They had loved him so much. They wanted to love him. When he showed himself to them they could forget the bad times and relive the ecstasy – for the time being.

Delegates' support for the enterprises had been so great that opponents had not even bothered to demand a vote for or against them. Hawke now had a mandate to move quickly. For more than a year before the Congress he had been devoting much of his time to discussions with businessmen and state and federal governments about possible enterprises, and earlier in 1973 had established a second joint venture, ACTU–New World Travel. The partnership was with Thomas Nationwide Transport, whose managing director (later chairman) was Sir Peter Abeles. Abeles was one of the most intelligent industrialists in the nation, and by 1982 was one of the richest. He was a big man – over 1.88 metres – and smoked big cigars. He spoke softly and moved with that unexpected lightness of step that big men sometimes have, while his smoothly plump face revealed little of a complex personality and a sophisticated mind. He wore heavy-framed spectacles, and behind them his dark-brown gypsy eyes were alert, worldly, and passionate. In conversation Abeles described himself as 'a romantic' and 'just a truckie'. Indeed, his suits are drab and so crumpled sometimes that it seemed he might have thrown them on the floor the night before; his hair looked often as if he had mislaid his comb. Abeles was born in Budapest in 1924, to a wealthy, totally assimilated Jewish family. His father was a steel merchant. His mother was an excellent pianist, and as a child and youth he studied music and Italian art, though his heart was set, he says, upon becoming a doctor. 'My father was a very strong personality and was all business ... I had the idea that one could not be a businessman and stay a human being', he said. Abeles' father had insisted that he learn a metal trade. But before he could enter medical school, the war broke out.

He recalled,

> I survived, at first, because of the trade: I was a specialist welder, so although I was a Jew I got an exemption and was employed in the garage of the German military staff. Then we were all conscripted and put into Jewish labour battalions in the Hungarian army, under German control. A lot of people in our camp were killed. We lost quite a few during bombing attacks, for instance, because we were not allowed into shelters but were left in the open. And later on it became even worse. But I was young, and I didn't have any notion that I'd perish. We worked very hard, repairing rail lines and doing work behind the troops. While we were not in a concentration camp and weren't behind wire, we were still always under German control, so there wasn't much future in it.

The Hungarian Jewish battalions did not wear uniforms, except for the yellow armband. When, in 1944, the Russian army overran the Hungarian–German-held position in Czechoslovakia where Abeles was working, he and many other young Jews took their chance and escaped. Officially they were deserters. Abeles' mother tongue was German; physically, he did not resemble the

Nazi stereotype of the Jew. He removed his yellow armband and, speaking German, hitched rides back to Budapest with German and Hungarian Gentiles. His family managed to find their way back to Hungary and after the war Abeles' father got his steel business back. Abeles said,

> In 1947, when it was clear that the Communists would take over, I decided to leave Hungary. I had a permit to go to the United States, but in Australia I had some relations, an uncle and a grandmother from my mother's side. I decided to go there first, and have a look. My father gave me £4000, which was a lot of money in those days. I had married in 1947, so I had to work. I thought I would work for a while, then go to medical school.

European migrants in the late 1940s were like gold from heaven for Australian shysters: a Sydneysider had managed to relieve Abeles of a quarter of his capital within a few weeks of his arrival. Abeles, who was a born entrepreneur, assessed his possibilities and decided to become a salesman. He bought 50 000 paperback novels – remaindered detective stories and westerns – and sold them to Gordon & Gotch newsagencies. He made a profit of £400. He then began to sell knitwear, and was still selling pull-overs and cardigans when, in 1950, a Hungarian friend arrived in Australia. This was George Rockey, whose family had owned one of the biggest forwarding agencies in Hungary. Rockey was eight years older than Abeles and had been the particular friend of Abeles' father, with whom he played poker. Rockey, too, had suffered during the war when the authorities had discovered that one of his grandparents was Jewish. He had been brought up as a Catholic. He was an officer in the Hungarian army but on the discovery of his Jewish grandmother, 'my uniform was stripped from me', he said. Rockey worked in his father's business before the war, rather unwillingly. He was a social democrat, in rebellion, he said, against 'the way I was brought up. As a child I was not allowed to fetch a glass of water for myself; I had to ring a bell for the maid'. He, too, had hankered for a medical career and described himself later as 'a frustrated psychiatrist'. At the end of the war he went to Vienna, 'and had a complete Jungian analysis', which took about three years. He arrived in Sydney with £150, moved into a boarding house in Neutral Bay and contacted the one friend he had in Australia, Abeles. Abeles said,

> In those days a lot of migrants bought a truck. I said to George, 'Tell me. You know transport. Don't you think we could do something in transport? I've heard if you buy a truck you make a good living.' So we walked around and we finally bought two trucks. They cost £6000 each, and as a deposit I put down all the money I had. But we didn't know much. George knew forwarding and shipping but not trucks, and within two months the trucks were out of commission, and we were both broke. And we still had to pay off the trucks. So, we decided to become contractors. We got the trucks repaired and hired people who could drive them properly.

Abeles and Rockey founded Alltrans on 11 December 1950. In 1954 they opened Sydney Coal Merchants as well and began to encroach upon the market of the coal giant, Sir Roderick Miller, undercutting his prices. Abeles approached Miller and asked if they might not have agreement about prices, in return for which Sydney Coal Merchants would have one-third of the city's coal market. Miller responded by sending Sydney Coal Merchants and Alltrans broke: he bought every mine that was supplying Sydney Coal. Abeles recalled, 'I am not being facetious: it was only the fact that neither George nor I could read a balance sheet that saved us from going out of business altogether. We'd lost everything we had and everything we didn't have.' Fourteen years later Abeles bought RW Millers. He said, 'Sir Roderick always thought it was my vengeance, to such an extent that one day he sat down with me – we had become friends – and said, "Tell me, how did you plan this? For how long did you plan it?" And truly, I had never considered vengeance: I just saw

RW Millers as good business.' In the mid-1960s Abeles moved in on Thomas Nationwide Transport. By the end of the 1970s he had a transport empire stretching around the world.

Until his business interests grew too vast Abeles himself had managed the industrial relations of his various companies. When Hawke became president of the ACTU, Abeles asked for an interview but on the day of the appointment Hawke was ill with one of his respiratory tract infections. Abeles went to Sandringham, where Hawke was in bed playing rummy with Rosslyn. Abeles said,

> He was completely different from what I had expected – I had imagined he would be just an aggressive man, but here was a very human, very nice man. I think we formed an immediate rapport. I think we became friends soon after, and we began to be together a lot. We became trusted friends, and the thing I especially liked – it is best expressed by the German writer, Stefan Zweig, who wrote: There is nothing more beneficial than two people with goodwill towards each other having an argument. Well, Bob and I have been arguing ever since, but always with a feeling of friendship. Bob shows his emotions, and more than his intellect, more than arguing, I find that most attractive about him. It is only the Anglo-Saxons who say a man cannot show his emotions, but I am a European. When I've had personal problems, I cry. If I've had problems with my children, Bob will listen to me. And I will do that for him.

Abeles, in fact, was Hawke's friend in time of need when, in 1976, there was a family crisis.

The idea of an ACTU–TNT joint venture grew quickly after this initial rapport had been established. In the ILO Hawke had picked up many ideas about the possibilities for trade union enterprises that confirmed the view he had held for years, that the ACTU had been blind to opportunities for improving services for its members. In West Germany and in Israel he had seen the

magnificent achievements of trade union organisations that provided womb to tomb security, plus holidays, housing and other
credit, entertainment, education and sporting contests for their
members. There was a big difference, however, between the
West German and the Israeli trade union movements and the
Australian one: Hitler had destroyed the German unions and,
reborn, their unofficial motto is 'Never Again'. Similarly, every
citizen of Israel has this motto engraved on her or his heart.
On Hawke's invitation representatives of both West Germany's
DGB and Israel's General Federation of Labour (Histadrut)
visited Australia in early 1972 to study and advise on the possibilities here for trade union enterprises. Both groups expressed
very cautious optimism, but offered to help the ACTU if they
were asked. The Israelis were astonished that Hawke had such
public power – one of the Histadrut delegation said, 'He was
treated like a prime minister, people felt honoured when he
spoke to them' – yet, because of the structure of unionism in
Australia, so little real power: 'He is the prisoner of the national
leaders of your big unions'. Both DGB and Histadrut pointed
out that the dispersion of capital among the Australian unions
was an immense problem for any ACTU undertakings. Abeles
had capital.

He recalled of the ACTU–TNT venture:

> It was a case of Bob's and Peter's over-optimism. There is
> no doubt that the ACTU's affiliated unions represent an
> enormous market. TNT was inexperienced in travel, but
> we knew everything about transport and, at the time, that
> seemed enough. Bob and I talked about it for weeks and
> weeks and sold the idea to each other more and more. We
> started to dream and by the time we had finished, we had a
> huge dream ... TNT had good industrial relations with all
> the unions; George and I were very friendly with Bob. We
> began to see something fantastic in such a joint venture.

At the ACTU executive meeting of August 1972 Hawke reported on his discussions with Abeles about a joint-venture travel company that would provide travel and holiday packages, general travel and, later, holiday accommodation for trade unionists and their families – all at slightly cheaper than normal rates. The executive, still enthusiastic about ACTU enterprises (with the exception of the far Right), was edgy. Earlier in 1972 Abeles had attempted to take over Ansett Transport Industries but the Premier of Victoria, Sir Henry Bolte, had obliged Sir Reginald Ansett and had had the law changed in Victoria to thwart the takeover. This had been a cause célèbre for months. Abeles had also been knighted that year. Soon afterwards a very senior business knight had drawn him aside to say, 'Now that you're one of us, you really should stop being seen around with that Hawke fellow'. (Sir Roderick Carnegie had similar warnings when it became known to his colleagues that he and Hawke were friends.) Whatever the misgivings at that end of the political and social spectrum about a relationship between Hawke and Abeles, at the other end, in the labour movement, they were much deeper. Lionel Revelman had been one thing: he was a businessman battling bigger businessmen. Abeles was a big businessman and by definition for the trade union movement, big businessmen are enemies. One can form non-aggression pacts, even have alliances with them, but beneath politeness and expediency there is fear and often its cousin, hatred. The Brotherhood of Man is a limited concept in the labour movement: it is the Brotherhood of Us. Hawke had been bewitched by this idea himself when younger – there had been his swaggering contempt for the rich that had so embarrassed Kirby in the 1960s – but at the same time, creeping through his consciousness, there had always been a fascination with the Other Side. Abeles fascinated him: he was subtle, sophisticated, cosmopolitan, immensely wealthy, a foreigner – his English was good, but non-idiomatic and with Hungarians he spoke their own language – and had suffered tribulations that Hawke could only guess at, sympathetically. Hawke's refusal to reject Abeles' friendship, despite many warnings from his political colleagues that it was viewed as consorting with the enemy, was to cause him massive political damage. Abeles' companies donated handsomely to Labor campaign funds; he also gave fund-raising dinners for the Liberal Party, one of them unhappily timed, for it took place within days of an announcement by Hawke that the ACTU and TNT were in business together.

A decade after Hawke had formally told his executive that he had a personal association with Abeles, that he wanted the ACTU to have a business association, and that Abeles was waiting outside, ready to enter the boardroom and address the executive himself, people still remembered the frisson that this created. 'I think Sir Peter found it easier than we did', Ducker recalled. At first some executive members objected to receiving Abeles, but others overrode them. It was, however, a weird moment when 'the very personification of big monopoly capitalism', as one executive member, speaking for many, described Abeles, entered the room. (Abeles himself dislikes being labelled a capitalist and says, 'I am not big capitalism – that is the government of Russia. I am big free enterprise.') Ducker recalled, 'There was a great deal of suspicion and unease'. And Pat Clancy:

> I objected to the idea of linking the ACTU with really big business. And I objected to the man. I was all for the enterprises. But I think on the arrangement with Sir Peter Abeles, Bob had moved ahead too quickly, without giving time for proper consultation with the unions, and without understanding the trade union movement. I was the only one opposed outright to the proposition of an ACTU–TNT joint venture. But since the proposal had to go to the labour councils for endorsement I said, 'All right, I won't record any vote against it'. And I think my judgment in doing that was wrong.

Abeles recalled, 'At first I found the executive members sceptical. But they did not seem hostile. Anyway, after about twenty minutes I found them most co-operative and I was surprised by the goodwill they showed and the friendly reception I got.' Ducker commented, 'I always wondered if Sir Peter were not buying himself a bit of industrial relations insurance' – a sentiment voiced by some other executive members also.

ACTU–New World Travel began business in March 1973, as a travel agency. The next step would be a holiday village. From the outset, the enterprise failed to thrive. Right-wing union officials whose members were low paid objected to it because holiday travel was a luxury beyond the means of their members. The AMWSU and other Left-wing unions objected on various ideological grounds: the 'big capitalism' argument; rejection of any association between the unions and capitalism, big or small, except in a master–servant relationship. Abeles said,

> The Left never felt comfortable with the idea. What should have happened was that we concentrated a lot of energy into it, to make it a success quickly, because if we didn't do that, the Left would say, 'There's proof it can't work'; and then they would begin to make sure that it would not work. Well, we didn't go about things in the right way. I am very critical of TNT, not so much of Bob. TNT was inexperienced in travel, which is a very different industry from transport, as I learned over the years. So, there were unions against us, and travel agents against us. And we did not put the time and energy into it that was necessary. One day Bob told me that Jetset [Australia's largest travel agency] had visited him officially, proposing that it could do things better. So we climbed out.

In 1978 ACTU–Jetset replaced ACTU–New World Travel and was from the beginning a success. The chairman of Jetset, Isi Leibler, is also a successful businessman but he does not have a diverse empire of companies. He had begun work in his father's diamond importing business and, from frustration with the way travel agencies had mismanaged his trips, had founded Jetset. He had none of Abeles' instincts for an Alexandrian sweep through the business world; his major preoccupation, since student days, was the plight of Jews in the USSR. By the time Hawke was preparing to leave the ACTU it was cash flow from ACTU–Jetset and, to a lesser extent from ACTU–Solo, a joint venture founded in 1975 with an independent petrol retailer, David Goldberger, of Solo, that was keeping the ACTU afloat.

Every ACTU executive meeting during 1973 discussed the enterprises and Hawke maintained enthusiasm for them by constantly publicising the progress of plans. Hot on the heels of an announcement about travel, Hawke would be talking of holiday villages, insurance, cheap housing, consumer credit. Throughout 1973 and into 1974 the news media carried stories of wonders about to be unveiled. Cliff Dolan, the man who succeeded Hawke as ACTU president, said:

> Personally, I thought we were trying to do too much in a hurry, and I didn't completely agree with Bob's enthusiasm. I felt he was forgetting that the trade union movement is very conservative and that there is as much conservatism in the Left as there is in the Right. On the other hand, it was no fault of Bob's that some of the schemes didn't get off the ground: the superannuation and general insurance ideas, for example. We looked long and hard at those and the executive as a whole believed they were goers. But unfortunately, the companies we were dealing with weren't substantial, to put it mildly.

In mid-1973 Hawke was severely embarrassed when, having announced that the ACTU would go into joint venture with an insurance company, journalists told him the company was under investigation for malpractice. Sinclair, who was unaware of the proposal and had many contacts in the Melbourne business community, said, 'I nearly had a fit when I heard Bob's announcement. I'd been hearing stories about that particular company since I was a schoolgirl. People told you on the tram.' An hour after announcing the ACTU insurance venture was on, Hawke had to announce it was off, saying blame for the error was entirely his. He repeated this explanation to the 1973 Congress. Dolan continued:

The housing scheme was different. We were to go into partnership with Lend Lease and the MLC. It was a real goer – and I know this, because I finally did the negotiations, and the bloke who stuffed it up was Tom Uren [Minister for Urban and Regional Development in the Whitlam government]. Uren would not give us the land for the housing scheme, which would have provided good, cheap houses for trade unionists. I think it was just incompetence in the Department of Urban and Regional Development. Tom Uren blamed other people – he said it was Lance Barnard's [Minister for Defence in the Whitlam government] fault, because the land was part of an old ammunitions complex, at St Mary's, west of Sydney, and was still under the control of the Department of Defence. But the real problem was inside the bureaucracy, and largely DURD's. Lack of expertise within the ACTU was not an issue because Lend Lease was handling all the expert decisions and had Tony Powell, later the chairman of the National Capital Development Commission, in charge of things. The plans were all drawn up and Lend Lease spent a helluva lot of money. Then Uren and Barnard got cold feet about that particular block of land and offered us some scrub over towards Liverpool, and the Lend Lease people were most unhappy. They pointed out that they would have to entirely redesign. So we went back to Uren and said, 'For God's sake!' One of the other problems was that Gough had made the initial promise of granting land to us, but by then we didn't have very good relations with Gough, so we could not go to him and say, 'Get the whip on to Barnard and Uren'. And he had other problems and wouldn't have done anything, anyway. Then we lost government, so that was the end of the housing.

On the holiday village, Bob was dealing with Askin [Liberal Premier of New South Wales] and a bloke up at Tweed Heads, and I think they both let Bob down. I told him not to trust Askin too far, but Bob seemed to think there was no real problem with Askin, despite political differences and personal differences, and that Askin would come good on his promise. But he didn't. There was never any decision not to proceed – the holiday village just drifted away.

Then there was the plan for developing a complex in Lygon Street. We owned the old ACTU building there and the idea was we would buy the corner pub [the Lygon] and the building next door, owned by the Builders' Labourers. Bob and Harold were both very keen. But there were problems right from the start. For one thing the Builders' Labourers were snaky and there were doubts that they would sell, and Bob's best mates on the executive were very unhappy about the idea of the ACTU being a pub owner. Bob and Harold argued that we wouldn't be going into the hotel trade, that we would buy it for the real estate, and keep the pub for just a couple of years, then redevelop the whole block. But we said, 'Oh, no. We won't agree to going into the pub business at all.' And then a certain union heard about the idea and made the publican a bigger bid, which we could not match.

The union's action seems to have been made to undermine the ACTU plan, for when the ACTU rejected the idea of buying the Lygon the union withdrew its bid.

Souter and Hawke, whatever their other differences, were in accord on the need for the ACTU to have enterprises. Souter knew, much better than Hawke, that the ACTU's financial situation was desperate, and in the 1950s had tried to persuade Monk to begin enterprises. Although a teetotaller, he had always been in favour of buying the Lygon Hotel. Hawke said,

When I first went to work in the ACTU I realised that it was pathetically weak financially, but that it had undoubted potential resources. It seemed to me absurd that the unions were pouring money into the Lygon – it was *the* union pub and an awful bloody place, though full of character – and getting, as it were, no return. If the ACTU bought it, the money could be recycled into the union system, and we could make it a better pub. There was also a garage in Victoria Street, across the road from the Trades Hall, which was used by the ACTU and a whole lot of trade union people. I went to Albert and suggested that we should buy both those things. The publican wanted only £30 000, which made the Lygon an unbelievably good investment. But Albert flatly refused. It was never my idea, then or when I became president, that the ACTU should be financed in its traditional areas by income from enterprises, because that would be trade unionism on the cheap. If the union movement wanted the ACTU to function effectively, and if individual members wanted their unions to function effectively, they would have to pay for that. I saw the enterprises as providing better services and cheaper services to unionists and the income for extra activities: like scholarships for kids. My attitude was not a matter of 'socialism in action', as was sometimes reported; it was functional.

At the ACTU Congress of 1971 the executive had recommended that union members pay 1 per cent of their wages as membership fees, to try to overcome the general problem of under-financing of the whole movement. Short-sighted self-interest won the day. Many large unions were holding elections for their leadership positions at that time and, as Edgar Williams put it, 'Nobody was willing to say, "Vote for me and I'll put up your membership fees"'. The recommendation was rejected. At the 1973 Congress the ACTU again recommended it, this time successfully – in theory. In practice, the majority of unions refused to demand higher fees from their members. A constant fear for union officials is that if fees are too high, their members will resign. 'Union shop' awards are their protection against defection, but there are few union shop awards in Australia and those that exist have been won only after battles with employers *and* other unions.[10]

Hawke said,

Until the unions themselves have an adequate fee structure we cannot get the ACTU into financial shape. My error, and there's no point saying it was anything else, was that I did not understand quickly enough that the ACTU's resources were so pathetic that it was unrealistic for us to try to do more than one or two things. What we needed was a department within the ACTU which would do nothing but run the enterprises: it would have needed a staff of lawyers, economists and finance people. And for too long I was unwilling to accept that we were incapable, because of our limitations, of responding to the opportunities and challenges that arose. We were inundated with proposals, and I worked tremendously long hours on them – and Harold did an immense amount of work, too, but ...

By 1981 the trade union movement had accepted the principle that 1 per cent of wages was a reasonable membership fee and consequently was willing to increase financial support to the ACTU. Also, the concept that unions should expand their horizons and shift, for example, into superannuation, had been established. Hawke had been a decade too soon, far too optimistic and much too publicised – for when the movement turned against the enterprises, the main reason given was that they were 'all Hawke's ideas' and that, as years earlier with International House, 'Bob hogged the limelight'.

With Hawke's two hats, publicity was becoming a disadvantage.

A few weeks after the 1973 Congress a Liberal MHR resigned, opening the way for a by-election in the seat of Parramatta. The Liberals had only just managed to hold the seat in 1972; with the new government still on its honeymoon with the electorate, Labor was confident of winning. Indeed, the Whitlam government needed to win the seat to confirm its 'mandate'. But suddenly Cabinet performed a miracle of bad timing: it announced that Sydney's second airport would be built at Galston, close to the Parramatta electorate.

Hawke went campaigning in the Parramatta by-election. He recalled, 'I was at a meeting there just after the federal government's announcement of the Galston airport. People rushed up to me and complained bitterly about it. They were talking of nothing else.' When asked by the news media for his views, Hawke said that to make such an announcement in the middle of a by-election was 'political insanity' and 'an act of imbecility'. The Liberal Party won Parramatta with a 6 per cent swing and Hawke, again wearing his ALP president's hat, commented,

> I think the parliamentary party and the Cabinet have got to be more finely attuned to the electorate. They are becoming removed from the realities of day-to-day politics. They should be keeping their ears open a bit more. They are not keeping in touch with what is happening at the grass roots.

Caucus and Whitlam were irate. Hawke had swallowed his conscience publicly over the tariff cuts, but now, in just a couple of months, he had reverted to form: liberty of conscience is the very foundation of puritanism, and Hawke was, again, exercising it with vigour. The ALP has been for decades a hybrid beast. With Whitlam as its leader and Hawke as its president it began publicly to resemble something monstrous: a two-headed calf. The Caucus was beginning to hate Hawke, to reject his criticisms of its actions as wilful embarrassment, even traitorous. Other party faithful disagree. David Combe, the federal secretary, said,

> Bob was the bloke who had the courage to stand up and make a bastard of himself by pointing out how crazy some of the government's decisions were, and trying to get Caucus to change its mind by making a fuss. You would not believe how difficult it was for people who were responsible for the Labor Party to get a hearing from either Caucus or Gough. They just would not listen. After the Parramatta by-election I called on Gough, as secretary of the party, to voice my concerns about how we

were performing politically, that we'd just had a disastrous by-election, it need not have been a disaster, we could have won the seat, and tiddly-dum. Gough was lying full-length on his settee, reading papers and throwing them over his shoulder as he finished them while various senior public servants danced attendance. He heard me out, still prone. Then he sat bolt upright and stared at me. He said, 'David. You have often told me that this government has one thing going for it. You are wasting its time!' That was the end of our interview. In the whole three years the Caucus never once met as a political caucus, to discuss how it was performing politically.

On 3 November 1973 Whitlam aired his displeasure with Hawke when, at a National Press Club luncheon in Canberra, in reply to a question about Hawke's opinion that income tax should be increased to help combat inflation, the Prime Minister said: 'Mr Hawke's advice was not sought. It will not be sought ... The president of the federal executive of the Labor Party does not determine such matters – is not consulted in such matters.' As he sat down Whitlam made an aside to journalists, along the lines of 'That will show the little runt'.

He had spoken too soon. A few weeks earlier there had been a dramatic development in international events and on the issues that arose Hawke and Whitlam were to be in disagreement not merely about method – a perennial problem in any reformist party – but about principles. War, said Marx, is the locomotive of history. The Vietnam War had helped to drive Labor in to office; it had showered the nation with gold and good times and good causes. On 6 October 1973, Judaism's Day of Atonement, a period spent in prayer and communion with God, when no fires may be lit nor cars driven nor work performed, the armies of Egypt and Syria invaded Israel for what later was called, after the Hebrew name for the day, the Yom Kippur War. And in five weeks the world was changed.

SIXTEEN

J ERUSALEM IS ONE OF the world's most beautiful cities. It is small, set high in the Judean hills and built from a pale honey-coloured stone that, at certain times of day, glows gold. The desert air is clean. Standing on the Mount of Olives, looking across at Jerusalem's walls and domes, one can pick out the churches that celebrate the life of Jesus, and his last hours – the place of the Last Supper is on a hill to the left, and the Garden of Gethsemane, its foliage surprisingly dark green and luxuriant, is just below, to the right. The sky above Jerusalem as seen from this hilltop has an unusually brilliant, pure light. It is, people say, the outermost garment of the Lord.

Hawke first saw the city in 1971. He came upon it suddenly, rounding a bend in the mountain road. He recalled,

> The physical impact of Jerusalem on me was almost, in the literal sense of the word, indescribable. It conjured up so much from my background, my knowledge of the Bible ... I don't know how often I've been there since, but every time I've felt a thrill as the car rounds a brow of the hill, and there it is!

Jerusalem: City of David; execution place of Christ; the town from which Mohammed's soul, resting a moment upon a rock, soared upwards into Heaven. 'Next year in Jerusalem', Jews in the Diaspora prayed for almost 2000 years and, if they were Orthodox, left a part of their houses unbuilt, to signify temporary residence outside the Holy City of the Holy Land.

The city has changed owners often, for it has the sacred sites of three great reformist religions. When Hawke first went there Israelis were still exulting that they had recaptured east Jerusalem and the Wall, all that is left of the Second Temple, from Jordan. The Wall looks like any old wall except that at the height of a man's head and hands, on the left side, and slightly lower – the height of a woman's – on the right, its stones are darkened and have a buttery glaze from the pressing of millions of humans against them. And between all the stones within human reach there are strips of paper, hundreds of thousands of them, each one a prayer. Hawke was taken to the Wall and inserted his own prayer: May Labor win the 1972 election. A few years later at least one Israeli inserted a prayer: May Bob Hawke become Prime Minister of Australia.

Hawke is loved in Israel. Initially, Israelis were sceptical of him.

He went there when he did, and in circumstances that obliged him to take a more than usually active interest in the country, almost by accident. In 1969 the ALP Senator Sam Cohen died during the election campaign. His widow, Judith (later Justice Cohen), and friends wanted to celebrate Cohen's memory and achievements. At the urging of Clyde Holding (leader of the Opposition in the Victorian Parliament, later Labor MHR), a Gentile with the status of 'a Jew among Jews' in Australia, it was decided to reject a plan that would have made Cohen's memorial some gift to Israel – a building at the Hebrew University in Jerusalem was favoured – and instead to send a trade unionist or a member of the Left-wing of the ALP to visit the country. On return, the visitor would be required to give a Sam Cohen Memorial Lecture about Israel to an invited audience. Holding was of the generation, as was Hawke, that in youth had been stunned by news of the Holocaust and then exhilarated by the founding of the state of Israel, in which H. V. Evatt, as Australia's Minister for External Affairs and Chairman of the General Assembly of the UN, had played a leading role.

Holding showed an uncanny foresight about a change in ALP attitudes to Israel in the 1970s and the need to encourage prominent Labor people to speak out in Israel's defence. He remarked later,

> With the decline of that whole heady, awful business, the Vietnam War, a lot of the younger radicals were a bit lost for a cause. They were on the lookout for the next wretched depressed victims of American capitalism – and there were those benighted Palestinians.

The choice of Hawke as the first Sam Cohen Memorial Lecturer seems, in retrospect, uncanny also. It is impossible to think of another gentile Australian in public life whose upbringing had made him so open to the appeal and difficulties of the state of Israel and who, at the same time, would be so ready to shout about it from the rooftops – and be heard. Hawke's whole career has been shaped by a sense of indignation. All his successes as a trade union advocate, a strike negotiator and a political campaigner have occurred when he has been able to heat others with his own belly fire – that old Methodist anger he had got from Ellie and from Will Lee before her, and which, as a small, sickly boy intimidated by bigger children, had become concrete and personal in his own life. The institutions and problems of the state of Israel were to seize upon the core of Hawke's being: his admiration for achievement, his capacity for anger, his identification with the 'little man', his instinct to rescue. Israel was – still is – the very image of David defying Goliath.

Israel had not been an issue in Australian politics before the escalation, in 1964, of the Vietnam War. In that year the Palestine Liberation Organisation (PLO) was founded with the major aim of its charter the total destruction of Israel. This aim was inspired by rankling over injustice: the United Nations decision of 1947 to divide British Mandated Palestine, a colony of the Empire, into two countries, allotting one to Palestinians and the other to Jews as a national home, was, from the Arab point of view, both a colonial act of theft and an insult to the whole Arab world. The Arabs had never accepted the Balfour

Declaration of 1917 that such a Jewish national home should be created in Palestine; they discounted the fact that already, before World War II, Jews who had been returning to live in Palestine since the 1880s had bought a great deal of land there from Arab and absentee Turkish landowners. That by 1947 European Jews were desperate for somewhere to live was of little concern to the Arabs for it was not they who had set up the gas chambers and slave camps. They saw the partition of Palestine as a European attempt to assuage European guilt. The Arab policy was to reject half a country and gamble upon winning by force of arms a whole country – or to lose the half they already had. But despite four major wars, 87 000 killed in action, hundreds of thousands wounded, billions of dollars spent on armaments that could have been spent on improving the lives of people, orgies of propaganda to encourage hatred, there is no Palestinian state and Israel has increased its territory.

On the day in 1948 when Israel was declared an independent state the Arabs launched a war and as a result lost territory to Israel. They continued to harass until 1956 when Israel launched a war and won more territory. The Arabs continued to harass, and after 1964 became better organised in their campaign for the total destruction of Israel, which in 1967 made a pre-emptive strike. In six days Israel won a victory that astonished the world. The Arab nations reacted to defeat by increasing the price of oil to what was at the time a staggering $US5 a barrel, more than double the old price. Israel, by now, had the image of permanent military invincibility, and slowly its status as underdog began to change. In the years after 1967 the Arab nations, with a population of 120 million, were able to cast themselves as the plaintiffs against Israel, with a population of three million, as defendants. The Palestinians, refusing to acknowledge the legality or the reality of the state of Israel, lived in refugee camps. In the early 1980s, children in the Palestinian camps born there and born of parents who were born there would reply to the question 'Where do you come from?' with the name of a village, now part of Israel, that their grandparents had once lived in and that they had never seen.[1]

The primary attitude of the Left everywhere is an amalgam of fellow feeling (for the weak) and hostility (for the strong). The Palestinian cause was tailored, after 1967, to Left emotions, especially since by then Israel was firmly in the American camp and, partly because of the Vietnam War, America represented All Evil. However, within the ALP the moral stature of Sam Cohen, which was towering, and the activities of other Jews who were active in the ALP Left, had managed to prevent an outbreak of anti-Israel feeling. With Cohen's death and the passing of the heyday of the Vietnam moratorium marches, in which Jews played a leading role, there was a gap. Holding had foreseen that the party was likely to become increasingly anti-Israel – at least, among those Left-wing, and younger, members who could not remember newspaper pictures of the Holocaust and the joyful relief that had greeted the founding of the state.

For anyone in the trade unions or the ALP, Israel in 1971 was a fascinating country. It had had Labour governments since its founding in 1948 and it had an egalitarian atmosphere that was an unachieved ideal in Australia. Its trade union council, Histadrut, controlled 25 per cent of Israel's GDP; it was one of the country's largest employers; it had 70 per cent of the population as members; Histadrut had the largest health fund; the second largest bank; the biggest construction company; holiday villas; a shipping line ... There are no demarcation disputes in Israel because workers – including doctors, diplomats and the president of the country – join Histadrut direct and are then allotted to unions. While other countries have a trade union council, Histadrut got itself a country. It had existed almost thirty years longer than the state of Israel, having begun as a workers' co-operative in British Mandated Palestine, and had provided the first framework of government in the new state. Everybody who was anybody in Israeli politics, aside from the religious, was a member of Histadrut. The Israeli Establishment was, in the broad, Labour.

In 1971 Hawke had, he said, 'a general knowledge about Israel, but no particular interest'. His eldest child, Susan, had recently read the best-selling novel *Exodus*, and was intrigued by Israel. When he accepted the invitation to be the first Sam Cohen Memorial Lecturer he asked if Susan could accompany him, explaining to the sponsors, with an incuriosity about the thinking of others that, by now, was habitual, 'I don't know why, but she'd like to come'. Arrangements were hastily made for Susan to stay on a kibbutz for six weeks. Hawke was to be in the country only a fortnight, before continuing on to Geneva for an ILO conference. He would collect Susan on the way home.

Dramatic complications to this bland scenario quickly arose. There was the bomb scare on their flight from Perth because of Hawke's role in the Springbok campaign, but this, as things turned out, was a mere gentle prelude. Hawke's love of Israel and his willingness to fight for it were to cause problems that veered close to wrecking his life and career. Havoc was created in the lives of his children, who became hostages to his public activities. Created, too, were the circumstances for an awful courage.

Hawke recalled his first impressions of the landscape of Israel as if it were reaching out from the books of childhood to embrace him: 'It was as I'd imagined, dusty roads and olive trees'. From the moment of arrival Hawke and Israel were *en rapport*.

Histadrut, which has a large international department that, among other things, looks after foreign guests, had provided an officer, Michael Siew, and a Tel Aviv taxi driver, Ari Tel-Shahar, to escort him. Relationships, emotional bonds, are everything to Hawke, the rest – including people's names (he could never remember Ari's surname although he loves him) – is detail. The three men formed an immediate bond. Tel-Shahar, who is sandy-haired, as wide as he is high and, in Hawke's words, 'one of the great rogues of all time – would take anyone down', said, 'When the three of us met, it was like a match to petrol'. He and Siew were astonished by Hawke's drinking and his ability to keep going for days with virtually no sleep. 'We learned', Tel-Shahar said later, 'when Bob comes, forget sleep'. Siew, who used to be a BBC journalist and, like Tel-Shahar, was in a tank unit, recalled Hawke at first meeting:

Initially I was impressed by his Mephistophelian eyebrows which he would twitch at me. Then, the fellow was asking too many questions – and very pointed ones, at that. And his arrogance! He actually hinted he was more intelligent than I. And then, his frankness – he told me that while in Oxford he realised one day that he had a prejudice against Jews. Then there was his sardonic impatience with some of our high-sounding, stuffy diplomats, who tried to impress our uncouth guest with Shakespeare. And there was his enthusiasm upon seeing and analysing some of our achievements in social experimentation. And he was a *real* humanitarian: he was disgusted at the suggestion that El Al should fly to Australia via South Africa. There was his sense of humour. His great taste in sheilas. And there was his all-consuming love for Australia, and his grief about the gap between what is and what could be ... After fourteen harrowing days and nights with him I was so exhausted I could hardly remember the brand of my favourite beer. I volunteered to take him to the airport to make sure he would leave, and en route he had the nerve to assure me he thought I had done my homework on Israel ... When he left I was besieged by my curious colleagues. They were sceptical about him. After all – shame! – he wasn't Jewish. There must be, they said, some ulterior motive to account for his friendliness – the man has yet to be tested. I told them, 'You can't even tell a friend when you see one'. Until this day people ask me about his blood. I tell them, it's hot, but he's not Robert James Lee Rosenblum. He is Israel's friend.

Hawke said,

I'm sure I would have developed a love and affection for Israel and its people, but the relationship that was so quickly forged between me, Michael and Ari and has remained ever since, created a beautiful initial environment. The first impression is one that has remained: here was this fantastic blend of informality – in dress [Israel lives in blue jeans], in arranging things; an irreverence, a cocking a snook at authority – *combined with* a very profound awareness of the ever-present threat. It seemed to me that in many people the threat would have produced paranoia, craziness – but here were these people delightfully relaxed in so many ways, and yet sharply attuned. You felt it was like a relaxed spring, that could coil into action very quickly.

The correspondences with his own style were striking.

He had arrived in Israel at a period when the country was exuberantly self-confident: Israelis had the Arabs licked. Or so it was thought. Hawke was taken on a tour of territory captured in three wars: to Sharm-el-Sheik, where Egyptian cannon had once blocked Israeli shipping through the Straits of Tiran; to Syrian bunkers on the Golan Heights from which machine-gunners had hosed the Israeli villagers below with bullets. Standing in the bunkers and looking through a slit in the side of the hill one can see, with a pair of binoculars, the faces of Israelis in their houses below and the shelters in which they had slept every night to avoid bullets and mortars. As Hawke's guides told him, 'We fought like Russians, just throwing away lives, to capture these positions'. Lists of the names of Israelis who died to capture a particular bunker are engraved on stones at their entrances. The bunkers themselves, a network of tunnels through the hillsides, are meticulously maintained; around them, above ground, there are heaped in nests old Syrian tank obstacles – great black iron thorns that look like the spiked eggs of some monstrous reptile. All Israeli war memorials have the same plain, brutal design of rock and jagged metal. They are horrifying to those with an eye for symbolism, for they all tell one story: this celebrates nothing; there has been no catharsis; this stands not for national glory but as a reminder that the war continues. Hawke quickly realised that the Israelis were deadly serious about the security of their borders.

He was impressed, too, by the achievements of Histadrut, and the argumentativeness and humour of the people he met. For the first time he was encountering a whole nation of individualists – tradition has it that every Jew is 'son of a king' – who had more jokes and as many opinions as he. There is a saying: when three Israelis meet they form eleven political parties; and another: the only reason I don't make love in Dizengoff Square (the most fashionable area of Tel Aviv) is because every passer-by would give me advice. Hawke said, 'It's the only country I've been to where every citizen reckons that he or she could be prime minister and would do a better job'. Hawke's love of all-night arguments had found a permanent home. But, more compelling than these attractions, there was a spot in his consciousness that Israel burnt into, ineradicably.

When he was taken to Jerusalem to visit the holy places he was taken to see Yad Vashem. This is a museum built to the memory of those who died in the Holocaust. It is on a hilltop, with a short avenue of trees leading up to a couple of squat buildings and a bronze mural depicting the Warsaw Ghetto Uprising. Each tree in the avenue has a name beside it and has been planted for a Gentile who, during the Holocaust, defied authority and saved the lives of Jews. Such people are known in Israel and throughout the Diaspora communities as The Righteous. Inside the buildings there is a collection of photographs and objects of surreal horror. They are displayed simply, with low-key, informative captions. Some people walk through the museum, read the captions, look at the display and after half an hour continue on the next part of their tour. Others are struck dumb with an inner howl of rage and shame. Hawke was among the latter. Tel-Shahar, who had been waiting in the car outside, said, 'Bob's face was very grave. He sat in the back of the taxi and lent his head against it and couldn't speak. I could see there were tears running out of the sides of his eyes.' Some time later Hawke said, 'The whole of Christendom bears the guilt for that'. He will talk for days about Israel without ever referring to Yad Vashem. For him, finding it always difficult to mention the horrible, the Holocaust is almost taboo in speech, if not in thought. One day in 1981 when the subject arose he said suddenly, 'I can't understand anybody who doesn't weep when they see that. Whenever I think of Israel that's what I have in my mind.'

A few days after Hawke's visit to Jerusalem he, Siew and Tel-Shahar were in Beer-Sheba holding one of their all-night drinking and talking fests, when the question of Israeli–Soviet relations arose. Hawke said,

> The yarning led to my first visit to Moscow on Israel's behalf. I argued to the others that the Israelis hadn't properly explained to the world, but most particularly to the Soviet Union, their position. And the parallel immediately struck me: Israel and the USSR were both creations of the twentieth century. Their viability had been put at issue immediately – there had been an attempt to destroy them at birth, and subsequent attempts. And that the whole concept of the need for security, for recognised boundaries, was something that was uniquely relevant to both countries. As a passing observation I said, 'You know, I really would love to make those arguments to the Russians'.

Hawke had already met the president-to-be of Histadrut, Yerucham Meshel, a man old enough to be his father, who said of Hawke:

> It was love from first looking at each other, from the first sentences. I realised that this man was very open to the tragedy of the Jewish people and the Jewish nation. I realised that he's a dreamer, emotional, spiritual, that he loves people. That he was dedicated to the Labor movement, and the trade union movement, not because he was a real trade union man, but because he wants to improve the standard of living of people in general . . . With all that intellect he has, Bob is also naive. Absolutely naive.

Hawke's desire to 'put those arguments to the Russians' revealed, perhaps more than anything else, the strength of his idealism. It was a combination of naivety – in the sense of his faith in goodness and logic – and his dreaming to improve the human condition, the quality that Bob Rogers had noticed when Hawke returned from India.

The USSR had supported the creation of the state of Israel but this had little to do with goodwill towards Jews. It was stimulated by Soviet desire to hasten the decline of Britain's power in the Middle East, to the advantage of the Soviet Union. Russia's initial expressions of warm feelings for Israel quickly cooled, then chilled and in 1967 became frigid. Soviet disinformation had triggered the Six Day War and the Russians, in high dudgeon of embarrassment, broke diplomatic relations with Israel. Tens of millions of dollars worth of Soviet armaments, sold to Egypt and Syria, had been destroyed by Israel in the war. By 1971 the USSR was massively rearming Egypt and Syria and had that year signed a Treaty of Friendship with Egypt, which was still formally committed to the total destruction of Israel.

Hawke's initial thinking about the arguments he might put to Moscow had sprung from his deep-seated belief in the Brotherhood of Man and his instinct to find common cause and mediate conflicting positions. On further reflection he realised a more sophisticated debate would be necessary; he proposed to make one of his complicated carrot-and-stick arguments to the Russians, a combination of morality and threats to self-interest: that the USSR, having worked for the creation of Israel, would lose credibility if Russian weaponry caused its destruction; that if Israel were destroyed the Arabs, who hated the Russians on political and religious grounds, would turn away from the Soviet Union, therefore it was in Russian interest that Israel continue to exist so that Arabs would continue to look to the USSR for support. He did not intend to state the too obvious: that if Russian weapons employed by Arabs destroyed Israel, the Jewish lobby in the USA would put an American president under immense pressure to intervene, either against the Arab destroyers or against the USSR.

By 1971 détente was underway and the Soviet Union was concerned about international public opinion, so there was some reason for Hawke to be optimistic that the Russians would heed his argument about morality and consistency. But given the freezing relations between Israel and the Soviet Union, it was a long shot. However, Hawke could aim at the bull's eye: he was already friendly with Alexander Shelepin, head of the Soviet trade union movement and a man who was among the top officials in the Soviet hierarchy, spoken of in the Western press as a potential successor to Brezhnev. Before becoming leader of Soviet workers, Shelepin had been head of the KGB.

Siew passed on the word that Hawke was interested in presenting a case for Israel in Moscow. Events started to move quickly. As yet Hawke had not realised what a godsend he was to the Israelis. One country wishing to communicate with another with which it is not on speaking terms must use clandestine methods or envoys from a third nation, usually ambassadors or heads of state who, as a matter of course, extract some payment for their own nation in recompense for the favour they are doing. Hawke had access to one of the highest in the land in the USSR, and his services to Israel cost only the price of his airfares.

He said,

> I was taken to meet Golda Meir, in her prime minister's office in Tel Aviv. On the personal side a fascinating dichotomy in her character came out. Susan was with me and had been given the inevitable drink of orangeade. Golda was sitting behind her desk, chain-smoking, and she and I were seriously talking about Israel. Suddenly, Susan knocked over her drink and the glass smashed on the floor. There was an immediate transformation in Golda from a stern stateswoman into a grandmother. She jumped up and came from behind her desk to put her arm around Susan and tell her that it didn't matter about the glass. That spontaneous and unaffected warmth of the human being, the woman, immediately coming out, had a big effect on me.

Hawke's friends said later, 'Bob had the greatest platonic love affair of his life with Golda'. One day, years later, when Hawke was talking to Kate Baillieu about the tribulations Mrs Meir had suffered in childhood, 'he began to weep – he was not drunk'. On their first meeting, scheduled for fifteen minutes, the conversation ran on for more than an hour, and touched on Moscow. Later, Hawke met the Foreign Minister, Abba Eban.

A delicate process of testing Hawke for soundness was in train. A Histadrut official said, 'We couldn't quite believe him – a man with such an intellect, such a forceful personality, a politician . . .' At length, the Israelis were convinced that they had met a rare character: a Righteous Gentile. Whatever the Israeli leaders thought of Hawke's proposed arguments and their chances of success, they had a different submission for him to make in Moscow: they wanted Hawke to argue for the release of Soviet Jews. But for him to do this on Israel's behalf it would be necessary to make him privy to confidential matters of state.

The position of the Soviet Jews, who number 3 million, is one of the most emotional and diplomatically sensitive issues for Israel and world Jewry. Soviet Jews are known as 'The Silent Jews', 'The Prisoners of Zion' and 'The Beautiful People', and have the status of living martyrs among their co-religionists outside the USSR. Little was heard of them during the 1950s and 1960s in the councils of world Jewry. But following the Six Day War many asked permission to emigrate from the USSR. Anti-Semitism is rife in the Soviet Union. It was pogroms in Russia in the late nineteenth and early twentieth centuries that had forced some Russian Jews to flee to Palestine and dream of establishing a Jewish homeland there. When exit visas were requested more frequently after 1967 some were granted, some were not; some Jews were sacked for asking, some were not; some Jews were harassed by the KGB, some were not. No explanations were given. Two hundred were allowed to emigrate in 1968, 3000 in 1969, but in 1970 only 1000. Then on Christmas Eve 1970 a group of three Jews and two Gentiles, who had been refused exit visas and had talked about hijacking an aircraft, were sentenced to terms ranging from fifteen years imprisonment to death. There was an international outcry. The Queen publicly implored clemency. The hijack plan was so widely known that Israeli officials were aware of it before its proposed date and in these circumstances it was doomed in advance, for the KGB must have known of it also. However, just as PLO hijacks were raising the national consciousness and indignation of Arabs, the Russian group's very plan and their draconian sentences had a great impact upon the consciousness of Soviet Jewry. Throughout 1971 the demand for visas increased dramatically although, as an Israeli remarked, 'It was like playing Russian roulette'. The Israelis were fearful that a false move would mean a loaded chamber for their kin in the USSR.

Hawke said,

> At some point as the trip went on the Israelis put it to me that they would like me to do a job of representation – in terms that I had proposed to them, to discuss with the Russians the attitude of the Soviet Union towards Israel, and also on the question of the Soviet attitude towards the release of Soviet Jewry.

Hawke flew to Rome and telephoned Alexander Shelepin. A year earlier Hawke had gone on from an ILO Conference to Moscow on a fraternal visit, as Shelepin's guest. They had taken a liking to each other: Hawke said,

> While I detested all that he stood for, the fantasy about a free trade union movement, and particularly his background in the KGB, I found him a fascinating and likeable bloke. He had an acute intelligence and was extraordinarily well informed. On my 1970 visit he had brushed aside his aides to ask all his own questions about Australia, revealing an unusual depth of knowledge and understanding. Physically, Shelepin could have been the twin of [Sir Henry] Harry Bland [former head of the Australian Department of Labour] – short, dark, sharp.

We had a strange liking for each other. I had no doubt that in an ultimate sense he was totally ruthless.

One of the pranks Shelepin had played on Hawke in 1970 was to try to trick him into vodka-drinking contests. Hawke said,

> There would be toasts for everything, and suddenly the cry, 'Bottoms up!' I noticed that I seemed always to have the biggest glass of vodka, and while the two comrades standing closest to me would do a 'bottoms up' and would look at me as a challenge to do the same, the real heavies weren't bottoms-upping at all.'

After a number of international telephone calls it was established that Shelepin, who was on holiday at the Baltic Sea, would be delighted to receive Hawke there. Hawke went on to the European conference, returned to Israel to collect Susan and have further briefings, then flew to Moscow. He arrived there on the evening of 21 July and was met by Boris Averianov, head of the international department of the USSR trade union movement, and others. Next morning they flew to Palanga, on the Baltic, where Shelepin was waiting in welcome. They had to communicate through translators.

Hawke was extremely cautious, as revealed by the report he dictated as soon as he left the USSR. He spent four hours on a *tour d'horizon* of international events with Shelepin, who opened talks with an exposition about recent USSR–USA discussions in Helsinki; the end of the Cold War; the obstacle of East Germany; the role of Norway, and so on, and set forth an overall view of international relations that was optimistic, in Soviet terms. They had lunch. Hawke then said he wished Shelepin to be under no misapprehension: he wanted to discuss specific issues 'which even by Right-wing standards transcend politics'. Hawke had reduced his arguments to note-form and kept his notes 'on my person for the whole period before and after this'. He made a general introduction, then 'submissions' – first on the Arab–Israeli question. His report says, 'While I put these Shelepin listened with absolute intensity and made copious notes. I proceeded to conclusion without interruption.' He said later,

> Often when you're talking to important people from other countries you know it's only a game you're going through, that the exchange of views is a charade of listening. There was no question that Shelepin was just being polite; his attention and seriousness were for real ... I put the altruistic argument about Soviet consistency, then I tried to impress upon him that the Israelis were just as serious about the security of their borders as the Soviet Union was, and, Christ Almighty, look at what the USSR had done in the cause of its security. It had enslaved the peoples of Eastern Europe, kept its own living standards appallingly low to spend billions upon armaments – naturally, I did not advert to specifics ... Then I moved on to Soviet self-interest in the Middle East – their capacity to bargain with and keep the Arab states dependent upon Russia for this very fact: that Israel existed.

Shelepin heard him out and began his reply with an insistence that everything he said must remain confidential.

In broad terms he tried to justify Soviet sympathy for the Arab cause and warned Hawke that he and the Israelis ought not to be deceived, that since their dreadful defeat in 1967, 'the Arab armies have been transformed'. He assured Hawke that the Soviet Union did not want another war in the Middle East and had 'expended kilos of salt' in attempting to convince the Arab states that they must abandon their plans for 'liquidation' of Israel. Hawke argued to him, 'You are backing the wrong horse', and a year later his remark was justified, when President Sadat expelled all the USSR advisers from Egypt. (Five years later Sadat unilaterally broke the Treaty of Friendship and severed diplomatic relations with the USSR.)

Hawke said in his report,

What Shelepin really seemed to grasp was my repeated pushing of the analogy between the Israeli determination about
the security of its borders, and the same Russian determination. He emphasised the need for time. That he would need
time to talk to his peers about this; then, if they accepted the
point, time for the Russians to talk to the Arabs. I believe it is
crucial to develop a diplomatic crescendo about the security
complex – use the German analogy, albeit in muted terms,
and create the equation: *What is* the difference between the
Soviet desire for territorial integrity and the steps it has been
prepared to take, and the position of Israel?

They then moved on to the topic of Soviet Jews. Hawke's report
said,

I put the argument, then Shelepin produced some strained
statistics and when I pointed out that they were strained, he
reacted. He said the exact statistics could be provided for me.
Then he said, 'The Jews are less than 2 per cent of our population, but they constitute at least 15 per cent of our scientific
people and those with access to state secrets essential to our
security'. He looked at me across the table and said with his
hand raised almost plaintively, 'What do we do? You tell me
what we do.' My first rejoinder was, 'Do these people want to
leave?' To which he replied, 'Yes!' My answer was, I suppose,
inadequate. I certainly gained the impression that it was for
him. I said, 'These people are merely identifying with a wider
cause. If you are humane to the less important Jews and allow
them to leave, then the ones you are really concerned about,
those with access to state secrets, will not feel the pressure so
much and will not want to leave.' Perhaps you [Jews] pay too
high a price for your ability.[2]

In 1971 the USSR allowed 13 000 Jews to emigrate. In 1972,
32 000; in 1973, 35 000. It is widely accepted by Israeli officials
that Hawke's 'submissions' to Shelepin had helped to achieve

this result. The reason may not be as straightforward as it appears – a matter of Hawke, as advocate, convincing Shelepin, as judge. A senior Australian diplomat who claims expertise on Soviet affairs made the point that because anti-Semitism is so great in the USSR, Soviet officials tend to have paranoid fears about Jews, which include an overestimation of the power of world Jewry. Further, that the KGB (Shelepin's former field) is especially prone to such attitudes. This certainly would explain the extreme seriousness of Shelepin's behaviour towards Hawke in 1971, for it suggests he would have seen Hawke as the emissary of a mighty and devious foe.

There was immense gratitude to Hawke in Israel. On every trip abroad he began to call in there. A Histadrut official said, 'In Israel, people really cared for Bob. We cared about his drinking problem and his family and his political problems, and he knew it. Here, everyone was his friend.'

But meanwhile, in Australia, relations with Israel were beginning to sour. The Australian Jewish community had donated lavishly to the Whitlam government's 1972 campaign, much of the money being channelled through Hawke, who, on returning from Israel in 1971, had become a favourite Gentile. Hawke had not told people about his trip to Moscow on Israel's behalf, but news had seeped back from Tel Aviv and Jerusalem that the government of Israel looked with particular fondness upon Hawke. Australian Jews inclined towards Labor, for it was the Chifley government that had offered them asylum and Evatt who had helped to establish Israel. They expected great things from the Whitlam government. During the election campaign Whitlam had promised that Qantas would fly to Tel Aviv. This was especially important for Israelis and their relations abroad because there are many airlines that will not fly to Israel and many countries in which Israelis dare not have stop-overs, so that travelling in and out of the country is a complicated process of picking out routes and airlines that only stop in neutral or friendly nations. Whitlam did not keep his promise about Qantas and the Israeli government was becoming testy, the Australian Jewish community uneasy.

Given the government's desire to play an active role in international affairs and to assume leadership of Third World and radical causes, disillusion was inevitable. Power was flowing towards radical Arab nations. There were various reasons: a renaissance of Islam had been underway since the 1920s, worldwide. It had swept through Africa and into the black population of America. The decay of the Christian colonial empires had given it room, and encouragement. Since the end of World War II the world production (and consumption) of oil had expanded from 5 million barrels a day, in 1945, to about 60 million in the early 1970s and the Arab oil-producers were black with black gold. Their societies were suffering psychic shock from the challenge to traditions that sudden wealth imposed, and were febrile. Importantly, the Palestinians and others were beginning to win the propaganda war against Israel. The world community would not tolerate their assertion that Israel must be obliterated, but to the less dramatic claim, that a great injustice had been done to the people of Palestine, there was growing attention.

Communists of all persuasions were hostile to Israel and in the Left of the ALP hostility was increasing. Hawke widely advertised his plans for Histadrut–ACTU joint ventures; he was invited to speak at what a leader of Australian Jewry called, 'every Jewish mothers' club in the country'; he was, inevitably, seen as an enemy of the Palestinian cause. His position on Palestine was straightforward: that a Palestinian state should be created; that Israel and its neighbours should recognise Resolution 242[3] of the United Nations. He complained later, 'I have made my position clear many times and I don't think I have ever been given any credit for it by the supporters of Palestine. They have simply refused to listen to what I have said.'

The problem is that in his speeches on the Middle East, Hawke has devoted only a small percentage, if any, of each one to the plight of the Palestinians, while highlighting the violent physical and verbal assaults upon Israel by its neighbours. He thus projected the impression that, for him, the Palestinians were irrelevant.

By 1973 tension was steadily building in the Middle East. Hawke went to Israel in the first half of the year and by mid-year was convinced that a crisis was looming:

> I felt very tense about it all. Then on the eve of the ACTU Congress there was a death threat, purporting to come from the Black September Movement. I think I was so nervous at the Congress because I had a sense that something was going to break.

By late 1973 the pace of Hawke's life had turned his life into the panting of a revolving door.

Then on 6 October, the Day of Atonement in Israel, the most holy day of the year, Egyptian forces surged across the Suez Canal and captured the Bar Lev defence line while, simultaneously, Syrian tanks pushed deep into Israeli-held territory north-east of the Golan Heights. It was a massive assault. At first it seemed that Israel had been swept into the sea, but by 12 October it had recaptured territory taken by the advancing Syrians and three days later had thrust between the Egyptian armies on the eastern bank of the canal, crossed the canal and established a bridgehead into Africa. On 17 October the Organization of Arab Petroleum Exporting Countries (OAPEC) announced it would reduce oil production by 5 per cent a month until Israel withdrew from all occupied Arab territories. Saudi Arabia put a total embargo on oil sales to the United States. The war continued. The USA and USSR worked out a ceasefire resolution that was passed by the Security Council of the UN. This broke down immediately, and on 25 October the Israeli forces on the west bank of the canal surrounded the Egyptian Third Army. Israel now had the Egyptians in checkmate on one front and, on the other, was in a position to destroy Damascus. The USA went on worldwide strategic forces alert, warning both the Israelis against further advances and the Soviet Union against intervention. There was a ceasefire. OAPEC announced further cuts in production of oil. On 6 November the nine members of the European Economic

Community endorsed a statement that called for an Israeli withdrawal from the territories occupied in 1967. The long campaign of forcing Israel down to the status of an international pariah had begun.

Hawke had been in Geneva at an ILO Governing Body meeting. He flew to Tel Aviv on 18 November and was met by Tel-Shahar, who was summoned from military duty to escort him. Michael Siew had disappeared, fighting in the Golan Heights. With an army spokesman, a journalist, and Siew's father, they set out for the north, Hawke determined to find Siew. The Golan Heights were 'a cemetery of tanks' – hundreds upon hundreds of them. Bodies had been removed and the barren mountains were eerily quiet, littered with wreckage. Hawke said, 'The tanks were brand new and had Russian writing on them – inside some of the ones I looked in there were bits and pieces of what had been men'. They drove all day, kilometres into Syria, stopping at Israeli army camps to ask news of Siew. It was bitterly cold and Hawke sat hunched up and swearing, increasingly distressed as they failed to find his friend. (Siew was alive; he turned up a few days after Hawke left Israel.)

Hawke recalled,

After hours of wandering through this evidence of carnage we drove down to Jerusalem, arrived there late in the afternoon, and I immediately met Golda, in her office. I think that was the most emotional meeting I've ever had in my life with anyone. There was an old woman who had just been through the most unbelievably traumatic experience of having the survival of her country in question – if the Egyptian and Syrian advance had lasted another twenty-four hours Israel would have been finished – and she was tormenting herself. Because, as she said, all the intelligence reports for days before Yom Kippur had indicated a massive build-up of Arab forces. So the pressure was on to do what they'd done in 1967 and make a pre-emptive strike. But, as she said, the overwhelming factor was that the Americans had warned they would not tolerate another first strike attack by Israel, and there had been a great fear that if they did attack first they would be left without the sustaining flow of ammunition and replacement weaponry. And she was just emotionally and spiritually shattered, because ultimately she had to make the decision, and she'd lost the lives of 2500 men. She was blaming herself. There was this great human being, in tears. She hadn't lost control of herself – in fact, the opposite, there was still a great strength in her – but tears were running down her face. It was in that circumstance that she showed me photographs of young Israelis who'd been captured in the Golan Heights by the Syrians, had their hands tied behind their backs and had their heads shot apart. And she was weeping and saying she couldn't understand how people could behave like that. I asked her if I could have copies of the pictures. I made up my mind that I'd do what I could for Israel.

When Hawke emerged from the Prime Minister's office Tel-Shahar said, 'I did not recognise him. He was trembling. Pale.'

Hawke's sense of duty had been stimulated as never before. And probably, too, his belief in his destiny – that he was an instrument that must be used for the good of humankind. He recalled later,

I had been uniquely privileged to have seen what I had – I was the first non-Israeli to have been taken so far into the war-zone to witness what *had* happened and what could have happened. The Israelis were shaken beyond belief by the war, not just emotionally but in the confidence they'd had in their strategic strength. That confidence was gone. But it had been replaced with a determination, which I cannot overemphasise, that, 'This will never happen again'. I must make this point: I have never been told by Israelis either in confidence or out of confidence that they have nuclear weapons, but it was not unreasonable to think in 1973 that they might have them, or might acquire them. In my conversations with people outside the leadership I made the suggestion, based on my observation of their utter determination, 'If Israel had tactical nuclear weapons and was again faced with obliteration, she would use them'. And there was no dissent from this view. So what we were looking at, if there were another round, was the possibility of nuclear war. I had already decided to return to Moscow to talk to Shelepin if the Israelis wanted me to. They did, and had already made arrangements before I talked to Golda. There was no question of the Israelis wanting me to convey the message to Moscow, 'Next time it's nukes'. But by then we knew each other very well – I had a relationship with people there in which the nuances and the unspoken were as significant as the direct and the spoken. I think they knew I would be talking about nuclear war to Shelepin. Certainly, they wanted me to tell him just how much determination there was in Israel, the same message as before, but now even louder. And, of course, they wanted me again to put pressure on him for the release of Soviet Jews.

On 22 November he flew to Moscow and was met at the airport by Shelepin. They talked during the late afternoon and into the night. Hawke recalled,

I had the sense that this was one of the biggest moments in my life, that I was uniquely placed in terms of knowledge and understanding of Israel to try to get this very powerful man, whose country's equipment I had seen smashed to pieces, to understand the enormity of the situation that had loomed and could return. And to try to make him realise that Soviet policy, resulting in the destruction of millions of dollars' worth of its most modern technology, was just insanity! The Arab armies had not been transformed by the USSR. The Israelis had surrounded the Egyptian army, and the bloody Syrians could have lost Damascus. And if it had gone the other way, against Israel, what did he think the USSR would gain? War with America, maybe?

Hawke quickly told Shelepin of his worst fears, the possibility of a nuclear war. Shelepin replied, one can only hope untruthfully, that Egypt had a nuclear device already installed and this could be activated in twenty-four hours. He maintained that the USSR was determined Israel would not be flung into the Mediterranean and that, if this had seemed likely, Moscow would have ordered the Egyptian and Syrian armies to halt their advance. Hawke replied 'rather strongly' – which means, he shouted – that such an assertion was idiotic, that the Arab armies could not have been halted by a command from Moscow and that Shelepin was insulting his intelligence with this assertion.

Hawke recalled,

There was a big difference in Shelepin since 1971. By late 1973 he was totally absorbed, fascinated and worried by China. Australia had a unique position because of Gough's opening of diplomatic relations with China and Shelepin seemed to think that we therefore were able to speak with particular authority. He talked to me as he would talk to very few people. He was paranoid about China. Full of fear and contempt. He said they were rubbish, nothings, but at the same time he manifested an enormous apprehension. He was terrifically concerned by the rapprochement between the USA and China and in this context, talking about Nixon, something weird happened. I'd said to him, 'You can stop thinking about Nixon – he's finished'. One did not need to be brilliant to know that by late 1973 Watergate had destroyed Nixon. But Shelepin became vehement that Nixon was safe. He said that the whole Watergate episode was a concoction by 'reactionary capitalist forces who are angry with Nixon because he initiated détente with the USSR'. He was totally insistent that Watergate would soon be revealed as a capitalist plot. It shows the strange relationship we had: I said to him, 'Would you care to put your money where your mouth is?' He was puzzled by the translation for a moment, then he realised what I was saying and grinned. We bet two dozen bottles of best vodka.

By the time Hawke had won the bet Shelepin was on the verge of disgrace, so Hawke did not collect his prize. For reasons unknown, Shelepin was removed from the Soviet hierarchy in 1975; there has been speculation since that his fall may have been due, in part, to his meetings with Hawke.

While Hawke was abroad, Whitlam had announced that the Australian government had an 'even-handed policy in the Middle East'. The party's policy, based on Resolution 242 of the United Nations, and adopted in July 1973 at the Surfers Paradise conference, stated:

> The situation in the Middle East remains the greatest threat to the peace of the world. There can be no peace until the Arab States respect and recognise Israel's sovereignty and right to exist. Equally, there can be no peace until Israeli forces have withdrawn from occupied territories to secure and recognised boundaries and a just settlement of the refugee problem is achieved.

Hawke returned to Australia on 24 November 1973 and in a Perth news conference made an impassioned plea for Israel. Clem, for the first time in twenty years, was alarmed by the vehemence of his son's manner. Hawke showed to the news media the photographs Golda Meir had given him of murdered prisoners of war. They were screened on nationwide television. On his part it was an act of questionable wisdom: there is no such thing as a war in which troops maintain military discipline at all times. Hawke's implication that the enemies of Israel had a monopoly upon barbarity was both unjustified – one must recall the activities, just for example, of the Irgun – and reckless, for atrocity feeds upon atrocity.

He said, 'Showing the photographs was, I think, the start of the real hate campaign against me'.

Hawke had said in his news conference: 'For the Australian government to say our position on the Middle East is one of even-handedness is not an intelligent approach to the situation'.

He also made reference to an assumption that the Whitlam government's attitude was based on fear of loss of oil supplies. He said, 'That's all right for the politicians, but I understand what truth and democracy are all about and I don't put my knees on the same altar as the politicians'. As a result, there were questions in parliament for Whitlam, and more questions at his weekly press conference. The Prime Minister said, 'Australia has a bipartisan policy, a policy of neutrality in the Middle East. The ALP policy is substantially the policy which governments have pursued for the last quarter of a century in Australia', and that Hawke was speaking as 'a private citizen', not as president of the party. The following day the *Sydney Morning Herald* in its editorial wondered, 'How long Mr Hawke, holding the views he does, can sustain his current balancing feat as ALP and ACTU President'. That question was to be tested at the next meeting of the ALP federal executive, due in February 1974.

On 28 November 1973 a senior journalist, Adrian Deamer, delivering the national broadcast, *Notes on the News*, said:

> This is another vicious attack on the Prime Minister and on the politicians of the Labor Party [by Hawke]. It maintains his early form when he criticised the Government's announcement during the Parramatta by-election that Sydney's airport was to be sited at Galston as 'political imbecility'. He followed this up with his public statement that the trade union movement would not support the Government at the December 8 referendum on prices and incomes, and just before he left for Israel he said that the Government should have increased income tax ... He has emphasised that on this occasion he is speaking as a private citizen, and this explanation was accepted by Mr Whitlam ...
>
> The real issue that emerges from this controversy goes far beyond whether Mr Hawke should or should not criticise his party and Mr Whitlam ... What we need in this country is more information on which we can act, and greater diversity of views, not less. We need to encourage people like

Mr Hawke to speak out and to tell us what they know and think, not condemn them for going against the official line ... Like him or not, Mr Hawke breaks through this apathy and dispels the dullness [of Australian politics], forcing a lot of people to rethink the issues they have taken for granted.[4]

That night Hawke went to see Abeles, who happened to be in Melbourne. Abeles recalled, 'Bob was tremendously upset. He needed to let off steam and talk and talk. He was in an agony. He talked the whole night, until dawn, crying sometimes, and shouting. I was terribly worried. I thought he was at a breaking point.'

Next day in the ACTU office Hawke answered the telephone. A man with a foreign accent said, 'I am from Black September. We are going to kill your children', and hung up. Hawke went into the boardroom to open an executive meeting. His old friends knew from his appearance that something was wrong. After a few minutes Hawke blurted out what had happened and began to weep, saying, 'Must I give up my beliefs to save my children?' The crisis that had been developing all year had been triggered.

A doctor was called. He gave Hawke a sedative injection. Hawke was driven home and put to bed. Police collected the children from school. Police guards were stationed at the house. Policemen accompanied the children to and from school and stood guard in their playgrounds. They opened letters that came to the house.

On 5 December the Friends of Palestine published a full-page advertisement in the *Australian* headed, An Open Letter to Bob Hawke. It refuted that the death threat had come from the Black September movement and went on to say:

We suggest that Mr Hawke is appallingly ignorant of the real issues in the Middle East dispute. *If he can support Israel on morality grounds, then the traditional meaning of the word 'morality' has ceased.* Mr Hawke is prostituting morality in the services of a fascist regime, sacrificing the noble ideals of the

Labor Movement and slaying the Australian 'fair go' principle on the altar of a racist government which imports Jewish
citizens from Russia and elsewhere, but consistently denies
the indigenous Palestinian Arabs the fundamental right of
citizenship in their country of birth.

As soon as Hawke was on his feet again he bought a rifle and
would check that all the house windows and doors were locked
before going to bed. In the office, 'he looked like death warmed
up – he was pretty much a wreck for four months', Cliff Dolan
said.

Meanwhile, letters and telegrams had flooded the ACTU.
There were hundreds from churchgoers, from 'Liberal voters'
and, of course, from Jews. Some said:

> God bless you in your work, and as you take this stand I and
> my church are remembering you in prayer.

> Neither my wife nor I are ALP supporters but we both sup-
> port your views on Israel ... delighted that at last a public
> figure has the courage to state what is morally right even if
> unpopular.

> In our church service this morning our pastor led us in prayer
> for you, your wife and family and for the people of Israel ...

> Australia needs men like you who will stand firm for what
> they believe to be right ...

> In your role as Trade Union leader, I have never felt there
> would be anything in which I could support you, but your
> public stand on this matter has changed my views.

> I am not on your side politically but loyalty to principles
> transcends political differences.

> For the first time I find myself in agreement with you.

> I beg you to use your position and your voice to pressure the
> Government into reversing the policy of neutrality ... I am

ashamed to live in a country which will even *consider* putting economic security before the right of a brave little country to exist, let alone live in peace ... I have no voice. Tell of my anger, I beg you.

I am not normally an ardent supporter of 'Bob Hawke' but ... after tonight I think I will be ... You will have I am sure a multitude of Australians behind you if they have the opportunity to make their voices heard.[5]

Many of the letters were from businessmen and academics; some drew attention to the fact that the writers were not Jewish. The response from the Jewish community was passionate. The Yom Kippur War had terrified world Jewry. Jews who had little interest in Israel were suddenly suffocated by the fear that genocide could recur, and without Israel there would be nowhere to flee. Saul Same, an ALP member, chairman of directors of Glo-Weave and chairman of the United Israel Appeal, was one of those in charge of fund-raising in Australia to help Israel during and after the war. He said,

People who had never given a penny in their lives to Israel came to us. Money poured in to the United Israel Appeal. There are plenty of poor Jews in Australia. They sold things to give us money. People mortgaged their houses, and came to us with their jewellery, even their wedding rings ... I can tell you that there were those among us who would give their lives for Bob Hawke. If anybody had harmed a hair of his head, that person would have been killed.

Among the letters and telegrams from Jews there were many offering Hawke their houses and cars as refuges for his family. Non-Jews made similar offers – a Western Australian businessman telephoned to offer his private aeroplane to fly the family to safety in the west. A Supreme Court judge wrote, '... you have had the moral courage ... while others in high places, known for their articulate professions of the Brotherhood of Man, have remained silent'. Another senior lawyer and an ALP member wrote,

> Gough will never know what chills he sent down our spines . . . with that 'even-handed neutrality' statement of his. It was so cold and so lacking in insight . . . I suddenly felt insecure here, for the first time in my life.

There were very few unfavourable letters. Some began, 'Mr Jew Hawke'. A regular critic, who signed himself 'Joe the Worker', wrote on this occasion: 'Your invitation to Zionists to take over your well-planned homes and holidays for the Australian worker is a clear indication that you also support the multi-national corporations and enterprises who [sic] dominate our finances.' Meanwhile, in the trade union movement and in the ALP there was anger: 'You have no right to pursue your personal views about Israel when Australian workers finance your trips overseas.' 'You [and Whitlam] have a duty to the people of Australia to control yourselves. Otherwise you will be guilty of sabotaging the Labor Party and the people, as did Billy Hughes and Lyons years ago.'[6]

When Hawke returned to work in January 1974 it was to plunge straight in to the predicament within the upper echelons of the ALP that his outspokenness as president of the party had caused. He was told that the Prime Minister and other members of the federal executive had exhausted their patience with him, and he would be sacked. 'The phones were running hot, all through January', a senior ALP man remarked. In mid-January Hawke gave a television interview to Mike Schildberger in the office of Eddie Kornhauser, at the time a Melbourne hotel owner. Kornhauser was a shrewd businessman and one of Hawke's close friends. When the interview was over Hawke had a violent argument with Schildberger, a non-Zionist Jew, over Israel. Kornhauser, a strong Zionist, was so astonished by the passion of Hawke's commitment to Israel that, he said,

'For the first time I realised, "This man is real". And that night I determined to try to do something for him.' Hawke had told Kornhauser that he was going to be removed from the presidency of the ALP. Kornhauser had a number of IOUs out in the party, which he had supported handsomely over the years. He decided he would call them in.

Meanwhile, Hawke refused to keep silent on Israel. On 26 January he addressed a conference of the Zionist Federation of Australia and New Zealand in Sydney. He was still being escorted by bodyguards and the hall where the meeting was held was under heavy police surveillance. Hawke wore the traditional Jewish skullcap as he spoke to a group that was already hyper-charged with emotion. He scorned the even-handed interpretation that Whitlam had given to ALP policy on the Middle East and went on to say,

> Oil is a murky substance and it has, I believe, blurred the vision of men of goodwill ...We cannot be even-handed in judgment between states, any more than between individuals, when one side is bent upon the physical destruction of the other. In the 1930s appeasement under threat and blackmail permitted, among other things, the holocaust in which six million of our fellow human beings, who happened to be Jews, were exterminated. All mankind was diminished by those events. I do not speak here for my party or for the industrial movement which I lead. But as an individual Australian, I know that I am not an island and I know that if we allow the bell to be tolled for Israel it will have tolled for me, for us all.[7]

There was a standing ovation.

On 14 February the ALP federal executive was to meet. It would be the first meeting to discuss the government's failure to win Parramatta and to win the referenda. The Hawke camp had decided to bring up the question of the Middle East. The numbers would be close but within the party those who were

furious with Hawke for his criticisms of the government and
the Prime Minister were confident they could force Hawke to
resign. This has been one of the better-kept secrets in the ALP.
Even in 1981 executive members were unwilling to talk about it,
including Hawke, whose only comment is, 'I can't really remember that'. Others too have developed amnesia. However, a letter
dated 19 February 1974[8] to Eddie Kornhauser suggests that the
move against Hawke was serious and failed because of the hard
lobbying conducted by Hawke's supporters. It appears that the
attitude of Egerton was critical, for if he would not agree to accept
the presidency there could be no smooth transition, but a party
brawl. As it was Egerton (most unwillingly) recalled, 'Gough
was saying to me, "Mr President, Mr President". Well ... I've
never had any time for Gough. I stuck by my mates.'

The executive minutes reveal little: merely that on a motion,
moved by Egerton and seconded by David Combe, to debate the
situation in the Middle East, the executive tied 8–8, and it was
therefore resolved in the negative.[9] The voting line-up seems
to show that before the meeting opened, a Left–Right alliance
against the Hawke group had come to an agreement with the
latter, and that the alliance itself aborted the plan. One person
who reluctantly spoke of the affair gave an explanation that has
the ring of realpolitik truth:

> They tried to take Bob head on and saw it would be very dif-
> ficult. So they called that off and went underground against
> him – used the news media, the smear campaign in the party.
> They're the sort of people who don't much like the light of
> day and prefer to work in the dark.

The speaker made clear that he did not include Whitlam in this
group.

Hawke escaped with a reprimand about his outspokenness.
But his problems within the party were only just beginning for
he had now earned the enmity of many Caucus members and all
the Left-wingers.

A prominent Left-wing figure on the federal executive was Bill Hartley, former secretary of the Victorian branch, and as devoted a supporter of the Palestinians as Hawke was of the Israelis. Hartley is a friendly, personable man who, after being a Liberal in his youth, made a change to radical politics. He was active in his opposition to state aid for non-government schools and the Vietnam War and after that turned his attention to the Palestinians. Later he became an employee of the government of Iraq and championed the 'People's Revolution' in Iran. He and Hawke had fallen out in 1970 over federal intervention into the Victorian branch of the ALP but were still on reasonably friendly terms in 1974. Hartley was, and still remains, at the extreme perimeter of the Socialist Left faction of the Victorian ALP and was for many years the faction's representative on the federal executive, one of the two Victorian delegates to the executive.

Hawke was in such poor shape before the 14 February meeting that Hazel, stalwart as ever, had accompanied him to Canberra. That night Hartley came to their room and he and Hawke had a long, 'fairly amicable', Hawke said, argument about the Middle East. It was the last fairly amicable meeting between them. Hawke developed during 1974 a hatred for Hartley because of the latter's published assertions about Israel, which included comments such as 'International Zionism collaborated with the Nazis';[10] and 'Israel is a huge Ghetto founded on a monstrous injustice [to Palestinians, which] should be replaced by a State containing virtues which Israel has never had, and never could have: an open society, equality, political and religious pluralism, freedom, democracy and amity with its neighbours'. Hartley's notions about the Middle East enjoyed currency in Socialist Left circles, and Hawke's determination to contest them at every opportunity was to intensify his struggle with the Left. The Yom Kippur War, which marked the beginning of Israel's conversion by the international community into a pariah state, was also the beginning of Hawke's pariahdom in the eyes of the Left. By the end of the decade he had, among radicals, the image of a monster: a corrupt and greedy man, a friend to millionaires and a 'fascist regime', an enemy of the poor and weak.

That night in the Canberra Rex Hotel Hawke had drinks with party officials and a group of journalists, during which he expressed the views that he had been unable to, earlier that day, in the federal executive. He said,

> I had these feelings: an enormous sense of frustration that people thought that the Yom Kippur War was just another war – so what? I was also horrified by the callousness of attitudes: people were almost blaming Israel for having been in a scrap, and, ho-hum, it might happen again. And following from that, I wanted to try to get home the message that if an attempt to obliterate Israel recurred and if Israel had tactical nuclear weapons, they would be used.

It appears that only Hawke's last point – which he illustrated dramatically by saying that if he were Israel's prime minister and were faced with the destruction of his country, he would feel bound to employ tactical nuclear arms in self-defence – got through to his audience. His agitate-and-educate conversation with the group was not an interview, and was therefore off the record. But on 16 February Sydney's *Daily Telegraph* carried a front-page story headlined, 'I'D A-BOMB ARABS, SAYS HAWKE'. Three days later the popular television program, *A Current Affair*, broadcast a jingle to the tune of the Jewish folksong, *Hava Nagila*, which implied that Hawke was nuclear-bomb happy. He sued on both accounts for libel and won costs against the *Telegraph* and a settlement from *A Current Affair*, but the damage to his reputation had been enormous.

Throughout Hawke's career many of his failures, like this one, have arisen from the same source as his successes: that behind what he says there is an attitude of mind and a system of values that people either grasp spontaneously, or not at all. It is often not the fault of Hawke's audience that he is misunderstood, for he talks in a sort of shorthand, on the assumption that others share his thinking. In conversation with him it is necessary to fill in or to translate much of what he has left unsaid or has stated in his own brand of laconic communication: a twitch of his mouth, a pause, a shrug, a look of puzzlement in return for puzzlement. One early example of the lacunae in his communications was his attitude towards Cecil Rhodes and Rhodes scholars, which none of his peers understood. A later example came from a very senior public servant who was involved in Hawke's first strike negotiations: the man recalled being initially confounded by Hawke's verbal shorthand. He commented, 'Bob said that "for obvious reasons" such and such could not happen. Those reasons were not at all obvious to me. It was only after lunch that Bob explained. His sincerity, his conviction and his total honesty then came through.' The public servant, who requested anonymity, is a man of unusually sharp intelligence and subtlety; less gifted people are more likely to be bemused by what Hawke says. Good journalists who attempt to maintain objectivity and therefore deliberately resist falling into rapport with Hawke often achieve this at the expense of understanding him.

A second aspect, which is both an advantage and a disadvantage, is Hawke's direct expression of anger. Clyde Holding recalled an evening when he and Hawke were arguing about Hugh Gaitskell:

> Bob wanted me to agree with him that Gaitskell was a bastard. I wasn't really interested, but Bob got intense about it. When I wouldn't agree with him he grabbed me and began shaking me or banging my arm on the table, I can't remember which, saying, 'Go on! Say it! Admit Gaitskell's a bastard!' People who aren't used to him, who don't know that's just the bloke's style, get very upset.

Many people are half-deafened by Hawke's intensity and find it difficult to follow what he is saying because their emotional reaction to him has partly shut down their thinking processes and Hawke's arguments come through to them simplified by the flood of adrenalin he has aroused.

One of those present in the Canberra Rex on the night of 14 February recalled that when Hawke had spoken of nuclear weapons, and had been challenged: 'You cannot justify the use of nuclear weapons under any circumstances', Hawke had replied,

> Why? Because of world morality? Be damned to world morality – the world has stood by for twenty-five years and watched attempts to push Israel into the sea without lifting a finger. If I were the Israeli prime minister I wouldn't give a damn about world morality – I would use the atomic bomb to protect my own.[11]

Had Hawke gone through the steps of his argument, beginning at Yad Vashem and leading on to the Israeli war memorials, his audience may have had a better grasp of his ideas. As it was, he simply expected them to *know* the effect the Holocaust has had upon Israeli attitudes, to *know* that Israelis have never forgiven and, perhaps, will never forgive the rest of the world because of the Holocaust, and to *know* that Israelis regard Gentile morality as bankrupt. They grasped, it seems, none of this background but remembered only the vivid foreground of his anger.

The months from the end of November, when the death threat was made, through to April, when Hawke gathered himself together for a federal election campaign, were terrible ones for the whole family. Hawke had been an absentee father for years; suddenly it had come home to him how dear the children were, and for the first time since his early days at the ACTU he decided he must make time for a family life. A doctor who was a long-term friend and who had treated Hawke after he had been on drinking benders owned a farm in Gippsland and had offered it to the Hawkes as a weekend retreat earlier in 1973. A police guard put on duty there in 1974 noted that Hawke was pitifully overwrought.

There were other symptoms: one night in early 1974 Hawke was drinking in the Boulevard Hotel in Sydney with a friend when he suddenly thought that a waiter, walking towards him, intended assault. Hawke threw a punch at the waiter and had to be forced to leave the bar and go to his room. Next day the friend upbraided Hawke for his behaviour:

> He looked appalled when I told him all the things he'd done the night before. We were having lunch in a restaurant. He said, 'Oh, God, why do I do these things?' and started to cry. But he had the guts to go back to the Boulevard, find the waiter and apologise to him.

The Attorney-General's department spent months investigating if indeed a terrorist group was operating in Australia and intended to murder the Hawke children. Its officers came to the conclusion that neither Black September guerrillas nor other Arab terrorists had reached Australia, and that the threat was, therefore, probably from a crank – which is not to say that cranks are incapable of murder. Hawke said later with bitter anguish, 'It worried me that, maybe, the kids had been through all of that for nothing'. When questioned further his demeanour becomes threatening, with a look that says, 'I refuse to discuss that'.

By April 1974 the worst period was over. Hawke's recovery was speeded by national political concerns, for the Opposition – emboldened by the government's failure in Parramatta; with the referenda; and by its mismanagement of an attempt to play political thimble-and-pea (the Gair Affair) – had summoned the nerve to delay Supply in the Senate. Whitlam decided to hold a general election. Hawke's popularity rating was very high and the party decided to use him to the utmost in the election campaign. He was especially useful because of the disillusion with government in the trade union movement, which was so great that a number of unions had disaffiliated from the ALP. This had depleted the party's campaign funds. Another of Hawke's uses was that he was by now an excellent fundraiser. David Combe said later,

I don't know how much Bob has raised for the party, but it is certainly hundreds of thousands of dollars. We could be confident that he would pack any hall. And he got a lot of dough from businessmen. There was always an irony that the Left would shriek about Hawke's being friendly with big businessmen but when he got big cheques from them there was no suggestion that the money should be sent back, or that he'd done the wrong thing.

During the campaign Hawke was anxious that Whitlam should win back the hearts of the Jewish community. Kornhauser gave a breakfast in his hotel, the Chevron, at which the Prime Minister was to address Melbourne's Jews and calm their fears about the government's joining the rush away from Israel. Unfortunately, the soothing turned into a confrontation, for during the meeting Whitlam demanded, 'What do you people want?' Years later Jews were still wrathful that Whitlam had called them 'you people'. Saul Same said,

Gough lost the Jewish vote when he said those words. But people made a distinction for Bob. If there were a fundraising function and Bob was speaking everyone wanted to come. I remember organising a dinner and being doubtful about approaching a particular man, one of the most senior industrialists in Melbourne. I rang him and he said, 'What! For Bob Hawke? I'll cancel a wedding.' And he did.

Even Hawke's enemies acknowledged that his efforts during the 1974 campaign were heroic and that the government's victory, with five seats in hand, owed as much to him as to Whitlam.

His determination to spend the weekends undisturbed in the country had of course been abandoned during the campaign. When the election was over his weekend peace was never completely restored. By May 1974 it was obvious that the economy was seriously ill; inflation was surging forward, thanks in large part to the sharpest weapon in Middle East politics: the price of oil. There was an epidemic of strikes; wage claims were extra-ordinary and fed back into the inflationary spiral; the Treasury restrictions on money supply were biting hard on business; and unemployment was increasing. After a while the demands on Hawke were such that a telephone had to be installed at the farm. He was called back to town more and more, and gradually the dream of a 'normal' family life drifted away.

Hawke had cancelled two ILO meetings, fearful that if he were in Europe, where Arab terrorists were most active, he could be killed. But in June he decided he must keep an appointment to address a conference in Oxford. Before he left he called on Kornhauser to ask him to look after Hazel and the children for him if he were murdered. Hawke had no idea what his exact financial situation was, except that he was in debt. He did not know if he had any life insurance policies, for Hazel looked after such matters. Kornhauser recalled,

> Bob was giving me a heart attack! No money, a wife, three children! What am I going to do? It's Saturday night and he's leaving the next morning. We owed him so much ... I assured Bob that if anything happened to him Hazel and the children would be cared for.

The Israelis also considered it their duty to protect Hawke, and when he arrived there en route for London, a bodyguard was waiting for him. Governments normally provide bodyguards only for ambassadors or heads of state. An Australian diplomat in Israel described the bodyguard as 'nine feet [2.75 m] tall and nine feet wide, covered in weapons and muttering into a walkie-talkie all the time. It wasn't very pleasant.' In England Hawke's back gave way again after a two-year remission of trouble and he had to board his aircraft home as an invalid in a wheelchair.

By August he was warning that the government would not survive unless it brought down the rate of inflation within a year. Meanwhile, throughout 1974, one after another of Hawke's ACTU enterprise schemes had been neglected and the enterprise ideas were fading away. There had been an outright rejection from the unions of any joint ventures with Histadrut, because of the odium now attached to Israel. Other schemes had vanished because Hawke had been too ill or too distracted with strike negotiations and other work (he was already a member of the Jackson committee as well as on the Board of the Reserve Bank), to give them time. All round, it had been a miserable twelve months.

Hawke was personally consoled when, in September, he was re-elected unopposed as president of the ALP and the federal executive paid tribute to the efforts he had made to have the government returned to office. Some office. Inflation for the year was 16.3 per cent, strikes had cost 6 292 500 working days lost and more than a quarter of a million were unemployed. Before the Budget was introduced, a month late, Hawke held pre-Budget discussions with the government, arguing for cuts in indirect taxes and the income taxes of the less well paid; a reduction in interest rates; the introduction of quarterly wage adjustments to curb wage claims; and indexation of income tax. At a special conference of ACTU affiliated unions he had managed to wring from delegates a commitment to try to pull together with the government, even to the extent, as the meeting's resolution stated, of giving 'sympathetic consideration to supporting attempts by the Government to acquire ... powers' to deal with economic problems. This was almost a reversal of the unions' previous policy on the incomes referendum.

By October he and Whitlam were friends again, lunching together at The Lodge. It was the calm before the next storm.

SEVENTEEN

IT MAY BE THAT future historians with a fondness for the convenience of dates will note 6 October 1973 as the day on which the centuries of world domination by the values and laws that arose from Christendom ended. Just a year afterwards, on 13 November 1974, in the General Assembly of the United Nations, Christianity's younger cousin-faith, Islam, revealed the triumph of its reinvigoration: with a gun holster visible on his hip, Yasser Arafat, leader of the PLO, entered the hall, strode to the podium and said, 'Today I have come bearing an olive branch and a freedom fighter's gun. Do not let the olive branch fall from my hand. I repeat: do not let the olive branch fall from my hand.'

It was the first time a man had addressed the international parliament with such dramatic symbolism. The most dangerous weapon previously displayed there by a speaker was Nikita Khrushchev's shoe, with which he had banged the lectern. Arafat's gun holster was a sign of the changing times: as a British diplomat had quipped in earlier days, 'The Kingdom of Heaven may run on love, but the Kingdom of Earth runs on oil'. The PLO was admitted to observer status in the UN; before the end of the decade an interesting term had entered common speech: 'the Islamic Bomb'. Nuclear weapons had once been 'American' or 'Russian' or 'Chinese'. Abruptly they were not only national, but religious.

For the rest of the 1970s Hawke fought against the crusades of a new era. He tried to be a mediator: in the PLO, in Israel, in Egypt and Jordan – extraordinary, but futile, efforts. He even

381

tried to meet Yasser Arafat when, in late 1974, a senior Egyptian journalist who had contacts with the PLO visited Australia and offered to sound out the possibilities for such a meeting. However, by then the PLO was riding high and had little need or desire to hold discussions with such a committed Zionist as Hawke. The increasingly bitter exchanges between Hawke and Hartley made it all the less likely.

Early in 1975 Hawke learned that, with Hartley's encouragement, a PLO delegation had been invited to visit Australia and that the government had agreed to issue visas. Hawke was outraged. The Australian government would not, for example, allow representatives of the Ustashi, the group dedicated to the overthrow of the government of Yugoslavia, to enter the country. The PLO visa issue was, for Hawke, another example of the Whitlam government's dual morality. Hawke's diary notes for 29 January 1975: '8.25 a.m. spoke to Whitlam about PLO visas'. Many others spoke, too. The trip was cancelled.

The next day Hawke had to chair an ALP federal executive meeting that would finalise business for the party's biennial conference, due the following week, in Terrigal.

Terrigal is a holiday resort town on the north coast of New South Wales. The choice of a hot weather playground for the party's meeting was ill advised, for matters of state should never be seen without neckties, or in the company of bare shoulders. Hawke said,

> The Terrigal conference would have been the worst the ALP ever had. The whole thing was a schemozzle. Ministers were writing their policy statements hours before going up to the conference. The assembling of an economic policy statement was – oh, ludicrous. There was no wages policy debate. There was an unreal air to the whole show; the government clearly felt that this was an ALP conference that was irrelevant, because *they* were in government, *they* were running things, *they* knew what they were going to do – or didn't know what they were going to do – but at any rate, it was for *them* to

decide. So what was the use of this conference? And matters were worsened by the determination of the press to convey the whole thing as an exercise in hedonism. The photographs of people sitting around the swimming pool, being thrown in the pool . . .

Hawke himself was guilty of playing into the hands of those sections of the press that were now extremely hostile to the government and were eager to project an image of it that was undignified. He agreed to assist the promotion of the government-sponsored Old Sydney Town project and, allotted the part of a convict, was photographed shirtless, his hands bound, and apparently being whipped by an attractive young woman who worked in the office of the new federal Treasurer, Dr Jim Cairns. Egerton complained about the photograph at the time, and said later that Hawke had been distracted from his duties during the conference by his own streak of hedonism.

Hawke gave the address that opened proceedings, a rallying cry for solidarity, but he was still writing it minutes before he delivered it, so the opportunity for having the speech distributed to the news media was missed. He had the valid excuse that he had no speech writers, no support staff at all, as president of the ALP. Ministers had plenty of hired hands – rather too many, and of the wrong type, in the view of the press.

For some months the news media had been focusing upon the person and position of a former air hostess and director of some failed companies, Junie Morosi. Morosi had in late 1974 become the personal assistant to the Deputy Prime Minister and federal Treasurer, Dr Jim Cairns. Their relationship had aroused curiosity. Cairns had been subjected to a barrage of attack and innuendo, but his fine response to the Cyclone Tracy disaster on Christmas Eve 1974 had served to recoup his prestige. People had temporarily forgotten about Junie Morosi. Then on the second-last day of the conference that, while it had produced little of value in terms of policy, had at least avoided any Left–Right brawls or motions demanding the nationalisation of BHP,

Cairns gave a personal interview. The journalist he talked to, Toni McRae, happened to be the wife of an aspiring Liberal politician. He admitted to this woman that he had 'a kind of love' for Junie Morosi. The news media went wild. Only once in a generation can editors hope for a comment as fey as that from a senior politician. The silly photographs aside, the Terrigal conference had been depicted generally as a dull turn-out, which is how the government wanted it to be seen. Overnight, Cairns' candid comments turned it into a farce.

George Rockey who, along with Abeles and Kornhauser, had helped to nurse Hawke through 1974, had driven to Terrigal to collect him. Rockey described himself as 'a very low-profile person'. He was small, neat and rather introverted, in marked contrast to his partner's, Abeles', largeness and ebullience. He and Hawke already had the type of easy friendship that Hawke can form in an instant, but between them there was a deeper attraction, an almost shy drawing together of opposites. Rockey was a gambling man and had been 'a bottle of Scotch a night' drinker, but had become teetotal in 1971 because he had reached the stage when every time he drank alcohol he fainted. He was thirteen years Hawke's senior and their relationship, much more than that between Hawke and Abeles, was another father–son affair. For all his gentleness and interest in psychology and metaphysics, Rockey was also worldly, even world-weary. He had worked as an intelligence agent during the war and perhaps because of this, and his later experience as a Jungian analysand, was not inclined to take people on face value. He had known plenty of betrayals. Early in their relationship he had decided to put Hawke's honesty to a test with a 'five-figure cheque', made out to Hawke, mentioning that it was for the ALP campaign fund. Years later he remarked, still with an echo of that first pleasure in his voice, 'And you know, next day I got a receipt for it from the secretary of the party'.

When he collected Hawke at Terrigal, Hawke was depressed about the state of the government and the farcical image that, in the end, the conference had had forced upon it. Rockey recalled,

I said to Bob the political situation was hopeless and told him that he had better bail out now. I offered him a sort of bribe. I said he could have any job he wanted in industry – he could be earning $100 000 a year, instead of living hand-to-mouth, with not enough money to educate his children. I said, 'Look, leave the party. Leave the trade unions and think of yourself and Hazel and your children.' He became so angry with me. He said, 'George, stop the car. I'm getting out.' I knew then that I'd met a good man, a person of real honour.

Another matter of honour soon arose for Hawke. In early May 1975 Francis Blanchard, the new director-general of the ILO, sent his senior assistant, Bernard Fortin, on what Fortin described as 'a secret mission' to Australia to elicit Hawke's help for the ILO. Blanchard had not met Hawke at this stage, so it was a measure of Hawke's reputation within the ILO that the director-general approached him to assist the organisation – in the affair that was later known as the Crisis of 1975.

The ILO had been the first of the United Nations bodies to feel the sting of Arab vengeance against Israel and the old colonial powers. In June 1974, at the annual conference that Hawke had not attended because of the death threats, delegates had voted overwhelmingly for a resolution condemning 'the policy of discrimination, racism and violation of trade union freedoms and rights practised by the Israeli authorities in Palestine and in the other occupied Arab Territories'. There had been no investigation by the ILO to discover if in fact such abuses existed in Israeli-occupied territory. In the past, when a state had been condemned, there had been a formal ILO investigation beforehand. However, times had changed. The Islamic countries of the Middle East, Africa and South-East Asia, joined by the Soviet bloc states and a few Europeans, in this case Spain and Greece, as well as Mexico, had an automatic majority. Having passed a resolution condemning Israel, they then passed a second: to have the ILO investigate conditions of workers in Israel. The resolutions, coming from nations in which trade union freedom was a joke, were staggeringly cynical and, legally, ranked with the adventures of Alice in Wonderland: sentence first, then judge. At the same conference the PLO had submitted a request to the director-general, Blanchard, to be admitted as an observer to all the activities and meetings of the ILO. The PLO could not request membership because the ILO constitution limits membership to states. The Americans had let it be known that if the PLO were admitted to observer status – a question that would be decided in June 1975 – the USA would withdraw from the ILO. George Meany, who had chief say on the issue, was intransigent. If the Americans withdrew it was feared that America's allies – for example, West Germany, which had the most important trade union movement in Europe – would also withdraw. Blanchard recalled,

I was desperate to find a solution that would allow the PLO some sort of status in the ILO but which would occur in a way that would not violate the constitution or the standing orders of the International Labour Conference. On one side we had the Arabs saying their demand was absolutely justified; on the other, the Americans, totally intransigent; and in the middle a lot of the European nations very embarrassed. Everything was complicated by Vietnam.

By early 1975, after a decade of American fighting there, the North Vietnamese armies were sweeping south; in late April North Vietnamese tanks rumbled into Saigon and, amid horrendous panic, one of the Indo-Chinese wars ended. At home and abroad American morale was at a nadir. Uncle Sam was in an irrational frame of mind, and was not yet accustomed to the idea that the non-Communist global community, ordered about by Washington since the end of World War II, had changed, and that there were, now, many centres of power outside the USA.

Blanchard continued,

Nations were using the war to insult and attack America and so, of course, the Americans were particularly sensitive. I thought of Bob Hawke as someone who could help because of several factors: he was totally orthodox on Israel and I knew he had a lot of credit in Washington and in the American Federation of Labor. George Meany liked him. I believed Bob was a man to get the Americans to listen, although I must say that Meany, a fascinating man, was absolutely The Chairman, the boss ... I had the impression, which I later found to be true, that Bob was fascinated by the world at large, beyond the shores of Australia, and fascinated by foreign policy. To me that meant he would not look at problems in a narrow way, but in the wider context of world politics. Bob had criticisms of the ILO, which he would make in private, but at the same time he understood, he had strong feelings about, its importance as an institution. And he could realise what a real crisis, as an institution, it was facing.

Fortin relayed Blanchard's request to Hawke, who agreed to fly to Geneva via Washington. Before arriving in Australia Fortin had gone in secret to Cairo, to ask the leader of the Egyptian workers' delegation, Anwar Salama, a former Minister of Labour, to try to seek a compromise also. Salama had readily agreed. The Yom Kippur War had been a catharsis for the Egyptians, for their armies' vast incursions into Israeli-held territory had exorcised the humiliation of the 1967 war. The Egyptian leadership had announced, and the nation believed, that they had won a great military victory during the 1973 war, and now that Egyptian pride was purring they were thinking more peaceful thoughts. The Egyptians agreed to lean on the Syrians and other hardline anti-Israel delegations so that a compromise on PLO observer status could be reached in the ILO's Standing Orders Committee. The International Labour Conference would then, automatically, pass the committee's resolution.

Clyde Cameron was to lead the Australian government delegation to the International Labour Conference, but on the eve of his departure Whitlam sacked him as Minister for Labour. Cameron, however, refused to be sacked and the Prime Minister had to ask the Governor-General, Sir John Kerr, to withdraw Cameron's commission – a somewhat ironic circumstance, at least for Cameron, in view of later events. His dismissal was one of a growing number of changes in the Whitlam ministry that added to the government's appearance of confusion. The drama over Cameron forced Hawke to abandon going first to Washington.

He set out in late May, breaking his journey to Switzerland in Athens, and from there went for a day's sightseeing to Delphi. At Delphi he received the news that Whitlam had performed a second miracle of bad timing.

Lance Barnard, the defence minister, had been miserable since he had lost the deputy prime ministership to Cairns. Barnard was a close friend of Whitlam. He had told the Prime Minister he wanted to leave politics and, since the post was becoming vacant, to be the next ambassador to Stockholm. This would mean a by-election in Barnard's seat, Bass, a Tasmanian electorate that had been egregiously affected by the tariff cuts. Whitlam had conceded to the request of his old friend, and so a by-election would be held in Bass on 26 June 1975. Hawke recalled, still stuttering five years later,

> I – I literally couldn't believe it! It was insane. And the reasons why it was insane were just so obvious. You had Malcolm Fraser [the new leader of the Opposition] looking around for a justification to bring the government down short of its term, and not having a justification – because, simply to assert that a government is doing badly is no reason to force it to the polls. So what do we do? We give a by-election gratuitously which Fraser was obviously going to use to say, 'Here is an opportunity for the nation to express its view about the Whitlam government'. And what were the circumstances? The economy in bad shape; the unions disaffected generally, but particularly in Bass, where the textile industry had been

decimated. On top of that Bass was a rural electorate and the rural lobbies *hated* Whitlam – they'd been throwing tomatoes at him – and further, Bass was not basically a Labor seat, but owed an enormous amount to the personality and position of Lance Barnard. So when you added all those things together, you could guarantee a huge swing. I hoped that if I kicked up enough fuss immediately, and was tough enough, there may have been a chance of turning Gough's decision around. There was no way in the world that I was going to allow, as president of the party, a position to be established where Whitlam or anyone else could act in a way which conveyed the impression that the ALP or the Labor government was his possession, in respect of which he could make decisions that could destroy it, and do so without criticism. I believed that the government was in the process of being destroyed by that decision about Bass, and that the Labor Party was being mortally hurt. The Galston decision had thrown away the seat of Parramatta; Bass was throwing away the Whitlam Labor government.

Hawke had one of his 'outbursts' to the news media: the Bass by-election was, he said, 'an act of Galstonian madness'. He returned quickly to Athens where the switchboard of his hotel had fifty telephone calls from Australia for him. He repeatedly told the news media that the decision was disastrous. He said later,

Gough never forgave me. Because what I said then and later, when I returned to Australia, proved to be right. Liberals confirmed my opinion – several of them told me afterwards that it was the Bass result which had made up Fraser's mind to go for our throats.

By the time Hawke arrived in Geneva he knew that his efforts to have the decision reversed were in vain; he began drinking heavily. People in Geneva who had known him for years and were used to his argumentativeness when drunk were shocked

by him, now. He was seething with bitterness and would verbally attack anyone. He bailed up a junior staff member in the
Australian embassy to ask sneeringly, 'Do you ever criticise your
boss? Do you just shut up and cop it when you know he's doing
something wrong? Have you got any guts?'

He kept working during the week, however, and took part
in confidential discussions between the representatives of the
United Arab Emirates, Kuwait, Jordan, Egypt, Israel, France, and
Australia, represented by him. The discussions were chaired by
Blanchard, and were promising, since all the Arab states were from
the soft-line camp and all agreed to lobby their hardline brothers.

On 3 June Blanchard had invited Hawke to a private interview,
their first meeting. Hawke had arrived half-drunk and, declining
an offer of afternoon tea, had asked for beer and drunk three bottles of it in quick succession. His language had been coarse but
fortunately Blanchard, who is very much the dignified French
mandarin, had not been able to understand much of Hawke's
swearing and Fortin, who was also present and whose English
is idiomatic, had not translated for him. Blanchard had formed
an unfavourable impression of Hawke from this encounter, but
nevertheless was willing to act upon the assurances of others that
Hawke was a better man than he appeared. During the interview
he had invited Hawke to lunch at his country estate in Gex the
following Sunday. By then Hawke had come to terms with his
misery over Bass. Barry Watchorn, a senior Australian diplomat
in Geneva, recalled, 'On Sunday morning there was a knock on
my door early and there was Bob, wreathed in smiles. He was
making an apology for the way he had behaved all week.'

At the luncheon in Gex the guests were Hawke, Fortin and
Parodi, the leader of the French government delegation. Their
purpose that day was to work out an amendment to the Arab
resolution that 'liberation movements be admitted to observer
status in the ILO', which would satisfy both the Arabs and
the Americans and would not violate the rules of the ILO. The
resolution, as it stood, was a monstrous piece of provocation
and a precedent that could turn the ILO into a political circus.

The PLO was committed in its charter to the total destruction of Israel, an 'illegal entity'. But Israel was a member of the ILO and the admission of the PLO – even with observer status only – could reduce the proceedings of the organisation to the level of a bear-baiting spectacle.

Bargaining is necessary for transcending differences of opinion; in Hawke bargaining (a prime political skill) is second nature. It was he who, during the luncheon at Gex, hit upon the words that could force the PLO, if it deeply desired to have observer status at the ILO, to bargain for that status. His amendment to the resolution was: 'that the liberation movement in question recognises the principles of the ILO and its Constitution and the right of all member states to continue in existence and participate in the work of the Organisation'. It was a masterstroke, for if the amendment were passed, the PLO would have to commit itself, before the world community, to rewriting its charter and withdrawing from it the demand that Israel be smashed – or, to abandon its plans to enter the ILO.

The four men were overjoyed. They had two and a half days left to sell the Gex amendment to the opposing camps. Blanchard recalled that by Monday evening, 'We felt we had sealed the thing. The Americans in private conversations accepted our formula, as had many of the Arabs.' The next step was to shepherd the amendment through the Standing Orders Committee of the Governing Body. Then, on 12 June, in plenary session of the International Labour Conference in the Palais des Nations, delegates would make their formal votes, having been advised how to vote by their factional representatives in the Standing Orders Committee, and everybody could get on with the business of the conditions of work, the status of female employees, child labour and other appropriate concerns.

It was the Americans, specifically George Meany, who set in process a chain reaction that ended all hopes. Meany, from Washington, instructed that the American delegation was to reject both the resolution and its amendment. There ensued, in the words of Francis Wolf, the ILO's legal adviser, 'a terrible battle in the Standing Orders Committee'. The Arabs flew into a rage because of the American attitude and announced that, in these circumstances, compromise was anathema. Salama and Hawke tried valiantly to bully and cajole the committee meeting to consider the wider context of its actions, but to no avail.

On the afternoon of 12 June Hawke rose with, as usual, just a few lines of notes, to address the plenary session. The Palais des Nations was packed; all the international galleries were filled; the world press was overflowing its gallery. After Arafat's triumph in the UN General Assembly six months earlier, this was the second great show of strength by the Islamic world. Tony Street, the shadow Minister for Labour, was attending the ILO for the first time and recalled,

> The atmosphere was electric with tension. Bob Hawke made a truly great speech. And it was like a Greek tragedy, because he stood there and pleaded, on international and humanitarian grounds, with those hundreds of delegates – and yet he knew, we all knew, that it was a lost cause. It was a tremendously moving speech, a magnificent piece of oratory – the best speech I've ever heard Bob make, one of the great speeches I've heard. And all for nothing.

Hawke, as he always does when the numbers are overwhelmingly against him, had wound himself up to believe that if he spoke forcefully enough he would be able to persuade some of the delegates to change their votes. He pressed hard on 'my friends from the continent of Africa', reminding them that 'members of the Australian trade union movement ... were prepared to face jail if necessary, in the early 1970s, to take industrial action to support the people of Africa'. He went on to stress that the ALP government had 'gone beyond sweet words in assisting liberation movements' and referred to the financial contributions the Whitlam government had made to the liberation movements of Africa. He continued,

So, I am speaking here with clean hands in terms of an absolute, practical and dedicated commitment to genuine liberation movements. It is in that sense that I plead with this Conference ... All that we are asking in this amendment is that you say to the PLO, as to any other movement: 'You are welcome to come into the ILO, provided you change your position about the right to exist of an existing member State'. And that is all we ask ... Delegates, you will never know how close we appeared to come in the work of the Standing Orders Committee to arriving at a position which would recognise Israel's right to existence ... unfortunately, the reasonableness of [the Egyptians] was overcome by the blind commitment of some people to the destruction of Israel ... In making a passionate defence of Israel no one is more conscious than I am of the fundamental problems of the Palestinian people and I believe that they have a right to a State, a right to a peaceful existence in that area of the world, but not at the expense of the obliteration of Israel.

Hawke concluded by warning that if the amendment were rejected,

Delegates, you are going to be the initial actors in the destruction of the ILO – no organisation can have its noble purposes emasculated by being made a political forum which is going to be used for the purposes of advancing the cause of the destruction of a member State. I appeal to you as earnestly as I possibly can ... if you take this step without voting for the amendment to the proposal before you, then I repeat that you will have taken the first steps down the road to the destruction of the ILO.[1]

The brilliance of the speech had been in Hawke's delivery, in his timing and intonation, and the passionate conviction he had conveyed through his voice and body language. People were unanimous that it was one of the best speeches ever made in the ILO and ranked with those of Leon Juro. But there was no clapping at the end of it, just a tense silence. Hawke returned to his seat beside the other Australians for one of the more bitter moments of his life: the only countryman who lent forward to shake his hand was his political opponent, Tony Street. Hawke said,

> I knew the Australian voting position in advance, but it was bloody devastating just the same to go and sit down with your mates, with the representatives of your government, and have them all looking the other way. I was disgusted by my own government.[2] And others. The leader of the British government delegation came up to me, backslapping and smiling, and said, 'My word, we'd love to vote for that'. And I replied rather sharply, 'Well why the hell don't you?' And he backed off – 'Oh, dear boy! Our vote would have made no difference . . .' Even a Cuban bloke told me and told other people in the ILO that, had he been free to make his own decision, he would have voted for the amendment.

Fortin said later of Hawke's warning that rejection of the amendment would have dire consequences for the ILO, 'Bob said what we – the ILO hierarchy – wanted to say, but could not'.

The PLO was admitted to observer status in the ILO, without any provisos. At Blanchard's request Hawke flew to Washington to try to persuade Meany to change his attitude about American withdrawal. It was fruitless. In November 1975 the US Secretary of State, Henry Kissinger, wrote formally to Blanchard telling him that the USA was withdrawing.

In 1980, a few weeks after Meany died, America announced that it wished to rejoin the organisation, but in the interim there had been a second drastic curtailment of ILO functions. Hawke was often the emissary between the ILO and the United States: 'He was one of my main channels of communication', Blanchard said.

While he had been abroad, and Australians at home had known little of his work in Geneva and Washington, a Gallup poll had been published showing that Hawke was now the most popular man in the country. Whitlam's popularity was declining inexorably; every week was bringing a new episode in the saga of the Loans Affair;[3] politics had turned into a national blood sport, with the government a frantic, panting fox. On 26 June the electorate in Bass swung by 15 per cent against the ALP, and the government knew it was done for. The only question now was the time of death.

Within the electorate Hawke became an object of increasing curiosity and, for those sympathetic to Labor, of hope. A month after the Bass by-election he agreed to give Mike Schildberger a national television interview that would focus upon Hawke, the man. Schildberger had known Hawke for a decade and like most other journalists in the country knew that he was objectionable when drunk, but this had never been publicised. Among journalists themselves there is a tradition of becoming as drunk as princes: perhaps this, and Hawke's reputation as a man who was quick with a libel writ, had inhibited the news media from referring to it. However, by 1975 Hawke's popularity made his heavy drinking a matter of legitimate public interest. Schildberger had drawn up a list of questions, based upon the assumption that Hawke would in the future be leader of the ALP, questions that covered his political and social ideas and his personal strengths. The penultimate question was 'What are your weaknesses?' The final one, 'It is said you have a drinking problem: comment?' The show was going to air live. Schildberger offered to tell Hawke his questions in advance but, with his typical self-confidence, Hawke replied he did not want to see them. At Schildberger's second-last question, Hawke hesitated for an instant then, to the horror of his friends and the disbelief of other political observers, replied that, as for weaknesses, he had a drinking problem. Schildberger could see what the television screens did not show – that Hawke's hands shook with nervousness as he spoke. Schildberger said, 'It was probably the most emotional interview I have ever had'. The cameras were switched off and Schildberger passed Hawke his clipboard with the list of questions, pointing to the last one. Hawke gasped, 'Thank God I told the truth!'

Only those who knew Ellie's detestation for alcohol, and knew that Hawke, even now at forty-five, was embarrassed if she saw him drinking, realised what an effort it had been for him to admit that he had a 'problem'. He said later, 'When we were in Maitland, when I was five to nine years old, and my mother first started work for the WCTU, she had made this connection: that alcohol was death and corruption, that it was destruction'. He had defied her and now had publicly admitted the consequences: he was the captive of alcohol. In his reply to Schildberger, Hawke had gone on to say that if he were to become leader of the ALP he would give up drinking.

The next day and for weeks later the press was full of the story. Hawke's supporters believed he had made a gaffe equal to Cairns' 'kind of love'. On 31 July, two days after the Schildberger interview, Whitlam arrived at Parliament House. Journalists were used to being brushed off by the Prime Minister on the steps of the parliament, and held back. But there was a gleam of merriment in the leader's eye and his imperial head was turning this way and that bestowing smiles of welcome. Reporters realised the Prime Minister wished to say a few words, and approached him. Someone asked about his drinking and Whitlam, with that straight-faced wit of which he is a master, drew a deep breath and replied, 'I intend to turn over a new leaf and undertake steady drinking from now on. I realise, of course, that to hold my position I have to undertake a rigorous program of social drinking.' He added that he expected future ALP executive meetings to be 'like gatherings of Alcoholics Anonymous'.

The public contempt that Hawke's supporters feared his admission would arouse did not eventuate. Instead, his popularity increased. In a country of heavy drinkers Hawke had admitted to a national sin. A couple of weeks later a record company released 'The Bob Hawke Drinking Song', which referred to him as 'champion of the underdog' and had a chorus, 'Let's drink to Bob Hawke'. His very ordinariness – his flashy suits, flat voice, friendly manner and vulgar humour – had been among his greatest advantages with crowds, because he appeared so like everyone else, only more so: the quintessential Australian, the little Aussie battler. It was an image that was partly true. But as Hawke had told Schildberger and other Jews many times, 'If I were to have my life again, I would want to be born a Jew'. And when in high spirits, talking of Israel, he would say, '*I'm* an Israeli'. He knew himself to have many facets. While at home Australians thought of Hawke as a 'true Australian', abroad people saw him as a cosmopolitan. Blanchard remarked,

> He brought things that were Australian with him – he spoke very fast and used all sorts of expressions which people could not understand – but at the same time he behaved as if he were at home always. I realised he was a man who was at home with the world.

In July Hawke, in a blaze of publicity, launched ACTU–Solo, a petrol-retailing venture that offered large discounts. Souter had done most of the work to establish ACTU–Solo, but left the public relations to Hawke, who reaped immense popularity from it. The petrol discounts saved the motoring public hundreds of millions of dollars – at first, directly, through ACTU–Solo; later because other retailers were forced to discount also. While it is impossible to quantify the effect on prices that the outlawing of retail price maintenance (thanks to Bourkes) achieved, Hawke believes that, like ACTU–Solo, Bourkes saved customers hundreds of millions of dollars. He regards these two enterprises as among the major achievements of his presidency.

The public at large, especially a growing number of people who, in letters to Hawke, drew attention to the fact that they were Liberal voters, had come to see him as courageous and concerned for the national interest, and had abandoned the idea – which had been bandied about constantly in his first two years as president of the ACTU – that Hawke was the cause of industrial unrest. However, within the Victorian ALP his problems were increasing. As the membership of the Whitlam ministry continued to change, rumours flew that Hawke would contest this or that seat of a disgruntled or disgraced former minister at the next election, and every bout of speculation about a seat was followed by warnings from representatives of the Socialist Left faction that Hawke could not win preselection in Victoria. Hawke said,

> As we moved into 1974–75 I was one who was, perhaps earlier than anyone else in the party, pointing out the change in economic circumstances and saying that we needed to adapt our thinking and our time-scale of expectations to various objectives. A lot of the Left didn't like that. They thought it was a sell-out position.

There had been row upon row between Hawke and the Socialist Left in Victorian meetings and one in the federal executive when, earlier in the year, Hawke had made what others described as a 'magnificently venomous' attack upon Hartley for an article criticising decisions at the Terrigal conference. The executive strongly censured Hartley. Significantly, Hawke's major ally in the attack on Hartley was John Ducker. That, in the Left's eyes, was another black mark against Hawke. Quietly, and as yet without a public name, the Stop Hawke campaign was operating.

Meanwhile, in the trade union movement, Hawke's position by late 1975 was one of unequalled authority. At the ACTU Congress that opened in Melbourne on 15 September he was at the height of his strength in the movement. For the first time since the Congress of 1939 there was not a single division involving a count of delegates' votes for or against recommendations by the ACTU executive. In the days leading up to the week-long meeting unionists had been subjected to an unprecedented barrage of comment from the news media and politicians about their responsibilities. Already there was talk that the Opposition, led by Malcolm Fraser, would block Supply in the Senate and thus force Whitlam to the polls again. After the scandals, real and counterfeit, that had dogged the government since the election of 1974, nobody in the Labor movement imagined that it could win a third time. Congress had assembled in a thoughtful mood.

Hawke's presidential address was an appeal for solidarity couched in sombre, Churchillian terms. He told delegates that, since the 1973 Congress, unemployment had increased by 266 per cent, that economic growth had declined by 158 per cent, that inflation had risen by 106 per cent, and that

> We ignore these facts at our peril ... [They are] a reflec-
> tion in this country of the fundamental malaise which has
> occurred [since 1973] in varying degrees in every advanced
> capitalist economic system. Whether their governments have
> been conservative, as in the United States, or social demo-
> cratic as in West Germany, all these countries have witnessed
> acceleration of inflation, rising unemployment and reduc-
> tions in growth rates.

He devoted nearly all of his speech to developing four themes. First, a defence of the government, in which he refuted the continual assertions that inflation and unemployment were all the fault of Labor. Second, he addressed the responsibility of the trade union movement, asking union leaders to 'restrain wage pushes well in excess of prices and productivity', and arguing 'our affiliates must recognise the full implications of their actions ... we must balance the self-interest of particular groups against the interests of workers as a whole'. Third, he spoke of the responsibility of the government, and in this context argued that it was up to the government to 'create the conditions within which [union] co-operation can be maximised'. He went on to ask (for the umpteenth time) for tax indexation and that the government avoid rises in indirect taxes and government charges, and that it expand the Regional Employment Development Scheme if unemployment remained high. And fourth, he spoke of the rights of the unions to free collective bargaining. This is the fundamental tenet and the primary function of trade union movements everywhere. It may seem illogical that Australia has a centralised wage-fixing system while at the same time we have – and have always had – collective bargaining. It is illogical, but then the system has grown haphazardly. Since the introduction of the total wage, in 1967, the illogicality has become more burdensome. Hawke, in reasserting the freedom of the unions to bargain collectively, was soothing their fears that wage indexation would mean a wage freeze. Beneath the surface of his message there lay another appeal: because we are free, we can choose, for a while, to be unfree. It was a skilful piece of manipulation, and it worked.

The Congress followed the sobering tenor of his opening address. In contrast to 1973 there was little open criticism of the government, while defiance and baiting of the ACTU executive, which is a normal Congress pastime, was at a minimum. As chairman of the meeting of 600 delegates, Hawke was at his best: decisive, good humoured and gentle, often offering speakers an extension of time instead of telling them to wind up. The Congress elections returned him an executive weighted twelve to six in his favour. He had taken a deliberate decision to play a small role in debates so that Charlie Fitzgibbon could shine. Fitzgibbon did. By the end of the week he was established in people's minds as the heir apparent. As well, Hawke had finally won his argument for extra administrative staff, and the appointment of a full-time assistant secretary was approved. Also, delegates voted to increase affiliation fees. By 19 September 1975 the ACTU was healthy enough for Hawke, in good conscience, to leave it and at long last to make his transfer to parliament. The next federal election was due to be held in late 1976 or early 1977.

During the rest of the month and throughout October the crisis in parliament continued to build. The Opposition, controlling the Senate, was there deferring the Budget bills for Supply, and the government's options for action were decreasing. Hawke's view was that the most prudent method of breaking the impasse would be a half-Senate election. He discussed this with

many Labor colleagues. On 10 November he met Whitlam at a
ceremony to lay the foundation stone at a club in Broadmeadows,
an oppressed suburb of Melbourne. Hawke, Clyde Holding
and Bill Landeryou, the secretary of the Victorian branch of
the Storemen and Packers' Union and an active member of the
Centre Unity faction of the Victorian ALP, to which Hawke and
Holding also belonged, buttonholed the Prime Minister. They
urged a half-Senate election upon him. When Whitlam left
Broadmeadows Hawke, Holding and Landeryou were all satisfied that the following day Whitlam would announce this solution to the constitutional crisis.

Hawke had objected to Whitlam over the appointment of the
man he used to call 'Goldilocks', Sir John Kerr, as Governor-
General. Several weeks earlier Hawke had asked the Prime
Minister and others, 'Can we rely on Kerr?' He recalled, 'From
my years of dealing with Kerr in the Commission I had no love
for the man. But everyone was sure he was reliable, and I was
convinced.'

Hawke had meetings on the morning of 11 November and
at 1 p.m. went to lunch at the Hotel Cecil, on the corner of
Queen and Lonsdale Streets, with Jack Kornhauser, the brother
of Eddie. Hawke said,

> I was feeling a tremendous weight off my shoulders because
> of the decision, which I thought Gough had made the day
> before, to break free of the Opposition's bloody-minded
> obstructionism and hold a half-Senate election. So I went off
> to lunch in a great mood and had an onion soup, and had
> ordered a steak to follow. It had just arrived – I can still see
> it now, a beautiful T-bone – when the telephone rang. We
> were sitting at a corner table, beside which Jack Kornhauser
> had a private phone. Jack answered and his face dropped.
> His voice sounded incredulous. He passed the phone to me
> and his daughter said, 'Kerr has sacked Whitlam'. She had
> to repeat it before I took it in. I think I said, 'Oh God' and
> got up, left the steak and went back to my office. Within an

hour I was on a plane to Canberra. We'd gathered up a lot of
union blokes and went immediately to John Curtin House,
the ALP headquarters, and into an ALAC meeting ... From
the moment the news had spread there had been calls for
a national strike. People were ringing me, demanding that
I call one. Demands were broadcast on the radio. And I obviously had to think seriously about it. I had to make a judgment very quickly. It was quite clear in my mind that the
idea was nonsense – for a couple of reasons: first, we were
arguing that the Opposition was violating the constitutional
and parliamentary processes of government, therefore, how
could one logically take over the processes of government by
bringing the nation to a halt? Second, and a more pragmatic
consideration, was that I did not believe we could call a successful national strike. And there would have been nothing
more futile and counter-productive than calling a national
stoppage which failed. So, there was the consideration of
principle and of pragmatism. In the ALAC meeting there was
a consensus that there should be no national strike, but that
we should mobilise the trade union movement to support
what we still called the government. The ALAC meeting was
like a group of stunned mullets, stunned by the enormity of
what had happened, while at the same time feeling as if it
were unreal. Gough was still furious, but he had slipped into
a different gear. Now that he had a real fight on his hands the
professional campaigner in him came out. So, while he was
still tremendously angry, he was talking coolly about tactics
for the election campaign. The rest of that day is a bit of a
blur – I think we organised a protest rally in Canberra and
that I spoke at that. Maybe I went to Sydney ...

Hawke did go to Sydney, either that evening or the next, and
addressed a rally called by the New South Wales Labour Council
at the Town Hall. Pat Clancy, who was already estranged from
Hawke, remembered,

Bob gave a magnificent speech: a stinging attack upon capitalism and a declaration in support of socialism, a classic Left speech and beautifully delivered. The Town Hall was packed and when he walked in there was a standing ovation, and throughout the speech people were clapping and cheering. There's no doubt that the workers in New South Wales hero-worshipped him, Right and Left. I only wish I'd taped it so that I could ask his views about it now.

Hawke recalled, 'I got back to Melbourne and went straight into the process of arranging a campaign'. On the nationwide radio program *AM*, on 12 November, Hawke, speaking in a voice described as uncharacteristically 'light and clear' appealed for calm and urged 'controlled and orderly involvement' by the trade unions in the election. He called upon unionists not to strike, but instead to 'give a day's pay for democracy', the same plea he made to the Sydney union rally, and that had been agreed upon at the ALAC meeting. He was in dire fear that the emotional reaction to the government's sacking could lead to riots. Whitlam, still flushed with rage, had stood on the steps of Parliament House in the early afternoon of 11 November and roared to the crowd that had spontaneously surrounded the entrance to the building, 'Maintain your rage!' Later that afternoon Hawke, in marked contrast to the Prime Minister, had given a news conference, saying, 'Australia could be on the verge of something terrible ... We don't want to substitute violence in the streets for democracy.' As far as the Left were concerned, Hawke's determination to try to calm the situation was another black mark against him. Even in early 1982 members of the Socialist Left were quoting the leadership Hawke gave to channelling anger into calmer modes of expression as another of his perfidies – although one of their number, Jim Roulston, had been at the ALAC meeting and had expressed no opposing view. In their outrage over the sacking people forget, or perhaps have never known, that it was the massive, botched strike campaign of the 1890s that desolated the Australian trade union movement. Sir Richard Kirby, who by 1975 had a half-century's experience of industrial affairs, said later that Hawke's finest contribution to the union movement was that then and throughout the bitter months that followed, Hawke kept an iron grip on militancy: 'I've no doubt', Kirby said, 'that without the leadership Bob gave, the unions would have pulled on a national strike which would have fallen to pieces and Fraser would have stepped in and smashed them. I don't think the unions have ever realised what Bob saved them from.'

Hawke recalled of the election campaign that began immediately after the dismissal:

> I was up to my ears in it. The things that were most striking were the overflowing, overwhelming enthusiasm of the audiences and the composition of the audiences. They weren't the normal party faithful, but people from all walks of life who had been deeply insulted by what had happened. Party membership soared. The meetings were the biggest and most enthusiastic of any in the 1970s. From the crowd response I thought right at the beginning that we would win, but the longer the campaign went on the more clear it became that the circumstances surrounding the government's sacking were being subsumed by disaffection with the government. By the end of the campaign, I knew that we'd lost.

Again, even Hawke's enemies acknowledged that next to Whitlam he had done more than any other during the campaign to try to win government.

On the evening of polling day, 13 December, Hawke, Hazel and the children all flew to Canberra. Hawke was to be a television commentator on the election result. He said,

> I didn't have any perception of the magnitude of the defeat we were facing. That election night was one of the longest and loneliest nights in my life. I couldn't get up and walk away from the TV cameras, but had to sit there for the whole horrible performance. It was obvious by 9 p.m. that we'd lost, and

I conceded defeat very quickly, but then it just piled up and up, defeat after defeat.

At one stage Hawke began to weep and told the television audience, 'We've had the guts ripped out of us'. He said,

> There I was looking out at the shattered remains of all the hopes of 1972 and 1974, and being surrounded by gloating Tories. The only redeeming feature of it was that for quite some time Bill Snedden was the commentator sitting next to me and I was able to point out to him that if he had been a little more patient and not blocked supply in 1974 he perhaps would have been Prime Minister ...
>
> I remember the moment when Gough arrived in the tally room: when people saw him, a sense of tragedy spread through the hall. I felt terribly sorry for him as a person, a sorrow separate from what had happened to the Labor Party. There was this giant of a man, smashed to pieces – you know, greatness brings its own set of emotions. Including, I suppose, jealousy, envy. Whatever feelings one had about Gough's mistakes at particular times one could not but be enormously sad for him. It wasn't just defeat that night; it was the end. It was a question of time, but he knew it was the end. And he conducted himself admirably: he acknowledged the dimensions of the defeat and then, fairly quickly, withdrew. We drove back from the national tally room and on the way passed The Lodge, where Whitlam was still in residence, and thought about going in and trying to give some consolation. But there was no sign of life there.

Next morning David Combe telephoned Hawke to say that Whitlam wanted to see him at The Lodge. They sat by the swimming pool. Hawke recalled,

> The essence of what Gough said to me was that his leadership had been rejected and that he had to accept that he was

finished. And that in his view Bill Hayden was the man to take over as leader, that he'd spoken to Hayden already, and Hayden had rejected the leadership. So that now I was the person to lead the party, and that we had to talk about getting a seat for me as quickly as possible. I was surprised, on two counts: first that he'd so quickly accepted that his leadership should come to an end. I think he was right, but was still surprised that he'd decided so quickly. And I was also surprised that he'd turned so quickly to me. Not because I disagreed with his judgment, but because I wasn't even in parliament. I thought Gough was quite right in wanting Hayden to take over – Bill had been an excellent minister and had gone through the hard grind of getting Medibank established, then, as Treasurer, had begun to turn the economy around. Gough's jump from Bill to me, while I could see a logic in it, was surprising. I understood quite clearly, as did David Combe, that the leadership was not Gough's to bestow, and that we would face some difficulties. We discussed a few seats. The general thrust of the conversation was that if it was going to be on, then getting a seat would not be an enormous difficulty – that someone would be prepared, in the circumstances, to step aside. Well, things started to go wrong.

The chain of events and actions following Hawke's discussion with Whitlam remains unclear.

Bill Landeryou was in Canberra and returned to Melbourne with Hawke; Landeryou, who strongly supported the idea that Hawke should lead the party, was anxious to prevent the issue becoming public before detailed plans could be made, and a seat arranged for Hawke. It would seem that Hawke was highly excited, for Landeryou later said that he stayed at Hawke's side that afternoon and evening, and next day, in order to prevent him talking to the press. He knew Hawke well and was familiar with his impatient overconfidence and his tendency to confide his hopes, as if they were realities, to journalists. Landeryou also knew Hawke's enemies. However, on the afternoon of the

Whitlam–Hawke discussions a statement was issued by some-body either on Whitlam's staff or working for the party in Canberra, to the effect that Hawke would be replacing Whitlam as leader. The following night Hawke was invited to appear on television in Melbourne. There he confirmed that Whitlam wanted him to lead the party. He went on to say that with his leadership the party would be back in government in three years. It was an error to have made any comment.

A Caucus outcry greeted the news: indeed, the leadership was not Whitlam's to confer, nor was it Hawke's to claim. And in Victoria, the place where the notional seat for Hawke should, obviously, be located, the Socialist Left was furious. They had hated Whitlam. But as their actions were to reveal, they now hated Hawke more. After all that Whitlam had been through he was now the underdog and therefore a just object of sympa-thy. Hawke was pictured as a man snatching at the crown of a mortally wounded king. At last the Stop Hawke campaign had a name and was out in the open.

Hawke said,

Besides the natural reaction of groups of people in Caucus, Gough himself changed his mind. Quite clearly, what he had said on the day after the election was post-operative shock, and once the patient had settled down he assumed a different view ... The Left said later that it was wicked of me not to have called the Revolution on 11 November, but the real guts of their dislike for me was my stand on the Middle East. Conversely, Whitlam was their hero, for the stand he had taken on the Middle East. The Left found it convenient to blur their reasons; much of the criticism I copped at that time, on the leadership issue, was a cloak for other things. And, of course, I did not know then, and was in blissful ignorance for another two months, that there had been certain hanky-panky with Iraqi money, and that a number of people must have been apprehensive, by then, about the facts emerging. I think it was very convenient to have a diversion and a figure, me, upon whom to vent hatred.

Whitlam decided he would continue to lead the party.

His moment of opportunity vanished, Hawke went off for a holiday and returned in late January 1976, 'all fired up', in the words of Jean Sinclair, 'about getting the Liberals out. Bob's view was that politics in Australia were now unstable and that the electorate could easily switch back to Labor at the next election.' It was a widely held view. What it discounted was that the ALP was now a demoralised, embittered party, led by a man who had lost his self-confidence – the vitals, the heart and liver of political leadership. Commentators made much of the fact that Whitlam had once said, 'You must crash through, or crash', as if such a daring attitude were unique to him, and some fatal flaw, but in fact the words could have come from Curtin, Chifley, Menzies, Gorton, McEwan and, most certainly, from Malcolm Fraser. Compared to Fraser, Whitlam had lacked daring.

There was an ALP campaign committee meeting in Canberra on 28 January that was a sad and pedestrian affair. Then, on Thursday, 12 February, Hawke noted in his diary: '3.25 – Egerton rang re financial trouble'. Hawke had no time to talk, for he was rushing to catch a flight to Canberra where he was to tape a *Monday Conference* television program. He went from the airport direct to the ABC studio. When he arrived at his hotel in Canberra at about 9.30 p.m. there were several telephone messages for him, including an urgent one from Egerton. Hawke returned the call. What Egerton had to tell Hawke sounded

> like a fairy story. Jack said that Whitlam and Combe had arranged to get $500 000 from the Iraqi government, to pay our campaign costs. The dough had not arrived, and the party therefore was in deep financial trouble. David Combe was on a holiday cruise. Ken Bennett, the assistant federal secretary, was waiting downstairs to see me, in a state of nerves ... I said we'd have to get Combe off his cruise ship and have a

meeting of the senior officers – the president, vice-presidents, the secretary and his assistant, to find out what the hell was going on.

In brief, this is what had happened: some weeks before the government had been sacked Bill Hartley, who was a Senate candidate, had the idea that the ALP's slender campaign purse could be plumped up with money from the government of Iraq, for which he worked as a press correspondent. He had a friend, Henri Fischer, who offered to go to Baghdad and raise the money – between a quarter and half a million dollars. It would not be a loan, but a gift from the Ba'ath Socialist Party, which was in government in Iraq, to the ALP. Had the Ba'ath Socialist Party been composed of seraphim with six wings the idea would have been improper; as it was, the Iraqi government was notorious for certain blood-curdling executions of its political enemies. For example, in the early 1970s a group of Iraqi citizens who had spied for Great Britain had been hanged by piano wire, in public. Currency black marketeers were shot. Iraq's legal system was different enough from Australia's to make any close association between the ALP and the Ba'ath Party an embarrassment in Australia. However, the more important point was that it was a violation of ALP principles even to consider financial indebtedness to a foreign government, whatever its complexion. But in the confusion and fury that followed the sacking, Whitlam and Combe agreed with Hartley's suggestion that he could tap funds from a special source. It seems that details were vague: the money could come to the ALP, Whitlam was told, via the Reuben Scarf Foundation. Scarf was a respected Sydney clothing manufacturer, who had made donations to the party in the past. Fischer was associated with the foundation. He recommended himself to party officials, and especially to Hartley, as a fundraiser, because of his often-declared loathing for Rupert Murdoch, the news baron and enemy of the Whitlam government. Fischer was a man of persuasive charm.

By 12 February Combe knew that the money had not arrived from Iraq but neither he nor anyone else knew the reason as yet. Combe assumed he would be sacked for being among those who had agreed to involve the ALP in such an unseemly venture – though, as he commented wryly later, 'I often wondered what view the party would have taken if the money had arrived and we'd been able to use it to pay our debts'. As it was, the ALP election campaign had been run on the premise that a massive injection of dollars was on its way, and the real budget had been overspent by some $300 000. Hawke took the view that Combe had made an appalling error of judgment but one that, in the secretary, was forgivable. At first, when Hawke reached Combe by telephone and told him to abandon his holiday and return immediately, Combe refused, saying that since he was going to be sacked anyway, he may as well enjoy himself. Hawke replied that if Combe would co-operate he would do all that he could to save him. Combe said later,

> Bob's a helluva loyal bloke. He'd stood by me in the past. I didn't have much hope about this one, but he was very strong in saying that, while I'd been a stupid bastard, I'd been trying to do my best by the party in a crisis.

Combe flew to Melbourne and the meeting of senior officers was held in secret, in Hawke's house, on Sunday, 15 February.

By then Hawke had heard some more of the fairy story and was dismayed for the ALP. During the meeting he argued that a special conference of the federal executive should be summoned immediately, for two reasons: first, the issue was grave, and second, it was not a matter that could be kept secret long. Already it had been necessary to involve bank officials and employees of the party's advertising agency, which was owed a fortune, in the affair. Hawke was due to leave a few days later for the ILO. He feared that the story would break in his absence and would be allowed to run wild, worsening the image, created by the Loans Affair, that the Labor Party was of its nature conspiratorial, devious and incompetent. Egerton and Ducker argued that it was safer to let matters rest for the time being, and to deal with the problem, in secret, at the next scheduled federal executive meeting. Hawke said,

> I was vigorous in replying to them that they were bloody crazy, that there was no way in the world that the news wouldn't leak, and when that happened it would be even worse for the party, for it would look as if we were trying to cover up.

Hawke lost the argument, but there was a certain savage pleasure for him in the meeting, for when Combe arrived he told the others that the scheme had originated with Hartley. Hawke saw his chance to have Hartley expelled. Other officers agreed that this should happen; Combe, however, they all agreed, should be allowed to stay on as secretary. They doubted that the federal executive would want Whitlam to remain leader.

Combe disagreed. He said if the officers were serious in wishing to see him continue as secretary they must adopt the principle of equal culpability and not distinguish between the gravity of his error on one side, and Hartley's and Whitlam's on the other, and that all should be punished equally. In Hawke's mind, however, Whitlam had for the last time 'played around with the future of the ALP', as he put it. Hawke was convinced that Whitlam should and would be sacked as leader. The discussions broke up with an agreement on secrecy.

That night or the one after, Combe and Egerton went to dinner at Eddie Kornhauser's home and told him of the scandal. Kornhauser was horrified: by the facts, because he was fearful that the story would break in the press and he could be blamed as the leak; and for another, special reason. After the argument between Schildberger and Hawke in Kornhauser's office two years earlier, Kornhauser had decided that Hawke should be given a lasting honour in Israel and had hit upon the idea of a forest. After months of planning he had arranged for a gathering of distinguished members of Australian Jewry, who had pledged to contribute to the cost of the forest that would be planted in Israel and named after Hawke. The gathering at which the plan for a Hawke forest would be formally unveiled was to be held on Thursday, 19 February. Kornhauser feared that if it became known in the interim that the ALP had been prepared to accept $500 000 from Iraq, a country demanding the obliteration of Israel, his guests would think twice about donations for the president of the party.

Kornhauser recalled,

> Bob said nothing to me and I didn't tell him that I knew about it already. I was having heart attacks on Tuesday, Wednesday, Thursday. Finally Thursday night came and there had been no story in the newspapers. Bob came to the function and was very subdued. He had to make a speech to all the people I'd invited to be supporters. He gave his speech without once lifting his eyes to the audience. People thought he was reading from a prepared speech, but I was sitting behind him and could see that he had no speech, just one line of notes. Later, when the story broke, he told me: 'I was too ashamed to look at them. That my party had done that . . .'

A day or so later Hawke left for the ILO, stopping first in Singapore, where he lunched with an Australian diplomat, Richard Butler. Butler told Hawke, in confidence, that he had applied for the job of Whitlam's private secretary. Hawke told Butler, in confidence, that he had better reconsider before resigning from Foreign Affairs, for Whitlam was unlikely to be leader much longer. He told Butler why. Hawke continued his journey towards Geneva, stopping next in Israel.

The morning after his arrival in Jerusalem he was in the lobby of his hotel chatting to a group of students who were the first beneficiaries of another eponymous honour in Israel: Hawke was one of the twenty-four Gentiles in the world, up to the time of writing, after whom a research fund at the Hebrew University in Jerusalem has been named. He was summoned away from the students to take a telephone call from, he thinks, London, from Rupert Murdoch. Hawke said,

> I thought, 'Oh, just as I predicted'. I didn't feel smart about having been right; it was just so bloody obvious that the story would break. Murdoch said enough to me for it to be clear beyond question: he knew. He asked me to comment and I told him I had no comment. At that stage I didn't know where he'd got the story, but as we discovered later, Henri Fischer had told him. I thought, 'Well, we're done for – it will be in the Australian press in a day or so'. I was going to lunch with a group of senior Israeli Labour Party people and decided that now the cat was out there was no point in pretending.

One of the Israelis at the luncheon, which was at a famous restaurant in Jerusalem, was the defence minister and later leader of the Labour Party, Shimon Peres. He recalled,

> When Bob told us, we could not believe that a fraternal party would do such a thing. Bob was depressed about the state the Australian Labor Party had reached. He said it had lost its character and ideology, and that he would stand for parliament soon because he wanted to bring back character and ideology to the party. But, he had personal problems ...

Hawke contacted Blanchard in Geneva to tell him he could not, now, attend the International Labour Conference, and caught a plane to Athens that evening. From there he telephoned 'either one or all of Combe, Ducker and Egerton'. They confirmed that Murdoch's flagship newspaper, the *Australian*, had a front-page story about what was already known as 'The Iraqi Money Scandal'. Hawke returned to Australia, arriving back during the final week of February.

The senior officers of the party had a succession of discussions to decide upon a recommendation to the federal executive,

a special meeting of which had been summoned for 5 and
6 March. The Iraqi Money Scandal was, beyond debate, a genuine scandal. For more defensible errors Whitlam had sacked
Rex Connor and Jim Cairns from his ministry. The officers
recommended that the federal executive of the ALP should expel
Bill Hartley from the party and severely reprimand Combe and
Whitlam.

Then, on the weekend before the federal executive was due to
meet, Hawke made a faux pas. He allowed a news conference
to be held at his house and after his tight-lipped formal announcement of a thorough inquiry, continued to talk, off the record, to
a few journalists who stayed on, drinking. During the conversation Hawke, in conveying the common belief of the officers
that Whitlam would not survive as leader, remarked, 'Gough's
gone a million'. The next morning Sydney's largest-circulation
daily newspaper, the *Telegraph*, had a front-page story headlined
'Hawke to Axe Whitlam'. It was the second breach of journalistic ethics from which Hawke suffered. Matters were made worse
by the fact that he was seen as pre-empting the decision of the
federal executive. The reporting of Hawke's remarks helped to
create a surge of sympathy from ALP branches for Whitlam,
who suddenly was the very image of pathos: sacked as prime
minister and now to be sacked as leader of the Opposition. The
party, wallowing in self-pity for its defeat, transferred that pity
to Whitlam – and not without logic. For if he were sacked as
leader that would seem to justify his sacking as prime minister.
For the second time in less than three months Hawke appeared
to be overstating his importance, and this time deliberately
humiliating further a humiliated man. Already, back in January,
he had stimulated a frenzy of paranoia in the Left by calling
on Fraser in Canberra, wearing his ACTU president's hat. It
was proper for Hawke to do this, as ACTU president. It was,
however, objectionable that the ALP president be photographed
smiling and chatting to the new Prime Minister. Under a Liberal
government, Hawke's two hats were as difficult to wear as under
a Labor one.

Whitlam's staff made many photostats of the 'Hawke to Axe Whitlam' story, and distributed them widely. Hawke was harassed by the news media to confirm or deny. 'It was a very windy moment for Bob', John Ducker recalled. Hawke made a statement that came perilously close to tarnishing his deserved reputation for truthfulness. Meanwhile, Hartley rushed in to the breach. During interviews with the print and electronic media he suggested that it was Hawke who had leaked the story to Murdoch, and went on to imply that the CIA and Israeli Intelligence were really behind the whole thing. The public could be forgiven for thinking, from what Hartley said, that Hawke was an agent of the CIA or Israeli Intelligence, or both, and had at their instigation set up Hartley and Whitlam for a phony deal, in order to bring them down, which he had then tried to accomplish by using Rupert Murdoch. It is a measure of the paranoia that the names 'Murdoch' and 'Hawke' could arouse in the Left that many believed this demonological nonsense, for years.

A further complication was that on 25 February, the same day as the Murdoch story had broken, the Melbourne *Sun News-Pictorial* also had a version of the scandal, written by a political journalist and author, Laurie Oakes. It was well known that Oakes and Hawke were friendly. Hartley announced, 'I know who gave the story to Oakes', which suggested to many ALP people that Hawke had. However, from certain details in Oakes' story, Combe and Ducker were convinced that an official of a state branch had been responsible, especially because the man had been overheard talking to Oakes. The man later left his job in the ALP, with a little help from John Ducker.

The federal executive met in Canberra on 5 March in an atmosphere of acute distrust. David Combe, since returning to his home, Canberra, had been besieged by the news media. He recalled,

> We had journalists camped on the front lawn and were under police custody for the best part of a week, with paddy wagons out the front and the family unable to leave the house.

It was terrific! I first went out on the night of 4 March, for the officers' meeting. Then the next morning, when the federal executive meeting opened, everyone was as jumpy as hell. There was a buzzing noise. We were all so spook-conscious that we thought the room must be bugged. Bill Hartley clambered around trying to find bugs. After a while [Senator] Arthur Geitzelt owned up. He had a new hearing-aid and he didn't quite know how to work the thing, and it was that which was making the noise. I moved that the meeting be taped, because X was there and I knew he had dudded me to Oakes. In case I was going to be dismissed, I wanted the tapes as an accurate record of proceedings. The meeting rejected my request, but as things started to unfold Egerton made one of his masterful interjections. He said, 'The secretary asked us to tape proceedings. We refused. We should have bloody well sold the film rights!'

Indeed, with a theme song and some special effects, the story that emerged could have been *A-L-P, The Musical*.

Hawke recalled,

It was a meeting that defied imagination. People were punch-drunk by the revelations. For instance: during the election campaign Frank Crean was still occupying the rooms of the Deputy Prime Minister of Australia, and Hartley had installed in this office the telex machine he used as the Iraqi press correspondent in Australia. So while the election campaign is going on, telex messages from Iraq about hundreds of thousands of dollars are pouring into the office of the Deputy Prime Minister. We heard all this, then I said, 'Are there any more questions?' and there was one, directed to Hartley, who then told us that the telex messages started going astray – to some major business office. Messages about the ALP were coming off a machine in Westinghouse! Then there were the stories about Henri Fischer. They were told to ring him in London; London said he was in New York; New York said he was in South America. It was Keystone Cops! That the Labor Party's future was being played around with, like that! We gave each of the three people involved, Combe, Hartley and Whitlam, the opportunity of making a full statement.

Combe said,

Hartley, in his statement, said things like, 'But I don't think the leader would have been aware of that' and 'I'm sure the leader didn't know ...' It became obvious from fairly early on that a deal had been done to save Gough and to dump me. During Gough's statement he said, 'It was perfectly proper for Reuben Scarf to give a donation. I thought we were only talking about ten, twenty or twenty-five thousand dollars'. I went white, and gawped. We broke for morning tea. Bob and I were furious. Bob called Ducker over and I said, 'If we're breaking from the principle of equal culpability, then the gloves are off. I'm going in to give fresh evidence.' Ducker said, 'I'll talk to Gough'.

So a great earnest discussion between Ducker and Whitlam took place, then Whitlam came over and said, 'Well, comrades, John seems to think that you're concerned about the amounts'. I said, 'Yes, Gough. You've conveyed the impression to the executive that it was just a normal donation. I must insist that you knew that we were talking about a very large sum of money.' Gough replied, 'I should clarify that'. So from then on the whole thing was run on equal culpability. Each of the three of us was as guilty as hell of gross lack of judgment ... I should mention that I don't think Reuben Scarf ever knew about the Iraqi money ...

The motions ranged from the officers' recommendation that Hartley be expelled, to one from Neil Batt and Ken Wriedt that we all three be expelled, through various alternatives. From the time that the principle was established that we must all be truthful and tell the whole truth the executive operated magnificently. There was a genuine endeavour on the part of everyone to face up to the problem and resolve it, and to forget about factional differences. Bob played a big role in preventing a faction feud. While he had strong personal views about Hartley, and while he would have liked to pursue them, he didn't. He backed off very quickly from the idea that Hartley be expelled. He kept that executive under a tight rein for two days, determined to elicit all possible information about what had happened, determined to get a genuine, non-factional discussion. If only Whitlam had handled the Loans Affair in the same way that Hawke handled that executive – getting everything out in the open, admitting there had been an error – then the Loans Affair would never have damaged us the way it did, with bits and pieces of information dragged out like teeth, and the suspicion in everyone's mind that the full story was never revealed.

Within two days the drama was over. The party knew all that it could know from Whitlam, Hartley and Combe about what had happened. The federal executive decided that the three men be severely reprimanded for what they had done and that it should tell the nation the facts. After some discussion about whether it was safe to allow Hawke to speak about Hartley, the executive decided that Hawke's sense of justice could be trusted, and he was given the task of divulging information to the public. The news conference was the biggest ever held by the ALP, and Hawke was at his best: he was frank, decisive and just. He did not go into any of the *opéra bouffe* details but revealed all the important elements of the affair. The paper on which was written the officers' recommendation to the executive that Hartley be expelled had been shredded, as had other pieces of paper recommending expulsion for all three. Hawke was alert in his handling of the news media: the best journalists in the country did not sense that there was a chink in the armour-plating of party solidarity that Hawke projected, or if any did, none had a chance to ask questions that would expose it. Hartley attended the news conference and at the end of it congratulated and thanked Hawke, saying he could not have wished for fairer treatment.

Hawke said,

> I had no doubt about the integrity of Combe and Whitlam, I merely thought they had been stupid beyond belief. But I believed one could distinguish between their actions, and Hartley's. I think there were other considerations in Hartley's mind. The surprising thing was that he seemed unable to comprehend the magnitude of his actions. When he told us those Keystone Cops stories people began to laugh, they couldn't help themselves. And Bill joined in the laughter, but he did not seem to know that we were laughing at him, and not with him. I realised that he honestly did not understand what he'd done ... I was quite happy to go along with those who thought that it was unfair to make a distinction between the three. I didn't feel, as I have on some occasions, that those opposed to me were just wrong and stupid.

The Iraqi Money Scandal was, literally, a nine-day wonder. The *Australian* story appeared on 25 February; Hawke's press conference was held on 6 March. The speed with which the federal executive had dealt with the issue had minimised the public damage to the party. But within the upper echelons of the ALP the little self-confidence that remained had suffered further attrition, for members of the federal executive suspected that as with the Loans Affair, the Gair Affair and the Kerr sacking, the Whitlam government had been the naive player in a very sharp poker school. They believed that the Iraqis had donated about $250 000 to the ALP, the money had been sent via Beirut to Tokyo for laundering, and got lost in the laundry.

The whole affair had affected Hawke much more deeply than he cared to admit later or, publicly, at the time. He loved the party and felt keenly protective of it. Privately, he was outraged that Hartley had remained an ALP member. He began to think of Hartley and other extreme members of the Socialist Left as malignant growths within the body of Labor politics, and among friends would have outbursts of invective against Hartley, during which he shouted, 'I will destroy him!'

Hawke fell ill with a respiratory tract infection soon after the special federal executive meeting. David Combe and his wife, Caroline, sent him some flowers and a message thanking him for all he had done on their behalf. Combe recalled,

> Next time I spoke to Bob he mentioned the flowers and then went into a *tirade* about how unfair it all was, that the only person who'd suffered out of the whole deal was himself. What had happened was that the Murdoch press had run a massive campaign promoting Bob, against Gough. Within the party anybody who was in favour of the Murdoch press was, ipso facto, a louse. In those days it was not only purists who refused to buy Murdoch newspapers – ALP members in general boycotted them.

Murdoch had barracked hard for Whitlam in 1972. During one of the campaign meetings Hawke had said to Whitlam, 'You're going to regret the day you got into bed with Rupert', a prophecy that was speedily fulfilled. Murdoch's news empire became the nemesis of the government it had once promoted and Murdoch himself was elevated, in the party, to membership of a trilogy of demons, the other two being Malcolm Fraser and Sir John Kerr. As Combe remarked, 'To be a friend of Murdoch was a sin'.

Hawke did not stop buying Murdoch newspapers, but few party loyalists knew this. All were aware, however, that Hawke was opposed to the party's obsessional hatred of Kerr. On several occasions early in the year he said publicly that he believed it was futile to dwell upon the past, and that the party should be concerning itself with the future. But hell hath no fury like a true believer scorned. Hawke's attempts at encouraging the ALP away from negativism towards a positive and expansive frame of mind were more black marks against him. Stroke by stroke, the picture of a traitor was growing. Hawke was now, for the Left, protagonist in a play plotted by unknown forces, all his actions taking place under a lurid light, or in deep, sinister shadows. For them he was turning into a Demon King himself.

Since he had become president of the ACTU Hawke had sometimes, when in his cups, shown exaggerated sensitivity to slights. For example, Richard Carleton, the television journalist, recalled Hawke arriving late and drunk at the Taiping Restaurant in Sydney for a dinner celebrating the 1972 election victory, and asking loudly of the Chinese waiter who blocked his path, 'Don't you know who I am?' His sense of power had grown bigger when he became president of the party in government, so much so that Hazel was worried that he had lost his sense of perspective in relation to others. An air of vulgar self-importance often surrounded him, and was accompanied by a discounting of other people. He had come to treat much criticism as humbug; he was habituated to flattery. Few had the temerity to object to Hawke's face when he was rude to them, but when, very rarely, someone would tell him afterwards of some outrageous act of his, he would at first refuse to believe he had behaved so badly, asserting, 'That's not me!' If he could be convinced he would slump into melancholic silence.

When Rupert Murdoch invited Hawke to dine with him in early 1976, in a Sydney restaurant, Hawke did not feel inhibited about accepting, although they were destined to be overseen. The meeting was widely reported and caused a scandal within the ALP. There was a detectable whiff of opportunism in Hawke's reception of the press baron's overtures, but his meetings with Murdoch were also an example of Hawke's consistent behaviour pattern of attempting to transcend differences and to reconcile opposites. He wanted Murdoch's support not merely for himself, but for the institution that Murdoch had so mercilessly savaged, the ALP.

By late March, Whitlam had made public his change of mind about the leadership, saying that Hawke's support in Caucus had declined in the past fifteen months and that, 'He is not, I believe,

as intellectually well equipped for leadership as I know Bill
Hayden to be'. By April, Hawke's popularity rating was 62 per
cent, compared with 53 per cent for Fraser and 41 per cent for
Whitlam.

For pragmatists within the party, the figures spoke for themselves: if the ALP were to win back government, Hawke would
have to enter parliament. A pressure campaign upon him began,
and was to last for the next three years. Countering it, there was
now the openly declared Stop Hawke campaign of the Socialist
Left. The period between 14 December 1975 and 23 September
1979 were the most difficult years of Hawke's life. He was
severely overstretched physically; emotionally he was becoming
unstable from physical exhaustion, political battles and a deteri-
orating personal life; intellectually, he was weary.

He read at least four newspapers every day and stacks of
committee reports, but it was years since he had read thought-
provoking books, and the effect of a barrage of shallow ideas and
trivial facts was becoming obvious – in his speeches, for example,
at the National Press Club in June 1976; in the few articles he
wrote, for example, in *Heyday or Doomsday: Australia 2000*;[4] and
in his conversation. His mind was still extraordinarily quick and
logical, and he could still perform astonishing feats of absorbing and analysing quantities of information at a speed that awed
those who worked with him. However, his natural inclination
to solve immediate, practical problems had caused a narrowing
of interests. Hawke fell silent, or looked bored, when discussion moved away from current events or politics. Paul Munro,
Hawke's friend from New Guinea days, said,

> Bob is without small talk. If people can't talk to him about
> things he's interested in, he can't talk to them about things
> they are interested in – you know, theatre, books. He's often
> plain awkward in company until he's figured out what role
> he can play. He needs to have a defined purpose in any social
> situation.

Hawke's social values were sound – like second nature to him – but his ideas often flimsy. A major cause of his physical, emotional and intellectual weakening was his gregarious drinking. Hawke would rarely drink alone, but he spent hours drinking with mates and he had come to depend upon alcohol to help him relax. Hours that could have been passed in thought were given over to the bogus intellectual stimulation of boozy argument. The fact that the Anglo-Australian legal system is one based upon debate about right and wrong in the eyes of the law and not, as for example in the French system, upon determining truth, encouraged in Hawke, as it has in all our lawyer-politicians, a love of scoring points in arguments.

While the forces upon him to enter parliament – and those threatening him against trying – built up, the more serious dilemma for Hawke was a private one: alcohol. He had made a public promise to eschew it were he to become leader of the ALP, and his sense of honour made fulfilling the promise unavoidable. But with or without a promise, he knew that he could not achieve his dream unless he moderated his drinking. Already television interviewers were covering up for Hawke, by scrapping film of him recorded when he was drunk. When he was to be broadcast live, or to take part in important pre-recorded debates, Hawke by 1976 would sometimes mutter, 'No. I mustn't drink. I mustn't drink.' He had arrived at a stage when he had to confront a conflict that was as old as he was: his relationship with Ellie. It was she who had inspired him to seek power, to seek the prime ministership; it was she who had instilled in him an image of the bottle as black god.

By June 1976 he had replied to the importunate press that 'this might be the year' he would enter parliament. A week later he led an ACTU delegation to Canberra for talks with Fraser and the Cabinet, held in the Cabinet room. Out of the meeting sprang one of the most unfair of the Socialist Left attacks upon Hawke. He said, in the presence of ACTU executive members, the Prime Minister and some senior Cabinet ministers, that if wage claims were to be moderated the trade union movement would require a reform of taxation, to guard its spendable income; Hawke proposed that if the government would change the taxation structure it could anticipate a lessening of wage claims. Fitzgibbon, a member of the delegation, turned to another ACTU executive member, Jim Roulston of the AMWSU, a leader of the Socialist Left in Victoria and Fitzgibbon's senior in the ACTU executive hierarchy, and asked, 'Do you know about this? Do you agree with it?' Roulston replied he did not. Fitzgibbon asked, 'As a senior officer of the ACTU are you going to say something?' and Roulston replied he would not. Fitzgibbon then addressed the meeting, saying he disagreed with Hawke's proposal, that it would be difficult to persuade the rank and file to accept such a trade-off. Fraser, the Cabinet ministers, Hawke and others formally took note of Fitzgibbon's warning. That evening Fraser invited Hawke, Ducker and Dolan to dine at The Lodge.

Earlier in the day the ACTU team had learned, from a note sent in to the Cabinet room from David Combe, that Egerton, president of the Queensland branch of the party, had accepted a knighthood from the Fraser government. The news was another stunning blow to Labor morale. John Ducker was so distressed that he drank a good deal before dinner; he, Dolan and the other guest, Tony Street, who was now Minister for Labour, all left The Lodge early. Hawke stayed on, drinking with Fraser, engaged by the Prime Minister in what Hawke believed was a challenge to last the distance with bottle after bottle of port. At last Mrs Fraser appeared in a dressing gown and said to her husband, 'Dear, it's time you went to bed'. Hawke recalled, 'Tamie Fraser was the most beautiful sight in the world. By then my legs were pretty wobbly, but I'd been determined not to give up.'

The next day Roulston announced that Hawke had cooked up a $650 million tax–wage trade-off with the Prime Minister. The story was spread, and reported, that this had been done tête-à-tête over dinner at The Lodge. It was even believed by some more gullible members of the party, and hinted at by the press, that Hawke's meeting with Fraser had occurred in secret, without the knowledge of the ACTU. At the next ACTU executive meeting Fitzgibbon angrily denounced Roulston and recounted Roulston's refusal to speak against the proposal when he had had the chance to do so in the Cabinet room. But the damage to Hawke had been done. In the next major meeting of the Victorian ALP the Socialist Left faction was joined by the Right faction to pass a motion condemning Hawke for his supposed 'deal' with Fraser. Handbills appeared in Victoria headlined, 'HAWKE HAS SECRET MEETINGS WITH FRASER AND MURDOCH TO BETRAY WORKING PEOPLE' and saying:

> Hawke is a most despicable person. Hawke cannot be called a 'traitor' because he has never belonged to or supported the working class. He was selected by the capitalist class to be President of the ACTU in order to strengthen the control of that class over the trade unions. Hawke is a close confidant of US labor attaches (CIA) and the greater part of his activity is secret. Who knows – apart from his bosses – what he does overseas? Who knows his precise relations with the fascist Israeli leaders? Who knows what he talks about with Fraser? Who knows what he talks about with Murdoch? Who really knows what his business connections are? This despicable person whose rotten outlook is reflected in his private life should be exposed for what he is ... DRIVE HAWKE OUT![5]

The garbage bins at his house were searched for evidence about Hawke's lifestyle and the readers of a radical newspaper were informed that Hawke had 'disgusting' rubbish: cartoned orange juice, for example. The house itself excited a frenzy of condemnation for its size, location and the fact that it had a tennis court and swimming pool. One night in mid-1976 somebody painted in black on its front wall: 'WEALTHY PIGS LIVE IN LUXURY'.

Such sentiments were not confined to the new breed of semi-educated baby puritans, bearded-up like Victorian curates, whom the 1970s had spawned. One evening in 1980 a clean-shaven, middle-aged professor of history from a Melbourne university delivered himself of the opinion that it was 'disgraceful' that Hawke lived in Brighton. When informed that Hawke lived in the less expensive suburb of Sandringham, the professor replied that made no difference: Hawke's life was luxurious. Upon inquiry, the professor divulged that he lived in the fashionable and expensive suburb of Kew, adding, 'But I'm only renting'.[6] Whatever that reveals about the quality of intellect of a senior academic, it is a demonstration of the success of the smear campaign against Hawke, who, until the end of the decade, was continuously in overdraft. Only when Hazel began working full time could they afford to hire somebody to do the heavy household cleaning and the ironing.

The paranoia of radicals about Hawke was matched by enthusiasm among non-radicals. In July 1976 the Reverend Lillian Livingstone, a Congregational minister, asserted during a sermon in Sydney that Jesus Christ resembled Bob Hawke more than 'the gentle Jesus meek and mild' of popular fancy. Letters and telegrams arrived at the ACTU urging upon Hawke various actions:

Should you enter Parliament the people of Australia will be exposed to the risk of having their greatest hope taken hostage. The Australian has needed a mate for nearly half a century.

Although opposed to your political views I sincerely believe your destiny is on the world scene, for God and the Good of all kind.

You have got a definite spiritual character about you that is hard to define . . . I say a special prayer for you each Sunday at church . . . I've got a photo of you from a local newspaper and I always carry it with me wherever I go. It gives me spiritual and emotional strength . . . I'd gladly die for you, if I had to. It's guys like you who make the Labor Party a great party.

For the sake of your Party and the country I urge you to go for pre-selection.[7]

By September 1976 speculation about when and if Hawke would enter parliament had reached such outlandish proportions that he decided to hold a news conference on the issue. The Victorian branch of the ALP had forced a showdown by deciding that nominations for preselection for the election due in December 1978 must be lodged by 30 September 1976. Normal practice was to call for nominations twelve months before an election was due. The rule change was designed to nobble Hawke, because if he put himself forward as a parliamentary candidate he would be a 'lame duck' president of the ACTU for – as it was then believed – two years. (As events turned out, Fraser held the election one year early.) Two days before his news conference was scheduled the Socialist Left announced, presumably in case some deaf person had not heard the sound of the grinding of axes, that they would 'oppose completely any bid of Hawke's for preselection'.

Fifty journalists gathered in the Melbourne Trades Hall on 15 September to learn Hawke's decision: Not this time. The *Age* commented editorially,

> Mr Hawke said . . . his move would create a lame-duck ACTU presidency for the next two years. We suggest the logic of that argument can be taken a step further: if his effectiveness as the leader of the trade union movement would be destroyed by his becoming an officially declared candidate, it will surely be at least diminished by his remaining a potential candidate.

It was a perspicacious comment. Hawke had been standing, unchallenged and unchallengeable, on a mountain top of trade union support: beneath his feet the rock was to subside.

By late 1976 senior officers of the ACTU were so alarmed by the campaign against him, and by Hawke's drinking, that they agreed he needed a chauffeur–bodyguard. The ACTU had no funds for such an extra staff member, so it was arranged that a job be found in ACTU–Solo, and that the man employed would work for the petrol discounting company when not driving and protecting Hawke. The person chosen was Chris Crellin, a young, physically beautiful giant – he weighed 100 kilograms – who had been a policeman. While still a member of the force he had been chosen as a bodyguard for Fraser during the 1975 election campaign, which was cause for hilarity among police, since Crellin was known for his Labor sympathies. He speaks quietly and moves with the silent grace and menace of a panther. He told Hawke he would feel honoured to work for him, then when Hawke asked him to wear a pistol, refused – 'with passive resistance, and after a while Bob didn't mention it any more'. Hawke doted upon Crellin; when Crellin would appear noiselessly in a doorway Hawke's eyes would soften. 'Chris. Chris … he loves me', Hawke would say sometimes.

Hawke has always craved love, and those he loves he trusts wholeheartedly. Kirby remarked,

> Once Bob accepts you, that's it. I could say to him I thought the Earth was flat and he wouldn't fly off the handle at me, but would say, 'Well, Dick, I'm sure you have some reason for believing that'. There's a special quality in his friendship.

By the end of 1976 John Ducker and Hawke were friends. It was a friendship that saved Hawke's political life in 1977.

EIGHTEEN

THE BROAD CHALLENGE TO authority that had begun in the 1960s had brought liberty. And liberty had brought confusion: by the mid-1970s Australian society was divided by a host of issues. Especially painful was the fight over the rights and status of women, an upheaval that had affected the whole community. There were questions about Australia's moral authority vis-à-vis its closest neighbour, Indonesia; education – for academic excellence or for personality development? permissiveness – in sexuality, dress, manners; debate about the citizen's duties to society – was unemployment 'dole bludging'? – and the government's duties to the citizen: should it artificially create jobs, and if so, how much should it spend? In private lives there were discovered, afresh, old arguments about emotions and awareness versus logic and cogitation: guidance for conduct was sought in astrology, and clearer perception through inhaling, injecting or eating vegetable extracts. Senior members of society despaired of the nation's youth. Preservation of the environment (an economic and moral question dressed as a purely moral one), was pitted against a frank economic question: jobs. There were demands for ethnic distinctions in Australia versus demands for a coherent cultural core; there was abortion: murder or mercy or none of your business? What to do for Indigenous Australians? We could not even agree upon a national anthem.

Malcolm Fraser had been elected to change all that. He was an authoritarian, with an authoritarian's disdain for human frailty, and he inspired confidence among the confused. While few people liked him, millions were willing to vote for him because Fraser promised a return to certainties, however unpalatable. He had the strength of a political leader who knows that his personality is matched to the inchoate yearnings of the electorate: frightened by liberty and uncertainty, people wanted a patriarch who would put an end to the bickering of national life and point them in the right direction for the Promised Land. He had won 57 per cent of first preference votes in the 1975 election, with a kind of decalogue, the first commandment being 'sound economic management' and the second 'fight inflation first'. The corollary of the first meant breaking up the handiwork, the great public spending programs, of the Whitlam years, while that of the second meant worsening unemployment. In theory, unemployment would worsen only in the short term; within a few years prosperity would return to all. In practice, the government found its program was as difficult to implement as that other one engraved on tablets of stone. Years of economic meandering began.

The percentage of votes cast for the conservative government in 1975 showed that a goodly number of those who would define themselves as working class, or who were members of blue-collar unions, had rejected Labor and chosen Fraser. Of itself this suggested that within the labour movement a period of self-hatred had begun. What the voting figures suggested was further revealed by the behaviour of the ALP and its demoralised representatives in federal parliament – they cursed the name of John Kerr, they maintained their rage, in the end a rage at themselves for having been tricked – and by the angry dejection and confusion within the trade union movement.

The unions had won great gains in the 1960s in wages and in liberty, culminating in the sweeping away of the penal powers in 1969, thanks, finally, to Kerr's mishandling of the O'Shea case. Fraser was determined to reintroduce 'pains and penalties', as the unions called them, into Australian industrial life. Hawke's jobs, as president of the ALP and of the ACTU, became exquisitely difficult. For the former he had to take the role of optimistic, inspirational leader to a group that had, as he observed, 'had the guts ripped out' of it. He had to stand as a party signpost pointing expansively forward. But as leader of the unions he had to demand a diminution of hope and an increase in self-discipline, in the pursuit of survival. He needed to be cheerful and soothing, and aggressively determined, by turns. His personality equipped him for the performance of both roles.

Fraser's vote in 1975 was, unlike Whitlam's 1972 poll of 49.6 per cent of primary votes, a genuine mandate, which gave the new Prime Minister the right to pursue whatever policies he chose. Once the new government was safely in office it began a campaign of 'union bashing', a procedure made easier by the fact that the Whitlam government itself had, in its confusion and panic, led the way. There had been Cameron's famous remark, when he was still Minister for Labour, about public service 'fat cats', and scores of speeches from Labor ministers inveighing against wage demands and strikes. Fraser was determined to take the issue much further, to mount a direct assault upon union freedoms.

To aid the process, the new government needed to bring the trade union movement into disrepute. Beginning in mid-1976 Fraser's ministry progressively introduced a legislative program designed to weaken the unions financially and, especially, to undo the liberty of action they had enjoyed since the O'Shea case. He and his ministers took every opportunity to blame inflation upon union greed and irresponsibility. Their assertions about wage claims causing inflation were not wholly true but nor were they entirely false – they were, rather, a confusion, similar to confusing a fever, symptom of disease, with its cause. Wage claims were a fever and, fed back through the arbitration system, were making inflation worse. They were not the cause of inflation but a response to it.

Fraser had not been elected for nice debate or for stating the facts – indeed, his disregard for facts was already well known in Canberra and was to become a national byword. Yet from him, this was acceptable to the electorate, at least until the period of acute fear had passed. The damage done by the electorate's acceptance that its federal government was led by a man who did not regard veracity as necessary in political life is difficult to over-estimate, for it generates cynicism and cynicism leads to apathy. It must be added that the Whitlam government's record in this matter was chequered: the Fraser government bulldozed along a track already marked out by its predecessor. By November 1975, the electorate had countless examples of the mendacity of politicians and their contempt for the people at large. The old anarchist saying, 'Whoever you vote for, a politician will get in', had come to have particular relevance.

It was Hawke's job to protect the trade union movement from the Prime Minister, and to carry the flag for honesty.

Fending off the attacks upon the trade union movement launched by the Fraser government required of Hawke all the political skill and authority he had, for the legislative wing of the labour movement, the federal ALP Caucus, had been reduced to a stump and was unable to assist the industrial branch. Souter recalled, 'The party could give us no help at all in parliament against Fraser's legislation. We were fighting it on our own and the ACTU just had to push and pull the best way it could.' Hawke needed to push at the government with one hand and to pull in the unions with the other; his life became a series of dramatic public threats to the government and private efforts at conciliation.

In mid-1976 when it became obvious that the Fraser government, in the teeth of its election promise, intended to dismantle the Whitlam government's most popular bequest, Medibank, the ALP Caucus was powerless to prevent the attrition of Medibank and the struggle to preserve the national health scheme became the responsibility of the union movement. Hawke was loud in his public denunciations of the government while privately he was trying to hold back the more radical unions from rushing to strike action, and behind the scenes was attempting to force the government to bargain with the ACTU over the issue. A large section of the Left of both the unions and the Party thought it shameful to negotiate with the Fraser government at all, and wanted immediate confrontation. Hawke had no doubt who would win: the government would, for the voting figures alone had told him that the union movement was deeply divided in its attitudes to Fraser and could not be relied upon to stand shoulder-to-shoulder in a confrontation. He stalled for weeks, requesting longer talks and more debates with the government before the ACTU could make a decision. At length, the activities of radicals sabotaged him. Fraser perceived the vulnerability of Hawke's position and decided to challenge the unions to defy the government. Very unwillingly, with no room left to manoeuvre, Hawke called the first national stoppage in Australia's history, in June 1976, to protest for one day about the changes to Medibank. It went quietly. The government proclaimed the Medibank strike had been a failure, and took courage.

Hawke was extremely bitter. A few weeks later he used the opportunity of a meeting with union representatives in the Brisbane Trades Hall to upbraid radicals and to try to beat into their consciousness the danger to hard-won wages and liberty that the unions now faced, and the consequent need for disciplined action. He told them:

In the Cabinet room – and this was a rotten, terrible bloody experience I had to go through – I had the Prime Minister saying to me, 'Mr Hawke, if we move to your position on Medibank, even if we do so because we are persuaded that you are right and that yours is a better position, we would possibly have the worst of both worlds, because you couldn't say to us that your trade union movement would accept it'. And that happened because *you* in your lack of wisdom and your snuggling under slogans and your non-thinking, tried to lead the trade union movement. You jumped the gun. You hadn't done your homework, you wouldn't know anything about what it was about. We [the ACTU] had done our homework, we'd got the government to the edge of agreeing to a better deal on Medibank. Then, you jumped in. And so, we had the Prime Minister saying, 'All right, the government won't agree for one reason: because, Mr Hawke, you can't control the trade union movement'. It wasn't the vast membership of the trade union movement who behaved in a way to enable the Prime Minister to say that. It was you!

Hawke knew from his meetings with Fraser how formidable he was in will power, if not in intellect and, being only an average-sized man himself, was particularly impressed by Fraser's massive 1.95-metre frame. 'You ought to see his thighs!' Hawke exclaimed.

> They're like tree trunks! ... The man is a bastard – he's a liar and he's got a second-rate mind, as was noted at Oxford. He needs to work tremendously hard to get on top of information. But he's a fascinating bastard ...

Hawke's remarks revealed as much about himself as about the Prime Minister: he adores intelligence – 'the God-given brain' that, in childhood and youth, he had been constantly urged to use – and his commitment to truthfulness was almost equal to Ellie's, but in much more difficult circumstances than any she had needed to withstand. Hawke spoke so often of his intellectual prowess that Chris Crellin, his chauffeur, picked up what *he* referred to as 'Bob's belief in his God-given brain and his duty to use it'.

It was many more months before the unions realised that they now faced a prime minister more intimidating than any in living memory and that if their lives were not to become harder, Hawke was their major hope. His public esteem was crucial, for it was the one weapon he had to use in bargaining with the government on one hand and, on the other, with those more wild-eyed sections of the union movement which did not admit that vis-à-vis the new government, the trade union movement was weak. Hawke became known as the Fireman, because of his constant rushing around and hosing down disputes, for which he enlisted the assistance of George Polites and other leaders of the organised employers, and of Sir John Moore and other arbitration judges. He also set out to establish rapport with the new Minister for Labour, Tony Street. Publicly, Hawke and Street would snap at each other. Privately, they were becoming warm friends.

In 1976 and 1977 Hawke made several public relations trips abroad to seek to improve the image of the Australian unions with the major trading partners, particularly Japan, urging that contracts for iron ore and other goods be signed, for the cargoes would be delivered, not held up by strikes. It was the government's own tactic of reviling the unions that had, in part, necessitated such exercises by Hawke: at home ministers abused the trade union movement for irresponsibility and ruining the country, and their speeches were reported in Japan and elsewhere. They would then arrive in Tokyo and expect Japanese business leaders to believe the truth: that since the appalling year of 1974, Australia's strike record had moderated,[1] although, unlike America, the timing of strikes was unpredictable. However, the government's constant harping upon the wickedness and greed of the unions was having its effect: the electorate at large, which had once accepted that the unions, for all their faults, had done more for decency, honesty and the betterment of society than most other organised bodies of men, was changing its mind. The unions *were* falling into disrepute.

In January 1977 Hawke began publicly to call for a meeting of unions, employers and government to discuss, without inhibition or party political considerations, the state of the Australian economy, and from such discussions to agree upon methods of improving it. He was convinced that the government was mishandling the economy; he knew that the employers were far from happy; and he knew that the unions could never be persuaded to co-operate in a national economic revival until the government had won their trust. So far it had only won their mistrust. The government and its institutions – such as the Reserve Bank and Treasury – had access to a wealth of information on the national and international situation: if only they could be persuaded to share it with the employers and the unions simultaneously, and in an atmosphere of frankness, the first step towards reform would have been taken. Hawke repeatedly demanded a consensus approach to the nation's economic problems. But politics is too often a game of winner take all, and his pleas and demands were rejected. Years earlier Albert Monk, who as ACTU president had co-operated with the Curtin, Chifley and Menzies governments to help to achieve and maintain full employment in Australia, had remarked to Sir Richard Kirby,

> You know, people say now that Hawke is a mad radical. Wait a few years. They'll be saying, 'Dear old Bob – he's trying to get a consensus. He's turning out to be just as conservative as Albert was.' There'll always be unemployment, and Bob's a responsible fellow. Wait and see.

Monk was dead by now; Hawke's commitment to seeking consensus was regarded as something new and within the ALP, if not in the trade union movement, was much disliked. The Prime Minister did not like it himself: a senior employers' representative who knew Fraser well remarked, 'Every time Malcolm looked at Bob he saw the president of the ALP and he just could not bring himself to trust Hawke'. There were no tripartite discussions. Instead, in March 1977, the government agreed eagerly to a half-formulated plan from the premiers to put a brake upon wages and prices. Don Dunstan, the Premier of South Australia, said, 'Being party to that was one of my errors. Bob Hawke came in and stitched up a compromise which saved the bacon of us Labor premiers.' After a few weeks the scheme was abandoned and wages, prices and unemployment all increased. The government blamed the unions.

Hawke was already so adept at strike negotiations that some unions had reached the stage of planning strike campaigns – without Hawke's knowledge – around him: they would calculate that they could reach a certain point in the bargaining process by themselves, but would then get stuck and would need to call upon Hawke to be their negotiator. This was a major change from the old days, under Monk, when officials would only turn to the ACTU as a desperate and unplanned measure. To resort to the Council was to seek to distribute the humiliation of a lost campaign: throughout the trade union movement the ACTU had been known in those days as the Graveyard of Strikes. Now, in a period when the unions were weakening, as unemployment continued to rise inexorably, month by month, and their membership figures were static or decreasing, Hawke's ability to bargain and win settlements for them was of major importance in keeping up morale. His mystique increased. He was seen to be the real Labor leader while Whitlam, in parliament, sat seemingly brooding – isolated and resentful.

As Hawke became in the public's eyes the equal of the Prime Minister, and far more popular than either the leader of the government or the leader of the Opposition, the Left's and the ALP Caucus' envy of him grew.

By mid-1977 Hawke was supremely enviable in Labor eyes. Alone of their leaders he had survived November 1975 with all his titles and privileges intact, and his prestige – now that Whitlam was off centre-stage and a mere shade of the Olympian he once was – had increased. The sweet perquisites of office had been ripped from the Caucus without ceremony. But Hawke now had a personal chauffeur and an LTD limousine (both paid for by ACTU–Solo), with a desk in the back seat where he could work. Even Hawke's supporters on the ACTU executive had been embarrassed by the size of the car – although the alternative, his continuing to drive the ACTU-supplied Holden, was both a waste of his time and a risk to his life, considering his drinking. There had been spirited criticism about the new car in an executive meeting, and much muttering within the party: Hawke looked too grand for a Labor man. And he was treated like a grandee. Crowds fawned upon him; mobs of nouveaux-riches rowdies attached themselves to him as cheer squads and Hawke did not discourage them – to the annoyance of his older and more serious-minded friends, who complained that he was surrounding himself with toadies who lacked both

social virtue and intellect. Hawke has always been indiscrimi-
nately friendly, giving and receiving love and admiration in
lavish quantities. In the years when his career was particularly
stressful and when his future was uncertain he seemed to need
his band of hero-worshippers to shore him up with yea-saying.
His real friends were not afraid to disagree with him and often
reproached him when they thought he behaved intemperately.
Abeles frequently prefaced remarks to Hawke, 'I must say to you,
Bob, you are being stupid'; Rockey, as host of a reception, had
once asked Hawke to leave when he was rude to another guest.
Hawke's closest friend in Melbourne was Colin Cunningham,
a small businessman, an excellent golfer, a good snooker player
and a keen punter. Racegoers describe Cunningham as 'a character out of Damon Runyon'; he calls himself 'a knockabout
bloke'. He is long limbed and laconic. Cunningham grew up,
son of a taxi driver, in the slums of Melbourne – 'a Labor supporter all my life' – and has a working-class wiseguy's sense of
irony. He is a couple of years younger than Hawke and said of
their relationship,

> Bob sort of latched on to me – it was a big deal for me, back
> in 1972 when everybody was staring at him – because, I think,
> he hadn't been out in the world all that much. He wanted
> to know more about life ... general knowledge, sayings. He
> loves sportsmen, and I knew a few: Frank Sedgman, Neale
> Fraser, Garry Sobers – I'd take them round to his house.
> I had golfing friends like Bruce Devlin and Jack Newton
> playing over in America, and I'd tell Bob what was going
> on ... I love the guy. He's a free-giving person ... I like look-
> ing after him, you know? Years ago I said to him, 'Pal, you're
> going to kill yourself – you need a chauffeur'. He wanted me
> to do it, to look after him. I was tempted. But my wife said,
> 'Do that, and don't bother coming home' ... He was very
> anti-Establishment, back in 1974 or 1975. He and I were on
> holiday in Surfers Paradise, and went for dinner in a famous
> restaurant there. Bob gave the owner a helluva time – he was

really misbehaving. I said, 'Pal, I'm going home. You can do what you like, but I'm not putting up with this situation.' We both packed our bags and left Surfers Paradise at 6.30 the next morning.

Recognised wherever he went, Hawke moved in an aura of power. Foreign dignitaries who visited Australia wanted to meet him: an official of the American embassy commented, 'We had to make a cut-off point of seniority. For those below the line we would not even consider trying to arrange an appointment with Bob.' Any news release of his was reported, while Labor shadow ministers had to cajole journalists for attention. People hurried to serve him in shops; chefs emerged from restaurant kitchens to ask if he were enjoying his food and would prepare dishes, at his request, that were not on the menu; airline staff shepherded him into VIP lounges; bowls of fruit and flowers, with a note from the manager, welcomed him in hotels (and one regularly supplied book matches with Hawke's name printed on them); artists of variable talent dedicated songs, books and paintings to him. Hawke was always immaculately dressed in public; he wore a single piece of jewellery: a gold ring set with a large topaz on his left hand. By his late forties he had grown handsome, much better looking than he appeared to be on television. His face was chiselled with character and his hair was grey, gleaming and luxuriant. One could often catch middle-aged men eyeing it enviously.

While sections of the ALP hierarchy could find reasons for condemnation of the party's president in his style, there was now a special area for argument with him: uranium. The Whitlam government's policy had been to mine and sell uranium ore, but since losing office the ALP had been rethinking its attitude. The Left of the party, plus a large minority of people outside the Labor movement, formed into protest groups and were intense in their fear of the mineral and its uses. They demanded that it should be allowed to lie sleeping in the bosom of the earth, its only safe guardian. Attitudes to uranium seem to be determined by personality and individuals' attitudes to humankind: is human

nature trustworthy or unreliable? Is history tragic and imper-
sonal, a progress towards enlightenment, or a divine comedy of
errors and angelic leaps? Or none of these?

Depending upon their answers, some people were convinced
that uranium would be misused and were passionately opposed
to disturbing it; others believed it could help to solve the world's
energy problems and thereby return the prosperity enjoyed
before the Yom Kippur War; others were simply baffled. There
was also the argument, ever fashionable, for venality – from those
who owned uranium leases, from those who were highly paid to
mine yellowcake, and from governments avid to collect revenues
from it. By 1977 the uranium debate had become radiantly hot
on the side of the objectors and, on the side of the supporters,
sullen and suave by turns. A large section of the community was
agnostic.

Hawke had publicly said that he 'wished the bloody stuff had
never been discovered', but since it had and since, whatever
Australia did or did not do about its massive deposits of uranium
ore, yellowcake elsewhere would be mined, refined and used,
he thought it futile to take an isolationist position. Therefore,
he believed that, given safeguards about its handling and use,
Australia's uranium should be mined. His was the pragmatic
agnostic's position. However, agnosticism is invariably confused
with atheism in the minds of excited true believers, and with
timid theism in the minds of excited atheists. Hawke had earned
himself another bunch of black marks in the Left of the party
and among radicals outside it.

Some of his closest supporters, including Clyde Holding and
Bill Landeryou, two of the leaders of the Centre Unity faction
in the Victorian ALP, were opposed to his view that uranium
mining should continue in Australia, as was one of his best
friends on the ACTU executive, Cliff Dolan.

For Hawke, much more distressing than disagreements with
his friends were arguments with his children on the issue.

His household was unusually liberal. Other teenagers had
been astonished by the subjects, taboo to them, that the Hawke

children raised with their parents and by the atmosphere of freedom in the house. Adult visitors were often shocked by the liberties in speech allowed to the children. Hawke was the obverse of an authoritarian father; as well, he was determined that his offspring would not suffer the tight social constrictions of his parents' milieu, against which he had spent half a lifetime in rebellion, and with which he had yet to come to terms. His son, Stephen, was opposed to uranium mining and his elder daughter, Susan, was an anti-uranium activist. Susan, who had resembled Ellie so much in infancy, now, aged twenty, looked uncannily like her father and had his fiery debating style and acute intelligence. He was extravagant in his admiration for her and had been boasting since she turned fourteen that he could have more stimulating discussions with her than with many of his adult male colleagues. However, as a law student at Monash University, Susan Hawke's politics had taken a radical turn. Her arguments with him were becoming embittered as, increasingly, their social views diverged. Hawke was dismayed by the rift that was opening between them. He was also anguished by his arguments with Stephen, whose personality was calm and full of tenderness, like Clem's. Family friends said, 'Bob would put his head on the railway line for Stephen'. Just before the ALP conference of 1977 Hawke flew to Tasmania to talk to Stephen, who had matriculated with excellent marks but was resisting the idea of going to university. Stephen wrote a ten-page letter imploring his father to change his attitudes to uranium mining. Hawke caught a plane for Perth on 29 June, agonising over his looming estrangement from the older children. There was no question that he would change his mind about uranium to please them.

For the time being, however, uranium was the least of his problems. Unbeknown to Hawke, he was about to be deposed as president of the ALP.

He was still extraordinarily selfish. He said of himself a couple of years later, with misery, 'I'm the most selfish man in the world'. He had selfishness' assumption that people would do as he wanted them to, and so was incurious about the wishes of others. If he thought about such matters at all, it was to assume that most people had the same good motives as he did.

Unfortunately, trust in good nature, applied in politics, frequently translates as naivety. Hawke had been trapped by naivety in the past; travelling to Perth, he was flying straight into an elegantly constructed ambush.

When he had become president of the party in 1973 he had said he thought he would hold the job for only one term (until the 1975 Conference) but he had already held it for two and had been shilly-shallying – assuming, again, that others would be in accord with his wishes whatever they turned out to be – about how much longer he wanted it. There were many arguments for his stepping down. A major new one was that his ALP presidency stimulated the combative spirit of the Prime Minister. The senior employers' representative who noted that Fraser could not help seeing Hawke as a political enemy because of Hat II added, 'A lot of things Malcolm did were to get after Bob as ALP president, and that meant getting after him as president of the ACTU as well'. Hawke, however, cherished the extra prestige that came with his second hat. Although the way he wore it continued to damage him within the Caucus, it was of great benefit to him personally, as a public figure, and, he believed, beneficial to the party. Hat II doubled his potential for publicity; he was the most popular man in the country. These two facts were interdependent and, he thought, generated a third: national affection for the ALP. He wanted all of these things. He had, therefore, decided to continue on as party president. He was especially keen to be chairman of this conference, in Perth, for that would give particular pleasure to Clem and Ellie. It had not occurred to Hawke that anyone would stand against him.

The ALP federal executive of eighteen members began its traditional pre-conference meeting on the morning of Thursday, 30 June, at the Sheraton Hotel, with Hawke in the chair. Executive elections would be held the following day; over the weekend interstate delegates would arrive and on Monday the conference proper would get underway.

At the morning-tea break on Thursday, New South Welsh-man Tom Uren, the leader of the Left in Caucus, deputy leader to Whitlam, and a champion of the anti-uranium cause, took David Combe aside. Combe recalled:

Tom was very chummy. He said, 'You and I agree on this uranium question. You know, you're not a bad bloke. I don't always agree with you, but you're not a bad operator. You've got a bastard of a job.' I said, 'Oh, sometimes, Tom. But I enjoy it.' He said, 'Yeah. Sometimes you've got to do things you mightn't like.' I said that was true. He said, 'Well now, you're a good mate of Bob's. A few of us have been having a talk and we've decided we want Mick Young[2] to be president. And we've got twelve votes to say he becomes President. You're the bloke to pass the message on to Bob.' I said, 'Bob's going to run again'. Tom said, 'We think it would be bad for the party if he did. He doesn't want to run and get knocked off. We've got twelve votes to say he shouldn't try – the whole of the Left, plus some others. It's not even close: Bob has had his chips. He's to step down and make way for Mick.'

Then Tom added, 'It's not a one-way street: we're going to support John Ducker for senior vice-president'. That was no concession at all, because Ducker was going to win anyway. Tom said, 'We're telling John the same thing. You're to tell Bob not to run.' I said, 'Why don't you tell him yourself?' Morning tea was over. There was no time to say anything to Bob.

We returned to the meeting and John [Ducker] and I exchanged sign language to indicate that we both had been spoken to, then we passed a note to each other saying we would give Bob the word at lunchtime. As soon as we broke for lunch John and I told Bob we had to talk to him. When we told him what had happened, Bob was devastated. It was inconceivable to him to be treated like that. He became very quiet. He was obviously terribly hurt. I guess what was going through his mind was *who* the twelve people were. Some were pretty obvious, but there were others he'd thought were friends. He was very distressed that Mick Young was involved, because Mick was his mate. Anyway, we agreed to talk it over when the afternoon session had closed. Bob was extremely subdued after lunch, visibly so. At afternoon-tea time Uren came up to me with a grin from ear to ear and said, 'Well done! You've obviously told him. How did he react?' I replied, 'He hasn't decided yet if he'll run or not. We'll discuss it later.'

That evening Hawke, Combe and Ducker assembled in either Combe's or Ducker's hotel room. Ducker took up the story:

I didn't realise that Bob was going to go under, because I'd got used to the fact that Hawke never went under. I think it was Graham Richardson [secretary of the New South Wales branch of the ALP] who told me the facts of life. Bob was saying, 'The West Australians are on side – they won't do me over'. He was very upset – overwrought – not in tears, but so close to tears it was indistinguishable – and still clinging to hope. So I had to say to him, 'Bob, you're done. Please understand that you are *finished*. Please understand the consequences of that: *you are a failed leader*. You're out!' And he replied, 'After all I've done for the party! Worked my arse off, battled and struggled. Sacrificed my family. And that's what they're going to do to me!' So I said to him, 'You've helped to create this yourself. You've been playing footsie, saying maybe I will continue, maybe I won't. You've got to make up your mind. Do you want to be president of the ALP?' And he said, 'Yes! Just for one more term.' So I said, 'Right. Let's get the list [of executive members]. You get on to your mates, and leave the rest to me. We'll call in every bloody IOU you ever had.'

There were two thoughts uppermost in my mind: one was friendship and loyalty to Bob. The other was the absolute disaster for the labour movement of his standing and being defeated. As well, I had my blood up, because in the final analysis, this was a fight between the Left and the Right. So for all those reasons I was willing to go to the wall ... Looking back, I think I was already wondering if the worst came and we were done, if that would be such a bad thing. Because, we'd live to fight another day, and on a pretty good platform: those for Hawke, and those against him. At that time especially Bob was a saintly figure in the labour movement – he was a figure of awe, of reverence, tremendously strong. Even among the Left in New South Wales. A helluva lot of the younger Left there had unbounded admiration and affection for him. So there was a potential in that. Now my thoughts about the possibilities for the future were not at the front of my head, but knowing myself, they were there in the back somewhere.

Time was critical: it was already about 6 p.m. and the federal executive would meet at 9.30 the following morning. Hawke is unused to fighting for himself, as distinct from fighting for others: the battle for the ACTU presidency had been a power bloc battle; when he had almost been sacked as ALP president in 1974, it was the trade union faction on the ALP executive that had weighed in to save him. Except for the most malicious, nobody doubted that Hawke had courage, but he was known as a man who was courageous in pursuing causes, while expecting fraternal generosity for himself. In the Victorian Left it was a frequent complaint that Hawke expected preselection for a winnable parliamentary seat, 'on a plate'. Indeed, the Socialist Left's ability to frighten Hawke off, apparently, from a fight over preselection had convinced people that he was a man who would not fight for himself. Therefore, if only he could be demoralised (by being treated shabbily), he would quail and give up. Ducker and Combe both feared that this would be his reaction. Combe said,

I learned that night that Bob was a fighter. I think it was the first time that he had been forced to get into that grimy arena in which Ducker and I, for example, had to operate often, the nasty nitty-gritty of actually getting on the phone himself and asking for support. He had always had such a machine working for him. His intellect and his stature were such that he'd never had to get down to that level that the rest of us were used to. Other people had always done it for him ... Ducker said to him, 'Listen, you're to get on the telephone to these buggers and say that you are running for president and can you count on them for support. Don't listen to how they hedge. You've got to force a commitment out of them – Yes or No.'

So we began running a couple of phones at once. Joan Taggart [executive delegate from the ACT] had joined us early on, and was on side. We had people all over the joint, finding other people. Poor old John Waters, the delegate from the Northern Territory, had just arrived and was checking in at the reception desk when we barrelled him and said, 'We want to talk to you. As soon as you get to your room, ring this number.' And upstairs Bob was on the blower, saying, 'I understand there's going to be a contest for the presidency tomorrow. I want you to know that I'm running for a final term. Can I count on you for support?' He got some pretty funny responses. You know, people who *obviously* had promised Uren that they would go along with the Young move, and who were now backing and filling to Bob.

Essentially, Hawke's lobbying was soft, an appeal to old colleagues to stand by him. The leaders of the move against him, Uren and Senator Arthur Geitzelt (brother of Ray) had not, it seems, counted on his lobbying at all. Their more serious miscalculation was that they had not counted on the loyalty of that wily myrmidon, John Ducker. It was well known that Ducker was keen to become senior vice-president of the party, so it was thought that Ducker would do nothing to ruin his own chances. But while Hawke was appealing to the sweeter instincts of his colleagues, Ducker, elsewhere in the hotel, was verbally thumping them witless.

He recalled,

I said to people, 'You realise that this will be a fundamental split between the party and the ACTU? You realise that we're dealing with the most popular man in the country and we are going to dump him, publicly?' And they came back with, 'Oh, can't we persuade him not to run? He hasn't said he's going to run yet.' And I said, 'Well, he's going to. And the party will be seen to have knocked him off – the president of the ACTU, a man with the esteem he's got. And if you're happy to wear that, OK. But I want you to know that we'll make sure you are personally accounted for, in terms of the part *you've* played in getting rid of Hawke, and you can go back and talk to your mates in the Trades Hall about the fact that you sold out the trade union movement ... Haven't we had a thousand bloody battles about the trade union movement's right to have a fair go in the Labor Party? And *you're* going to be one of the people who've destroyed that!' And I'd get the arguments: 'Hey, listen. You know he's gone off the deep end. You remember when he bucketed the [Whitlam] government! You remember the number of times when all of us were bloody angry about the things he did. Why have we got to cop that, forever?' And I'd say, 'Well, he's been going a lot quieter, hasn't he? And if you do the balance sheet adjustment about Bob, which way does it go?' And to that I'd get, 'Yeah. All right – he's done more good than bad.' So then I'd be nice and friendly, and would say, 'Do you carry as much bloody stress and pressure as that bloke does? Look what it's done to his wife and kids. And he's done it for the party and the trade union movement. Now, where do you stand?' And, then I'd have to say, 'I'm a reasonable man. But I'll make sure that the lines are drawn in this bloody party and trade union movement between who stands for Hawke and who is against him. And I'll be on one side of that fence, and you'll be on the other, chum. And if you're satisfied that the rank and file will support you for stabbing Hawke in the back, have a go, mate!'

And to Mick: 'Mick. You want to stuff yourself for all time? You're a man with many ambitions. Don't forget that Hawke, in intervention in Victoria, stood up for what was right. Just count your debts, Mick. Just count the number of times he's been a mate for you. Just consider how you'll feel about cutting his throat. Do you think, after that, you'll be able to ring him up and talk about which horses to back, like in the old days?'

And then I had another point to make to a few people: 'If you want the parliamentary party to be seen as anti-trade union, if you want to run the risk of an absolute split – because, I tell you something, friend, the trade union movement and the workers of this country are getting to a point where they're wondering whether they can afford the bloody Labor Party. And it wouldn't be all that bloody impossible to see the trade union movement decide to go independent. You realise that, I hope? And I hope you realise that if the trade unions were to abandon the Labor Party, well ... You haven't got too many resources left, have you?' It was a friendly sort of light chatter ... To the people from New South Wales I had a particular message. I told them, 'We've always in the end had a bit of tolerance in New South Wales with the factions. There will be *none* if this happens. I'm prepared to go all the way on this one. Because, quite frankly, I don't altogether mind a situation in which the Left has destroyed Hawke and the Right has backed him. If you want the battle lines drawn on that basis, then I'm prepared to go to our next [New South Wales ALP] conference and have a bit of cleaning up.' Well, they didn't like that sort of proposal.

Not surprisingly, for Ducker was threatening frontal assault by the Right on the Left in New South Wales, and there could be no doubt about who would win that. The outcome could be a split in New South Wales. If the party split there it would almost certainly split in Victoria as well.

By about 8 p.m. Hawke had spoken to those whom he knew were not his sworn enemies and Ducker had bailed up the same people and many others for his friendly chat. But Hawke was still far from safe: promises are one thing, votes another. More importantly they wanted to avoid, for the Labor movement's sake, a brawl on the eve of the conference. Obviously Uren also wanted to protect the party from a brawl. David Combe said, 'I think *we* finished up with about twelve votes', but Ducker was not convinced and said later, 'I wasn't confident that when the moment of truth came the numbers would be there'. The Hawke camp, now a Gang of Four – Hawke, Ducker, Combe and Taggart – decided that they had to seize the weapon of their opponents and turn it against them. Uren had tried to use psychological warfare to frighten Hawke out of standing for the presidency: the trick now was to frighten Uren out of attempting to execute his plan for running Young as president. Combe recalled:

> We had to decide how to get the message through to Uren. We tried to find him and he'd gone into bloody hiding. So had Geitzelt. We tried to telephone him several times and there was no answer, then we got on to the hotel switchboard who told us that Mr Uren was not taking any calls. So we came up with what was a brilliant strategy: everyone would be listening to [the national ABC radio broadcast] *AM*. We'd give John Highfield of *AM* an exclusive interview. We'd get him to do an interview with Bob, ostensibly about the conference and then – I would have primed Highfield up – he'd throw in a question at the end asking, 'By the way, Mr Hawke, have you decided yet whether you're running for the presidency?' And Bob would say, 'Well, John, you've caught me at a weak moment. Yes, I am going to run.' It would be obvious to anybody who heard it that he had the numbers. The important people would know that Hawke was fighting back. So we tried to get Highfield but he'd gone out to visit relations. We left messages everywhere for him. We were all feeling

absolutely euphoric about our brilliant plan and went and had a marvellous dinner to celebrate. By the time Highfield got back to the Sheraton we were as full as boots. Bob was no worse than the rest of us: we were all full, with the exception of Joan Taggart, who has an amazing capacity to hold her liquor. It was a tremendous dinner! The interview with Highfield took place at 1 a.m., on John Ducker's bed. And then we rollicked on for the rest of the night: I don't think any of us went to bed at all – maybe we had an hour's sleep. Uren complained later to the executive that he'd been harassed at 4 a.m. – he claimed he looked through the peephole in his door and there was a little bloke with crinkly hair and a big bloke with curly hair standing outside, thumping on the door. Joan Taggart swears it's not true. She stayed with us all night, and is positive that Bob and I didn't do that to Tom.

Before eight o'clock, when *AM* is broadcast, the Hawke camp had reassembled around a radio. Combe said,

I remember the *AM* linkman saying, when the interview was over, 'that was an obviously tired and emotional Bob Hawke telling John Highfield ...' Well, we needed a bit of a heart-starter. I think Bob had a brandy for breakfast. Then we went into the executive meeting. And they were furious! You could have cut the air with a knife. They'd all listened to *AM* and knew they were done. So the vote was taken quickly. Ducker nominated Hawke as president of the party – there were no other nominations – and that was it. Unanimous re-election for Hawke. The whole episode was one of the most exciting I've been involved in.

Hawke's comment about the affair was:

It was all a bit nebulous. There was a brief push that developed around Mick Young. By the time we arrived in Perth it was clear that there was a move to try to get Mick up and knock me off. I didn't want to hold on to the ALP presidency forever, but I particularly wanted to chair the conference in my home state ... Oh, but a bit of talking here and there and we were able to fix things up.

This description was given years later, when Hawke's barricade of defence mechanisms was in place. He especially wanted to forget that Mick Young, of whom he is very fond, had been a party to the plan. In 1978, when Hawke voluntarily stepped down as ALP president, he lobbied hard for Young to succeed him, but the numbers for Young could not be raised a second time and Neil Batt from Tasmania won the position. Talking of other matters, Hawke remarked in the early 1980s, 'I suppose that thinking the best of people has done me a lot of harm over the years. But I still believe it's the right way.'

On Friday, 1 July 1977, he was scheduled to address a luncheon at the Perth Press Club, and set off in an elated mood, positively swaggering with renewed self-confidence. He began his speech to the news media, assembled from all over the country, and all aware that there had been moves afoot to oust him, by announcing his unopposed re-election as president of the ALP. Earlier he had told journalists that he might have an 'important announcement' to make about his future, creating the impression that he was about to announce his move to parliament. There was some surprise that his speech – which was peppered with jokes, including one about the Queen's horse breaking wind – had no mention of this. During question time, journalists raised the matter. Hawke replied, 'If I am going to change from a position which I enjoy and do well [the presidency of ACTU], it would not be sensible for me to put my bum on a backbench seat', and went on to say that, were he to enter parliament, he would want to be leader.

There was an instant scandal. The *Sydney Morning Herald*'s headline of 4 July best summarised the Caucus reaction: 'HAWKE SELF-DESTRUCTS'. The country's major political commentators announced that day and for weeks afterwards that Hawke, by implicitly demanding the leadership of the Opposition as the price of his entry to parliament, had destroyed his political future.

On the same day, under a headline, 'Hawke hogs the spotlight again', Michelle Grattan of the *Age*, in a long, thoughtful analysis of the party's mood, wrote:

> ... he is putting the terms of his entry so high [people are saying] that they cannot be met within the Labor Party's democratic norms. Therefore he can explain his failure to enter Parliament as due to factors outside his control. Friday's behaviour can also be seen as showing the essential Hawke style ... An unmistakable Hawke characteristic – both a limitation and a strength – is the so-called larrikin streak, the recurring tendency of the Congregational minister's son to break out and say 'to hell with the niceties' ... [Like] Whitlam, Hawke also uses [the] device of appealing over the heads of his immediate circle to a wider audience. Mr Hawke must know Caucus's knee-jerk anger and resentment at anyone's attempt to claim the leadership as some sort of right (or destiny). But perhaps he believes, consciously or not, that the electorate sees it as refreshing honesty, a willingness to dispense with the false modesty politicians assume ...

Phillip Adams, the humorist and social critic, wrote in the *Sydney Morning Herald* of 7 July,

> Mr Hawke said today he would only enter the Catholic Church if he became Pope. 'I'm in a pretty powerful position now, as spiritual advisor to the Butchers' Union, and wouldn't want to waste my time going to the Vatican unless my colleagues in the College of Cardinals promised to come across with the puff of white smoke. Similarly, I don't propose dying unless suitable arrangements are made in heaven. I'm not knocking God. He's done a pretty good job in recent aeons. But it's about time he stood down in favour of a younger, more talented bloke.'

There was a consensus among political journalists that Hawke's parliamentary career was finished before it had a chance to begin. Combe remarked in late 1981, 'I wonder how those characters can live with themselves, having written him off so often, now saying that he is the best thing the ALP has going for it?'

The conference, which opened on Monday, 4 July, was not a happy one for Hawke. Conferences are traditionally occasions for social drinking; a number of women – delegates and journalists – complained later that Hawke, drink-taken, had propositioned them with his usual frankness and on rebuff had become sarcastic. He was bad tempered for much of the week. He had been prevented from speaking on the uranium issue but had made a vehement speech in support of the building of the Omega navigation base in Victoria – to which the Left was strongly opposed, believing it to be linked with the darker side of American international defence. The conference decided by one vote that Omega should be constructed. Hawke took satisfaction from this, for Peter Cook, a delegate from Western Australia, told Hawke later that his speech had persuaded him to vote for Omega, against instructions. Hawke is probably justified in believing that his intervention decided the policy. The uranium policy that was proposed stated that there should be a ban upon uranium mining and export 'until the ALP national conference so determines'. But Clyde Holding, Don Dunstan, Combe and others conceived an ingenious amendment, which they persuaded the Left to support. It was that uranium mining should be banned 'until the ALP so determines, recognising that the authority of the Australian Labor Party can be vested in: the Conference, the executive, the Caucus'. Combe said,

> It was very bloody clever. While Bob and I and the others knew what it meant, the Left didn't quite realise what it was getting itself into – because, should we win government, it would be a very simple proposition for the Caucus to say 'the ALP has now decided ...'

Most of the media also did not quite realise that there was a loophole in the wording of the ALP ban on uranium that would allow a future Labor government to overturn it. The policy was widely reported at face value, as an unlimited ban on uranium.

Hawke's argument, which was stated privately to the executive then restated by him publicly, to an ALP gathering, was:

> I am not convinced as a matter of intellectual integrity by the arguments for leaving uranium in the ground. If we leave it in the ground we have done nothing about the dangers – the disposal of nuclear waste, terrorists acquiring weapons – nothing about the people occupied in the generating plants in West Germany, Japan and the United States. We have done nothing about that, except to make it more expensive, and in the process, it seems to me that what we have done is to forgo the opportunity as Australians to have a voice in safeguarding the world in the processes of the utilisation of uranium.

The anti-uranium lobby was furious. When the conference was over the Socialist Left's newspaper, *Labor Star*, ran a story asserting that 'some prominent ALP people believed themselves immune to policy' and that they could 'please themselves what they said publicly'. It singled out Hawke as a major offender, then concluded, 'If our leaders do not wish to accept this principle [of loyalty to policy] they should get out or be removed. The Party cannot afford this luxury.'[3]

A few days later Hawke was addressing a public meeting in the Town Hall Square, Sydney, attacking the latest federal Budget, when a demonstration organised by the New South Wales Teachers' Federation was staged. People bearing placards that read 'No Nuclear Hawks' marched onto the platform and others in the audience began to boo and heckle him. Hawke lost his temper. Indeed, the anti-uranium propaganda campaign had grossly misrepresented his views on the issue, and over a period of months had suggested that Hawke was in cahoots with captains of the mining industry, among them Sir Roderick Carnegie, to assist them in their uranium ventures. (An irony was that Carnegie and Hawke disagreed about the virtues of uranium: Carnegie found Hawke's lack of enthusiasm irritating. But the anti-uranium forces did not know that and were scandalised to have recently discovered, twenty years after the event, that Hawke and Carnegie were friends. Vile motives were read into their relationship.) Hawke accused the protestors of being 'enemies of the working class' and 'henchmen of Fraser and Lynch' (then deputy Prime Minister) and stormed off the platform.

On 25 August, the government announced that mining and export of uranium could go ahead. The ACTU Congress was due to open just over a fortnight later, in Sydney, and the uranium issue would be paramount, whether Hawke liked it or not. He did not.

Hawke's ability, learned in childhood, to put out of his mind matters that he found unpleasant has been a major factor in sustaining him physically and psychologically over the years. Under pressures that would have caused others to have nervous breakdowns, heart attacks, or to give up in despair, he has remained cheerful or, when he has suffered some serious reversal of fortune, has recovered quickly. He banishes the negative, as Ellie banished any doubts about divine mercy when Neil met his horrible death. Uranium was a factor in the tensions of Hawke's private life – while the ALP conference was in progress Susan had been in an anti-uranium demonstration that was ridden down by mounted police – and of his public one. Colleagues in the party had warned him that, as president, he must either remain silent or toe the party line. He wanted to be allowed to forget yellowcake.

At the ACTU executive meeting that preceded the Congress, Charlie Fitzgibbon read through the agenda of recommendations to be put to delegates and was taken aback to see that there was no mention of uranium. He said to Hawke, 'We have to formulate a policy on uranium. No matter what it says, *we've got to have one*. And Bob replied, "It's not an issue. Don't worry about it."' The ACTU executive prepared for the 1977 Congress without a uranium policy, but was then forced to accept a motion from delegates that the uranium issue be added to the agenda. As well, forty ALP Caucus members signed a petition to the ACTU requesting that it uphold ALP policy. The executive scrambled together a recommendation demanding, first, that the federal government agree, within two months, to hold a referendum on uranium mining; second, if no referendum undertaking were given, that the unions 'after proper reference to rank and file meetings and subject to their endorsement' place a ban on the mining and transport of uranium. This double-barrelled recommendation did not amount to an ACTU point of view about uranium. It was, rather, a barrister's argument against the government, which had chosen to adopt some of the recommendations of the Fox Inquiry into uranium while rejecting others. The ACTU's recommendation wore the hallmarks of Hawke's legalistic carrot-and-stick puritanism. It was logically watertight, morally spotless and evaded the big issue: emotional prejudice. It also evaded ALP policy. The party has no right to order the trade union movement around, but it often behaves as if it thinks it should have.

Hawke was supremely confident about the ACTU Congress. Since he had been written off as a future parliamentarian in June, his status as leader of the trade union movement had strengthened. Unionists were not at all dismayed that Hawke had offended most of the ALP Caucus, for the ancient hostility of workers for 'their' politicians is a constant undercurrent in labour movement affairs, and becomes a rip tide whenever 'their' politicians are seen to be useless in protecting the workers against legislative assaults by anti-Labor governments. Hawke had been fighting against the Fraser government's industrial relations legislation for a year, with some success, for while the Bills were being introduced, their laws were not being enforced. The government was arming itself against the unions, but so far had not summoned the nerve to launch a material, as distinct from verbal, attack. As well, 1977 was the fiftieth anniversary of the founding of the ACTU, and a cause for general good humour, sentimentality and congratulations.

Hawke's confidence was well founded: the 1977 Congress turned out to be his most resounding personal success. After eight years he managed, in that Congress, to achieve a major aim of his election platform – agreement to the merger of white-collar unions with the ACTU. As well, he trounced the extreme Left, which had been harassing him since the moment he had been elected president. And he got a new secretary.

Souter was retiring. A new secretary and a new assistant secretary would mean that ACTU administration would be different in future, run by younger and less strict men. Souter's replacement was the assistant secretary, Peter Nolan; Bill Kelty, who had been a research officer, would move up to become assistant secretary, and was to become the most significant element in ACTU administrative affairs. Kelty was from a working-class Melbourne family, university educated, and like Hawke had rejected a promising academic career – Kelty's professor of political science said he was one of the brightest students he had ever had – to work for the trade union movement. He had first joined the Storemen and Packer's Union. In Lygon circles that union had once been known as the Poormen and Slackers, but the leadership of Bill Landeryou was transforming it into one of the best organised and most progressive unions in the country. Landeryou himself was a product of the New Look unionism that Hawke, by his successes as ACTU advocate, had helped to create. Kelty was Landeryou's protégé. Souter, whose eye for good staff was unusually sharp, had hired him in 1974 and had trained him. Kelty was justly described as 'a little factory' because of his capacity for work.

By 1977 Hawke and Souter were reconciled to each other and there was even the warmth of nostalgia between them, but their working methods still drove each other mad, and their mutual irritation affected other ACTU employees. Souter and Jean Sinclair, Hawke's right arm, had not been able to work easily together, but Sinclair and Kelty were buddies.

The new secretary, Peter Nolan, had a traditional trade union background – he had been a printer – and was a large,

well-dressed and agreeable man whose personality and appearance equipped him to take some of the burden of public performance from Hawke's shoulders. Souter had eschewed the news
media and speech-giving. Nolan's relaxed manner fitted him
for public appearances of all sorts; he projected the image of a
modern, reasonable union leader. Even Tories could not dislike
Peter Nolan, while Hawke still sent them into fits of anger.

In Hawke's opening address to the 632 delegates (representing, because of a new card-voting system, 864 votes) he devoted
most of his time to an attack on the government's policies and
made only fleeting reference to uranium. It was not one of his
better speeches, being spangled with superlatives, many of them
theatrical-sounding exaggerations. Since the election of the
Fraser government there had been a notable change in Hawke's
speeches to union audiences, a reversion to the dramatic oratory he had used in his early days as ACTU president when,
with anti-Labor governments in office, he had described every
federal Budget as 'the worst', 'the most hypocritical', 'the most
blatant ...'

It was his role to fire the troops with conviction. His own
conviction – that the new government's policies were socially
disastrous and economically futile – was deeply felt, but his
speeches by 1977 were running against the social current: people
were fatigued by political drama, the electorate at large did not
possess his emotional stamina to continue arguing. The press,
affected like others, was wearied by Hawke's language of crisis.
Andrew Clark of the *National Times* reported, 'Hawke showed
during the conference that the considerable intellectual fat he
built up during his days as a student at Oxford, and later the
ANU ... is diminishing ... Hawke's opening speech was verbose
and sloppy ...'[4]

Indisputably, however, Hawke's speeches during the uranium
debate, which took up most of Thursday, 15 September, were
brilliant displays of jury barrister's art. By the time the uranium
issue arose it was clear that the ACTU executive was in deep
trouble with its recommendation, for the Left and Centre had

organised and were determined to force the executive to argue on a different ground – not on legalities, but on the emotional issue: the dangers of uranium. Charlie Fitzgibbon quickly drafted an addendum to the executive's recommendation to try to save the leadership, and specifically Hawke, from defeat. A major problem for the executive was that members of the AWU and the Federated Ironworkers were already employed in uranium mining at Mary Kathleen. They were very well paid. No matter what the Congress decided, they or other men would mine yellowcake, for the money was too good to resist. If the unions of which they were members decided they must obey a ban on uranium mining and removed the uranium miners from their books, other unions would move in and sign them up, or non-union labour would be used. All of this opened the way for bitterness, demarcation disputes between different unions vying for members, and, worse, a public demonstration that the ACTU was incapable of enforcing its policies upon its affiliates. It would, in short, be a show of weakness, and to a government already determined to weaken the union movement. Tony Street had told Hawke that if the trade union movement barred transport of uranium, the government would use troops to do the work.

The Left's amendment was moved by Ralph Taylor of the Australian Railways Union and seconded by Jim Roulston of the AMWSU. Their proposal echoed ALP policy and went on to demand an early meeting of unions 'involved in uranium mining ... for the purpose of seeking the endorsement of the union members concerned' of a total ban to prevent the Mary Kathleen mine from filling existing contracts. Hawke, in his first speech, emphasised that the issue before Congress was not uranium mining as such, but the ACTU executive's recommendation about a referendum. The anti-uranium faction refused to be sidetracked and four hours of vehement debate, most of it from the Left, ensued. Their speakers included Taylor; Roulston; P. Cavanagh of the Northern Territory Trades and Labour Council; and the Left's lion, John Halfpenny, who provided a 'brilliant piece of atmospheric oratory'.

There is no contest between the oratory of the trade unions and that of the federal parliament: as public speakers, union officials excel parliamentarians in their sincerity of feeling and their robustness of language, and an ACTU Congress battling over a serious issue is one of the great pieces of theatre in Australian political life. Unhappily, it is all allowed to dissipate, unrecorded, except for a paragraph here and there that is reported by the news media.

Hawke, having moved the executive's recommendation, had the right of reply. He had taken some notes of his opponents' arguments during the preceding hours of debate. When he took the rostrum he spoke for almost an hour, pouring out refutations of the major points of those who had supported the Taylor–Roulston amendment. Professor Ross Martin of La Trobe University, who had attended ACTU congresses for two decades, wrote:

> His reply in the uranium debate was a *tour de force*. [I] could not recall any Congress contribution during the last twenty years in which a range of opponents was attacked in terms of their own remarks quite so cuttingly and with such command ... If there were any votes still swinging at the end of that debate, Mr Hawke must surely have swung them his way ... It is impossible adequately to summarise such a long and complex speech ... but its varied flavour may be suggested by a sample of comments (necessarily abbreviated) on specific points made by opposition speakers:
>
> The 'people should examine the issue' (Taylor): [Hawke] 'Examine but not decide; this is a nonsensical position'.
>
> Anti-uranium demonstrators are not 'louts or long-hairs' (Taylor): [Hawke] 'Don't use this argument to me, Ralph Taylor', a reproof administered with evident emotion and followed by remarks about 'Those sincere young people', involving an implicit reference to the President's own daughter.
>
> Likening a referendum on uranium to one on heroin (Taylor): [Hawke] 'an absurd analogy', the distinction between

uranium and heroin, in terms of views about their consequences, being elaborated [by Hawke].

The unions should not leave it to others to determine
their position (Halfpenny): [Hawke] 'Don't put up that nonsense that we're dodging the issue'; the executive recommendation committed the ACTU to campaign for a 'continuing
moratorium'.

The task is to protect workers and Aborigines (Halfpenny):
[Hawke] 'We'll be in an infinitely stronger position to protect the trade union movement' if, when the Government
tries 'to put troops on the wharves and on to the railways ...
we can be seen to have adopted the processes of democracy'.

Statistics of worker fatalities in North American uranium
mines (Cavanagh): [Hawke] a 'bad and improper argument'
because the figures related to underground mining not open-
cut, as in Australia.

A written account, let alone a short one, cannot hope to
convey all the nuances of such a speech – the changes of tone
and tempo, the flashes of raillery, sarcasm and jocularity, the
spurts of emotion and the calm appeals to reason. It was a
speech that drew jeers as well as applause, boos as well as
cheers. It also drew blood in unusual quantity ... Irrespective
of reaction, however, the President held his audience completely captive for the entire forty-nine minutes of his speech.
At the end he reiterated that there were 'people of integrity'
on both sides of the uranium issue, and quietly asserted that
there had been 'no more important decision in our whole
fifty years of history ... and about the sort of society in which
this trade union movement operates'.

Fourteen minutes later, Congress had made that decision.
The Taylor/Roulston amendment was defeated by 493 votes
to 371 ... The great issue was settled – for the time being.[5]

Martin's final comment was prophetic: the uranium issue was to
resurface at the Congress of 1979 and to provide Hawke with
his most devastating defeat as leader of the union movement.

He had, in 1977, although he did not yet know it, made his last great speech to Congress as president of the ACTU.

The executive that Congress elected was weighted 13–5 in Hawke's favour; the significance of this lay in the new meaning of 'in Hawke's favour'. Once it had meant a coalition of Centre to extreme Left supporters: now it was an amalgam of old friends and former enemies, stretching from the Left to the Right. Ducker was Hawke's candidate for the junior vice-presidency of the ACTU, in contest with the Left's candidate, Jim Roulston. Ducker won. The alliance that had brought Hawke to victory in 1969 was, by 1977, formally broken, and Hawke had bid good-bye to the hard Left for good. The parting was not of his making, but rather that of the Socialist Left faction in Victoria: Labor politics in that state had forced him in to alliance with the Right.

Hawke could now choose to continue as president of the ACTU for the rest of his working life, or he could seek to enter parliament. The impediment to this latter course was, as it had been in the early 1960s when it had first been suggested to him that he should aim for the presidency of the ACTU, that he did not have many feathers to fly with. He had no effective power base, no machine, only – as then – the affection and admiration of ordinary men and women. By 1977 there were millions of Australians who held him in high regard. But millions of citizens could not guarantee that seventy people, members of the Victorian ALP's electoral committee, would vote for Hawke's preselection as a Labor parliamentary candidate.

He had little time to consider his future, for from the time the Congress ended he was busy with dispute negotiations and con-tinued arguments about the uranium problem. The government had rejected the idea of a referendum on uranium within days of its adoption by Congress; Hawke entered negotiations with Street and the government on one hand, and the unions on the other, searching for a compromise. He overworked and by the first week of October was in bed with a respiratory infection, so severe that some newspapers reported he had pneumonia. While he was still convalescent another federal election was called.

Hawke rallied his energy and set out on the campaign trail. The party had arranged an electioneering schedule for him that, just to read, creates a sensation of fatigue: 15 November: Goulburn; 16–17 November: ALP campaign, Sydney; 18 November: Perth; 19 November: Kalgoorlie; 20 November: Brisbane; 21 November: Sydney and Melbourne; 22–23 November: Sydney; 24 November: Brisbane; 25 November: Queensland; 26 November: Melbourne; 27 November: Launceston and Hobart; 28 November: Hobart and Burnie; 29 November: Melbourne, Australian Farmers' Union; factory gate meeting, Melbourne Ports; lunch Windsor Hotel; Box Hill Town Hall; 5 December: Melbourne, Canberra, Orange; 6 December: white-collar rally, Her Majesty's Theatre; Kadmiah Hall, Elsternwick; 7 December: Melbourne, Hobart, Melbourne; 8 December: Sydney Chamber of Commerce; book launch; Fitzroy Town Hall; ethnic meeting.[6]

In fact, his electioneering began three weeks before this formal schedule. Senior party officials commented during the campaign that Hawke was working so hard they feared he would drop dead. He recalled:

> As the campaigning went on I knew that we were not going to win, and that has a physical as well as an emotional impact. I was – you know – miserable inside … From early on I was very apprehensive about our economic policy. I remember sitting in my office at the ACTU, not long before Whitlam was due to deliver our policy speech, when Ralph Willis [who had left the ACTU in 1973 and been elected member for Gellibrand] telephoned me. He said, 'Have you heard what's happening?' And I said, 'No, what do you mean? And he told me that Whitlam, in the policy speech, was going to announce that Labor would not give tax cuts – which Fraser had promised, and which the Libs were using in their advertisements, with photographs of a fistful of dollars – but instead of that Gough would promise to abolish payroll tax. Gough was going to say that abolition of payroll tax would

stimulate economic recovery and provide more jobs. I said to Ralph, 'You're bloody joking!' And he replied, 'I'm not. You'd better ring Bill Hayden, because Bill is not opposing it.' So I rang Bill and he said that he'd talked to Whitlam and Whitlam seemed absolutely committed to it, so there was nothing Bill could do. That was about Tuesday. On Thursday or Friday, Whitlam was to launch our campaign at the Sydney Opera House. The night before I flew to Sydney and stayed in the Boulevard Hotel. Gough's Sydney office was next door, in the Westfield Tower. I spent about half an hour with his advisers, explaining to them that this was just *lunacy*, unbelievable lunacy – that if they thought they could persuade people that abolition of payroll tax was better than tax cuts, and get the electorate to believe that, they were just bloody crazy. I persuaded them that I was right. So off they went to talk to Gough about it – he was closeted upstairs somewhere. After about half an hour they came back and said, 'Aw, we're sorry, Bob', and I'll never forget the next words, 'We're sorry, but Gough feels that he must have something dramatic'. And I replied, 'Well, you can tell him that he's got it!'

Then we went out on that campaign trail and everywhere I went I was hit between the eyes with the payroll tax. I remember one particular meeting in Tasmania, at a factory. It got a good reception and when the crowd had dispersed one of the shop stewards, a stalwart Labor bloke, came up to me and said, 'That was a great speech, Bob. But it's tough. This tax thing – they just won't buy it. Not half of them are going to vote for the party.' At a factory meeting! The more I went around the country, the more I knew we were gone. Gough was a giant in so many respects, but in terms of understanding the political implications of decisions ... Even so, I was surprised by the enormity of our defeat. It was a gruelling night in Canberra, in the tally room. The defeat was even worse in terms of votes than 1975.

Labor polled only 39.6 per cent of primary votes, its worst result since 1931. Whitlam's political career was dust and ashes and it seemed he was leaving behind him crippled heirs, a party whose sense of failure was such that it would espouse defeat as romantic, its inevitable fate. David Combe, seated in a corner of the tally room was almost in tears. Earlier in the evening Kate Baillieu, who was reporting on the election for a television network, had asked him to comment when the results were clear and Combe had agreed to do so. When she returned with her cameraman Combe dissuaded her from going through with the interview by saying, 'Do you really want me to show my humiliation to the people of Australia?'

Baillieu recalled,

A while later Bob left his chair in front of the TV cameras and I saw him go over to Combe, who was alone, and put his arms around him … At the end of the night Bob, Hazel, I and Geoff Gleghorn [who had returned to the ACTU as press officer] all went out to get in the car and be driven to the Canberra Rex. Geoff was so upset that he began banging the roof of the car with his fist, then beating his head on it. Bob was very depressed, but his reaction was extraordinary. He immediately started to cheer Geoff up, and to talk about the future. He said, 'Come on. We mustn't despair. We've got to think about the future, about winning.' And he went on talking like that for the rest of the night.

Hawke said,

As president of the party I had the obligation to attempt to counterbalance the proportions of the defeat. I had to say, 'Look, we're down – but we can win from here'. And I believed that. Also I thought it was imperative that we prevent people from thinking, 'Oh, Labor's out of office most of the time, and now it's out for another twenty-three years'.

It was a foregone conclusion that Whitlam would resign as leader and be replaced by Bill Hayden. Hayden had been the most able of Whitlam's ministers; he had displayed true grit as Minister for Social Security, in his negotiations with the medical profession over the introduction of Medibank; in the few months he had been Treasurer he had shown decisiveness and an understanding of economics otherwise lacking in the Cabinet; he was a hard worker; reserved, pleasant. Political journalists respected him. But Hayden was not a forceful speaker, and he had neither Whitlam's grandeur of vision and wit, nor Hawke's larrikin panache and large sympathies. Whether Hayden would be able to compete successfully with the bull-like strength and monkey cunning of Malcolm Fraser and lead the party back to office was debatable. The popularity polls said that Hawke could.

Hawke had been delaying his dream now for fourteen years, since the Corio election. Since 1974 he had frustrated his political supporters and his numbers man in Victoria, Bill Landeryou, by refusing to make a decision about parliament. There are metres of newspaper cuttings, from 1974 onwards, reporting that Hawke had or would decide to became a candidate for one safe Labor seat after another. Landeryou and others had been scurrying around behind the scenes, negotiating on Hawke's behalf, only to discover that he was not, today, as keen on the idea as he had been yesterday. For all Hawke's impetuosity in small matters, in large ventures – for example, finding employment, running for the ACTU presidency – he can take an interminably long time to act. In the interim 'he blows hot and cold', as Jean Sinclair noted. She had learned to discount Hawke's sudden spurts of enthusiasm, knowing that by the following day, he would as likely as not have thought of reasons why a certain course was unwise.

But now the time for decision making was running out. Hawke would have to make his parliamentary move before the next federal election, or not at all. And the problems he faced were daunting.

Politically he was a man under siege, hated by the best-organised and most disciplined faction of the Victorian ALP, the

Socialist Left. The Right faction was in its social complexion and attitudes a very different group from the New South Wales Right, which was solidly working class and union. The Victorian Right was middle class and professional and had no great love for the trade union movement. It had often joined forces with the Socialist Left to defeat Hawke's Centre Unity faction, and to attack Hawke. The Right regarded the Centre as 'lacking in principles', mere pragmatists.

Hawke had never cared for the time-consuming niceties of local politics: he did not attend branch meetings; he rarely went to the weekly Labour Council meetings in the Trades Hall, as Monk had done, religiously. People complained Hawke operated 'at the top level', and resented this. It was conceivable, given the neurotic and vengeful nature of much of Victorian Labor politics, that the branch would reject him if he put himself forward for preselection. The Victorian party would make itself a national laughing stock if it took such action – but it had done some impractical things in the past.

Preselection for a winnable seat was only the first impediment to Hawke's ambitions. In the federal Caucus he had a mere handful of supporters, too few to carry him within touching distance of party leadership. He could abandon leadership of the trade unions and all that meant in terms of power, prestige and striving for the public good, only to sink into obscurity. His other problem was personal: alcohol. The difficulty was not that Hawke drank but that he was and had been for years a loathsome drunk – poisoned, savage, a man possessed. He was not like this every time, or even a quarter of the time when he was drink-taken. Usually, especially if he drank only beer, he would remain a boisterous, good-natured man. But it happened often enough, noticeably if he drank too much champagne, that Hawke would transform. A colleague of the 1960s recalled,

> You could never tell when it would happen. Bob could be his beautiful self, then suddenly he'd take a dislike to someone. It might be a taxi driver or a lift attendant, anybody at all,

a face or a voice or some remark a person made – I never knew what it was that would affect him – and he would launch into horrible abuse. There was nothing one could do to stop him. As far as I know he was never like that with anybody he was fond of – he could be aggressive, of course, but that was part of the excitement of debate ... By the mid-1970s I'd see Bob ringing up Jean [Sinclair] to ask her if there were any cocktail parties or dinners that he had been invited to, and had turned down, which he could attend. Partly, it was his gregariousness. But really, he was looking for opportunities to drink.

Another colleague remarked, 'I can remember Jean going almost mad with anxiety because Bob was setting out for some public performance, and she knew he was drunk or was going to get drunk, and she'd be trying to head him off'. Hawke could live with his drinking problem as head of the ACTU, in Melbourne. He could not live with it in Canberra. It is a small, sharp-eyed town, with a limited number of restaurants and bars, where political and social gossip runs from tongue to tongue as quickly as the news of a miscarriage runs through a village. Behaviour tolerated in a trade union leader would, if he were a parliamentarian, incite the Canberra press gallery to pillory him.

In November 1977, during the federal election campaign, Ellie had had a stroke. A couple of weeks later Hawke went on the wagon. He had taken the first step of what was to be a traumatic, three-year struggle with the very roots of his personality. Of all Hawke's battles this one was to be the most harrowing, for the enemy was himself. As an act of will he had to smash up the old Bob Hawke and create a new one, stalked by the anxiety that if he succeeded it may be at the cost of his magic touch – his popularity, his enthusiasm for life, his expansive sympathies – and that the new Hawke may be colourless and empty, denatured. He set off whistling loudly, into the dark. He announced at every opportunity that he was not drinking, and the press duly reported this astounding news.

Hawke poses with the first Medicare card at Parliament House in Canberra, 1983.

The Hawke ministry, 1984, on the steps of Parliament House.

Hawke with Senator Susan Ryan in 1986. Ryan was the first woman appointed as a Labor minister.

Hawke with Pam O'Neill, the first sex discrimination commissioner, in 1984.

The dream team: Barrie Cassidy, Hawke and Craig Emerson in Dubrovnik, 1987.

Hawke and Bill Kelty, 'the sorcerer's apprentice', at the disastrous ACTU congress, 1979.

Hawke and Dr Bob Brown enjoy a 'Mad Hatter's Tea Party' in the grounds of Parliament House in Hobart, Tasmania, to discuss the proposed Hydro-Electric Commission (HEC) Gordon-below-Franklin Dam project in Tasmania, 1983.

Hawke plants the first of a promised one billion trees, with ACT Chief Minister Rosemary Follett, and the premiers of Victoria, NSW and SA: John Cain, Nick Greiner and John Bannon, 1989.

ACTU president Bob Hawke meets with Gurindji leaders Donald Nangiari and Vincent Lingiari in the fifth year of the Wave Hill walk-off, 1971. The strike ultimately led to the first successful land rights claim in Australia.

Hawke receives Barunga statement, 1988.

Hawke jokes with John Farnham at the official opening of the new headquarters of Ausmusic Training Centre, 1989.

The Hawkes with Cathy Freeman, Young Australian of the Year, and Professor Fred Hollows, Australian of the Year, at Admiralty House in Sydney, 1990.

Hawke with Midnight Oil lead singer Peter Garrett at the opening of the Australian Conservation Foundation's new office in Melbourne, 1989.

With US actress Heather Thomas, television personality Bert Newton and entertainer Barry Humphries in character as Dame Edna Everage at the twenty-sixth Annual Logie Awards in Melbourne, 1984.

Hawke and Labor MP Kep Enderby are interviewed by Norman Gunston (actor Garry McDonald) on the steps of Parliament House following the dismissal of the Whitlam Government in 1975.

Hawke was a guest reporter for a *60 Minutes* profile on Aussie golf legend Greg Norman, 1993.

Hawke's first and last foray into working as a foreign correspondent in Somalia, 1991.

Hawke is struck by a cricket ball, shattering his glasses, 1985.

Hawke returns serve to Chinese vice-premier Wan Li, 1986.

Hawke with swimmer Lisa Curry at an official farewell for the Australian Olympic Team at the Boulevard Hotel in Sydney in 1984.

Two working class heroes: Hawke with rock legend Jimmy Barnes, 1986.

THE AUSTRALIAN *magazine*

December 2-3 1989

HAWKE AT SIXTY
BY BLANCHE d'ALPUGET

Hawke with his granddaughter Sophie in 1989 on the television series *Beyond 2000*. He used the opportunity to appeal to the Australian people to care for their environment for future generations.

Hawke with grandchildren David, Sophie and Paul, at the Lodge, Canberra, 1989.

Hawke meets his impersonator, Max Gillies, at the North Melbourne Grand
Final breakfast at the Southern Cross ballroom, with former Prime Minister
John Gorton.

The prime minister and treasurer were regular characters on the hit satirical puppet show *Rubbery Figures* during the late 1980s.

Hawke as Napoleon created by Peter Nicholson, part of a caricature sculpture exhibition that toured during 1985–86 and later went to the National Museum in Canberra.

Hawke during his emotional speech on the Tiananmen Square massacre, 1989. Without even consulting with his Cabinet colleagues, Hawke offered Chinese students studying in Australia asylum.

By early 1978 he was recidivist: just a glass of wine with dinner had become just a glass at lunchtime also. Then two. Then a bottle. Then cognac with coffee. Ellie had partially recovered from her stroke and Hawke had partially recovered from shock and remorse. His mother had a magnificent constitution: in the early 1970s she had suffered a heart attack but one week after she had been released from hospital Ellie was so spry that, conducting her favourite niece on a tour of the University of Western Australia, her headlong rush had forced the niece, almost thirty years Ellie's junior, to beg to be allowed to rest. Ellie had spent a couple of weeks in hospital after her stroke then had returned home and begun to recuperate. She continued to attend church, but she had to walk on a frame. It was tragic to see this lioness of a woman dragging herself around, wounded.

Hawke telephoned his parents at least once a week and took every chance to fly to Perth; during the 1977–78 Christmas holiday period he and Hazel went there together. Ellie, who had prayed daily since 1949 that he would give up alcohol, saw that he was drinking again. She was very distressed and talked privately to Hazel about her anxiety. From this point on Ellie's health declined, so sharply that Clem began to despair of his capacity to care for her. He was a competent housekeeper, but he was in his eightieth year. In late January or early February 1978 he told Ellie, 'I'm sorry, my dear, but it looks as if you'll have to go into a nursing home'.

Some weeks later, following several days of heavy drinking, Hawke again became teetotal. Then on the eve of Mother's Day, 1978, he learned that Ellie had suffered a second stroke and was not expected to survive until dawn. He went immediately to Perth, where his mother was alive by a thread, sometimes conscious, sometimes not. There would be no recovery this time, and no easy death. Ellie was moved into the Home of Peace for the terminally ill, in Subiaco, and there entered a long twilight. Hawke drank less during 1978 and into the early part of 1979 than he had for years, sobered perhaps by thoughts of mortality. In 1979 when he was visiting his mother one day he knelt by her bedside and said, 'I want to thank you, Mum, for everything you've done for me'. She had recognised him, but he was not sure if she had heard him. Ellie suddenly spoke. 'It was a pleasure, son', she replied. Those were her final words to him.

The change in Hawke on his second attempt to give up drinking was remarkable. During his five teetotal months in 1978 a man whom many had never seen began to emerge: Hawke was considerate, sweet-tempered and serious-minded. These qualities had always been in him, but too often blurred out by the roller-coaster speed at which he lived. Sober, the rush of his life eased in pace and noise. The change was especially evident to those who saw him infrequently and whose attitudes to him were not shaped by the Australian news media and Australian political life. An official of an international trade union federation based in Geneva recalled:

> I had first met Bob in 1975 when I was on a union visit to Australia, and had not liked him. I'd found his behaviour most unimpressive. In 1978 I began to talk to him seriously. He was a different man from the one I'd met before. He was a man with a great heart and a great strength ... At the time I was going through a crisis, with my job and my personal life. I don't know how, but somehow Bob Hawke gave me strength. I think if it hadn't been for him I may not have survived. He said once, 'In Geneva, you can see me as a human being. In Australia, people don't see me as human any more – politics has distorted everyone's vision.' He was sad about it, because he loves people, and he'd been for years in a position of power, never allowed to forget that he was important. Even his close friends, maybe even his family, could never forget that he was important.

However on that or a later visit to Geneva during 1978 he angered the senior ILO official, Bernard Fortin, by aggressively questioning an American guest of Fortin. Hawke demanded that the American state his ideas about American society in the year 2000. The Frenchman said, 'I wanted to poke Bob in the eyes, by making him answer a difficult question. I asked, in the same tone he had used, "What do you enjoy most?"' Hawke answered, 'Power!' The remarks of the union official, above, and Hawke's reply to Fortin reveal the depths of his ambivalence – his dislike of the effects of power and his craving for it.

He and Fortin then moved on to a discussion of personal power, its uses and the limits to exercising it, Fortin questioning whether Hawke had ever, in fact, been able to exercise power as an individual, as distinct from the power of a group representative. Fortin recalled that Hawke reflected for a while before replying. He then said that he thought his speeches during the ACTU Congress of 1977 in the uranium debate had been an example of personal power exercised for the public good. He offered Fortin no other example, which suggests a weighty discontent with the balance sheet of his career.

On a different visit to Geneva, when Hawke was drunk, he told Fortin 'that when he was prime minister he would appoint me to his Cabinet. Bob said I could become an Australian citizen quickly', Fortin recalled. This assertion of Hawke's was more than a little outlandish, one of many examples during the 1970s of his attacks of grandiosity that would infuriate colleagues and irritate friends, whose complaints ranged from 'Bob thinks he's God' to 'He's behaving as if he were Superman'. Essentially, they were attacks of childishness: the child believes, until it learns not to, that wanting something will, magically, make that something materialise – a bicycle; a cricket bat. The adored child of Bordertown, Maitland and Perth was still alive inside the adult, and another of Hawke's problems. But the boy – affectionate, daring, vulnerable and imaginative – was also the charm of the man, and one of his strengths, for through him Hawke had kept the capacity to dream. He dreamt of reform. His remark to Fortin about appointment to Cabinet was indicative of the continuing growth of Hawke's ideas about parliamentary reform that he was to take up in the Boyer Lectures of 1979.

Despite his talk about parliament during 1978 – which included telling close friends, categorically, that he would stand at the next election, and assuring non-Australians that he would be the next Labor prime minister – he had not yet made up his mind. He would jump forward a few steps then dart backwards again, like a juggler. The four hoops he was juggling were his prime minister dream; the pleasures of life at the top of the union movement; the Stop Hawke forces; and drinking–teetotalism. He was able to relieve the tension of mental acrobatics by undertaking during 1978 more international work: the Crown Prince of Jordan had invited Hawke to Amman to discuss Middle Eastern affairs.

In mid-1977 the Israeli Labour Party, after twenty-nine years in office, had lost government to the Right-wing Likud Party, in coalition with minor groups. The new Prime Minister, Menachem Begin, was loathed in Israeli Labour circles. As a leader of the Irgun he had planned, among other atrocities, the bombing of the King David Hotel in Jerusalem in 1948. He was a man known still to harbour the terrorist's attitude of mind: that history can be changed by dramatic, manipulative actions. The world was amazed when in November 1977 Begin was co-author of another dramatic event. President Sadat of Egypt had announced, with that theatrical flourish so popular in non-democratic societies, that he would go 'even to Jerusalem' to seek peace in the Middle East. Begin instantly responded and days later the two were kissing each other, in the holy city. The door to peace had been unbolted, by a most unlikely pair.

Hawke had met Begin in late 1977 or early 1978. He had no comment to make on the Israeli Prime Minister. However, an Israeli who was Hawke's escort during his first meeting with Begin said afterwards,

> I knew our new Prime Minister was crazy. But even I could not believe the things he said. I felt embarrassed and ashamed, as an Israeli, by what Begin told Bob. When we came out I was bowing my head. Bob put his arm around my shoulders

and said, 'Don't worry. I'll still support Israel, no matter what your Prime Minister says.'

Hawke discussed the Crown Prince's invitation with Israeli officials, some of whom were alarmed. Fear of betrayal eddies in the depths of Israeli consciousness, for millions of good reasons. Since the Yom Kippur War one former friend after another had abandoned the country: embassies and consulates had been closed, votes in the UN, the ILO and other international bodies had switched to abstentions or to open support for the Arab side. A senior Israeli said, 'We feared that Bob would fall under the charm of Arab hospitality'. In diplomatic parlance 'hospitality' can mean seduction and blackmail, although this may not have been what the Israelis feared, for throughout the world Arab charm is justly famous. The Israelis put aside their concern and primed Hawke up 'to convey to the Jordanians the *mood* in Israel'. Hawke is one of fewer than half a dozen non-Israelis who have undertaken such an unofficial Israeli–Arab go-between role. Another was the Austrian Chancellor, Kreisky, and a third the former British prime minister, Jim Callaghan. Hawke was to be the houseguest in Jordan of a leading businessman, Rauf Sa'd Abujaber, who was a supporter of the Palestinian cause and was close to the royal family.

Hawke entered Jordan by walking across the Allenby Bridge,

with very strange feelings: I just did not know what sort of reception I would get on the other side. I was met by a chap who was equivalent to the secretary of the Department of Labour, a very bright young man who had been trained in the United States, and we formed a close relationship immediately. We drove up to Amman, and there and elsewhere I had meetings with the Crown Prince, Hassan, who was in charge of the country, because his brother, the King, was abroad. I made a crack to my escort that the King was probably out looking for a new wife, and as I learned later, the guess was right: Hussein was away courting the daughter of the Jordanian head of Pan-Am. The first meeting I had with Hassan was in the palace, and I was very very favourably impressed. He was enormously well informed and involved with his people. Clearly there was a division of labour between him and the King, with the Crown Prince predominantly concerned with the internal economy, the operation of the country and its development. He talked in great detail about sectors of the economy and plans for development in rural and secondary production, and was particularly worried by the bleeding of talent – of skilled labour and professional people – out of Jordan and into other higher-paying countries in the Arab world. The following day he invited me to lunch at a big oil refinery town about eighty kilometres north of the capital. There was a lavish luncheon for a group of foreign guests, but Hassan and I had a chance to continue talking during lunch, then he invited me to drive back with him to Amman. He drove himself; there were just two of us in a big Mercedes, the bodyguards were somewhere behind. After a while he said he wanted to show me something, and what happened next was fascinating. He drove into a refugee camp.

There were hundreds of thousands of Palestinian refugees in Jordan. Sporadically, from the mid-1960s up to late 1970, the PLO had launched attacks on Israel from its bases in Jordan, until the Israelis told the King if it happened again Israel would retaliate not just against the PLO, but against Jordan itself. In September that year Hussein expelled the PLO from his country. The Black September movement, in whose name so much mischief had been done to Hawke's life, formed in revenge. King Hussein was at the top of the Black September assassination list. When it had been announced that Hawke was going to Jordan there were reports that, in Australia, Hawke was No. 1 candidate for murder. He was astonished that the Crown Prince, without a bodyguard, had stopped his car and was about to enter a refugee camp where there could be Black September agents. He recalled,

The camp was extremely crowded and squalid. He just walked in and started talking to people, and two things struck me immediately: he was very popular with them, and totally fearless. When we got back in the car I said, 'Well, you and your brother have a reputation for fearlessness, and certainly that was evidence of it'. He replied, 'Oh, well, Mr Hawke, I am the President of the London Jujitsu Club'. And I remember I said, 'I don't know what good that might do you, in terms of stopping a bullet', but he just laughed and shrugged it off. So we returned to the palace and had another very long yarn, about the whole situation in the Middle East. By this time the process that led to the Camp David talks[7] was underway. Part of the documentation of Camp David referred to Jordan and expressed the desire that Jordan would join in negotiations.

There was no question about Hassan's commitment to the desirability of peace. Also, he accepted without question the right of Israel to exist. But Jordan has no oil of its own and is totally dependent upon subventions from Saudi Arabia for its economy, so quite clearly cannot take any significant initiatives, independent of the Saudis. The Crown Prince was forthright in saying that Jordan could not afford to associate itself with the processes that were emerging from Sadat's visit to Jerusalem. The Israelis had asked me to find out just what the Jordanian attitude was, and it boiled down to this: existence of Israel; commitment to a Palestinian entity; and, long-term, the possibility of an economic federation between Israel and Jordan while leaving open the possibility of a relationship between that potential Palestinian entity and Jordan. Naturally, he expressed some apprehension that an enlarged Jordan would become the new Palestine.[8] His position about the borders of a Palestinian entity was that Israel would have to withdraw to its pre-1967 boundaries. He accepted that Jerusalem [which until 1967 had been divided by barbed wire, with its eastern sector and – most significantly – The Wall, belonging to Jordan] would prove to be the most difficult part of the negotiations. In total, I thought the reaction from him was very positive. And, arising from that, I began to turn over in my mind the crucial question of security for Israel's borders.

Her great fear was that if she withdrew to pre-1967 lines, which meant reducing her territory to just a few miles in width at its narrowest point, overrunning the country would be easy – much easier in the 1980s, with more modern armaments, than ever before. The Egyptians were saying that Israel need have no anxiety, that Egypt would not use the territory returned to it as a launching pad against Israel. Hassan said the same thing to me about the West Bank. So it occurred to me sometime in late 1978 or early 1979 that an undertaking should be written in to the peace treaties, but in this form: should Israeli-occupied territory, returned to its pre-1967 owners, be used as a launching pad for assault upon Israel, any gain in territory that Israel made as a result of going to war would be non-negotiable. Israel would keep the lot, and there could be no argy-bargy afterwards, with the Arabs saying, 'Aw, come on, give it back to us'. There would be a clear agreement on ground rules: if this happens, then that follows. I elaborated it a bit more in my own mind, going into the details of non-military zones and what would constitute *casus belli*. I thought that if the major parties could be persuaded to accept this concept formally, and before the world community, there would be a magnificent opportunity for establishing peace in the region.

Hawke's idea was constructive. Maybe one day it will be a protocol in a peace treaty between Israel and Jordan or Palestine–Jordan, and between Israel and Syria, but that day has not yet dawned.

He did not have an opportunity to discuss his proposal with Israelis until early 1979, and it was another year before he could advocate it to the Egyptians and Crown Prince Hassan.

Meanwhile, this first trip to Jordan had stirred up his instinct to help people; he thought up a modest, easy to implement scheme. In Jordan he had been impressed that

there was something in the country which you could reasonably, genuinely, think of as a trade union movement.
Not in our sense, but there was a Department of Labour,
and there was a concern to improve the conditions under
which people worked. Not free collective bargaining or anything like that, but there was more reality in the relationship
between employers and employed than in many other non-
democracies. It struck me that it would make a lot of sense
if Australia attempted to help the Jordanians. The Crown
Prince and the Department of Labour people had talked
in particular about industrial accidents – the prevalence of
them – and industrial health. I thought it would be worthwhile
for Australia to provide one or more mobile industrial health
units. The Jordanians were enormously responsive. There
were two elements in my thinking: first, the intrinsic value of
improving industrial health;[9] second, that Australia had good
relations with Israel, that Jordan was a critically important
state in the Arab–Israeli situation, and therefore it would be
useful for Australia to have a practical and warm relationship
with Jordan. And that this would be one way of establishing
it. When I got back to Australia I talked to Tony Street. He
was totally responsive and arranged for me to see Fraser, and
the three of us had a long yarn in the Prime Minister's suite
about it. I've got to give the government full marks: Fraser
was *perfect* about it: he saw the point and responded positively,
without any equivocation. He said it could go ahead.

As often happens, the politicians were willing but the bureaucrats were weak. Hawke's Jordanian scheme echoed one he had
evolved on his first visit to Indonesia, in 1970, when he had been
appalled by the lack of training facilities for skilled tradesmen
and the resultant impediment to Indonesia's economic progress. He had suggested, then, that Australia could strengthen
its friendship with Indonesia and improve life in a country where
unemployment was, at a conservative estimate, 30 per cent, if
the Australian government established a large skilled-trades

school in Java. Nothing happened. Similarly, the Jordanian scheme was allowed to lapse: it seems there was a bureaucratic power struggle in Amman and Jordanian responsiveness to the proposal dissipated.

Hawke's great success during 1978 was in the ILO.

Namibia had requested membership of the organisation. Namibia was also known as South West Africa, and was controlled by South Africa – illegally. In 1966 the United Nations had terminated the old League of Nations mandate given to South Africa over Namibia, and in 1967 had created the UN Council for Namibia and established this as the legal administering authority for Namibia. South Africa ignored the UN, and continued to occupy the country. In 1971 the International Court of Justice declared that, its presence being illegal, South Africa was under obligation to put an end to its occupation. South Africa ignored the International Court of Justice. Finally, in resolution 32/9E of 4 November 1977, the United Nations asked all its specialised agencies as well as all international conferences to admit Namibia as a full member.

When the UN Council for Namibia requested that the country be admitted as a full member of the ILO, the organisation's Selection Committee sought advice from the International Labour Conference's legal counsel, Francis Wolf. Wolf gave a long written opinion, the key phrase being 'that Namibia cannot be admitted as a member of the ILO until it attains independence'. He had drawn on the precedent of the Free City of Danzig (now known as Gdansk, the birthplace of Solidarity), which had been created by the Treaty of Versailles in 1919 and in 1930 had applied for membership of the ILO. The matter had been referred to the Permanent Court of International Justice for an opinion; the Court had held that the Free City of Danzig could not participate as a member of the ILO. Danzig was not admitted.

Wolf's opinion on Namibia was circulated on Monday, 12 June, to members of the Selection Committee, of which Hawke was Workers' vice-chairman. Wolf recalled,

By any legal definition, Namibia was not a state, and only states may be members of the ILO. The difficulty was that virtually all members of the ILO wanted Namibia to be admitted – many of them passionately so, for one-third of our members are Africans. The problem appeared insoluble and for the ILO secretariat was an extreme embarrassment. Bob Hawke accepted that my legal opinion was correct; he appreciated that a political disaster was looming for the organisation. He got himself elected to a small subcommittee of the Selection Committee, which organises the work of the International Labour Conference, and there he produced a draft proposal of great ingenuity: it did not refute the ILO's formal legal opinion, but stepped around it. The crux of Bob's draft was that the ILO 'should not let the illegal action of South Africa frustrate the aspirations of the Namibian people'. It was a master stroke! From the abstract legal point of view there was no solution, but Bob had the imagination to break the impasse. His formula was one of the best examples of constructive imagination we have seen in an international body. What he had done was to change the question around: instead of being asked to vote *for* an illegality [violation of the ILO Constitution, by calling a non-state a state], the conference would be asked to vote *against* an illegality [South African occupation].

Hawke gained unanimous agreement from the Workers' Group for his Namibian proposal. On Friday morning, 23 June, he made a stirring speech to the plenary session, assuring delegates of the uniqueness of the situation:

> I ask you to note the words [of the resolution] ... 'That Namibia is the only remaining case of a former mandate of the League of Nations where the former mandatory Power is still in occupation'. I stress that, should there still be any delegates who are legitimately concerned that in passing this resolution we may be creating some precedent for the future, they should have confidence in the fact that the resolution

itself quite clearly and specifically spells out why this [deci-
sion] is absolutely and totally unique and cannot in any way
constitute a precedent for any other set of circumstances ...[10]

The conference voted 368 in favour, none against, with
50 abstentions, to admit Namibia.

Another major step towards freeing the people of Namibia
from South Africa had been taken, and African gratitude to
Hawke was lavish. The same International Labour Conference
had before it a resolution condemning Israel. When the vote was
taken it was the Africans who defeated it. Oscar de Vries Reilingh,
a former secretary of the Dutch trade union movement and later
the secretary of the Workers' Group in the ILO, said,

> Bob swayed the Africans back from condemnation of Israel.
> He could influence not only the African workers, but African
> governments. His influence was very great – much greater than
> his presence. He exercised influence on the chairman of the
> Workers, Joe Morris; on the British; the Anglophone Africans;
> the Commonwealth delegates; the Asian Anglophones; the
> Caribbean Anglophones; the Americans – sometimes even
> the Russians because of his personal friendship with Peter
> Pimenov of the USSR. He was the best orator in the ILO and
> he flowered in conferences, before a big audience. He electri-
> fied the atmosphere.

By 1978 Hawke was the most popular Workers' delegate. The
Workers' chairman, a big gruff Canadian, Joe Morris, was one
of Hawke's closest friends in the ILO and another of his father
figures. Morris was due to retire and in 1978 he began to urge
Hawke to declare himself a candidate for the post of Workers'
chairman – that is, to be the spokesman of the workers of the
world. Morris said,

> Bob had everything – an analytic mind, courage to fight,
> qualities of leadership, and capacity as a speaker. But he was

torn by the conflict of where he could make the greatest contribution: in the trade union movement, or in politics. I think
he'd become mesmerised by politics. I kept at him, though.
That year and all the next.

The temptation that Morris held out to Hawke was an additional complication to the decision he had to make, soon, about
his future. Were he to become Workers' chairman, Hawke
could press forward on an issue of international importance that
in the past few years had been occupying much of his attention:
the hypocrisy of the Soviet bloc trade-union system.

Hawke had a minimal interest in the technical work of
the ILO. Many people noted that he was 'bored to tears in
Governing Body meetings and during technical discussions,
and would often sit there reading the Australian newspapers, or
taking a nap'. Much of the ILO's most creative work takes place
informally – at the receptions and dinners that are a permanent
accompaniment to conference life, and during breaks for conversation in the coffee bars that are scattered throughout the ILO
headquarters building. The place is a market for ideas. Hawke
was one of those who had noted that the Russian tripartite team
of government, employer and worker was an artificiality: the
government delegate could just as easily announce he was the
worker, or the employer. People had become used to this, but
in doing so had overlooked a major principle, a legal convention
of the ILO, and a matter that lay at the heart of trade unionism:
freedom of association. Clearly, freedom of association did not
exist in the USSR or in other Soviet bloc countries. For several
years Hawke had been taking the opportunity of informal discussions to draw attention to the fact that the USSR was violating ILO conventions about the treatment of workers and human
rights, which it had promised to honour. Tony Street said,

In my view Bob had a significant influence on people's thinking about the meaning of ILO conventions. He identified
with great precision the inherent contradictions in the Soviet

bloc ratifications of those conventions, and the Soviet performance. He talked constantly about the Soviet system – and that became crucially relevant in relation to Solidarity, in Poland.

In 1978 the ICFTU, within which Hawke was highly respected, submitted a complaint to the ILO about trade union rights in Poland. The Polish government said it would apply ILO standards. In May 1980 the ILO sent a delegation to Poland to investigate the application of ILO standards in the country. In August 1980 Solidarity was formed, with a major aim of forcing the Polish government to implement ILO conventions. In November 1980, after a long court battle, Solidarity was registered as an official trade union body and included in the documentation of registration were ILO conventions 87 (on freedom of association) and 98 (on the rights of collective bargaining). Nobody makes the claim, least of all Hawke, that he was involved in any way with the birth of Solidarity and the revolution in Poland that followed. However, his efforts as an agitator and educator in the ILO helped to create an atmosphere in which recognition of rottenness could surface. Heribert Maier, the general secretary of FIET (the International Federation of Commercial, Clerical and Technical Employees) remarked,

> Hawke was very active during his eight years on the Governing Body as an advocate for applying the basic human rights conventions of the ILO – that is, 87, 98, 100 (equal pay), 111 (non-discrimination in employment) and 105 (forced labour). His major concern was that human rights be respected.

In 1981 the ILO Application of Standards Committee took an extraordinary step: without putting the issue to a vote the committee condemned the fact that Soviet Union law does not allow freedom of association. If ever the workers of the USSR have the nerve to challenge Big Brother, that international condemnation of the Soviet system will be one of their most telling arguments. Street commented, 'In my view George Polites, the leader of Australia's employers' delegation, was the greatest single influence. Hawke, in the workers' delegation, also played an important role in bringing about that finding by the Application of Standards Committee'.

Hawke's work in the ILO was unknown in Australia. Nevertheless, his stature at home was growing. Earlier in 1978 he had been a negotiator in one of the most ugly industrial disputes in the nation's life this century: a row between meat workers and farmers over the export of live sheep. Once more, the origins of the problem lay in the Middle East. Islam requires special methods of slaughtering animals for food (halal in Arabic) and, for some major festivals, the sacrifice of animals. The massive oil wealth of Middle Eastern countries had created an upsurge in demand for meat there for everyday eating, and for sheep to be slaughtered in religious observances. Although meat-exporting countries, like Australia, gave assurances that carcases were being prepared in accordance with Islamic requirements, there was an understandable preference in Middle Eastern countries for meat that was killed by Islamic butchers. What is more, halal meat should be freshly slaughtered. For these reasons a live animal could fetch a far higher price than a dead one. The Australian rural industry had been severely depressed for several years: the sudden demand for live sheep was a life raft for them. But for meat workers, it was disastrous: it meant a loss of work. Negotiations between farmers and unionists had been dragging on for more than a year without any resolution to the argument about how many live sheep, in relation to sheep carcases, could be exported.

Hawke happened to be in Canberra, continuing discussion with the government on the uranium question, when he was given a message asking him to go urgently to Street's office in Parliament House. The dispute had abruptly shifted towards flashpoint. Unionists were picketing wharves in Western Australia and South Australia to prevent sheep export. In South Australia a convoy of sheep trucks had already set out and was only a few hours away from arriving at the wharves; both the picketers and the farmers were carrying weapons. Hawke recalled,

> I got to Tony's office and he told me what the position was: we had only a couple of hours. The situation was appalling – the union blokes and the farmers were armed, and when the trucks arrived at the wharves that was going to be it. We got on the telephones and managed to get a message to Ian McLachlan, who was the leader of the farmers' group in South Australia. McLachlan is a very able bloke and one of the toughest I've ever had to deal with in negotiations. Finally, we were able to talk to him in a telephone box at Wallaroo. I had a very tough conversation with him – I pleaded then demanded that he had to call his people off because otherwise there would be bloodshed, maybe death, and if that happened then there was no way the thing could be unravelled, and at any rate, it was just too horrible to contemplate that people might be killing each other. He was very tough – his side undeniably had a case: the farmers were really scratching financially and were fighting for their livelihood – but to his credit he responded. He called his men off. That was just the first step.
>
> The next was to try to resolve the conflict. He, Street, I and [Sir] Sam Burston [president of the Australian Woolgrowers and Graziers Council], who was magnificent in his co-operation, then had to work something out. We set up an inquiry. Everything happens in such a rush in these situations – you're going on television and flying backwards and forwards – I think I flew to Sydney and to Adelaide once or twice, and then in Canberra I was operating out of Street's office for a couple of days. Fortunately, the government had given Street a free hand in reality, although I think for public consumption there was a bit of nonsense going on, requiring Tony and me to argue with each other on TV. But Doug Anthony [leader of the National Country Party] had flown

up in the air, and was a damned nuisance. You can always rely on Doug to do his block and start blazing away from the hip. Fortunately Burston, for the farmers' side, understood the enormous danger of the situation, and he's a generous-minded man: he could understand the union side, that the meat workers were fearful that they would lose their jobs. Another man who was very helpful in calming things down was Wal Fife, who was acting as Attorney-General.

I must add that the whole situation was made more difficult by two facts: there was an internal blue in the Meat Industry Employees' Union, and there was an element within the union which was violently anti-Hawke. The South Australian branch of the union was unhappy with the way the federal body was handling the dispute: there was a background of intra-union rivalry and jealousy. Then Wally Curran, the Victorian secretary [an activist in the Socialist Left and ardent supporter of the PLO], was pathologically anti-Hawke. He and his group, at a meeting we had in Adelaide, paraded gross absurdities and falsehoods and prejudices – that I was selling out the unions, enemy of the working class – all the usual stuff. It wouldn't matter what I was doing or what the issue was, those blokes would misrepresent it. Then we had the Western Australian government, and the ever-unhelpful [Premier] Sir Charles Court.

A senior government official, who requested anonymity, said later that Hawke's handling of the dispute had averted not just a brawl on a wharf in South Australia but the development of a widespread violent confrontation. Both sides had access to weapons – the farmers were carrying iron clubs and batons gnarled with barbed wire, and are rifle owners, while the meat workers could lay their hands upon a murderous variety of skinning and boning knives. The live sheep dispute is generally regarded in industrial relations circles as the most potentially dangerous since the Depression. Sir Richard Kirby commented, 'The only dispute that I remember being anything like as serious was the Rothbury Disaster of 1929. I think for the country as a whole, we had a very lucky escape in 1978.'

Hawke was the negotiator in two other major but less dramatic disputes in 1978: one was a six-week Utah miners' strike; the second was a month-long dispute between Telecom and its employees that silenced telephones throughout the nation.

He had just returned from the International Labour Conference when he was pitched in to the Utah row, which was a straightforward argument over wages. Utah's profit had risen from $8 million in 1971 to $158 million in 1977. As the Queensland Coal Board noted in its twenty-sixth annual report, each of Utah's 2000 employees had contributed $79 150 to the company's profit for 1977. Yet Utah, which exported most of its profits for 1977 to the USA, had refused to negotiate a new award with its miners since 1972. By 1978 Utah miners needed an extra $50 a week to be in the same position as they had been six years earlier. If their pay were increased by $75 a week, that would merely restore to them the $23 award loading of 1972. They worked in harsh conditions on remote sites and were now demanding a $100 a week increase, and had already rejected an offer from Utah of $83.30. Hawke proposed that, in return for a 5 per cent increase in coal production at Utah's mines, the company pay an increase of $95 a week, made up of a $63 production bonus; a work clothes allowance; money for medical and dental expenses; an accident contribution scheme; and a Christmas bonus. After three days of talks, both sides agreed to the package deal. The company had sought government approval before committing itself to the new award, since $95 a week sounded an outrageously large sum when stated baldly, and out of the context of Utah miners' conditions. The government agreed that the increase was reasonable. But as soon as it had been announced the Prime Minister publicly attacked Hawke, referred to the 'outrageous' size of the award, asserted that union greed was rampant and that Hawke was its instrument. Hawke was furious. Fraser's remarks were one of the clearer examples of his somewhat paranoid attacks upon Hawke, the potential prime minister, under the guise of attacking Hawke, the president of the ACTU.

By this stage the Telecom dispute was underway, grinding slowly forward through a series of bans and limitations, and little by little Australia's telecommunications system was breaking down. Hawke had already arranged to go to the Northern Territory to discuss with Indigenous leaders the issues of land rights and uranium mining. He was particularly anxious to spend some time alone there with his son, who was working for Indigenous people.

Stephen Hawke was following the tradition of social commitment that had marked out the Lees and the Hawkes for generations and that, in each generation, had required a rebellion against parental values. Will Lee had rebuffed the clannishness of the Cornish miners; Ellie had fought for the right to be educated; Clem had rejected his ancestral church. Stephen was rejecting his parents' urgings that he attend university. Clem had ministered to Indigenous communities in South Australia in the 1920s and 1930s; Hawke, as a student at the University of Western Australia, had agitated for Indigenous rights and throughout his presidency of the ACTU had highlighted the plight of Indigenous people. He was delighted that Stephen had decided to take up the cause of Indigenous people, but he disagreed strongly with his son's methods: 'I wanted Steve to be properly – as I thought then – equipped', he said. Hawke was hoping to persuade Stephen to enrol for a university course the following year. He wanted, too, in the calm of the outback, to reflect on the question of his future career: he could be spokesman for the workers of the world; or he could be Australian prime minister; or he could lose the lot. Before he set out he remarked to a friend, 'Let's see how that fount of industrial wisdom, the Prime Minister, handles the Telecom dispute. I've not forgiven the bastard for what he did to me over Utah.'

By the time the Telecom dispute had reached a crisis, Stephen Hawke had convinced his father that further arguments about attending university were futile, and that he was going to pursue his chosen career in his own way. The seriousness of the rift that had existed between them was revealed in Hawke's comment to journalists, 'I think we got closer then than we have been for a long time'. Hawke had also taken another step forward: he had decided – almost – to enter parliament.

He recalled,

I was at an ALP fundraising dinner in Darwin, where I was to be guest speaker, when a telephone call came through from Street's office, asking me to return to Melbourne for a National Labour Consultative Council [NLCC][11] meeting next day. The government had got itself into a fine mess. It had not allowed Telecom management to negotiate with the union, which is the first ingredient for disaster. Fraser was doing his tough guy act, 'We shall never surrender'. Meanwhile, there were two pertinent facts: the union had a valid case and one which concerned the community, for its argument was over the introduction of new technology. There were millions of citizens who were frightened by the surge of technological change that was sweeping through Australia and that was, obviously, going to put tens of thousands of jobs at risk. Word processors, electronic cash registers, massive changes in banking – the technological revolution was starting to rumble over people in the white-collar sectors, and here, with Telecom, was the first real fight about it. The ATEA [Australian Telecommunications Employees' Association] leadership had very effectively got this message through to the public: 'It's our jobs today – it'll be yours tomorrow'. So there was public sympathy for the union. The second thing was that the business community was going berserk, and was screaming at the government to do something. But Fraser was carrying on with his Tarzan act. So now the government was saying: 'Come back, talk'.

We met on Saturday morning [26 August] in the Department of Labour Building in Bourke Street. Tony Street was sitting in the middle with his people around him, and

I was seated opposite, with my blokes. And it was beautiful: Tony gave a rundown on the dispute, then said, 'We must be able to talk about this'. I grabbed hold of that sentence and replied, 'You say, "Talk". The guts of it is that Telecom management is not being allowed to talk to the union. Now, will you say to me unequivocally that Telecom management is allowed to talk, to negotiate?' There was a silence. Then Tony turned round to his advisers and they all whispered to each other.[12] At last Tony said, 'Yes'. And I said, 'Right. Let's close this meeting. We're going to Telecom.' So my mob went round to the Telecom office, to talk to top management, including Jack Curtis, the managing director. The atmosphere was very taut, because Telecom believed that the introduction of new technology was a management prerogative, and rejected the idea that the workers should have any say in how it was to be introduced. Telecom management had welcomed the government's support; they were feeling undermined by the change of government position which I'd forced from Street. We had some pretty tough talking: I had to put it hard and clear to Telecom that it was facing a Luddite position, that if it went ahead and introduced the new equipment in disregard of the wishes of its employees that the danger of sabotage was real. My second argument was that this was a fundamental social issue, and that the trade union movement was *not going to budge*. Ducker was with me, but he had to leave early. Just as he reached the door he turned back to the room, put his hand on his heart and said to the Telecom people, with that marvellous, rueful look he can assume, 'Please, please don't make me pull out New South Wales'.

By Saturday afternoon Telecom had agreed to conciliation and arbitration by Justice Mary Gaudron of the Commission. Hawke again was the union's tactician, while its federal secretary, Bill Mansfield, presented the complicated technical submissions. After thirteen hours of argument the month-long dispute was ended, but for the formality of mass meetings to endorse the agreement between ATEA and Telecom about the manner in which new technology would be introduced and jobs protected.

The news media covered Hawke in glory. By this stage his reputation as a strike settler was such that the mere announcement that Hawke was about to intervene in a dispute created an expectation in the parties that their troubles would soon be over and, psychologically brightened, they were already prepared to consider a compromise. His skill as a negotiator arose from those aspects of his personality that he had inherited from Clem – capacity to listen, patience and soothing diplomacy – and those inherited from Ellie – honesty and determination. He was often asked by business groups to tell them the secrets of successful dispute negotiation, and singled out three basics: patience, honesty and authority to make decisions.

Although Hawke was awarded the kudos for ending a strike that had caused appalling public inconvenience and had seriously disrupted the business community he said later that Justice Gaudron, the first female federal arbitration judge, deserved much of the credit.

> We all knew she was an extraordinarily intelligent woman, but she has an unnerving manner: she giggles. It was even more unsettling for management than it was for our side, I think. However, everyone soon realised that the judge knew exactly what she was doing. In fact, her sense of humour was a big help in keeping things together. In conferences of that length fatigue and frustration cause short tempers, and often the whole thing breaks down. It's a tremendous plus if the mediator can keep the atmosphere light.

Two years later Hawke for the union side (which is consulted on appointments to the Conciliation and Arbitration Commission) championed Judith Cohen, widow of Sam, to become a federal judge.

Hawke had never doubted that women are as intelligent as men; from the time he had joined the ACTU he had publicly espoused the principle of equal pay for women. In his first year as president he had excited comment by hiring for wage-case research a young woman graduate, Jan White (later known by her married name, Marsh) who, like Jean Sinclair, had also worked for the investment counsellor, Jim Cowan. Hawke was promoting her as the next ACTU advocate, an idea to which many members of the trade union movement were still having difficulty accustoming themselves. Distrust of female competence runs deep in the unions. At ACTU congresses in the 1970s, whenever one of the handful of female delegates spoke, male delegates would leave in droves and broad grins would spread across the faces of those who remained. At the end of her speech – however good, bad or indifferent – there would be long, indulgent applause. Few if any of the clapping men realised how insulting it was to treat a speech made by a woman as something extraordinary. Hawke, on one hand, had a strong sense of justice but, on the other, his attitude was trammelled by the effects of his milieu.

His intellectual conviction about the equality, or potential for equality, of women was one thing: emotionally, he was yet to come to terms with his old ambivalence of simultaneous love and resentment for the other sex. Women who worked with Hawke often feared him, for his general impatience was (and remained) more noticeable with females than with males and he seemed to find conventionally feminine women irritating. He paid a sincere compliment when he remarked of a woman, 'She's got balls'. It would appear that the pressures upon him in early childhood and later, at school, caused him to exaggerate his virility. By the time he was in his early thirties masculinity was so strongly established in him that he had the freedom to behave in conventionally 'unmanly' ways – crying, for example, or kissing his men friends. Once on a long aeroplane trip, accompanied by Bill Landeryou, Hawke noticed that a child, whose mother was asleep, had vomited. Without waking the mother, Hawke cleaned up the child himself. His friends have scores of examples of his kindness, many of them, like this one, 'unmasculine'.

During his months without alcohol in 1978 he had been, at some unconscious level, sorting out the turmoil of his attitudes to women. Again, it was people abroad who noticed more quickly than those in Australia that he was now less aggressive with women.

In his own odd way Hawke was a faithful man, devoted to Hazel. By her late forties she was a strikingly handsome woman, her gaiety and quick wit melded with strength of character, warmth and a certain worldliness. People who met her for the first time remarked that she reminded them of the French actress, Simone Signoret, when she was in her forties. When, very rarely, he broke his silence about intimate matters, he spoke of Hazel with Biblical passion: 'Out of *her* loins she has borne me children'. One had the clear impression that any man who dared to look speculatively at Hazel in the presence of her husband would be in trouble. However, his own refusal to behave as the possession of any one woman evoked female anger and jealousy, and within the ALP it was widely asserted that 'Hawke treats women shamefully'. One long-term friend, a mystically religious woman, remarked, 'People crave to own Bob, but he is a Big Soul and cannot be owned by anyone else'. Abeles made a similar point: 'Bob is such a blithe spirit'.

Moreover, Hawke's artless self-relevation as a harem male was a social affront, especially in the extremely prudish atmosphere of traditional Labor circles. There was much prurient gossip. Newspaper editorials had been referring for several years to his 'flamboyant lifestyle', a euphemism for philandering, and articles about him were now more often using the term 'playboy'. By late 1978 Hawke had come to recognise that, if he were to enter parliament, he would have to conform to accepted mores about women as well as drink. The two were linked, of course. He had managed to deport himself staidly during his teetotal months but in September 1978, on a trip to China, he began to drink again. He assured everyone that he was drinking now only in moderation – and so he was, for a while.

The new year opened on a high note for him, as a public

figure: on Australia Day he was to be made a Companion of Australia. Another source of satisfaction was that he and others had worked out a scheme for having Bill Hartley expelled from the ALP. But in Hawke's private life forces were gathering that were to make 1979 the nadir of his existence.

Hazel, who said later, 'At home we mostly saw Bob when he was beat', had been to see a divorce lawyer. The story that the Hawkes were going to be divorced was around Melbourne and soon reached Sydney. Bob-and-Hazel were still the bonded pair they had been since they were teenagers, but their relationship had been under acute strain for years and now that the children had left home they had both come to terms with changed circumstances. Doing so was traumatic: Hawke, the great negotiator in other people's affairs, was helpless to renegotiate with Hazel the shape of their marriage now that the enforced stability of parenthood was removed. Fortunately George Rockey, who had been married three times, was as close to Hazel as he was to Hawke, and was a source of sympathetic advice. He had no doubt that beneath the turbulence their marriage was sound; that they were, as he put it, 'still deeply in love'. Rockey set out, patiently and quietly, to help them both. Hazel referred to him as 'my father confessor' and Hawke as 'Uncle George'. Other friends were supportive: Sir Roderick Carnegie, who had perceived that Hawke was in bad shape emotionally, gave him a copy of *Seasons of a Man's Life*, a major study of patterns of change in male existence, which set out to demonstrate that, at certain ages, crises are inevitable.

All Hawke's behaviour, from September 1978 when he abandoned teetotalism, to September 1979, when he formally made his decision about parliament, was affected by the dramas of his personal life – the upheaval in his marriage, his sense of inadequacy as a father, Ellie's slow dying, fears for Clem's health and, perhaps most of all and arising from these pressures, the beginnings of a long-delayed introspection.

He had stepped down as ALP president in mid-1978 but was still a Victorian delegate to the federal executive. Its first meeting for 1979 was due in late January, in Canberra.

Hawke arrived a few days beforehand in a buoyant mood, for everything was arranged for the federal executive to expel Bill Hartley of the Socialist Left. In 1978 there had been a row in the Western Australian branch of the party in which Hartley had intervened, making accusations about the state secretary, Bob McMullan, other branch officials, and Hawke. Leaders of the Centre Unity faction in Victoria saw their chance. Hawke said,

> Hartley had been an electoral albatross around the party's neck for years but the argument always was, 'That's Victoria's problem'. Here was a matter of sufficient significance and relevance for the federal executive to be involved. A number of Centre Unity unions in Victoria talked it over and Bill Landeryou decided that the Storemen and Packers would lay a formal complaint against Hartley with the federal executive. We got the numbers. But a state election was due some time in the first half of 1979, so in the circumstances it was only fair and appropriate that Frank Wilkes, the Victorian leader of the ALP, be informed and have right of veto. The argument would be: If you expel Hartley you could split the Victorian branch, and Wilkes, with an election coming up, might adjudge that as a net minus. And if that were his judgment, we wouldn't go ahead. Also, if Wilkes lost the election the blame could be laid on those who had expelled Hartley and created party strife just before polling. So I invited Wilkes to my office. Landeryou was also present. Wilkes' response was simple and, I think, right. He said, 'Have you got the numbers?' I said, 'Yes' – I'd spoken to Hayden about it and a number of other people, and there was no doubt. Wilkes said, 'If you've got the numbers, that's good. The worst thing would be to have a go and miss.' So we accepted that. I went to Canberra and had lunch at the Lobby with Landeryou and his secretary, and they had the letter to the federal executive with them, typed out. It was to come up next day.

Meanwhile, plans had begun to go awry in Melbourne. The Victorian branch of the ALP somewhat resembles in its intrigues the courts of the medieval popes. The Socialist Left faction is not, as many outsiders think, composed entirely of wild-eyed radicals but has, rather, an extreme wing more interested in ideology than in forming a government, and a pragmatic wing concerned with winning elections. The state secretary, Bob Hogg, a former engineer, was among the pragmatists of the Socialist Left. On Boxing Day 1978 he had heard of a move involving Hawke, Landeryou, Combe and others to expel Hartley, but had discounted it as 'Christmas drinking'. Then on Monday, 15 January, he had been asked by someone he did not name to come to a 'private meeting' in, curiously, the Lygon Hotel. There are few places less private than the Lygon: the windows of the Trades Hall overlook its door; one walks past the old ACTU building, which is now the headquarters of the Storemen and Packers' Union, to enter the pub. Inside, there are no private rooms. Hogg realised that he was being observed by a group of union officials and that the 'private meeting' was designed to be a public one. In the hotel he was told that the numbers were there for Hartley to be expelled. The next day the agenda for the ALP federal executive meeting would be finalised and Hartley's expulsion would be an item. Hogg said,

> Those who wanted Hartley expelled gave as their reason that it would be worth a 3 per cent electoral swing in the forthcoming state elections. This was a simplistic argument, for it ignored the behaviour of the Left wing of the ALP, both in Victoria and elsewhere. The Left would have united: there would have been a Save Hartley campaign. The Victorian branch would have talked and thought of nothing else for six months. It was exactly what we didn't need, with a state election looming. I rang Combe and a few others. The New South Wales people, including Ducker, had a meeting. On 15 January the Expel Hartley forces had the numbers. By 16 January, they didn't.

On 16 January Wilkes told Landeryou and Hawke that the situation was too dangerous. The agenda for the federal executive meeting was drawn up, without any mention of Hartley, who once again had survived. Hogg was criticised for his 'policies of containment'; loathing for Hawke increased. Frank Wilkes failed to win the election, and in due course was replaced as leader by John Cain. Hawke has maintained since that

> If Wilkes had not made his misjudgment, or the people around him hadn't made the misjudgment, he may well have become Premier of Victoria. The nervous nellies! I thought all the talk about a schism was rubbish and that expelling Hartley would have won us seats. Once Wilkes had told us the deal was off I just put the thing out of my mind.

Defeated, Hawke had decided to fight another day.

The ALP Victorian state conference was held in late March. Its Industrial Affairs Policy Committee presented a report to which a very long amendment, moved by Percy Johnson and seconded by Bill Hartley, had been added. Item 3 of their amendment read: 'The revolt of the Third World as reflected in the events in Iran is likely to intensify these [economic] contradictions which are an inherent part of the contemporary capitalist system'. The Shah of Iran had recently gone into exile and an elderly Islamic religious leader, the Ayatollah Khomeini, had returned from exile to become head of state. Iran was in the early stages of chaos, a massive social bilious attack brought on by the nation's inability to digest an overdose of oil wealth, and other problems. Hartley and other extreme members of the Socialist Left were hearty in their applause for the Iranian revolution, which increased Hawke's contempt for them: he swept into the Fitzroy Town Hall, where the conference was held, exhaling fumes of sulphur. Hawke's speech during the industrial affairs policy debate, delivered off the cuff, was in the tradition of the hellfire-and-brimstone harangues of his Methodist ancestors.

He described the Hartley group as 'a canker' and, in lighter vein, 'a telephone box minority'. He recalled,

> There was *unbelievable* stupidity during the debate. The mad Left had bans on the building of Newport power station – yet Newport was being built, growing each week. So when were they going to remove the bans? The day Newport's doors opened? But people got up and endorsed a continuation of bans. That is the sort of lunacy which does nothing but bring the party into disrepute and create divisiveness within the trade union movement. Then Hartley, this great expert on foreign affairs, made a speech about Iran – that here was a marvellous example of revolution in the Third World, another case of the democractic forces in the Third World bursting forth. And, oh my God, it would make you sick! The whole thing stuck in my gullet. So I gave them a bit of a serve, and asked in passing whether Hartley's female supporters, the Joan Coxedges of this world, would, as members of the women's movement, find the Iranian revolution such a glorious event. Returned to purdah; civil liberties, human rights, stripped from them. It was so obvious what was happening in Iran, but there they were cuddling up with their warm little slogans. And again, some of our weak brothers and sisters thought I'd done the wrong thing. Centre Unity people came up to me after and said, 'That was a very good speech, but you shouldn't have done it'. I said, 'Why not? They're bastards – but you don't tell them?' It was just too much, part of this weakness syndrome: You're allowed to *see* the canker, but you're not to say or do anything about it. For a decade we'd been putting up with the SL and I was sick and tired of the number of times I'd been told that they were changing, they were becoming more reasonable; but every time they opened their mouths they became less reasonable.

Peter Blazey, the political biographer and journalist, described Hawke's 'bit of a serve' as one of the most excoriating attacks heard within the Labor movement since the 1955 Split. It was more contemptuous and satirical than speeches made by Whitlam against Hartley's Victorian Central Executive in the late 1960s and historically represented the destruction of the [Socialist Left's] ability publicly to embarrass the Parliamentary wing [of the Victorian ALP].[13]

But the headline of Blazey's double-page analysis of the Victorian conference read: 'SuperHawke Proves He Is No Heavyweight', and was accompanied by a cartoon of Hawke as a demonic Superman, hitting Bill Hartley over the head with a phallic-shaped weapon, in a telephone box.

The speech, and the amalgam of praise and condemnation that it evoked, both from commentators like Blazey and from Centre Unity faction members like Gareth Evans (later the federal shadow Attorney-General), who took Hawke to task about it, encapsulated Hawke's difficulties within the Victorian ALP. Many have remarked that Hawke does not understand the Victorian branch, that he is unfamiliar with the intricate web of friendships, hostilities, grudges and debts that twine through the factions and across the factions, and that therefore an intervention like the one he had just made, disturbed, unbeknown to him, both enemies and friends. The point that even Hawke's close friends in the branch were slow to recognise was that, if a principle were at stake, Hawke would not give a damn about whom he offended. His speech had done the party a service by damning a foolish proposal close to a state election. Labor's chances of winning Victoria in 1979 were enhanced by his assault upon the Socialist Left, for Hawke had been address-ing the electorate at large when he described Hartley's group as a 'telephone box minority'. But simultaneously Hawke had injured himself: the very force of his assault helped to create unity in the Socialist Left, when it had recovered from shock. As well, people were uneasy that Hawke expended so much pas-sion on what, to them, was a trifling cause. Yet passion had been a feature of the Hawke style for his twenty years as a public figure. Blazey wrote:

> At the Napier pub everyone was crowded around Hawke congratulating him on his speech. He was beaming, drinking and filling the air with contempt for the Socialist Left. Surrounded by admirers, he had got such an adrenalin blast from the speech that it was obvious he would love to be back in the fray ... There was almost a sexual glamour to him in the Napier pub ... He had just 'done over' his worst enemy in the most humiliating manner possible. And everyone approved – they had to. But his victory was too easy, too set up. It was beneath him in a way – or perhaps it wasn't ... Really classy fighters don't fight out of their class.[14]

Blazey's observations were a fair example of the sort of ambivalence that Hawke's outsized passions aroused. They suggested an apprehension that people had felt since he was a small child that in some way that they could not quite express, he was uncontainable, like a genie escaped from its bottle. Blazey's article also predicted that Hawke would not enter parliament because he lacked the character to do so:

> He lacks . . . the one characteristic by which all his other brilliances are reduced to histrionics or mere charm – it is the quality in leaders which Churchill called mettle. Menzies, Stalin and Mao had mettle. So do Whitlam and Fraser, but not Bob Hawke. All have done their lonely, unpopular long marches in politics. But Hawke, at the age of 50, is not prepared to undertake such an uncertain slog. Why should he? He's the most popular politician in the country without really being one. He loves the applause too much to give it up now.[15]

It was a widely held view. In 1982 political journalists and Hawke's colleagues in the Caucus were still harping upon this theme: 'Hawke is always looking in the mirror of the polls – he's

only interested in his popularity' and 'he has no self-discipline'
were the expressions used. (Even Hawke's closest friends had been
convinced that he would be unable to give up alcohol.) People
sneered at some of his fixed indignations; they were derisive,
for instance, about his passionate hostility for the Minister for
Industrial Relations, Ian Viner; there was a Canberra press gallery
jest: 'Not another Hawke statement about Ian Viner's lies!'

Hawke spent much of April campaigning in the Victorian
election and in May flew to Israel for briefings in a venture that
was, as events turned out, to tear him in half. He had agreed
to go to the USSR for a third time, to plead for the release of
Soviet Jews. On this occasion he would not be making a general
submission, but would go requesting that twelve people in jail
or Siberian exile, and their families, plus other Jewish families
who for more than five years had been refused exit visas from
the USSR, should be allowed to leave the country. For the first
time he would be meeting, face to face, Soviet Jews who were
forbidden to leave the USSR. Hawke had never contemplated
suicide: he was to do so after leaving Moscow.

Some hint of what was happening to Soviet Jewish dissidents
came in snippets of information that seeped out. A letter to
Hawke in 1979:

> I beseech you to take up my cousin's cause ... In January this
> year I sent a parcel of new winter clothes for X, who is in exile,
> to his mother's address. It was returned in May with a stamp
> 'Forbidden' on it ... He has been sentenced to seven years'
> hard labour and three years' exile.[16]

A radio broadcast from London, also in 1979, incorporating
tapes smuggled out of the USSR:

> A, who displayed a banner reading, 'Allow me to join my
> family in Israel', was sentenced to four years' exile for 'mali-
> cious hooliganism'. There she lived in a hut with sixty former
> male convicts who 'behaved like apes' and attacked her in

the night. She fortressed herself in one room, with a dog for company. 'Sometimes I don't know what to do – to cry or laugh. My life here is so miserable, so meaningless ... Even the children when they played with my dog were questioned by police.'[17]

A report smuggled out to Australia, following interviews in the late 1970s with 'refuseniks', as those who are forbidden visas, are called:

She appeared pale, sad and desperate. Her husband is in gaol, living in a room with three others in temperatures 50 degrees below freezing. He has been convicted of 'parasitism'. He spent two years in exile, returned to Moscow, then was sentenced to three more years' exile to the Far North. It took two months' travelling to get there.

B was sacked from his job as an electrical engineer after applying for a visa to Israel. He was gaoled for drunkenness, although he is a teetotaller. He now drives a lift.

C said, 'If they deny my sons a visa again I think that by September no matter how terrible it must sound to you, I will leave without them. I cannot take it any longer. I don't want to die here. The problem we ask ourselves all the time is who makes decisions? We don't know. Probably Brezhnev himself.'

D said, 'When the US Senators were here the authorities permitted Yiddish theatre performances, which are usually forbidden, to take place in major urban centres. It was incredible. One couldn't get tickets ... It was a great occasion for Moscow Jews, it was a holiday, people were excited and cried.'

Mrs E queued for four hours to buy fish for my [kosher] lunch. They were so hospitable. We loathed eating any of the food they offered us.

F, a cyberneticist, author of twelve books and a total of 160 scientific works, some of which have been translated into English, German, French, Chinese and Japanese. World renowned in cybernetics. Applied for a visa in September 1971. Refused on the grounds of 'State interest'. Dismissed from all his elected bodies and duties. His name has been deleted from all his publications in the Soviet Union, he was forbidden to teach and deprived of membership of the Communist Party. Medical aid facilities at the Academy of Sciences were also withdrawn. His children were expelled from post-graduate studies.

G, H and J have been sacked for applying for exit visas. They are teaching Jewish culture, Hebrew, and so on, but have had to find menial work, because they are not allowed to declare their tax on earnings from teaching Jewish culture, and if one does not pay tax one can be gaoled for 'parasitism'. This is the only country in the world where people desperately fight the bureaucracy to be allowed to pay tax.

The temperature was below freezing on the Sabbath, but an extraordinary number of people gathered in the synagogue. The KGB stood around, watching and taking notes . . . I have been trailed by the KGB all the time, even at the ballet. I had had a drink and was a little light-headed. I walked up to him and showed him my ballet tickets. He shouted at me and then walked off. I paid for my foolishness later that night: every hour the telephone rang and when I answered it, they slammed down the receiver at the other end . . . I feared being charged with 'hooliganism'.[18]

Hawke was to meet some of these people and hear from them much more about their lives. Among them are the most famous names in world Jewry, people who in Israel and the Diaspora communities have the status of supernatural beings because of the persecutions they have suffered over many years, and their refusal to surrender.

Hawke had a long-standing invitation from the Soviet government to pay another visit to the country. It was Isi Leibler, the head of Jetset and a world activist on behalf of Soviet Jews, who persuaded him that 1979 was the time to return to Moscow and while there to apply pressure on the authorities for the release of refuseniks. The hour seemed ripe: the USSR had recently allowed some Jews, who had been in jail, to leave the country. Rumour said that this was done in exchange for Soviet spies held in the USA. Strategic Arms Limitation Talks (SALT) II between the USA and USSR were in progress; there was a Bill before the American Senate that could veto Most Favoured Nation treatment in trade with the USSR unless it observed human rights. Since the initiation of détente the Soviet bloc economy had become intertwined with Western economies and the trading partnership with the USA was of special importance to the USSR. Another vulnerable area was the Olympic Games, to be held in Moscow in 1980. It was known that the Kremlin was anxious that the Games should not be marred by demonstrations about human rights.

The Australian Olympic Federation had awarded Leibler's company, Jetset, accreditation as the official Australian tourist organiser for the Moscow Olympics, in recognition of its handling of the Montreal Olympics in 1976. Leibler had gone twice to Moscow in 1978 on Olympic business and while there had quietly suggested that the Olympic Games could progress more smoothly if the Russian government would allow exit visas to Soviet Jews. A senior Australian diplomat remarked, 'The Russians were furious. They saw that Leibler had a lever over them, and they regarded that as a dirty trick.' Leibler wanted to accompany Hawke to the USSR in 1979, but he had been refused an entry visa. 'I am, of course, an agent of the International Jewish Conspiracy', he remarked with a weary smile.

By 1979 Isi Leibler was one of Hawke's closest friends, although for many years he had deliberately remained distant from Hawke out of political delicacy. Leibler had been born in Belgium, the eldest son of a diamond merchant who had escaped from Europe just in time. The Leiblers had arrived in Australia in 1938, when Isi was four years old. By his early twenties he was working towards an academic career in political science, his special study being Marxism, when he became aware of the plight of Soviet Jews. In those days and for years afterwards conventional wisdom had it that, since the Revolution, Jews in Russia had suffered no discrimination. The ALP Left, including Sam Cohen, was committed to this view, as was the World Jewish Congress. Leibler became the *enfant terrible* of the Australian Jewish community and alarmed international Jewish leaders because of his audacious insistence that Soviet Jews were harassed as a policy of state. He was saved from being dismissed as public relations chairman of the Victorian Jewish Board of Deputies only by the intervention of the communal leader, Maurice Ashkanasy. His continuing fight for his kinsmen in the USSR led him into close contact with the Menzies government: Australia was the first country in the world to raise in the United Nations, in 1962, the question of Soviet anti-Semitism, and this occurred thanks to Leibler's tireless lobbying of Liberal politicians, especially the Minister for External Affairs, Garfield Barwick. Because of his heresies about the Soviet Union at a time when the ALP Left was sympathetic to it and his contacts with the Menzies government, Leibler was regarded as an enemy of Labor.

In 1965 Leibler published a Marxist analysis of the plight of Soviet Jewry that Rex Mortimer, a leader of the Australian Communist Party, and other important Communists, publicly endorsed. The book and its endorsement caused a furore in the Communist Party; more importantly, it influenced pro-Soviet groups throughout the world. They used its information and conclusions to dissociate themselves from Russian anti-Semitism.

Leibler's social manner is mild and charming but manifestly determined. On first meeting he could be mistaken for an ordinary, agreeable, successful businessman, who has carried over into middle age an interest from his youth. In fact he is a man of extravagant feelings. Of all Hawke's friends, Leibler is the one who most resembles him in passionate commitment. By 1979 he was the president of the Executive Council of Australian Jewry.

Leibler knew of the turmoil in Hawke's private life in 1979 and insisted that Hazel accompany her husband to Moscow, to look after him and to share what Leibler guessed would be a harrowing experience for Hawke – who, by April, was again drinking as heavily as ever. He said,

> Bob is a genuine ideological social democrat and I think only an ideological social democrat can be truly appalled by the Soviet Union. He understands the extent to which the system has moulded the country, that beneath the pseudo-civilised mask there is a very ugly animal, that you have there a world of pretence – fake history, fake unions . . . Bob *hates* the Soviet system. I think the only time he is ever frightened is when he is in the USSR. On something like this there was nothing in it for him, politically – which is a totally different situation from that of the American senators who have lent their support to the cause. There are votes in it, for them – but the Jewish vote in Australia . . . ? It's inconsequential. I knew he would be deeply affected by actually meeting the refuseniks – Bob makes life such a passionate experience, all the time. He is incapable of neutrality.

The three of them flew to Israel, where Hawke had briefings and again met with Begin, then the Hawkes continued on to Moscow and Leibler went to Rome for a meeting of the Praesidium on Soviet Jewry.

Before he left Australia Hawke had told the Soviet ambassador that he would be raising the refusenik issue – 'I thought it was better to be frank with them' – and had discussed it with Andrew Peacock, the Minister for Foreign Affairs. Peacock had been sympathetic and promised Australian embassy support in Moscow. A further oddity in the bizarre nightmare of life for the refuseniks is that, while they live under surveillance, they have contact with the outside world – one woman has a telephone, others use public telephones to make reverse charge calls. They had been alerted to Hawke's arrival. He had the address of a flat in Moscow in which they gathered, but given the circumstances he did not want to travel there in a Soviet government car. Something peculiar had recently happened to an Australian diplomat posted to Moscow, and it appeared that he had been drugged. Peacock arranged for embassy transport.

It was only in the evenings that Hawke and Hazel had a chance to meet the refuseniks: during the day he had a rigorous program of talks. One of these was a lengthy discussion with Professor M. S. Kapitsa, head of the First Far Eastern Department of the Soviet Foreign Office, and an expert on Asian affairs. The summary of their meeting, made by an Australian diplomat who accompanied Hawke, fills twelve pages and covers Sino-Soviet relations, Soviet perceptions of future Chinese development, USSR–USA relations, political developments in Western Europe, China's role in South-East Asia, Vietnam and Kampuchea. The record of conversation concludes: 'Professor Kapitsa ... complimented Mr Hawke on his wide knowledge of international affairs. He added he now knew why knowledgeable people were saying Mr Hawke was the future prime minister of Australia.'[19] Hawke was gratified by the professor's final remarks, for they encouraged him to think that elsewhere in the Soviet hierarchy his reputation would be enhanced and the real purpose of his visit moved forward.

He had already had one meeting with the refuseniks, and had given his heart to them. They called him 'Bobba' and later asked Leibler: 'Isn't Bobba really Jewish? How could anybody understand us and have such rapport with us after such a short time, and not be Jewish?' 'He made a tremendous impact on them – they are not naive simpletons, those people the USSR is holding back, but are men and women of unusual intellect, probably encompassing some of the most outstanding Jews living in the world', Leibler said.

Even before he arrived in Moscow Hawke was tense with anxiety about what he was attempting to do. Once he had met the refuseniks his anxiety twisted tight. On the next day of his visit Hawke broached the subject with Alexei Shibayev,

Shelepin's successor as head of the Soviet trade union movement, and with Peter Pimenov, another senior official. They said that a decision would have to be taken 'at a high level'. Hawke made a second evening visit to the little flat on the outskirts of Moscow; on the final day of his visit to the USSR, in the late afternoon of Friday, 25 May, he went for a third time with astonishing news: one of the Soviet officials had said that Hawke's requests would be met. The gathering that night was euphoric.

People wept with joy. Hawke drank a lot of vodka and was in tears on and off. It was, the refuseniks told Leibler afterwards, 'like a family reunion'. At some stage during the celebration it was suggested that a press statement should be prepared because, as Hawke said, 'The refuseniks and I thought this change of Soviet policy should be presented to the West as a *good* decision, and the West should be invited to welcome it'. At seven o'clock next morning one of the refuseniks, Professor Alexander Lerner, arrived at the Hawkes' room in the Sputnik Hotel with the news release already typed out. It read:

> We welcome the position which we believe has been conveyed on behalf of the Soviet Authorities in regard to the emigration of Jews from their country. Our understanding of this position, as conveyed at the end of last week to an Australian Trade Union Official, Mr Bob Hawke, was summarized to three issues. First, people who have had their application for visas denied for more than five years will be granted exit permits. Second, the twelve in prison or in exile will be released. Third, as to the future, five years will be recognized as the maximum period for refusal of exit permits, consistent with the concern of the Soviet Authorities for security in regard to State secrets. We understand that the processes necessary to give effect to these changes are to be initiated in the near future. These changes are of profound importance and when given effect to, will call for appropriate positive response on our part.[20]

Hawke took a copy of the statement and showed it to Pimenov, who had come to the airport to farewell him. In the presence of a number of Russian and Australian officials, including the ambassador, Hawke asked Pimenov, 'What should I do with this?' to which Pimenov replied, 'Do as you will'. Hawke had earlier asked if he might telephone a friend to convey the good news, and Russian officials had agreed that he could and should, and had arranged the call. It was, of course, to Leibler in Rome, who said, 'I was frightened. I thought, oh, Christ! It's too much! Bob said to me on the phone, "This is the greatest contribution to a humanitarian cause I've ever achieved". He was intensely emotional.' When, next morning, Pimenov read the press statement and raised no objections to it, Hawke – who said 'I still felt staggered by the whole thing' – was convinced that the matter was sealed.

It was inconceivable to Hawke that Pimenov would allow a public promise to be made, through a press statement, and then retract it because, as he reasoned, 'They would be revealed to the world as liars. And with the international situation as it then was, that could only harm them.' At the airport Murray Bourchier, the Australian ambassador, warily agreed with Hawke that it appeared he had pulled off a magnificent coup. What became known in Moscow as 'The Hawke Incident' was just unfolding.

NINETEEN

A PHOTOGRAPH PUBLISHED on the front pages of Australian newspapers and in other papers around the world tells some of the story: Hawke had just disembarked from his aeroplane in Rome, six hours after leaving Moscow. He is walking towards the photographer with Hazel beside him. His expression is angry and confused. Hazel has turned towards him, her eyes full of alarm.

Unknown to Hawke, Professor Lerner had distributed the news statement to the Moscow press corps that morning, convinced that Hawke had authorised him to do so.[1] By the time Hawke arrived in Rome journalists from all over the world were waiting for him. Hawke barged through them, saying only that the Moscow statement was correct. It was an embarrassment that the story had broken before Hawke had had a chance to talk to Leibler and other international Jewish leaders on publicity tactics.

Leibler recalled,

I've never seen Bob quite as shattered as he was when he got off that plane in Rome. He looked like a dead man. I've never seen a person so completely pulverised as he was, his emotions were smashed in. He was out for twenty-four hours.

Much of Hawke's exhaustion was due to vodka. He said,

I was absolutely whacked. The Russians entertain extremely hard and I'd made a point of staying with them – there was no

way I was not going to be entirely with them – so I was tired
and worn out by the time I got to Rome.

By the next day he had slept off the effects of six days of entertainment and tension, and was brimming with optimism. At a
lunch given by the world Jewish leaders he reported in detail
on what had transpired in Moscow, his personal conviction so
intense that it swayed his audience. Zvi Netzer, a senior official
of the Israeli Foreign Office, whose ancestors were Russian Jews
and who had served as a diplomat in the USSR before the 1967
war, happened to be in Rome and recalled, 'I *knew* the Soviet
system, but even I was convinced. We were all very optimistic.'
Even the premature press release appeared an advantage: Hawke
argued that it would lock the Russians in to their promise. His
view was accepted. The president of the World Jewish Congress,
Phil Klutznick; the president of the Jewish Agency and the
World Zionist Organisation, Leon Dulzin; and the chairman
of the United States Jewish Presidents' Conference, Theodore
Mann, all publicly expressed their appreciation for Hawke's
efforts. In Australia the Victorian Jewish Board of Deputies
unanimously passed a vote of thanks to Hawke 'for his extraordinary and courageous efforts on behalf of our brethren in the
Soviet Union'.[2] There was an atmosphere of exhilaration, not
just in Rome but for Jews around the world. In the same week
as the refusenik announcement, Egypt had opened its borders to
Israel – for the first time in thirty-one years.

The next step was to take place in Geneva, at the ILO: there
Peter Pimenov, the leader of the trade union delegation, would
give Hawke a list of those who were to be issued with visas.

Hawke arrived in Geneva at the end of May in an exalted
frame of mind. George Rockey, who had resigned from TNT
when it became a public company (he complained, 'A public
company! Every time you wanted to have a pee you had to ask
the secretary'), was a resident in Switzerland now. He met Hawke
in Geneva and they went off to France for a few days to indulge
Rockey's passion, gambling. Rockey had introduced Hawke to

casinos in 1977; by 1979 Hawke was a blackjack fan. He refused to play roulette, but he had 'a system' for blackjack and for the third year in succession won handsomely.

When he returned to Geneva and saw Pimenov he had the first inkling that his winning streak had run out: Pimenov, on catching sight of Hawke, dodged him.

The following day the international press carried a story quoting Pimenov as saying that Hawke had 'misunderstood' what had been said in Moscow. He conveyed the impression to journalists, and Soviet officials in Moscow made similar suggestions to foreign diplomats, that Hawke had gone to the Soviet Union resolved on some stratagem the depths of which were unknown, and had finished up leaving the innocent Russians in a state of honest perplexity. The conclusion to be drawn was that Hawke was a devious customer.

Then on 7 June at the opening of an ILO Governing Body meeting, Pimenov arrived with a translator. His English had been satisfactory in the past: suddenly, it seemed, he could only speak Russian. Hawke bailed him up but Pimenov, using sign language, indicated that the situation was too delicate to discuss in the presence of the translator. Hawke appealed to Joe Morris, chairman of the Workers, to intervene. Morris, too, discovered that Pimenov could not understand English. Later that day, in the Governing Body meeting, Hawke sent Pimenov a sharp note, stating that while they had in the past had disagreements, he regarded as 'monstrous the suggestion that I have in any way misrepresented the unequivocal commitments made to me in Moscow'.[3] He demanded a private discussion with Pimenov. The Russian read the note (without the assistance of his translator), rose and left the meeting. Hawke could not find him.

A day or so later Boris Averianov, the man who had accompanied Hawke on his visits to Shelepin in 1971 and 1973, approached Hawke. Averianov was a senior official of the World Federation of Trade Unions, the Soviet-dominated version of ICFTU. Averianov had with him a document relating to the

SALT II talks, and asked Hawke to endorse it. Hawke replied, 'Before asking me for any favours, consult Pimenov'.

A few days later the Soviet delegation to the ILO was giving a cocktail party, which Hawke attended. He was standing alone, willing Pimenov to stop ignoring him, when he was approached by a smiling, personable young man who introduced himself as Eugene Arapov. Arapov explained that he was based in Geneva as a Soviet ILO liaison officer with the news media. When Hawke questioned Arapov further the Russian said, 'I have been here for four years. You don't think we would have someone insignificant in this position, do you?' In plain English this meant, 'I am from the KGB'.[4] He suggested that it would be useful if he and Hawke could talk to each other, soon.

By this stage Hawke was growing desperate. On Friday, 15 June, following a session of the Resolutions Committee that he was chairing, he was approached once more by Arapov who invited him to go outside the building 'for a confidential discussion'. They went out to the Russian's car and as soon as they were inside Arapov switched on the radio loudly, remarking, 'You know why I'm doing that, don't you?' The cat was playing with its mouse. Arapov said he wanted to speak to Hawke privately and confidentially, at a place where neither the Soviets nor Hawke's colleagues could see them. However, driving Hawke around in his own car, in daylight, was hardly the right way to begin what is known in the trade as 'a deniable meeting'. With one part of his mind Hawke realised that what was happening was fantastic, but by now he was so anxious that he was willing to suspend his incredulity. Arapov drove to a small restaurant in Geneva, the Monte Cristo, and there they talked for three hours.

A transcript of Hawke's oral report to Jewish leaders, made soon afterwards, says:

> Arapov advised Hawke that ... It would be counter-productive for Hawke to have any further discussions with Pimenov about the Soviet Jews unless Pimenov himself raised it, which was highly unlikely. All future discussions should be directed

to him. Secondly, he asked Hawke to recapitulate everything that had transpired, although it was quite clear that he was fully in the picture. Thirdly, he advised Hawke that the matter was of such a nature that he would have to revert to Moscow and possibly go to Moscow personally for discussions.[5]

Arapov then raised the SALT II meeting in Vienna between President Carter and Brezhnev. He emphasised the importance of SALT II and asked Hawke if he believed, in the event of exit visas being granted to Soviet Jews, that it could be guaranteed that the American Jewish lobby would 'give a positive response' – that is, pressure the Congress to ratify the SALT II agreement that Carter and Brezhnev had signed in Vienna. He ended by telling Hawke that he must wait until discussions with Moscow had been finalised, when he would again make contact.

Hawke's anxiety and misery brought on a bout of heavy drinking. A couple of nights later he telephoned a friend in Australia and talked for more than an hour, expressing his fears that he had, all along, been duped. At one stage he said, 'If I've let those people down – I've never thought of this before – I think I'll kill myself. I really think I could commit suicide.' Leibler, with whom Hawke was keeping in contact, said later,

It was heartbreaking. Bob was in the weakest negotiating position he's ever been in, and he was clutching at every little straw, every little word. Intuitively, I felt the Russians were playing a game just to keep him quiet, to prevent him from attacking them in the ILO. But like him I was also looking for miracles.

Already General Vladimir Grigorievich Borisenko, the head of the Passport and Visa Office of the USSR Interior Ministry, had given an interview in Moscow saying that Hawke had no authority to broadcast reports that refuseniks would be released, and nor did Alexei Shibayev have any authority to make such claims. Borisenko added, 'We in the Interior Ministry have not authorised anyone to make a statement about decisions coming within the competence of the Ministry of the Interior. No maximum period for refusing exit visas has been set. We will never set any.'[6]

After his first long discussion with Arapov, Hawke had twelve days left in Geneva, time in which he could cause severe embarrassment to the Soviet delegation by publicly attacking the USSR on the general issue of human rights and on the particular question of the refuseniks. Arapov, however, had adroitly silenced Hawke: he had warned him that he should say nothing, lest he jeopardise the delicate, secret process now underway. Leibler confirmed Hawke's belief that he must avoid a confrontation with the Russians. Then on 26 June, the day before Hawke was due to leave Geneva, Arapov invited Hawke for lunch – again at the Monte Cristo.[7] Their luncheon lasted almost two hours. According to Hawke's report, Arapov told him that

> He had been advised by Moscow that there was a probability of Brezhnev becoming personally involved in the situation, but that the most important prerequisite from the Soviet viewpoint ... would be a quid pro quo if the Soviets delivered.
>
> Arapov stated that he would still have to get final authorisation (presumably on the level of Brezhnev) and if that were forthcoming, Hawke would be contacted either directly from Geneva or via the Russian Embassy (in Canberra) with a message stating, 'Go on Bob'. If such a message were received it would mean that the following quid pro quo situation would come into effect:
>
> a. Hawke would have to go to the United States and convince the American Jewish lobby to support strongly the [view] that the SALT II talks were beneficial, and ensure that key Jews would be prepared to lobby (openly) for Senate ratification, without amendments.
> b. If SALT II were to be fully ratified without changes, the Soviets on the day of ratification would release the fifty

refuseniks and twelve prisoners and their families and provide them with a special flight.

Hawke pointed out to Arapov that it was more than feasible that even if Jewish groups could be persuaded to lobby for SALT ratification, it could still fail because of other factors. Arapov responded that ratification was imperative; that Soviet delivery of the package would be more difficult but still possible in the event of Jewish lobbying failing to succeed in ratification. After ratification of SALT II [which would be followed by] the release of the fifty refusenik families and the twelve prisoners, Jews should then extend support for Most Favoured Nation status for the Soviet Union, and extension of credits to the USSR. If this succeeded, the Russians would then formally ratify their commitment regarding a maximum five-year term for all Jewish emigrants denied visas on grounds of their having had access to State secrets.

Arapov also discussed at length the Olympics and stated that in the event of the above scenario moving smoothly, the Russians would expect an undertaking that there would be no problems encountered during the Olympic Games.

The oral report made by Hawke continued:

Arapov was evasive and embarrassed as to reasons for Soviet repudiation of promises made in Moscow, although at no stage did he suggest that Hawke was misrepresenting what had been conveyed to him. He emphasised that [the quid pro quo] scenario still had to be confirmed through discussions on the highest level, involving contact with Brezhnev. He indicated that he considered the likelihood of package endorsement at the highest level to be very good and he hoped to revert to Hawke in the not too distant future.[8]

Hawke told Arapov that he would give him until the end of June to make contact. If he had heard nothing by then he would make one final effort to contact Arapov through a Geneva intermediary.

The message 'Go on Bob' never came. It is unlikely that anyone outside the USSR will ever know what happened, but there are some interesting points to the Hawke Incident. An Australian diplomat's comment: 'Hawke was trapped between two powerful forces – the KGB and International Zionism which, in the Russian mind, because of Russian anti-Semitism, is a huge and dangerous adversary'. From an Israeli diplomat:

> The Russians had not been serious from the beginning, but had been anxious to avoid embarrassment – a denunciation of them by Hawke in the ILO – so had kidded him along in Moscow, then in Geneva, playing for time. The Russians require payment, and Jews are bargaining chips. Australia, an insignificant country, was in no position to 'pay' for the Jews. SALT II was the payment and Hawke was unable to deliver on that.

It was almost a year, and one of the chessmen in the game was dead, before a more complex analysis of what had happened emerged. Another very senior Australian observer of the Soviet scene wrote to Hawke:

> ... the 'nekrolog' [necrologue] of Peter Pimenov [published in *Pravda* on 30 May 1980] ... confirms the views of those who said that [Pimenov] was personally very close to Brezhnev ... This suggests that Pimenov who was, it seems, stage-managing developments during your visit was pursuing a stratagem known to very few others. My tentative conclusion ... is that everything turned out exactly as intended by the Soviet side. I think they may well have been worried that the meeting between Brezhnev and Carter in Vienna on 1 June 1979 might have been made the occasion of a demonstration by Jews dissatisfied with aspects of Soviet policy. Pimenov may have been told to do something which would make a

Jewish demonstration in Vienna less likely, for instance to get a credible report circulating that good news for the Jews was on the way, leading them to think that a demonstration might be not only unnecessary but actually against their interests. If my supposition is right then one can only say that as a disinformation operation it was cleverly done – at some cost perhaps to the USSR's future relations with Australia, but meeting the demands of the moment very well![9]

Hawke was comforted by this 'tentative conclusion', since it vindicated his integrity. But if the analysis is correct he had been victim of a most subtle undermining and the worst traducement of his career, for the Soviet Union had successfully portrayed him as a devious incompetent – to the world: the refusenik release story had made the front pages of all the great newspapers of the West. There is no suggestion of any malice towards Hawke: the issues at stake were too important. He had simply arrived in Moscow at a convenient time, making a convenient request.

Meanwhile, the effect of these experiences on his morale was grave. He was both wrenched with guilt for having falsely raised the hopes of Soviet Jews, and fearful that because of the incident they might be punished. He felt humiliated before his Diaspora and Israeli friends. Leibler was staunch and did not doubt that Hawke had got his facts straight, but there were others, especially non-Jews and Australian journalists, who made Hawke their butt and tormented him about what he had failed to do for the Russian Jews. The most distressing result was that the episode brought fear and distrust to the surface of Hawke's mind. In the past, paranoia had risen occasionally when he was drunk, but even roaring drunk Hawke had remained affectionate and trusting with friends. In the period after his sojourn in Geneva in 1979 up to the time he became a teetotaller, Hawke, when drunk, made accusations of treachery to some of his best mates.

He left Geneva on 27 June 1979 in an agony of hope and despair. As usual he was able to disguise his feelings with his public mask of bonhomie, but misery was having its effect and within two months, his life complicated by other problems, he felt 'relieved' when told he might have a brain tumour.

Hawke flew from Geneva to Rome, where he was to have a private audience with Pope John-Paul. His Holiness was keen to talk about Australia, Poland, the USSR and trade union matters and their interview overran its allotted time. Hawke has never lost his simplicity of heart: as Ducker remarked of him, 'a giant in many ways, and also in many ways an ordinary bloke'. He felt deeply honoured by the Pontiff's interest in what he had to say. The audience had been arranged at short notice by Hawke's friend, John Hogan, a much-loved figure in the New South Wales ALP, who farmed in the Tweed River district and was nicknamed the Planter. Hawke had been reading without break on the flight back from Rome but then, as the plane approached Jakarta,

> I put my book down and began thinking about John, wondering about my schedule and how I could get to see him to express my enormous gratitude. I was filled with very warm feelings for him. When we landed in Perth I rang Hazel, who told me that John had died a few hours earlier. It had happened at the very time I had begun thinking about him, coming into Jakarta. I was terribly upset – and I couldn't go to the funeral because there was a dispute on Christmas Island that I had to fly out to immediately. I sent a long telegram from Perth and Hazel went to the funeral, representing both of us.

On Christmas Island the workers garlanded his shoulders with flowers in thanks for what he had done for them. But in Australia miseries and problems were awaiting him. In Perth he visited Ellie. A few weeks earlier she had spoken to him; she was now beyond speech. In Melbourne his domestic life was still strained: a front-page newspaper photograph of Hawke and Hazel, at home, published a few weeks later beside a quote from Hawke saying that 'lack of privacy had also affected his family' hinted at the difficulties.[10] The children had all left home and were living in various states, Stephen using a fictitious surname. Furthermore, there was discontent within the ACTU, for Hawke's continuing inability to reach a formal decision about parliament was unsettling to staff and executive members, who complained that he was often distracted from the real concerns of the presidency. There were complaints that he did not fully have his mind on the job and that the Council was not functioning properly because he was absent from his office so often – frequently because the burden of his normal representation of the trade union movement on a wide range of committees was increased, at this time, by his membership of the Crawford Committee.

On return to Melbourne from Christmas Island he went straight into a new Telecom dispute and was still engaged in a rush of travelling to and from Canberra for negotiations with the government, which had proclaimed the *Commonwealth Employees (Employment Provisions) Act* and was threatening to sack tens of thousands of public servants, when the ALP biennial conference opened in Adelaide.

It was Bill Hayden's first conference as leader of the ALP and naturally enough he wanted to make an impressive showing. Hayden was in an invidious situation: he was leader of a demoralised party and his own position was being continually undermined by news media speculation that Hawke would enter parliament, usurp Hayden's leadership and sweep Labor to victory at the polls. Barely a day passed without the news media goading Hayden about his leadership, vis-à-vis Hawke, while Hawke was constantly pinched and prodded with questions about his political career, causing him, around this time, to exclaim to journalists, 'If the reindeer were moulting in Lapland you would want to know how that affected my attitudes to entering parliament!' The result was inevitable: two men who had liked each other and worked amiably together had forced upon them the roles of antagonists. If the news media did not exist, this would have happened anyway. The difference the media, especially television, made was that it transformed political rivalry into a Roman circus, at once creating and catering to an appetite for blood.

While Hawke had been abroad Hayden had made a veiled public attack upon him; the deputy leader, Lionel Bowen, had followed up with a less veiled one. In the days prior to the ALP's conference there was much broadcast speculation that Hawke would give a more dazzling performance than Hayden.

For more than a year Hawke had been chairman of the ALP's federal economic policy committee, among whose members was Ralph Willis, now the shadow Treasurer. They had drawn up a series of recommendations to put to the conference, the most controversial being that a future Labor government would hold a referendum to gain control over prices and incomes. Six years earlier the Whitlam government had failed to convince the trade union movement to support government control over incomes, but at the time the idea had been presented to the unions brutally, without consultation, and during a period of booming employment – the last loud flash, as people had come to realise, before a twilight stillness descended upon the economy. Had the Whitlam government been empowered in December 1973 to restrain prices and incomes, its handling of the economic crisis of 1974–75 would have been easier; it may even have survived.

Hawke and Willis were now convinced that a future Labor government must have such powers. However, persuading the trade union movement, even six years later, to agree to such a proposal would be difficult. Hawke's strategy was to have the ALP adopt as policy a prices and incomes referendum at its July conference in Adelaide. He would then be well armed, at the ACTU Congress in September, to argue to the unions that they, too, should adopt this policy. By September 1979 the ACTU would have 2 million affiliated members; if such a large number of citizens were morally bound to the referendum proposal, a future Labor government would have the best chance any government has ever had of winning a controversial referendum.

The matter was scheduled for debate on Monday, 16 July, in Adelaide. Meanwhile it was known that the Left had drawn up seventy amendments to the ALP's economic policy recommendations, and that it would reject outright the referendum.

The ALP federal executive held its pre-conference meeting in Adelaide on Thursday and Friday, 12 and 13 July, but because of the Telecom dispute Hawke could not attend. He said,

> On Sunday night Neil Batt [the ALP president] telephoned me and begged me to come over to Adelaide because of the wages policy debate that was coming up the following week. He said it was absolutely vital that Bill have a good win at the conference on this issue, which would be so important to a future Labor government. Then on Monday night Batt rang me again and handed the phone to Bill who said, 'We've got the numbers, but we want to make sure we win well'. He said he really wanted me to come to Adelaide, although as I'd explained the Telecom dispute was at such a stage that I felt I should stay with it, and that there was a danger that I'd have to pull myself out of Adelaide to return to negotiations. The federal executive had decided to put the economic debate off by a day to give themselves more time to lobby delegates for support. I told Bill on Monday night that I'd get over to Adelaide on Tuesday morning. The debate was due to begin at 9.30 a.m., but there was no flight that would get me there early enough. So it was agreed that Ralph Willis would open the session and when I arrived, around eleven o'clock, I'd take over. I had a speech prepared, attacking the Left's position on the issue, which would have devastated them and shown up what a pack of bastards they were. When I arrived Ralph was already speaking. I went up on the platform and sat down behind him. Hayden was seated in the audience, on the left of the hall. We broke for lunch and I went down to say g'day to Bill. He made an extraordinary remark. He said, 'This was never my idea', referring to the recommendation on wages. I was in a hurry to get to a luncheon at state parliament. I said, 'What are you talking about?' I was staggered by what he had said, but I just thought, 'Oh Jesus'. When I returned from lunch I was given the message that Hayden had done a deal with

the Left. They had an amendment to the wages policy and Hayden was going to support it.

Unbeknown to Hawke, his old adversaries Tom Uren and Jim Roulston had buttonholed Hayden the day before to tell him that the unions would not accept the referendum proposal. Uren had said, 'We've got the numbers to roll you'.[11] On Tuesday morning Hayden had called a breakfast meeting with about nineteen delegates to lobby them to support the referendum proposal. By lunchtime Tuesday Hayden had come to the conclusion that he could not muster the numbers to have the referendum idea passed: he was therefore, as leader of the party, forced to choose between defeat at his first conference, or a compromise. He chose to compromise. Unhappily – in the broader view – he did not warn Hawke that he believed himself trapped and was therefore changing his tactics. Instead, he embarrassed Hawke, who had only two minutes warning before the debate resumed after lunch that the leader had dumped him and the economic policy committee recommendation. Willis and Mick Young, the shadow Minister for Industrial Relations, were similarly caught off guard for they, too, had been given no warning. Neither had the New South Wales Right. Hawke believes that members of Hayden's staff had persuaded him that a sudden undercutting of the president of the ACTU was a smart tactic to strengthen his leadership of the party. He was furious – on his own account, and on the larger issue of what he believed was best for the labour movement and the Australian economy.

He asked Neil Batt, 'What will I do now?' Batt told him to say nothing, to avoid confrontation. Ducker, who was beside Hawke, gave the same advice: there were only seconds in which to confer, then Ralph Willis had the unpalatable job of continuing the debate, deserted by Hayden and unsupported by Hawke, who was seated behind him, fuming but silent. The amendment, which committed the party to a 'dialogue' with the unions, but not to an incomes referendum, was duly moved, supported by Hayden, and passed into ALP policy – as formidable as a resolution in favour of motherhood. Hawke did not speak all afternoon.

At the end of the session journalists asked Hayden when Hawke had been told of the compromise. He replied, 'After lunch', then added heatedly, 'Listen, I make up my own mind in these matters and I carried the conference. I think that's the thing that counts and it's not such a bad result' – remarks that revealed, unwittingly, the leader's jittery feelings about Hawke.

Hawke himself was already raw-nerved and deeply fatigued. The previous week, during the Telecom dispute, he had slept on average only three hours a night. He was vulnerable, especially at this stage when he was still throbbing with pain from the duplicity of the Russians, to exaggerated feelings of betrayal. Add an atmosphere of hostility towards him, then alcohol, and he would be primed for an outburst of self-righteous anger. Unhappily his old protector, John Ducker, was not well enough to force Hawke to evade danger. Ducker said later,

> If only I'd been able to persuade Hawkey to come upstairs with me to talk to the Queenslanders. He could have said what he liked to them, got it all out of his system. But he wanted to go and sound off in the bar.

Ducker, after years of 'fighting and struggling for purity and goodness', as he referred later, with a cherub's smile, to life in ALP politics, was going through a period of traumatic emotional change: 'a tremendous pressure of contradictions – trying to keep oneself afloat and do something useful'. His blood pressure was high; his doctors had ordered him to have more rest; he was torn, he said, between his political career and wanting to spend time with his family.

Ducker had spoken vehemently against the amendment inside the conference, stating the view of the New South Wales Right, which was furious about the deal. When the session ended he joined Hawke in a makeshift television studio only a metre or so from the conference floor. Journalists had not yet realised what complicated emotions had been unleashed: at Bill Hayden's conference, Bob Hawke was being cold-shouldered. Ducker said, 'Everybody walked away from Bob. I was the bloke who stuck with him. Others simply found they were engaged elsewhere.' Hawke gave a low-key television interview, saying that the compromise 'was something which occurred over lunchtime. I haven't had time to consider it.' Asked about his political future, he replied that if delegates thought he could serve the party better in another capacity he would expect them to come to him and express their view 'and so far they haven't'. At the end of the interview Ducker and Hawke hugged each other. Paul Kelly and Stuart Simpson of the *National Times* continued:

> The ABC, sensing they might be on to a story, brought in some bottles of beer to keep the duo around ... Hawke and Ducker stayed in the studio watching replays of the Hawke interview, punctuating their stay with frequent displays of comradeship, as more and more people, sensing the drama of discontent, came into the studio.[12] But after an hour or so John Ducker, realising Hawke's capacity to exaggerate was leading to overkill, began to play down the incident, telling colleagues, 'It will all be over after a good night's sleep'. But to no avail. Sleep was low on Bob Hawke's priorities. He walked into the Rotunda Bar of the Gateway Inn at 9.10 p.m. Journalists, delegates and other hotel guests were sitting around in the plush red chairs of the small bar. Hawke was quiet at first, mingling with delegates ... But his temper warmed when he spotted Hugh McBride, original author of the amendment moved by Bill Hayden, and Simon Crean, also a member of the Victorian delegation.[13]

Hawke called out to McBride and Crean, both Centre Unity faction members, 'You're all bloody gutless!' He added, 'As far as I am concerned Hayden is dead'. Limbering up he went on to describe Hayden as a liar with a limited future.[14]

The next morning Hawke's outburst was national news. His potential career as a parliamentarian was written off, comprehensively, by the press. The *National Times* devoted its whole front page, plus pages 3 and 4, to a cover story: 'Hawke: The End of the Road?', remarking,

> His behaviour probably rules out any chance he will ever have of becoming Leader and suggests that he will never run for Parliament anyway ... The most significant point of the Adelaide Conference was that it brought on prematurely the long simmering, inevitable clash between Hayden and Hawke ... [and] resolved [it] in Hayden's favour ... The irony of Adelaide was that Hawke's undoing was entirely his own ... Hawke, through dint of sheer perseverance, transformed a minor setback for himself into a major one ... despite his brittleness and lack of political nous, Hayden emerged with the imprimatur of leadership. He put his own indelible stamp on Labor's future direction, formally ended the era of Whitlamism, and ushered in a new era of his own based on the twin themes of sound management and limited reform.[15]

The page 3 headline read: 'How Bob Hawke Blew It – Again', above a cartoon by Patrick Cook of Hawke, pacing, hands behind his back, thinking to himself, 'And some have self-destruction thrust upon them'.

By the next day Hawke was very shaken. When harried by a TV crew while trying to telephone Jean Sinclair about the Telecom dispute he shouted, 'Piss off!' and film of this remark, with Hawke flailing his arms at the cameras, was put to air. He recouped some of his ground with mild television interviews, given later on Wednesday, and broadcast on the evening news, but he was hunched up and haggard. He had to return that night to Melbourne for the Telecom dispute, and arrived back at the ACTU office at 8 p.m. He recalled, 'The staff were beaut. They gathered around me, sort of protecting me ...' He had been in the office only a few minutes when Rosslyn telephoned from inter-state to comfort him. Hawke was so upset that when she had rung off he left his desk and went to a corner of the room, pretending to look out the window, so that those gathered in his office would not see the tears in his eyes. His miseries, however, were not over yet.

Publicly, he had recovered his poise within a few days. By the end of the following week an amiable, cheerful Hawke was launching a book at the National Press Club in Canberra and announcing that a future Labor government would limit the powers of the Governor-General. Ten days was time enough for the news media to forget that Hawke's political career was ruined, and speculation on the topic resurged. Every major article evoked a flood of letters from the public. Throughout 1979 hundreds, maybe thousands, of people wrote to him, urging him to enter parliament; a small number asked him to remain with the ACTU. It was years since he had had time to read his mail; he relied on Jean Sinclair to tell him the trend of opinions. Excerpts from individual letters give some hint of his standing with the electorate by mid-1979:

> I have always looked on you as a kind of Messiah ... God bless you.

> When you become Prime Minister you will enrich our lives and inspire our hearts.

> You have been a strong leader of men.

> You are the saving grace for our country.

> There are hundreds of people who pray for you and your family.

> You can be likened to a type of Christ.

> As I was working through the day's work called 'Confidence and Faith' your name kept coming into my mind. The pos-sibility for Australia of a Prime Minister living his life to the limit of the potential given by the Creator and without limit

when lived in perfect harmony with the Creator made my heart leap for joy.

You are such a brilliant, honest and humane man.

You are the hope of Australia and the future of our land lies in your greatness.

I cannot compare your style of English, *the matchless words*, to anyone but to the late Sir Winston Churchill, who used very choice words in times of crisis.

At present there are many thousands who do not know where to turn. You are the one ...

The young people of Australia need you.

Old people, recalling the Depression and stating that they found Hawke a source of hope in new, harsh economic times, wrote many of these notes as, obviously, did the religious. Despite the discounting of political commentators the Australian public continued to believe in Hawke, for somehow, through the miasma of information, misinformation, gossip, myth, scandal and simplification he had managed to reach out and touch the people. In a selfish epoch of shrinking opportunities and insecure status, Hawke's generosity of mind and his confidence were a balm for mass anxieties.

A remarkable number of letters expressed patriotic fervour – 'this great country', 'this beautiful country' were phrases that recurred – and revealed a link in correspondents' minds between Australia and Hawke: that he was the authentic expression of our society. This was particularly interesting sociologically, given Hawke's public commitment to Israel and to such an abstruse issue, for the majority of Australians, as Soviet refuseniks. Mick Young noted, after Hawke had wept in parliament in late 1981 when a Liberal backbencher had accused him of deserting Israel to please the ALP,

If I'd cried I wouldn't have had the nerve to return to my electorate. I would have been dead, politically. Soon afterwards I went with Hawkey to a public meeting. You would have thought that people would give him a roasting but they were trying to touch his hair, touch the sleeve of his jacket. There isn't another politician in this country who could arouse that response.

Perhaps the explanation is that Hawke is not a politician in the sense in which this label is generally understood.

Sir John Crawford, who first began advising Australian prime ministers in the 1940s, knew Hawke well by 1979, having met him regularly for more than a year on the inquiry into manufacturing, of which he was chairman and Hawke one of three committee members. He saw striking correspondences between Hawke and John Curtin, the Labor leader whom Hawke most reveres and who, like him, was a bad drunk. However, it was another quality, common to both men, that Crawford singled out: 'Sensitivity and associated deep feeling'. He said,

> Curtin was not a professional politician – and for that matter, neither was Ben Chifley when he started out as prime minister – Curtin was a humane man, a man of very deep feeling, but not a professional in politics. Neither is Bob Hawke. Compared with someone like [Sir] Phillip Lynch [the former deputy leader of the Liberal Party] Bob is a novice politician. But he could get the people behind him, like Curtin did, for a great national effort. My fear, and I choose my words advisedly, is that the strain of office would prove too much for Bob Hawke, as, in my view, it did for John Curtin.

There is a curious resonance between Crawford's sober concern and the ecstatic outpourings from ordinary men and women, describing Hawke in their letters as 'Messiah' and 'type of Christ': the ultimate purpose of such figures is that they be destroyed, for the community.

Skimming through Hawke's fan mail, the poetry and prayers sent to him, observing hands yearning to touch him, one begins to suspect that some ancient, inchoate force is at work in Hawke's relationship with the Australian public and that this middle-aged boyish man represents something else – perhaps something lost but cherished, and recognised in him. It is curious that in a period when the trade unions were falling in public esteem Hawke, their representative, continued to rise: in the community's mind he was placed apart.

By August 1979 his inner struggle with what he was and what he could become was moving towards a point of critical decision: he had only a few weeks left to declare his candidature for parliament. The seat that his Centre Unity supporters had marked out for him was Wills, in the industrial heart of Melbourne, a blue-ribbon Labor electorate. But within the Victorian ALP Hawke's opponents begrudged him a safe seat: it was widely asserted that he should stand for a marginal electorate, and that he had no right to demand special treatment from the party. His insistence that he would consider only a safe seat (which would leave him freer to meet the demands of electioneering for the party as a whole and for national issues) was said to be another example of Hawke's 'top level' attitudes.

Meanwhile, he had other problems. Since he had returned from Geneva he had been having trouble with his hearing, which he had thought at first was due to the effects of a head-cold, and flying. When the cold had cleared he had remained partly deaf. In the third week of August Hawke sought medical advice and was told he might have a brain tumour. By this stage he was so intensely miserable, in such a state of conflict over his private life and his future, that he said, of hearing the news, 'I almost felt relieved'. It was another week before further tests revealed that he had nothing physiological wrong with him. In the interim, and for weeks afterwards, Melbourne buzzed with the rumour that: 'Hawke is dying of cancer'.

He was dying of indecision. Night after night he was awake until the early morning, drinking, talking, driving himself and his friends mad about his future career. Many of them believed he should not enter parliament: they feared that he would go to Canberra only to be torn apart by the press and the party. Michael Elitzur, the Israeli ambassador to Australia at the time, a man who was very close to Hawke, told him, 'You would be like Uriah with David. I didn't have to remind him of his Sunday school lessons; he understood immediately.'[16]

The Stop Hawke campaign was now in full gear. The Socialist Left had decided to try to frighten Hawke out of standing for preselection, and handbills, called by those who produced them 'shit sheets', were circulating in Melbourne. Some made their way interstate to other Left-wing branches. They elaborated the familiar themes that Hawke was an enemy of the working class, the stooge of big capitalism and Rupert Murdoch, lived in luxury, and would betray Labor principles. One had a drawing of a large, cigar-smoking 'capitalist' who bore some resemblance to Sir Peter Abeles. The drawing suggested that whoever it was, Hawke in parliament would be his creature.

Abeles himself was strongly opposed to Hawke's stand-ing for preselection. He had been abroad for some weeks but had learnt of the Adelaide debacle. On 5 September he visited Hawke, who was in Sydney to attend the next day a Reserve Bank board meeting. Abeles pleaded with him not to run, for the same reasons as Elitzur had given. George Rockey accom-panied Abeles and similarly urged Hawke not to abandon the safety of the trade unions. Elsewhere, pressures on Hawke's few supporters in Caucus were already intense. Clyde Holding, who had moved from leader of the Opposition in Victoria in 1977 to federal parliament, recalled,

> The kind of pressures that were placed upon me were amazing. Bob and I were old friends, our kids had grown up together, we have a very close relationship, we'd gone through God knows how many battles together. It was said to me, 'You've got to stop him getting into parliament'. In Canberra I was adopting political positions which were very attractive to the

Left. Lots of my ideological positions I would regard as more progressive than, say, Uren's and the Left's. I was also getting, I suppose, a lot of promotion from the leader. It was put to me quite directly and very hard that I would have a crucial role, that it was not in the interests of the party that Hawke should be in parliament, and as I was someone from Victoria I could make that clear. I was told – it's demonstrable – if you go through the pages of Hansard you'll see a whole range of debates on important issues: there would be the shadow minister or the leader, and me; the leader, and me. All of a sudden, nothing. I was told subsequently that I had behaved in an awful way – the implication of the carrot was always there. There were all those pressures to keep Bob out, and much of that has carried over. There's an example: one of the issues that Bob and I don't agree on is uranium. He knows my position; I know his. I believe that within the framework of his position he has behaved with integrity. Certainly, during the 1980 election, he *didn't put a foot wrong*. But during that election, as soon as we started looking like winning, who were the blokes up in the Northern Territory and South Australia and elsewhere, who were saying, 'Well, if we're the government we will have to look at our uranium policy'? It wasn't Hawke. He'd played it straight down the line: he'd had his argument, and he'd lost, and that was it. The blokes who were proposing to throw out Labor policy were the people in the leadership. But that doesn't stop people saying, today,[17] 'Aw, you couldn't trust the bastard'.

Hawke's supporters in Caucus numbered about twenty and there was no aid to be sought now from John Ducker. A few weeks after the Adelaide conference Ducker had resigned from all his positions in the ALP and the trade union movement.

Meanwhile, Hawke refused to fight those campaigning against him. He said later, with scorn, 'Personally, I did nothing about it. I regarded it as ridiculous bastardry. My own people in the electorate were working on numbers, doing the job, so I left it to them.'

The Socialist Left's candidate for Wills was an energetic young Socialist Left organiser, Gerry Hand.

By 6 September Hawke, still in Sydney, had decided that he would not run. He telephoned Jean Sinclair, who was convinced that he should enter parliament, to obtain Bill Landeryou's telephone number so that he could alert Landeryou, his chief organiser, to halt his lobbying efforts. A few days earlier Lord Mountbatten had been murdered by the IRA; it was publicly admitted that some IRA assassins were trained in their craft by the PLO. While explaining his change of mind to Sinclair, Hawke said, 'I'm the guy who's copping everything and I'm expected to go on copping everything, including the proposal that I must justify myself as an ALP candidate to the preselection committee in preference to the likes of that unknown Gerry Hand'. He went on to say that the Socialist Left formed 'a party within a party' and that this had been sufficient in the 1950s to cause the Split: why was a party within a party tolerated now? He added,

> I hate Hartley more than I hate Fraser and yet I'm expected to appear on platforms with him and others, as brothers. Mountbatten was assassinated with the help of people [the PLO] whom Hartley supports, and I find that abhorrent ... I'm worried about the State of Denmark. The ALP has got to begin a process of self-criticism; it's got to purge itself of this rottenness.

He had cheered up as soon as he had decided against standing. For the first time he cancelled, without notice, his Reserve Bank board meeting, saying 'I can't come today, I'm celebrating'. This was a figure of speech, for he went immediately into a meeting with representatives of the Seamen's Union, attempting to persuade them to agree to reduce crew sizes in return for an expansion of employment through the founding of an Australian-owned overseas shipping line, in which the ACTU would be a partner. For sixteen years, since the Corio election, Hawke had urged a reform of Australia's maritime transport; in the early 1970s he had made strenuous efforts to form a shipping partnership between Don Dunstan's South Australian government, the ACTU and Israel's ZIM, a shipping subsidiary of Histadrut, but the Australian trade union movement's rejection of things Israeli and other difficulties foiled the plan. Hawke continued to dream of it and in 1979 had a new burst of optimism when George Rockey, retired from TNT and equipped with a wealth of experience in the industry, agreed to act as an agent. It was, and is, extraordinary that Australia, economically reliant upon overseas trade, does not own an international shipping line: a major disincentive to establishing one is that Australian crew costs are so high. Hawke had been arguing for weeks with shipping union officials that if they would accept a reduction in employment per ship, they would have guarantees of greater employment in future because there were companies ready to start an international Australian line, if the price were right. He was so exhilarated that before going to the meeting he said, 'I'll fix this in half an hour'. After two hours he had been unable to clinch his argument. However, his spirits were still buoyant.

The next day, Friday, he appeared at the opening of an ALP electoral office in the Melbourne suburb of Coburg, smiling and relaxed. He stood on a butcher's box so that those at the back of the hall could see him and remarked, 'I got a box. I thought it might have been a seat, but they're hard to come by.' When journalists asked him if he would seek preselection he grinned and replied, 'I may'. This was taken to mean that he would. Late that evening he was at home in Sandringham when Hazel, who had answered the telephone, approached him softly. 'I have some bad news', she said. Ellie was dead.

For almost two years he had been mentally preparing for this blow to fall, even saying sometimes, 'I almost wish she could die – what's the use of living in the state she's in? Just breathing ...' Now that it had happened, he was stricken. Over the weekend, during which he had been scheduled to work on final preparations for the ACTU biennial Congress that would open on Monday, he spoke to many of his friends about Ellie's death, and was frequently in tears. Rockey said later, 'Bob couldn't believe his mother was dead. It was weeks, at least, before he began to accept that she'd gone.'

There was much rearranging to be done: Hawke would deliver his opening presidential address to Congress on Monday then he and Hazel would fly immediately to Perth for the funeral, on Tuesday.

Harold Souter, retired now, had come for the opening day of the Congress, which was held in the Dallas Brooks Hall in Melbourne. He seemed to be one of the few people there who realised what Hawke was suffering, and who sorrowed for him. As delegates milled around in the foyer, laughing, joking and lobbying, Souter stood aside, shaking his head. 'This is a sad day for Bob', he said. 'For a great man like him ... his mother's death.' When Hawke walked on to the platform to address the 755 delegates he looked an old man, stooped, grey, haggard. But for his luxuriant hair, he could have been seventy – and he was not yet fifty. Hazel had come to the Congress and sat in the visitors' gallery watching him roaring out hope and determination to the audience below, his feet dancing, his hands gesturing with light, dramatic movements. From his words there was no hint that he was grieving. He was like a toy figure on the stage: wound up, he worked. 'A millionaire with words', someone sneered loudly. Already the atmosphere was hostile.

In Perth, he spent the whole night talking to Clem and the next day kissed Ellie goodbye. He murmured to Hazel, 'She's so cold'. Hazel tried to comfort him but the chill of death preyed on his mind and for the next few days he referred to it, grimacing. Straight after the funeral he flew back to Melbourne, for the worst fortnight in his life: in Adelaide Hawke had been sent to Coventry by his party, but at the 1979 ACTU Congress he was rejected by the trade union movment.

On the night he arrived back from Perth, Tuesday, there was an ACTU concert at which a range of prominent artists were performing, free. Unfortunately the audience was small.

Ray Geitzelt was worried by Hawke's appearance and at about 9.30 p.m. told him, 'People will understand if you leave early. You're exhausted. Go and get some sleep.' Hawke replied, 'I can't walk out'; he had about three hours sleep that night.

Had his mind been at ease; had he not been exhausted; had he not lost four days of Congress organising time because of Ellie's death … disaster may have been averted. Hawke failed on everything at the 1979 ACTU Congress: he failed on the executive elections, on the uranium debate, and on affiliation fees. By the afternoon of Friday, 15 September, he was left standing alone on the stage of the Dallas Brooks Hall from which the roaring crowd of men had vanished, contemplating the losses: the ACTU was facing a cash shortfall of $400 000 and Charlie Fitzgibbon, arguably the most able ACTU executive member, had been tipped out of office. It was, however, the uranium debate that had occasioned his worst defeat.

The debate, the most controversial issue before Congress, was scheduled for Thursday, 14 September. By Wednesday morning the thrill of a rout for Hawke was in the air: the executive elections were in progress and news was spreading that there were two Left–Centre tickets, both entitled 'Official Progressive', but one coloured white, the other yellow. The 'Hawke ticket' was white; the yellow ticket was a ring-in. The vice-presidents, senior and junior, of the ACTU are elected by a complicated system of preferential voting: first the senior vice-presidency is established, then through an exhaustive method of distribution of preferences, the junior vice-presidency quota is reached. The two 'Official Progressive' tickets, one of them not official at all, and the Right–Centre ticket all nominated Cliff Dolan as senior vice-president. The Hawke ticket nominated Charlie Fitzgibbon as junior vice-president. The ring-in ticket nominated Jim Roulston of the AMWSU. There were yellow and white Official Progressive tickets for other elections, also. The far Left and the Right had done a deal to support Roulston – although he was a member of the Socialist Left – in favour of Fitzgibbon, who was an ALP moderate. Part of the background to the Left–Right deal was that the Right was angry because it had failed to get extra ACTU executive seats for its bigger unions, like the Clerks and the Shop Assistants, while the middle-class ACSPA group was to be rewarded for joining the ACTU with special executive positions. As well, a faction fight was stirring in the New South Wales ALP, where a middle-class New Left was gathering strength, to the irritation of the industrial Old Left and the fury of the industrial Right. And importantly, Fitzgibbon was a more intelligent and strong-willed man than Roulston. Geitzelt commented, 'The Right knew it couldn't control Charlie, while Jim Roulston would be much easier to deal with'.

It was the familiar story of strange bedmates. Until too late Hawke's camp was unaware of the yellow tickets that, as Geitzelt noted, had been carefully designed to take advantage of this complex preferential voting system: 'I believe that –, from the AMWSU, used the union's computer to calculate how preferences must be distributed to defeat Fitzgibbon.[18] The yellow tickets were handed out by marshals to trusted delegates who then voted according to instructions', he said. By midday Wednesday, Fitzgibbon was gone, running last in the race. Simon Crean, a very able Centre–Left Hawke candidate, had also been defeated, in favour of a Right nominee.

The elections were a stunning setback for the Hawke camp and for Hawke personally. He had lobbied hard on Tuesday evening for support for Fitzgibbon who, besides being one of the most capable union leaders in the country, and therefore a desirable member of the ACTU executive, was the man Hawke wanted to succeed him as president. If Hawke were to change his mind about parliament, he now had no obvious successor as ACTU president. Dolan, although next in line, lived in Sydney, and did not want the job.

The Left was ecstatic about its cleverness in the elections. By Wednesday evening Hawke had been told that the executive's recommendation on uranium mining would be defeated. He had three choices: to dump the executive's policy; to run dead; to fight.

The ACTU's recommendation was that delegates accept the existing and future operation of uranium mining at the Ranger, Mary Kathleen and Narbalek sites, while opposing any further development. There was nothing, in reality, that the ACTU could do to prevent mining at those sites: if union labour were withdrawn, blackleg labour would move in. The transport of uranium ore could, perhaps, be prevented: but the government had already said that it would use troops to move yellowcake, if necessary. Military trucks could carry the mineral just as effectively as the railways; it could be loaded on to ships berthed at naval wharves. The executive's recommendation recognised these facts of national life – plus a harsher truth: in Hawke's words,

> If you want to damage the trade union movement, commit yourself to a policy that you can't deliver; ban mining, then watch unionists go in and mine it, and unions fight each other to get the miners on their books. My major concern was an industrial one, a concern for the movement.

The crucial amendment to the executive's proposal came from the Left; it demanded 'continuing opposition to the mining and export of uranium and the present programme of development'. Late on Wednesday night the assistant secretary, Bill Kelty, said to Hawke, 'They've got the numbers and we're going to get done. Let me lead the debate so that it's not a defeat for you, personally.' Hawke replied, 'You know I don't operate like that. If we are going to be done, I won't walk away from it.' He would move the executive's recommendation and would thereby have the mover's right of reply. As usual he screwed up his optimism to a point where he was declaring, 'It's worth a go!' It was, again, David against Goliath.

Outside the hall there was a large crowd of anti-uranium demonstrators; a room inside the building had an anti-uranium display. Susan Hawke was among the volunteer workers there, in what was called by delegates 'Sue's Room'.

Hawke gave a fiery, three-quarter hour speech on Thursday morning, emphasising the impracticality of outright opposition. He characterised this attitude as 'a sloppy exercise in ineffective morality'; he stressed the divisions among unions and their members on the issue; the failure of the unions to prevent uranium mining so far; and the doubtful impact on the international use of nuclear energy of even an effective Australian union embargo: if Australia would not supply uranium, South Africa, Gabon and the USA would. When the open debate began there were hours of splendid oratory but this time, although there was a sense of déjà vu, the atmosphere was more hostile, both to the executive and to Hawke personally. When Kelty rose to support Hawke's motion, Jack Marks, a swashbuckling greybeard from the AMWSU in Western Australia, shouted, 'The sorcerer's apprentice!'

It was an inspired interjection – for when Hawke came roaring back to the microphones to make his speech in reply he seemed transformed into some blood-curdling spirit escaped from the underworld, cursing men on earth. The glinting sword-play of his address in reply in 1977 was abandoned: Hawke was swinging an axe. He was like a man possessed of holy rage – shouting, taunting, his feet in a boxer's dance, his arms flailing the air, his fists banging the rostrum to emphasise points. Had he turned aside and spat on the people who were yelling back at him, his contempt and fury could not have been more savagely stated. As a performance it was, literally, stunning: the force of his harangue, which went on for almost an hour, at deafening volume, had people pressed back in their seats. And at no point had he lost control of himself, although he attacked opposition speakers in personal terms that would take them months to forgive. He assaulted one of his dearest friends, 'Cliffie Dolan', and his young supporter from Western Australia, Peter Cook, both of whom had spoken in favour of the Left amendment. Cook had privately told Hawke that he did not believe in the anti-uranium case. Hawke hurled this back at him, scornfully, and from the visitors' gallery people could see that tears were standing in Cook's eyes. It was as if all the anger and frustration that had been building up in Hawke for months were now being given catharsis. The experience was frightening for observers, the more so because it was directed by a mind that had not stopped thinking, but that was in the grip of inflamed audacity, of moral outrage and logic locked together.

He sat down, the vote was taken and lost 512 to 318 – the executive's defeat was even greater than it would have been had he not intervened. Hawke grimaced as if in agony. Then as the hall erupted into cheering he dropped his head in his hands. People seated above the dais could see what delegates could not: he had gone to sleep. He slept for about a minute then woke up, looking relaxed. A few minutes later he was imperturbably telling journalists, 'You win some, you lose some. I cop it sweet.' The public mask was back in place and stayed there that night when Hawke was host to a large reception, and next day when the executive was rebuffed on the question of affiliation fees: the Left and the Right combined to defeat a recommendation that fees be increased by 75 cents a member, and indexed to rises in average award wages, in favour of an amendment to increase them by only 6 cents, without indexation. That meant the ACTU would be deeply in debt within a few months. *Tribune*, the Communist Party of Australia newspaper, celebrated the Congress with a front-page announcement that 'Left and centre forces scored important victories'.[19]

Judged by the prejudices and preoccupations of the hour the 1979 Congress was a slashing defeat for Hawke. But in the longer view it blazoned a major achievement. In his opening address he had said, 'This is an historic Congress, for it marks the definite emergence of one central trade union organisation in this country'. And so it did, for after ten years as president, Hawke had accomplished the major aim of his campaign platform of 1969, a goal he had described then as 'some form of organic co-operation' between the ACTU and the white-collar union councils. At the 1979 Congress the Australian Council of Salaried and Professional Associations (ACSPA) had formally affiliated with the ACTU; at the next Congress the Commonwealth and Government Employees' Organisations (CAGEO) would do so.

Ironically, it was the Left-wing ACSPA votes in 1979 that had decided the uranium issue: temporarily. By early 1982 the ACTU executive had been forced to accept that Hawke's exposition of the problems of banning uranium mining and export was accurate, and had acknowledged the policy he had espoused two and a half years earlier by waiving export bans. Meanwhile, the affiliation fee decision had been overturned in favour of the executive's original proposal, and Charlie Fitzgibbon was once more on the executive.

Before these reversals of Hawke's 'defeats' had occurred Professor Martin wrote:

> ... once the dust of contemporary controversies has settled, the 1979 Congress is likely to be remembered principally as marking the beginning of the end of the independent existence of the two main white-collar peak councils ... the effective incorporation in the ACTU of the Australian Council of Salaried and Professional Associations ... for the first time took the ACTU's official total of affiliated unionists to more than two million ...
>
> In his 1969 acceptance speech, Mr Hawke had also spoken of expanding both the policy concerns of the ACTU and its administrative expertise. A decade later, Congress considered executive recommendations which not only covered an unprecedented range of policy issues, but were formulated with a care and an eye to detail that owed most to a greatly enlarged and highly qualified full-time staff ...
>
> The 1979 Congress was also distinguished by two noteworthy innovations, both of which reflected the President's inclinations. One was the invitation extended to M. Young, shadow Minister of Industrial Relations in the federal Parliamentary Labor Party, to address Congress. Mr Young is the first Labor parliamentarian, other than a prime minister, to be accorded this privilege in at least twenty years.

The other innovation was the special effort made ... to encourage the attendance of observers at the Congress. This is in line with what is, perhaps, Mr Hawke's most remarkable talent, his extraordinary flair for publicity. There can be little doubt that it will be in relation to projecting a public image of the ACTU that his successor as president will find him most difficult to follow.[20]

In the week following Congress, Hawke's schedule was that he would set to work writing the Boyer Lectures. These are an annual series of ABC radio broadcasts given by eminent Australians, the majority of them scientists. It was a unique honour that Hawke, a party political figure, had been invited to be the Boyer Lecturer of 1979. He had accepted eagerly early in the year and nominated his subject, the 'Resolution of Conflict', but had as usual delayed writing his talks. He was due to record the programs in mid-October. Mid-September, when he was to begin writing, could not have been a worse time for him to attempt calm reflection. He was exhausted physically and was daily flaying his spirit with doubts: the closing date for parliamentary preselection was 1 October – which happened to be Ellie's birthday. Earlier in the year, when she was still alive, he had mentioned this coincidence of dates to journalists: descendants of the Lee family, who read his remark in the newspapers, saw in it an unconscious statement of how firmly, still, Ellie's hand rested on her son's shoulder.

He spent the week from the end of Congress to Saturday, 22 September, in an agony of irresolution, drawing up lists for and against daring the parliament, becoming increasingly distracted and self-pitying. Finally, it was Hazel who persuaded Hawke that he must come to terms with the forces that had shaped him and his career. She knew, as Hawke later also acknowledged, that he would live the rest of his life with a sense of failure if he 'squibbed it', as his Uncle Bert had done in 1945.

Hawke had arranged a press conference to announce his decision on 23 September; on 22 September he telephoned

Eddie Kornhauser and asked him to come to Sandringham. It was Saturday, and the Jewish New Year, when the Orthodox may not drive cars. Kornhauser had to organise a ride to Hawke's house. When he arrived Hawke asked his opinion. Kornhauser urged him to run. Hawke replied, 'That's my decision'.

After his experience in Adelaide with Hayden, Hawke's distrust of the leader was acute: he feared to give Hayden advance warning. However, Kornhauser insisted that he telephone Hayden immediately and tell him. Hawke rang Hayden, told him he thought he had made up his mind, and would be announcing his decision at 3 p.m. on Sunday. On Sunday morning he rang Hayden again and told him he would be standing.

There were sixty journalists gathered in the ACTU boardroom that afternoon and Hawke's voice was trembling as he announced, 'I have done what I believe is best in all the circumstances ... I will be a candidate for preselection for the seat of Wills ...' Hazel had accompanied him to the ACTU and sat in the boardroom composed, beautifully groomed, her expression revealing nothing of what they had both endured before this moment had arrived.

Hawke continued, plainly stating his position in the centre ground of politics, 'I want now through the [ALP] to help provide a position which will match the thoughts and aspirations of the great majority of Australian men and women, which will help weld Australians together', then added a swipe at the Socialist Left, 'We cannot be a vehicle for advancing the fantasies of any extremist group'.

When the news was broadcast his trade union colleagues had mixed feelings. Joe Morris of the ILO said, 'I thought it was a tragedy'. Charlie Fitzgibbon said to Ray Geitzelt, 'If he thinks he must, I suppose he must'. Both men had known for years that Hawke's dream was to become prime minister. They doubted that he could achieve it: he had alienated the Left of the party and it was questionable that the Right would support him. Unlike his drive for the ACTU presidency, Hawke had no major power-base within the ALP.

The support he did have was from the people. They wrote:

I gave three cheers when I heard [the news]. It's just wonderful ... you may be emotional, but emotions are sincere and deep.

I'm quite excited and have gone up and down the corridors of this large hotel broadcasting the good news – and the response? 'Good on him' and from others – Liberals, too – 'Really, well that is good news for all of us'.

A born Liberal voter ... but your Party will certainly get my votes from here on.

You will be a great Prime Minister, for a great country.

Your actions are Christ-like – helping those who need help, labouring for the betterment of our nation and, above all, a peacemaker.

Our Party desperately needs practical leadership by men with a wide mental horizon and the ability to gauge what the electorate requires – and I believe you are one of the very few with those qualities.

Thank you for being a Christian leader, who stands up for the right.

Once the fever of indecision had broken he began to recover. But he had burned many bridges in the party and in the trade union movement – the uranium speech in reply was generally held to be 'the worst speech Bob ever made' – and he had yet to conquer alcohol. His friends nagged and cajoled him to stop drinking; they telephoned Hazel and Jean Sinclair to propose stratagems for persuading Hawke to give up grog. Abeles told him, 'I will always be your friend, but if you won't stop drinking I will cease to speak in support of you'. Hawke continued to drink. Meanwhile he had to undo some of the harm he had done to himself and, with a very little time left, write the Boyer Lectures.

His diary records that at 5.45 p.m. on 2 October he 'spoke to Peter Cook' – that is, apologised to Cook for his remarks during the uranium debate. He had also to make peace with Dolan, who was now the most likely successor to the ACTU presidency. Dolan accepted Hawke's apology; he rejected the presidency. In early October the final drama of preselection closed. The Socialist Left waged a spirited campaign for Gerry Hand, but Hand was sunk and they knew it. Bob Hogg, the Victorian secretary, and a Socialist Left member, said later, 'Once Hawke had decided to nominate, the matter was decided. The party could not afford to defeat him.' On 14 October, following interviews with the selection panel, Hawke won ALP endorsement for Wills by 38 votes to Hand's 29.

In between all this politicking, and distractions like continued negotiations with the Seamen's Union and press conferences, Hawke had been trying to write, in the Boyer Lectures, a major statement of his social and political ideas. The Boyer Lectures of 1979 have been lauded as visionary and scorned as glib. They were the work of a man who was very tired and short of time.

For twenty years Hawke had been making speeches about constitutional reform; be began his series of talks with two that were concerned with the question, 'How We Are Governed'. These were the lectures that most excited commentators to praise or condemnation. In them Hawke proposed an adventurous rethinking of Australia's political system in the light of changes that had occurred since 1901:

> We are daily witnesses to the fact and impact of change unparalleled in our memory, change which is being reflected in the structure of our economy, our capacity to provide employment and in the very cohesiveness of our society. And yet we are constitutionally and institutionally immobilised – in the framework for the conduct of our affairs, nothing changes. It is not change itself of which we should be afraid, it is this paradox of change/no change, the total lack of symmetry between our innovative capacities as technical

and political human beings, that should cause us alarm ...
no one is more conscious than I of our tendency to conservatism, as a people, and of the need, therefore, for those who
would advocate change to temper their fervour with a sense
of gradualism ... no one ... would believe that the men and
women with the best available administrative capacity for
the government of the country repose exclusively in the two
Houses of Parliament ... I would advocate that as an initial
step one quarter of the positions in the Ministry should be
open to be filled by persons not elected to the Parliament ...
These Ministers would not be members of the Parliament
but would be responsible *to* Parliament ...

Hawke developed his theme of parliamentary reform at
length. A reviewer, Professor G. S. Reid of the University of
Western Australia, writing in *Quadrant*, asked:

What would a government do if a strongly held opinion of
an appointed Minister was electorally unpopular – would the
Government defer to the Minister and run the risk of political annihilation; or would it reject the Minister's point of
view and run the risk of his resignation? If the Government
took the former course the public would ask – why have electorates or elections? And if it took the latter view the public
would ask – why appoint expert Ministers? Mr Hawke does
not appear to have thought through the problems his scheme
would create.[21]

He went on to say:

From the scholarly point of view Hawke's best lectures were
the two called 'Australia In Crisis' (his third and fourth). In
these he discussed the nation's unemployment crisis, the
problems of equality for women, alternative lifestyles and
industrial relations. These chapters reduced the flow of [his]
rhetoric in favour of a few statistics ... These two lectures

rescued the intellectual standing of the series ... Hawke's lectures on *The Resolution of Conflict* were interesting for the conflicts they ignored. For example, there is nothing in them about uranium exports, nuclear power, mining, Aboriginal landrights, law and order, environmental crises, defence expenditure, the American alliance, abortion law-reform, the structure of taxation and so on – subjects which attract the major social and political conflicts in Australia today. They were ignored in favour of subjects more amenable to the projection of a positive man. Hawke chose his subjects with precision.

In conclusion, Professor Reid commented:

Bob Hawke's Boyer Lectures did not measure up to a scholar's predilection for tight logical thinking ... The former Rhodes Scholar obviously decided he was speaking to an audience which would not demand precision and exactitude in argument ... [The] 1979 Boyer Lectures were obviously designed to foster the speaker's public profile. In that respect the lectures were highly successful.[22]

Reid's conclusions were an accurate assessment of Hawke's political strategy, beleaguered as he was in the ALP: he was addressing the group who could, perhaps, outweigh the Caucus – the Australian people. Reid had also identified the shortcomings in Hawke's working habits, shortcomings which George Rockey complained of as 'Bob's leaping from A to Z, without worrying about the details'. Changing his habits – from thriving on pressure to dreary diligence; from painting in bold brush to paying attention to petit point; from relying on quickness of wit to resigning himself to the tedium of background reading – were problems Hawke would have to face in parliament. The job of ACTU advocate had forced him to develop steady working habits, contrary though they were to his impatience, his confidence in heroic energy and his 'streak of hedonism'. The question was whether, in his fifties, after a decade of riding a roller coaster, he would have the strength of will to discipline himself once more. If he could stop drinking, that would be the first sign.

By December 1979 he was talking about resigning from the ACTU around Easter 1980. This would give him about six months before the next federal election in which he could rest, read, think and, he said, learn Italian. There are many Italians in the Wills electorate: Hawke's desire to learn their language had little to do with winning votes, since the seat was unchallengably Labor's, but it had everything to do with his instinct to be *en rapport* with people. He had time for none of this, least of all learning Italian. Jean Sinclair, who had to cope with Hawke's estimation that every day contained forty-eight hours and that he should be awake and occupied for all of them, remarked that a good week for her was one in which she dissuaded him from committing himself to a major scheme: agreeing to write a book, for example. In late 1979 she took six months holiday to accompany her husband on sabbatical leave. Hawke had thought he would need Sinclair's help when he moved to Canberra. The experience of being six months without her convinced him. He also wanted Bill Kelty to accompany him to Canberra as a research assistant and administrator, but at length Kelty decided he could not abandon the trade union movement. He was in tears as he made the farewell speech to Hawke at an office party.

Hawke had to delay his departure from the ACTU until two major difficulties were solved: finance and the presidency. By December 1979 the ACTU's financial difficulties – a cash shortfall of $400 000 – had become public. Two years earlier, when Peter Nolan had taken over as secretary he had reported to the executive that by 1979 there would be a deficit of $27 000. Just before the 1979 Congress some executive members who were familiar with balance sheets suspected that the financial situation was much worse than anyone realised, but it was not until after the Congress and further auditing that the seriousness of the position became clear. Hawke, Nolan and Kelty knew that delegates' refusal to increase affiliation fees by a reasonable amount was due largely to two factors: the mistiming of the fee debate – which was held the day after the uranium debate – and the traditional Congress caper of plaguing the executive. Once tempers had cooled they were confident that the ACTU's state branches, the trades and labour councils, would vote for the 150 per cent fee increase needed. By the end of the year this process was underway. On Christmas Day 1979 Hawke turned his attention to the presidency. He telephoned Ray Geitzelt, asking him to have dinner in Sydney the following week to discuss what could be done. Geitzelt recalled, 'I'd had dinner with Cliffie Dolan the week before Christmas and he'd told me he was not interested in the job. Between Christmas Day and 2 January Bob had changed Cliff's mind.'

When Hawke had become president of the ACTU it had a membership of 1.4 million, 107 affiliates and a total staff of eleven. Dolan would be taking over an organisation with 139 affiliates, 2 million members and a staff of forty. In 1970 its income had been \$162 000; by 1980 it was more than \$1 million. In a decade the ACTU had established a social welfare research unit; a legal department; an occupational health unit; an industrial information co-operative; a migrant workers' office; a union child-care centre; a working women's charter; an arts department; ninety petrol discount outlets; and a travel branch that had catered for 20 000 people. Bourkes–ACTU had forced the introduction of legislation banning retail price maintenance, which saved Australian shoppers untold millions of dollars and saved the ACTU \$1.2 million in rent. The Council's research staff no longer had to devote nearly all its energy to preparing wage cases, with a little time left over for Budget submissions. During Hawke's final year as president, the research staff wrote forty-seven separate submissions and background papers to government departments and government-sponsored inquiries and authorities. The executive had been reorganised into a committee system; the committees were supplied with background papers in advance of meetings. In Monk's day there had rarely been an agenda for executive meetings. During Hawke's presidency the ACTU had helped to establish the Commonwealth Trade Union Council and the Australian–New Zealand Trade Union Co-ordinating Council; it had also joined the Trade Union Advisory Committee of the OECD. Perhaps the greatest difference that Hawke had made to the ACTU was in its image: he had firmly established it as a major institution in Australian public life. Yet in a spasm of invective or ignorance the *Financial Review* editorially summed up the years of Hawke's leadership of the Australian trade union movement as 'a decade of barren failure. He leaves the ACTU with nothing more than he brought to it.'[23]

In February 1980 Hawke left for Geneva to make his last major contribution to the ILO. On Christmas Eve 1979 the Soviet Union had invaded Afghanistan, an action that, among other things, spelt doom for hopes of early recovery in Western economies, for it quickly stimulated a diversion of capital into armaments, at a time when industrial nations were just surmounting the financial disaster that had ensued from the Yom Kippur War. Hawke had been appalled by the invasion and the consequences he foresaw, but he was out of step with the major trend of ALP thinking, which inclined to the view that the USSR's activities were of little concern in the antipodes. In Geneva he had an opportunity, denied -- or, at least, muted – in Australia, to express his thoughts, and did so in a speech to the Governing Body. He was the first Governing Body member to raise the Afghanistan invasion, for the matter was not on the agenda and was, in fact, irrelevant to the business in hand. Observers described Hawke's speech as 'electrifying'. Having damned the invasion, he went on to inveigh against the USSR's refusal of human rights to its citizens and its flouting of ILO conventions: one more step had been taken towards the formal ILO condemnation of the Soviet Union that was to follow, in 1981.

While Hawke was tidying up the loose ends of his public life, his private life remained badly frayed. Alcohol. And not alcohol *tout court*.

He had been trying to ameliorate his problem by drinking only white wine, but whenever he was in a public place in

Australia where alcohol was served people would press him to drink; strangers would send drinks to his table – sometimes triple whiskies. One could see the struggle on his face as he stared at a glass of spirits; suddenly he would reach for it.

By May 1980 his drinking problem was as bad as ever – he was drinking less but was a more unpleasant drunk. He looked ill. In three years his face had aged many more; his cheeks were deeply scored with lines and his complexion, when he had been a week or so without sun, had an unhealthy sallowness. He had been used to be able to go to sleep as if throwing a light switch, but during 1979 he had become insomniac and this had persisted. Waking, he moved in a deepening shadow: George Rockey, the man he loved almost as much as he loved Clem, had just learned that he had a malignant secondary tumour on his brain and Hawke had been affected by this news as if Rockey were, indeed, his father. Neither of them was able to articulate his feelings for the other – Rockey said, 'My little daughter, she's three years old, I called her Roberta . . .' Hawke turned much of his psychological energy into schemes of diversion for Rockey's last months of life: for example, that Rockey should collaborate in writing a company history of TNT; that they go travelling together to exciting and unknown places. Hawke spent time he could not afford, professionally, with Rockey, flying to Sydney frequently to visit him and accompanying him on trips to the Wrest Point Casino in Hobart. Rockey was a true gambler: he returned to the tables until he was too weak to walk; on their final trip Hawke had to carry him back to bed in the hotel. Every meeting and conversation with Rockey would bring on a fit of gloom in Hawke. He complained frequently of fatigue and talked about taking a holiday – on Hayman Island, on a yacht in the Mediterranean, 'just somewhere where I can lie in the sunshine and *sleep*'.

At the beginning of the third week of May he flew to Hobart for an ACTU executive meeting and was joined there, later in the week, by Rockey. On 21 May they went to the casino together. Hawke had a good win on the blackjack table, slept for a couple of hours then returned to Melbourne to appear before the Conciliation and Arbitration Commission as advocate in the ACTU's national wage case. The more radical metal trades unions were campaigning for a 35-hour week and the Bench had threatened to discontinue the national wage case hearing unless the strike and bans campaign stopped. Hawke had less than two hours to assimilate the ACTU's arguments about why the Bench should continue with the case. Ranged against him, asserting that the Bench should carry out its threat, were more than half-a-dozen advocates, representing the employers, the federal government and state governments. Hawke succeeded in persuading the Bench to delay its decision about hearing the case until he had negotiated with the metal unions. Next evening he flew to Canberra and instead of resting, went to a journalists' party, where he stayed until about 1 a.m. The following morning he had to go shopping early to buy curtains for the apartment he had bought in Canberra, then fly on to Sydney for talks with the metal unions. He was ashen when he set out for Sydney, but successfully negotiated a change of tactics on the 35-hour week campaign, thus opening the way for the Bench to decide to proceed with the national wage case.

Hawke returned to Melbourne that evening. He was to leave the next day for Egypt and Geneva. He recalled,

> Sometime that night I was having a leak and I said to myself, 'Well, bugger it. You'd be better off not drinking. Why don't you give it up?' So I went and washed my hands, and that was it . . . I never thought of myself as an alcoholic and I don't think I was in the sense that I could not do without it. I didn't get up in the morning and have a drink. There were days when I did go without it. It didn't have hold of me in that sense, but it was really too much of a crutch to me. I'd gone through enormous pressures about making up my mind about what I was going to do – it was driving me absolutely bloody crazy. That year, 1979, was an awful one; a terrible year . . . I couldn't quantify this, but the whole thing

about my mother dying was gnawing away at me, the uranium question was driving me mad, and all of that horrible period had spilled over into 1980. I suppose the very fact of deciding to go into parliament started to do things inside me. I knew I would have a big, new set of pressures on me and a lot of people wanting to destroy me if they could ... I didn't relish life without grog. I embraced Churchill's observation: I've taken more out of grog than grog has taken out of me. I enjoyed especially the way it could break down barriers with people – I've got close to a helluva lot of people through drinking. I loved it. But I knew what the minuses were, and I just had to admit to them.

For months he had been, as he called it later, 'climbing the mountain': abruptly he had wrenched himself up to the summit. By curious coincidence it had taken nine months and two weeks since Ellie's death for Hawke to struggle his way out of drunkenness – curious because he had earlier lived nine months and two weeks unborn: it was as if an intimate, slow rhythm of growth had pulsed through him, unhurriable, its span determined, and now here he was, delivered at fifty, as unprepared as any newborn creature is, after butting its head for an eternity in the dark, to meet daylight.

From the time he had decided that his drinking days were over he had 'a total certitude' that he would not fall back again. Others were sceptical, waiting for a collapse of will: there were constant rumours that, 'Hawke's back on the grog', despite the fact that one only had to see him to know he was not. However, in time even the cynics were convinced that Hawke had climbed a mountain. Within months he was looking younger, his gestures and expression lightened by a surge of vitality. The glowering, demon-possessed demeanour that had been familiar by late or early evenings when he was boozing had gone – although he still appeared older and tougher than other men of his years. Standing beside contemporaries who had become academics, judges and senior executives in business or the public service

Hawke could have been a generation older than they, but he had an animation and vigour that contradicted the impression one first gained from a gnarled, grey head. His manner was more gentle and more often light-hearted. He had always been a kind man; however, it had often been difficult for people to perceive it, on the other side of the intelligence in his eyes and his raspy voice. Men and women who met Hawke for the first time in the early 1980s frequently remarked, their tone incredulous, 'He's so nice. He was polite; he didn't snap ...' A Labor feminist, who shared the sisterhood's hostility to Hawke in the 1970s, said in early 1982, after he had given a paper on the economic problems of women, 'He understands it. Broadly. He actually understands the social and economic implications of sexism. The radicals almost fell off their chairs ... I talked to him later and got the impression that he was a man who was at peace with himself.'

Almost as soon as Hawke stopped drinking he started sleeping properly and began eating, on his estimate, 'twice as much'. In the early months of teetotalism his craving for sugar was so strong that he ate kilos of confectionary, but in time this need decreased to 'normal' – for a sweet tooth. (Hazel said later she thought he had always been allergic to alcohol; scientists are only beginning to decipher the cryptograms of biochemistry: it may be that a physiological cause and effect relationship existed between Hawke's appetite for sugar and his later abuse of alcohol.)[24] In the early months, too, he suffered acute discomfort when in the company of drinkers: he was bored, ribbed and needed to explain repeatedly why he wanted orange juice or mineral water. He said afterwards,

The first months were pretty rough. The worst thing would be sitting through dinners where people were drinking beautiful wines, talking about vintages and bouquets, and I'd be hanging on to a glass of mineral water – surely the most boring drink ever created.

He began to turn up at social functions with his own two-litre container of orange juice, until his new condition was widely enough known for hosts and hostesses to have on hand soft drinks for him. He avoided pubs and left dinners early, at first because of discomfiture, later because he had, after a lifetime of gregariousness, come to value solitude. At home, his teetotalism was a revolution; Hazel often confided to friends her admiration for what he had achieved.

In late August Hawke stepped down as president of the ACTU and within a fortnight was campaigning for the federal election. Since the Adelaide conference, ALP officials, especially the Victorian secretary, Bob Hogg, and the national secretary, David Combe, had worked hard behind the scenes to achieve a rapprochement between Hayden and Hawke, and had succeeded. Before the campaign was launched the leader and the candidate had established a working relationship and a degree of intimacy. Hayden had promised that Hawke could go straight to the front bench (Caucus permitting); Hawke that he would campaign as hard as he could to make Bill Hayden the next prime minister. The party's national campaign team was Hayden, Hawke and Neville Wran, the new ALP president and the most popular state premier in the country. During the election period Hawke had an unexpected bonus from teetotalism: 'I travelled as much and I made as many speeches, but physically it was the easiest campaign I've done. Instead of staying up after meetings, talking and on the grog, I went to bed early.' Ten days before the poll, due on 18 October, it seemed as if the unimagined were happening and that the swing to Labor would bring them back to office. Hawke was wildly excited, although a Labor victory in 1980 would have ruled out for years, or forever, his own chance of the prime ministership. However, when the counting was finished Labor had lost – by only several thousand votes in a dozen electorates, but by 23 seats in the House. Hawke was the Member for Wills and a couple of weeks later became the shadow Minister for Industrial Relations.

Parliament resumed in November 1980. On the evening of

the 26th, the galleries of the House of Representatives were full: word had spread that Hawke would, sometime that night, make his maiden speech. Clem and Hazel were seated in the visitors' gallery. At 8.52 p.m. the Deputy Speaker called on Hawke and reminded the House that, because this was a maiden speech, interjections were out of order. His reminder added to the slightly unreal atmosphere: maiden speakers are supposed to be hesitant and to need protection from the experienced, tougher members. Listening to maiden speeches is one of the tiresome duties of a new parliament, from which ministers usually excuse themselves. Hawke had just risen and approached the mace when Malcolm Fraser and the rest of the government front bench strode into the chamber. In the press gallery above journalists came hurrying in.

He began lightly, saying to the Deputy Speaker, 'As one of the tardier maidens to appear before you I express the hope that I shall do nothing in the future to upset unduly the even tenor of your ways'. He then moved on to his reasons for entering parliament:

> I come to this House after twenty-two years with the Australian trade union movement, an organisation often denigrated by our opponents in this Parliament ... but the existence of which is a *sine qua non* of a free and democratic society ... I have become increasingly conscious that in such a democracy ultimately it is only in and through the Parliament that decisions can be made which will fashion for all our people the opportunities to release their talents in work and in leisure – the opportunities to be well-rounded, constructive human beings, the opportunities for happiness for themselves and in relation to others, which seems to me what government should be about.

He then turned to the theme he would pursue relentlessly:

> In his election policy speech of 30 September the Prime Minister, in describing a situation where over 100 000 kids between fifteen and nineteen could not find work, found

it sufficient to say of those who leave school: 'Some move smoothly into a job; others have difficulty'. Even more insidious is the attempt to blame the victims, to make them appear indeed the victims of their own inadequacies ... the crying need is to create cohesion, a sense of common purpose leavened by a constructive compassion for that growing body of our fellow Australians who are underprivileged ...

As we have moved into the 1980s under this Government, we have moved inexorably towards that destabilised and dangerous position described by Disraeli as 'two nations', the nation of the privileged and the nation of the poor ... we face an enormous challenge to combine those human and natural resources in an economically and socially productive manner, in a manner which will eliminate the pathetic spectacle of the importing of skilled and semi-skilled labour while our young in growing numbers are untrained and unemployed, and in a manner which will eradicate the canker of poverty in the midst of opulence ... Our tragedy is not that we, as Australians, do not have the capacity to meet this challenge. It is that we have a Prime Minister and a Government whose natural instincts are not for cohesion but confrontation, not for truthful exposition to serve as a basis for mutual understanding but for partisan propaganda calculated to set Australian against and apart from Australian ...

We will, from this day, work to provide Australia with an alternative government which will match not only the resources and the challenge but also what we believe to be the innate sense of fair play of the great majority of the Australian people.[25]

It was a grand beginning yet soon it seemed, as pundits had maintained for years, that Hawke had delayed too long – that he should have entered parliament in 1974 or 1976, in a by-election, for now he would have to serve years of apprenticeship and in the interim his ambitions would be withered by forces he could not control. In government, Fraser's giant frame overshadowed political life; in Opposition, Bill Hayden had earned respect for rebuilding the party since 1977, plus the prestige of almost toppling Fraser in their first contest. And increasingly, the opinion polls showed a trend towards Labor so that, at the next election an ALP led by Bill Hayden seemed likely to win. Most importantly, while the Australian people continued to admire Hawke and stated consistently that he was their preferred political leader, Hawke was failing to impress the would-be kingmakers of the press gallery and the real kingmakers: his colleagues in parliament.

His public-speaking style, which for more than a decade had been shaped by the robust requirements of the union leader, sounded overly hot and aggressive in the cooler, jacket-and-tie atmosphere of the House. In Caucus meetings he was often fidgety and distracted, or bored. His supporters, a group of about ten, mostly Victorians, were bewildered by his patchy performances as a parliamentarian and complained privately that Hawke 'simply isn't contributing in Caucus'. When challenged later (but before he had become ALP leader) that he seemed to be 'idling, not in gear' during his first two years in parliament, Hawke acknowledged that his showing during that time was uninspiring: 'I don't *have* a gear for being in that position, unable to make decisions', he said.

> All my adult life, since I was at university and became president of the Guild, I've been used to leadership or being my own boss – as I was all the years as ACTU advocate, when I made decisions about conducting cases, and took responsibility for them. I've felt at a loss …

For the period from November 1980 to May 1982, Hawke nominated (for this book) three personal successes in parliament that at first seem curious, even shallow, but that in the light of later events reveal how soundly his political intuition works. One success was a straightforward matter of performing effectively in his job as shadow minister; Hawke helped take the scalp of the real Minister for Industrial Relations, Ian Viner, a man whose sobriquet was Sid Vicious, and whom Hawke loathed. Viner was moved to a minor portfolio. The other two 'successes' were much less obviously cause for satisfaction: Hawke had forced the establishment in Hansard of his description of the Prime Minister – 'a liar'. This label, applied to an MHR, had never before been allowed to stand and Hawke's pleasure in it arose in large part from the intuition that he had dealt Fraser, a man whose assertions of rectitude were immensely important to his self-respect, a piercing psychological blow. The third success Hawke nominated was this: Lionel Bowen, the deputy leader of the Labor Party, had declared in parliament, 'It appears that whenever the Honourable Member for Wills, Mr Hawke, decides to do anything in this House, the Government takes fright'. In the daily vilification of parliamentary debate Bowen's remark sounds little more than a throwaway line. But Lionel Bowen had the power, finally, to decide who would lead the Labor Party; at the time his loyalty to Hayden was unquestioned. When Hawke signalled out this trifling comment of Bowen's as a personal achievement, he was doing so as one who has seen a straw in the wind.

With nothing of great moment to point to from his first year as a parliamentarian Hawke added to the uneasiness about his capacities in the new arena by a classic gaffe, in late 1981. The ALP had decided to oppose the government's decision to send an Australian contribution of men and helicopters to the American-sponsored peacekeeping force in Sinai, the establishment of which was a protocol of the Camp David Accords. The Australian public objected to contributing to the force and it was in large part this objection that determined Labor's attitude. Hawke did not share the public's or the party's view. He argued against this in Caucus, accepted defeat, then admitted openly that he had changed his mind because public opinion was set against him. It was the first test of his relationship with Israel under the strains of parliamentary life and Hawke was less than happy with himself about it. As he left his office to go into the

House where the issue was to be debated and where, he knew, government members would take the opportunity to attack him personally, he said to Jean Sinclair, 'I hope I'm going to get through this'. He did not. When a Liberal backbencher taunted him with abandoning Israel – a gross overstatement but a very accurate emotional dart – Hawke became so distressed that he walked out of the room, in tears. The only other case of weeping in the chamber in MHRs' memories had occurred twenty years earlier when Garfield Barwick had witnessed one of his prize pieces of legislation being destroyed, and even then he had only appeared to be weeping, people could not say for sure. Hawke's tears made front-page headlines. One year in parliament, it seemed, had ended his ambitions, in the light of two accepted truths: that leaders must be strong men and that strong men don't cry. Hawke's support in Caucus waned immediately; politicians of both sides, with blood-curdling hypocrisy, declared they had been disgusted or appalled. But then, after a few weeks, it became plain that the people were less mesmerised by some laws of masculine mystique than had been supposed.

Hawke was downcast and shaken by the incident for about a fortnight but by Christmas 1981 he had recouped his self-confidence and began telling friends that he could be the leader within six months. It was an assertion he had been making privately for almost eighteen months, to increasingly sceptical listeners. Only those who were prepared to believe that if Hawke said something, it must be so, or those who, like Kirby years before, had realised that the sheer force of Hawke's conviction could penetrate a power structure and crack it internally, gave much credence to his claims. But just as his drive for ACTU presidency was founded upon his certainty that unionists would reward him for his work as advocate that won increased rates of pay, so, in considering the ALP leadership and his position vis-à-vis Bill Hayden, Hawke's confidence owed less to wishful thinking than it seemed. Before the 1980 election Hayden had told Hawke that even if Labor lost 'only two seats', he would step aside for Hawke. Hawke had understood from the discussion that Hayden would abdicate immediately on failing to win government, but in twelve months Hayden had shown no sign of doing so, and rather, the reverse. However, the conversation of 1980, kept confidential by both men, had cast a psychological die – indisputably for Hawke and apparently, too, for Hayden, in the light of later events. Hawke was indignant that Hayden, by his silence, had seemingly forgotten the promise.

During 1981 he had taken stock of Hayden's attitude and of his own meagre support in Caucus and had decided upon a tactic of using popularity polls as a psychological weapon to gain the leadership. He did not have a moment's doubt that, if he were the ALP leader, he would beat Malcolm Fraser in an encounter at the polls. His conviction about this was so strong that he mentioned it only in passing, as a matter too obvious for discussion, or in irritation that all his political colleagues and political journalists had not come to the same conclusion. But he was less certain about the necessary first step – the leadership – because his electors in that competition would not be the Australian people, with whom he felt *en rapport*, but the raw-nerved small group of men and women, prey to melancholy and wild swings of mood, who made up the Caucus.

By May 1982 he believed he had a 50–50 chance of displacing Bill Hayden before the end of the year: that month Hawke learned the results of a poll that showed that on a range of personal qualities he rated in public esteem well ahead of both Hayden and Fraser. Importantly, although the ALP was outpolling the government, its figures were not so handsome as to assure a Labor electoral victory.

In the latter part of May, Hawke supporters gave the poll findings to selected newspaper journalists, members of Caucus and senior officials of the ALP; throughout June a movement to make Hawke leader gathered speed, its initial impetus given energy by other opinion polls, publicity and Left-wing anger with Hayden because of his determination to soften Labor's objections to the mining and export of uranium. There were few policy differences between Hayden and Hawke. The Hawke challenge was based on a single blunt argument: with Bill Hayden as leader a Labor government is not guaranteed; with Bob Hawke, it is. By the beginning of July there was mounting excitement within the party and the news media about the possibility of a leadership contest.

On 5 July, the party's national policy-making conference opened in Canberra – under a theatrical glare of television lights, in a conference room made portentous, even jingoistic, by giant displays of national and party symbols. The motto of the conference was 'Preparing for Government' and the policies it espoused were mild – for there was in the air an impatience with the impotence of Opposition and an unfamiliar pragmatic, even crafty, mood that said, 'The head must rule the heart'. But glaring over the words, in red, white and vivid blue were the extravagantly large symbols of a resurgent nationalism. They announced an unspoken and seductive message: patriotic Australians vote Labor. (Within nine months this conference's symbols would be haunting the Fraser government: knowing his party would lose the election of 1983, a Liberal official complained, 'And Labor has taken over the Australian flag'.) The Canberra gathering was so well dressed and sensible that some wits wondered loudly about the difference, these days, between a Liberal and a Labor Party conference. Indeed, business was progressing so smoothly, with such decorousness and sobriety, that the ALP's 1982 conference could have been boring. But from its opening day it was febrile with tension, for hour by hour the Hawke challenge was growing, under a momentum of its own, now that television and radio had taken up the issue.

On Wednesday, 7 July, the *Bulletin* published a new poll that showed that Hayden's popularity had slipped sharply while Fraser's had increased somewhat, and that 50 per cent of people questioned thought Fraser would be a better prime minister than Hayden, while only 31 per cent thought the reverse. Early that morning, asked to comment on television, Hawke remarked that the poll results were worrying for the Labor Party. His implied criticism of Hayden's leadership ended the weeks of shadow boxing.

The next afternoon, following thirty hours of wild surmise, Hayden acted. At three o'clock, just as Hawke was to deliver his major speech of the conference – on industrial relations – Hayden issued a statement that complained of 'a deliberate campaign … to destabilise' the party, 'serious damage to [its] morale and credibility', 'this destructive exercise' and 'insidious destabilisation'; he then called a special meeting of Caucus for the following week 'to put an end to this matter'. Journalists had rushed from the conference room at the news of Hayden's statement and Hawke was left addressing a small audience that was too excited to listen to him, and had to be called to order. If points were to be given for upstaging tactics, Hayden had won hands down.

On Friday, 9 July, the editorials of the country's major newspapers declared for Hayden; throughout the week the press mounted a hostile campaign against Hawke, reverting to fears and suspicions about him that it had first expressed, using different epithets, in the early 1960s ('Mr Inflation', 'Communist') and early 1970s ('Napoleon', 'Dictator'). The *Bulletin* had gone to the trouble of mocking up a photograph of Hawke's head upon the opulently gowned body of an actor who was posing imperiously and dressed as the Emperor of Rome.

There were alliances and broken alliances all week. Within days the Left, which had pledged itself to Hawke before 7 July, had deserted and for twenty-four hours Hawke faced ignominious defeat – until some trade union leaders of the extreme Left made the astonishingly naive error of publicly demanding a Hayden victory. At this, the New South Wales Right swung from Hayden to Hawke. By the morning of 16 July, both camps were claiming they would win, although Hayden told Hawke later that he thought he – Hayden – would lose and Mick Young, on Hawke's team, had 'a feeling in his bones' the night before that some of the promised votes would not be honoured, and that Hawke would 'just miss'. Young's Celtic bones were right: three people switched sides and soon after 11 a.m. the Caucus, by 42 votes to 37, re-elected Hayden as leader.

Praising Hawke's 'honourable ambition' to lead the party, Hayden was as magnanimous in victory as Hawke, who had immediately declared loyalty, was gracious in defeat. But within two hours, in Hayden's presence, Hawke told a news conference that his ambition for leadership remained.

After the challenge, many Caucus members complained that they did not know Hawke, they had never spent any time with him socially, and that they were puzzled or offended by the fact that he had not lobbied them for support but had delegated the soliciting of votes to lieutenants, or had simply relied upon a belief that they would 'do the right thing' by him. This behaviour was unconventional, but from Hawke to be expected. It had a singular advantage for any leader-to-be: by holding himself aloof, Hawke had very few debts in the Caucus. Meanwhile, the eruption of hostile publicity had taught him and his supporters a lesson about silence. The challenge damaged relationships within Caucus, for after the first relief of victory, the victors had set to, punishing the vanquished: at least two shadow ministers who had supported Hawke became seriously ill from stress; a poisonous bitterness infected the air.

Some time after his defeat Hawke was alone in a washroom in Parliament House when John Button happened to walk through the door. Button was Labor leader in the Senate and the head of the Victorian Independents. The Independents are descendants of the Participants, the right-wing group that forced federal intervention in the Victorian branch a decade earlier; with a new name they were now celebrated as the faction that had organised a coup in Victoria to install John Cain as state Labor leader – and soon after, premier. The Independents characterise themselves as pragmatists with principles. Button had been, along with Bowen, Hayden's most senior marshal in beating off Hawke's challenge. Suddenly alone together, Button said to Hawke, 'I told Bill he had to win well. And that five votes weren't good enough'. Hawke responded coolly, replying merely, as he remembered, 'Is that so?' Despite his show of indifference Hawke saw the exchange as of great significance and during the next six months recalled it, in private, as a pillar for his next challenge: Button had served notice on Hayden that it was only a matter of time before he would be displaced.

In more than eighty years in federal politics, Labor had never dumped a leader. However, the mood of professionalism that had distinguished the national conference had marked a turning point in the ALP: the conference had revealed that, after its long night of anguish caused by the events of 1975, the ALP had returned to life and the world, a tougher creature than before.

Politically, the latter half of 1982 was entirely taken up with government and social scandals, speculation about an early election, and, from September, concern about an acutely worsening economic situation that boded to deteriorate further during 1983. Despite this, Labor made little headway against the government in parliament and in the public mind, in part because Hayden mishandled the Opposition's attack on the government over tax evasion. Information about massive public fraud and sharp practice came to light in the second six months of the year and proved, at length, what Labor politicians had realised for some years but had felt helpless to change: that the nation's communal values were decaying. Safe, fat and on the edge of the world, the country was sliding into carelessness. The trade union movement was becoming increasingly selfish and bloody-minded; the rich were selfish and bloody-minded; the petit-bourgeois aspired to be rich and selfish; tax evasion and disregard for the poverty-stricken unemployed were symptoms of the national disease. Successive governments, beginning with Whitlam's, had educated the public to realise that the Australian economy was a pawn on the table of international economics, but the reaction to this perception of overriding, alien forces had been, 'Every man for himself'. Some renewed sense of community, of national solidarity, was essential if Australia were to halt its degeneration into a nation of white-collar criminals, thuggish labour bosses, sharp lawyers, pettifogging tax cheats and a mass of ordinary people enervated by cynicism. Inchoately, perhaps, those who had designed the symbols for the ALP conference had realised that an appeal to nationalism would be a string to pull the country around. However, it was Malcolm Fraser who, by November 1982, had clearly understood the mood of self-disgust and had devised a policy to capitalise on it. That month, before a by-election in the Victorian seat of Flinders set for 4 December, he proposed a wage freeze that would, he announced, help the economy and therefore the unemployed. Using logic and statistics, economists quickly advanced arguments that proved that the wage freeze was *a*, the perfect solution, or *b*, useless and damaging. The correct answer belonged to the Prime Minister who, as ever, had calculated on the political abacus of psychology. The wage freeze was welcomed by the electorate, for it gave a sense of national purification through suffering.

Labor had expected to win the Flinders by-election. It lost. A mood of inevitable defeat, if Hayden continued as leader, set in. At Canberra Christmas parties held after the Flinders by-election, leading political journalists who had campaigned savagely against Hawke in his July challenge were saying that sometime in the new year he would become leader. Only one, Greg Hywood of the *Financial Review*, had enough information to present a factual story: just before Christmas, he wrote that John Button had gone on holiday to Fiji, where he would decide whether or not he and his group would continue to support Hayden. It was unknown to the press that the issue was much further advanced than that: a disciplined Hawke machine was already at work and, barring bad luck and bad management, Hawke would be the leader by February. The Hawke machine had decided upon secrecy: Hawke himself was to take merely a passive role and was informed of achievements or setbacks only when necessary. One reason for secrecy was to maintain in the Prime Minister and government the sense of security that had overtaken them on winning the Flinders by-election. Speed was also essential. When Hawke learned the Flinders result and considered it in combination with the foreseeable trade union reaction to the wage freeze, he was convinced that Fraser would hold the earliest possible election. By mid-December he was forecasting in private that the wage freeze, opposed by the ACTU, would give rise to a big strike, 'perhaps in Telecom', as soon as the Christmas holidays were over, and Fraser would thereby have a popular issue to take to the country. (Telecom, along with the oil industry, was the area of industrial disputation that most enraged the public. As events turned out, it was the oil industry that obliged – or disobliged – Malcolm Fraser.) Hawke also believed that if the ALP leadership did not improve, Fraser would win such an election and that, because of the likely upturn in the world economy during 1984, the Liberals could win the next election after that, and possibly another, thanks to national good-temper arising from the bicentenary celebrations of 1988. What the ALP was facing by December 1982 was the possibility of disintegration.

The Prime Minister, who had spent the final weeks of 1982 convalescing from an operation on his back, returned to work in the second week of January with a vigour that astonished. In his weeks of recuperation he had refined still further his intuitive grasp of the public mood, its yearning for solidarity and purposefulness. With days of returning to his desk, he had abandoned the rhetoric of small government, announced an array of grand national building projects and had articulated the concept, magnificent in its flourish, 'Australia won't wait for the rest of the world!' President Sukarno of Indonesia – 'Go to hell with your aid, America!' – would have been proud of him, and could have offered a little extra advice about the danger of coups. On 6 January, before Fraser had returned to work, John Button had flown to Brisbane and asked Bill Hayden to step down. Hayden had refused. On 19 January, while Fraser was still in the process of announcing nation-building schemes, Lionel Bowen, by his demeanour in a Labor executive meeting, had indicated that he, too, now rejected Hayden. By this date Hayden had mishandled ALP–ACTU dealings over the wage freeze. Without consultation, he had switched from the agreed position of opposition, to one of cautious support, when it appeared he was backing a politically unpopular cause. The ACTU was extremely angry and demanded, through Hawke, that Hayden switch back again – or the party's prices and incomes agreement with the trade union movement would again be scuttled. Hayden and Hawke had a blazing row in the executive meeting. While Hayden was defending his actions, Lionel Bowen rolled his eyes. Hawke, watching Bowen's face, knew that the last domino had fallen. It was abruptly a contest between the cunning of Hawke's machine, and the Prime Minister. The Hawke group had to persuade Hayden to abdicate quickly and silently, for as soon as the Prime Minister got wind of the upheaval in the ALP, he would sprint for Yarralumla. For months the government had possessed the constitutional reasons for an early election – from thirteen sales tax Bills rejected by the Senate – and a strike in the oil industry was threatening right on cue. Senior members of the Labor Party believed that Fraser had already planned an election for 19 March, so by mid-February at the latest the leadership change would need to be made. Caucus was not due to meet until 21 February.

The twelve days from 19 January moved in tantalising slow motion for Hawke; he thought he had the numbers, Hayden thought Hawke had the numbers, but Hayden was refusing to resign and was proposing to force the issue to a party-room fight. The consequences of that could be disastrous for Labor's electoral prospects. By the last weekend in January, Hawke's machine had decided that, beginning on Monday, 31 January, Hayden was to be systematically pressured by the other parliamentary leaders to desist and go quickly. Button had already written to Hayden telling him he should step down: the latest opinion polls showed that at a time when Labor could expect to be ten or fifteen points ahead of the government, it was only four; under such circumstances, it would lose the unannounced but imminent election. The context, by this stage, was that inflation was running at 10 per cent and almost 650 000 people were unemployed. The ALP hardly had any business in politics if it could not beat a government with such a blighted record.

It was not until 31 January that the seriousness of the leadership struggle moved from the shadows of journalists' guesses and snippets of information into the glare of publicity. That morning, Bowen, asked if he supported Hayden's leadership, gave a noncommital answer to the press. The next day Button flew to Brisbane to talk to Hayden again. He gained the impression that Hayden would resign if he were guaranteed the Foreign Affairs portfolio. This shadow ministry was held and cherished by Lionel Bowen who, in a separate conversation with Button, agreed to relinquish it. The day afterwards, Wednesday, 2 February, Hawke and Button met in Melbourne to discuss what would happen the next morning in Brisbane where, at an ALP executive meeting, they both expected that Hayden would step down.

None of these events was known to the news media, the Prime Minister or, indeed, to any but a tiny group of senior Labor people and some of their staff members. However, on the evening of 2 February, somebody apparently hoping to change Hayden's mind informed Fraser's office of what was afoot. The Prime Minister decided to call an election the next day, thereby expecting either to short-circuit Hayden's resignation, or to catch the ALP, once more, 'with its pants down'.

By a quarter past midday on Thursday, 3 February, there was an eerie feeling of crisis around Parliament House, an atmosphere that revived memories of 11 November 1975. Rumours from the news media in Brisbane had reached the capital that something momentous was happening inside the ALP meeting there, while the Prime Minister had just set out in his official limousine for Yarralumla, having told the press he soon would have an announcement to make. Fraser, as he had done before, was dashing off to use the Governor-General, but this time nothing went smoothly: fifteen minutes earlier, in Brisbane, Hayden had formally told Hawke he was resigning immediately; in Canberra the new Governor-General, Fraser's own appointment, had not been informed of the Prime Minister's visit and when Fraser arrived at Government House he was told he would have to leave his letter requesting an election until the duties of a diplomatic luncheon had been fulfilled. By the end of lunchtime

on 3 February, Fraser had, like Whitlam at the end of his lunchtime seven years earlier, thrown away his government and his
career. Hawke, by then, had taken over the ALP.

On election day, 5 March, having campaigned on a slogan
that expressed his own struggle away from a divided personality,
towards wholeness – 'Bob Hawke, Bringing Australia Together' –
Robert James Lee Hawke became the prime minister.

With only two years in parliament and three weeks as leader
of the Opposition, his rise to power is the most spectacular in
the history of Australian politics.

PART II
The Prime
Minister

TWENTY

NOTHING IS AS ENIGMATIC as the wheel of history: some it favours, some it will crush – but who, and why, is a guessing game. Aware of that yet ignoring it, every political leader embraces an irresistible urge to try to take hold of history. Gough Whitlam, brilliant, imperious, an inspiration to a generation, was the greatest leader of the Opposition Australia had ever known. He laid his hand on the wheel and it flung him, chariot and all, over a cliff. The Prime Minister and the government he led were politically destroyed, but history favoured Whitlam with the radiant legacy of a social and cultural reformer. Had the Governor-General not dismissed him and he had simply been voted out after a term and a half, he could not have become a Labor hero.

Malcolm Fraser, a giant with a mirthless laugh, snatched the steering wheel from Whitlam, only to shrink. His achievements were minor, and he ended walking from the stage of public life in tears.

Now there was Hawke, whose entry into parliament in 1980 caused Bill Hayden to declare, 'The disaster of my life'.

Hayden, who had lost one election to Fraser, had been leader of the Australian Labor Party for six years and had rebuilt it from the Whitlam wreck of 1977, which had been a political catastrophe for Labor even worse than that of 1975. Hayden constructed a fighting force with a chance of winning the 1983 election. Senator Gareth Evans, shadow Attorney General, had spent his time in opposition reconstructing the relationship between Labor's cabinet, caucus and national conference.

Whitlam had struggled with a rebellious mess. Hayden now had a disciplined militia with a clear chain of command. Hawke, from the moment he decided to overcome his weakness for alcohol, control his social behaviour and stand for preselection for the seat of Wills, was determined to seize the leadership for himself. He would not wait for another election to pass before he did so. But always impatient, optimistic and boundless in self-confidence, he made his grab too soon and lost a Caucus challenge to Hayden in 1982.

Hawke's solution to his setback was a change of tack, setting out on a chess game in the upper echelons of the party, allowing him to bypass the Caucus, for he had realised, a little too late, that Caucus' mind was set in parliamentary traditions. As a new member, Hawke did not fit them. He had not served his time. Two decades of fighting for Labor ideals, first as the advocate, then as the president of the ACTU, did not count for much in parliament, where nobody became leader of a party without first serving a good five to ten years in the House. Hawke's only virtue, and questionable at that as far as Caucus was concerned for it was a nest of envies, was that the Australian people loved him and would vote for him if given the chance. At the time, nobody in Caucus believed he possessed the wisdom, the foresight and the toughness of a statesman. But he did, and his leadership would bring Australia the greatest standing in the world it had ever experienced. Back in 1982 most Caucus members thought of him as a show pony. As they would discover, Hawke exemplified Walter Bagehot's view of great Prime Ministers: 'Men of commonplace opinions and uncommon administrative abilities.' Through his two decades in the trade union movement and his perpetual mixing with all classes of Australians he had an encyclopaedic knowledge of how the nation worked.

The pieces Hawke set up on the chessboard were his national popularity, the political force of the unions inside the Labor Party, and sections of the news media. With these he plotted to capture not only all of Hayden's pieces, but to trap his king. The pragmatic

New South Wales Right swung behind Hawke but the Victorian Right, less pragmatic, more idealistic, was still for Hayden. The game dragged on through the torpid Christmas–January holiday of 1982–83. Hayden's friends and advisers were away. Nobody could find the key man, Senator John Button of Victoria, nor know that he was on an island in the South Pacific with his colleague, Michael Duffy. Both were Hayden men. Away from the hectic emotions of parliament and in the balm of the tropics, they discussed the future of their party and its leader. Button had known Hawke for years and did not like him much. But he returned from Fiji convinced that Hawke, not Hayden, must lead Labor at the next election. He wrote Hayden a letter urging him to step aside for the good of the party. It was a devastating blow for the leader. Hayden had difficulty in trusting others, but he had considered Button a friend on whose loyalty he could rely.

Hawke now had Hayden in check. The only move through which Hayden could succeed needed total self-confidence that *he* would win the 1983 election. But Hayden, a thoughtful, honourable, gentle man, was easily assailed by self-doubt.

On 3 February 1983, behind closed doors, in the secrecy of an ALP executive meeting in the Commonwealth Offices in Ann Street, Brisbane, Hayden resigned as leader of the Labor Party. Away to the south in Canberra, just hours earlier Malcolm Fraser sensed danger and rushed to Government House for permission to call an election. As Fraser had snatched the prime minister-ship from Whitlam by a well-timed dash to Government House in 1975, he was to repay his debt to history by an ill-timed one. When he arrived at Yarralumla unannounced, the Queen's representative declined to receive him: the Prime Minister needed an appointment.

By the time Fraser returned several hours later at a time convenient to the Governor-General, he was too late. A few hours earlier he would have been fighting Hayden, whom he felt confident of defeating once more. Now he was matched against Hawke. When a messenger entered the executive meeting in Ann Street, Brisbane, with urgent news, the room, until that moment filled with passionate acrimony, exploded with laughter. 'We've tricked the bastard!' someone shouted.

Hawke had usurped without a Caucus vote, without a drop of blood spilt in public. Behind the scenes, where the struggle had been conducted, Graham Richardson noted that Hawke had been ruthless and 'there was a smell of blood ... more blood ... than the entire stage at the end of *Hamlet*'. He said, 'There are many people who want to be the leader – there were eight or ten of them in the Caucus at the time – but very few have the courage to challenge.' Richardson was the New South Wales Right's numbers man, busy for months putting to the sword enemies of his hero. 'I worshiped Hawkey,' he recalled wistfully. 'I would have killed for him.'

With the nostalgia of a love cherished now only in memory, he added, 'And I did. I did.'

For his part, Hawke already subscribed to the political axiom: 'A statesman never stoops into the gutter, but makes sure he has around him those whose loins are suppler.'

That night, a live television interview took place that made Hawke's supporters wonder if they had just made an egregious mistake. The old Hawke, the wild man who would shout down a crowd when sober and when drunk shout obscenities in a bar, the man they believed was dead and buried – or if not dead, at least prisoner in some dungeon far from the light of television cameras – suddenly seemed to have escaped. Hawke was teetotal now: how long, they wondered, would that last under pressure? ALP polling, never publicly released, had revealed that the electorate thought him brilliant – a rolled-gold Aussie larrikin, but a super-sized one – but at the same time was apprehensive that his behaviour could embarrass the nation. They confided to pollsters their concern that a Prime Minister Hawke may not deport himself appropriately with the Queen. Mr Fraser, unlikeable as he was, nevertheless knew how to behave as a gentleman; Hawke's larrikinism could be sufficient reason not to vote Labor. Unaware of the polling, Hawke well understood that his demeanour from the moment he became leader was of critical importance.

The dramatic events of 3 February – Fraser's double dash to the Governor-General, Hayden's sudden resignation, the charismatic new Labor leader, a federal election just weeks away – seemed to have sprung out of the air. That night the public thronged to their television sets. There was a huge audience for Hawke's first in-depth interview as leader, to be shown live on ABC. Hawke was tense; the day, although victorious, had been emotionally draining: there had been hard bargaining over the division of spoils before Hayden would give way. It had required Lionel Bowen, who had converted to Hawke's side only recently, to give up his dream of being Foreign minister. Hayden insisted on that, and he insisted that his closest allies, John Dawkins, Peter Walsh and Neal Blewett, be given the ministries they wanted. For a while in the Ann Street meeting there was a stalemate as Hayden and Bowen shouted abuse at each other. Then Bowen gave way. The deal was done, the doors were opened, and a group of smiling men presented a united front to the waiting media.

Richard Carleton, a star television journalist, was the interviewer that night. Carleton was tall and dark-haired with a slightly condescending manner. His long teeth, long nose and small chin gave him the appearance of a handsome, glossy rodent, one ready to bite. A professional to his back teeth, he was a master of tricks of sleights-of-hand that astonished children and disarmed adults. He had reported from Asian countries where he used magic to break down cultural barriers. After a few desultory questions, he turned on his journalistic magician. He leaned forward, lowered his voice to a suggestively insinuating tone and asked, 'Mr Hawke, do you have blood on your hands tonight?'

Around the nation hundreds of thousands of viewers were transfixed by his effrontery, on tenterhooks for Hawke's response.

Hawke seemed momentarily stunned. His eyes narrowed and became hooded. He sat perfectly still, focusing his gaze on Carleton's face. Then there was a flash of such fury from Hawke that Carleton appeared to have been hit in the solar plexus. It was not what Hawke said – 'You haven't improved, have you?' – that was shocking, it was how deadly in aggression he appeared. His close supporters were appalled. Bob Hogg, then the secretary of the Victorian ALP, recalled,

> There was a campaign committee meeting that night – the first for Bob and the last for Bill. They were both there, so it was awkward. But what had just happened had to be addressed. I said to Bob, 'If you go on like that, you can kiss your arse goodbye.' And he copped it. It would have been better to say it in private, but there was no opportunity. We were straight into the campaign.

Apart from one interview in Brisbane with John Barton during which Hawke became testy, the rest of the campaign went without a hitch. As his press officer, Geoff Walsh, said, 'The thing about Bob is he's obviously very intelligent and he's incredibly disciplined, and once he was convinced that what had been put to him made absolute sense, he acted on it.'

Hawke had a vision for Australia that he captured in the slogan: 'Reconciliation, Recovery, Reconstruction'. It conveyed his attitude to power: 'The knowledge that what you do is going to have an effect, not just immediate, but perhaps lifelong effect, on the happiness and wellbeing of millions of people. I think the essence of power is to be conscious of what it can mean for others.'[1] The party under Hayden had built a platform of policies to take to the electorate, but it was Hawke's vision that fired the campaign. 'Reconciliation' gave it a churchy ring, evoking Jesus reuniting God and man, but it was authentic Hawke. He promised that, if elected, he would hold an economic summit of employers and employees, state governments, social security groups and churches, to work out some new co-operative arrangement to help the country out of the hole it was in. It all sounded to the hardheads in the party kind of fluffy, but they were not willing to argue. Their leader was fighting an election in the midst of a national crisis – and if he won he would have to fix the country any way he could. The economy was stalled and New South Wales, Queensland, Victoria, Tasmania and South Australia were in the grip of the worst drought on record. It lasted 334 days, affected 4 million people and destroyed and damaged $3 billion (in 1983 terms) worth of property. Dust storms caused the loss of millions of tons of topsoil; a total of 86 million sheep and 14 million cattle were without adequate food and water and many had to be destroyed. Wheat production fell by 37 per cent, with similar falls in barley, oats, rice, cotton and sugar. Unemployment in some rural areas was 40 per cent. An unknown number of destitute farmers died 'by accident', in sheds, under the wheels of tractors, in the shallow brown water left in their dams. On the mid-afternoon of 8 February, a dust storm covered Melbourne in choking darkness, and eight days later, on Ash Wednesday, a conflagration destroyed more build-ings and property – including some of Australia's most beautiful paintings – than any other bushfire. It claimed seventy-five lives. Hundreds of thousands more lives were being slowly destroyed by unemployment and inflation, both just under 11 per cent. For eighty years Australia, once one of the two richest counties on earth – the other was Argentina – had been sliding slowly down the economic ladder. By 1983 it was feeble. The nation was full of social cracks and fissures, without common pur-pose, adrift, and with no new ideas about how to rescue itself. If Hawke wanted a summit, it was worth a try. Even those who disliked him recognised that the nation's happiness was his motive.

On a hot night in a suite at the Lakeside Hotel in Canberra, sur-rounded by his wife, Hazel, his father, the Reverend Mr Clem Hawke, a few close friends and staff, Hawke learned from watch-ing television that he was officially Australia's twenty-third prime minister. The atmosphere was happy, relieved and subdued: everyone was conscious of the wild euphoria of the Whitlam victory a decade earlier, and the disasters that had followed. 'Our win was tempered by a good deal more realism than the

Whitlam victory,' Hawke said. By odd coincidence his election was fifty years to the day (adjusted for international time), since Franklin D. Roosevelt had offered the frightened and wretched people of the United States a 'New Deal'. Hawke, similarly, wanted and needed to rebuild Australia, and recognised his task would be difficult. Already his mind was tinged with the knowledge of tragedy with which, Max Weber wrote, 'all action, but especially political action, is interwoven'. For the new Australian leader the moment was also tinged with sadness as he reflected aloud several times what a pity it was that his mother, Ellie, the only photograph he carried in his wallet was hers, had missed seeing the fulfilment of her dreams. But it was a personal comfort that his father, whose eighty-fifth birthday it was, was with him, and brimming with joy.

Bill Hayden, according to his friend, John Dawkins, who was 'as close as anyone could be with Bill', had sulked during the campaign and was sulky for some months after it. Asked on television what he thought about Hawke's seizing of the leadership from him, Hayden remarked that a drover's dog could win the election. It was hard to know if his scorn was directed at himself, at Hawke, or at his colleagues who had pressed him to step aside. For many, perhaps a majority, of professional politicians the unspoken apprehension was: Hawke's an election winner, he has the ruthless courage of a leader, but does he have good political judgment?

John Button, whose letter to Hayden had ended the chess game, had also written in it,

> I must say that even some of Bob's closest supporters have doubts about his capacities to lead the party successfully, in that they do not share his own estimate of his ability. The Labor Party is, however, desperate to win the coming election.

Button was short and sharp, a thimble of wit, vitality, charm and scepticism. He was a very attractive character who, as a university student, was wildly popular for his knowledge of scores of bawdy songs, and, according to Hawke, the most consummate liar he ever met in politics. In the same letter to Hayden, Button dismissed Hawke as 'a media performer and winner of popularity polls'.

Hawke's political judgment – in every successful political leader an intuitive quality, observable but unteachable, apparently inborn – would determine if his government would survive and prosper or crash and burn. The magnificent Whitlam's political judgment turned out to be so inept that Hayden, who admired Whitlam's capacious intellect and oratory, said of him, 'He should have handed over to someone else to run the government, because he couldn't. He just couldn't. He had no idea.'

The omens for Hawke were mixed: he was possessed of an abundance of courage, the cardinal political virtue, since the first job of a political leader is to *fight*. But Whitlam was courageous too. Political leaders have to inspire confidence and they must not only possess courage but also the flair to display it theatrically. Like justice, courage in politics must be seen to be done and the leader must be a good actor. Hawke was – but so was Whitlam. And Fraser, through his sheer physical dominance – his giant's body, brass forehead, iron jaw, deep-set eyes – achieved the same effect: he embodied the patriarch come to restore order to a chaotic family. Another essential of leadership is a steely will, a true intransigence – perhaps the most dangerous of a leader's qualities for, if combined with poor judgment, intransigence can lead not just to political defeat but to national catastrophe (as citizens were to learn, all over again in the twenty-first century, from the case of George W. Bush). Whitlam, Fraser and Hawke had steely wills, but Hawke's had only recently been tested by giving up alcohol, and usurping Hayden. His philandering, though potentially dangerous, had not been a cause for censure in the Men's Union of the Labor Party – or any Australian political party, since by mutual consent such matters were either forgivable, unexceptional or taboo. Parliament House was and always had been a place of intrigues and *liaisons dangereux* and #MeToo was not even a distant cloud.

By Hawke's own estimation, one of his strongest attributes as a leader was the one John Button had scorned: his popularity. Hayden recalled campaigning in a shopping centre with Hawke:

> a dumpy little woman held up her baby – it was no more than six months old – held her baby over the head of the crowd so it could see the Great Man. She seemed to be telling the baby, 'Look at the Great Man! His feet don't touch the ground when he walks.'

Already tokens of admiration were arriving in Hawke's office, as they had been for years: cards and letters, portraits done in oils, in pencil, in watercolours, his face embroidered on cushions, even woven into a rug. His pottery head served as beer mugs. In plastic, he became a wine cask.

Hawke had a clear, simple-sounding, ambition: to improve the lives of ordinary Australians by reforming the economy and the social security system. His motivation sprang from his deepest feelings of what he believed in and what was sacred to him. After his childhood and youth in the Congregational church, in his early years at university, Hawke had been a Sunday school teacher and had preached sermons at Young Christian Movement camps. His brand of Christianity had been dull, worthy and teetotal. It was untouched by ecstasy. By his late twenties he had abandoned the church, did not know whether he believed in God or not, and had rejected all Christian dogma. But Christian principles were in Hawke's bones and he found their expression not in lifeless Sunday ritual but in the vibrant, communal, morally cohesive and uplifting labour movement. As for many others, this was his new and true religion. And it was ecstatic: the ecstasy of drinking together in bonded fellowship with men who shared broad ideals for society and would fight as a band of brothers to achieve them.

The Australian Labor Party of Hawke's childhood and youth was the glorious union-based party of John Curtin and Ben Chifley. Curtin, a man with a serious drinking problem, like Hawke, and a West Australian, steered the nation to safety through World War II. Chifley, calm, simple and wise, prepared Australia for prosperity in peace. The ALP of Hawke's childhood and youth was the party of national pride, led by honourable, compassionate men – among them his uncle, Bert, who was Premier of Western Australia. There had been Labor governments in almost every state.

As Hawke turned twenty, it all collapsed. For most of the next thirty-four years Labor was the party of Opposition: impotent, angry, scarred with the wounds of disappointment, a party of energetic pathology. Hawke wanted to regain Labor's honour, and restore Australia's prestige among the nations. But what he wanted to do would run headlong into cherished popular attitudes and the money and muscle of vested interests. Only with the Australian people behind him could he hope to succeed.

On 5 March, when Hawke's television would confirm that Labor had won that day's election and he was now prime minister, the national mood became hopeful, but apprehensive. The Liberals had run a fear campaign, saying that if Labor won people would be better off hiding their money under their beds than entrusting it to banks. Fraser had screamed into a megaphone at a Melbourne rally that Labor would 'rob' the Australian people 'to pay for their mad schemes' and repeated this threat in other venues. Andrew Peacock, who was to become Liberal leader after Fraser, predicted a 15 per cent devaluation of the dollar. Promptly, $2.7 billion in capital fled the country and on Monday, 7 March, another $200 million left.

The intellectual elite, of which Hawke was a member, knew that the economic system under which Australia had operated since its birth as a nation was dying, and was dragging the country with it towards the grave. But they were a tiny few. The mass of Australians did not realise that the entire system, bit by bit, would have to change. They knew that something was wrong, that a ten-year cycle of boom and bust, of inflation, wage hikes, then unemployment, had beset national life. In the 1960s middle-class Australians could afford a holiday in Europe, returning with prêt-à-porter designer clothes and other luxuries.

No more. The nation lurched from crisis to crisis, each wave of wage rises and unemployment growing higher. In 1980 Lee Kuan Yew, the Prime Minister of Singapore, remarked, 'If it goes on in the same way, Australia will become the poor white trash of Asia.' To be berated by Singapore, a nation the size of Sydney, dependent for its water supply on Malaysia, was indicative of the scant respect Australia commanded abroad.

At the beginning of 1983 Australians felt divided, uncertain of themselves and insecure. Although Malcolm Fraser was an ardent anti-racist, an upholder of human rights and the creator of national multiculturalism – his greatest achievement and a lasting legacy – tragically for him his method of seizing power poisoned his image in the electorate. He seemed to have more compassion for an impoverished black African than he did for an impoverished white Australian. He became a divisive leader, setting group against group. His government pilloried the unemployed as 'dole bludgers'; women demanding equal rights were dismissed as 'lesbians'. There was constant industrial strife. It was a harsh, uncivil time.

Hawke's solution was the 'Economic Summit', at which he would fully unveil an 'Accord' with the trade union movement. Through a summit, he believed he could put into effect the slogan of the campaign: 'Reconciliation, Recovery, Reconstruction'. He wanted to end the dog-eat-dog temper of the Fraser years and restore the Christian ethos of tolerance and respect for human brotherhood in which he had been raised. In those days secularism was virtually a religion in itself. No Australian political leader could afford to talk openly in churchy language without being labelled wet. Hawke himself now thought in a different terminology, but those with sharp noses got a whiff of the theology behind it. Neville Wran, Labor Premier of New South Wales, summed up what the hardheads thought when he said of the summit, 'If the greedy bastards want spirituality they should join the fucking Hare Krishnas.' The conservative side of politics, and the public service, considered the idea simply odd. 'They were all sceptical,' Hawke recalled. 'They went along with it just to humour me.' He was, for the moment, Mr Charisma, so exceptional that he was almost a fetish object. He was a multimillionaire in political capital, and while it lasted he could spend it as he wished. The Summit, he decreed, would be held in Parliament House before the first sitting of the new government.

Before any action could be taken, on the Sunday morning after the election, the secretary of the Treasury, John Stone, called on the new Prime Minister. The message he brought was hair-raising: the projected budget deficit for 1983/84 was $9.6 billion dollars (in 2019 terms about $80 billion). It was the largest budget deficit in history and, in its percentage of GDP 'almost without precedent among the major OECD countries in the post-war period', Stone's official note said. Someone in Treasury had leaked this news of a huge deficit to Hawke during the campaign, but he had decided to keep it secret until he had been officially informed. He commented, 'I was painfully aware of the implications of the figure for our program, and for our economic management of the country.'

While painful for Hawke's election promises, the deficit was political gold. Hawke had a huge economic headache but also a huge stick with which to beat the Opposition, and a huge lever for reform. Australia was one of the world's oldest and at the time feistiest and most argumentative democracies. All democracies demand explanation of policy. In Australia no leader could hope to persuade the people to accept something they did not like without explaining the very good reason for it. With the drama of a national economic crisis to announce because of the deficit, Hawke could begin the economic education of the electorate. On that foundation, he could successfully reform.

The same day that Stone visited, the weather changed. It began to rain. In a country town during the campaign Hawke had joked to some locals, 'Elect me, and I'll fix the drought!' By the end of the first week the whole of the parched east coast of Australia was awash with life-restoring water. The nation rejoiced. Hawke, laughing, said, '*I* did it!' The press began calling him 'The Messiah'.

But unknown to the new Prime Minister, on the night before the election something had happened that could smother all his hopes for national rebirth.

In 1983 the Cold War was being fought in deadly earnest, but it was almost invisible in Australia and analogous to a greenhouse gas – undetectable unless one was aware of it, and went looking. George Orwell had coined the term 'Cold War' in late 1945, when he warned of a 'peace that is not peace'. Since then the Cold War had become the toxic air the planet breathed and to which it had become accustomed. Hawke's entire adult life and almost all his enmities within the trade union movement and the Labor Party, stretching from the 1960s into the 1980s, were infected with the unseen poison of a peace that is not peace. After the bitterness of the Vietnam War, disillusion with international military adventures took hold of Australia, so much so that foreign policy played almost no part in the election campaign and almost no part in politics. During the Fraser years, little had been done in foreign policy terms: there were no major military deployments and hardly any minor ones – except a small force sent to Afghanistan, which the Soviet Union had invaded on Christmas Eve, 1979. In those days few, on either side of the chamber, could have pointed to Afghanistan on a world map. Paul Keating, the physically beautiful, sharp-as-a-whip bovver boy from the New South Wales Right, spoke for them when he interjected in parliament 'Where is Afghanistan?' Indonesia's invasion of East Timor and America's bases in Australia were left-wing issues, boring for the rest of the electorate. But in January 1981 the idiosyncratic and strangely gifted Ronald Reagan took office as President of the United States, and almost immediately announced his goal of confronting the Soviet Union. His aggressive stance, combined with his amiable manner, mellifluous voice and previous career as a movie actor, made him in Australia a figure of incredulity and fun. His obsession with the Soviet Union, which he dubbed the 'Evil Empire', seemed to opinion-makers in the media and academia both inscrutable and dangerous, although not to Hawke who, despite his loathing of the Soviet Union, held his tongue. The government was young and could afford no Whitlamesque grand gesture. And there was something else: public ignorance.

Until Reagan, there was virtually no national recognition that, if the policy of mutually assured destruction (MAD) between the United States and the Soviet Union broke down and a nuclear war ensued, the bases in Australia would be targets. Nuclear-armed Soviet submarines standing off the north and west coasts would attack them, and probably sooner rather than later. Australia, as a United States ally and a central cog in America's military intelligence machine, was both a Cold War and a hot war target. Consequently, since the 1950s the Soviet Union had spied on Australia. Unfortunately – or fortunately – not only did Australians not realise the country would be attacked in a nuclear war, they did not believe in the reality of the world of espionage. Australia had an internal counter-espionage service, ASIO, and a little-known external one, ASIS. Labor had established ASIO but the party had grown fervently hostile to it, thanks to the Petrov Affair in 1954. Petrov was a Soviet spy whom ASIO persuaded to defect, but Labor, in an unbelievable act of folly, managed to turn what was a political plus for Menzies into a total disaster for itself. The Petrov Affair was the fine crack that opened a chasm in the Labor Party, the split that would keep it out of office for almost two decades and sear the words 'ASIO' and 'Russian spy' through Labor foreheads into its tribal consciousness as symbols of danger, defeat and humiliation. Members of the Labor Party's Left and, especially, clandestine members of the Communist Party who had succeeded in infiltrating the ALP, felt personally threatened by ASIO. During the Whitlam years Labor hostility and paranoia about ASIO had been so severe that the Attorney-General, Lionel Murphy, had in person 'raided' its offices in Melbourne, searching for information that, supposedly, it was withholding from him. Labor's platform for many elections had been to abolish ASIO completely and in the last mad days of his government, Whitlam summarily dismissed the head of ASIS over a trifle that had been beaten up in the press. There was institutionalised contempt and distrust on both sides.

On Friday, 4 March 1983, the night before Hawke and his inner circle gathered to watch the election result in the Lakeside Hotel, David Combe, the former secretary of the ALP, had dinner with the first secretary of the Soviet embassy, Valeriy Ivanov, at Ivanov's house in Canberra. Dinner began rather early, ended late and David Combe had a lot to drink. He also had a lot to say. He disparaged Hawke's 1979 visit to Moscow, 'at the height of his drinking', he recalled to Ivanov, during which Hawke had asked for, and had believed he had achieved, the release of Soviet Jews. As prime minister, Combe asserted, Hawke might restrict Australian–Soviet trade were he to attempt once more to have Jews released, and to fail. Combe was certain that Labor would win the election scheduled for the next day – the same day, by the time he left Ivanov's house – and his excitement for his party was mingled with a certain resentment that he had put in eight years as national secretary, years of struggle and grinding disappointment, only to be relegated to bystander status for the victory parade. Eighteen months earlier he had resigned as national secretary to set himself up as a lobbyist and business consultant. It was a career move that a half-dozen smart young-men-about-town, former political staffers from both sides of politics, had already made. They were considered trendy, but not quite respectable.

Combe's wife, Meena Blesing, was a partner in the company and mother of his four sons. (In 1981 Caroline Combe, as she then was, had become a follower of Rajneesh and changed both her names.) Combe was eager to foster trade with the USSR, which, until recently, had been one of Australia's largest trading partners, the balance being heavily in Australia's favour. He was a member of the Australia–USSR Friendship Society, and in 1982 had visited the country as its guest. While in Moscow Paul Dibb, an Australian defence and intelligence analyst, had warned Combe that a senior official of the umbrella organisation, the

Union of Friendship Societies, Andrey Parasteyev, was 'a bad bastard' – by which Dibb meant he was from the KGB. Both Combe and his wife suspected that Ivanov was a KGB officer. Why they did not take the next step of imagination and consider that, if this were the case, there was a chance that Ivanov was under surveillance is explicable only in the context of the contempt in which Labor people held ASIO. A nightmare for the Combes and their children was taking form.

David Combe was a tall, gangling man with a mop of black curly hair and a personality so open, so hearty, so expansive, so obviously good-natured, so essentially innocent, he put one in mind of a huge puppy. There was something of the soft sweetness of a child in his nature, as if he had carried into adulthood the Anglican chorister and altar boy he once was. He had grown up in a conservative Adelaide family with staunch Liberal-voting parents. 'My mother,' he recalled, 'used to take the Labor "How to Vote" card on polling day and very ostentatiously tear it up.' The family was socially respectable, his cousin on his father's side being a former archbishop, but they were not well off and David could only attend a private school, Prince Alfred's, thanks to winning a scholarship. The school was associated with the Methodist church and unlike St Peter's, the Anglican college, had no record of notable left-wing alumni, but boasted a long menu of Liberal parliamentarians. At university, Combe joined the Liberal Club. His study of politics, and the 1961 election campaign, began his rebellion. He was working part-time in a service station to help the family finances. During 1961, he said,

> guys whom I'd been serving for years would come in asking if they could have ten bob's worth of petrol on the slate, so they could go looking for work. Then I'd go home and see Menzies on the television say, 'The only people who are not working are those who will not work.' This was terribly wrong, to me. It upset me greatly.

Soon afterwards he met the state Labor MP, Don Dunstan,

> and I was totally captivated by him. He invited me to lunch
> in Parliament House ... [and this started] a long association.
> Most Sundays I would go to his home in Norwood, sit down
> and learn at the feet of the master.

In those days Dunstan was married and he and his wife were
both superb cooks. In August 1962 Dunstan persuaded Combe
to join the Labor Party. 'So I went home and told my parents
that I'd joined the Labor Party and my mother took to her
sickbed. Neither of them would speak to me for several days.'
Finally one night when Combe and his father were washing the
dishes after dinner, they had a man-to-man talk. Combe senior
said, 'This has come as a great shock to your mother and me,
but I suppose we have to accept it.' Then he added, 'But promise
me one thing: promise me you'll never come home and tell us
you've decided to become a Catholic.'

Around 1964 Combe met Hawke when the star trade union
advocate was scheduled to come to South Australia to address a
Young Labor seminar, and Combe was designated his chauffeur.
He knew that Hawke was the son of a Congregationalist minister and assumed he would be teetotal.

> It was a stinking hot Adelaide day, and I had been playing
> tennis for the ALP tennis club, and I was determined to say
> to him, 'Look, Mr Hawke – I don't know about you, but I've
> got to have a beer.' We met at the TAA counter and the first
> thing he said to me was, 'Jesus Christ! Where can we get
> a beer?

A friendship began immediately. From the start their relationship was familial – Combe took Hawke home to meet his parents
that very afternoon – and accepting. Bill Hayden recalled 'going
to Combe's home one day and Bob was there, coming out of
a bender, and he was in a terrible state. Combe had been that

kind of friend to him.' In the Labor movement, through a century of hard times and disappointments, 'mateship' and 'sticking by your mates' had developed the status of a blood bond.

But by 1983 Hawke had already on two occasions been angry with Combe, once justly, once not. The first was over the Iraqi Loans Affair, perhaps the worst folly of the dying Whitlam government when Combe, as secretary, and Whitlam, as leader, had agreed to borrow money for the ALP from the Ba'ath Socialist Party of Iraq, already then a heinous organisation given to torture, murder and public executions. Hawke, as president of the party, was beside himself with rage when he learned of the plan, but his handling of an ALP national executive meeting in 1976 that was held to decide how Combe and others be punished – expulsion from the party was a strongly suggested option – was deft and generous, leaving Combe deeply grateful to him. Then in early 1980, when Hawke (who had not yet become teetotal) was already set upon overthrowing Hayden, he berated Combe in a bar in front of others, including Stuart Hornery, the chairman of the building and development conglomerate Lend Lease, over his support for Hayden. It was an ugly scene but they got over it. It would be fair to say that Hawke doubted Combe's judgment.

Despite believing the Soviet First Secretary was a KGB agent, the Combes were confident it was nothing to worry about, although his very name may have given them pause to reflect. Meena was particularly well read and most certainly familiar with the classic novel of Soviet oppression *Darkness at Noon*, in which the unfortunate character under suspicion is entangled by a man called Ivanov. In a book she wrote about the affair when it was over she noted, 'we both knew that Ivanov was not dangerous'.

Sadly, they knew no such thing.

Not without reason is espionage known as the second-oldest profession: its lineage stretches to the fall of Troy and further back in the mists of prehistory. Over millennia the world's intelligence services have developed an assembly of sophisticated skills, but spy movies and books presented espionage as so whacky that nobody outside the loop took it seriously. In the early 1980s, there was little understanding of how a spy could, by patient cunning, turn an honest but humanly flawed citizen into a type of slave. It happens through grooming or 'cultivating' as it is termed. Combe was a superb target to cultivate: he knew everyone in the new government, knew their quirks and weaknesses, knew their staff members and their oddities, he was keen to make money, he loved to eat and drink. He was the perfect Trojan horse to penetrate the fortress of government. He needed no access to secret documents – that might or might not come later and almost certainly not from him. All he had to do was *talk*. Over dinner on the night before the election, he boasted of the access he enjoyed to the men who were about to become Labor ministers. He suggested that at their next meal together, Bill Hayden, the soon-to-be Foreign minister, and his wife, Dallas, should be invited along. He also revealed he thought the party owed him something substantial for his years of service, telling Ivanov, 'I'm entitled to something. I want my job for the boys: Ambassador, Moscow, will suit me – thank you very much.' He also mused on being appointed chairman of Qantas. And in what must have been Tchaikovsky to Russian ears, he spoke bitterly against the United States, saying he believed the CIA had destabilised the Whitlam government, and had gone unpunished for it. He wanted, he said, to 'really nail the Americans'.

Unconsidered by Combe but not, it seems, by Ivanov, there was a nest of scorpions in the house; ASIO, whose name in cable traffic for many years was SCORPION, had bugged the residence (as it had a number of other diplomatic buildings in Canberra, to the astonished, sometimes sour, approval of the new Labor ministers when they found out). It already knew Ivanov was from the KGB. Its job was to catch him seducing someone. On reading the transcript of Combe's conversation that night, the case officer monitoring Ivanov realised that ASIO had an exquisite dilemma: the organisation was about to trap a Soviet spy, its first since 1963 (a man named Skripov), but how would the new Labor government react to the news that a favoured son was being cultivated? Harvey Barnett, who had been an ASIS officer, now ran ASIO. He decided to keep listening and see what developed. Neither Hawke nor the Attorney-General, Gareth Evans, was to be told anything – yet.

Hawke and his staff were flat out planning the Summit, scheduled for the following month. 'I had been aghast at the way Fraser was setting Australian against Australian,' Hawke recalled.

> In the period after my first challenge to Hayden I started thinking deeply about what I could do to really change the country. I believed in the goodness of the Australian people, I believed they did not want to be attacking each other, and from those thoughts I got the idea of 'Reconciliation' in the campaign slogan and of turning this into something practical by calling a summit to bring representatives of all sections of society together, from the wealthiest to the poor.

In this he was following in the footsteps of Curtin, whose first great achievement was to reconcile a frightened, divided nation to the single purpose of fighting the war and saving the homeland from Japanese invasion.

Although the drought had broken, the misery of unemployment continued. Hawke's grand plan was that the Summit, besides giving practical effect to 'Reconciliation', would deal with the problem of unemployment *without* causing a new round of wage rises and inflation. His instrument for this was an 'Accord' with the trade union movement. In his chess game for the leadership, the Accord had been a winning gambit. The ACTU had refused to sign off on it until Hawke replaced Hayden as leader. Hawke then announced it during the election campaign.

While the Summit was Hawke's idea, the Accord was the brainchild of his former ACTU assistant, Ralph Willis, a quietly spoken, gentle, self-deprecating man of strong intelligence. Willis had entered parliament in 1972, experienced the rise and the crash of the Whitlam government and, as an economist, understood that the whole Australian industrial and tariff system was collapsing: from the end of World War II until 1973, with only a couple of ripples, there had been full employment, low inflation and steady economic growth, an environment that could, with relative ease, accommodate the uncoordinated and adversarial pursuit of wage claims and price rises. Those comfortable days were gone. When Hayden became leader, he had promoted Willis to shadow Treasurer and in that role Willis visited the UK, where the Callaghan Labor government had managed for two years to control wage rises through an arrangement with the Trades Union Council. But in the third year the government tried to keep wage rises down to 7 per cent and, as Willis described it,

> the TUC just walked away, went out in the field and got an increase of about 15 per cent which basically blew the Callaghan government out of office and ushered in Thatcher in 1979. I was there in '78 when this had all blown up and I had long talks to people like [Denis] Healey and others who had been involved in it, and it seemed to me that we could learn from their mistakes, because for a couple of years it had served them pretty well ... At home Labor's credibility on inflation was not good, we were tagged with the Big Spender line from the Whitlam days so we had to develop some sort of credibility that we could keep inflation down whilst growing the economy at a rapid rate ... I could talk easily with Bill Kelty [secretary of the ACTU] and Jan Marsh [the advocate] and Bob [still president], so we started doing some formal work then, but Bill Hayden was always uncomfortable and didn't trust the unions, didn't really have a rapport with unions ...

Hayden observed,

> Unionists have a narrower agenda than politicians. At Labor conferences the trade union people weren't much interested in anything other than industrial issues – but on those

they would fight like bloody tigers ... They're like a big family, they're looking after their members and they've got a whole lot of things to look after: industrial battles, medical problems, housing – they're expected to be half-baked priests in some ways.

Indeed, trade unionism performed the functions of social cohesion and defence of the group that are fundamental to religion.

Willis recalled, 'Bill never really wanted to push the Accord along. At the 1980 election we had a very generalised expression of some sort of agreement to co-operate, but nothing more than that.'

After the 1980 election when Hawke entered parliament, he moved into an office next to Willis, and they 'talked about the Accord all the time'. Gradually, its acorn started sprouting into the mighty oak it was to become: one of the grandest pieces of social and economic reform in Australian history.

The key negotiating team was Kelty, Marsh and Willis, with input from many sections of the union movement, especially the Left. Laurie Carmichael, the highly respected, wiry, fierce and fiercely intelligent Communist leader of the Metal Workers' Union, was a major influence. Carmichael, Willis said,

[insisted on] a decent industry policy. The unions were saying if it's okay for us to accept conditions on incomes, we want to talk about the *social* wage. We want to make sure a Labor government delivers on other areas that are in our interests – we want to see Medicare [a Whitlam initiative castrated by Fraser] reformed, we want educational reforms and social security changes. It became bigger than *Ben Hur* ... The context seems almost foreign now. Our economy at that time was replete with anti-competitive behaviour. We had high tariffs, which meant there was no competition from imported goods in lots of areas so people could charge what they liked. We had lots of anti-competitive arrangements internally in

Australia, we had regulations and controls everywhere ... In
that situation it was very easy for employers to cave in to wage
demands, push wages up and push prices up, creating inflationary take-off which would then be crunched by monetary
and fiscal policy, leading to unemployment ... It was a hopeless situation. I thought if we got into office we didn't want
to be blown out of it by inflationary take-off, crunch then
unemployment.

Willis, as shadow Treasurer, believed he would be Treasurer
in a Labor government led by Hawke. But, in what were to
be the final days of his leadership, Hayden decided to punish
Willis for his open support of Hawke by demoting him. In an
effort to shore up his support in Caucus, Hayden promoted Paul
Keating into Willis' place. Willis was deeply upset. Keating was
the brilliant young leader of the New South Wales Right and
had the might of the machine behind him. It was as putative
Treasurer, therefore, that Keating went to the polls, against the
experienced Liberal Treasurer, John Howard. Hawke was confident that after the election he could re-promote Willis and give
Keating some other portfolio. This confidence was misplaced:
before his government was sworn in, Hawke was to have a personal demonstration that the New South Wales machine was a
big family, too, and had its own religion, and would fight like a
bloody tiger for its tribe. With a prime minister from Victoria,
the second most prestigious job, Treasury, had to go to New
South Wales. Keating was to stay Treasurer, although at that
time he had scant knowledge of economics.

For his part, Keating was sceptical about the Summit, the
Accord, and his new job. He considered the Accord was very
underdone and it was up to him to cement it. 'I've been handed
the poisoned chalice, mate,' he remarked.[2]

While Hawke had made some speeches about an accord with
the trade unions during the election campaign, just how expansive it would be was too complex to explain. Hawke was certain the only way to gain understanding of its potential and to

win wide acceptance by rank-and-file unionists and employers (many of whom found the existing arrangements to their taste) was to inform them how dire the situation really was. He proposed to give to the Summit participants (representatives of government, business large and small, unions, the welfare sector and churches) all the relevant information the government had about Australia's economy. These were statistics that until that time had been mostly secret.

The public service was appalled.

Public servants did not like the sound of the Accord. Willis said,

> It was impure policy, an arrangement that went outside Treasury control, Finance control, the control of the Prime Minister and Cabinet department. The public service likes to control things and this was something they didn't understand, had no control over, no involvement in and no say in, and never really came to grips with. But they learned to live with it.

It was scandalous for many – public servants, politicians and journalists – that the Prime Minister had insisted the Summit be held in Parliament House, in the Chamber of the Representatives. Their reason for disdain? *It had never been done before.*

'There were,' Hawke recalled, 'many humorists, sceptics, agnostics and doomsayers – but few true believers.' Clyde Cameron, the former Whitlam Minister for Industrial Relations, wrote to him,

> Your economic conference will fail; the participants won't be able to deliver and will be addressing the record. If you can succeed in making a worthwhile compact with the unions, you'll go down in history as the greatest Australian Prime Minister ever.

The final flourish aside, Cameron's assessment was the general view: what was planned would turn into a vapid talk-fest.

The Summit opened on 11 April, ten days before the newly elected government and its equally new Opposition would take their seats in parliament. In his opening address, Hawke said that the minimum measure of the Summit's success should be,

> first, a heightened appreciation of the need to work constructively together to meet the great challenges now confronting our country; and second, an increased likelihood of all participants tailoring their expectations and claims upon the community's resources to the capacity of the economy ...

He continued,

> Australia can no longer afford to go down the path of confrontation and fragmentation which has embittered and disfigured so many aspects of the national life ... It is not only a question of the need for national reconciliation in this current economic crisis ... It is a question of the shape of the future of Australia.

The hand Hawke laid upon the wheel of history was pleasing to it: his Summit was a stunning success.

As Curtin in 1941 had set out to forge a national consensus to save the nation, so Hawke, after a decade of bitterness and eighty years of economic mediocrity, was re-civilising public life and founding a modern Australia.

In his opening speech to the Summit, the Prime Minister said that the participants needed to recognise they had a common goal, and therefore a common interest: an improvement of their standard of living due to real economic growth.

He had wondered to himself before the Summit how traditional foes, captains of industry and trade union leaders, would comport themselves when brought face to face, taking morning and afternoon teas together, lunches and dinners under the same roof. He recalled,

> It was fascinating to observe the 98 delegates ... time and again leading industrialists would take me aside and say, 'You know, Bob, this is the first time I've really talked to a trade union leader; they're not bad blokes.'

Trade unionists made the same discovery about captains of industry: they were not, after all, ogres, but responsible citizens. Hawke said, 'Those simple observations excited me because, after all, that was what the whole thing was about.' (Not every trade unionist was a convert: 'Stormy Normy' Gallagher, the burly ruffian who led the Builders Labourers' Federation, when asked by a reporter, 'Mr Gallagher, what did you think of the Summit?' replied, "I'm still tinkin'".' Ralph Willis, as Industrial Relations minister, was later to deregister Gallagher's union for illegal behaviour.)

On the Summit tide, a sea change in national life swept in. The managing director of BHP, John Prescott, in thanking Hawke some years later for the new approach he had brought to the steel industry in particular and to the economy generally said, 'In BHP we preferred it if our workers left their brains at the gate. Now, in this new atmosphere of industrial relations we realise that is absurd. They are, in a sense, our best resource.' The unions agreed to wage restraint. 'This took the employers somewhat by surprise ... but they also rose to the occasion,' Hawke wrote.

There were many practical spin-offs from the Summit, one of them being the shock of employers on recognising how disorganised, compared with the unions, they were. In response they formed the Business Council of Australia, to this day an important wheel in economic policy formation. Out of the Summit too, the Economic Planning and Advisory Council (EPAC) was established. This body, unprecedented in Australia, created a forum for co-operation between federal and state governments, business, unions, the rural sector and community groups. Its main role was to analyse medium- and long-term economic performance, and the factors that influence it. EPAC's secretariat proved so skilful in analysis that in 1985 it also became the secretariat for the Cabinet committee on long-term growth; it was later named the Structural Adjustment Committee.

Thanks to the Summit, for the first time since World War II the state premiers agreed to a joint communiqué on national economic policy. And from the time of the Summit onwards, the number of industrial disputes began to fall. It kept falling – to the point where Australia's international reputation of the 1960s and 1970s as an unreliable supplier and a poor bet for investment turned 180 degrees.

The ripple effect of the Summit's success was further demonstrated when other nations began copying it. First was New Zealand, in 1984. In March 1985 the new Canadian Prime Minister, Brian Mulroney, held a national economic conference, modelled on the Australian Summit, to which he invited Hawke as keynote speaker. In 1989 the new government of the Republic of Korea asked Australia to brief it on the Accord and in December 1992, President-elect Bill Clinton held an Australian-style summit in Washington. In Zurich, gnomes clapped their manicured hands. Bryan Kelman, the general manager of CSR, was a summiteer who travelled to Europe immediately afterwards for meetings with bankers in Frankfurt, Basel, Zurich, Brussels, Paris and London. 'The interest expressed was quite extraordinary,' he told Hawke. 'Many of the Swiss bankers volunteered the opinion that a strong and unified Labor government would be better placed than a Coalition government to guide Australia through the economic difficulties ahead.'

At international conferences into the twenty-first century, government and business leaders were still approaching Hawke for informal discussions about the Summit and the Accord.

Another positive outcome was that the young, green Treasurer, Paul Keating, 'embraced the Accord with the fervour of a convert'. If Keating loved something, he loved it madly. Hawke was delighted that his Treasurer had begun forming a close association with the ACTU and its secretary, Bill Kelty. Kelty was a well-trained economist and would help balance the views that the Department of Treasury, under its flint-faced conservative, John Stone, were seeking to hammer into their young minister's head.

The Summit's final communiqué was unanimous but for the abstention of Sir Joh Bjelke-Petersen, Premier of Queensland, a personally charming redneck who, like his state in those days, waltzed a couple of beats behind the music.

Within months the Accord bore its first fruit: the Conciliation and Arbitration Commission granted a wage rise that was only the size of the increase in the CPI, and the vast majority of unions made a written undertaking to forgo additional claims. In years to come – first in 1986, when the dollar collapsed, then during the boom of the late 1980s – real wages fell but nominal wages rose. Inflationary expectations had been swept away on the tide of change.[3] The new leader of the Opposition, Andrew Peacock, felt obliged to acknowledge the Summit's success (before launching into criticism of things he did not like about it), telling the House at the beginning of May,

> I think that all Australians have recognised that the National Economic Summit Conference was a valuable opportunity for Government Ministers, trade union leaders and the leaders of industry to exchange views, and I am certain that all participants found that that aspect of the Summit was of great value. I also acknowledge the many thoughtful, pertinent and useful contributions made at the Summit by a number of participants; in particular, some of the employers ...[4]

Hawke had time to savour his Summit triumph for just twenty-four hours. Unknown to the Labor Caucus, the news media and the public, the government had a crisis on its hands.

On the afternoon of 20 April the head of ASIO, Harvey Barnett, was granted his request for an urgent meeting with the Prime Minister 'on a matter of national security'. Barnett considered it so important he wanted to tell Hawke before he told his own minister, Gareth Evans (an action many in the Caucus deemed sinister when they heard of it). The Prime Minister and the head of ASIO had never met before but Hawke had little or none of the ALP's paranoia about ASIO and liked Barnett on first meeting. Barnett was a slim, refined, conservative man in his late fifties, his manner of upper-middle-class restraint offset by an open, velvety smile. He appeared, and was, a person deeply at peace within himself. Hawke was unaware of Barnett's spiritual life but recognised something about him that recalled his father's peacefulness. There was nothing tricky about Barnett, to Hawke's eye. A number of his ministers, large sections of the Caucus and, of course, the news media, thought otherwise. Barnett was a *spook*. To them this meant he was not a patriot but treacherous. Such was the temper of the times.

The only other person in the room that afternoon was the Prime Minister's principal private secretary, Graham Evans, permitted to be in attendance because he had a top-secret security clearance. Barnett told them about Combe and Ivanov. 'I was very surprised,' Hawke said. A couple of weeks earlier Combe had annoyed the Prime Minister when he had walked uninvited into his office behind the Chief Minister of the Northern Territory, a man with whom Combe had a business association. Hawke had considered Combe bumptious on that occasion. Barnett explained that since Combe's dinner with Ivanov there had been further contacts, and that Ivanov was showing skittish signs – as if he suspected that his house was bugged and he wanted Combe to shut up. The head of ASIO pointed out that Ivanov's next step with Combe would be to suggest they stop meeting in public and in his house – that is, to begin a clandestine relationship. If Combe were to agree he would be a lost man, literally and metaphorically. As Prime Minister, Hawke had two paramount responsibilities: first, to defend the nation; second, to defend the government. He found it distasteful that Combe was assuming entitlements thanks to his mates in government, and alarming that Combe felt so friendly towards the USSR, a country whose political system Hawke detested.

Combe, Hawke decided, was toxic. 'Here was a clear security risk,' he said. 'And I immediately thought of what it meant for the government.'

His government had not yet sat a single day in parliament – that would happen the next afternoon – but already a time bomb was ticking. There were two electoral death traps Labor had to avoid. One was mismanaging the economy, which Hawke believed his team would avoid; the other was security. Graham Evans said, 'It's probably impossible to think of anything that could have been more challenging early in the period of a Labor government.'

As Barnett talked, Hawke thought, 'If this blows, we'll only last one term.'

He would say later, 'The Tories have been the myth-makers of Australian politics: they created the myth that Labor was a bad economic manager, and weak on security.' Unfortunately, at that time there was a truckload of historical grist to the mythological mill. There was the insane reaction of the ALP's leader, Dr Evatt, to the Petrov Affair: in 1954 Evatt wrote to the Soviet Foreign minister, Vyacheslav Mikhailovich Molotov, asking Comrade Molotov if it were true there were Soviet spies in Australia. Molotov had, in his long career as an acolyte of Stalin, claimed the bombs he was dropping on Finland in World War II were actually 'food baskets for the starving Finns'. (The starving Finns promptly invented 'a drink to go with the food' that they named the Molotov cocktail, and threw at Soviet tanks.) Comrade Molotov wrote back to Dr Evatt, assuring him there were no Soviet spies in Australia. Evatt announced this news from Moscow to the Australian nation. Had he done so a few years later people would have asked each other what he was smoking. After Petrov, there were the party's anti-Vietnam War campaigns, which conservative governments used to assert Labor was an unreliable ally for the US and to suggest it was 'soft on Communism'. The Whitlam government follies of the 1970s and the widely believed and later confirmed fact that the party had been infiltrated by Communists added to the charge sheet. Being anti-war had been Labor's signature through the 1960s and 1970s and was still in the 1980s – although Australia, like the rest of the West, was in the midst of an undeclared but violent war, in which espionage and counter-espionage were on the front line.

As Barnett talked, what Hawke immediately understood was that the Opposition would have a weapon in parliament and through the press to beat his newborn government to pulp. He could imagine the headlines already: 'ALP Official Russian Spy!'

In 'Politics as a Vocation', Max Weber noted that a successful politician must have passion, a feeling of responsibility and a sense of proportion. He described 'the decisive psychological quality of the politician: his ability to let realities work upon him with inner concentration and calmness. Hence, his *distance* to things and men.' Within Hawke's warm and passionate nature, *his distance to things and men* had already formed. He asked Barnett what his options were. There were three: to counsel Combe quietly; to expel Ivanov quietly; or to expel Ivanov publicly. Hawke rejected the first out of hand, as he believed Combe, a member of the anti-ASIO wing of the party, would not respond positively and, anyway, to do so would be a security breach. The second he also rejected 'because it would leak'. They settled on the third option, plus bugging Combe's phone to monitor further contacts with Ivanov or other Russians, as there was the chance that Ivanov was not the only KGB officer in town, and he could hand over Combe's grooming to a colleague. Barnett assured Hawke before he left that nobody but ASIO, Hawke and Graham Evans knew of the situation.

In any circumstance, a prime minister's staff is important to the smooth functioning of government; in a crisis, it is critical. Hawke's principal private secretary, Graham Evans, ran the Prime Minister's office. He said later, 'It was a joy to come to work each day. Bob generated respect, trust and loyalty from his staff.'[5]

Evans had been a diplomat who had taken time out while in Washington to do postgraduate economic studies, later working in the Treasury. He was a calm, good-humoured, highly organised man of the finest type of public servant. He gave polite, thoughtful, frank advice. He and Hawke had sounded each other out in Washington and Canberra in 1982; when Hawke offered him the job, other senior men in the public service – Stone from Treasury, Sir Geoffrey Yeend from the Department of Prime Minister and Cabinet and Michael Cook, also a former diplomat and intelligence analyst who had been Fraser's principal private secretary, encouraged Evans to take it.

All three said they thought there were significant advantages having a public servant running the office, because it made the liaison a lot better. But in fact, Bob had already thought about that. It was clear that he had in mind the Whitlam experience: he said, 'You know, a lot of the issues the Whitlam government encountered were a consequence of not having as good a relationship with the public service as they could have had without compromising on their policies.' He welcomed the fact that I had a background in both economics and foreign policy.

Of Barnett's briefing, Evans recalled, 'My first reaction was great surprise, but my next was "Oh, my God. The buck stops with Bob and, to some degree what I say to him about whom he should talk to next."' 'Loose lips sink ships', as the saying goes. The problem was to decide on whom to bring into the loop.

Hawke called a meeting of the National and International Security Committee for that evening at which he laid out what had been discovered and called Barnett back in to brief the ministers and discuss expelling Ivanov. 'Hayden was apprehensive,' Hawke said. 'He wanted Ivanov out of the country, but quieter than quiet, without so much as a word to the Soviets. To Mick Young, this was a nonsensical idea.' Hayden recalled,

Bob was always a dramatist, he was in a great drama. He told us what had happened, and we were all shocked. And when we walked out I said to Mick Young, 'Why would Combe do that?' and he said, 'Just bloody greedy.' And I remember going home and sitting on the edge of the bed and telling Dallas. I was really upset.

But by the next morning, after another briefing from Barnett in the Prime Minister's office, Hayden came to the conclusion that Combe was 'just big-noting himself. He comes on so strongly – and he has nothing to offer.' Gareth Evans, too, was becoming doubtful. When he asked Barnett for the transcripts of Combe's dinner with Ivanov, Barnett refused to hand them over. His refusal was correct in terms of 'trade craft', since raw intelligence is notoriously difficult to interpret. Politically, his refusal was of questionable judgment. Barnett's agenda was security and the prestige of his organisation. He did not yet grasp the government's political agenda. And Combe, third leg of what had turned into a triangle, had his own pecuniary agenda backed by his network of mates in the party, the press and the Canberra lobbying business. From these three forces, a thunderhead of suspicion would explode.

The Australian Capital Territory, which consists of Canberra and some paddocks, in those days was a pampered enclave, living comfortably on federal largesse, a showpiece for national pride. Its roads were as smooth and as charcoal grey as a diplomat's cashmere suit. Its lawns were neatly clipped; its civic buildings, although lamentably unimaginative, were immaculately maintained. It was the best paid and most highly educated city in Australia and small enough for the citizens to be forever running into someone they knew at the shops or in a restaurant or cinema. Socially liberal, Canberra residents were allowed to possess small quantities of marijuana for personal use to be consumed in private. The national capital was also the Australian distribution hub for the pornography industry. It had the amenities of a quiet, high-minded university and foreign embassy city, which it was, and the mentality of a colonial outpost, with its expatriate pukka sahibs and memsahibs, its cliques, intrigues, storms in teacups, rules of behaviour, parties, clubs and affairs so numerous that Canberra hostesses were plagued with indecision when compiling dinner-party guest lists. Gossip ran from tongue to tongue as in a village. Parliament House was Gossip Central, for this was the place of work not only of politicians and their staffs, but also of the press gallery. Senior members of the gallery were the sahibs and memsahibs of Australian journalism and the most expatriate; as standard bearers of free speech they saluted a higher civilisation than the one they observed, that of the natives: the members of parliament. It was the role of the sahibs to keep the natives in line – and especially the wily new sultan, who had snatched the throne without any of them being tipped off in advance.

As the Combe–Ivanov Affair was to reveal, those making the transition from Opposition to government traverse a minefield. Unknown to any of his colleagues, a member of the National and International Security Committee had leaked. On 21 April, in a car park outside the 19th Hole Restaurant, he had confided to Eric Walsh, a former Whitlam press secretary, now a lobbyist, 'We're going to kick out a Russian.' The minister had gone on to warn that David Combe was involved with the Russian and that Walsh should be wary of doing business with Combe. He also disclosed that the deputy Prime Minister, Lionel Bowen, had expressed hatred for a third man, X, another person involved in the Russian trade.

The friend confided in X. But X, as it happened, was an ASIO informant. The minister's indiscretion would in due course find its way back to the ears of the Scorpion. And there, as the raw intelligence of a 'report of conversation', it would lie for months: a second time bomb for the Hawke government.

The next day, at lunch, the same minister told Rod Cameron, the ALP pollster, that the government was about to expel a Russian. Two hours later Bill Hayden announced Ivanov was *persona non grata* and would be leaving the country within days.

This was an exciting event for the media and the prestigious win for ASIO that Barnett wanted. He returned to his headquarters in Melbourne a happy man. His organisation, which 'in fact was *good*', according to Bill Hayden and others who had top-secret security clearances, was about to enjoy one of its very few public successes.

The most realistic of espionage writers, John le Carré, had one of his characters remark of political journalists 'they put out their tongues and fart and think they've invented democracy'.[6] On news of Ivanov's expulsion and rumours about Labor figures being involved, gusts of hot wind began blowing from both ends of the press gallery.

Meanwhile, following accepted precedent, the government gave Andrew Peacock a two-hour background briefing on the expulsion and Ivanov's relationship with Combe. Peacock gave his word that he would tell nobody about Combe's association with the spy.

On the evening Ivanov was publicly revealed as an enemy agent, David Combe had discovered from Rod Cameron, the ALP pollster, who heard it at lunch from the minister that day, 'that Ivanov was expelled because he was too close to people who had influence with the government'. Meena Blesing exclaimed to her husband, 'But that's you!'[7]

At that moment the Combes realised that their business, which depended upon David being *persona gratissima* with government, was in great danger.

A formal decision to blackball Combe was only days away but already Parliament House, the bars around town and the Journalists' Club were hives of rumour and paranoia. There was bitter division in Hawke's own office, between those who thought the Prime Minister had acted correctly and those who hated ASIO as something both impure and bumbling, and who felt Combe was being badly treated. Bob Hogg, Hawke's political adviser from the Victorian Left, was accused by ASIO of having breakfast with Combe after the Prime Minister had expressly told him not to. Hogg vehemently denied the accusation when he discovered what ASIO had reported, but until then he recalled, 'It was as if I had plague. I walked into the office and people wouldn't speak to me. I didn't know why.'

A problem confronting the Prime Minister's office, as Graham Evans explained,

[was that] there was no recognised process to follow … at the time we had to move forward step by step in how people were brought in, and how [giving secret information] was managed. There was no precedent, no standing process that we could turn to. Bob and I had been having conversations about 'How on earth do we manage this issue? We can't let David Combe go on talking to ministers because down the line someone will say, "Why did you let him do that, knowing what we'd been told by ASIO?"' On the other hand, Bob couldn't go in and say to the ministers, 'You're not to have anything to do with Combe, because of this.' That would have been a breach of national security. So he had to stop one without doing the other. Bob had been thinking about the risks of having heaps of lobbyists dealing with the government and how to get around it, and there had been some general discussions, but nothing had been done.

John Dawkins, the new Minister for Finance, had also been pondering what to do about lobbyists, and may have discussed the problem with Hawke. Certainly, he had a constructive suggestion.

The night before the Cabinet meeting in Adelaide at which Hawke was scheduled to inform the rest of Cabinet about Combe, Graham Evans was getting ready for bed when the Prime Minister, dressed in pyjamas, knocked on his door and said, 'We need to resolve this issue.' Evans, also pyjama-clad, recalled,

And it was at that point that we came up with the idea of a register of lobbyists and that ministers were not to engage in the use of lobbyists until the rules of engagement had been worked out, and a register had been established.

It was one in the morning by the time they said good night. Exactly how events unfolded is not clear, but later that day in the Cabinet, Dawkins proposed a register of lobbyists, which his colleagues endorsed. Everyone was henceforth constrained from dealing with *any* lobbyist.

Evans added, 'It would have happened at some point anyway, but I was the only person who knew it was because of Combe.' The Cabinet meeting was on 26 April.

Combe recalled,

> By 29 April I knew I was under surveillance, because Richard Farmer [a former journalist and ALP press officer] and the other guy who was coming into partnership with me [David Butler] came round to tell me [they would not be joining the business]. It was pissing with rain and they wouldn't come inside the house. So they obviously believed it was bugged ... they didn't say that, but I just knew.

The Prime Minister, in a fish restaurant in Adelaide, had himself told both Farmer and Butler to avoid Combe. Somehow the conversation leaked and was gleefully reported in the press as a breach of national security by the Prime Minister.

Soon after the visit from Farmer and Butler, a letter arrived from Combe's old friend, John Button, now Minister for Industry, which said:

> Dear Mr Combe
>
> As you will undoubtedly appreciate my ministerial duties make it impossible for me to discuss with you the business of your client.
>
> Yours sincerely
> John M. Button[8]

By now Caucus was full of rumours. Hayden supporters, who would never forgive the Prime Minister for overthrowing their leader, were lining up against Hawke. In the Prime Minister's office, and the Cabinet, there were suspicions that Combe had been tipped off by an insider. Distrust was pervasive.

On the day he received Button's letter, David Combe, 'in a highly emotional state' according to his wife, had dinner with his friend, Brian Toohey, for many years an anti-ASIO crusader and also editor of the *National Times*. Combe poured out his heart to Toohey, begging him, Toohey said, to write his story. It was, as Combe saw it, one of betrayal of himself and dark right-wing forces taking over the government. A number of teasing, Delphic stories appeared in the *National Times*, whetting the appetite of its leftish intelligentsia readership for more.

On 10 May the first bomb exploded. In the House of Representatives, Ian Sinclair, deputy leader of the National Party, asked if Hawke had instructed members of the government 'to dissociate themselves from the former secretary to the Federal Australian Labor Party, Mr David Combe? If so, why?' Hawke answered 'that in respect of any lobbying activity there is to be no association', and immediately asked that further questions be put on notice. He was furious and had a strong suspicion about who had given Sinclair his information: Andrew Peacock.

'RUSSIAN SPY! LABOR OFFICIAL NAMED' was the front page of the *Daily Mirror* that afternoon. The subheading read 'ASIO Briefs Hawke'.

From the tenor of Sinclair's question and two other questions in parliament that day, the government was convinced that Peacock *was* Sinclair's informant and that the Opposition was bent on a strategy of attacking Labor's 'weak spot', just as Hawke had feared.

In politics and in certain sections of the news media, bad faith is a given: attacks are made in full knowledge they are baseless. It was suggested to Hawke that Mick Young, his closest friend on the National and International Security Committee and one of his closest friends in the party, had leaked. Hawke called Young in, asked him if he had been indiscreet, and Young assured the Prime Minister that all he had done was mention to Rod Cameron that a Russian would be expelled in a couple of hours. Hawke took him at his word, and in parliament vigorously defended Young, noting

> that from the moment he made that comment at about 12.30 to the point at which the Minister of Foreign Affairs announced, about two hours later, the expulsion of Mr Ivanov, Mr Cameron had been with him [Young] at all times.

He went on to add that Young had 'in all other respects acted ... with honour and propriety'.

But Young had lied to Hawke; as a result, the Prime Minister had just misled the parliament. Why did Young lie? Presumably from fear. It was the first indication that the most popular man in the party, the jester whose wit had buoyed up Caucus spirits during the long, grim years of Opposition, had not yet made the psychological adjustment to being in government.

On 11 May, the day after the first public explosion, Gareth Evans called in David Combe, read his remarks to Ivanov to him, asked him to acknowledge that he had blotted his copybook so badly he would just have to realise he was no longer acceptable as a lobbyist, to put up and to shut up. The government would make no more comments; Combe was to make no more comments.

Combe agreed.

But within hours he changed his mind, urged to do so by journalists. They persuaded him he had been betrayed and abandoned by his erstwhile mates, and he should resist. 'PM faces backbench revolt over Combe', the *Australian* reported on its front page next morning; there was a 'Flood of support from ALP' to Combe. The electronic media was running hot with the Combe story. As Bob Hogg, a close friend of Combe's, remarked, 'They were willing to fight to the last drop of David's blood.' Combe's case was that the Cabinet, and the Prime Minister in particular, had trampled his civil liberties. The sahibs and memsahibs of the gallery seethed with indignation on his behalf and with the excitement of a great story. They could see themselves giving that sultan a good flogging.

On the same day as Combe was asked, and agreed, to remain silent, Hawke tried to calm the situation with a statement to the House setting out the reasons for the government's decisions and defending it against the charge already being made, that individual civil liberties – Combe's – had been trampled. He concluded,

> It is perhaps inevitable that there will always be elements of doubt and suspicion in the minds of all Australians in circumstances where there can be less than full disclosure of information. This is a responsibility a government must accept, and for my part I accept it. But I trust this statement will put to rest the uncertainty of the last few days. A climate of innuendo and deceit is not one which my government will be guilty of creating or permitting to flourish. Finally ... in no way will my government be compromised when matters of our national security are at stake.

But the storm gathered force.

Combe was winning the battle for public sympathy. Less than a week after Hawke made his statement to the House, hoping to bring calm, the atmosphere grew so hostile that the Prime Minister announced a Royal Commission. Michael McHugh of the Sydney bar, husband of a Labor backbencher, Jeanette McHugh, would represent the government, with Neil Young, from Melbourne, as his junior.

McHugh recalled,

> Combe was very clever. He was running his case in the press. He was obviously in daily contact with the press, probably at the Journalists' Club. Richard Carleton was very pro-Combe, the press generally were very supportive of Combe. And that persisted for a long period of time ... I was sort of running

the case as just an ordinary, straight legal proceeding. But one day Jeanette said to me, 'You think this is just another court case. This is really an extension of a parliamentary debate.' And that really woke me up.

The barrister suddenly understood the politics. McHugh now realised the government's life depended on Mr Justice Hope, the Royal Commissioner, finding that Hawke and the National and International Security Committee had acted correctly in expelling Ivanov and in blackballing Combe as a lobbyist.

McHugh said, 'The government had not been shown the transcript of the tapes [of Combe's conversation with Ivanov] until weeks after Harvey Barnett first called on Hawke. Barnett had only given them a summary.' When McHugh and Neil Young read the transcripts they were taken aback: they had a very weak case to argue.

Such was the hysterical farrago that by now it was assumed and being asserted in the news media that Combe was suspected of espionage. ASIO and the National and International Security Committee suspected him of no such thing: the very idea was absurd. But that was the public perception, and that was what now had to be legally tested in the Royal Commission. McHugh asked for a meeting with the Prime Minister, at which Gareth Evans, Mick Young and Sir Geoffrey Yeend (the departmental head of Prime Minister and Cabinet) were also present. McHugh asked that the government and ASIO be separately represented,

I've always remembered Hawke's decisiveness about this. Gareth Evans wanted a government counsel to control the case for the whole government. But I could see big problems, a conflict of interest between ASIO and the government. In the end, ASIO might have to wear the blame from the government's point of view. I didn't want to be in a position where [I was representing both parties]. I would have a conflict of interest. And Bob said to me, 'Is it your professional judgment that ASIO be separately represented?' and I said,

'Yes.' And he said, 'Well, it will be' – and Evans didn't seem to like that. It was obvious from his face. But it turned out to be the right thing. There were a number of reasons. First, I realised that there were going to be two climaxes to the case: one would be the cross-examination of Bob, if he was called, which I thought was only a remote possibility, but obviously, the cross-examination of Combe was going to be a great climax. And although this is not a legal consideration – good lawyers take into account things outside the strictly legal application – I thought the government was going to have big trouble within the Labor Party itself if their counsel was the one who did the major cross-examination of Combe. So it would suit the government's purpose, I thought, to have ASIO's counsel do the major cross-examination of Combe.

Stephen Charles, QC, was appointed to represent ASIO. In McHugh's opinion ASIO, by not showing the transcripts to the government immediately, 'had really made a bad mistake and the government was going to have to wear it'.

The Royal Commission got down to business on 14 June in a frenzy of publicity. Headlines of the time read: 'I Have Been Destroyed: Combe Speaks Out'; 'Labor In Revolt Over Bugging'; 'I'm No Spy'; 'David Combe, Sacrificial Lamb'; 'Your Dad's A Spy'. The effect on Combe's family was appalling – at the time and for years to come.

Because much of the evidence being put to the Commission was confidential or secret, the hearings were frequently in camera, for hours or even days at a stretch. David Marr, whose book *The Ivanov Trail*, is authoritative, wrote, 'Like a great whale, the royal commission surfaced briefly from time to time only to descend once more beneath the waves where it remained almost all through July.'[9] Combe was still winning the sympathy war.

In the middle of July, the second bomb exploded. Jovial Mick Young, the man considered the heart and soul of the Labor Party, one of the funniest men who ever pulled a laugh in the

Caucus or the House of Representatives, the one you could rely on to restore good humour in the most tense situation ... *Mick*, Hawke's mate of twenty years, his drinking buddy who went blind man when women appeared in Hawke's hotel rooms, was unmasked as the leaker.

It was the other Mr Young, Neil, McHugh's junior, who was doing the legwork for the case, reading ASIO documents and conducting his own interviews, who found him out. Neil Young asked to see Hawke and laid out the facts. Hawke was devastated.

'I had asked Mick a question [on 10 May] and he'd looked me in the eye and lied,' he said.

Sir Geoffrey Yeend was called in, then hurried out of the office to get a copy of the *Crimes Act*. Yeend, Hawke and Graham Evans pored over the Act. It was obvious Young had breached section 79(3), for which the penalty is two years jail. There is always a personal price to pay for leadership: Hawke knew what had to happen next. 'It was the hardest thing I ever had to do in politics,' he said.

That afternoon he called Neil Young back to his office. Neil Young had with him a record of what Mick Young had said, to whom, when and where. Hawke asked Neil Young to stay in the room and called in Mick Young. Neil Young recalled,

> Bob asked Mick Young whether he'd had a conversation with Eric Walsh [lobbyist and former press secretary to Whitlam] and what he had told him. And Mick told Hawke exactly what he'd told me [earlier]. Didn't beat around the bush. He was quite frank and candid, and then Mick said he'd been considering his position and he thought he should resign from Cabinet. And my recollection is that Hawke did not ask for his resignation but Young said he'd been thinking about his position and he'd made that decision. It was a very professional and amicable discussion. I don't remember Bob being upset or angry at any point. The conversation was very professionally handled by Hawke and there was a very professional response, no nonsense, no bones about it, by Mick

Young. The whole conversation would have taken probably fifteen minutes.

The sangfroid of the politicians in the presence of the young lawyer is remarkable, because both were dying inside. Mateship was the highest value in life for Young. He had just reached the pinnacle of his career, had been a minister for only six weeks – and his mate, Bob, had not just let him fall but would have pushed him had he not jumped. Like Shakespeare's rupture between Falstaff and Prince Hal, it was a tragedy unique to politics.

McHugh, more worldly than his junior assistant and more familiar with Hawke, recalled: 'Bob was very distressed about it all – whether it was because of his friendship with Mick, or whether it was the problems it was going to create for the government. He was certainly shaken by it.' In Caucus, Young's resignation caused uproar. Hawke was blamed for it.

Meena Blesing wrote,

[Young's] resignation ... caused great shock waves in the Government, the press and the labor movement. Young was seen as a sacrificial lamb or goat – a John the Baptist – in this murky affair and it was feared that more heads would roll. There was talk of more Ministers being involved and it was all publicly a rather frightening and hush-hush affair.[10]

Young resigned on a Friday. Over the weekend Peacock, knowing how loved within the party Mick Young was, accused Hawke of 'hiding behind the facade of a Royal Commission' in the Young affair, asserting Hawke had 'sacked' Young.

Within a week the *Australian* published an editorial asking, 'Is this the way to run a country?' Hawke was under attack from every side. McHugh, who had thought to bring him into the witness box, if at all, as last of the ministers, decided, 'things were going too badly in the press and it was important that the Prime Minister come in first ... I thought if Bob Hawke made a very impressive performance then the whole atmosphere would change.'

The national media were in a frenzy of excitement when it became known Hawke would be going into the box. This was the moment when the sultan would get his flogging.

Hawke recalled, 'When I walked into the room to give evidence you could have cut the air with a knife.'

McHugh said,

It was one of the best tactical decisions I ever made in any formal case, because Hawke was a superb witness. There's no doubt about it. And that was really the end of Combe. At the end of the day [Hawke spent almost three days in the witness box] it was all over. After his performance there was no way that Combe was going to succeed.

David Marr, the most pukka of the press sahibs, a trained lawyer and no fan of the Prime Minister, wrote,

No one present had seen a prime minister in the witness box before ... Hawke here was facing professionals, hired guns of the Bar. But he was at home. Hawke had spent more of his career in the roughhouse of arbitration tribunals than he had in parliament. The forum of the royal commission suited him perfectly ... [he] had drilled himself superbly for the occasion and had the facts, down to tiny details, at his fingertips ... Hawke was an exceptional witness ... he could always see the question coming, and chose at times to answer a slightly different question.[11]

Cross-examination is one of civilisation's darker arts, but Hawke understood it. Poor David Combe did not.

McHugh recalled,

I felt very sorry for Combe and the position he was in, and I didn't like the job of cross-examining him, however I was going to have to do it. But when he was giving his evidence he actually volunteered this statement about Bob getting $1500 for some speaking engagement, and I thought to myself, 'You bastard!' There was no need to say that. It was an irrelevance, it had nothing to do with the Royal Commission; it was just saying that Bob was greedy and charging money and it wouldn't go down well with the hoi polloi in the Labor Party. My mood changed from sympathy to neutral. It steeled me, and put me in a better mood to cross-examine him.

Combe's volunteered information, inaccurate as to the sum (which Hawke had declared and on which he had paid tax), did indeed have the effect Combe had anticipated: there was more anger in the party and the press, and questions in parliament against which Hawke had to defend himself. But Combe, having moved from a position of being unable to win, had, by raising the combative spirit of a skilled cross-examiner, assured himself of a horrible defeat. He spent eleven days in the witness box and left it a shattered man. His wife noted in her diary,

> he had been forced into agreeing … that he was indiscreet, self-aggrandising, greedy; he wanted to get rich. He had practically concurred with the whole ASIO argument in his efforts to go along with [ASIO's counsel] in the vain hope he could still clear himself.

Their marriage broke up; Combe fell into a slough of despond. 'I was deeply depressed during the case,' he recalled years later.

> I felt betrayed by the party and by people I'd known for years. The media was camped on the front lawn and you know, you'd put on a happy face, but feeling like shit. But that's how I was raised: stiff upper lip.

In the first week of December 1983, the Royal Commission's report exonerated the government of all its presumed malfeasances and found that David Combe's relationship with Ivanov had 'serious implication for national security'. It found that there was no further reason to blackball Combe's lobbying, but it also found that Mick Young had breached the *Crimes Act*. The Attorney-General, Gareth Evans, recommended Young not be charged. There was a storm of abuse in parliament – 'a stench about this government, a stench of dishonesty, a stench of duplicity, a stench of downright deceit, subterfuge and cover up', said Andrew Peacock. He was attacking the Prime Minister especially over Mick Young, whom, having taken his punishment, Hawke proposed should now return to the ministry. The wound to their relationship had not healed and never would completely, but Hawke, who so shrank from hurting vulnerable people that he could be emotionally timid himself, was doing all he could for Young. He defended him in parliament, but he was at a psychological disadvantage because he was traumatised about sacrificing Young in the first place. His speech was hot but off-key. Hawke was not and never would rise to become a great parliamentary speaker. It was the young Treasurer, Paul Keating, who had spent all year immersed in economics and had played no part in the spy drama, who strode into the fray and skewered the Opposition. Keating turned the attack back onto Peacock with the vehement contempt for which he was to become adored in the Party and loathed in the Opposition. Peacock, he said,

> could not rise above his own opportunism or his incapacity to lead. He made a public issue of the matter ... The Opposition [took] a decision to drag David Combe's name into the public arena. That is why there is a Royal Commission report. There would have been no Royal Commission, no report and no briefing of Mr Combe ... had the leader of the Opposition not breached the commitment he gave ... [at the security briefing] to the Prime Minister ... the Government did everything to protect Mr Combe's name. It was only after exposure by ... Jumping Jack Flash from the National Party ... [Ian Sinclair]

The Treasurer went on to refer to Peacock as 'slinking' and 'crawling'; he raised the Opposition leader's past embarrassments over his wife's behaviour and his resignation as Minister for the Army in the Fraser government.

Mr Justice Hope had exonerated the government; Keating beat the Opposition into mush.

John Dawkins, both hard-nosed and soft-hearted, had been troubled by Combe's plight but had no way to help him – until the end of 1985, when as Minister for Trade, he offered Combe a job abroad. In December 1985 David Combe accepted the post of trade commissioner to Canada. Combe's broken marriage had repaired, and his wife and four sons accompanied him. He had, at last, his 'job for the boys'.

TWENTY-ONE

WHILE THE ROYAL COMMISSION into the Combe–
Ivanov Affair was making its inquiries, Australia
became, on 26 September 1983, the first country to
beat the United States for the most prestigious yachting prize
in the world, the America's Cup. For most of its 132-year history, the race series had been a refined addiction of American,
British and European multimillionaires, virtually unheard-of by
the Australian public. But in the early 1960s, Sir Frank Packer,
the Sydney press baron, became an addict himself. He publicised
the sport in his newspapers and magazines and by 1983 the race
had captured the public's imagination. Australians were proudly
supportive of the national boat, *Australia II*, which needed to
beat yachts from the UK, Canada, Italy and France to become
the official challenger. There was a renewed sense of pride in
Australian abilities and potential.

The final series of races was held off the east coast of the
United States and when it seemed that Australia had a chance of
winning, hundreds of thousands of people from Sydney to Perth,
from Darwin to Hobart, stayed up most of the night to watch
a live telecast. Serendipitously, Cabinet was scheduled months
earlier to meet in Perth on what turned out to be the day after
the last race. Hawke spent all night watching the decider in his
hotel room and later that morning went to the Royal Perth Yacht
Club where, at the request of members from the club, he donned
a jacket of red, white and blue, with *Australia II* and the Union
Jack printed all over it. Photographs and television footage of
the Prime Minister in the flamboyant jacket, cheering wildly,

flashed across the country. 'I'll wear it to the next Cabinet meeting!' Hawke said. When a journalist asked if he feared people might be sacked for taking a day off work because they were tired and hung-over, Hawke responded: 'Any employer who sacks an employee for not turning up to work today is a *bum*!' There was sanctimonious tut-tutting from the usual suspects, but the electorate at large was delighted. More than three and a half decades later, people who had been children at the time would recall being thrilled by the Prime Minister's naughtiness. Hawke's star continued its rise. 'He bestrides us like a Colossus,' a public servant noted at the time.

When parliament closed on 6 December, with the Hope Royal Commission successfully concluded, Hawke gathered a couple of his economic advisers together to focus their full attention on something much more daring than a sickie.

When the Labor Party won office, a newspaper headline had asked, 'Will Hawke Cast the First Stone?' It was a reference to John Stone, the permanent secretary of the Department of Treasury, whom Hawke had known and disliked since their school days at Perth Modern. The feeling was mutual. Stone was a highly intelligent, fierce right-winger with a dominating manner. Senior bureaucrats are selected after rigorous academic exams – Stone was a Rhodes scholar – and are experienced in bureaucratic infighting. But no bureaucrat can stand up to the aggression, developed over decades of training in the struggle for power, that attends a political leader. Both sides know this; politicians often see bureaucrats as employing the weapon of the weak – manipulation – and can be apprehensive of their nimble manoeuvres. They can also be driven half-mad by bureaucratic passive defiance. Chairman Mao, it is said, launched the Cultural Revolution in 1966 in a frenzy of frustration with his own mandarins' refusal to implement reforms. (The Chinese mandarins, it should be noted, understood economics, while the Chairman did not.) John Stone's overt aggression made him an unusually scary mandarin. A senior government economist recalled,

Graham Evans and I were having a leak in the urinal at
Parliament House, right at the end of the Summit, saying
to each other how good it had been and what a good base it
had laid for policy things we wanted to do, and a gruff voice
yelled out from behind us, 'You blokes should be ashamed of
yourselves!' It was John Stone.

For Labor, Stone was a Number One Class Enemy.

Hawke, having long reflected on how important the public
service was to effective government, decided to trust Stone –
if not his political judgment, at least his honour and integrity.
Being incorruptible and a guardian against corruption, being
truthful and objective no matter the circumstances – in short,
having honour – is to good public servants what a fighting spirit
is to good politicians. Hawke believed that Stone, whom he
described as 'a very good technical economist' was honourable,
that he would serve a Labor government as diligently as a conservative one. The Caucus, with an indrawn breath, accepted
his decision on Stone. The public service greeted news that he
would remain head of Treasury with delight: to them it demonstrated that the new government had learned from past mistakes. For his part, Hawke was completely confident he had the
means of keeping Stone's headstrong and domineering nature
in check. Not only was he himself more economically educated
than any former Australian prime minister, he had on his staff
an economist whose intellect he found exhilarating. The Prime
Minister enjoyed his conversation above all others – loved his
mind and liked him physically: his tall, virile physique – he was
a talented Australian Rules footballer – his candid light brown
gaze, his frequent laughter that a wide gap between his two front
teeth made as engaging as a happy child's. He sported a magnificent, almost Viking, beard. He was Dr (later Professor) Ross
Garnaut. Garnaut, too, had attended Perth Modern; he had
been the school captain. As a seventeen year old, in 1964, he had
remarked to Kim Beazley Senior that Hawke would make a good
future prime minister. Beazley Snr corrected the boy: after the

usual parliamentary apprenticeship (five to seven years), Hawke would make a good Minister for Labour.

Hawke had met Garnaut in New Guinea in 1966 when he had been invited to lend his talents to an industrial dispute that became known as the local officers' wage case. Garnaut, an ANU postgraduate student, was in Port Moresby doing a research job in the vacation. Garnaut said,

> The next and more substantial contact was when Bob was working on the Crawford Study Group for Structural Adjustment, in the late 1970s, and John Crawford used to bring me along at lunchtime to meet people, and I had a few yarns to Bob then. He was very much engaged in the ideas that both Crawford and I were bringing before the committee ... [ideas] on the positive opportunity in Asia for Australia.

There had been a tendency in public policy discussion to see the beginnings of rapid growth in East Asia as being an economic threat to Australia, but Garnaut presented an alternative perspective that Hawke found both attractive and persuasive. Garnaut's generation of students at the ANU viewed the deeper engagement of Australia in Asia as a change that had to come. The key issues for students interested in policy in the late 1960s involved undoing the historical mistakes Australia had made in relation to race: the treatment of Indigenous people, the White Australia policy, apartheid in South Africa, and a fearful approach to Asia. These were all in accord with Hawke's personal views, pursued through the trade union movement. The same issues led Garnaut to study trade. His PhD thesis had been on Australian trade with South-East Asia; trade issues had been the whole of his professional life.

Of the economy – as it was when Hawke took over – Garnaut said, 'We'd made a historic mess.' Protectionism, once such a nice idea, had become counter-productive. Like a lot of young Australians, Garnaut had been excited by the election of the Whitlam government and gratified with what Whitlam did for

Australian foreign policy. But he was deeply disappointed by Whitlam's mismanagement of the economy. 'I spent a fair bit of time thinking, and some time writing, about what needed to be done about our macroeconomic situation,' he said.

> It always included a need to open up more in the financial sector and in trade, and it always included a need for more budget discipline, a lot more care in what we spent money on, and always included the need to have a more flexible wage and industrial relations structure, supported by a social democratic budget. But I felt fairly pessimistic that Australia would ever do anything about it.

Fraser was always enlightened on racial issues and far ahead of his party in this area, but he had set back the economic debate and he and his Treasurer, John Howard, had run an undisciplined budget process. Early in the 1983 election campaign Garnaut wrote to both Hawke and Keating about the likely problems that would emerge in the regulated exchange rate system, quoting the enormous flight of capital that had occurred in the Mitterand government (elected a few months earlier in France), and the destabilising capital flows in Sweden after its new government's announcements of social democratic programs. In Australia, at that time, each month a note would be hand delivered to the prime minister, telling him what the secretary of the Treasury, the governor of the Reserve Bank and the main economist in the Department of Prime Minister and Cabinet had decided the exchange rate of the Australian dollar was to be. 'The focus required on this area of policy was quite ridiculous,' Garnaut said. The antiquated practice had also created a competition in the business community for outguessing the government officials, thus causing speculative capital flows.

In his letters to the putative Prime Minister and Treasurer, Garnaut also said that an anticipatory devaluation at the very start of the government would probably be necessary. It would need to be supported by a high degree of wage restraint to ensure that the inflationary effects of the devaluation did not pass through into the cost structure of the economy. 'I thought there was a risk of a lot of destabilising capital flows at the time of the formation of the new government. Now, as it happened, that capital outflow began during the campaign.'

When Hawke and Keating met on the Monday after the election, a feeling of crisis had already developed among bankers and the business community. The new Prime Minister and Treasurer decided to devalue the currency by the amount that Garnaut had suggested: 10 per cent.

A day or so later Graham Evans rang Garnaut to ask him to come over for a chat with the Prime Minister. They had a long conversation on the issues facing the new government, at the end of which Hawke asked,

Is there anything I've been saying, or in our program, that would make you uneasy about taking on the role as my economic adviser? You don't have to worry about protection: I know your views on that, and we'll get there, but not until we've got employment moving in the right direction. We have to do that first.

Garnaut recalled,

I said, 'Well, I'm pretty uneasy about the whole macro-economic framework that you've been elected on – this big fiscal expansion. Malcolm [Fraser] has already fired up the Budget so much that before long public expenditure will be putting a lot of pressure on things, and if you put in place the whole of your existing expenditure program on top of that, you'll blow the head off the place.' Hawke replied cryptically, 'You don't need to worry about us doing that.'

It was only days since Stone had given him the note warning that Labor was heir to a deficit, kept secret by the Liberals during the campaign, of $9.6 billion. Privately, Hawke had already decided to jettison most of the spending promises in Labor's platform. But ditching election promises was a matter of great delicacy, with ministers, in the party and in the electorate, which he intended to reveal only as necessary.

Garnaut said, 'So we agreed there were no inhibitions to my taking on the role as his adviser.' Hawke would describe him later as 'the co-architect' of the government's landmark economic reforms. The Prime Minister's other economic adviser was the very able and influential Ed Visbord from the Department of Prime Minister and Cabinet.

Garnaut and Visbord were set to work immediately on ways of reducing the huge projected deficit and Garnaut spent Easter 1983 at the Hawkes' house in Sandringham, where he and the Prime Minister worked together from early morning to midnight over several days on what turned out to be the government's first budget statement, delivered in May. Their only interruptions were for meetings with a succession of state premiers.

In his initial letters to Hawke and Keating, Garnaut had raised the issue of the exchange rate system. It sounds Dickensian these days, and it already was in 1983. From early in the year discussions began on how to reform the antiquated, dysfunctional system for determining the exchange rate. 'In the end the only change that would clean it up was a floating of the dollar and a lessening of exchange controls,' Garnaut said.

But this could not be achieved without first psychologically preparing the business community. In May 1983 when discussion began in earnest, floating the dollar was not seen as urgent. In the second half of the year, there were larger speculative capital inflows, and they continued to grow. Speculative investment is destabilising, and these ever-greater inflows, attracted by the artificial exchange rate, caused things to come to a head in October. There was a meeting in Hawke's office with Keating and Stone. Stone was against a float on principle, for the cogent reason that once the currency floated, Treasury would lose control over monetary policy. Garnaut recalled,

Hawke in the prime ministerial plane during the 1987 election campaign.

Hawke addressing the troops on the campaign trail.

Hazel and Bob with the Governor-General, Sir Ninian Stephen, his wife, Valery, the Queen and Prince Philip during the royal visit in Australia's Bicentennial year, 1988.

The opening of the new Parliament House, Canberra, in 1988 had a special significance – 61 years earlier the Queen's father had opened the first 'temporary' Parliament House.

With Princess Diana, Canberra, 1983.

With Pope John Paul II
during the papal visit to
Australia, Perth, 1986.

From left to right: Peter Barron, Graham Evans, Sir Robert Cotton, Hawke, Neil McInnes, Ross Garnaut and Tim McDonald at the White House with Vice President George Bush, President Ronald Reagan and Secretary of State George Shultz, Washington DC, February 1985.

Commonwealth Heads of Government review meeting regarding South Africa, London, August 1986. Front row (left to right): Margaret Thatcher, Lynden Pindling, Kenneth Kaunda. Back row (left to right): Rajiv Gandhi, Brian Mulroney, Shridath S. Ramphal, Hawke, Robert Mugabe.

Richard Woolcott (bottom left) and Craig Emerson (top right) were among those present with Hawke at a lunch hosted by President Mitterand, Palais de l'Elysée, Paris, June 1989.

With Margaret Thatcher at the Commonwealth Heads of Government Meeting, Vancouver, 1987.

At the White House with President Ronald Reagan, February 1985.

Hazel Hawke with Nancy Reagan.

With President George Bush, Barbara Bush and Hazel.

Hawke with President George Bush, Barbara Bush and Hazel at the US Embassy,
Canberra, January 1992.

With Benazir Bhutto, Prime Minister of Pakistan, 1989.

With Rajiv Gandhi in
New Delhi, 1989.

Hawke welcoming Nelson Mandela to Canberra, October 1990.

With German Chancellor Helmut Kohl, Bonn 1991.

At Tiananmen Square on a state visit to China in 1984.

Hawke and visiting General Secretary of the Chinese Communist Party, Hu Yaobang, 1985.

Hawke with President Jiang Zemin, Beijing, October 1993.

With Bill Clinton, watching the President's Cup golf competition.

Hawke with Israeli President Chaim Herzog and Prime Minister Yitzhak Shamir, 1987.

Jacques Cousteau and Hawke joined forces in 1989 to have Antarctica declared
'A Nature Reserve – Land of Science'.

With actor Paul Eddington, who played the British PM in the political satire *Yes Minister*, 1986.

Meeting the Queen Mother in London, 1983.

Hawke with Singaporean Prime Minister Lee Kuan Yew, 1986.

With Sheikh Khalifah ibn Salman Al Khalifah in Bahrain, 1988.

Distressed but dry-eyed, Hawke announces his defeat as leader of the ALP by
Paul Keating in Canberra, 1991. Keating became the new prime minister.

Paul wasn't against it per se, but he was still pretty dependent on Treasury through that first year, so he let Stone carry most of the argument. At the meeting I suggested floating the forward rate, which would give a clear signal [to business] that soon we would float the whole thing.

The next day, at a meeting of business economists in Melbourne, Hawke announced the government would float the forward rate, 'and from that time we were just waiting for the best moment', Garnaut said. But money kept flowing in, in waves.

The next crisis came at the end of the first week of December 1983. It was obvious to Hawke and Garnaut that the float could not wait any longer: the question was whether Keating and the Treasury could be persuaded to act. There was a long discussion in Hawke's office, ending about midnight, which was inconclusive. Garnaut said, 'We in the PM's office were disappointed that it hadn't been decisive, and after Paul had left we said, "You know, we can't keep buggerising around like this."' Hawke's chief of staff, Graham Evans, wrote of:

Peter Barron [one of Hawke's political advisers] meeting with the then Treasurer on the night before the decision to float the exchange rate . . . to establish whether or not 'he was in the cart' (an event which has since given rise to enough works of fiction to start a library!)

Garnaut recalled,

So Peter Barron was sent down to bring Paul back. And Bob said something like, 'We're buggerising around!' and Paul said, 'Well, I've just had the Reserve Bank in my ear saying a similar thing – so yes, we'll do it.' By then it was well after midnight. Paul phoned the bank people and said, 'Come up to Canberra tomorrow.' There was a series of meetings, the bank announced the markets would be closed all day Friday. It was announced, and by Monday the dollar was floating.

There were surprisingly few objections because few people understood what had happened. Garnaut said,

> There was some muted anxiety from the industrialists; the farmers hadn't worked out what it meant. It was sort of breathtaking, and so the main commentary was from positions of awe, rather than criticism. The people who understood it best were those in the merchant banks, the investment banks, who liked it and took the benefit from it. And they immediately came in with plenty of positive commentary. My memory is that once it was done and was positively received it gave Paul a lot of confidence. He had taken a position contrary to John Stone, it had turned out to be a political success, and I think that was crucial in building his confidence.

Bill Hayden, who had been Treasurer in the Whitlam government, recalled, 'I wrote in my autobiography that it was Keating's idea, because Keating said it was. And Peter Walsh [Finance Minister] got in touch with me and said, "You're wrong, you know. It was Hawke who did those things."' Hayden added,

> Keating was terribly worried about it, because Stone was against it. He came and saw me and said, 'I want to talk to you about floating the exchange rate. How do you feel about it?' I said, 'I've always supported it. I've made speeches about the way Fraser used to rig the exchange rate to keep the dollar up and he did that through high interest rates. So count on me. I'm on side.' But I had misunderstood Keating's reason for coming to talk to me. He wanted me to be on side with him to *oppose* it.

Until this time Hawke had hankered after having Ralph Willis as Treasurer, for Willis' skill and knowledge, and had raised the issue with his political advisers from time to time. They told him it was non-negotiable: the New South Wales Right, which had overturned Hayden in Hawke's favour, still insisted on Keating. Paul Kelly, the political commentator and author, recalled, 'This is a hyper-sensitive issue which I don't think ever came out at the time, but the discussion [in Hawke's office] was, "What do we do if Paul's not up to the job?"' Keating had confessed to the Prime Minister that he was terrified during Question Time in case the Opposition asked him for economic details he would be unable to give. Fortunately, the Opposition was in too much disarray to realise it could severely embarrass the Treasurer and the government, and the dreaded questions were never asked. Unknown even to close advisors, a great friendship had sprung up between the Prime Minister and his young Treasurer, a friendship that would last eight and a half years, a partnership that drove the longest reform period in Australia's history. Hawke set out, according to an insider, to 'strengthen Keating, give him confidence and win his friendship'. John Bowan, the Prime Minister's adviser on Foreign Affairs, recalled,

In the old Parliament House we'd be in those little cubby holes of offices and at Question Time Paul would put on one of his virtuoso performances and then he'd come walking down the corridor to go and have a session with Bob. And Bob would tell him how wonderful he'd been. They would bask in this mutual admiration.

The relationship between Prime Minister and Treasurer was on Hawke's part warm and avuncular. His elder daughter, Sue, recalled, 'Paul was the only man Dad encouraged to take the limelight from him. He had an indulgent feeling to Paul.' He called the Treasurer 'Paulie'; Keating called him 'Uncle Bob'. Hawke was proud of Keating, fourteen years his junior, and regularly introduced him to foreign leaders as the future of the Labor government. Keating had plenty of rough edges, for in his bones he had the Irish Catholic anger of how it hurt to be pushed to the margins of society for generations, to be humiliated into second-class lives – deprived, even in egalitarian Australia, of a place at the table in matters of social importance. Hawke was keen to expand Keating's geopolitical grasp and invited him to come to Asia, the initial leg of Hawke's first overseas visit as prime minister. It was Asia that had first opened Hawke's eyes to another world, one so foreign it had made him question the core of his identity. Keating was still green. Graham Evans, running Hawke's office, noted: 'The Treasurer informed us he would not be joining the prime ministerial party in Asia, "because Asia was somewhere you flew over on your way to Europe".' Keating would change his mind later, and became an Asiaphile. He sparkled with intelligence and had a natural elegance of movement that made him visually pleasing as a foil for Hawke's shorter, stronger body and hard jaw. 'Paul's a mixture of a hired killer and someone you could imagine as a parish priest,' Bowan said. 'A terrific guy. Very warm and decent. And charming.'

The relationship of Prime Minister and Treasurer, while warm and strong with the cement of comrades in arms, had from the outset an undertone of rivalry, to be expected from two such competitive men – politicians by nature being highly combative. Unrecognised by most outsiders, this rivalry did not negate their shared respect, nor conviction that their partnership was uniquely able to make a wholesale policy reform of the Labour Party, and the nation.

Hawke had ruined not only Hayden's plans for his future, but Keating's also: Keating had backed himself to succeed Hayden after a term and a half, or two – as he had told Hayden to his face – and had been a late, unwilling convert to Hawke's ascendancy. Keating recognised in Hawke a leader much tougher to unseat than Hayden, if at all.

Garnaut recalled,

I knew Paul better than Bob at the beginning, because when Paul had been shadow Minister for Resources and Energy he took a lot of interest in my work. One of the big policy issues Paul pushed then, in fact the biggest one, was the resource rent tax, which I had designed. Paul used my material, and whenever he needed a battering ram in Caucus he would drag me over to play that role. So we had a fair bit of contact. When he was putting his staff together Bob set up a process requiring a couple of references from others for each new staffer, and Hayden and Keating felt they knew me well enough to provide references. And on my very first hour in the office Paul Keating came into my room, a small cubicle in the old Parliament House, and closed the door and said, 'Ross – if you and I play our cards right, we'll run this show.' So he was inviting a close relationship. And it was a close and productive relationship through that first year. But I must say I was taken aback by his remark. A little bit surprised. I didn't know how to interpret it, so I just tucked it away as one of those things you think about.

Not long after the election, the doyen of columnists, Peter Robinson had noted that Hawke was an anomaly in Labor politics:

By history and by definition, the Labor Party is a party of conflict – a political movement aimed always at 'fighting' – fighting what used to be called 'the class war' ... Its passionate oratory almost invariably centres around the righting of wrongs, the correction of injustice, the battle against overwhelming capitalist power. The entire thrust of the Hawke philosophy is, in fact, foreign to these basic Labor assumptions ... His rhetoric ... concentrates on national unity, the pride of all Australians in their nationhood and the need to work together for future generations ... It is a theme he has been hammering away at ever since he came into public life ... which he has pursued with such evangelical zeal that many political cynics concluded he was just too good for the real world and would never get anywhere in politics. So much for cynicism.

By the end of that first year in power, the government and the Prime Minister were more popular than ever. Hawke was named Australian of the Year. In January 1984, the *Australian* ran a headline 'Hawke Is the Man Who Is Bringing Us Together' and inside, 'People believe there is change, there is hope.' There was an excellent team of ministers, probably the most talented in Australian history, becoming even stronger later when Hawke moved young Kim Beazley into Defence. In those days a Labor Prime Minister had to accept as ministers men and women chosen by Caucus; his only discretion was in how he allotted portfolios. But his personal office was at his own discretion: there Hawke assembled a cast of erudition, sophistication, cunning and power. Most importantly, all of them saw it as their job to call the shots as they saw them and not as the Prime Minister wanted to hear.

There was Hawke's chief of staff, Graham Evans, and his chief economic adviser, Dr Ross Garnaut; his Foreign Affairs adviser, John Bowan, a passionate, witty, well-read former diplomat, a self-described 'music lunatic', whose ear had won him the apocryphal reputation for knowing every note of every symphony ever written. He was also a sports fanatic, which created a strong bond between him and the Prime Minister. Hawke decided to revive a tradition that had died with Menzies, a Prime Minister's XI cricket team. Evans, assisted by Bowan, helped him select it. 'I think if cable TV had existed then,' Bowan said, 'the government would have fallen to pieces because Bob would have been up all night watching the golf and the tennis.' Hawke had two political advisers: Peter Barron, of the New South Wales Right, and Bob Hogg, of the Victorian Left. Barron was one of the most fascinating characters in Labor politics, for he had an octopus' knack of invisibility, rarely giving interviews or allowing an opinion to be attributed to him and never writing anything down. But his tentacles were everywhere. He later went to work for Kerry Packer. Communications ministers and shadow ministers spoke of seeing Barron 'flit out of the room' on their approach – having already advised Packer, they realised, on how to handle them. Barron was stocky and fair-haired, with a pudgy face and blue eyes in which, from time to time, an imp could be seen turning cartwheels and laughing. As a youth he had worked in Paddy's Markets in Sydney before becoming a tabloid journalist, then a press secretary to the New South Wales Premier, Neville Wran. The fruit and vegetable markets, a ragged, poetic, semi-criminal world of hungry expectation and quick wits, had helped form Barron's intellect and sympathies. He was shrewd, straight talking, funny, very likeable – and would never step back from a fight. One of his jobs early in Hawke's time in office was to close the door to people who, because of past association, presumed they had as much access to the Prime Minister as in the old days. The millionaire industrialist, Sir Peter Abeles, a friend with whom Hawke did want frequent contact, quickly ran foul of Barron, whom he urged Hawke to sack. Abeles was a large, dignified man of deeply serious demeanour, who bore himself with the same quiet majesty as his Rolls Royce. He had a heavy Hungarian accent. He would pause in conversation and in the silences one could almost hear the wheels of some mighty machine turning; when he next spoke, a deeper, unanticipated layer of thought would be revealed. But while Abeles knew a lot about business and the world, he was unversed in Labor politics. He complained 'That Barron is not –' searching for the expression in English, but ending with a literal translation from Hungarian '– not *room clean*.' He meant 'house-trained'. Being not house-trained was exactly how Barron was most useful. A very senior public servant observed of Barron,

> If he's got a point to make, he can make it in three words where most people would need three sentences. He's very direct and you can't miss the message he's giving you. He's a combination of being really, really smart and astute politically and in other ways, but also of knowing if there was a bad decision coming

down the line. He would kill it in three words. Bob used Peter to deal with issues that arose with some of the really strong ministers. It was a very strong Cabinet, and some of them had very strong views. When there were issues bubbling, especially from the New South Wales Right, or Keating, they would talk to Peter first, and if he thought what they were telling him was crazy he'd just say so and they'd go off with a flea in their ear and would think again. He protected Bob from having to deal with a lot of stuff that was going on.

Ross Garnaut recalled,

It was a relatively small office by modern standards but it was a pretty interesting group. The work environment was made much more productive by Bob's very open approach. He had from the beginning what I think is a very important characteristic for a prime minister, but a rare one, he did actually want to hear what people were thinking, whatever that was, whether it was positive or negative. We presented truth exactly as it was, unspun, and often loaded with awful political management challenges ... It was a very open office in terms of exchange of views. Sometimes shockingly so. Although I was used to being open and candid, I was open and candid in a gentle way. Peter Barron would use the language that I later learned was characteristic of the New South Wales Right. I remember after one Caucus meeting Bob came back shaking his head, saying, 'Those bloody troglodytes from New South Wales!' and Barron said, 'Bob: they might be troglodytes. They might all be as thick as planks, but I don't want ever to hear you call them troglodytes again. You're Prime Minister because they put up their hands when we want them to.'

(In retelling, Garnaut almost certainly deleted Barron's favourite adjective, 'fucking'.)

Barron understood the way bureaucrats would return with an issue that a political adviser believed was settled with the Prime Minister, and change his mind. 'Peter was very good at knowing when to have the last word. He'd make sure somebody didn't get let in to the prime ministerial presence after a decision had been made,' a colleague recalled.

All agreed that Barron was sometimes crude in his language.

At a time when it was such a bad word even red-blooded men in anger rarely used it, Barron regularly called people 'cunts' to their faces; he was allowed outrageous behaviour rather in the fashion of a Shakespearean king's fool. Like the fool, Barron was always the politically smartest guy in the room, the one to speak unwelcome truths. Once, travelling interstate, he was so frank and fearless in his advice to the Prime Minister within the hearing of the Commonwealth driver that Hawke summoned him to his hotel suite and verbally decapitated him. Hawke's temper when unleashed, which it rarely was, was ferocious. But always, as soon as the storm was over, sunshine returned, with no hard feelings. Michael Duffy, known as 'Black Mick', a Minister for Communications, recalled, 'I had rows with Bob and I'd think, "Jesus, he'll never speak to me again." But the next time we met he had completely forgotten about it.' As Graham Evans noted, 'Bob was not a hater and he would move on from any disagreements.' Hawke was, all his staff agreed, a very amiable and fair-minded boss. They were loyal to him, and to each other.

Bob Hogg, from Victoria, had been given the job of weeding out undesirables from among Hawke's associates before he became party leader. Power brokers in the Victorian branch of the party wanted Hawke rid of, Hogg said,

> sycophants and back-slappers, some of them just grubs, others of dubious value, people who made him feel comfortable, put him in too much of a comfort zone, rather than in a critical zone. Politics is about ideas, and these people had no ideas.

Hawke, ever optimistic about himself and human nature, was and would remain vulnerable to toadies and the company of people who praised and apparently adored him. 'If somebody was nice to Bob, he thought that person liked him,' an observer remarked. 'If somebody was nice to Keating, Paul thought, "What's he after?"'

The risks from adulation and lies are a constant danger to people with power. The vanity of political leaders is tempted day and night, for everywhere they go they are flattered. It was all the more important that Hawke surrounded himself with men (and one woman, Jean Sinclair) who spoke frankly. Hogg had been an enemy. He had despised Hawke over the question of uranium mining, which Hawke supported, and which at the time was still the most bitterly divisive issue in the ALP. Kim Beazley recalled being spat on as he walked down the steps of his Canberra hotel in 1984 by anti-uranium activists attending a party conference. ('How we got ourselves into such a knot over uranium is a mystery – when you consider that Jim Cairns, Whitlam's Minister for Trade in the early '70s, was trying to sell Australian uranium to the Shah of Iran,' Beazley said.) The ALP, so long out of power, was filled with people whose political idealism had become reckless and unreserved, untouched by any pragmatic need to maintain economic order. Hogg said,

> I was a product of the Cold War period, of the left persuasion on social issues especially. After I went to work with Bob when he became PM, very sane, rational leftish people said, 'How can you work for that shit?' I said, 'He's the fucking *Prime Minister*.'

Hogg's political fire was concealed by a diffident manner and a soft, kind face under a Beatle haircut. He resembled a stocky brown-eyed pixie. He recalled, 'After about three years the same people said to me, "You were right, you bastard." When you look back on those years [the 1970s and early 1980s] you wonder, "What on earth were they going on about?"'

Geoff Walsh was Hawke's press secretary, but also functioned as a de facto third political adviser, and was another quietly spoken good-looking young man, with a wry sense of humour and sharp political nose. Walsh later made a tribute to Hawke, describing his time with him as 'the richest work experience in my life ... Your optimism and ambition for this nation and its people ... your compassion and genuine delight in the company of your fellow Australians was a source of wonder and inspiration.'

In addition, the Prime Minister had two lieutenants, each in control of a large faction in the Caucus. One was Senator Robert Ray of Victoria; the other Graham Richardson. Ray was a former teacher, a calm, pipe-smoking, brown-skinned man who projected an aura of quiet menace. He had a very dry wit and, and, as a lover of junk food, an ample girth. Keating referred to Ray as the 'Fat Indian'. The Victorian Right was smaller and less important than the New South Wales Right, so Richardson had a larger role to play with Hawke, although the Prime Minister respected Ray in a way in which he could never respect Richardson.

If Garnaut was Apollonian in intellect and temperament, measured and restrained and of unimpeachable character, Richardson was his dark opposite: Dionysian. To the Left wing of the ALP and Left-leaning journalists, there was little to distinguish between Richardson and Mephistopheles except, perhaps, the devil cut a more dashing figure. Richardson's face had been lacerated in a car smash when he was sixteen and stitched back together without expert cosmetic skill. It was Richardson's personality that was intensely attractive. Full of vitality and brisk intelligence, shrewd, earthy and humorous – although given to gloating on how clever he was – he kept bad company, was guilty of numerous moral delinquencies, was loyal to friends, a fighter, frank, a man determined to claim his right to avoid the disappointed life he had seen the men of his father's generation live. He was also a gifted liar. Most importantly, he could 'count': that is, he could discern, by tone of voice, by light of eye, who was lying and who was speaking honestly when he asked for support. He was, in a way, an archetypal trickster, a man who knew that, despite fervent belief to the contrary, the world was essentially irrational. He seemed to understand the bottomlessness of human desire. In his youth in ALP headquarters in Sussex Street, Sydney, he was nicknamed 'Consumption Man' because of his appetite for junk food. He and Barron were best friends, very alike in their shrewdness, wit and irreverence, but Barron was more playful and blithe of spirit.

There were two other key members of the Prime Minister's inner sanctum: Sir Geoffrey Yeend, the secretary of the Department of Prime Minister and Cabinet, a dignified mandarin who had served Whitlam and Fraser and whom Whitlam praised as 'the *second-best* politician in Canberra'. (No prize for guessing the best, in Whitlam's mind.)

Last, and importantly, there was Graham Freudenberg, Hawke's speechwriter. Freudenberg had been Arthur Calwell's speechwriter, Whitlam's and Neville Wran's. He had a love of history and the party, a lovely, prosodic writing style, a rather fey manner, and an addiction to cigarettes and drinking cans of beer while he worked. He and Jean Sinclair were very close. Jean, who had been Hawke's secretary and personal assistant since 1973, was the most low-profile member of Hawke's staff, but she held in her memory more than a decade of his life, habits, family problems, friends and indiscretions, and in this respect was senior to all the others. A sophisticated, well-travelled economics graduate, she was Hawke's 'office wife', a woman to whom Hazel never warmed. The wives' relationship was one of civil aloofness; but as her discretion was legendary, it was to Jean whom staffers turned when unusual problems arose.

According to all the staff, it was a very happy office. On a typist's birthday, there would be a cake and a song and a kiss from the Prime Minister. When there was tension between Sir Geoffrey Yeend and the politicals – especially Barron – it was diffused with humour. Yeend had, Hawke said, a love–hate relationship with Barron, whose political brilliance Yeend recognised. For his part, Yeend's gravitas caused Barron's imp agonies of temptation. On an official visit to the Cook Islands, Barron, having arrived before Yeend at the hotel in which the Australian party was to stay, took the manager aside to warn him an international conman would soon be arriving, claiming to be 'Sir Geoffrey Yeend': under no circumstances should he be checked in or the manager would never see his money again.

Barron installed himself in a large armchair in the lobby to observe what ensued at the reception desk. Yeend turned up and announced himself. Unfortunately, he was not booked in, he learned. Puzzled, he persisted. Finally, asserting his natural authority he had the manager summoned. The manager confirmed the hotel was full, and there was no booking in his name. At this point Yeend broke the habit of a lifetime and insisted that the Australian Prime Minister be informed. With a po-face, the manager gave way to the sheer force of conviction of the knight. Barron, hiding in the armchair, was in stitches, but vanished just as Hawke, dragged away from reading in the sun, arrived in the lobby.

Walsh recalled,

It was a fabulous place to work. There was such a sense of purpose. It was a team that didn't need any artificial, contemporary team-building exercises to create it. There was mutual respect for the qualities that each person brought to the task. Where there were difficulties, they didn't linger ... There were tensions because you had Left and Right, New South Wales and Victoria, idealistic and pragmatic, and lots of neat divisions, but there was more that Peter [Barron] and Bob [Hogg] agreed on than they differed on. Because in the end they were always thinking, 'How do we turn this into votes? How does this get us re-elected? How is this going to be perceived by all the small interest groups?'

This team of invisibles was the dramatis personae who played their roles in the wings and behind the set, working the stage machinery, dressing, coaching and prompting.

Garnaut said,

> It was a respectful office. Bob used to drag us into all of the
> discussions, especially on the economic things. It was some-
> times uncomfortable, because he'd bring together people he
> thought needed to be part of a discussion and would, with
> everyone present, ask them to put out their views. And he'd
> sit back, sometimes with his feet up on the desk, smoking
> a cigar, listening. On economic policy matters that often
> required me to say things that were the opposite of what the
> Treasurer was saying, which wasn't great for my relationship
> with him, but Bob wanted to hear both sides. 'What do you
> think about that, Ross?' 'What's your view, Paul?' And this
> brought us into direct conflict. I always said exactly what
> I thought; I had no doubt what the Treasurer was think-
> ing. Bob would get the discussion going, listen to everyone,
> and after thinking about it for a while would sum things up.
> Sometimes he'd say, 'Well – I agree with Paul.' Or, 'I agree
> with Ross.' It was all right for my relations with Paul if Bob
> had agreed with him, but if he had summed up against him,
> that was very bad for my relations with the Treasurer …
> Bob handled discussions with [other ministers, such as]
> Button [Industry], with Susan Ryan [Education], Walsh
> and Dawkins in the same way. Paul was the only one who
> resented it. And he did resent it.

Keating had an intuitive, artistic mind that arrived at
conclusions through leaps of insight of dazzling originality. But his formal education had not reached the end of high
school. Garnaut was an academic intellectual head to toe, his
speech diffident, nuanced and expressive of deep complexities.
Keating's speech was of rapier wit and thrust. In seconds he
would arrive at a point that Garnaut could take half an hour to
tease out, layer by layer. Keating often complained to others
about the presence and influence of Garnaut on the Prime
Minister. For Hawke, Garnaut had a beautiful mind. The

fact was that he and Garnaut were mind brothers; Hawke and Keating were brothers-in-arms.

But these tensions between the Prime Minister's office and the Treasury were ephemeral in the context of the major work of reforming the nation upon which all of them were bent. Paul Kelly said,

> Keating had been infused with a great sense of confidence after the float. It really made him as Treasurer. It was a good period for [the government]: Hawke was a confident Prime Minister, Keating was now confident about the Treasury job. You had a constructive and co-operative phase in their professional alliance.

By the end of 1983 Hawke had launched a national conversation on the importance of change, including science, technological innovation, education and trade as part of the economic structural reform story he elaborated. Hogg, Barron and Walsh had urged him from the outset to be frank with the electorate, which chimed with his own inclination. Hogg said,

> The thing that, by far, made him the best prime minister I've ever seen is that he took to heart the early advice that you had to explain to the people what you were doing. Why were you doing it? Is there going to be pain? He did that across the board. He was an educator. And that educative role was essential.

In his speeches Hawke connected all areas of the economy, pointing out its weaknesses and potential weaknesses, strengths and potential strengths, so that, over a period of years, and with the help of financial journalists, the Australian electorate became one of the most, if not the most, economically literate in the world. Keating backed him to the hilt with his own salesmanship. Bill Hayden recalled, 'Paul was a super salesman. If he wanted to persuade you of something with which you disagreed, you'd have to hang onto the arms of your chair. He was the most persuasive bloody salesman I've ever come across.'

At the time of Federation, Australia was one of the two richest countries on earth but had gone steadily downhill until the 1980s, when the Hawke government halted the decline and the nation began climbing back towards the rich list. Hawke's first years of government were spent stripping the economy of hangovers from the past. Kim Beazley recalled,

> Basically, we were still in lock-step with the paradigm established in the 1950s under Bob Menzies. It had been tinkered with at the edges, there had been lots of studies done on what was the problem in Australia, there was endless chatter about how the structure on which we had survived and prospered had basically run out of steam, but there was no will or policy direction in the Australian political process. Bob changed all that.

Hawke was assisted by talented ministers but, as many noted, he encouraged their talents. Other prime ministers before and since have had cabinets that were never allowed to reveal their talents. As soon as the ministry was selected Hawke called them together to say: 'There are only two circumstances in which I will become involved in your portfolios. First, if you ask me, and second, if an issue arises that has a whole-of-government implication.' His method was to talk individually to each minister about priorities and the direction of the portfolio. The road map being clear, he then left the minister to get on with the job.

Peter Walsh, Minister for Resources, dismissed at a stroke a system for setting the price of domestic crude oil that had been in place since the days of John Gorton's prime ministership (1968–71). Walsh was a dour, tough character, an economic rationalist, robust and down to earth. His management style was blunt. He never much appreciated Hawke's open, blithe and lively character, and was not the sort of minister to be defied or mystified by bureaucrats, but in Trade and Industry, the bureaucracy was able for months to stonewall their new minister, Lionel Bowen, on changing a practice that had been introduced by the Whitlam government and left in place by Fraser. The Department of Trade had to approve the price of any export contract in the resources sector. It provided plenty of work for the bureaucracy – which engages endlessly in turf battles for more staff and more authority – while many businesses also found it congenial. A staffer recalled,

> It was a comfortable sort of arrangement where companies didn't have to be very clever at negotiating. They were told what the price was. In that area Bob really had to say to Lionel Bowen how things were going to be in future. It wasn't quite a meeting of minds, but Lionel never made a big issue about it, he just accepted it.

The forum in which ministers learned they would have to curtail their budgets was the Expenditure Review Committee (ERC). The ERC was established soon after the government took office and was in full swing by May 1983. Its purpose was to cut all the fat it could from the government's program. Hawke chaired it. The other members were Keating, Walsh, Willis and Dawkins, at the time Minister for Finance. Dawkins, from a wealthy West Australian family, was an intelligent, complex man whose nature combined courage, strong sympathies for the underdog and in his convictions a certain brutal rage. Like Walsh, he was a head kicker. These two were the hard cops of the ERC. Ralph Willis was the soft cop. ERC meetings were held in the Cabinet room. Dawkins, as Finance minister, was in charge of the one department that shadowed every other department and knew more about what was happening financially in the government than any other minister, on occasions even more than the Prime Minister. He frequently knew more about a department's expenditure than its own minister did. He recalled,

It was a matter of bringing these new ministers in and pinching their money. It just had to be a fairly brutal process but it really was done with a great deal of co-operation, and was a very important part of making the new government. It established the discipline we needed.

On occasions Garnaut would be called in to explain to a minister the economic necessities the government was facing. In May 1983, in the midst of the Combe–Ivanov distraction, the ERC produced its first expenditure review statement, announcing a big reduction in spending, but also reintroducing a universal health care system, Medicare. He told Bill Kelty, secretary of the ACTU, 'Our job is not to implement medicare but to put it into concrete.' Hawke had to leave the ERC from time to time to attend to other business but it sat almost daily for six weeks, from the end of the Summit, until the statement was ready. 'We were hardly ever out of the bloody Cabinet room,' Dawkins recalled. 'We'd start in the morning and quite often go through late into the night.' In June, July and through to the first week of August, the ERC sat again, almost daily, preparing for the Budget which, in those days, was delivered in early August. Hawke began calling ERC sessions 'Erk!' meetings.

Sector by sector, Hawke worked through the economy. It was clear at the time of the election that Australia had serious problems at both the micro and macro levels. Macroeconomic policy balances the economy's total demand with its capacity to supply; if the macro balance is out of kilter it is impossible for the nation to improve overall. Hawke's view from the outset was that the macroeconomic situation had to be going in the right direction, and employment growing, because that was the necessary base of everything else. Microeconomic policy reform is concerned with efficiency at the level of an industry or a firm, or a union or the labour market, and is the engine of economic growth.

While the Summit and the Accord had as their first focus the macro economy, behind that and simultaneously there was recognition that barriers to efficiency had to be removed across the board. In steel production, in research and development –

miserable by international standards – and in education. Australia's proportion of children completing high school, 37 per cent, was the lowest in the OECD. Changes in attitude in the labour market, with an end or at least a diminution of confrontations and strikes, were essential to raising productivity. Hawke knew this only too well from his decades in the trade union movement. He was determined that attitudes and relationships within individual industries had to change, that government policies had to be adjusted to achieve higher productivity. With higher productivity, the nation could become prosperous again.

But there were many instances in which good economic policy could not be reconciled with good politics. Hawke had *an* answer to this problem, but there is no complete answer. Geoff Walsh recalled,

> Bob insisted that if people were impacted for something that was in the medium- or the long-term good of the country and the economy there was a responsibility to ensure that they were adequately protected. But there is often a crunch, when you can't get that neat resolution. For example, Bob's speech in Japan in early 1984, announcing tariff cutting: in the Labor Party there were a lot of people who had a deep interest and commitment to the continuation of the manufacturing sector and the membership of their unions, and all the consequences that had for the internal dynamics of the Labor Party.

He added, 'Garnaut won that one.'

Hawke knew that reforms made in 1983–84 would take up to a decade to have their main effects, but as Garnaut noted, he 'underwrote long time-perspectives in policy ... he expected his government to be around to absorb the benefits [of reform]'. The benefit of the tariff cuts and the general economic reforms were paid to the nation in the late 1990s. 'People just couldn't see the benefits earlier,' Walsh lamented. By the time the reforms did start to make the economy soar, Hawke was out of office.

Garnaut recalled,

Bob had ideas on what needed to be done in each of these areas [of science, technology, education, resources, etc.]. Typically, a couple of members of staff, with Bob, would have a chat about the sort of agenda he would try to lead, we'd get the department to get together some basic material, then have a lengthy discussion with the minister. After a fair bit of focus there would be an understanding with the minister on the way things would go. And that worked very well, with one minister after another. Bob's role as the leader of Cabinet is often described as being chairman of the board and giving ministers a lot of rein, which is certainly a fair characterisation – but it was in a framework that had been worked out fairly elaborately earlier on, before the issue ever came to the Cabinet room.

By the winter of 1984 Hawke had reason to be delighted with the progress his government had made. The recession was over. Unemployment was falling; job vacancies were growing; strikes were fewer; the Opposition was having problems adjusting to its diminished status. The *Sex Discrimination Act* of 1984 was a landmark achievement, for the first time providing protections for women from discrimination in the workplace, including sexual harassment. It was born thanks to Senator Susan Ryan, and led to Australia's first female High Court Judge, Mary Gaudron; it paved the way for other women to achieve high office, including the present Governor of NSW, Margaret Beazley, Q.C. Hawke was a champion of women's rights; a corollary was his horror of prostitution, which he saw as female oppression. With exceptions, the news media were somewhat awed and certainly respectful. The party's national conference had seen another bitter anti-uranium fight, which Hawke had won, and most importantly the conference had agreed to opening the banking sector by allowing in fifteen foreign banks – a huge win for the pro-Hawke, modernising, anti-protection forces.

Government was still strenuously hard work: sixteen hours a day was normal for the Prime Minister, but there was a mounting number of small and larger goals successfully achieved. And always, he could tune himself into the glorious, exhilarating sensation of holding in his hands the nerve fibres of historical action. His popularity rating was 75 per cent, the highest in Australian history.

Then, in a moment, it collapsed in ashes. The staff had to struggle to keep the Prime Minister politically alive.

Fame is the enemy of family life. The Hawkes' family life had been unusual from the time they moved to Melbourne when Hawke took the job of ACTU advocate. 'From that first wage case, in 1958, I had pretty much rock star status,' he said. He worked hard, drank hard and played hard while Hazel stayed in the background, running the house and rearing the children. She was a down-to-earth woman who kept her emotions under firm control and had no illusions about her husband's philandering. Their earlier, romantic relationship had matured to the ancient, transactional tradition of married couples in which partners do not expect of each other super human powers of virtue and devotion (as seems to be the case today). She was proud to be the wife of a man of outstanding ability who, materially, was a good provider. In an era before mothers worked outside the home, this carried much weight. They owned (with a mortgage) a large house with a tennis court and an in-ground swimming pool and Hazel drove a second-hand but handsome Mercedes. She shared her husband's dream of one day living in The Lodge and years later explained why she had not divorced him for his many affairs: 'When you're on a good thing, stick to it.' Neither was happy in the marriage, however, and the household tended to dysfunction. After the firstborn, Susan, the Hawkes had a son, Stephen, then a daughter, Rosslyn. Rosslyn was an adorable toddler whom Hawke liked to keep on his lap or close by when he was studying for wage cases. She grew to be pretty, quick-witted and empathetic, looking exactly like Hazel in her youth. She was full of gaiety and humour: 'Don't touch me! I'm a work of art!' she exclaimed after having her hair and make-up done professionally for a party. Friends doted on her. She adored her father, but threats to his life, public attacks and sneering at him in the media were the constant background to her primary and early secondary school years, causing her acute anxiety. Police guards were posted outside her school when a man threatened to murder Hawke's children.

By the early 1970s huge numbers of schoolchildren were experimenting with cannabis; parents were apprehensive, but more or less powerless against the force of peer pressure. Hazel knew both her daughters were smoking dope and, encouraging them to be open rather than secretive, making a joke about it by having a marijuana leaf pinned to the kitchen notice board. At the time it was unknown and unsuspected that weed could have a lasting effect. Hawke disapproved of marijuana, which he never tried himself, but he had no scientific ground to argue against it, and as his own drinking was reprehensible it was left as one of those family issues best avoided. At the age of fifteen, Rosslyn left school and home for a gypsy life in the drug houses of Sydney. Hawke and Hazel lived in a state of denial that she was taking hard drugs, but there was no denying the spectral waif Hawke went searching for and eventually found, with the help of Sir Peter Abeles, in a squat house in a Sydney lane. Back at home, her teenaged indiscretion became a family secret. She regained her lovely appearance, fine skin and glossy hair, married a young man from a respectable family and presented her parents with their first grandchild, a son. On 1 August 1984 she gave birth to a second son.

Meanwhile her elder sister, Sue, living in Japan at the time of the 1983 election, had returned to Australia and to Left-wing political activism, and had recently been convicted for possession of marijuana. She was waiting on an appeal.

It was obvious to everyone who knew Rosslyn and her husband, who partied with the Brett and Wendy Whiteley crowd, that they were using heroin – everyone, that is, except her parents, who clung steadfastly to the belief that their daughter did not use hard drugs. The news from the hospital in the first week of

August that the new mother was so wasted by heroin she could soon be dead fell on Hawke like an axe. Although he saw less of his children than many fathers, and from the late 1970s there had been a civil war between him and his two elder offspring over uranium mining, his children were, nevertheless, sacred to him.

The news about Rosslyn was like tumbling into a nightmarish fable: at the height of his power, the king's daughter is cast under a spell; a demon is taking revenge on him, on her, on her children, because he failed as a guardian of the sacred.

Hawke told only Jean Sinclair, Paul Keating, a few of his most intimate friends – Abeles being one, plus a couple of others in the Jewish community on whose devotion to family and discretion he knew he could rely. He told no one else on his staff. But most noticed that something was wrong: the Prime Minister was unusually quiet and seemed distracted and nervous. He shrank in on himself.

At this moment there arrived a weird confluence between Hawke's private life and national public events. By the beginning of September 1984 a public storm about drugs was brewing. In 1980 Malcolm Fraser had set up a Royal Commission into the Ship Painters and Dockers Union (SPDU), in the hope of uncovering the nest of vipers that union certainly was, and of embarrassing both the union movement and the Labor Party. He appointed Frank Costigan, QC, to head it. With zeal appropriate to a Jesuit, Costigan pursued his inquiries, unearthed the vipers but then, to the horror of many supporters of the Liberal Party, discovered their billion-dollar eggs: a vast tax avoidance system known as 'the bottom of the harbour scheme'. It was the tax evasion of choice of thousands of prosperous Australian citizens. During the Fraser years avoiding tax had become a middle-class sport: the tax system was so ramshackle and so full of holes that the temptation to cheat was irresistible. In the chatter of tens of thousands of dinner parties, tax cheating was rebranded as financial savvy. One's doctor and lawyer were doing it. But respectable citizens did not know, or care to know, that a direct line led from their tax accountants to the thieves, thugs and murderers of the Ships Painters and Dockers Union. It was SPDU men who enabled the whole rotten system to operate.

There was huge embarrassment and anger in the Liberal Party when John Howard, the Treasurer, passed retrospective legislation to outlaw the bottom-of-the-harbour and other tax rorts.

But then the situation got messier. Costigan himself had suffered the anguish of a drug-addict child and like every parent in the same predicament nursed a burning hatred for drug dealers. When he stumbled over the fact that the multimillionaire press baron Kerry Packer was having huge amounts of cash delivered to him, Costigan demanded Packer appear before the Royal Commission, which Packer did in February 1984. Costigan's time was running out: the Attorney-General had told Costigan he must wind up by June 1984. (This may account for the shoddiness of the 'case summaries' that were handed to the National Crime Authority, the permanent body established to replace Costigan.)

Enter Brian Toohey of the *National Times* (the journalist who had first floated the Combe–Ivanov story). Someone from within Costigan's team gave Toohey cases of material, including copies of case summaries that asserted Kerry Packer, whom the *National Times* called 'The Goanna', was a drug lord, the importer of pornography and involved in the death by shotgun of a former Queensland bank manager. There was a frenzy of gossip and speculation; Packer was publicly abused by strangers; once, immobilised under a cape in a barber's chair in the window of a Double Bay hair salon, he had to endure the finger pointing and screamed abuse of a group of young people on the street outside.

Andrew Peacock, meanwhile, had found, he believed, a site from which to launch an attack on the Prime Minister: the winding up of the Costigan inquiry, with investigations to be passed over to a national crime authority, was happening against a background of accusations of corruption against police and politicians in New South Wales. Peacock, who had been rather limp as Opposition leader, used letters asking for a time extension from Costigan to Hawke to launch a censure motion in parliament. He accused the Prime Minister of undermining the fight against the drug trade, of protecting 'some of the most powerful criminals in Australia', of being 'a perverter of the law' who 'associates with criminals and takes his orders from criminals'. Hawke stalked from the chamber in fury: if anybody hated drug dealers, he did. As he left, Peacock called after him 'little crook', a slander for which Hazel would never forgive Peacock.

The *Costigan v National Crime Authority* debate ranted on, with Hawke threatening legal action if accused outside parliament of criminality. Already the *National Times* had run a story that the Prime Minister's daughter, Sue, had a drugs conviction that by now had been overturned on appeal; it insinuated corruption of the legal process. At a press conference a week after Peacock's censure motion a journalist asked Hawke 'if it made a mockery of the political system if politicians [i.e. Peacock] felt inhibited in making statements because of threats of legal action [i.e. by Hawke]'. With television cameras trained on him, Hawke replied, 'In public life you cannot, it seems to me, entirely abandon the rights that you have, because it is not only a matter affecting yourself,' he said. His eyes filled with tears. 'You don't cease to be a husband. You don't cease to be a father. My children and my wife have a right to be protected in this matter.' Tears began flowing down his cheeks. He was then asked if he was upset by the *National Times* article about Susan. Openly weeping he replied,

> Of course I was, because like any father I love my daughter. I trust her and she was completely exonerated by the processes of the law. I had no contact with the judge or anyone involved in it and yet you have this insinuation that affects her. Of course, I'm upset.

The question had referred to Susan, but Hawke had answered thinking of Rosslyn. He was thinking of her day and night, of how to save her and his infant grandsons, who could soon be motherless.

Geoff Walsh shut down the conference as soon as he could and, mystified, shepherded Hawke away. Laurie Oakes, writing for the *Age* commented,

> politicians on both sides were unsure about the electoral impact of yesterday's prime ministerial weeping. There is no doubt, though, that it changes the nature of the organised crime debate ... The tears were real and it made extraordinarily moving television. The millions who saw it will be less likely to give credence to Opposition claims that the Prime Minister deliberately curtailed the Costigan Royal Commission to protect people financing drug importations and distribution.

The press conference was the start of a full-scale crisis in the office because Hawke, after a month of silent self-flagellation, could no longer conceal the family secret. Nor could he function as national leader. He had gone straight from the interview to a meeting with the Malaysian Prime Minister, Dr Mahathir Mohamad, who hanged people for possession of heroin, and burst into tears, weeping in Mahathir's arms as he told him the story. The staff were appalled. When Hawke called them together to explain the situation they were more annoyed than sympathetic. The Prime Minister had collapsed.

It was as if the guiding hand of destiny in which he had so long and so fervently believed had suddenly bunched into a fist and punched him in the face. Both his elder children, Left-wing in their sympathies, especially Stephen, had argued bitterly with him over uranium at the ALP conference two months earlier. Stephen, eponymous with the first Christian martyr, had suffered a kind of martyrdom all his life as 'the son of ...', repeatedly flattered or abused on account of his father, to whom he bore a striking physical resemblance. He had taken his mother's side in the dysfunctional family and when he left home changed his name to her maiden name, Masterson, until people recognised him anyway and began calling him 'Steve Wink-Wink Masterson'. Then, having reverted to 'Hawke', he gave his own children their mother's maiden surname so there would be no grandchildren named 'Hawke'. Their grandfather did not comprehend how galling it was to be perpetually labelled the son, or even grandson, of a rock star, and was deeply hurt that the Hawke name would die out in two generations.

After Hawke's public tears, Peacock was criticised within the Liberal Party for having 'gone too far'. His deputy, John Howard, tried to defend him, saying, 'Mr Hawke should remember that he is not the only parliamentarian who has a wife and children.' The ever-vicious Wilson Tuckey from Western Australia weighed into the fight with:

Australians are entitled to the guarantee that their national leader has the moral fibre to carry the pressures of national calamity. After the Prime Minister's 'I want my mummy' performance today, it is clear Australia has no such leader at present.

Keating, a savage team fighter at any time and in an emergency especially dangerous, deflected the attack from the Prime Minister and turned it back on the Opposition with scalding invective. From his upbringing in the Catholic church, he was as familiar with the mighty language monuments of Christendom as with contemporary gutter slang, and he pressed both into the service of his oratory, describing the Opposition's attitude to tax avoidance as 'a dog returning to its vomit', a reference of fascinating horror to those unfamiliar with the second Book of Peter 2:22. To Howard, Keating said, 'I will squash you like a rat.'

Meanwhile in Hawke's office the staff were slow to realise that the Prime Minister was in the grip of depression. They were so used to him riding like a horseman whom some talisman protects from every fall that they were almost blind to what was in front of them. Hawke was contemplating resignation, and at one stage, even suicide.

How long his depression lasted is contested. Hawke says he was 'down' for about six weeks; some staff members thought six months; Richardson, after he had turned against Hawke, said more than a year. Garnaut said, 'I think a year, or even six months, is bullshit: you just have to look at the record of what was happening: Bob's work in Asia, against protectionism, in education – where he needed endless discussions with [Education minister] Susan Ryan, who was nervous about the teachers' unions.' With disdain Garnaut added, 'They were solid reforms which Richardson wouldn't have noticed.'

As yet no explanation had been made to the electorate about the Prime Minister's emotional state. During a radio interview in Sydney with John Laws, Hawke choked up and did so again with another well-known television and radio man, Clive Robertson. Rosslyn, who unlike her brother enjoyed the excitement of publicity, volunteered to go on national television and explain she had been the cause of her father's distress. The hardheads in the office vetoed the idea immediately. One of them remarked,

> She was too naive to realise they would have crucified her. She wouldn't have had a day's peace for the rest of her life: the media would be watching her every time she stepped out the front door.

Her husband, Matt, then volunteered for the job – but it was discovered he did not own a suit, and for such a serious occasion a suit was deemed essential. Geoff Walsh was a similar size: he was to lend Matt one of his suits. Finally, Graham Evans realised that the best spokesperson would be Hazel and it was she who, with dignity and self-control, explained that their daughter had a drug problem. This was the first time the country had seen her strength and fighting spirit, seen a woman emerge from the shadow of her husband into the limelight, a champion for the vulnerable, a mother whose instinct was to nurture and protect. The nation took Hazel to its heart from that moment on.

Political reporters, who had sat staring at their laps when Hawke wept, seemed relieved to be let off the hook of needing to ask more questions; the public treated the episode 'as one of those things that can happen in any family', Walsh said. Hawke won a large measure of public sympathy.

But behind the political scenery, things were going from awful to frantic. The Caucus was panicky because their jobs depended on the Prime Minister's charisma and it seemed to be evaporating. A leader's authority lies in his *personal* responsibility, which, as Weber noted, 'he cannot reject or transfer ... Ultimately there are only two kinds of deadly sins in the field of politics: lack of objectivity and – often but not always identical to it – irresponsibility.'[1] Hawke, unable to control the dam-burst of emotion, had fallen into deadly political sin. The staff were increasingly annoyed in private, while in public defending him. After Walsh's explanation to journalists that the Prime Minister had not choked up again during a speech, he just had a bit of a frog in his throat, a grim joke went around the office about 'the optic frog' – as in: 'we had another optic frog moment today'. Barron was appalled at what he saw as self-pity.

If any of the staff, beyond the security men, were present when Rosslyn, distraught and hysterical at being separated from her infant children, was loaded on to a private jet and flown to the United States for treatment, all were too loyal to their boss to admit it, even decades later. For Hawke the moment was lacerating. Normally he could switch off from subjects as easily as flicking a television channel, but from this episode he could not.

By September 1984, the government had a technical excuse for calling an early election. Hawke decided to have an eight-week campaign. Richardson said, 'We thought the length of the campaign was crazy, but he just wouldn't listen.' The staff and the election committee tried to convince themselves that a long campaign was worth the risk because the Prime Minister, being so extroverted, would benefit from getting out among people. *They* would cheer him up.

There is a reason that politicians of all persuasions refer to their work in military terms: battles, campaigns, strategy, tactics, troops, rank and file. It is equally obvious that, if launching a war, one should design it to be as short as possible. Richardson said, 'Hawkey thought, "The longer it goes my mastery over Peacock will show, and I'll increase my majority." And everyone said, "That's bullshit, Bobby. We're a government, we don't give the Opposition room to shoot at us."'

What's more, by now Peacock had some targets. Middle-class abuse of welfare payments had built up over decades in Australia and become egregious during Fraser's years. There were instances of millionaires claiming aged pensions. The government was determined to undo middle-class welfare in favour of giving more to the needy. The 1983/84 Budget introduced an assets test for pensions that inaugurated needs-based welfare as a central theme of the decade – but caused outrage from the Coalition, the Democrats and even some sections of Caucus who had large numbers of retirees in their electorates.

Grey Power was born out of the 1984 election.

Peacock pressed relentlessly on the issue, loudly assisted by a campaign in the Melbourne *Herald*. People were deadly serious about the right of the affluent to government handouts, for Fraser had taken the view that once something had been given to the electorate, it could never be taken away. It was the perfect situation for a Liberal tax scare campaign, at which Peacock excelled. John Button accidentally helped him along on 17 October when, in the Senate, Opposition Senator Fred Chaney asked a series of scaremongering questions: 'Will the Government give an assurance that a capital gains tax, a wealth tax or death duties will not be imposed following any review of the taxation system ... ?' John Button replied, 'It is very difficult for me to give an undertaking in respect of capital gains taxes, wealth taxes and death duties.' The fat was in the fire and the Opposition fanned it vigorously. Hawke, campaigning in Perth, needed to quench it as quickly as possible. He announced on radio that there would be a 'Tax Summit' after the election, at which everyone would be entitled to put forward views about reforming the tax system, just as they had at the Economic Summit.

Geoff Walsh, travelling with Hawke, rang Graham Evans in Canberra, explained what had happened, and passed on the message that Hawke wanted Garnaut to begin work on an outline for the Tax Summit. 'It was,' said Evans, 'policy on the run.'

Geoff Walsh recalled, 'From a dream run in 1983, the '84 campaign was a nightmare.' The early election, little more than halfway through the government's term, irritated the electorate, and the enormous length of the campaign irritated it even more. But from the very beginning there was another irritation, and that was in the Prime Minister's right eye. Hawke had played cricket at Kingston Oval in Canberra on the weekend the election was announced and, batting, had mistimed a hook shot, with the ball smashing his own spectacles and driving glass into his eye. In agony and half blind, he was taken to hospital. The surgeon who removed the glass said had it gone a fraction deeper he would have lost the sight of his eye altogether. It was an event that seemed to echo Kafka's story, 'The Penal Colony', in which condemned men have a description of their crimes cut into their flesh with glass. Hawke had been blind to what was happening with his daughter. Now glass had inscribed 'unable to see' in his eyeball.

Hawke said, 'I was an emotional mess and my eye was driving me mad throughout the campaign. I found it almost impossible to concentrate.' But by now he was practising a stiff upper lip and few realised he was in pain. Geoff Walsh, who travelled with him, noted, 'He was clearly uncomfortable and at times a little short.' Hawke spent a minimum of time with the news media travelling with him, whereas Peacock and his new wife, Margaret, fraternised and had fun with their travelling circus.

Before the election was announced Hawke and the party had assumed Peacock would be easily beaten. In the *Bulletin* of 16 October Richard Farmer summed up ALP thinking in a cover piece headlined 'Hawke's Biggest Headache: A Record Poll Majority'. The summary beneath it read: 'With the prospects of a general election loss virtually disregarded, Labor's federal leaders are contemplating a quite different challenge – how to cope with a record majority.' Labor polling confirmed a Morgan poll that the government could win 100 out of the 148 seats in the House of Representatives. The years of existential outsiderness would soon be a distant nightmare and the party looked forward to a decade of Labor government, a political luxury that, until this moment, had been beyond their dreams. For Hawke, victory would be the vindication he yearned for: restoring Labor's honour as the natural party of government, one that could unite the nation in the cause of enlightened self-interest.

Farmer noted that an important part of Hawke's thinking was 'a belief the more the electorate sees of Peacock the less voters like him, and consequently, the greater Labor's likely victory'. Most of these opinions were in error. It is always an error for a government to assume it will win and, worse, to allow the electorate to know it holds that assumption. It is always an error to underrate an opponent. It is always an error to count chickens before they hatch. As Kim Beazley said, 'Had there been something of an expectation that we could lose, we would have changed strategy. Since then, many a Labor government has saved itself by crying poor, but we weren't so sophisticated in those days.'

Richardson recalled,

> At that stage Hawkey's ego was as big as all outdoors, and I think he had an extraordinary view of himself, that the longer the campaign went, the better he'd go. He saw himself as the emperor and his subjects would all dutifully bow down at the right time – except a lot of them didn't.

Peacock fought well and beat Hawke in their debate, largely it was said, by looking manfully into the camera, something that Hawke, with his sore eye, could not do. Walsh said,

> It was a campaign that lacked the energy and point and punch we'd had in '83. You couldn't repeat that, because the

circumstances were different, but Bob didn't do as well as he expected. We all had a share in the blame for that.

Besides Peacock, Keating campaigned well. Stone had taken early retirement in August and this may have contributed to the Treasurer's sense of freedom and strength. What he brought to a campaign in which pensions were a major issue was, in Kim Beazley's words,

> his love of old people. I've never seen anyone, even Bob, better with old people. Paul genuinely respected and loved them. He looked on old men as repositories of wisdom. And they responded to that. The election transformed him.

Keating had been the darling of his grandmother. As a youth he had gone, week after week, to sit at the feet of the aged giant, Jack Lang, a hero to Keating's father, a man old enough to be his grandfather; Keating was born, in a sense, thanks to the tutelage of Lang and to the respect Lang showed him, always addressing the young man as 'Mr Keating'. It was Lang who taught Keating to look intelligently upon himself, who opened the world to him. Theirs was that strangely intimate relationship between a student and a teacher when Sirens sing enchantment to both sides. It was Lang's strong old voice that unveiled to Keating the possibilities of what the world could hold for him. Lang had lived through, and was in power, in one of those incendiary periods of history, the Great Depression, and had been shockingly burnt by it, sacked as Premier of New South Wales, expelled from the Labor Party (by Curtin), humiliated and reviled. He was a man with a grievous sense of deprivation. It was Lang who warned Keating when he got into parliament, 'you haven't a moment to lose'.

On the Monday after the election, the *Age* editorial's headline summed up the situation: 'Hawke shaken, Peacock stirred'. In a cartoon Hawke was shown crowned, draped in kingly robes, but with sticking plaster on his cheek, a tooth missing, his robes torn and wearing a penitent's sandals. Michael Gawenda wrote, 'Nothing could disguise the disappointment. The smile looked like it had been sculpted on to his face ... He had won even if it had not felt like a victory at all.' Hawke's enemies would paint the 1984 election result as poor. More accurately, it was a realistic result, less than hoped-for, because rather than deliver a swing to Labor there was a 1.4 per cent swing against – but because of recently introduced electoral changes there was an informal vote of 12 per cent, mostly in Labor electorates. In addition, a redistribution meant a loss of two seats in any event. The government was still comfortably in power at the end of the night of 1 December, with a 16-seat majority. But the magic aura that had surrounded the Prime Minister had lost its brightness and he would never be 'Mr 75 per cent' again.

While his public life had taken a battering, his private life was improving. His little grandsons were living at The Lodge. They were to be a source of joy for Hawke and Hazel, bringing a springtime of family life and happiness. After months of hard work in a Californian clinic, Rosslyn overcame her addiction. She returned to live with her parents and care for her children. The fugue of death and despair was over, but its damage to Hawke would never be completely undone. In time, his right eye lost 95 per cent of its vision. Politically he was no longer a god.

But he determined he would win the 1987 election.

TWENTY-TWO

Ｉｎ mid-April 1984, on Palm Sunday, an estimated 600 000 Australians marched in cities around the nation 'Against Nuclear War'. The Nuclear Disarmament Party, whose only policy was expressed in its name, came within 6000 votes of winning a Senate seat in the election in December of that year. Hugh White, a defence analyst and journalist at the time, later an adviser to the Defence minister, then the Prime Minister, made the droll observation, 'Nuclear war wasn't actually *the policy* of the Hawke government, but somehow people thought it was a good idea to have at go at us about it anyway.'

The real issue was the American alliance, especially since Reagan had entered the White House four years earlier in 1980 (he would stay there until 1988). Hawke personally was determined that the Labor Party must establish its credentials to govern in the Cold War that, with the Reagan administration, had been growing noticeably warmer. Hawke's government had been elected on a platform that promised to 're-examine the ANZUS alliance to see if it still meets Australia's purposes'. Once the Labor Party had assumed office, the defence chiefs gave Hawke a briefing about what the American bases in Australia – Pine Gap, Narrunga and North West Cape – actually did. Hawke became, in Beazley's words,

immensely conscious about how vital the bases were to the United States and to the Western alliance generally and as a result, recognised two things: one was that the bases were basically useful for a whole range of stabilising policy

663

directions in the global political system – that they assisted in making things like arms control stability possible. The second was, he realised that with the United States, if you got too far offside there would be no half measures with them: you would end up in the doghouse. He utterly despised New Zealand's playing games with the nuclear warship visits. He thought that was pissant politics.

The bases, because they were American, and top secret, were a magnet for leftist activists. In the party, Beazley explained,

> The Right took the view that the US alliance was critical, that we needed to pay a price for that relationship and that we were prepared to pay a price. The Centre Left position [Hayden supporters] was: that's probably true, but we ought to be optimising the extent to which we leverage it. The Left position was: it's all just unacceptable.

In December 1984, immediately after the election, Hawke promoted Beazley to Defence minister. Beazley recalled,

> The next day a couple of my senior officials came to me and said, 'Minister, there is something we think you should know.' And they told me about this MX missile test which had to be supported by Australia.

It was the beginning of one of the worst crises of all the years of the Hawke government. John Bowan, Hawke's Foreign Affairs adviser, was to say later, 'When I die and they open me up, they will find "MX" engraved on my heart.' He felt personally at fault for advice he gave the Prime Minister, and for the way he handled the press.

Defence is the largest department of government and, because of its size, complexity and technical detail, presents the greatest difficulties for a new minister. The warrior's eternal mystique is part of the problem, but so too is the continuity of experience for war fighting: the Australian Defence department boasts a proud tradition of baffling and browbeating its ministers, especially about weapons it wants the taxpayer to buy. To add to the problem there is constant friction between the armed and civilian wings of the department, the civilians having perfected a subtle weapon known as 'the snow job': enormous numbers of papers, reports and analyses that need to be read. Beazley, who came to be internationally respected as the best Defence minister Australia ever produced – the best in the world, according to the United States Defence Secretary Caspar 'Cap' Weinberger – had come to the job after decades of personal interest in military matters. He was so intellectually and psychologically well equipped it seemed some field marshal of the past had been resurrected in the guise of a huge, genial West Australian politician. 'Kim was overwhelmingly good. It was like Snap! you could almost hear it happen when he took over,' White said.

> He always thought strategically. For Kim the armed force is never an end in itself. There's always the question: what are the political objectives we're trying to achieve with the armed force? One of the distinctions between people who do this well and those who don't is that the latter become obsessed with the armed force itself. They forget it's meant to serve a political purpose. Or they get obsessed with the operations themselves, and forget they're meant to be serving a political purpose. For example: what exactly are we trying to do in Afghanistan? Are we sending Special Forces there for fun? . . . With Kim, he never lost sight of the reason for action. His view was you had to act not just for domestic political, but for a national political strategic purpose.

On 14 December 1984, when Beazley was told of the proposed MX missile test, he recalled,

> I said to these guys, '*WHAT DO YOU MEAN BY AGREEING TO THIS! YOU KNOW IT'S AN AMERICAN TRY-ON!*

All they need to do is change the azimuth of the rockets and they can perfectly well test the MX. The Yanks are trying to assemble all flags.' And they said, 'Yes, we know that, but it was Bill Pritchett's [the secretary of the Defence department] idea and it was picked up by Malcolm Fraser and it went through your security committee ...' So I went up to see Bob and said, 'Mate: this is bad news.' And he said, 'Awww ...'

The background to Hawke's own support for the MX test was that, while Hawke was in Washington in 1984, George Shultz, the American Secretary of State and an old friend, had taken him aside and, out of the earshot of Hawke's aides, had asked him to agree that Sydney could be a staging base for reconnaissance flights to monitor the missile splashdown. Hawke had agreed. Weinberger and Shultz were delighted and thanked Hawke.

Beazley continued,

I said, 'Mate, this is a weapon that will be interpreted as a counter-force; it will be seen as an effort by the United States to achieve superiority in all their rockets. *We* are for MAD [the policy of 'mutually assured destruction' preventing any side from starting a nuclear war], a stable balance. We're going to have hell to pay on this. It'll leak, and there will be a scandal.' ... The Caucus in those days was a much more emotional beast than it is now. And Bob said, 'Oh well, that doesn't matter. We'll just get down and fight for it.'

Bill Hayden remembered,

Bob said he didn't see anything wrong with the Americans using Australian support to launch the missile. And I said, 'Jesus: I wouldn't do that! It's going to send the party into fits.' You see, a lot of moralising had developed in our long period in Opposition, and nobody had tried to straighten them out.

According to White, Hayden underestimates his contribution as Foreign minister to educating the party and the electorate about the American alliance. He said,

> Bill established a whole line of argument which had not been present in the Australian debate before and that was: our support for the joint facilities serves Australian interests directly, by supporting agendas we have in arms control and disarmament. There was an element of political convenience in that argument but it was true. Bill made the announcements. Bill's department produced the paperwork and so on. But as soon as Kim took over as Defence minister, Bill backed off and Kim reached out and grabbed it. It became Kim's issue.

But the situation continued to develop. Hayden recalled,

> Anyway, Bob wouldn't agree about the tests. No! No! He banged the table and said, 'Listen! I want you to get in there [the Caucus] and fight. *FIGHT!* Hold the fort. Don't back down.' And I thought, 'Jesus – that's all right for him.' And the whole issue opened up and all hell broke out.

Keating was strongly backing the Prime Minister. Richardson recalled, 'Paul was literally telling them all to get fucked. "We'll stand the Caucus up" and all that stuff. I remember having a huge argument with Keating over the MX. He was totally gung-ho.'

The journalist who broke the story was, again, Brian Toohey. In the *National Times* on Sunday, 1 February 1985, Toohey, reporting from Washington under the headline 'Sydney Role in U.S. Missile Tests', noted that the MX could deliver twenty times the explosive force that had obliterated Hiroshima. By the next day, every newspaper, radio and television station in the country was running the story, harping on the theme that Hawke would have to say no, since the test would fly in the face of the government's disarmament policies, and create ructions in the party. The media campaign continued all week.

Hayden continued,

Beazley came forward defending the decision in his way, which was quite intellectual, and then the weekend came up and I thought, 'Most things don't survive the weekend.' I was still going strong. I went on TV with Richard Carleton on the ABC on Monday and defended the decision very vigorously. Huh! Next morning my principal private secretary told me the declared CIA officer from the American embassy had rung to congratulate me. *Bloody hell!* Anyway, the thing just blew. Blew its head off. There was no way we could hold the line.

Frequently for Hawke, as for any prime minister, the fiercest battles in getting government policy accepted were against his own side. As the political apophthegm has it: 'Those opposite are our Opposition; our enemy sits behind us'. Hawke had been able to enforce Cabinet solidarity, a luxury Whitlam had not had, but the Caucus was another matter. It was the job of the faction bosses, Richardson and Ray for the Right, to keep the Caucus in line. It would be political death for Hawke to be rolled in Caucus, which was growing increasingly fearful; some of it was pumped up, Beazley said, 'by the KGB and Muscovite agents of disinformation who were floating around the place'.

At a news conference in Sydney, Dr Helen Caldicott, a leading anti-nuclear activist, described the agreement to co-operate with the MX test as 'a suicide pact'. The Victorian premier, John Cain, said federal ministers had no 'moral authority' to make the decision without consulting the rest of the party; the New South Wales branch called a rank-and-file meeting on the issue. Richardson said,

We couldn't hold the Right. If you can't hold the Right, you've got no chance of getting the Centre, and of course you'd never get the Left. At least a third of the Right would have broken. Alan Griffiths [a law and economics graduate from Melbourne, still a backbencher] led the charge – it was twenty-five years ago, but I've never forgotten. Alan Griffiths: one of our rock-solid blokes. He wasn't someone accustomed to revolution, but he was absolutely adamant. We were dead.

To cap it all, Sir Joh Bjelke-Petersen announced that if Hawke backed down he would allow the P3 aeroplanes needed to monitor the splashdown to fly from Queensland.

Beazley said,

Bill and I put endless pressure on it. We did press and radio interviews defending the position. The view the pair of us took was, 'The US won't let us off the hook.' In an environment in which the New Zealanders were kicking over the traces on the nuclear ships issue, when the Americans were bracing the Europeans to take Pershing missiles on the Continent and cruise missiles in Britain – this was *not* an environment in which the United States was going to back off. I remember meeting the Americans and saying, *'Just fire the bloody missiles!'* and they said, 'Oh, no. They won't be ready for eighteen months.' So we were going to have to put up with this crap for another eighteen months. Anyway, Bob was about to go overseas, to Japan and then Washington, and he got Richardson to do the numbers. I spoke to Richardson and he said he thought he had a majority of three votes in the Caucus. So I said to Bob, 'It's going to be pretty bloody tough in Caucus,' and he said, 'Aw, no: I've made up my mind we'll have to get out of it.' I said, *'Mate! You can't do that!'* The Americans won't let us off the hook.'

Neither Beazley nor Hayden realised that Hawke was holding out as strongly as he was because of his long-standing friendship with the American Secretary of State, George Shultz, whom he had known since his ACTU days. 'He didn't want to fail Shultz,' Richardson said.

Shultz was one of the great men of the twentieth century, and continued to be so in the twenty-first when, well into his ninth decade, he worked on international nuclear disarmament. As a marine in World War II, he had led the American forces ashore at Pulau in the North Pacific and was fond of remarking, 'There's no such thing as an ex-marine.' He was a warrior by nature, a Republican, a sophisticate who – way beyond the conventions of his status and class – had a tattoo somewhere on his body; he was politician, diplomat and a man of profound sagacity and shrewdness. He spoke slowly and thoughtfully, usually in a soft voice and often after a long pause during which his remarkable blue eyes, the colour of aquamarines, gazed like a sea captain's towards some distant horizon. Henry Kissinger, always sparing in his compliments about others, said if the United States were in danger, Shultz was the man he would like to see in charge. At Stanford University, Shultz taught a course in diplomacy that was famous for its insights. 'His knowledge of geopolitics was ency-clopedic,' Beazley said. Shultz and Hayden more or less loathed each other and had many shouting matches. Hayden referred to Shultz as 'the German pork butcher'. What Shultz called the Australian Foreign minister to his face was '*STOOPID*'. White recalled, 'In press conferences, when they had to sit side by side, the hostility was just radiating off both of them. It was right up there with John Howard and Bill Clinton in terms of negative chemistry. But it was quite effective diplomatically for Australia.'

Hawke, as so often in a tight corner, was about to turn his weakness – not wanting to disappoint Shultz – into a strength.

Beazley recalled,

Bob arrives in Washington. For some reason he decided to confide in me – reasonable, I guess, as I was Defence minis-ter. So I had one of those weird nights. I had my two little girls over from Perth staying with me in a hotel in Sydney and Bob was on the phone to me *all night* to discuss what had been said by whom and to whom. Each time the phone rang my little girls, aged about four and six, would wake up and crawl into bed with me and then start flicking through the television channels and get onto the X-rated movies.

I'm desperately trying to talk to the Prime Minister and to seize control of the remote from them, while on the screen people are shagging the arse off each other. Terrific! It was a *dreadful* night. But only Bob could have pulled it off. He convinced Shultz that if the test went ahead, then serious issues would come on the table about the joint facilities, and that there would be a groundswell of opinion in Australia against them.

Hayden recalled, 'Bob rang me at 4 a.m. and said, "Look, we're not going to allow the tests." And that was it.'

When Hawke announced that Australia would not be supporting the MX missile tests the news media frothed: 'Hawke caves in: No to MX tests' was on the front page of the *Australian*, which ran a side story 'Breathtaking victory for the anti-nuclear camp'. One cartoonist, making fun of the fact that American presidents of the past had called Australian prime ministers by the wrong names, had a flunkey announcing to the United States leader, 'Mr Bob Chicken to see you, Sir'. Others drew Hawke tied in a knot with his own arms and legs. Peacock announced that 'Australians would never again trust Mr Hawke in international affairs after his handling of the MX missile'. A poll showed that only 9 per cent of people thought Hawke's performance as prime minister was 'excellent', while 64 per cent rated it as 'poor' or 'average'. Reflecting anger in the party against Hawke, a cartoonist drew the ALP as a frog, its tongue flashing out at a fly: the Prime Minister.

Richardson said,

If a leader backs off something, the media present it as a disaster for him. But it isn't really. It's just a few days of bad publicity. The far bigger disaster is getting rolled and having your leadership totally undermined. Leaders have to cop a few days of bad publicity now and again. That's what being a leader is about.

The hysteria whipped up about the MX crisis was blamed for a dive in the Australian currency – 'Missile Confusion Undermines Dollar' according to the *Australian*, on 8 February – although the more likely cause was that markets were beginning to react to Australia's external payments situation; nevertheless, the dollar was down, and this had serious implications for inflation, and the Accord.

Hawke was blamed.

The day before the Prime Minister returned to Australia, Keating, who had played no public part in the MX Affair to date, stepped forward and told the party, through the news media, to '*Shut up!*'

In 2010 Beazley saw the crisis at its conclusion as one of the most positive turning points in Australia's relationship with the United States.

> These days everyone wanders around examining their navels, trying to work out the relationship between Rudd and Obama: is it going to be better than the one between Howard and Bush? or was that better than the one between Keating and Clinton? Nobody used to talk like that in the 1980s. Nobody was looking around for a close relationship between Bob and Reagan, Bob and Bush Senior. In fact, the view in Australia was, 'Yes, keep the alliance, and a degree of independence. Agree on fundamentals, but keep our national policies and the way in which *we* see the world.' So the first of those close personal relationships that I've come across historically between an American and an Australian politician was the Shultz–Hawke connection. It was the first. And it was deeper than any of the others because it did something that none of the others have ever done: it caused the United States to surrender a very important strategic policy to allow an Australian politician to get off the hook. What Bob managed was a miracle.

The MX crisis brought to the fore public debate in Australia about the American bases. Founded on the work Hayden had begun, Beazley steered discussion within Australia and with the Reagan administration; his imaginative power united with his depth of military knowledge transformed the bases issue from one of Big Brother–Little Nobody into one of equality between the United States and Australia. By the end of Beazley's term as Defence minister, the American bases had become the 'joint facilities' – in name and in fact. This is a relationship of equality that, even in 2010, had not yet been negotiated by the British for the American bases in the UK. In the late 1980s, Dick Cheney, the American Secretary of Defence, visited Australia and Beazley, instead of meeting him in Sydney, asked him to fly straight to Pine Gap for a briefing. The Australian Defence minister knew what was about to happen; the American did not. A beautiful woman stepped forward. 'She was gorgeous: a mane of blonde hair,' Hugh White recalled. She was the briefing officer. When she began to speak Cheney's head spun round to stare at Beazley. 'She's an Aussie!' he exclaimed in a stage whisper. White recalled, 'I was standing right behind Cheney. It was a *very telling* moment.'

After the MX crisis, the next major challenge for the government, and for Hawke in particular, was the 'Tax Summit', promised during the election campaign. There was now a mandate to reform the taxation system. Treasury was more excited than it could remember: with Keating, it had as its champion a politician who, once convinced on an issue, would fight relentlessly. Treasury was only too aware of how jerry-built the tax system was; for a decade its economists had been itching to dismantle most of it and rebuild on the firm foundation of a value-added tax, bringing Australia up to date with most of the rest of the OECD countries. The moment, it seemed, had arrived.

Garnaut had been working since October on a framework for the Summit (as had economists from the Department of Prime Minister and Cabinet, and Treasury). His original note on the framework included both a broad-based consumption tax and death duties – 'not that we would *include* those things, but that we should consider everything', he said. But the Treasurer and the New South Wales Right regarded death duties as a political suicide tax, and they were struck from the list as taboo, never again to be mentioned. Hawke had announced nine principles during the election: no overall tax increase; more cuts in personal income tax; a crack-down against tax avoidance and evasion; a simpler tax system; a more progressive system in which tax was paid according to capacity to pay; no disadvantage to welfare beneficiaries; no indirect taxation expansion that might prejudice wage restraint; a package that facilitated investment and employment; and, finally, proposals that had wide community support. It read like a list for Santa Claus. Out of delicacy, the really big present had been omitted. The *big* gift Treasury wanted was a broad-based consumption tax (its purer form, a value-added tax, being deemed too difficult even to consider). 'The Keating–treasury tactic,' Paul Kelly wrote, 'was to hijack the tax agenda. The treasury was not interested in an analysis of options; its mind was set.'[1]

Keating and his advisers believed Labor could win the next election, due in 1987, by outflanking the Opposition on tax reform: broadening the tax base and making deep cuts in personal income tax; appealing to the less affluent by an attack on the tax shelters of the wealthy and rounding this off with a well-aimed kick to the shins of the prosperous: a capital gains tax.

But within a few months Hawke and Garnaut began to suspect Keating and Treasury had helicoptered away into cloud cuckoo land. So, in the end, did most of the rest of the Cabinet. The scene was set for an internal battle.

Keating's tactic, Kelly wrote,

> was to destroy Labor's options ... Keating's aim was to generate such a momentum for reform that ... retreat would be seen as political cowardice and that biting the tax bullet would become the lesser electoral risk ... It was a classic hijack.[2]

Keating had frightening strengths and equally frightening weaknesses as a politician: his weapons of scorn and bias were unparalleled, seeming at times as refined as a civilised vice. His rhetorical skills for attack and salesmanship were of the highest order; he was a man of passion and imagination – and had he not been a politician would have been 'a mad inventor', according to Beazley. His intelligence and curiosity of mind had led him to hobbies, one after another, all his life: car engines; budgerigars; the life of Winston Churchill; rock music and, as his taste matured, classical music and its visible sister, architecture. He loved clocks and the decorative arts of the Second Empire in France. Especially these: over the years he was to collect enough for a small museum. He had begun life as a beautiful dark-haired child from a working-class suburb that struggled to become middle class and he had grown into a beautiful dark-haired political tough – 'that boy is a political killer', Kim Beazley Senior had remarked when first he had seen Keating, aged twenty-five, in Parliament House. And all the time the young man was assiduously transforming himself from his modest beginnings into the Bankstown version of a gentleman – with a good dose of Johnny Rotten, the punk band leader, up his well-tailored sleeve. Keating wore beautiful clothes; he had a natural eye for elegance both elaborate and simple; his wife, Annita, was a stately, multilingual European, with whom he enjoyed mutual devotion; he was courted by the rich and powerful, and revelled in the company of artists. His life was a dream come true. But it was even more than that, for it seemed as if Keating's very soul bore traces of the brilliant Second Empire: Paris – the capital city he most loved and studied so well he could draw maps of it from memory – had been rebuilt during that brief and shining age of Napoleon III when good music was promoted for its uplifting effect on the labouring classes. The emperor had wanted to transform his society, but unfortunately he had also declared war on the Prussians. France was left 'in pieces'. There was, in Keating's nature, something of the same lust for transformation as displayed in the Second Empire: he had transformed himself; now he would transform his country. He wanted a *different* Australia. Both aimed for reform: both wanted a *better* Australia, one in which all people would have equal opportunity to use their innate gifts, prosper, and have the opportunity to be happy. If Hawke had a motto for the nation it would have been that of the Roman Emperor Hadrian: 'Humanity, Liberty, Happiness'.

He was, in Paul Kelly's description,

> A balanced and diligent Prime Minister, assessing issues on merit. People today underestimate the extraordinary chemistry and atmosphere of the time: the crusading element in Keating was amazing. Hawke, I think, was concerned at how far out Keating had gone on this issue; Keating would talk in terms of 'putting his job on the line' over it. [The Tax Summit] was the first evidence we saw of a remarkable phenomenon of the Keating political character, which we saw later in his Prime Ministership – a really crusading element, wanting to move beyond the limits of the system to transcending new policies. Which he can then impose on the system ... In a sense, it's a variation of the Whitlam crash-through-or-crash.[3]

Keating's supporters were ever after to present the Tax Summit as a time when Hawke showed that, underneath, he was weak. It was a view important to their self-esteem, because the other explanation was that Keating was reckless.

Immediately after the 1984 election, the Prime Minister had held a meeting at The Lodge with Keating, Garnaut and other advisers. From this meeting a task force had been set up to draft a White Paper for the Summit. Kelly wrote, 'It was an immediate battle.'[4] Treasury was on one side, Garnaut and Ed Visbord from Prime Minister and Cabinet on the other. '[They] grew more hostile with each task force meeting.'[5] Peter Barron and Bob Hogg, Right and Left wings of the party, were dubious about the Treasury idea of introducing a series of new taxes, each one potentially alienating a part of the electorate.

At the outset, Hawke laid down a condition: whatever was finally adopted as the reform, it would have to be in place completely before the 1987 election, with no loose ends onto which the Opposition could attach a wrecking ball. Garnaut said,

> He wanted to be able to implement changes crisply, to have them all up and running a year or more before the next election. That was tremendously important. Bob made very clear that we needed crisp answers to the questions of income distribution. We still had high unemployment and high inflation and the big game was still macroeconomic reform: winding down inflation; economic expansion to mop up unemployment; wage restraint through the Accord and the support of the ACTU. If all that was to come out of the Tax Summit was a consumption tax added onto wages you'd bugger the rest of the program. But Treasury didn't hear that. They didn't want to hear the conditions.

Partly because of the hyped drama of the MX missile crisis, the dollar had fallen, which increased inflation, which in turn meant it would be more difficult for the ACTU to support wage restraint.

Garnaut, having himself put a broad-based consumption tax on the agenda, was convinced by April that it was more trouble than it was worth, a danger to everything that had been achieved so far.

> I started saying that the whole package was not going to meet Bob's conditions, pointing out that we had a big inflationary impulse but we really did have to deliver on wage restraint or we'd simply lose the big game.

Keating meanwhile was assuring the Prime Minister and others that the ACTU was on side. But Garnaut, who had his own sources, was hearing a different story, as was Willis, and they were reporting to Hawke that Keating was being misinformed. All factions expected that, at the Tax Summit, business would be supportive of the reforms. Keating, busy lobbying the ACTU and welfare groups, was confident he could take for granted the endorsement of the Business Council of Australia.

The White Paper, still including the option of a broad-based consumption tax, was put to the Cabinet in mid-May, causing disbelief. There were three meetings and, according to Kelly, twenty-three hours of discussion,

> before Keating emerged victorious with Cabinet endorsement of his option [C] as the preferred government position ... only Hawke, Gareth Evans, Kim Beazley and Susan Ryan supported Keating's position; it was carried against the numbers. Keating talked, seduced and intimidated the Cabinet into submission, leaving a legacy of bad blood. It was a decision devoid of conviction. Most ministers were unenthusiastic and some were horrified.[6]

Ralph Willis said,

> Bob's approach to Cabinet was consensus, to let people have their say and not to have his own say until he had the feel of the meeting – or if he didn't like the way it was going, he would steer the discussion and argue the points. Paul's was: 'Well, this is what I think – and you all should think the same.'

Hawke knew he had to back up his Treasurer to save Keating's face in Cabinet, while reasoning that the Summit, through a free play of ideas, would be the final arbitrator. But his less-than-ecstatic support for Keating's 'tax cart', as it had become known, annoyed the Treasurer who, in frustration, referred to the Prime Minister as 'Old Jellyback', a sobriquet invented by Peter Walsh. This, despite the fact that without Hawke's backing Keating's cart would be a write-off. Peacock picked up the 'Jellyback' tag and used it in parliament, as did Wilson Tuckey. Behind Hawke's back, Keating was speaking so vituperatively of him that Bill Hayden, not a man to carry stories, sought out Ross Garnaut, to warn the Prime Minister's office, 'Look, it doesn't matter to me what Keating says about Hawke, but I think it's bad for the government.'

Hawke opened the Tax Summit on 1 July, with an appeal to its 160 delegates to restore 'equity, efficiency and integrity' to the tax system, adding, 'All Australians require an assurance that the least privileged among us will not suffer as a result of the changes. I give that assurance unreservedly.'

Next up was Bob White, president of the Business Council of Australia (BCA) who, for a week before the Tax Summit had tried to contact Keating, but the Treasurer had been too busy to take his calls. That was a mistake, because what White had to say lobbed a hand grenade into the tax cart. The BCA rejected the proposed reforms holus-bolus, because they didn't go far enough – and once the BCA had bridled, every other sectional interest felt at liberty to do so too, each from its own narrow point of view.

John Hyde, the Opposition's intellectual leader, wrote,

> Like the cast of a Greek tragedy, Tax Summit participants remained true to their flawed characters destroying something that most of them wanted then or came to want within a few years. Keating should have anticipated the selfishness and political incompetence of the business community ... while he worked in detail with the ACTU, he did little to ensure that the business sector did not destroy his summit in a manner that was foreseeable.[7]

The cart was running downhill fast; to Hawke, who had been giving Keating his head for months, it was obvious that the Treasurer was no longer in control of his vehicle. That evening 'events moved with speed and drama as Hawke began a series of private talks to locate a compromise', Kelly wrote.[8] The talks continued on the second day, inconclusively, then, on the morning of the third day, the *Bulletin* magazine came out with a Morgan poll that showed the Opposition leading Labor by

8 per cent – and, for the first time, Keating being more popular than Hawke. This was the inevitable result of Hawke's lower profile and Keating's higher one during the months leading up to the Tax Summit. Kelly described the shocked mood within the party and the government over the Morgan poll: 'If debate about Keating's package had done such harm what fate for Labor after its implementation?'[9] The Prime Minister had given the Treasurer every chance to drive his tax cart home, had supported him during the drafting of the White Paper, in Cabinet and at the Summit – and the result was this: a looming electoral defeat. Hawke realised that he must take the power he had given Keating away from him.

Bill Hayden, who had been vociferous in his opposition to the consumption tax, said,

> Paul is a typical Irish political conniver … [but] I thought he was taking on too many fights at once. In politics, if you take on too many fights you can get done on the lot of them, instead of just the ones you should get done on.

Lined up against Keating and Treasury were business, the ACTU, the Centre Left and the Left of the party, the welfare lobby, John Stone – now, on the loose from his public service bridle, kicking down doors as a media commentator – and the canny populist, Sir Joh Bjelke-Petersen, who wanted a flat tax. Of these, from Hawke's point of view, the ACTU was of paramount importance because of the big game in which it was decisive: wage restraint.

That night the Prime Minister, without telling Keating – whom he thought had temporarily lost all sense of objectivity – visited Simon Crean, president of the ACTU, and Bill Kelty, its secretary, in their hotel rooms to work out a compromise. Keating and his advisers still believed they had the unions on side, although all week Crean and Kelty had been telling them the situation was very difficult. Hawke said,

When I arrived at the hotel that night I asked Bill Kelty to restate the ACTU's position for me. Bill did not mince words. The ACTU would not accept Option C . . . With that, the consumption tax was dead.

Eyes and ears are everywhere in Canberra and the story of Hawke's visit by night to his old colleagues leaked: Keating was to learn from the morning newspaper that, like a dream, his planned transformation of Australia's tax system had vanished.

Hawke, whose heart had been broken open by the shock of his daughter's plight, was still and would remain for years, easily prone to tears. His depression had lifted but there remained with him a deepened sense of the pains of life: he was a more sensitive man than he had been, which is not always an advantage for a political leader. He knew how badly he had hurt Keating and how deeply Keating bore hurts. His voice trembled with emotion at the Tax Summit that afternoon as he announced that Option C was dead because it did not meet the condition set out at the very beginning for 'wide community support'. Keating was gracious and reached out to pat Hawke comfortingly. He was the trusted colleague to whom, in his deepest misery, Hawke had reached out, father to father, to confide about Rosslyn. Until the end there would stay with them a subtle bond of affection that the news media, through ignorance or mischief, refused to acknowledge.

During the press conference that followed they did an impressive double act as brothers in arms. Hawke, feeling tense, was strident and Keating, feeling devastated, was funny. Referring to his 'tax cart' he said, 'It's a bit like *Ben Hur*. We've crossed the line with one wheel off, but we have crossed the line.' Nietzsche remarked: 'A joke is an epitaph for the death of a feeling.'

In private, Keating's slaughtered dream cried out for revenge not from Hawke but from Hawke's staff. Kelly wrote that Keating

abused Barron and complained about Garnaut. His loathing for Hawke's office . . . intensified. His senior advisor [Tony]

Cole had a screaming match with Barron ... From this night onwards Keating, typically, manufactured his own history. He insisted that he could have won – but for Hawke's betrayal.[10]

Ironically, eight years later Keating implicitly acknowledged that Hawke had been correct when he fought furiously against a consumption tax proposed by the Opposition.

But a line had indeed been crossed. Prime Minister and Treasurer would still fight side by side as a formidable duo, but their tender feelings for each other had weakened. In earlier days they could often be seen hugging, holding tête-à-têtes, touching each other's hands and arms with an easy rapport. Their friendship now was less overt, but it still ran deep, and intimate.

Meanwhile, from the wreckage of his cart Keating constructed over the next two months a new tax package that was, in fact, an impressive reform – so much so it convinced members of the Opposition that it would be electoral poison, especially after they mauled it in the Senate. Keating's tax reforms, the Opposition believed, would deliver to them the next election. Peacock had eagerly adopted the idea that Hawke was a weak leader and that but for minor reasons *he* would have won the 1984 election. Peacock was a vain man whose care of his appearance and dress gave the impression he spent more time on fittings with his tailor than on fitting himself for leading the nation. He had a reputation for laziness. On 5 September 1985 a plain, hard-working but more formidable politician inside the Liberal Party overthrew him. John Howard became leader. Now Hawke and the government had a serious adversary.

TWENTY-THREE

B OTH GOUGH WHITLAM AND Malcolm Fraser were well
regarded in China: Whitlam for opening diplomatic
relations with the People's Republic in 1972, and Fraser
for striking the first bilateral aid agreement. Fraser had invited
the Chinese Premier, Zhao Ziyang, to visit Australia in April
1983, supposing he would be the prime minister to greet the
Chinese leader. But it was Hawke – and from the moment of
Zhao's arrival the Chinese and the Australian leaders took to
each other *yi jian ru gu* (first sight, like old days) as the Chinese
proverb says. The times were opportune. Just over four years
earlier China's supreme leader, Deng Xiaoping, had decreed that
China would open to the West and move to a market economy.
He had done so against huge opposition within his own government. Psychologically, the country was still entangled in a puzzle
of ideological knots. Few of its leaders had ever been outside its
borders. Its people were forbidden to travel abroad. The bulk
of its gigantic population was backward, poor, superstitious and
paranoid after centuries of mismanagement, Western attack,
warlordism, two revolutions – the first republican, the second
Communist – occupation, the worst famine in human history,
and three decades spent in Chairman Mao's laboratory for social
engineering and intellectual adventure. An entire generation
had been robbed of an education thanks to the decade of terror
known as the Cultural Revolution. Like the religious of medieval
Europe obeying dictates of the Church, millions still embraced
suffering and poverty as virtues: the party had instructed them
to do so. But in December 1978, Deng had declared, 'To get

rich is no sin' and dismissed ingrained concepts of good and bad Communists with a proverb: 'It doesn't matter if the cat is black or white, so long as it catches mice.' China's third revolution in one century had been proclaimed.

By the early 1980s, the obstacles it faced were vast: in its own neighbourhood China had no diplomatic relations with Indonesia, South Korea or Singapore, while the Chinese people's feelings for Japan, the world's second-largest economy, were embittered with memories of the Japanese occupation that stretched from the late 1930s to 1945. China had very few interpreters of foreign languages, no system of commercial law – and thanks to its centuries of turmoil (although having once been a peaceful, law-abiding empire) – the country now barely understood the concept of the rule of law. It had state guest houses for foreign heads of state, but the hotels it needed for foreign businesspeople were still of a standard to give a Swiss hotelier toothache. Lacking foreign language staff and with cultural differences so vast they seemed planetary, phone calls and housekeeping were often pantomimes ending with Western visitors puce with rage while a smiling Chinese writhed in silent fury at them. (The Westerners, by losing their temper, had lost just as much face as the Chinese, but being unaware of this, kept going.) The 'Western food' in dining rooms was punitive. China existed outside the stream of history as far as the Western world was concerned, still regarded as Napoleon's 'sleeping giant'; in the twentieth century, it seemed a giant kicking around in a comic nightmare of little red books and running dogs.

During the 1970s Left-wing trade union leaders urged Hawke to go to Beijing but he refused until the Gang of Four were in jail or dead. (The Gang of Four was a group inside the Communist Party, led by Mao's wife, known in the latter stages of the Cultural Revolution for their cruelty and ambition to seize control of China after Mao's death. They were overthrown in a coup d'état in late 1976, tried and imprisoned. 'Four' in Chinese sounds the same as 'death', so they were, to Chinese ears, 'the death squad'.) When Hawke did visit the country, in 1978, he was captivated by the people and the potential he saw in them.

'My first visit was the beginning of a deep friendship towards the Chinese people,' he said. 'China was a poor and insignificant economy with hundreds of millions living below the poverty line, but I had the feeling that they would harness their mighty resources of human capital and become a great world power.' He was the first leader in the world to foresee China's re-emergence.

From their initial encounter the Chinese liked Hawke. Intuitively, it seemed, they recognised he was non-racist and had benevolent feelings towards their country. Physically, Hawke was not so big as to be intimidating; his body was trim rather than shambling like many Westerners; his high forehead was a sign of intelligence; his nose was curved at the tip rather than pointy, which is considered ugly; he had a warrior's hard, piercing gaze; prolific eyebrows of the correct, strong shape for a leader; ears with large fleshy earlobes, a sign of high status and good luck; his face was without unlucky moles, and he was very friendly. He allowed himself grey hair, a look that was both exotically Western and rather bohemian to the Chinese eye. Over the decades, thanks to many television and newspaper interviews, Hawke became one of the most recognised foreign faces in China and could not walk down a Beijing lane without people shouting 'Hou Ke! Hou Ke!' and calling friends to come out of their houses to look at him.

From Zhao's initial visit a rhythm developed: each alternate year a Chinese leader would come to Australia and in the intervening year Hawke would go to China. Australia was, from the Chinese point of view, a perfect gateway for its opening to the West. A developed English-speaking nation that had never been a colonial power was in alliance with the United States and had good relations with its Asian neighbours. China in 1983 was a land power. Although Communist, in Cold War terms China was an asset to the alliance because its adversary was the Soviet Union, which threatened China from the north and west, and also from the south, via the Soviet client state, Vietnam. President Nixon had 'played the China card' during his phase of the Cold War, bringing China under American protection vis-à-vis the USSR. It was a brilliant move, but the Americans remained nervous about their Communist ally, on tenterhooks that Nixon had been too clever, and that the Chinese may have a secret understanding with the USSR. For Republicans, the concept of alliance with *Communists* created mental nausea. They jumped at Chinese shadows. Hawke's good relations with the Reagan administration were known in Beijing and on several occasions the leaders, once their relationship with him had blossomed, asked him to take messages of reassurance to Washington. From Hawke's point of view, China was a highly desirable trading partner: it was in the same time zone as Western Australia and offered the biggest market in the world for Australian products. One of its ambassadors never tired of telling Australian politicians, 'If you sell a single pair of socks made from Australian wool to every Chinese, you won't need to sell wool to anyone else in the world.' But it was on iron for steel and, increasingly, black coal, not wool, that the commercial friendship was founded.

In his earliest days in office, Hawke had spoken about 'enmeshment with Asia', which at the time was greeted with cynical chortling from press sahibs and other gurus. With the exception of Japan, 'Asia' was poor, backward, overpopulated and had been asleep for a couple of hundred years.

Zhao's first visit to Australia had been a getting-to-know-you exercise at which nothing was decided. Chinese culture is intensely hierarchical, and Chinese leaders of those days and even now can be, by Australian standards, rivetingly formal. For centuries the motto of Chinese rulers has been 'First awe, then soothe'. Leaders observe a strict dress code of dark suit, subdued tie and black shoes. There is no mention of family, of recreations, of private interests. No personal issue is permitted to appear even fleetingly from behind the official mask of office – at least until feelings of trust are established. An agenda for discussion is worked out by aides in advance of a meeting; each side says their piece, there are pleasantries, an exchange of gifts, photographs and a banquet. If a leader is visiting a building, the aides will check it in advance so that the size and layout of the rooms, whether there are stairs, and how many, are known. Surprises can cause confusion, even loss of dignity, and the horror of loss of face.

In February 1984 Hawke visited South Korea, Japan and China and just before calling on Zhao told the Australian ambassador in Beijing that he wanted to raise with the Premier an idea for co-operation in the iron and steel sector. The ambassador was aghast: 'You can't do that, Prime Minister! There have been no preparatory discussions. The Premier will think we have ambushed him.' Hawke listened impatiently to a treatise on the protocols of the Middle Kingdom. At the end of it he took Ross Garnaut, who was travelling with him, aside. 'I'm going to say it anyway,' he said. Hawke had judged that Zhao liked him enough to accept a surprise.

When Hawke raised with the Premier the idea of closer links in the iron and steel industry, Zhao was fascinated. At the time, almost all Chinese iron ore and all its coal were domestic, but it was of low quality and consequently Chinese steel mills' productivity was poor. Australia was keen to find markets for its iron ore and steel, so Hawke proposed to Zhao that China could improve its steel industry, especially in the coastal provinces, by importing Australia's high-quality iron ore and coking coal. As Garnaut remarked, 'This was *radical* stuff.'

Mother China had a deep ideological belief that she must be self-sufficient in rice and iron, lest she once more found herself at the mercy of enemies who could starve her children or beat her to death. Hawke proposed the two countries ease into the new relationship through a joint venture in iron ore production as a way for China to gain confidence in using imported raw materials. Garnaut was taking notes of the discussion and recalled,

A few times Bob stopped for Zhao's response and Zhao said, 'No, no – keep going.' He wasn't taking notes himself at all.

So Bob talked through all his points, which took about half an hour, and at the end Zhao just started answering them in the order in which Bob had raised them. And on the iron and steel stuff he was very expansive, saying, 'It's a good idea, let's work together on that.'

Zhao proposed a joint study group as a way of China getting to understand Australia's capabilities as a supplier of high-quality material, and Australia getting to know China's needs for industrial development. From this conversation began the enormous trade in raw materials that was to fuel Australian prosperity and give jobs to tens of millions of Australians and Chinese as yet unborn.

Zhao was a reserved, serious man, a protégé of Deng Xiaoping, but as he and Hawke saw more of each other he increasingly relaxed. He was the leader of the reformists in government and deeply interested in the nuts and bolts of reform. As he felt more confident in the Australian leader, he allowed their conversations to move to discussion of the ideas that really excited him, inviting Hawke to share his own ideas and experience on reforming the Australian economy. They began moving further and further outside the confines of their strict, premeditated roles. It was a relationship that was as poignant as it was thrilling: two men from enemy ideologies striving to found modern economies and uplift their people through mutual co-operation. On Hawke's trip of 1984, Zhao engineered a meeting for him with his superior, the General Secretary of the Communist Party, Hu Yaobang. Hu was a tiny, excitable extrovert, 'like a bright-eyed sparrow', Hawke said, very popular with the Chinese people and one of the last of the great eccentrics of Chinese politics. As second in command of the largest country on earth, he was somewhat more important in world affairs than the Prime Minister of Australia. But he paid Hawke an unusual compliment. They were scheduled to have their first meeting in Nanjing when a storm made landing there impossible. Hawke had to fly on to Shanghai. Hu flew down to Shanghai himself so the meeting could still take place. It was obvious that Zhao had spoken highly of Hawke to his boss. Again, there was an instant rapport: *lao pengyou xiang yu* (old friends on first meeting).

Hawke invited Hu to visit Australia, which he did in April 1985, in the midst of the discussions about the White Paper for the Tax Summit. While he was with the General Secretary, he delivered by hand a reissued banking licence for the Bank of China, to facilitate trade.

Meanwhile, agreement had been reached on a Sino-Australian mining joint venture at Mount Channar in Western Australia, the first investment China had ever made in a foreign mine. Hawke repaid Hu's compliment by flying to Perth to meet him and his right-hand man, Hu Qili, after dinner in a restaurant overlooking the Swan River. The next day they flew to Mount Channar. Hu found it all highly exciting and exotic. China was grey and dusty. Australia was technicolour. Hu Yaobang marvelled at skies as blue as a Ming vase, at the endless red landscape and the huge, well-fed workers with their sunburnt faces and brawny forearms pelted in yellow hair. To everyone's delight he put a rock in his pocket to take home as a souvenir. The party then flew on to Whyalla to visit the BHP steel mill from which, in due course, China would buy 40 per cent of production, thus keeping the city going until the Australian domestic market improved. At Whyalla the word was around that Hawke would be visiting and most of the town turned out to greet him. Hu was thrilled. He assumed the people had come out to see *him*, and that the waving and smiling and cheering and photograph-taking were all being staged in his honour. He waved and smiled right back, his exuberance, Hawke said, 'was wonderful to see'. Australian informality was intoxicating for mainland Chinese of those days, burdened as they were by etiquette, protocol and fear of loss of face. The Chinese saw a young and innocent people living an insouciant, rapturous life amidst glorious natural beauty. In one sense, they saw us more clearly than we saw ourselves: by 1985 Australia was already living way beyond its means.

On Hu's return to China the bureaucratic machinery suddenly shifted up several gears, in Australia's favour.

In late 1985, after the tax reform package was finalised, Hawke appointed Garnaut as ambassador to Beijing. Garnaut said, 'Hu was politically really important. While Zhao was the one who managed government and made the reforms happen, Hu was cleaning out the old Cultural Revolutionaries from the Party, embedding the new approach.' (More than thirty years after 'The Terrible Decade', as the Chinese call the Cultural Revolution, what one did or failed to do during that time still determined how high one could rise in government in China, and often if one's business would prosper. Nobody says, but everyone remembers: you saved my grandmother from starvation; you beat my uncle to death.) After Hu's visit Australians in China who had been battling the bureaucracy suddenly found that doors opened and insoluble problems evaporated. Cultural and educational exchanges became easier; a group of Chinese was allowed to attend Writers' Week at the Adelaide Festival. Australians were allowed to tour China in supervised groups.

Garnaut said, 'People down the chain of command were saying, the Boss likes the Prime Minister of Australia, and likes Australia, so we'll make it happen.' In two years, from 1984, there were more than twenty-eight delegations at ministerial level and economic co-operation expanded from iron and steel to wool, non-ferrous metals, transport and communications, and to coal. Six technical co-operation programs had been concluded and fourteen more were underway.[1] Such was the amiability of the relationship, Zhao began teasing Garnaut about his beard. 'Here comes the Marxist economist,' he'd announce when Australia's ambassador was ushered into his presence. Garnaut shaved it off.

He was in charge of arranging Hawke's reciprocal visit in May 1986 by which time Australia was, in his description, 'flavour of the month'. In April 1986 John Bannon, Premier of South Australia, had visited Beijing and made a courtesy call on the general secretary, who had shocked everybody except Bannon, who did not fully grasp the significance of what was happening, by saying, 'Let's have a meeting in my house in Zhongnanhai.' Garnaut said, 'It was unheard of. Like setting out for an official visit to the Queen, and having her say, "Oh why don't you stay for a sandwich at lunchtime?"' Bannon duly went to the political holy site, Zhongnanhai. At the end of their meeting, Hu had said, 'It's spring, and the first blossoms have appeared. Why don't we walk around the lake?' During their stroll Hu had made it clear, by referring to issues he had discussed with Hawke, that this had been the reason for his pleasure in Bannon's company. He mentioned he would like to see Australia–China trade doubled by 1990. The Beijing diplomatic corps, Garnaut reported, 'were green with envy: a mere state premier had been treated better than any of their heads of government ever had'.

When Hawke arrived a few weeks later, Hu and Zhao made room in their schedules for unusually long discussions, and Hu set out to reciprocate Hawke's courtesy. Hawke had arrived in the west, in Chengdu. Hu flew across China to meet him there and arranged a banquet with *knives and forks*. He knew Hawke was at ease with chopsticks, but he was being hyper-polite in providing cutlery. He was also making a political point: Hu wanted the Chinese to give up the unsanitary tradition of plunging chopsticks into a communal food bowl, a known way to spread hepatitis, and thought the Western cutlery was a necessary reform. But in 1986 the knife and the fork were such rarities in China that only the social elite could manipulate them, so the Chengdu banquet, photographed and televised, turned into a lesson for the nation: knife, right, fork, left. Plunge fork into food, steady it with knife. Et cetera.

It was during the formal discussions on 19 May between Hawke and Premier Zhao Ziyang that Hawke raised the possibility of Chinese students studying in Australia. At the time only a handful of postgraduate students from China and Australia had studied in each other's countries. Hawke wanted Chinese schoolchildren to come to Australia to qualify to enrol in Australian universities as undergraduates. It would be good for bilateral relations, he believed, and a great financial boost to the tertiary sector, which had been desperately in need of funds since Whitlam made university education 'free': free, that is, for students, expensive for taxpayers. Hawke had talked long and hard to his Education minister, Susan Ryan, about the need for her to stand up to the teachers' unions opposed to the idea of fee-paying foreign students 'on principle'. Premier Zhao welcomed the suggestion and agreed that, when Ryan visited later that year, it could be further explored. None of them imagined then the bonanza Chinese (and other foreign students) would be for Australia. By the early twenty-first century education had burgeoned into a $35 billion export industry.

In China – then and now – leaders, both domestic and foreign, are accompanied by hordes of advisers, aides, bodyguards and general fusspots who watch over them with such solicitude for their welfare they could be little children who might suddenly, through inattention, trip and hurt themselves. Leaders will have their heads protected by a white-gloved hand each time they enter a vehicle; every step on a staircase will be pointed out to them lest they slip, and they may not go to the bathroom unaccompanied. A female leader will have her handbag held by one of several female assistants who wait outside the cubicle and prepare running water or a little wet towel for her hands. Honour guards of beautiful, long-limbed young women in cheongsams split to their thighs welcome and farewell leaders, one presenting a bouquet while thirty others applaud. No other nation displays respect with the dramatic panache of China.

When that Chengdu banquet with its knives and forks was over, Hu dismissed his army of aides and invited Hawke back to his apartment in the state guest house. There were three Australians: Hawke, Garnaut and another diplomat, Richard Rigby, fluent in Mandarin, who was to act as translator. The Chinese were Hu Yaobang and the Vice Minister, Zhu Qizhen. Their translator was Gao Qikai.

Garnaut recalled, 'They just talked and talked. It was completely unknown for the Chinese leadership to do this. It didn't happen with Khrushchev or Tito. Hu talked until midnight, and the conversation covered everything.' At first they discussed the United States, Hu saying that the Chinese leadership 'would like to have separate, in-depth discussions with members of the US leadership, but they are always in a hurry'. The theme of China's frustrated attempts to form a genuine friendship with America wove throughout the night, with Hawke listening sympathetically, while constantly making clear his unshakeable friendship with the American leadership; he offered to convey Hu's message to Reagan, and to tell his friend, Shultz, that Hu and Zhao craved serious get-to-know-you discussions with the United States. Hu told Hawke he had tried to point out to the Vice President, George Bush, that in the Third World (a term China had invented), American prestige was slipping because of United States heavy-handedness. He told Hawke he had said to Bush, 'You've got more money than friends.' It was meant as a playful opening to a serious discussion over United States foreign policy. But Bush stood on the dignity of American imperialism, replying, 'No we don't – we have more friends', and that was the end of that, Hu said. He went on to ideas about solving the issue of Taiwan, the most intractable problem between the United States and China. He described Chinese alarm at recent American arms sales to the Republic, asking rhetorically, 'were all these arms designed to allow Taiwan to launch war against the US, Japan or the Soviet Union? No! They [are] only for confrontation against the mainland.' The discussion turned to the problems of the Korean peninsula, of American support for the Contras (the anti-socialist counter-revolutionaries) in Nicaragua and the recent bombing of Libya by the United States. Hawke argued back to Hu that Libya was planning terrorist attacks against American targets wherever it could find them – including in Australia, thus revealing to the Chinese leader secret Western intelligence. Hu responded with intelligence on the situation in Cambodia and Vietnam. As Hu continued to fret over American foreign policy, Hawke gently pointed out that the United States had existential problems to deal with: 'The US has a sense of isolation,' he said.

> Power, and great power, causes many people who come into contact with it to feel uncomfortable, and this can lead to the United States feeling isolated. If the US feels that China understands what it has to face, this will help it to respond favourably.

Hawke had recently had an audience with Pope John-Paul II and told Hu that the Pope had mentioned he would like the Holy See to have relations with China. Hu said, 'Bob, that's not a problem. All the Pope had to do is recognise Beijing is the capital of China.' (The Vatican continues to assert that Taipei is the capital of China.)

Hu Yaobang then remarked, 'The Soviet Union thinks it's the Pope of Communism.' It was his opening to a long conversation about the USSR, and China's analysis of its future – which proved to be extraordinarily prescient, for the Chinese had studied their worst enemy closely and calculated it would collapse internally from economic mismanagement. Hu also spoke movingly of Chinese social history, saying,

> For more than 100 years the Chinese were oppressed by the three big mountains: Imperialism, Feudalism and Bureaucratic Capitalism. Chinese people will never allow oppression by another mountain. If the Chinese leadership does not respect the wishes of the people we will be toppled.

He added, 'It is often more difficult to deal with the Soviets than the Americans,' and concluded by saying, 'Well, Prime Minister, I have shown you all our cards.'

The next day they flew to Nanjing and walked around the city together, drawing crowds of people excited to see the General Secretary. Hawke pretended they had turned up to see him, waving and smiling like Hu at Whyalla; that evening he and his host again talked long into the night. During these discussions, at which the same group of people gathered, Hu spoke about Sino-Japanese relationships, on which Richard Rigby was an expert. At one stage Hu said, 'We have to get over our feelings against Japan. We need to develop peace and prosperity together with Japan.' His sentiments of forgiveness for Japanese atrocities during its long occupation of China were so generous that Rigby, a professional diplomat, had tears streaming down his cheeks as he translated. The Chinese leader asserted to Hawke that China, 'for a minimum of thirty years would be buying Australian iron ore, steel and wool' and asked Hawke to do what he could to increase Chinese imports to Australia, 'because we lack foreign currency'.

Although the fact of these talks remained secret, within the diplomatic corps the word went round that the Australian Prime Minister had received 'unprecedented courtesies'. Garnaut said, 'It was a wonderful time to be ambassador.'

But China had neither policies nor regulations to deal with the agreements its leaders had made for the iron ore and steel venture and an investment in the Portland aluminium smelter in Victoria – in fact, Chinese foreign exchange laws made such investments illegal. Zhao and Hu instructed the bureaucracy to grease the machinery and problem after problem eased away. Several times Garnaut went to see Zhao with obstacles that seemed insurmountable and Zhao would either telephone officials or, on occasions, take the matter to the State Council for new legislation to be passed.

Zhao Ziyang had told Hawke the Chinese proverb: 'Ruling a big country is like frying a small fish' – that is, it's easy to ruin. Shanghai, China's most cosmopolitan city, was and is the centre of avant-garde thought and action. It was there that the Communist Party had been born after student unrest in 1919. Deng's reforms announced in December of 1978 had created a surge of wealth in China, but with it came a surge of corruption – the latter endemic in any society lacking the rule of law. At the time, per capita income was $US400, while the Chinese Premier was paid only five times this amount (although provided with many perquisites). The country was used to a degree of economic equality that by the 1980s was rare in the rest of the world. The surge of prosperity after opening to a market economy threw this accepted and cherished situation out of kilter, and in late 1986 students in Shanghai began demonstrating over rising prices and corruption. Deng became alarmed that Hu was not dealing with the students firmly enough, and that the city could run out of control. Deng, like Hu, was a physically tiny man, a veteran of the Long March and a pragmatist with a deeply grounded horror of mob rule. He had been jailed and bashed during the Cultural Revolution; as additional punishment Red Guards had thrown his son out a window, crippling the boy for life. As well as Deng's horrific personal experience, there was an ideological gulf between him on one hand and Hu and Zhao on the other. The younger men believed that with economic reform would inevitably come demands for greater social freedom and political accountability that the government would have to deal with. Hawke and Zhao had spoken of this on several occasions. But Deng believed it was essential to do one thing at a time: economic liberalisation came first, politics at some later date. He described in a proverb how China was to manage its progress: like a man gingerly crossing a river, feeling out with his toes the river stones on which to step. Deng feared that the conservatives in the party, who loathed his opening of the economy to the West, would use Shanghai's social unrest as excuse to throttle economic reform.

Hu Yaobang had always been something of a loose cannon, another reason the Chinese people loved him: he was a leader they could relate to as a human. Others were distant, awesome demiurges. Around the time of the Shanghai unrest, Hu was on a trip to New Zealand where he announced the very big news that the People's Liberation Army would be cut by 1 million troops. The decision to slash the size of the army had already been taken, but was still officially secret. Mentioning it provided enough ammunition for Hu's enemies in Beijing to criticise him publicly.

Deng took the hugely unpopular decision of sacking Hu. He replaced Hu with Zhao Ziyang.

Shanghai got the message and the students, dismayed and sullen, left the streets.

But there was a much sadder aspect to the disgrace of Hu Yaobang: the party held private denunciations of him in which he was accused of the crime of revealing state secrets to foreigners. 'That was, I think,' Garnaut said, 'a reference to some of his intimate conversations with Bob. It wasn't the reason, but it was the excuse they used inside the party, after the event, once they'd decided to kick Hu out.'

Hu's disgrace jerked the wheel of history. It began turning in a stormy gyre. Its thunder would burst three years later, in 1989, in the very centre of Beijing, in the huge plaza in front of the Forbidden City known as Heaven's Gate: Tiananmen.

At the beginning of his 1986 trip to China, while he was still in Tokyo, Hawke had his own troubles. An economic crunch, decades in the making, had arrived. On 13 May the Bureau of Statistics revealed the trade figures for April: the national current account deficit had leapt to $1.48 billion, 6 per cent of GDP. The economy had been expanding, but to finance the expansion the nation was borrowing more than it was earning in exports. Australia was in debt up to its ears.

Hawke had been given the figures before he left for East Asia and had discussed the situation with both the Treasurer and the rest of the Cabinet. 'The figures were certainly no cause for celebration, but we were determined to deal with them without panic,' he said. Cabinet had agreed that funds to the states would have to be cut, but they would leave that argument until the forthcoming Premiers' Conference, when Hawke and Keating would make it in public. The decision was to do nothing to spook the markets and to buy time for grappling with the underlying problems that had caused the huge debt. Since February 1985, the Australian dollar had lost 40 per cent of its value. The loss felt all the more queasy because the nation was unused to its currency riding the waves of the international markets – rather than standing more or less still on the Treasury wharf. (Paul Kelly discusses these problems in fine detail in his magnum opus, *The End of Certainty*.)

In Australia, the day after the figures were publicly released, the Treasurer travelled to the semi-rural electorate of Burke and it was there, in a reception centre, that John Laws, reigning king of Sydney radio, tracked him down for an interview over the telephone. It was an era before mobile telephony was ubiquitous; Keating took the call in a kitchen, where the sound of plates and saucepans could be heard crashing in the background. But what currency traders heard was the sound of a crashing Aussie dollar. The Treasurer, making a spur of the moment decision to impress the electorate with how serious the situation was, let his supple tongue run loose, uttering a phrase which for evermore would be associated with his name. Australia, he said, could face the prospect of becoming 'a banana republic'. He may as well have used a twenty-dollar bill to light the stove.

It is the destiny of political leaders of every stripe to arouse disapproval and mockery by disrupting social stagnation, since they are, or should be, agents of social evolution. Their actions are to shock the community into reaction against prevailing beliefs. But the shocks must be administered in small doses, if possible.

Within hours of Keating's interview, the dollar had fallen three cents, and would keep on falling in the days and months ahead. It was not quite what the Treasurer had intended, but at this stage of his career it was difficult to know – some thought, even for the man himself – just what he did intend. Keating, after his successful reassembly of the wrecked tax cart into a reform package, seemed in the same combative state of mind as he had been before the Tax Summit. In combat, every action suddenly looks different: prudent hesitation appears to be specious cowardice, while reckless audacity is reframed as courage.

In private, Keating was metaphorically beating his own chest. That Garnaut was now out of the country and not available, with his steady gaze and long, smiling silences, to unsettle the Treasurer in economic arguments inside the Prime Minister's office may have lent extra weight to Keating's feeling that *he* was the silverback.

Keating shared his sentiments about Hawke's weakness with people from his office and some in the press gallery. Inevitably the stories found their way back to the Prime Minister's own staff, notably to Peter Barron, who had many sources of information inside and outside Parliament House.

Perhaps the real trigger for Keating's angry mood had been a succession of low blows from the Liberal thug, Wilson Tuckey. Tuckey had discovered the skeleton of a dead romance in the Treasurer's closet – in the early 1970s Keating had proposed to a woman then changed his mind. Since the very opening of parliament in February 1986 Tuckey had attacked the Treasurer inside the House with offensive insinuations, including that he had fathered an illegitimate child. Such suggestions were bound to disturb the feelings of Keating's wife and children. 'Paul was more devoted to his family than any other man I knew in politics,' Hawke said. Once Tuckey had discovered the Treasurer's Achilles heel, he bit it at every opportunity.

The Opposition, which had sunk back in the polls once the government's tax reforms were recognised as a success, seemed to have decided on the tactic of disrupting parliament, a common enough response to the frustrations of Opposition. In 1983 Labor had promised to create 500 000 jobs in three years, and had more than succeeded, creating 608 000 jobs by February 1986. Keating was trying to advertise in parliament the government's achievement when Tuckey hit his sore spot. The Treasurer struck back furiously, calling the Opposition 'animals', 'this rabble', and threatening them with 'a few New South Wales ALP rules'. And that was on the first day. The next day, during some cut and thrust between Keating and the leader of the National Party, Tuckey again leapt into the fray with an irrelevant reference to the Treasurer's former girlfriend. Keating responded with 'The loopy crim ... is at it again', 'you stupid foul-mouthed grub' and 'you piece of criminal garbage'. He was visibly shaken and outside the chamber ranted about Tuckey and what he would like to do to him. Tuckey continued using his weapon against Keating for years, the tongues of both men vigorously exercised for the injury they could do each other. 'The tongue is a little member and boasteth great things ... It is full of deadly poison,' the Bible warns. Tuckey's tongue, in due course, would bring ruin on his own party. Meanwhile, he tried to poison Keating's personal life with it.

Hawke was in Tokyo when he got the news on 14 May about the 'banana republic'. He was dismayed by Keating's clumsiness because of the panic he knew it would set off, and for the difficulties it would cause him in trade talks in Japan. 'Paul had turned a weak currency, as the Aussie was at that stage, into a collapsing currency,' he said. In addition the Budget process had begun, a period during which the government tries to keep economic decision-making to a minimum while prime minister and Treasurer concentrate on Budget strategy.

But while Hawke was angry with Keating, he was more sympathetic to him than was his staff. He knew from personal observation how protective of his wife and children Keating was and understood the impotent rage Keating felt towards Tuckey. Hawke still harboured avuncular feelings for Keating, who was his undisputed heir-apparent, and he was much more willing to indulge a man fourteen years his junior than one his own age. He was concerned about the Treasurer's health, both out of friendship and because he knew how much good health one needed as prime minister. Until the moment in December 1990 when Keating spoke disrespectfully of Curtin, Hawke would in private ask medical friends and others who used alternative medicine if they could help with Keating's small but debilitating physical problems. Hawke had been robust since his teenage years. Even during his heaviest drinking, in the 1970s, when he sometimes collapsed from overwork and lack of rest, Hawke would bounce back from exhaustion and respiratory infections after a good night's sleep. As everyone who knew him recognised, Hawke had the proverbial constitution of an ox, and the libido of a group one stallion, albeit a beast now stabled and held in check with a Chifney bit.

His work habits as prime minister delighted the public service. He always read his briefs, he could absorb quantities of detail seemingly without effort; he could concentrate on whatever he was reading in the noisiest environments, he travelled with ease, unaffected by time zones, heat or cold, he could fall asleep within minutes in cars, boats, trains and aeroplanes. The Lodge had a tennis court on which he and Hazel and visitors played on weekends, and he played cricket when he had time. Keating played no sport and was plagued by minor complaints, sore eyes and chest infections. Antibiotics for one such infection when he was rundown after the tax summit caused him permanent, debilitating tinnitus. He did not have the stamina to work as hard as Hawke, nor did he have the temperament for hours of reading briefs. But both Treasurer and Prime Minister shared a tenacity to complexity and nothing could interrupt their concentration once it had located its chosen difficulty. Keating loved to read figures, but how he gained the rest of the information he needed was, for many who worked for him, a mystery. 'I never knew how he got his information,' a public servant said. 'He read almost nothing.' Keating was a classic intuitive, able in a few minutes of observation or conversation to absorb as much as a non-intuitive collects in an hour. He could not work for long periods without physical depletion and needed to escape from the tension of high office by immersing himself in hobbies and music. Hawke would zone out from politics into the cryptic crossword puzzles that he carried with him and could do anywhere for a few minutes at a time. Keating needed to get away from people altogether, to refresh himself in the meditative solitude of a symphony. The Tax Summit and its aftermath had exhausted him; now Tuckey's attacks on a sensitive issue, the early Budget process and worry over the current account deficit were the cause, Hawke believed, for his mishandling of the Laws interview. What the Treasurer had actually said was,

> If in the final analysis, Australia is so undisciplined, so disinterested in its salvation and its economic well-being, that it doesn't deal with these fundamental problems, then the fall-back solution is inevitable because you can't fund $12 billion a year in perpetuity every year, and then the interest on the year before that, and the interest on the year before that, the only thing to do is to slow to a canter. Once you slow growth under 3 per cent, unemployment starts to rise again. And then you have really induced depression. Then you have gone. You know, you are a banana republic.

He had been quoted out of context.

Hawke was travelling with his politicals. Unlike their boss they were certain that Keating, although misjudging his shot, had nevertheless aimed to hit Hawke. They believed, because they were being fed information by press gallery journalists, that back in Australia Keating was presenting himself as the real man in charge, asserting there were two leaders now: one a figurehead, the other doing the hard yards. Both men knew this was nonsense, but Keating compounded the uproar over the banana republic and falling dollar when two days later he announced an unscheduled meeting of the Advisory Council on Prices and Incomes to discuss all aspects of the economy. 'Everything is up for discussion as it relates to economic policy, the economic outlook,' he told the media. Already in a febrile state, the media described the proposed meeting as a 'mini-summit'. The Treasurer issued no correction. There were three interlocked problems now: first, Keating had not mentioned to the Prime Minister his plan for a mini-summit; second, he had not discussed it with his Cabinet colleagues; third, his proposed mini-summit looked like a panic measure to divert attention from his banana republic remark.

This was all an enormous distraction for Hawke and his staff dealing with difficult trade issues with Japan.

From Tokyo, Hawke phoned the deputy Prime Minister, Lionel Bowen, and told him to take charge of the situation. Bowen, also of the New South Wales Right, was a former lawyer, a devout Catholic, a man of great calm, modesty, common sense, wit and good humour. Within an amiable exterior, there was a steel core. Hawke asked him to call a meeting in the Prime Minister's office for a conference call with him in Beijing. When the Treasurer and other ministers had assembled, Hawke announced there would be no mini-summit, no special meeting of the Advisory Council on Prices and Incomes, that there were not two sources of policy-making in the government – the Treasurer on one side and everyone else on the other – and that economic problems would be handled in the normal way, in Cabinet, upon his return.

Hawke's staff were unhappy that he had not been tougher on Keating, but he said, 'My main concern was *not* to be tough on Paul. I needed to settle things down and stop him taking the government off on a dangerous sidetrack.'

Sandy Hollway, who would later take over as Hawke's chief of staff, was on the trip in his then role as a Foreign Affairs officer. He recalled,

From the time we hopped on the plane at Fairbairn until we got off again, I was beavering away on speeches and notes for all the places we were visiting, but I became aware that there was some other issue running that was much more important than the China visit. I didn't realise at the time, but it was when Keating made his 'banana republic' statement. And I remember this distinctly: that whole issue was a subtext to the entire trip. Bob was getting on with the foreign policy and trade stuff very professionally, but this other issue was running. Barron was on that trip. And Hogg. I remember we got to the last night and I walked down the hotel corridor back to my room, all my work finished, and passing

Peter Barron's room there were clouds of cigarette smoke seeping under the door. I poked my head in and there was Peter with an ashtray full of stubs, working the telephone back to Canberra. And I said, 'Peter, what are you up to!' He replied, 'Just putting the guns on the hills, Comrade. Putting the guns on the hills.'

The news media, gazing into the mirror of cheap reflections that human malice so enjoys, had made much of the second falling out between Hawke and Keating. 'I was annoyed by Paul's looseness of language, and his presumption in calling a meeting. But I didn't regard either as an ongoing obstacle to our own relationship. I think Paul understood and accepted my reaction,' Hawke said.

The next day, when Hawke arrived back in Canberra, Keating came straight to his office, shook his hand, and they sat down together to talk. Keating told Hawke that on top of his other worries his wife needed an operation, but was holding off until the Budget was finalised. The Treasurer had four young children for whom he would be mother and father while Annita was out of action. Hawke assured him of his continued regard for him, and they got on with the business of framing the Budget. Whatever the intent of Keating's adventure, and there has been disagreement over his motives ever since, both men knew that disunity was death. They in fact enjoyed working in harness, knowing they were a brilliant team. Keating was one member of government for whom Hawke's door was always open, and who sought frequently to call in on him, not as often as in the first term, but still very often. They continued to discuss ideas and their personal lives right up and into 1991. Rosslyn, living in Canberra, saw Keating often in the course of her job in the business-class lounge at the airport and retained a strong affection for him throughout his dispute with her father. 'I loved Paul,' she said. 'He was always such fun.'

After Hawke left office a documentary series called *Labor in Power* negatively distorted the relationship of Prime Minister and

Treasurer (and almost completely discounted Hawke's achievements) but the series was so well produced it gained a specious authority as factual, being shown and reshown on ABC television and the History Channel. A friend of Hawke's, a senior lawyer who had persuaded him to trust the ABC producer and co-operate with him, wrote to apologise when he realised how misleading the series had been. In 2010 a TV docu-drama, *Hawke*, portrays the Hawke–Keating relationship as moving from twilight to dark, without showing the affection and years of sunlight that had shone between them.

Keating was embarrassed by the banana republic analogy, but ironically its effect in the longer term was a net gain, since he made the nation focus on its very real, chronic problems, thus creating an easier political atmosphere in which to introduce reforms. His point was rammed home a few months later in August 1986, when the international credit-rating agency, Moody's, downgraded the Australian government's AAA rating, effectively making it more expensive for the nation to borrow money. But by then an economic tempest was raging and Hawke and the government were in the fight of their lives to save the nation from a financial capsize.

The situation was so dire that finance journalists were forecasting the IMF was poised to intervene in running the Australian economy.

While Australia had created many of its own problems over decades by taking easy options – chiefly high tariffs that led to uncompetitive industries, and a protected industrial relations system that led to low productivity – the crisis of 1986 was brought to a head by external events. The United States had a huge trade deficit, due in part to its economy staying open during the Cold War years, for both economic and political reasons, and because it was already squandering money on oil. The post-colonial world of the 1950s and 1960s had descended into confusion and poverty for a decade or so, but by the 1980s many 'developing countries' were developing fast and their agricultural and mining products were both feeding their own people and flowing into world markets. The nations of Western Europe found themselves with 'beef mountains' and 'butter mountains' and other agricultural goods they could not sell, while parts of Africa starved. The Europeans' solution was to subsidise their farmers, which was politically sweet for governments in Paris and Bonn. Meanwhile, in the United States, Republican Congressmen were pitching to the mid-west, to seats to the west of Illinois, where grain and beef grew. Naturally, their farmers wanted subsidies too. For the first time since the 1930s, powerful elements in the American Congress began flirting with protectionism. There was a frightening groundswell of opinion for the United States to place import barriers across the board. This would have the effect of halting the American trade deficit, and of causing havoc in the economies of virtually every non-Communist country in the world. Reagan passed the Farm Bill, justifying it on the grounds that to overcome European protectionism America needed to take the fight up to them. It was electorally convenient for the Republican Party, and disastrous for Australia, caught in the crossfire between the United States and Europe, a war that Japan joined as a third force. By the early 1980s the world agricultural market was rigged. Just one incident exemplifies how rorted the system was: the European Community dumped sugar at US$0.05 a kilogram, wrecking the economy of the Philippines and traumatising sugar towns right up the Queensland coast.

Government was suddenly much, much harder. Hawke said, 'We had to face up to some really tough decisions: every minister was told he or she must cut costs and we spent *hours* upon *hours* in sittings of the Expenditure Review Committee.' Ministers reacted differently to the problems now confronting them, some unable to come to terms with what was happening. They had to go to the ERC, one by one, and argue their case for every dollar. Barry Jones, the Minister for Science and Technology, brilliant and original in many areas, was one who was unable to cope with the iron laws of economising. Ralph Willis, the gentlest member of the ERC, recalled,

Barry would come in and say, 'It's perfectly obvious why this money is needed for Science and Technology', and we'd say, 'You explain to us exactly why.' And he'd get in a huff and reply, 'Well – if you can't see this for yourselves, what's the point of talking to you!' *Sleepers Wake!* and all that stuff. And we'd say, 'Right. Piss off. That's one less issue on the table.' It was a pity, but Barry was just too emotional about his portfolio to be able to argue for it, and as a result it lost out. There were a number of ministers like that.

Hawke had the unpalatable task of persuading the unions to accept not merely restraint in their wage demands, but in fact a cut in real wages. He made a major speech on 11 June in which he explained that with Australian inflation now running at 9 per cent, when the rest of the world's was only 3 per cent, there was no way that wage earners could be compensated fully for increases in the CPI.

But just when things seemed as if they could not get worse, they did: on 28 July 1986 the dollar fell 10 per cent in twenty-four hours. Hawke recalled,

> We had just finished three months of grinding Budget deliberations in the ERC, and were about to put the Budget to bed. The ERC members were together in the Cabinet room when the dollar began to fall. There was Paul, Peter Walsh, John Dawkins, Ralph Willis, John Button, and me. Paul had a portable Reuters screen and he began calling the drop in the dollar like a referee calling the count on a boxer who's hit the canvas. It had been at 63 cents, then it went through 60, 59, 58 ... It finally stopped at 57.15. We felt like stunned mullets. It was very depressing.

Because of the floating of the Australian dollar, this was the first time an Australian government had practical knowledge of this experience. There was no precedent to guide them. Senator Walsh, by this time the Finance minister, said later,

I was closer to despair than I'd ever been in politics, because
I thought we'd been a good government … and yet we had
been hit with this, and we didn't really deserve it – and how
the hell were we ever going to get out of it?

The solution was to reconvene the ERC and 'slash and burn'
(in Hawke's words) their way out. It is difficult for a government
of any hue to cut costs, but for a Labor government it is especially challenging: the ALP balances exquisitely between ethos
and pathos, between its noble, dignified, universal moral aspirations and its inherent feelings of pity and sympathetic sadness
for the downtrodden of the world. Small gestures, let alone large
ones, can pitch Labor people from one extreme to the other.
Hawke said,

Philosophically, the party had been brought up on the notion
of government playing an expansionary role. The party
expected a Labor government to spend on health, education
and welfare. I had to tell them, as did other ministers, there
was no money to spend. It caused much discomfort among
the faithful.

During a horrible fortnight the ERC cut another $1.5 billion
from the Budget. One decision was to save $70 million by lifting a
ban on uranium sales to France. The French had made a contract
with Queensland Mines to buy uranium at a fixed price, but when
Labor policy banned uranium sales, France bought its uranium
elsewhere, and more cheaply, leaving the Australian taxpayer
obliged to compensate Queensland Mines for the cost of the ban.
Hawke despised what he had always seen as an unintelligent,
emotional fad about uranium mining, a field of disinformation –
much of it ploughed over decades by agents of the USSR – into
which were sown the deadly weeds of paranoia. He was personally delighted to have an opportunity to dismiss the ban –
an idea that had originated with John Dawkins, who was now
Trade minister – especially because, Hawke said, 'Labor's policy

was penalising the Australian people: our taxpayers were subsidising a prejudice that served absolutely no purpose. The French were simply buying cheaper uranium elsewhere.' But in the party there was anger. By small degrees more and more of the ALP faithful were feeling uncomfortable with Hawke. In the two previous years budget deficits had been 2.5 per cent and 3.2 per cent; now the ERC cut spending to zero, but only Hawke and Keating knew how drastic the surgery was. They kept it secret, even from the Finance minister, Senator Walsh.

The ERC also decided to levy fees on tertiary students on a capacity-to-pay basis. This too had been Dawkins' idea but Hawke backed it wholeheartedly, as he had always regarded the phrase 'free university education' introduced by Whitlam, as pernicious nonsense. 'It's never free,' he had argued.

> It's a question of who is paying – and most of the time it's working-class people, through their taxes, paying for middle-class kids to get the education their own children will not. I had the inequity of all this brought home to me one day when Frank Lowy [third-richest man in the nation] said to me how absurd it was that his employees, through their taxes, were paying for his wife to do a university degree.

The Vice-Chancellor of the University of Queensland, Professor Peter Høj, wrote in 2019, 'Were it not for Bob's government's vision and courage, it is unlikely we would have universities that are now the envy of the world, the mainstay of Australia's largest services export industry.'[2]

For many in the party, however, university fees in any form ranked as treachery both to the Labor ethos and to Whitlam's legacy.

The news media hammered the government – and the Treasurer in particular became fresh prey for the ever-questing vole, Brian Toohey. The *National Times* launched an investigation of Keating's friendships, creating an impression that the government from the top down enjoyed consorting with the wrong sort of person – namely the very rich. It published photographs of Hawke and Keating in dinner suits at a function where million-aires were also guests, with the insinuation that they were behaving improperly: by being present, by wearing dinner suits, by having 'rich mates'.

It was the same old sahibs-versus-the-natives (admittedly, the native rulers) mentality, but it was damaging to the government all the same. As Keating was to object, 'One photograph of me and the Prime Minister at one function in a dinner suit is republished and rebroadcast 1000 times.' The media made it appear that the Prime Minister and Treasurer almost lived in black ties after dark. However, dinner-suited leaders caused predictable outrage on talkback radio. By 1986 a new money class was already springing up, seemingly out of the cracks in city pavements: men who had been paper shufflers or 'on the tools' were now driving Porsches and taking skiing holidays in Aspen. Suddenly all kinds of people did not know who they were, or where they fitted in to the new social hierarchy – and this released the social poison of envy. Hawke was less vulnerable to it, because of his down-to-earth working-man's image, but Keating, with his elegant suits and beautiful ties, was so unpopular both in the electorate and in the Caucus that Hawke was warned that Keating could not win a contest for deputy prime minister if Lionel Bowen stepped down.

Politics on its surface is an ever-restless ocean. Its deep currents are mostly invisible. And, invisibly, while the Hawke government was doing much to reconstruct the economy and re-establish Australia's role in the world, the Opposition began tearing itself to pieces.

TWENTY-FOUR

O NE OF THE NEW money men of the 1980s was a Gold Coast developer called Brian Ray, friendly, charming, determined and generous, a mate of Kerry Packer, an enthusiastic risk taker, both in business and in life. Mostly he was a millionaire, but sometimes he was broke. He was a leader of Queensland's white-shoe brigade, a group of entrepreneurs whose patron saint seemed to be Jay Gatsby. They had made lots of money very quickly and enjoyed its conspicuous consumption: designer casual clothes worn with the classic 1930s accessory, white shoes. They were masters of a small, tropical universe – from just across the Tweed River then on and on up north for a thousand kilometres, anywhere there was land to develop for housing or tourism. Brian Ray had come to the attention of the Costigan Royal Commission in 1984 when, as a bankrupt, he lent Kerry Packer $250 000 in cash; this had led to the notion that Packer was a drug dealer and all sorts of other innuendo enthusiastically bantered about. But just how a bankrupt happened to have on hand a cool quarter to lend to a multimillionaire was to remain a mystery both men would take to their graves.

Another friend of Ray's was Queensland's National Party premier, Sir Joh Bjelke-Petersen, whom he had met in the early 1970s, and with whom he formed a strong friendship. Ray could rightly be called 'visionary' as a property developer; like many people who experience outstanding success in one field, he had confidence he could succeed in another. In the second quarter of 1986 when Keating was making his 'banana republic' statement, Ray, fired by hatred of Keating's taxation policies, his admiration for Bjelke-Petersen, and the premier's own ambition, envisioned an Australia with Joh as prime minister. Ray had a meeting with Joh to discuss what their next step might be. It was to bring into the loop Mike Gore, another white shoe, a former car dealer who had made it big time, and been bankrupt, who loathed the Hawke government and revered the capitalists' friend, Bjelke-Petersen. Gore, Ray and Bjelke-Petersen were of that cohort of successful men, shrewd in business but deeply ignorant of history and of how a national economy actually works, arrogant and parochial, who believed with almost touching innocence that they could run a country. Now it seemed that their day, the Day of the New Capitalists, had arrived. They would revenge themselves on the Canberra Socialists who had imposed the fringe benefits and other tough-on-business taxes, and who were hurting the battlers (the social strata from which these men had sprung) through the increasing cost of living.

Bjelke-Petersen was already seventy-five years old and, as an old political soldier, now gloried in memories of his salad days when, with a flash of brazen political cunning, he had helped destroy the Whitlam government by appointing a Trojan horse to the Senate in 1975. He dreamed of destroying Hawke – but more dramatically: *mano a mano*. He, Joh, would run for the prime ministership at the next election. There was a small hurdle to overcome first: John Howard was the leader of the Liberal Party and Ian Sinclair the leader of the National Party. It would be necessary to dispense with their services, but Mike Gore saw this as a marketing exercise. He paid for some high-quality market research that showed that Andrew Peacock and Joh Bjelke-Petersen were a winning team, compared with stolid, bespectacled Howard (not yet forgiven in conservative circles for outlawing bottom-of-the-harbour tax evasion) and the virile but shop-worn Sinclair. Hawke was leading Howard 70 per cent to 16 per cent as preferred prime minister in May 1986.

In July Mike Gore, now the organiser of the secret 'Joh for Canberra' campaign, as it became known, revealed the plan to astonished senior members of the National Party. Joh was facing a state election that polls showed he would win only with difficulty. To believe that, at his age, coming from the National Party, rather than the Liberal Party, he could go on to defeat Hawke and the Labor Party was, to say the least, imaginative.

It would be some months before the campaign would go public, but whispers of it came much sooner to the ears of Hawke, who was incredulous. 'I thought there must be a God,' he said.

He was back on top of his game, but he was facing a sea change in his private staff during 1986. Three years is usual for political staffers if they are to avoid burn out or loss of objectivity. During the banana republic spat, Keating, in tones of contempt, had named those who ran the Prime Minister's office, a 'Manchu court'. The description was reported in the press, leaving people somewhat puzzled, since the Prime Minister's staff were on good terms with the Treasurer. Graham Evans, Hawke's senior officer, recalled,

> When I first went to work for him in 1983 Bob said, 'I haven't been in Parliament long, so I will have to rely on you a lot' ... I never thought about Keating's calling the PM's office a Manchu court at the time it happened, but later I did. I wondered, 'Why is Paul [attacking Bob's staff]?' It wasn't that he had problems of access, or disagreement about policy issues: so why? What's the motive? And I think Paul was aware that Bob had a very good and loyal staff, and if he, Paul, were to push himself forward, a significant obstacle to that would be the people around the Prime Minister. Paul realised that while Bob had a competent and loyal staff he was not likely to make the sort of errors that would open him up to criticism of his performance.

Keating's staff, which also consisted of outstanding people, had nevertheless let him down badly by allowing the Treasurer to overlook submitting his tax returns at a time when he was thumping others over tax, and in miscalculating a claim for parliamentary allowances. Later, two staff members wrote books about Keating[1] that, while not intentionally derogatory, were not helpful to his reputation. Hawke's staff considered the authors traitors to their boss who, like Hawke, was considerate and affectionate with his office. Keating's jibe had most particularly been directed at Peter Barron, who had taken charge of managing the banana republic crisis in a way that would prevent the Opposition from driving a wedge into the government. In the process Barron had upbraided the Treasurer with a savagery that Keating was accustomed to hear coming only from his own lips.

By the end of 1986, Evans, Barron, Garnaut, Walsh and Hogg had all gone on to other jobs, their time spent on Hawke's staff setting up their careers for life. Somewhat quixotically, when the last of the courtiers, Hogg and Walsh, were about to leave, Keating arrived unexpectedly to thank them and the rest of the Manchus for their great contribution to the government. One of the newcomers, press secretary Stephen Mills, was to write,

> Their departures deprived Hawke of considerable accumulated experience and made him more susceptible to the increasingly dry economic advice flowing from the bureaucracy. But in a certain way it also liberated him. The first generation ... having been in their jobs as long as Hawke had been in his, they were quasi-equals; they had seen him when he was still a novice and they had seen him in his bereft phase in 1984. As they peeled off, Hawke seemed to gain in self-assurance; the longer he remained prime minister, the more comfortably he managed the responsibilities and workload of the job.[2]

Yeend had retired and in the new head of Prime Minister and Cabinet, Mike Codd, a fellow West Australian, Hawke had a magnificent strong right arm. Codd not only filled the gap left by Yeend, but in intellectual prowess added the delight that Garnaut once provided to Hawke's quiet hours of discussion.

Codd is a tall, reserved man with a quiet voice who had worked for prime ministers John Gorton, Billy McMahon, Gough Whitlam and, under Malcolm Fraser, had been appointed head of the Industrial Relations department. Someone very powerful in the trade union movement had taken such an intense dislike to him that, when Hawke won office, Codd was virtually the only senior public servant to be put out to grass. He was made head of the Industries Assistance Commission. By rumour, he was a blue-nosed Tory. But in late 1985 Hawke dispatched Peter Barron to look Codd over as a possible replacement for Sir Geoffrey Yeend, who was due to retire. When Barron returned after half-an-hour's chat with a favourable report there was shock in Hawke's office. John Bowan exclaimed, 'I thought he was the devil incarnate!' By 1987 the Prime Minister's staff recognised Codd for what he was: a highly intelligent, honourable, hard-working public servant with a good political nose.

Times were tough for the government. It was losing its electoral base in droves – those who had been subject to the enormous pressures of restructuring the economy and who, despite Hawke's best intentions, did not feel, and had not been, fully compensated for what they had lost. Graham Richardson noted,

> our fortunes were starting to decline; after three years of dominating the Opposition, our ascendancy was beginning to sink. The fallout from the [1985] tax package was considerable: workers felt short-changed by the taxing of staff canteens and employer-provided motor cars, employers were angered by the extra taxes they were having to pay to keep their workers happy. Virtually everybody ignored the benefits that flowed from the tax package, such as lower tax rates for all and the raising of the lowest tax threshold which meant that 100 000 people no longer had to pay any tax at all.[3]

An internal report by Bob Hogg noted,

> The electoral coalition of support we took years to build is almost completely alienated ... we have lost youth, the low income blue and white collar workers, to a lesser extent the aged, and we have lost the middle ground in a big way.[4]

Young people saw the government as cynical and lacking Labor idealism.

Hawke's response was to fight to win back the minds – the hearts had never really left him – of the people. From mid-1986 he launched himself into an intense schedule of visits outside Canberra – to schools, factories and shopping centres. His message was that the nation faced a hard slog. His speechwriter, Graham Freudenberg, recalled,

> The economic crisis of '86 was the other side of Hawke at the Summit: that is, Hawke at the Summit, the optimistic, outgoing leader. Hawke at the mid-'86 crisis was quite stern. No prime minister had spoken to the Australian people in those terms since Curtin.

Hawke was still so popular that at one Sydney shopping centre a crowd gathered in such a surge a Hawke staffer feared there had been an accident. Asking what had happened, he was told 'We're here to see the Prime Minister!' But while Hawke, in personal popularity, was a mile in front of Howard, the government was a mile behind the Opposition. In late November, Hawke convened a Sunday meeting of the full ministry at which he read out to his team of twenty-seven men and women just how big a battle they faced to win the following year.

> The mood we have to create for the next year in the conduct of government business is one of stability, certainty, decisiveness, cautious and realistic optimism ... It is essential that the government control the middle ground – and that

the Opposition be excluded. There need to be twenty-seven voices selling the government rather than twenty-seven voices selling twenty-seven pieces of government.

He told his ministers they needed to 'get out of Canberra more' and have as much contact with their electorates and with traditional supporters as possible.

By the end of the year the Coalition's 7.5 per cent lead over Labor had, on one poll, narrowed to 1 per cent. Hawke was still three times more popular than Howard. An important turning point for young people in late 1986 had been the government's renewed emphasis on the environment. In the 1983 campaign, Labor had fought hard against the building of the Franklin Dam in Tasmania, winning many votes on the mainland and losing every single seat in the island state, which, like Queensland at the time, danced a few steps behind the salsa.

But during 1986 a most unlikely character had turned green. In April Senator Bob Brown, a Tasmanian independent at the time, through the Tasmanian Wilderness Society, which he had founded, invited Labor backbencher Senator Graham Richardson to fly by helicopter over some of the Tasmanian forests that both the Liberal and Labor parties in Tasmania were keen to log. Richardson already knew from party research that there was a huge, untapped number of idealistic young people across Australia who wanted the environment protected. Neither of the large parties had tapped into their yearning and Richardson realised the Opposition, because of its ties to business and its contemptuous attitudes to 'tree hugging', would have difficulty in doing so.

He wrote of his first experience of the majesty of Tasmania's trees,

we flew over some of the world's most beautiful forests and stopped for a lunch of soggy sandwiches near a small mountain lake ... Bob Brown wanted chunks of forest, or preferably the whole area, put into World Heritage classification and protected forever ... by the time we arrived back in Hobart

I was a convert . . . I wanted to become a warrior for his cause.
That was a bad day for the logging industry in Australia but a
very good one for me, the environmental movement and the
Labor Party. It didn't take too long to work out that we had a
perfect convergence: what was right was also popular.[5]

Richardson always promoted himself as a tough operator,
which the Left took at face value, and loathed. But there was a
softer, genuinely empathetic side to him, best seen some years
later when he was Minister for Health and, in the words of Mike
Codd, 'became passionate about Aboriginal health. Genuinely
passionate. He could have achieved an awful lot in that portfolio,
but he had to resign.' His resignation was due to scandal, and the
shadow of scandal seemed to be Richardson's kismet, pursuing
him into his seventh decade.

But it would be insulting to Richardson to attribute his green-
ing in 1986 to purely idealistic motives – unless they were the
ideals of winning votes and keeping Labor in government. The
'perfect convergence' of which he wrote was even more exquisite than he suggested. As the New South Wales Right's faction boss, Richardson had counted the numbers and knew that
the current minister, Barry Cohen, was weak in Caucus support
and not highly regarded in the environmental movement. The
greens wanted a fighter, and Cohen simply did not have the fight
in him that Richardson had. Urban to his toenails, more at home
in a Chinatown restaurant than by a woodland stream, Senator
Richardson flying above the virgin forests of Tasmania saw not
just beauty, but his chance to be promoted out of the ruck: *to the
ministry.*

But there were pitfalls for an Environment minister: forestry
workers, who were traditional Labor voters, would lose their
jobs.

On returning to Canberra, Richardson took Senator Brown
to talk to the Prime Minister.

Just two days earlier Hawke had appointed a young economist, Dr Craig Emerson, to his staff, who, on hearing that Brown

would be talking to Hawke about environmental issues, asked if he could sit in. Hawke agreed, and from that moment Emerson became something new in a prime minister's office: the environmental adviser. There was a touchy issue to resolve: the Hawke government had signed a memorandum of understanding with the Liberal government of Tasmania to allow logging. Emerson recalled, 'Brown told the PM, "This logging means the destruction of the national estate."'

Hawke and Emerson studied the memorandum and to their delight discovered that the text said one thing, and the attachments said another – which allowed the federal government room to attack the agreement and begin intervening in the Tasmanian government's permits for logging. It was not quite cricket, but it was good politics. The government took a decision that it would protect the national estate. The Wilderness Society was thrilled.

Emerson recalled,

We were flying by the seat of our pants at the outset. Whether what we were doing was Constitutional was moot. Anyway, we said to the Tasmanian government, 'You've got to stop logging these places.' And it was on for young and old. A real shit fight. But the Wilderness Society backed us all the way.

By December 1986 a glimmer of optimism for a Labor victory in 1987 had appeared.

Then at the end of the month, at Christmas, the change in Labor's fortunes became surreal. On Christmas Day the white-shoe brigade set out in one of their privately owned helicopters to fly to Sir Joh Bjelke-Petersen's farm at Bethany to deliver the premier their special Yuletide gift: the blueprint for how he would take over the Australian government in 1987.

New Capitalism's Saviour mulled things over until New Year's Eve.

On 1 January, in the *Australian*, came the astonishing news that Sir Joh Bjelke-Petersen would be running for federal parliament, that a hundred groups were supporting him, that he would introduce a flat-rate tax – and that any time the Canberra Socialists wanted to call an election, he would be ready to take 'em on.

Sir Joh had launched a populist crusade to appeal directly to the people; he intended to sidestep party structure as a trifle beneath his contempt. For good measure he attacked former and current leaders of both the Liberal and National parties: Malcolm Fraser, John Howard and Ian Sinclair.

The sahibs and memsahibs of the press gallery were ecstatic: here was a story better than any since Combe–Ivanov: a home-grown People's Revolution! The downtrodden of the earth, uneducated white men and women in horrible jobs or without jobs, and millionaires who were having taxes extracted from them by the Canberra socialists as unwillingly as if their money were their fingernails, would join in a mighty tide rising across the nation to sweep away socialists and milquetoast leaders of the Liberal and National parties as so much flotsam after a storm. Des Keegan of the *Australian* described Sir Joh as: 'this remark-able man [who] is clearly going to shift the debate substantially towards personal freedom after 20 years of weak, grasping and undemocratic leadership'.

On 1 February 1987, Sir Joh told a rally, 'I'm starting the bushfire here today and the media is going to fan it.' He was certainly right about that. The Joh campaign was page one for weeks on end and talkback radio ran wild. Most journalists restrained themselves to simply reporting what was happening, which was astonishing enough, but some of those went for Joh's throat. On 3 February, Richard Carleton announced on ABC radio,

> The Premier of Queensland, a man who can't string together three words in the English language, a man who believes in water-powered cars and quack cancer cures, this man is stomping the country preaching voodoo economics and flat earth finance and he's being listened to.

And so he was, but his audience was not confined to rednecks. Members of the left-wing intelligentsia were so alarmed there were some public and many private expressions of anxiety about the possibility of concentration camps for homosexuals and the need to flee abroad.

The 1980s were, for many, already a decade of anxiety and uncertainty not simply because of the vast economic reforms the Hawke government was instituting but because people did not know what to believe in any more. The traditional churches had become lifeless relics, the morality and social cohesiveness they once embodied wasting as the power of their rituals faded. By the 1980s the women's movement of the 1970s had disrupted the emotional basis of personal life at a deep psychological level by altering the power relationship between men and women. This accompanied a disruption of power relations between parents and children and a drug culture, begun in the optimistic innocence of the 1960s, which had by the 1980s grown mad, demonic and criminal. Adding to nervousness about society at large was a terrifying new disease: AIDS.

It was a mystery epidemic first noticed in Australia in 1982. By 1984 it was known to be a virus spread through blood, mostly from anal intercourse, among homosexual men, and through shared needles, by intravenous drug users. There was no treatment and no cure. In America conservatives seized on AIDS as a moral and political weapon, 'God's punishment' for sinners. The idea began to gain traction in Australia; such was the terror of the disease, local gay men became lepers, thrown out of homes and jobs, shunned by families and friends. The Minister for Health, Neal Blewett, explained to Hawke how the virus was transmitted and together they set out to do something extraordinary: to educate the public and to refuse to allow the medical community a monopoly on the process. Hawke, who gave his ministers their head unless there was sound reason not to, allowed Blewett to choose Ita Buttrose, editor of the *Australian Women's Weekly*, as the inaugural chair of a National Advisory Committee on AIDS, appointing her over the objections of eminent doctors who were appalled that she was 1. a woman and 2. a journalist. Then the government got to work on making a change in behaviour of radical proportions. Blewett's senior private secretary, Bill Bowtell, said, 'We had to get people using condoms, and clean syringes had to be given to all drug injectors – people who were breaking the law. With sex workers we had to get all the women to wear condoms. We had to clean up the appalling hygiene standards in doctors' and dentists' practices.' And, critically, the other political parties had to be persuaded to support the campaign. To his credit Andrew Peacock did, and leaned on his partner, Ian Sinclair, leader of the Nationals, who was inclined to weaponise the issue, to maintain a united front. On 5 April 1987 a series of shockingly confronting bulletins, known as The Grim Reaper advertisements, were televised. They were designed to terrify, and they did. But they worked. Australia's response to the AIDS epidemic was the best in the world. Had Hawke not thrown his weight behind it, Australia would have dithered along, bickering, like America. As the current Prime Minister, Scott Morrison, said in 2019, 'Tens of thousands of people are alive today because of those efforts.' And not only in Australia: our model was adopted by a range of countries, including China, so over the three decades since the grim reaper appeared on television screens, those tens of thousands could probably be counted as millions.

Lives were saved, but it was a frightening time.

Money seemed the only security, the only way for people to measure their value to each other, to belong. The new money class, the cutthroat merchant gentlemen driving Italian and German sports cars, squiring flashy women and ordering Bollinger at lunch, seemed to show the way forward. A lifetime of certainties about Australian society had been overturned in a few years.

On 7 February, Sir Joh announced, 'I am determined to turn politics upside down in Australia ... [I have] a lot of experience and I know what I am doing.'

Labor research showed that most of Joh's support was coming at the expense of the Coalition, but a disturbing percentage of it was from the ALP, from unskilled male workers with little education and low incomes. If it's a truism that a man with a fortune is in need of a wife, it's equally true that a poor man will be lucky to find one. Unskilled men had suffered most from the feminist revolution, and from economic restructuring. They felt abandoned to the scrap heap of society, without a hand to help them up. Until Sir Joh! A Channel Nine television poll showed 72 per cent of 204 000 callers supported Sir Joh. The figures were dubious, but could not be entirely ignored as Channel Nine was the most popular national station. On 18 March a credible poll, by Morgan, showed that an Andrew Peacock–Sir Joh team could win 52 per cent of the vote, while the existing Coalition leadership of Howard and Sinclair would win only 42 per cent. It was not clear if Peacock or Sir Joh would be prime minister, but the electorate did not seem to mind. They wanted a saviour.

Sir Joh was on a roll.

While Labor's research was pessimistic, the Prime Minister became increasingly annoyed with Labor's pollster, Rod Cameron, because Hawke believed Cameron was mistaken in his advice to the government. There was a large personal element at play: Cameron, whom David Combe believed had betrayed him in evidence he had given in the Ivanov Affair, had by now turned against his Prime Minister. According to Richardson, Cameron 'considered himself the equal of or better than pretty well all the politicians and party officials with whom he worked' and was openly backing Keating against Hawke. Relations between the pollster and the Prime Minister were by 1987 'poisonous' in Richardson's view.[6] In Hawke's office, the new political advisor, the very able Bob Sorby, had argued vehemently since January that the Prime Minister should call an election as soon as possible, which would be March 1987. But Hawke wanted to wait, and he had hit upon one of his unexpected manoeuvres: instead of the advertising company the party had used for the past thirteen years, he would arrange to appoint a brilliant maverick, an anti-Labor radio and advertising wild man, John Singleton, best friend of the white-shod Brian Ray, to run Labor's ad campaign.

When the Prime Minister first proposed Singleton ('Singo' as he became known throughout the nation) to the 1987 campaign committee its members were flabbergasted. Bob Hogg, working as a consultant at the national office, was horrified, and expressed himself vehemently opposed. Others concurred. Singleton was famous for his love of drink, beautiful women, racehorses, having fun and making and spending lots of money. On radio he had frequently attacked 'the socialists' and had actually founded a half-baked populist political party in the 1970s to attack the Whitlam government. The objections to him as Labor's champion for the election were loud, but Hawke hammered through his reasoning: Singleton was uniquely gifted in advertising, sharp as a scalpel, always original – and now he was on Labor's side ('to the death, mate', he had told Hawke). If Sir Joh was weird, Singo was weirder. And much smarter.

Sullenly, the Labor election committee agreed.

Hawke was focused on winning, and on restoring the good repute of the Labor Party in the process. He had decided that the longer he let the Joh for Canberra campaign run, the stronger Labor could become. But it took nerve. Bob Hogg said, 'Bob hung on and on, until July, which was the right thing to do, because the Joh campaign ran Howard ragged. If Bob had listened to his advisers and gone in March the outcome could have been different.'

As Hawke had calculated, the Coalition began hitting and biting each other in public. The Liberal president, John Valder, called Sir Joh 'a political terrorist in the Colonel Gaddafi mould'; Ian Sinclair called him 'the Norman Gallagher of the National Party'; Andrew Peacock, smooth and cynical after too many years believing in nothing in particular, announced, 'Sir Joh is a great Australian, a great patriot who always – and I mean always – puts his country first.' Sir Joh said Peacock would challenge Howard for the Liberal leadership and referred to Howard as 'a silly little boy'. Peacock denied he was about to challenge. Howard sacked Peacock from the shadow ministry. Joh then announced that his son, John, would accompany him in the storming of Canberra, which prompted Bill Hayden to request that Sir Joh on arrival in Canberra should also, in emulation of the Emperor Caligula, appoint to the Senate his horse.

By now the weather had turned cold and Canberra's lovely summer roses were blown. Hawke announced the election for 11 July – mid-winter, a time never before chosen for an election. This of itself was news, and a show of prime ministerial daring.

A few days earlier, Sir Joh had attended the Premiers' Conference in Canberra, which, the white shoes had planned, would be his real launching pad into federal politics. But Hawke, backed by Keating, savaged Bjelke-Petersen's economic proposal for a flat 25 per cent tax to a point of grave public humiliation for the Queensland premier. It was a tax welcome only to the rich. 'I remember saying to Paul: "This is too good to be true,"' Hawke said.

At that conference Sir Joh suddenly knew beyond doubt that he was fighting out of his class; he was on a hiding to nothing.

Then, on the day after Hawke's election announcement, Howard made a fatal political mistake. On 3 June, from fogbound Canberra, he set out to fly to Queensland to speak personally to Sir Joh. His plane had to wait hours on the tarmac before it could take off. Howard should have seen the bad weather as an omen, and disembarked. But instead of publicly dismissing Sir Joh as a populist ratbag, Howard believed he needed to appease the premier, to persuade him to make no more waves during the election campaign. When he finally arrived in Brisbane, Sir Joh treated Howard with contempt. The premier knew his own campaign was sunk; he believed Howard's was also – and that Howard and Sinclair deserved to lose.

For the government it was more fun than a circus. Hawke laid it on with a trowel, telling parliament,

> The desperate early morning dash ... by the Leader of the Opposition to Brisbane is the action of the weakest leader in the history of Australian politics ... This man, this silly little boy, goes up to see the thug, to see the Norm Gallagher

of conservative politics ... and he says, please, Sir Joh, will you anoint my campaign? Will you say no longer I am a silly little boy? ... He knocks on the door of the thug, the Norm Gallagher, and says: Norm, Norm, here I am, the silly little boy ... He says, 'I'll take it all back. Joh, I won't any longer call you a thug. I won't say you are ... the worst conservative Premier in Australia. Do you remember, Joh, that I said you were suspending the laws of arithmetic? I will now take all that back.'[7]

Mick Young joined the fray:

The Leader of the Opposition should not have gone to Queensland this morning; he should have gone to St Vincent's Hospital to see whether the staff could find his spine ... the Leader of the Opposition, helped by the fog at the Canberra Airport, rubbed ointment on his knees and went to the altar of the white shoes. He has carpet rash from kneeling in front of Joh this morning saying, 'Please, don't upset our campaign too much.'[8]

Singleton, as Hawke had predicted, fashioned a dashingly original advertising campaign, with a battle hymn that encapsulated the feeling of hard times for ordinary people, 'Together, Let's stick together, let's see it through'. The song and the ads, plus disciplined campaigning from the government, helped to deliver Labor a majority that increased from 16 to 24 seats.

Years later Howard remarked in a tone of gallows humour, 'Bob Hawke should contribute to the Joh Bjelke-Petersen Memorial Fund.' Although he felt cheated of victory in 1987, Howard was too realistic a politician not to recognise later that history had, in fact, been kind to him: had he succeeded in 1987, he would have been a one-term leader, in charge of a mutinous crew, trying to steer his ship through an economic storm that was building into a cyclone.

Hawke's election victory in 1987 was a high tide for him and the government. Graham Freudenberg, whose knowledge of federal government history was peerless, remarked,

> One of the outstanding things about Bob was there's never been a prime minister who enjoyed the job, had sheer joy in it, as much as Bob. He exuded the spirit of fun and sheer zest for it. I don't mean having power and the appurtenances, which of course he enjoyed, he loved. But just the sheer joy of being prime minister for THIS PEOPLE. *The Australians.*

Hawke surged with the renewed energy of a man who has stuck to his vow, and succeeded. His vision of the Australian Labor Party as the natural party of government, and his dream of ordinary Australian people leading lives of greater happiness, justice, freedom and prosperity was coming true. In photographs he appeared younger, more vital and buoyant than he had since 1984. In winning three elections, he had outdone his hero, Curtin. He was now, officially, the most successful Labor prime minister.

Hawke said,

> I was thrilled that the Australian people had endorsed the ideas I'd developed and, in many cases had had to persuade my party to embrace, in what was a historic event. I felt excited and ready for the challenge of a third term.

Hawke saw his task now as pushing through further economic and social reforms; like Curtin and his successor, Ben Chifley, he and Keating were laying the foundations of a New Australia.

The triumphant 1987 election was, in Paul Kelly's words, 'the big turning point' in the relationship of the Prime Minister and the Treasurer, for it was after that Hawke victory 'that Keating's mind really starts to turn to leadership ... and it starts to prey on his mind'.

In February 1983, Hawke had ruined Keating's long-laid plan for taking over the leadership from Bill Hayden 'after a couple of terms', as Keating told Hayden to his face. At the time Hayden thought to himself, 'Well, *how kind* of you.'

Richardson, who was close to the Treasurer in those days, wrote,

> Keating ... has never understood the concept of being in a position of weakness: he just keeps going and expects his position to improve by virtue of its inherent correctness; if it's his position, it must be right.[9]

Keating had the intransigence of a born leader. Together with his personal charm, his ferociously held convictions gave him powers of salesmanship of extraordinary force, and slowly this force would be brought to bear upon the Caucus.

At first, only those closest to Keating knew of his mounting frustration, but as Richardson noted, 'Keating cannot hide disappointment, so his private rhetoric on Hawke got worse and worse.'[10] Keating began sharing his sentiments with colleagues and a critical few of the gallery sahibs. Unlike Hawke, who enjoyed discussion but not talk, Keating was a relentless talker whose telephone calls to journalists and editors would sometimes stretch to an hour. Hawke was the most popular prime minister in polling history, even after five years of hard reforms, and Keating was highly unpopular. Hawke, as was his custom with bad news, chose to ignore it. He dismissed reports of Keating's remarks as gossip he did not want to hear. Publicly, he and Keating were a brilliant team; privately they continued to talk to each other as intimates, Hawke fretting about Keating's health, particularly his tinnitus, a cruel affliction for a man who so loved classical music. It was sections of the staff in both offices who were at fault in stirring trouble. Chris Conybeare, a distinguished career public servant, who was the Prime Minister's principal private secretary from 1986–88 said, 'There was great distrust between the two offices, but great stability in the government itself. In the subsequent commentary over the 1990s, for example, the development in the relationship between Australia and Asia and the APEC initiative, the re-writing of history by Keating's supporters sickens me. It's shameful.'

Unlike the Opposition, the government had not promised tax cuts during the election campaign; its message had been sombre and wintery to match the hard times the country had been experiencing due to the collapse in the terms of trade. There was only one area in which the ERC and Cabinet agreed more money must be spent, and that was on the children of poor families. It was to be, and was in fact, the greatest social reform of the whole Hawke–Keating era, a multimillion annual allocation to be added to existing social security child payments, integrating them into a single system that would significantly benefit 500 000 families and more than one million children. Hawke had announced it, the Family Allowance Supplement, as the centrepiece of his policy speech at the Sydney Opera House on 23 June. There was spontaneous, roaring applause in the auditorium as he described *con brio* what would be done. But unnoticed by everyone that day, and for many months afterwards, the Prime Minister had committed a grievous political sin. Later several staff members would claim the guilt was theirs – but it was Hawke who would have to take the punishment. In the behind-the-scenes madhouse of preparing for an election launch and condensing the policy speech to thirty minutes for television broadcast, those proofreading the final draft that Hawke would read from an autocue had missed the fact of a small but important change in wording. Hawke was meant to say, as was written in the printed speech circulated to the media, 'We set ourselves this goal that by 1990 there will be no financial need for any child to live in poverty.' (This was achievable, and the government delivered on it.) Instead, the speech Hawke read from said, 'We set ourselves this first goal: by 1990 no child shall live in poverty'. It would be two years before a thousand times over, and over again, the phrase 'no child will live in poverty' would be flung back in Hawke's face. The softening words, 'we set ourselves this first goal' were always omitted, making him seem an even worse political shyster. His speech writer, Graham Freudenberg, lamented, 'It was as if Gough Whitlam had never said anything but "nothing will save the Governor General".' If 'MX' is engraved on John Bowan's heart, 'no child will live in poverty' was engraved on Hawke's. 'I was deeply hurt,' he said,

> because the welfare community acknowledged publicly and told me privately that this was the most significant improvement in child assistance ever. Many mothers confirmed the official judgment. They wrote me letters of thanks. I remember one mother approaching me in a shopping centre to say the new entitlement had changed her life. She had tears in her eyes as she thanked me.

To this day, 2019, the Australian Council of Social Service (ACOSS) is thankful to the Hawke government.

In October 1987, three months after the election, there came the greatest stock market crash since 1929. It threw every government in the Western world into turmoil, with fears that it was the start of another Great Depression.

But in spite of the difficult times, being in government was glorious. Sandy Hollway, who had replaced Chris Conybeare in late 1988 as Hawke's principal private secretary, recalled it as 'the sweet spot'. The government was confident and cohesive, the faction system worked smoothly, the ministry carried no dead wood, the public service machine purred along, the Opposition was in a shambles and the Prime Minister could now afford to concentrate on his second great ambition: lifting Australia's profile in world affairs.

TWENTY-FIVE

OON AFTER FIRST WINNING office, Hawke turned his attention to foreign policy issues. By 1985 Australia was an
elected member, with a then-record majority in its support, of the Security Council of the United Nations. Much of
the credit was due to the professionalism and debonair charm of
Australia's ambassador to the UN, Richard Woolcott, a former
Rhodes scholar, an elegant, witty career diplomat with the even,
finely boned face that Americans call 'preppy'. He resembled the
diplomat of popular romance: with his beautiful Scandinavian
wife, Birgit, the Woolcotts cut a glamorous swathe through the
cocktail and dinner parties of New York. But Woolcott could
not have accomplished his feats of lobbying for Australia without the international respect the country was already commanding. Michael Costello, principal private secretary to the Foreign
minister, Bill Hayden, recalled being present at Hawke's first
visit overseas as Prime Minister: 'It was an incredibly exciting
time: a new Labor government. I've never forgotten, we walked
into the hotel in Jakarta and the foyer erupted into cheers.'

In 1983 Australia had voted in the UN to condemn the
United States for its invasion of Grenada. Hawke was not happy
with this vote – he would have preferred an abstention – but he
accepted Hayden's argument that there could not be one law for
the Americans and another for the Soviet Union, condemned
a only a few years earlier in the UN for invading Afghanistan.
The Soviet Union, which at the time seemed invulnerable in its
worldwide power, had invaded the most strategic point in the
Middle East, Afghanistan, at the end of 1979 while the United

States was distracted by the sacking of its embassy in Tehran. The Soviets took the opportunity to install a puppet government in Kabul.

Woolcott recalled (of the Grenada invasion),

> We thought that even a close ally shouldn't invade another country and expect our support, particularly if we hadn't been consulted. In the short term, the Americans were very cross with us ... Bob was extremely deft about the relationship with the United States. He sort of played the good guy and Hayden tended to play the bad guy. That worked pretty well.

Journalists and members of the Left liked to accuse Hawke of being a lickspittle of the United States but, as Costello – who was no Hawke fan at the time and who observed the relationship closely – remarked, 'I never saw him as such.'

The UN vote against President Reagan's decision to invade Grenada allowed Andrew Peacock to create a drama in parliament, accusing the Hawke government of being an untrustworthy ally of the United States. 'The Americans knew they had sort of broken the rules,' Woolcott said, 'but thought they had the right to act to prevent what they believed was a looming Communist threat, because the Communists, in addition to Cuba, had got hold of Grenada.'

At the time of Australia's election to the UN Security Council, the Iran–Iraq war was devouring hundreds of thousands of young soldiers, many as young as fifteen. As a member of the Security Council, Australia was among the countries that drafted a resolution, then in Woolcott's phrase, 'sold it' to the Big Five, the permanent members. This resolution paved the way for ending the war. Australia took on Malaysia, and won, in a major fight over the Antarctic Treaty, and the French over obstruction to independence for New Caledonia, another win but only after a 'highly abrasive' fight.

*

Two huge chess games were in play in the 1980s: one in the Middle East, worsening in this century, the other in South-East Asia.

It was in the South-East Asian game that Hawke decided Australia could play a constructive role.

Costello recalled, 'Bill came back from a meeting with Bob in 1983 and said, "Well, Bob tells me he wants me to take a big initiative to solve the Cambodian problem." I said, "Should be a piece of cake, Bill."' Costello, then in his thirties, had the tall, imposing body of a front-row rugby player, a shock of russet hair and an open, friendly face to which laughter came easily. He towered over every Asian he met, which in many Asian countries is considered offensive, but he would end up a trusted negotiator.

To describe the politics of Indo-China in 1983 as venomous is an understatement. Labor sentiment added to the government's difficulty in making any constructive moves in Indo-China, the party feeling being 'red raw', in Costello's description, on the issue of Vietnam and Cambodia. Indeed Cambodia stirred passions across the political spectrum.

In 1975 the Khmer Rouge had taken over Cambodia and launched an orgy of murder that included emptying the capital, Phnom Penh, of inhabitants and declaring the history of the country to have been abolished. They announced a new calendar with 1975 as Year Zero. Millions of citizens were tortured or slaughtered; everything Western was destroyed – even traffic lights, which had their 'eyes' ripped out. In the grip of blood lust, and with the acquiescence of China, the Khmer Rouge began raiding into Vietnam. The Vietnamese, toughened by years of warfare and almost giddy with victory over the United States, repaid their ancient enemy by invading. In late 1978 Vietnam installed a government in Phnom Penh, led by Heng Samrin. But waiting in the wings was a former brigade leader of the Khmer Rouge, Hun Sen, who would outmanoeuvre Heng Samrin and become prime minister in his place. Hun Sen had already swapped sides and also moved sideways, from being a Khmer Rouge fighter to fighting against the Khmer Rouge (a battle in which he lost an eye), then joining the invading Vietnamese forces. China denounced the Cambodian government as a Vietnamese puppet.

In 1983 Cambodia had a government that was the vassal of Hanoi; it had large Vietnamese forces occupying its territory and three factions of guerrilla fighters on its borders: the Lon Nolists, who, under General Lon Nol, had deposed the ruler of Cambodia, Prince Sihanouk; the Royalists who supported the prince (at the time in exile in Beijing); and the Khmer Rouge, who called themselves the Party of Democratic Kampuchea. These three made up a somewhat fractious coalition called the Coalition Government of Democratic Kampuchea, or CGDK. (The Khmer Rouge had renamed their country 'Kampuchea'.)

The United States had been furious over its humiliation in Vietnam. Militarily the South, backed by America, had been holding off North Vietnamese forces with ease. But after the disgrace of the Republican President Nixon over the Watergate scandal in 1972, the Democratic Congress voted to withdraw from Vietnam and within six months, drained of fighting spirit by the psychological collapse of its ally, the South surrendered.

Costello recalled that, even more than a decade later, in the mid-1980s,

> Reagan and the Republicans felt absolutely beside themselves with rage about this. Their sense of betrayal was almost like that of the German high command at the end of World War I. It was incredibly important in American domestic politics.

The Reagan administration took the stance: 'my enemy's enemy is my friend'. Despite the appalling atrocities of the Khmer Rouge, America supported the CGDK as the legitimate government of Cambodia. This suited the Chinese, for several reasons. All the neighbours of Vietnam were frightened of its fighting forces – even huge China, which had attacked it twice in the late 1970s and on both occasions received a horrible shock. As a Thai general explained to Bill Hayden, 'You always knew where the Vietnamese had been because there was blood everywhere.' Other Indo-Chinese were so terrified of the Vietnamese that in refugee camps Vietnamese refugees were accommodated in separate areas from the Cambodians and Laotians, who feared even the glance of their eyes.

The Thais were desperate for the Vietnamese to leave Cambodia, because just over the hills they were too close for comfort. Thailand had an army that looked very smart on parade, but its general staff had no illusions about how it would cope with a Vietnamese assault.

Added to all this was the tension between China and its dangerous next-door neighbour, the Soviet Union. All through the 1960s and 1970s, both the Soviets and the Chinese had worked hard to make Vietnam their ally, but centuries of Vietnamese resentment against China, whose vassal it had been, ended with an alliance between the Soviet Union and Vietnam, revealing to the West the bitterness of the Sino-Soviet split. The Soviet–Vietnam alliance became a nightmare scenario for China when the Soviet Union invaded Afghanistan, for China was now surrounded on its northern, north-western and southern borders by its enemy. The Soviet Union was obliged by treaty with Vietnam to support it militarily: China turned to its ancient text and the bible for contemporary Chinese businessmen, *The Art of War*. It set out to bleed its small enemy, Vietnam, in order to cut an artery in its big enemy, the Soviet Union. China voted in the UN in unison with the United States to uphold the CGDK as the legitimate government of Cambodia. More importantly, China gave material support to the Khmer Rouge: money and arms. The Chinese intended to destabilise the government of Cambodia and 'they did it very effectively', in Costello's view. Meanwhile the Thais were also doing all they could to work with the Chinese against the Hun Sen government in Phnom Penh. 'The Thais really didn't give a big rat's about the Khmer Rouge or the Cambodians, whom they'd dominated and exploited for centuries,' Costello said. 'They were just terrified the Vietnamese would come across the border.' To top it off, Singapore, buoyed by the sheer force of will and intellect of its prime minister, Lee Kuan Yew, was riding herd on the other ASEAN countries over Vietnam–Cambodia. Although Lee was not a military man, there was no other South-East Asian leader or Foreign minister who could stand up to his rapier intelligence and Western legal training. Singapore demanded that Vietnam–Cambodia be treated as a pariah, while 'Singapore-registered cargo boats dumped kilotons of consumer goods in Cambodia's harbours', Hayden noted in his memoirs.[1] He considered the Singaporeans 'sheer humbugs'.

For years Australia had been voting in the UN the same way on Cambodia as the United States and China: that the Khmer Rouge in its CGDK coalition was the legitimate government of Cambodia, that Vietnam had illegally invaded and it must withdraw. The Soviet Union and its allies voted the reverse. All this was occurring some years before the film *The Killing Fields* had exposed the horror of Khmer Rouge atrocities to the Western public. But among policy buffs it was such a passionate issue that in 1981 Andrew Peacock, then Foreign minister, had resigned over Australia's UN vote for the Khmer Rouge and had challenged Malcolm Fraser's leadership of the Liberal Party. In the ALP there were screaming matches about Australia formally supporting the Khmer Rouge. Personally, Hawke thought it disgusting, but like Fraser before him, he was conscious of the dogmatic and prejudiced position of the United States.

He wanted Hayden to find a way through.

When Hayden returned from that 1983 meeting with the Prime Minister, he explained to his secretary,

It's to do with Vietnam and the United States. We have in the party platform an absolute commitment to resume aid to Vietnam. If I do that the Americans will go absolutely nuts, and I don't want to start this whole government off by getting the Americans furious with us. If we undertake an initiative on Cambodia we can say to the Left and we can say to Vietnam it would be a very bad idea for us to resume aid to

Vietnam because we need the Americans on board to support a solution to the problem in Cambodia. And we need the countries of South-East Asia on board to support the solution: they'll all be very upset if we resume aid to Vietnam as our first act. So can we put it on hold?'

Hayden said Hawke had explained this as the background to what the Prime Minister described as 'just like a big industrial dispute. Mate, you get all the parties round the table and you just talk and pretty soon you'll have a solution.'

Hayden, always downbeat, was highly amused. But as Costello noted, 'It showed one of the best sides of Hawke: his optimism, his belief that if you try hard enough you can do it.' Despite misgivings, Hayden set out to try, noting 'the risk of total failure, and the dismissive hoots which would inevitably follow ... were no justification for fudging the challenge'.[2]

Foreign Affairs officers were aghast when their new minister explained what he and the Prime Minister wanted to do.

Hayden, accompanied by Costello, attended his first ASEAN Plus meeting, in Bangkok, in 1983. Shultz was representing the United States. Before the meeting a quiet word had gone out that Australia intended to raise the Cambodian issue. The Americans already had doubts about Hayden, who recalled, '[Paul] Wolfowitz [the assistant Secretary of State for East Asian and Pacific Affairs] was going around South-East Asia telling people in government that I was a secret Communist'.

Costello recalled,

I was sitting in the chair behind Bill, who was seated at the table. He puts his proposition on the table. He is highly apprehensive. The ASEANs, who knew what was coming, turned their faces to wood and said nothing. Obviously, they had set up George Shultz to do the talking – not that he needed much encouragement. So George launched into this bitter criticism of the initiative. 'Is Australia really part of this show? Whose side is Australia really on?' All the usual things they do. 'The whole of ASEAN was as one with the United States and Japan, and here was Australia ...' blah, blah, blah. And at the end of it he came up with this line, '*And you know, I've got to say, this proposal is just STOOPID.*' People think Bill is a little bloke – and he did look that way on television – but he's a big guy, an ex-Queensland copper, and at that moment he looked every inch his size. The back of his neck was going redder and redder. He said, '*Well, Mr Secretary, not as STOOPID as your efforts in Vietnam.* You created this situation! The United States of America, by its action in Vietnam and the bombing of Cambodia, created this nightmare!' He just gave it to Shultz: Boom! Boom! ... So it was a very bad start to the Hayden–Shultz relationship. But he had clear instructions from Bob that he wasn't to give up, because otherwise we'd have to resume aid to Vietnam, which would have created a bigger problem. Anyway, Bill being Bill, he just kept going from then on.

Hayden said,

After Shultz had had a go, the Korean Foreign minister ripped into me. Then Sit, the Thai Foreign minister, chose to disagree in a very elegant, Thai way. So there I was, the flak-catcher for Bob Hawke ... Shultz gave me a hard time for a few years, but then he settled down. The Americans didn't like me ...

Costello recalled,

We went round and round and we were getting nowhere. Then Bill went to Vietnam, which we'd been to a number of times and met with the Foreign minister, Nguyen Co Thach, a brilliant, smooth, sophisticated man. He persuaded Bill to go down to Ho Chi Minh City and meet the 'Foreign minister' of Cambodia, whom we officially regarded as an illegal Foreign minister. The Foreign minister was Hun Sen.

Hayden took up the story,

From Hun Sen's response I thought we might get somewhere. So I went to Bangkok, went straight to their Foreign Affairs department to tell them. I was waiting outside the meeting room and they began playing a tune I thought I recognised.

Hayden had quickly got the hang of how oblique Asian manners were.

I asked, 'Anyone know that tune?' 'Yes,' said one of the assistants, 'It's called "Bring in the Clowns".' I thought, 'Oh Hell!' I went in, and the Thai Foreign minister was white with rage. 'How could you do this to me! How could you! I just want to ask you a question, Bill: whose friend is Dallas? Is she Madam Hun Sen's friend? Or is she my wife's friend? And whose friend are you, Bill? Are you Thailand's friend? Or are you Cambodia's friend? Are you my friend?' . . . I got back to Australia and the Opposition put up a censure motion against me. And I was very tired, jet-lagged, and Bob said something like, 'Oh well – you're for it today. They're going for you. I'll lead our side.' And he was good. Defended me.

The press had persisted in trying to present the Hawke–Hayden relationship as tense, but Hayden added, 'Our relationship was always good, in my view.'

Hayden, after his interview with the Thai Foreign minister, with whom he and Dallas had until that moment enjoyed a warm friendship, decided he had done all he could about Cambodia; he was at a dead end. Costello said,

Regional balance of power considerations, global balance of power considerations and American passion and emotion meant that it wasn't possible to shift anybody. It just wasn't. The geopolitics wouldn't allow it. The regional politics wouldn't allow. American politics wouldn't allow it. Bill had got a huge kick in the arse for meeting Hun Sen – the Thais made sure of that.

Hawke turned to the Chinese to seek a lever. In his long late-night talks with Hu Yaobang in 1986, the Soviet Union was front and centre in Chinese concern, but Cambodia was interwoven with Sino-Soviet tension. Chinese intelligence on the Cambodian situation was of the highest quality. Hu, knowing Hawke's feelings about Pol Pot, head of the Khmer Rouge, tried to reassure him by saying, 'I can tell you, Prime Minister, that it is a real fact that Pol Pot has already retired from the leadership.' He went on to say that the CGDK forces had agreed that, were they able to defeat Vietnam and take over government, a free economy, not socialism, was the essential future for Cambodia. He was optimistic that the CGDK's 70 000 guerrilla army could better the Vietnamese. Hawke disagreed. There was in existence already an eight-point plan for peace talks, but as Hawke pointed out to Hu, in parts the plan lacked clarity. 'What,' Hawke asked,

> would be the status of the Khmer Rouge forces [if they agreed to] discussions? Would they still be armed? If so, people would fear a return to the excesses of the past … While we acknowledge the sincerity of the Chinese view, we have doubts about how much optimism we can justifiably have about the CGDK to force Vietnam and Heng Samrin to the bargaining table … We feel it requires too much optimism to believe that the CGDK can force negotiations. Perhaps, therefore, we should be applying our minds to an honourable and reasonable way of resolving this stalemate.

They went on to discuss the problems within ASEAN for any Cambodian solution. In April 1985 Malaysia had suggested there could be separate rooms for the CGDK and Heng Samrin, with someone acting as runner between them, but Thailand, Singapore and the Philippines opposed the suggestion and Vietnam flatly rejected it. So did Hu Yaobang. Hawke responded,

I can only express the hope that your optimism about the CGDK's capacities are justified. I must repeat, we have some doubt ... Does the General Secretary see any reason to believe that the Soviet Union will change its position [of expanding its presence in Vietnam, and propping up Heng Samrin]?

Hu replied, 'No.' Hawke asked, 'Do you see any prospect for change in Vietnam? They are having their party Congress later this year. Are there any grounds for optimism here?' Hu replied,

There is much dissatisfaction amongst the cadres and masses with the present Vietnamese leadership. It is also a fact that Le Duan [the leader of Vietnam who had approved his country's invasion of Cambodia], who is seventy-eight years old, is not in good health. It is now a race to see who can last longest.

They concluded the meeting with an agreement to keep in touch on Cambodia.[3]

The stalemate continued for several years. Then, as Costello remembered:

We come to 1989, and guess what? The Soviet Union is collapsing. And it's 'Bye bye, Vietnam. You're on your own.' The Vietnamese say to themselves, 'We can't afford to keep our army in Cambodia,' and they decide to fall back. And suddenly, everyone's confronted with this terrible situation: the people who are going to take over will not be Prince Sihanouk and the Royalists, will not be the Lon Nolists – it's going to be the Khmer Rouge. They have the weapons and the grunt. Hey, we don't like this! But nobody could work out what to do.

At a conference in Paris the French proposed a quadripartite interim government to run Cambodia until there could be free and fair elections. Costello said,

> Hun Sen, who was the prime minister by now, said, 'Three of you, and one of me? I don't think so.' So that didn't fly. By this stage, in Australia, the Caucus was going nuts, absolutely nuts. Caucus was saying, 'Australia has *got* to change its vote.' The Americans were saying, 'Don't you dare!' ASEAN was saying, 'Don't you dare!' So what are we to do?

Hawke appointed Gareth Evans Minister for Foreign Affairs on 2 September 1988, as Hayden had left parliament to take the office of Governor-General. On 1 September the Prime Minister had appointed Richard Woolcott head of the department. During their meeting Hawke had asked Woolcott to assist Evans until the new minister – in whose abilities Hawke had total confidence – had a grip on his portfolio. Costello was no longer working on Cambodia, but he remained interested, and he was close friends with Hawke's foreign policy adviser, John Bowan. Bowan was concerned by the pressure on the Prime Minister coming from Caucus. One night he invited Costello to dinner at his house in Canberra where they worried at the Cambodian issue. Costello was due to attend political–military talks with the Americans in Hawaii, before going on to Japan. He recalled,

> About halfway through the second bottle of port we dreamed up this mad idea that instead of spending four days on the beach in Hawaii, I should go to Hanoi and talk to the Vietnamese Foreign minister, whom I'd met several times when I was working for Bill. Meet him to see if he and I could come up with something. At that point in the evening it seemed we had a great idea: to create a supreme national council, and make that the representative Cambodian authority. Get it to delegate all its power under certain terms and conditions, to be negotiated, to Hun Sen's government as the interim

authority, and then have an election. For every ministry there would be a UN shadow minister and a UN shadow administration to oversee the Hun Sen regime and prevent it impairing the free and fair election. Plus there would have to be a substantial UN peacekeeping and peace maintenance forces, and UN control of all the factional armies. It was one of those ideas that only come when you're drunk. Anyway, we went to Gareth and he said, 'Why not? Try anything.' I presume he talked to Hawkey about it. So, we got the mandate, and off I went. I didn't have a single briefing note. Absolutely nothing.

In Hanoi, Nguyen Co Thach found the plan interesting. He told Costello,

We trust Australia on this because we know you're allied with the US and we know you're friends with the ASEAN and we know how you vote in the UN, but we also know you are trying hard. You showed you did with Minister Hayden, you did everything you could. So we trust you.

He suggested Costello go down to Ho Chi Minh City where he could talk to the Vice Foreign Minister of Cambodia, Sok An. Sok An, who was a close ally of Hun Sen's, whose children were to marry each other, told Costello, 'You may not believe me, but I'm telling you: Hun Sen is his own man. You will have to convince him.' Shortly afterwards Costello received the message, 'Hun Sen would like to see you. Come and see him.' Nobody from Australia, the United States or any of Australia's ASEAN allies had gone to Phnom Penh since the 1970s, when it had fallen to the Khmer Rouge. Cambodia was a pariah state. Hiding in its jungles was an army of guerrilla fighters armed by the United States and China. Costello requested permission from Australia; the delicacy of the issue demanded it be cleared not just with Evans, but with Hawke. A return cable said, simply, 'Go'. He was off into tiger country.

Costello plus a note-taker from the department and an Australian solider were driven from Hanoi to the Cambodian border, where a man on 'a very large white motorcycle in a funny uniform, with his gaiters sort of falling off, escorted us through the Khmer Rouge areas'. Costello had insisted on taking the soldier with him, and that the soldier come to the talks wearing uniform, 'because I knew they weren't going to believe some crappy civilian, particularly on the military stuff. Our soldier looked very fierce. He wasn't wearing formal military dress. He was wearing the stuff you'd wear in the field.' The roads were bad and it took two days to reach Phnom Penh but they did so without any sign of the jungle armies.

Finally Costello was face to face with Hun Sen, a slightly unnerving experience as it is difficult to know which of Hun Sen's large brown eyes is real, and where his gaze is directed. He was in military uniform, as Costello had anticipated, and looked every centimetre the war-toughened fighter he was. After the first day of talks, when Costello had explained the plan, the Cambodian leader responded, 'I am prepared to take this seriously. The only reason I'm seeing you is because Bill Hayden saw me all those years ago, and took such punishment for it.'

The peace process in Cambodia, which in due course would see Gareth Evans nominated for a Nobel Prize, was underway.

There were many more hurdles to clear – with the Chinese, who by this time were angry with Australia and with Hawke personally over his reaction to the Tiananmen Square killings – with the members of ASEAN, with Prince Sihanouk and with the Khmer Rouge. Their representative agreed to meet Costello but when the Australian asked his first question the guerrilla took out a notebook and read a forty-seven minute diatribe. Costello asked a second question. The Cambodian opened his notebook again and read the same diatribe for another forty-seven minutes. Costello tried a third time and received the identical response.

At least Thailand was no longer maintaining its rage. As soon as the Vietnamese army left Cambodia, Thailand was, Costello said,

> Keen to re-establish relations. They didn't give a damn who was running Cambodia, didn't care if it was Hun Sen or Sihanouk or the Khmer Rouge. They just wanted to get back in there and resume stealing their timber.

Throughout these tortuous negotiations, which dragged on for months, Hawke gave Evans his full support, which in turn empowered Costello to bravely go where no man had been before. One cable from the Australian Foreign minister to his negotiator read, 'Your instructions remain as they have always been. Follow your nose and see where it leads you.' Costello said,

> I wanted to talk to the Chinese, who were isolated at the time because of Tiananmen. Nobody was speaking to them, not the Americans, not us. And once again Hawkey came though. Straight away. 'Yep: we'll take the flak for talking to China.' It wasn't Gareth's decision, it was Hawke's.

Finally, after years of conferences and shouting, the goal was accomplished thanks to Gareth Evans' brilliance as a draftsman and a last throw of the dice by Costello. The Khmer Rouge were insisting on the framework for peace that had, largely, been drafted by Evans. But Hun Sen refused, saying he wanted to negotiate further. By now the Americans had moved away from the Khmer Rouge, but were still refusing to speak to Hun Sen. All the parties had arrived in Jakarta for a final conference. Costello recalled,

> I went round to see Hun Sen. The only reason I felt confident doing it was because I had this instruction to follow my nose. I said to him, 'What's your price to sign the treaty in its entirety?' He said, 'Get the American ambassador to pay

a formal call on me.' So I went to the Americans and said, 'If you'll do this we can get a signature tomorrow.' They cabled the President of the United States [George Bush] for permission and the next day the American ambassador called on Hun Sen. The leader of Cambodia emerged from the meeting to announce, 'I will sign.'

Costello added,

Remember this: officials do their thing. They can do it well or ill, they can bugger things up. But they suffer few consequences. It's the politicians who get the heat. They are the ones who have to answer for what's been done. There is no particular credit to me, but enormous credit to Hawke and Evans.

In early 1988 Hawke had been prime minister for five years and had almost completed the task of restructuring the public service, reducing the number of departments from twenty-eight to eighteen. This included amalgamating Foreign Affairs with Trade. In acronym-loving Canberra FA had become DFAT, presumably because FAT was too tempting for wits. Hayden was still Foreign minister. Woolcott recalled,

I was brought back [from the UN] by Bob Hawke and Bill Hayden [who would still be the Foreign minister for a few more months] with the specific instruction of trying to make this melding of two rather different bureaucratic cultures work. I think we did. I think the amalgamation was a great success. The philosophy behind it was very sound. It was that Australia was a major trading nation. It needed much closer co-ordination of foreign policy and trade policy, and it would work better if they were under the same roof. As time passes, people almost forget there used to be two separate departments. Creating DFAT was a very sound move because it really strengthened our position in the World Trade Organization, in what was then the Uruguay Round [of global trade negotiations], and enabled us to move ahead with the formation of APEC, the Asia–Pacific Economic Co-operation forum ... Australia's currency had collapsed in 1986, and that really motivated the Prime Minister to call for the establishment of an Asian-Pacific economic co-operation forum, because he was afraid that the way the global economy was moving there was a risk that the world would break up into three blocs: the yen bloc, the dollar bloc and the deutschmark bloc, and Australia – and New Zealand for that matter – would find themselves excluded. This was part of the driving force, the need to have better institutional arrangements, which led him in January 1989 on a visit to Korea to launch the idea of APEC.

Sandy Hollway, Hawke's principal private secretary from late 1988, recalled,

The idea of some sort of Asia–Pacific community had been kicking around the academic community for about nine months. It wasn't right on the radar screen, but the idea was there. And I remember we were preparing for a visit Bob was to make to South Korea, Thailand, Pakistan and India, and as was customary, many months before the trip we were sitting around in the office talking about how the trip would work: what appointments Bob wanted with ministers, what speech opportunities there were. And it became obvious there were opportunities for major speeches in Seoul and Bangkok. It's very important to remember that at the time a huge thrust of Bob personally and of the Hawke government generally was Australia's economic relationship with Asia. Bob had invented this phrase that he continually used, 'enmeshment with Asia'. Multilateral trade negotiations were also a constant pre-occupation: how to liberalise international trade? So the thing that naturally always sprang to our mind was economics. I was talking to Bob late one night in Canberra and one of us said, 'You know, this trip might be the time for Australia to stand up and say we should have some kind of community for the Asia–Pacific. It was a very embryonic conversation.

Hollway envisaged a kind of Asia–Pacific OECD; the OECD studied and issued reports on matters such as intra-regional transport, economic management and financial flows.

I remember thinking to myself, There is a model which is utterly defensible, and it's a no-lose proposition – even if we don't get anywhere – because *forever* the Australian government will be on record as having stood up and declared that it wanted Australia to be part of Asia.

Gareth Evans was not scheduled to accompany the Prime Minister on the Asian trip because he was due in Washington for talks with, among others, Jim Baker, President Reagan's Secretary of State. His right arm, Woolcott, was to stay in Canberra minding home base.

Hawke travelled with a team that included his head of Prime Minister and Cabinet, Mike Codd, who recalled,

The thing senior public servants *pray* for from prime ministers is opportunity: opportunity to offer a view and be part of any discussion around policy suggestions that are going forward – because if you're engaged in that process it not only inspires you, the message goes back to the department and to other people in it, who have the job of fleshing out what's being proposed, and they all feel they are part of the government machine. Bob was very good throughout his time at doing just that, and one example is the formulation for APEC. We flew into Seoul one afternoon for a meeting next day with President Roh Tae-woo. And as was Bob's usual way, that night he drew in people from the team to chew the fat and discuss what major issues he should raise with the

President next morning, and what we should try to get out of the meeting. John Bowan was there, Sandy Hollway was there and I was there. It was about 10 p.m. We talked about regional co-operation, the fact that the Asia–Pacific would be the growth region of the world in the next few decades, and how to get more cooperation. We talked about needing something a bit more than the OECD, but not a body that required a huge machine to run it. And the proposition about what might be put forward, initially to President Roh, emerged from that discussion. Everyone in the room felt they were engaged in the process of developing the idea. It was remarkable: you often have PMs or leaders who have a great idea, but rarely do you have people who do that, who then think, 'How can we successfully implement it? What are the hurdles? What are the issues that can come up?'

There were plenty, the first being China's towering hostility at the time to Taiwan, its 'renegade province', and the Chinese refusal to recognise Hong Kong as an independent state empowered to represent itself. There was also the problem of the United States. If Australia were to propose that the United States should be part of the group, thereby presenting itself as an American 'deputy sheriff', then the members of ASEAN would baulk. Malaysia, in particular, harboured strong anti-American feelings, partly based on its pro-Palestinian stance. Its Prime Minister, Dr Mahathir, often seemed possessed of a general aversion to white people. In former colonial countries a reef of fear and hatred of Europeans lay just beneath the surface and it was easy to raise anti-Western passion. Codd said, 'We decided to leave Taiwan out of it, because it was just impossible at that stage to talk to China about Taiwan; we decided we wouldn't say if we thought America should be in or out.'

Hawke already enjoyed a warm relationship with Roh, he and Hazel having been guests at the President's house where they played tennis with Roh and his wife. 'When I outlined the APEC concept to Roh it was to a man who was prepared out of friendship and trust to discuss seriously any proposal I raised with him,' Hawke said. At their meeting the next morning Roh 'gave immediate and effusive support ... going out of his way to make it clear ... he wanted to be seen to be identified with it'. Hawke and his staff thought an envoy from Australia should travel from country to country, explaining the concept to each leader. Roh agreed.

Based on the President's positive attitude, the speech Hawke was to give the next day at a luncheon of Korean business associations was rewritten to present a clear, strong case for regional co-operation on trade, economic and social issues, to be driven by an intergovernmental vehicle. The United States and Taiwan were not mentioned.

In Washington there was outrage.

Unfortunately for Gareth Evans, because of his flight and the time difference in the era before wireless technology, he arrived unaware of what had been said in Seoul. The smooth, hard-nosed, gentlemanly Secretary of State, Jim Baker, later to become famous as *consigliere* to the Bush family, treated Evans to a tongue-lashing. Woolcott recalled,

> Baker bawled Gareth out about how could Australia, a friend and ally, take a major regional initiative in the Asia–Pacific, not *only* without the required consultation with the United States, but not even *including* the United States in the list of countries involved?

Evans' red-beard temper was famous throughout the Australian government and public service. He was known for primal shouting and throwing things at walls. What he had to say to his staff and the department in Canberra after this interview has not been revealed but, as Woolcott remarked, 'He was rather unhappy.'

Meanwhile, Hawke flew down to Bangkok. Codd recalled, 'The Americans were going *bananas*. They were *so angry*. We were very keen that Thailand, as one of the ASEAN countries, should bless the general idea, which the Thai Prime Minister did.'

As the trip progressed everyone realised that if Hong Kong and Taiwan were excluded because of Chinese objections the plan would be empty, and would fail. Within governments and in the press, discussion and comment began to call openly for these two tiger economies to be members of the group.

Hollway continued,

> I remember arguing very strongly, not that it took much argument with Bob, that if we're serious and if we want to project the Prime Minister as a serious player rather than somebody who's just shooting the breeze, we need to be ready immediately to follow the speech up with some serious diplomacy. Richard Woolcott was the obvious man for the job.

For years Woolcott had enjoyed the reputation of being able to walk on eggshells. Hollway continued,

> Some of the ASEANs were nervous about the Americans because the Malaysians were so cranky about them. The Japanese were saying, 'Sounds interesting but we're pretty wary of this unless the United States is happy.' It took about a micro-second to realise that Dick Woolcott would have to go to Washington.

Woolcott said,

> The upshot was I was nominated as the Prime Minister's special envoy to go to all the countries concerned and deal with them. That worked out very well with two exceptions, China and Malaysia. In unfortunate timing I arrived in Beijing just before the Tiananmen Square issue and called on the new Premier, Li Peng, as the students were occupying the square.

Li Peng was the adopted son of China's first premier, Zhou En-lai, who had intervened to save the life of Deng Xiaoping when Red Guards wanted to execute him during the Cultural Revolution. Li had met Hawke on a visit to Australia in 1988 and for once the magic of Hawke's personality had made no impression. Li, widely described as very reserved, was alarmed by the speed of the vast reforms in China being made by Zhao Ziyang, Hawke's close friend and a man Li despised. He had advised Garnaut, 'I wouldn't waste my time with him.' Indeed, Li intended to depose Zhao and a palace coup was brewing in Beijing in 1989, well before the students occupied the square. Because the granite foundation of China's civilisation is inter-generational responsibility, Chairman Deng, owing his life to Li's father, owed a debt to Li. Li had far greater access to Deng than his superior Zhao Ziyang and it was Li Peng's advice that would persuade Deng to authorise the killing of the students in Tiananmen Square, and the permanent house arrest of Zhao Ziyang.

Woolcott said,

> I made my pitch about what the Hawke initiative was and he said, 'Well, you should inform Mr Hawke that this is not acceptable to China since it includes Hong Kong, which is a British colony soon to revert to China, and Taiwan, which is an inalienable part of China.' If it wasn't acceptable to China that would be the end of it. We had to think very quickly.

Woolcott was as quick as a cat on his feet. He said,

> I had a couple of guys from Foreign Affairs with me and we conferred for a moment, then came up with something slightly different. We said what Mr Hawke wanted was to have a ministerial meeting of major *economies*. Not countries as such, but *economies*. Premier Li sort of softened and said, 'We can think about that.' He asked me then to talk to the Foreign minister, Qian Qichen, along those lines, which I did.

Meanwhile, as Hawke and his staff had hoped, the ASEAN nations began to say publicly that the United States should join. 'It *had to* come from them,' Codd said. The leaders of the push were Lee Kuan Yew of Singapore and President Suharto of Indonesia. Having decided that a regional economic forum was a good idea, Suharto, the strongest, most suave, most respected and intimidating of the ASEAN leaders, exerted his authority over Dr Mahathir, who abandoned his fight against America. In Washington Woolcott explained Australia's apparent unfriendly behaviour. As there was a warm regard that had been established over more than five years between Reagan and Hawke, who loved telling each other jokes, and Hawke and Baker, who had a few fine stories of his own, the row blew over.

The first APEC meeting, attended by the United States, the members of ASEAN, Japan, South Korea, Hong Kong and Taiwan – but without China – was held in Canberra in November 1989. China by now was a pariah in the United States and other Western nations over the Tiananmen massacre, and it was not until 1991, at the third APEC meeting, held in Seoul, that China acceded. Woolcott said,

> China had made one more proposal, which was accepted. China asserted it was inappropriate that Taiwan be represented by its Foreign minister, because Taiwan was not a country, and therefore could not have a Foreign minister. But a Trade minister would be acceptable.

(There is no word for 'logic' in Mandarin, which perhaps explains the delicacy of Chinese reasoning.) The knot was undone: Taiwan and Hong Kong attended as major economies, not as countries. Woolcott said,

> If Bob had been at that meeting he would have been proud. It was the first time China and Taiwan had met at an international conference. It was an interesting moment, because once they got through the preliminaries, out in the corridors

they began chatting away to each other, and it went very nicely. APEC was basically Bob's idea. Twenty years on it has its critics, but it's been enormously useful in the business communities, in Australia and the other member countries, and in things like harmonising customs regulations, producing a major trade database and generally in being a useful pressure group for trade facilitation and liberalisation.

APEC over its three decades has assisted in the creation of wealth and welfare for millions of people in the Asia–Pacific region. Paul Keating built on APEC, taking the initiative in 1992 to raise it from an annual ministerial meeting to a leadership meeting. In 2019, APEC had twenty-one members representing 2.7 billion people, 40 per cent of the world's population, while its GDP was 55 per cent of the world's total. Throughout Asia, Hawke is known as 'The Father of APEC'. Garnaut commented, 'Bob's establishment of trust with Chinese and many other leaders created the launching pad for APEC.'

Hawke took another major foreign policy initiative in 1987, as daring as his ambition to try to fix the Cambodian mess, but an issue in which he was involved day by day and hands-on. This was the fight against apartheid in South Africa.

He had publicly fought against apartheid from the moment he was in a position to do so, on acceding to the leadership of the ACTU in January 1970, when he called for a union boycott of the rugby tour of Australia by the South African Springboks team scheduled for the following year. The pro-apartheid slogan of the time was 'Don't mix politics with sport'. As Hawke pointed out, the Springboks team was a perfect example of politics mixed with sport: no blacks were allowed in it. In the 1970s and in years following, there were violent protests for and against apartheid and Hawke was subjected to a barrage of racist hatred, including a bomb threat to an aeroplane on which he was a passenger. His predecessor as prime minister, Malcolm Fraser, had been as anti-apartheid as was Hawke, and like Hawke had been unable to make any progress against the adamantine will, backed by a huge treasure of gold, diamonds and oil, of the white South African regime. The biggest, richest, most heavily armed and strategically located country in Africa was immovable. Hawke realised he was in need of a lever, and preparing for the 1987 Commonwealth Heads of Government Meeting (CHOGM) the thought suddenly struck him of what such a lever might be.

At the CHOGM of 1985 a ginger group, made up of Prime Minister Rajiv Gandhi from India, Brian Mulroney from Canada, and Hawke, had formulated a communiqué that, with great difficulty, they persuaded the formidable British leader, Margaret Thatcher, to sign. The communiqué announced an Eminent Persons' Group to negotiate with the South African government over apartheid and, if this did not work, a stage-by-stage application of sanctions against the regime. Hawke nominated Malcolm Fraser as Australia's representative on the Eminent Persons, but the group got nowhere in its attempts at negotiation with the South African government. In 1986, to the disgust of Mrs Thatcher, sanctions began. She believed apartheid was the only viable system for the time being for South Africa, that sanctions would not work and to the extent they did, the only people to suffer would be the black population. Small as she was, and titanic as he was, Thatcher the Ice Queen seemed to tower above Malcolm Fraser in their meetings about South Africa. Brian Mulroney, built along the lines of an Aberdeen Angus bull, also received the Thatcher freeze. In a very uncomfortable meeting, held in Malborough House, London, in 1986, Hawke made life bearable for himself by a surreptitious exchange of notes with Geoffrey, later Lord, Howe, the British Foreign minister. They competed in lampoons of the Iron Lady. Hawke and Thatcher, both of whom enjoyed a fight, actually liked each other personally, while disagreeing about almost everything politically. On his return from London Hawke had to report to parliament on 21 August: 'Specific and meaningful action has not been taken to dismantle apartheid. A new State of Emergency has been introduced. Nelson Mandela and other detainees are still in jail ...'

Although the Eminent Persons had failed, international feelings against South Africa were now following the Commonwealth lead. In August 1986 the United States Senate voted in favour of strong measures against South Africa, the European Community was considering sanctions, and Japan was quietly adding its voice. Another year of sanctions went by and the South African government was, if anything, more intransigent. For a price, rogue traders and countries around the world were willing to break the sanctions. Thatcher, to date, was proved correct.

The tenth CHOGM was to be held in October 1987 in Vancouver. Hawke would be accompanied by various advisers, the most senior being his head of department, Mike Codd. Like Hawke, Codd was the son of a clergyman, an Anglican, whose ministry had been in Subiaco in Perth, the same district in which Clem Hawke was a minister for the Congregational church. He said,

> Long before I worked for Bob my father told me about his conversations with Clem, initiated by Clem, who was very interested in consensus on major social issues. He wanted to get the other denominations in the Subiaco area to be singing from the same hymn book, and approached my father about putting a joint letter forward to the local papers about not drinking on Sunday, which was one of Clem's passions. But my father actually liked a beer, including on Sundays, so he wasn't terribly encouraging on that issue. The other one was to do with sport on Sundays. Clem had this drive for achieving change in attitudes by having consensus views put in front of the community.

Codd recalled,

> A couple of days before the CHOGM started we were having a meeting, at night, and Bob started talking about the financial support for the regime, the bank loans they had, and if that could provide a lever. I got some work done and a

brief came back to Bob that said there are major loans from American and European banks that are due to be rolled over in about eighteen months. The view was, if the banks refused to roll over those loans it would cripple the South African economy. And the business sector, if it got some hint this was about to happen, would put *huge* pressure on the South African government to do something to stop it. So that was the embryo.

But these were views from within the Australian government, not those of professionals in the field.

Codd continued,

Bob said, 'We need a meeting with some of the other members to talk about this, but we can't have Brian Mulroney, because he's the CHOGM host and the tradition is you can't involve the host in a controversial issue. And obviously we can't have Thatcher, because she's out on an island about apartheid.' So it was to get together Robert Mugabe, who back then had not yet gone mad, Kenneth Kaunda, Rajiv Gandhi plus Sonny Ramphal and Chief Anyaoku from the Commonwealth Secretariat. So one night before the conference had started we gathered this small group and Bob, who had had further briefing on the loans situation, outlined the plan. They were all very enthusiastic about it. And Bob said, 'Well – now we've got this far, we must find someone who knows the financial system to come and tell us what is doable, and if so how? I know Jim Wolfensohn, an Australian [who had become an American citizen in 1980] who's running a small investment bank in New York. Will we try him?'

And they all agreed, so Bob rang Wolfensohn and without telling him much on the phone, asked him to come to Vancouver. Jim got on his private jet and was there by the following evening. They all sat down together and Jim was so helpful. He did think this would have a major, major impact on the South African economy and he felt it was doable if the

right people spoke to the right banks. He offered personally to approach some of the American banks, who were big
lenders to South Africa, but asked us to get somebody else
to deal with Europe. Then he got on his jet and flew home.

As Wolfensohn needed to return to New York as soon as possible, there was no opportunity for Codd to raise security issues
with Hawke. As soon as they were alone together Codd told
Hawke they had failed to alert Wolfensohn to something rather
important: if the South Africans, who had a wide-ranging intelligence service, were to discover what was afoot, not only could
Wolfensohn's own business be attacked, his life could be at risk.
The apartheid regime was not squeamish about assassinations,
either at home or abroad.

Codd said,

> We needed some follow-up with Jim immediately – first to
> alert him and to make sure he understood how serious the situ-
> ation was. We knew the South Africans were very active and
> that they would be trying to listen in to what was happening
> in Vancouver, or to pick it up in one way or another, so we had
> to act very fast. Second, we needed a secure channel to keep
> communications with him open, and decided the Australian
> consul general in New York, John Taylor, would be the man to
> use. We were to drive this on behalf of the others. So it was late
> on Thursday and the leaders were all due to go off together on
> the Friday afternoon for their weekend retreat.

The retreat is a leaders-only conference, without staff. Hawke
decided that Codd should fly immediately, on Thursday night, to
New York to see Wolfensohn. He had to travel commercially so as
not to draw attention to himself. As it happened there were only
economy seats available, and Codd, who is more than 1.85 metres
tall, was forced to hop from Vancouver to Seattle, to Chicago,
and finally New York. He met the Australian consul general at
10 a.m. on Friday morning, then met Wolfensohn. Codd said,

I wanted Jim to be absolutely clear what sort of stuff goes
on in the real world when these big issues are at stake: he
needed to get his head around just what he had let himself in
for, because he had generously volunteered and put his own
reputation at stake with the American banks he needed to
deal with.

Wolfensohn accepted the risk to his business and possibly his
life, and on Friday night Codd went to Kennedy airport to fly
back to Vancouver. 'But as usual,' he said,

> out of Kennedy on Friday night it was chaos and we sat on
> the tarmac for an hour, then we circled Chicago for an hour,
> so I missed the last connection out of Seattle to Vancouver.
> There were security perimeters around the hotel in Vancouver
> because Rajiv Gandhi and Margaret Thatcher, in particular,
> were targets [Gandhi was later assassinated]. I had to get on a
> bus then fight my way through security somehow.

Codd had spent his scant free time in New York in buying
what he modestly described as 'some flimsy gear' for his wife.
He recalled his excruciating embarrassment when, 'At every
checkpoint they pulled this stuff out and inspected it. Eventually
I got into the hotel at about 3 a.m. . . . . At no stage did Margaret
Thatcher discover what was going on.' The execution of the plan
to have international banks boycott South Africa was, Codd said,

> an example of the idea that you need expert advice about how
> to get something done. Within days we had appointed Tony
> Cole, who was my deputy on the economic side, a highly
> competent, respected fellow who went on to become head
> of Treasury, to deal with the European banks. He worked
> especially with the German banks, the biggest lenders to
> South Africa, and so between Tony and Jim we actually got
> the banks on board. We had very secure communications net-
> works set up with the other leaders to keep them informed

of progress. And the impact was just as we expected on the South African business community. None of us was there in South Africa, so we can't say for sure that this was *why* apartheid came down, or exactly what percentage of the reason it was, but there's no doubt in my mind that it was very, very significant because the business community was saying to the government, 'You've GOT TO move.'

In 1990 the South African Minister for Finance, Barend du Plessis, admitted that the banks' disinvestment was 'the dagger that finally immobilised apartheid'.[4]

Codd added,

I think it was a very, very clever idea in the first place. It was the most powerful individual weapon that had been used against South Africa, and the execution of it was done very effectively. If ideas are in the least bit controversial, and most good ideas are, just announcing them will never work. Bob had a good idea and he won other people over to it, he got the right group committed. Some leaders can't do that: they have an idea and just throw it into the Cabinet ring, without talking to anyone beforehand, and opposition sinks it. This was an object lesson in leadership by Bob.

In February 1990, President de Klerk announced that Nelson Mandela had just been freed from prison after twenty-seven years, that the African National Congress was a legitimate political party and that the government would negotiate with it. In October that year a tall, graceful African stepped into Hawke's office in Canberra, a smile on his face, his arms open to embrace the Prime Minister. Taking a seat he said, 'I want you to know, Bob, that I am here today, at this time, because of you.'

TWENTY-SIX

ANDELA HAD CHOSEN AUSTRALIA as the first country outside Africa to visit after his release from jail. The friendship between him and Hawke flourished and years later Mandela would become International Patron of the Bob Hawke Prime Ministerial Centre in Adelaide. But well before their first meeting in 1990 Hawke had known that apartheid was on its deathbed – it was formally buried in February 1991 – and began to think ahead to the problems South African could face. Sandy Hollway said,

> He was thinking ahead about it in a way that no other country did. It's a very important story. It wasn't an initiative that changed the world, but in terms of demonstrating an attitude about getting out ahead of a problem – if we're bringing this system down we've got a responsibility to help its successor up – of thinking creatively, it's a very good example.

Africa, which at the beginning of the 1960s seemed as economically promising as Asia, was by the 1980s a continent in precipitous decline, a mess of mismanagement, corruption, violence and – defeating all attempts at modernisation and decency – the knot of tribalism.

Hollway said,

> Africa economically, in too many places, was a basket case – and Bob said this couldn't be allowed to happen in South Africa. So he wanted to figure out what we could do to help a

future black government in South Africa to manage its economy decently. And he sent me and Ross Garnaut and Doug Sterkey from DFAT to talk to the ANC, to the business community, to the government, about what we could do by way of advice and assistance.

At about 3 a.m., when the flight from Perth was midway across the Indian Ocean, Garnaut, who had been reading the economic brief on South Africa, nudged Hollway awake. 'We may as well turn around now,' he said. 'This place is stuffed.' But they ploughed on and the assistance given at Hawke's instigation to South Africa during a time of critical transition was just one of many unpublicised initiatives, mostly in Asian and Pacific countries, that helped them and established Australia's prestige in the region as an intelligent, creative nation committed to benevolence. This was the Australia that Hawke wanted the world to see and to recognise as the *real Australia*.

Hollway added of the work Australian economists, bureaucrats and other advisers did in South Africa, 'Of course the difficulties were formidable because half of the people now running the country had been out in the bush fighting, or had been trained in Moscow.'

Hawke held strong views on Moscow's economic efficiency and especially on its trustworthiness in negotiations. In 1979 he had suffered his single-most mortifying humiliation as a negotiator at the hands of Muscovites. They had promised him that a group of Jews, desperate to leave the Soviet Union, would be allowed to emigrate and Hawke announced this joyous news to the Jewish world. There was an ecstasy of relief and happiness. But Moscow had played him for a sucker. The so-called 'refuseniks' were not allowed to emigrate after all and were still in Moscow more than eight years later when Hawke met the new tsar, Mikhail Gorbachev.

The international news media was in the early stages of turning Gorbachev into a superstar but, as Hawke knew, the media, like the wind, blows where it lists, one hears its sound but cannot tell whence it comes nor where it goes. He had good reports from both Margaret Thatcher and Ronald Reagan, both of whom were edging forward on arms reduction talks with Gorbachev. Hawke, as leader of a Cold War alliance nation that would be due for almost immediate attack in a hot war, was keen to judge for himself. But protocol decreed he should not meet Gorbachev, who was the Secretary General of the Communist Party, but instead the Soviet Prime Minister, Nikolai Ryzhkov. Hawke was determined to talk to the man who mattered, and before leaving Australia sent Michael Costello and Sandy Hollway to Moscow as an advance team whose job it was to arrange a meeting with the Secretary General and to ensure that no barrier would be put in the way of a meeting between the Australian Prime Minister and the refuseniks. They succeeded. Before leaving for the USSR Hawke also spent hours in conversation with Bill Lane, the United States ambassador to Australia, a Republican and fierce anti-Communist, reassuring him that his visit to the 'Evil Empire' would in no way be detrimental to the alliance.

John Bowan, Hawke's Foreign Affairs adviser, said,

Bob had this fantastic ability to adjust himself to the situation: if he had to spend four and a half hours reassuring Bill Lane, he'd do it. If he was with Lee Kuan Yew, who considered himself an intellectual master of the universe, Bob would turn into an intellectual master of the universe. And he could go to the pub with a bunch of wharfies. He wasn't drinking alcohol at all, but he would somehow give the impression that he'd had one or two himself and was really comfortable with these blokes who were boozing up.

Hawke's years of building Australia's international role got off to a good start in Jordan in January 1987, and on the same swing through the Middle East meetings went well in Egypt, Hawke being the first Australian prime minister to visit Cairo since Menzies' disastrous intervention in 1956. But he ran aground in Israel, where his brief, disagreeable meeting with the Prime Minister, Itzak Shamir of the right-wing Likud Party, instantly established that both men disliked each other.

On the very day in 1983 when Hawke was sworn in as Prime Minister, he had said in a radio interview he believed he might 'have a part to play' in negotiations between Israel and Arab nations by making an official visit to the Middle East. The holy grail was a Grand Bargain: a trade of land seized by Israel in 1967 in exchange for peace with the Palestinians, specifically their acceptance of Resolution 242 of the United Nations that stated Israel's right to exist within secure and recognised borders. The politicals on Hawke's staff and the Department of Foreign Affairs were appalled that the Prime Minister wanted to revive his passion for Israel. John Bowan, who took up his job as Foreign Affairs adviser just a couple of days after Hawke's 1983 remarks, said,

> Bob saw himself as a fixer and thought he could perhaps fix the Arab–Israel dispute. My job was to keep him out of the Middle East for as long as possible. There was a general fear among the powerful people in the office that if he got into the Middle East, God knows what he might do. I remember sending him a note letting him know that everybody – the entire staff – felt that he should not go to the Middle East.

Since the late 1970s Israeli intellectuals had been arguing that their country could have any two of three attributes, but not all three: it could encompass Greater Israel, the land it had seized from Palestinians in 1967; it could be a Jewish state; it could be a democracy. His conviction was naive. For Israel, the greatest virtue is survival. It could not be a Greater Israel Jewish democracy.

By the mid-1980s Hawke had come to this view himself. He believed Israel was trapped in a race against time and Palestinian population increase, in danger of losing its greatest virtue: democracy. His conviction was naive. For Israel, the greatest virtue is survival. As usual there was a 'peace process' underway; as usual, it was going nowhere. Israel's future, as Hawke perceived it, was so alarming he decided to tackle the issue in a speech to the Hebrew University in Jerusalem, where he was to receive an honorary doctorate. But when he showed the Australian ambassador a draft the envoy was horrified. He ruled thin red lines through page after page.[1]

From long experience Hawke knew that, beneath their macho swagger, Israelis were terrified of their Arab neighbours, especially the Palestinians who lived under Israeli occupation, and that they turned skittish and thin-skinned at any criticism from outsiders. He agreed to boil down his full message to one question: 'How will Israel solve the great issues of political principle and human rights, not to mention the demographic pressures, entailed in its role as administrator of occupied territories?' Abstract and academic, the speech caused no offence, and the Australian news media travelling with him missed its underlying significance: that Hawke's views on Israel had changed. The media was after an emotional story. They were hoping that the Australian Prime Minister would fall into a tearful state when confronted with imagery of the Jews' appalling history. Photographs of Hawke weeping were guaranteed for page one and the lead item on the television news. Stephen Mills, Hawke's speechwriter noted, 'After he inspected the Holocaust memorial in Jerusalem there was intense media speculation about whether there was a tear in his eye – and if so, whether it could be put down to emotion or to the cold morning.'[2] But Hawke had the present and the future rather than the past on his mind, and was determined to raise the issue of where he believed Israel was heading.

After he received his honorary doctorate, he was accorded a state dinner in the Israeli parliament, the Knesset, and intended to raise in that forum the issue of Palestinian self-determination and the future establishment of a Palestinian state. In an unprecedented breech of protocol the President of Israel, Chaim Herzog, insisted that Hawke censor his remarks. Hawke refused, pointing out that the speech had already been circulated to the media, but he agreed to soften the text by inserting the suggestion that a Palestinian confederation, rather than an independent Palestinian state, would be the most likely outcome of the peace process. The next morning, in East Jerusalem, he met a group of Palestinian leaders and was impressed by their realism: they were, he believed, people with whom Israel could, and should, negotiate, and that to refuse to do so was both immoral and would lead to violence. That night he dined privately with Shimon Peres, a Labor Party leader, and a man with whom he could talk unreservedly. Hawke proposed a simultaneous act of recognition by the Palestinians and the Israelis as a basis for negotiations. Peres wholeheartedly agreed. Bowan said, 'While Bob had started out [his prime ministership] with a partial view, skewed towards Israel, he ended up with a very well-balanced view.'

Hawke left Israel with an ominous sense that the nation he had admired and supported so long and at such expense to himself was now, under its right-wing government, moving in a direction away from not only peace, but from its own principles and ideals, the very qualities to which he and so much of the West had been so attracted in the first place. Israel was transforming into a country he found difficult to recognise. As Israelis remark sardonically, 'We live in a tough neighbourhood.'

The year ended in Moscow in December where, thanks to the efforts of Michael Costello and Sandy Hollway, he was to meet Gorbachev.

The interview was scheduled to last twenty minutes, but such was the leaders' rapport it stretched to three and a quarter hours. There was much at stake for Hawke. He had established Australia as a country for 'reality testing' between China and the United States. If the meeting with Gorbachev went well, Hawke would be in a position to play the same role between Moscow and Washington, passing on messages that neither side wanted to give directly to the other for fear of rebuff, but would do so through a trusted intermediary. 'You could make suggestions in good faith and could explore them without prejudice. And you could kill off bad ideas without fear of international embarrassment,' he said. Off his own bat he urged Gorbachev to push both the Arab states that were committed to the destruction of

Israel and Yasser Arafat, leader of the Palestinian Liberation Organization, another Soviet client, to accept Resolution 242 of the United Nations. At the time every nation in the Middle East, plus others including Malaysia, rejected Resolution 242. Hawke said,

> I argued to him he should use his influence with the Arab states and the PLO to recognise Israel *in return for which* Israel would recognise the right of the PLO to speak for the Palestinians. He accepted the logic of what I put, but made the wry observation, 'Prime Minister, you must understand, they don't always accept my recommendations.'

In his meeting with the Soviet leader, Hawke also brought up the issue of the refuseniks. He intended to persuade Gorbachev to consider the wretched group of Jews whose plight he had first raised in 1979. The excuse for refusing them exit permits was that, as scientists, they knew state secrets. One of them had been asking to be allowed out since 1971, had long since retired, and any state secret he might have known was by 1987 completely out of date.

Hawke emerged from his meeting with the Soviet leader so enlivened that for the first time since he had given up alcohol he felt like a glass of champagne. He was excited not because he believed Gorbachev was approaching his reform of the USSR in the right way – Hawke believed Gorbachev had put the political cart before the economic horse, and told him so – but because he had recognised the hand of history resting on the Russian's shoulder. 'I had been with a man of destiny,' he said. 'I knew he was *the indispensable man* for closing down the Cold War.' He found Gorbachev, he told the Australian media, 'engaging', 'stimulating', with 'a quickness of understanding', 'an attractive preparedness to recognise past weaknesses', and that he was 'sincere' about reforms. He said there had been 'vibrance' in their conversation. Gorbachev had told Hawke something he did not pass on to the media: that the Soviet Union was 'in a pre-crisis situation'.

Back home Hawke's comments caused John Howard, leader of the Opposition, to accuse him of looking 'through rose-tinted glasses'. Howard declared that the Prime Minister had made 'a monumental error of judgment' for declaring he would welcome 'constructive involvement' with the USSR. History put egg on Howard's face rather swiftly when a few days later there was a Gorbachev–Reagan summit from which the American President emerged smitten with admiration for the Secretary General.

Hawke did not reveal to the travelling media in Moscow that during their meeting Gorbachev had promised to give serious consideration to the list of refuseniks with which Hawke had presented him. On the last morning of his visit, amidst the splendour of the Australian ambassador's residence, an art-nouveau mansion once owned by a sugar merchant, Hawke had an emotional reunion with the group of old and shabbily dressed refuseniks he had last seen in 1979. Many were now ill and feeble. He told them his thoughts on Gorbachev and that the Secretary General had agreed to give consideration to their plight. Late that afternoon as the Australian entourage was preparing to leave the state guest house, Gorbachev's interpreter unexpectedly turned up. He was middle-aged, which is old for an interpreter, and a man whose thought processes it had seemed to Hawke were virtually a continuum of the Secretary General's, such was the lightning fluency, the flow and counter-flow of his translation. He brought wonderful news: five of those on the list Hawke had given Gorbachev would be allowed to leave immediately.

By the following May almost all, more than twenty refuseniks, were free. It was a triumph for human rights and for persistence. The Jewish communities in Australia and around the world were ecstatic about their release and the World Jewish Congress voted to award Hawke an honour. He stood at the pinnacle of respect in the Jewish community. His old friend, Isi Leibler, the founder of Jetset and a man whose passion for the release of Soviet Jews seemed to drive the very breath of his body, arranged a great celebration in Melbourne for Hawke.

Leibler was of aggressively sharp intelligence and for years Hawke had enjoyed mentally sparring with him. Leibler flew the liberated refuseniks to Australia for the grand occasion, which was envisaged as a homage to the Prime Minister, champion of justice and human rights. 'It was to be a lap of honour for him,' Bowan said.

Hawke, however, had what he considered a better idea. He intended to tell his audience what he had wanted to tell the Knesset seventeen months earlier: among other things, that Israel was violating the human rights of the Palestinians.

Years earlier, in the 1970s, his daughter, Sue, who was active in a number of left-wing causes, had asserted that if her father ever heard firsthand the Palestinians' side of the argument, he would be as sympathetic to them as he was to the Israelis. Hawke was such an Israelophile, especially after the Yom Kippur War of 1973, the idea sounded outlandish. But now he had heard the Palestinian side of the argument and he was determined not merely to rain, but to pour, on his own parade. 'They had to be told,' he said. 'I'd proved my friendship and I thought it the duty of a friend to speak the truth as he saw it – and that truth was the universality of human rights apply to the Palestinians as to the Israelis.'

John Bowan recalled,

Bob wrote the speech he wanted to give at the dinner, and you had this ironical situation that his staff, most of whom had a much more pro-Arab view of the Middle East than Bob did, trying to talk him out of saying what he wanted to. In one sentence he was comparing the Palestinians in the occupied territories with the blacks in South Africa and the Jews in the Soviet Union. His principal private secretary, Sandy Hollway, Bob Sorby, his political adviser, and I were all horrified.

By May 1988 the Palestinians had launched an uprising (the first intifada) in the West Bank and Gaza, exactly the violent

770 BOB HAWKE: THE COMPLETE BIOGRAPHY

reaction Hawke had feared would eventually but inevitably be the response to Israeli oppression in the occupied territories.

At his lap of honour ceremony in Melbourne, Hawke said, 'Our sense of celebration is necessarily muted ...' and referred to the intifada as providing proof that the principles on which Israel was built 'do not sit easily with the role of master of occupied territories and subject peoples'. Around the room there were sharply indrawn breaths. He continued,

> The Palestinian in the occupied territories, as the Jew in the Soviet Union and the black in South Africa, has his aspirations to be fully free. The friends of Israel around the world are fearful that in a real sense we may be witnessing again, after thousands of years, a giant eyeless in Gaza.

The temperature in the room dropped, Hawke's staff noted, 'about twenty degrees'. The audience began muttering to each other but their guest of honour went on, 'Is there not emerging the danger of Israel being blinded to the threat to its very soul and the vision of its founders?' The audience by now was so angry they were on the point of booing. The staff muttered, *'There goes the Jewish vote.'* Bowan said, 'Bob knew exactly what he was doing. Sometimes he just did these things.'

Leibler was dismayed and furious. When the ceremony was over, Hawke returned to Leibler's house in Caulfield, where they argued for about three hours. Their friendship, begun in the early 1970s, never recovered.

In the same month, May 1988, the Queen opened Canberra's new Parliament House, which had cost $1 billion and was the most expensive building in the country. Shaped as two huge boomerangs when seen from above, it had 4500 rooms and was, for both the upper and lower ranking inhabitants of the old Parliament House, a glorious new workplace. Hollway was the last chief of staff for a prime minister in the old House, and the first in the new. He said, 'We'd had people crowded together in ship-galley-width rooms, trying to handle phone calls, write speeches and hold meetings. And that was the Prime Minister's office.'

For junior backbenchers, independents and members of a splinter party, like the Democrats, the old House had been a ghetto: Senator Don Chipp, the leader of the Democrats, had been accommodated, with another senator and a shared staffer, in a tiny room in which the air conditioning did not work, where private conversation was unthinkable. In Canberra's 36-degree summers, Chipp would remove his jacket and tie and open his shirt four buttons down and still be perspiring. Hollway said,

> It was weird. My office was next to the PM's office and the way for me to know whether he was meeting with someone, or whether he was in the bathroom, was to look though this spyhole in the wall: it amplified the room and I could see a distorted figure in there. It was absolutely bizarre. It had been there since Curtin was PM, when someone had come up with this bright idea about how to know if the boss was busy. So when a staffer or a minister came and asked, 'Can I see the PM?' I'd go and have a look, and say 'Yes' or 'No'. In the new Parliament House, I had a monitor under my desk and I could glance down without anybody realising what I was doing. The physical environment of the new office was far superior for the good running of the government.

Hawke loved it. Unlike many parliamentarians who had spent most of their working lives in the old House, he had no nostalgia for it and he preferred contemporary domestic architecture and furniture.

After five years in government there were, Hollway said, 'a central core of ministers who were all extremely competent and by then pretty experienced, pretty confident, and not yet getting tired. They were firing.' The economic difficulties after the stock market crash of October 1987 meant that from early '88 economic advisers were just beating a path continuously back and forth across that corridor [from the PM's office] into the Cabinet room, and there were more and more ERC meetings. The economy was a *huge* preoccupation.

Nobody quite realised at first that a boom was gathering and that 'the most unpredictable year in an unpredictable decade' had begun. Like riding a bolting horse, it was a case of holding on, staying focused and hoping the beast would run itself out before hitting a wall.

In the calm of hindsight, it's easy to see that 1988, which caused economic chaos throughout the West, was the cloud of a storm that would burst in 1989, a year of shocks and wonders in which the world watched in astonishment as the proud towers of European Communism shuddered on their foundations, as the emperor of China, Deng Xiaoping, decided that bloodshed was necessary, as the death of Allah's Voice on Earth, Ayatollah Khomeini, threw Iran into convulsions, as Nelson Mandela would be secretly freed from prison, as the tyrant Nicolae Ceau̦sescu and his fearsome wife were executed, as Germans clamoured for reunification – and the ancient empires of the East would begin inexorably to rise.

The government had intended to tighten monetary policy at the end of 1987 or in early 1988 but, because of the stock market crash in October, delayed doing so. Ralph Willis recalled, 'everybody was worried that if you tightened monetary policy on top of the crash you might hammer the economy through the floor'. This was the mistake made in 1929 that had created the Great Depression. Willis continued,

> So we held off for something like nine months after the crash before a tightening cycle got under way – and it was too late. It became a case of making up for lost time, which is diabolical with monetary policy.

He used a simile to describe the devil in monetary policy:

> It's like a brick tied with a piece of elastic. You want to move the brick, and you pull on the elastic. Nothing happens. You pull harder. Still no response. And harder. Suddenly the brick jumps and hits you in the face.

At some stage during 1988 Willis thought, 'This looks traumatic.' For the Cabinet and the ERC, and especially for the Treasurer, managing the economy was as difficult as it had been two years earlier, during the trade and currency collapse, and by now Keating was fed up with playing second fiddle to Hawke. He was forty-four years old and it was time, he believed, for him to become prime minister.

All Keating's hopes were invested in Hawke's retiring during the third term so that he, Keating, could lead the government into a 1990 election. He believed Labor could not win a fifth election, but if he took over in 1988 he would have the satisfaction of being prime minister for five years, before almost certain defeat at the polls in 1993. He began to gather supporters for his cause, among them John Dawkins, the very able, aggressive and unpredictable Minister for Education and Training. Dawkins said,

> Bob had this great ability to engage with people in the broad, in this sort of matey way, and everybody thought he was their best friend. Keating, in contrast, had an incredible capacity to actually engage with small groups: he'd sit down at the table and he'd have them eating out of his hand in no time. There was an intensity about him, and an intensity about his discourse which was very engaging.

Dawkins held long discussions with the Treasurer on what the job of prime minister required. Dawkins said,

> You really only have to do one thing a day, if that. You have to do a couple of things a week, but they've got to be things that

matter. And you can do some of them from Canberra – you don't have to go around shopping centres, and all that stuff.

For Hawke, the idea was risible. *He* knew the hours he worked and was concerned that Keating did not have sufficient stamina. Compared to the prime minister's job a Treasurer's is relatively easy, most of the work being done by officials; a number of very successful Australian Treasurers have been famously lazy: after a learned or amusing performance in Question Time, they could mentally sign off for the rest of the day. Only around budget time or in crises did they have to work consistently. The Prime Minister's heir apparent presented him with a dilemma: brilliant in Parliament, the government's greatest weapon for verbally demolishing the Opposition, a good campaigner, Keating lacked the boundless vitality he would need, Hawke believed, to keep him going day after day. There were few people with whom Hawke could or did share this view, which he had developed over five years of observing his partner. He said,

> Paul had many outstanding and some unique positive qualities as a politician, but he lacked what I considered the sine qua non for doing the prime minister's job successfully. He did not have the constitution for the continuous hard work the job requires.

The mutterings and verbal backstabbing of Hawke, which had been growing bolder since his 1987 victory, grew bolder still. Geoff Walsh, former press secretary who had rejoined Hawke's staff as political adviser, was astonished when he walked into Keating's office one day and saw written on a large whiteboard, 'The Lodge in 88'.

It is hard to overstate the influence a senior politician's staff and advisers have in these affairs. In the years before he challenged Hayden, Hawke himself once remarked of his beloved and trusted confidante, Jean Sinclair, 'Aah – she just wants to be the prime minister's secretary.'

The staff stand to gain status in the same ratio as their boss, and their plotting, scheming and leaking to the news media, plus the encouragement they give their champion, are critical in political fights. Their vicarious lives tend to deepen staffers' pains and triumphs. So 'The Lodge in 88' was in the Treasurer's office. Keating believed he could persuade Hawke into giving him the leadership during the year. He held an ace: if he did not get the job he wanted, he would resign and go to Paris, he said. A Treasurer's resignation, unless on grounds of health or family crisis, is a blow to public confidence that governments must try to avoid. But, as Paul Kelly wrote,

> the Hawke camp ... had the challenger beaten before he began. Hawke and his advisers had operated on the assumption that Keating might mount some form of challenge ... [Hawke's] tactic was to keep the loyalty of the dominant NSW faction, Keating's own base. Hawke's political aide Bob Sorby, appointed on the advice of Graham Richardson, worked closely with Richardson during 1988 to ensure that there was no defection to Keating ... While Richardson stayed with Hawke, Keating was stymied.[3]

But Keating, who believed in his own point of view with unshakeable intensity, carried on as if the prize was already his. It sometimes seemed that within his heart there blundered about the huge old man, Jack Lang, Keating's political father, with iron will and iron muscles, his actions motivated by a kind of unrestrainable blindness. Keating devised the Budget he delivered in August 1988 as a vehicle for him to win the 1990 election. He characterised it as 'bringing home the bacon', announcing on the first page, 'the nation is successfully emerging from its most severe economic crisis in a generation ... we are now well on the way back to prosperity'. His career as Treasurer was about to end in triumphant flourish, he thought. But reading the budget papers, economists and economically literate journalists recognised it as better politics than economics. And worse was to come, for within three weeks Keating's own officials were to warn him his numbers did not add up. Kelly noted, 'Keating ... was looking for a virtual [landslide for himself in 1990], an election win which would increase Labor's majority and set up the Keating government for many years.' But the Budget, in fact, was a horrible mistake.

Hawke never attempted to micromanage the government nor interfere with his ministers but was now fed up with Keating's public rhetoric, and his private threats to 'take the Paris option'. He decided to bring the subterranean rumblings from Keating's supporters up into the light. 'My patience, which had been considerable, was not, however, limitless,' he said.

The morning after the Budget a Morgan poll showed Labor ahead of the Coalition 47 to 42 per cent, and Hawke leading John Howard as preferred prime minister 69 to 18 per cent. The Treasurer was still very unpopular with the electorate, despite his attempts, since 1987, to soften his image. The Prime Minister took three opportunities that day in answering questions to remark that there were many competent economists in the government and that if Mr Keating wanted to live in Paris he would not be irreplaceable. Keating was furious and, in a brief conversation with Hawke in the Prime Minister's office, announced their relationship was 'dead and buried'.

Richardson quickly organised a peace treaty of sorts, persuading Hawke to go back on television and recant about Keating's indispensability, which Hawke did, but as a very poor liar his effusiveness was unconvincing – certainly to Keating, who saw Hawke's praise as so insincere it was an insult. That night Richardson rang Keating from his car phone to persuade the Treasurer to bury the issue, pointing out that the Prime Minister had done the right thing. Keating objected that Hawke had not meant what he said. The cat's cradle of Richardson's loyalties – to the Prime Minister, to the government, to his political tribe in New South Wales – were demonstrated in this phone call, in which he and Keating fell into the male-bonding speech that members of the New South Wales Right use with each other.

Richardson referred to the Prime Minister as 'the cunt'; Keating gave Hawke a less obscene but very cutting character assessment. The phone call was intercepted, recorded and offered for sale to the press gallery. Hawke had a transcript of it within a day.

He read it on a flight to Sydney, where he was to address a dinner, but grew so angry he spent forty-five minutes beforehand on the telephone arguing with Keating, while the two hundred guests waited. Later that night he spoke to Keating again and suggested they meet on Sunday afternoon, 28 August, when Hawke was back in Canberra. Before their meeting Kim Beazley, whom Hawke loved like a son, and who loved and admired both the Prime Minister and the Treasurer, talked to each in turn. Both assured Beazley they would be civil with each other.

Keating arrived determined that Hawke should promise him a transition in late 1988 or early 1989. Hawke said he would stay on and win the 1990 election. He did not accept Keating's assessment that the 1990 election was virtually unwinnable; he said that if Keating made good his threat and went to Paris, Dawkins could replace him as Treasurer. What's more, Hawke believed that the Opposition was still in a parlous state. The Melbourne businessman John Elliott, a Church shoe rather than a white shoe, had taken over as Liberal Party president, and had told Hawke at a dinner at Government House what a mess it was. (Elliott, as it happened, was plotting to overthrow the current leader, John Howard, and become prime minister himself at the 1990 election. He neglected to mention this to Hawke.)

Keating did not accept Hawke's analysis of how weak the Opposition was; Hawke told Keating he had, with time and effort, established himself as an Australian leader who could play a constructive role internationally and he intended to do so right through until 1990. Keating said Hawke was neglecting leadership at home, and that if he had to keep being Treasurer until then, 'I'll be going ga-ga.' Keating's fear, according to Kelly, was that he would, indeed, be physically and mentally burnt out by the time he became leader, and that his whole team would be exhausted. The meeting ended in a frosty stalemate, with a promise by both men to keep up public appearances.

But Hawke's counter-threat to Keating to make Dawkins Treasurer in his place was evidently alarming to Keating, who took swift action. It seems he talked to Dawkins that night, for next morning on the *AM* radio program, Dawkins called on Hawke to set a timetable for transition. Dawkins then went a step further: he decided to front the Prime Minister and ask him to step aside to give Keating a clear run at the 1990 election. He had arranged to be accompanied by Peter Walsh and John Button, both ministers anxious about an orderly transition and to avoid a rerun of the internal ructions over Hayden's leadership. But at the last moment they changed their minds and Dawkins went alone. The Minister for Employment, Education and Training was a man with the psychological freedom that wealth may confer: he could walk out of parliament any time he wanted to (and would later, when he became disillusioned with Keating). His encounter with Hawke was, according to both men, friendly: for many years Dawkins had worked closely with, and had enjoyed support from, the Prime Minister when other ministers were attacking him. He was an attractive target because he belonged to no faction. In every portfolio he held – Finance; Trade; Education, Employment and Training – Dawkins was outstandingly effective, prepared to take hard decisions without fear of being disliked. 'I was the only minister Graham Richardson was frightened of,' Dawkins said, 'because he knew he couldn't manipulate me.'

Hawke listened then told Dawkins he believed that, as Prime Minister, he still had a significant contribution to make, especially in international affairs. To Dawkins' mind, international affairs were largely the problem: Hawke was focusing too much attention abroad. 'It's the curse of leadership,' he said.

> It happened to me when I was Trade minister. It's incredibly infectious to get involved in international stuff, to be rubbing shoulders with all these famous people and to believe you're making a difference. In some cases, you actually are

making a difference – but it takes an enormous amount of time and effort and personal commitment and personal relationships.

Oddly, Dawkins thought, Hawke used the current turmoil in Poland as an example of an arena in which he could help, which seemed 'to be a little bit off track from our point of view'. The Prime Minister was passionately interested in it because the Polish turmoil was due to the trade union, Solidarity's, struggle against Poland's Soviet-controlled government. At meetings of the International Labour Organization in the late 1970s Hawke had helped nurture the formation of Solidarity, then only an embryo, which came into the light in 1980. Now it was a mighty warrior in the Cold War, a conflict that Hawke, as leader of a nation at risk, fervently wanted to come to an end. Events in Poland were, however, as Dawkins said, an irrelevance to most Australians. He thought Hawke almost fey in talking about a country so far away that few in the electorate could have found it on a map. He and Hawke were speaking and thinking on politically different levels.

Hawke changed tack. He argued that Keating was not physically strong enough for the pressures of the job. The ministry was familiar with the plague of minor illnesses and potential illnesses the Treasurer endured, for some of which he sought unusual treatments. According to his biographer, John Edwards, Keating took up jumping on a trampoline as a prophylactic against cancer cells in the body. One of Keating's most notable, and often most attractive, characteristics was his refusal to accept received wisdom, including that of science. Dawkins did not seriously consider Hawke's assertion that Keating lacked the physical strength needed to be a successful prime minister. 'I came round more to Bob's view later,' he said in 2009.

They parted amicably. 'He at no stage demonstrated any kind of anger or irritation to me,' Dawkins said, adding,

I don't know what it was that led me to tell [Paul] Kelly about it. I suppose it was a kind of an instinct that, I don't know,

I just sort of talked to him about it and then of course it
ended up in the paper. It wasn't supposed to. It was supposed
to be off the record.

There is a touch of madness to all successful politicians,
especially on the Labor side, since their purpose is to shift
society and they can't achieve this aim if they agree with the
status quo. Hawke prided himself on being 'a little bit mad'.
Dawkins too scored well on the 'slightly mad' scale. His belief
that Paul Kelly, whose reputation for trustworthiness is immac-
ulate, may have quoted him when he was speaking off the record
is eccentric. Parliament was sitting and Kelly's report in the next
morning's *Australian* brought delight to the hearts and whimsy
to the tongues of the Opposition. One of Hawke's many nick-
names was Old Silver. The wittiest gibe during Question Time
came from Ian Sinclair, who said this was 'not a case of "Hi-ho,
Silver," but "Heave-ho, Silver."' Dawkins recalled,

Bob and I made it clear that we were friends, we were sitting
next to each other, sort of hugging each other, to deflect the
Opposition ... basically, after I'd spoken to him I accepted
that he wasn't going to move. I didn't set about to wreck the
government.

But in the view of the Hawke camp, he did.

Hawke was embarrassed he had so misread his Education
minister, while his staff were enraged: they too had not realised
Dawkins was already a Keating general in the war of succession
now taking shape. They dismissed the idea of Dawkins as a possible future Treasurer. Dawkins said afterwards, 'I did wonder
what I would have said, but it would have been a close-run
thing. If [Hawke] had asked me to be Treasurer and I'd declined,
I would have felt bound to leave the government.' Keating had
promised Dawkins the Treasury in a government led by him.

The noise from Keating's camp was that Hawke was not
giving leadership at home. Certainly, there had been a change

in atmospherics at the peak of government. After the 1987 election Caucus had promoted all the faction bosses – Richardson and Ray of the Right, Gerry Hand of the Left, and Peter Cook of the Centre Left – into the ministry. Hawke promoted them into Cabinet, where their presence altered the power balance of the government. Dawkins said that ministers were frightened to speak against a faction boss seated at the Cabinet table because preselection depended on him. Meanwhile, according to Beazley, the backbenchers were under the thumb of less formidable factional overlords, and were more prone to indiscipline. It was a flaw in the Labor system, not present in the Coalition, that the Caucus elected the ministry and the prime minister could only allot portfolios to the ministers he was given. In a Coalition government, the prime minister holds the whip over his entire government. John Howard later said that the most important part of his job as Liberal leader was choosing and discarding members of his team. This was a power that neither Hawke nor any previous Labor prime minister had ever held. (In 2007 Kevin Rudd simply announced he would be picking his own ministry, and so eager was the party to win no one raised a voice against him.)

Meanwhile, Keating's 'bacon budget' was transforming into a live and greasy pig. It was not his fault: both the Treasury and the Reserve Bank had badly miscalculated. They had all predicted lower inflation and a lower current account deficit. But both were rising. Catching the budget pig was going to be tricky and potentially dangerous.

Keating spent much of September abroad, during which he contemplated his future. He had failed to bluff his way into The Lodge and the Caucus was not supporting him, but as he believed in his bones he was destined to be prime minister he decided to take the option Hawke had offered: a handover after the 1990 election. Keating decided he must nail Hawke down to a promise, witnessed by another, for the deal to stick or else Hawke would string him along until he was totally worn out. It was impossible, even for Keating, not to recognise that Hawke's well of stamina was almost inexhaustible and that his skills of evasion were similar. It took more than a month before Hawke could find time in his diary for a meeting with Keating.

Finally, on the evening of 25 November 1988, three grave-faced men arrived at Kirribilli House, the Prime Minister's Sydney residence. They were Keating and his witness, Bill Kelty, secretary of the ACTU, and Hawke's witness, Sir Peter Abeles. The deal was that Hawke and Keating would work as a team until the 1990 election, which Hawke expected to win; then, after a suitable time, but before the end of 1991, he would step down. Keating would then, after the formality of election by Caucus, become prime minister. Hawke's one proviso was that if the deal were leaked it was null and void. Keating agreed. Nothing was put on paper.

For the Treasurer, the Kirribilli pact was a disappointment: his 'Paris option' card had not worked and the thing he had wanted so fervently to avoid, spending another two years grinding figures, while his wife and four children lived in a cramped Canberra house, would have to be endured. For Hawke it was a triumph: as Prime Minister, he had, after an initial error, successfully steered the government through treacherous waters; he had called Keating's bluff and won. He now had clear psychological air and could, without worry about disloyalty to distract him or his staff, pursue success at the next election. Privately he was elated by the Kirribilli pact. When every waking hour is spent in the grip of difficult and practical issues, both trivial and great, life becomes disenchanted. With his new-found freedom of action he recovered a sense of spaciousness. He had kept his extra-marital affairs on a tight rein since he moved into The Lodge, restricting himself to just a couple of women of great discretion. He decided he was feeling so good he could feel better still, and began to expand his diminished harem. Keating, for his part, manfully accepted the setback, but his language showed how psychologically rattled he had been: he made a weird, vehement attack on John Howard, likening himself and Hawke to a pair of black widow spiders weaving a web to trap the leader of the Opposition. To Keating's great credit, although he knew of Hawke's womanising and, as a devout Roman Catholic husband, no doubt deplored it, never did he use this knowledge to attack the Prime Minister.

But winning the 1990 election was looking more and more dubious inside the government: the nation ate, drank, partied, sported fast cars, big yachts and big shoulder pads, all with a feverish excitement that made economists' blood run cold. The boom the government had meant to avoid was gathering force. Hawke remained optimistic for he had set himself the goal of winning a historic fourth term – and this would cement Labor's reputation as the party of government, and his own place in history. Only Sir Robert Menzies, who fought a Labor Party crippled by its splitists, the DLP, would have won more elections than he. While Australia remained a democracy Menzies was unlikely ever to be outdone. So, although winning a fourth term would only win second place, it was of the utmost prestige for the party and the leader.

TWENTY-SEVEN

THE NEW YEAR BEGAN calmly enough with the former vice-president of the United States, George Bush, assuming the presidency in January. Bush was a tall East Coast multimillionaire of aristocratic bearing who had been a much-decorated navy pilot in World War II. He was personable, educated and thoughtful, with a broad knowledge of geopolitics. But as a leader he could never match the luminous power of Reagan's personality – the sunshine smile, the jokes, the actor's perfect timing with a line, the deft, ineffable charm – all tailored, as if by Providence, to soothe the troubled breast of the American people. With Reagan gone, so was George Shultz, whom Bush replaced with Jim Baker. Hawke had met and respected Baker, but did not enjoy with him the long, warm friendship he had had with Shultz. His friendship with Bush, however, was more intimate than it had been with Reagan; an extra benefit was that Hazel and Barbara Bush clicked when they met.

The year 1989 was the bicentenary of the French Revolution, of which it is alleged Zhou En-lai, when asked in the 1960s had it been a good idea, replied, 'It's too soon to judge'. It would turn out that 1989 was another revolutionary year that would reveal the long view of history of Chinese leaders – but in a manner the rest of the world found horrifying.

On 19 April, the General Secretary of the Communist Party, the sparrow-like Hu Yaobang, died, his death arousing grief the length and breadth of China. Ordinary citizens everywhere openly wept in the streets for Hu. The grieving populace ideal-ised their lost leader and began to yearn for change. They were angry with corrupt officials and their corrupt children. There had been a bout of inflation in 1988 that had raised the issue of corruption. In China's two-tiered price system of those days, the well connected could buy steel, for example, at the state price, sell it at the market price and pocket the difference. 'It was,' a foreign observer said, 'a very easy way to steal money.' In the big cities students, artists and musicians began discussing alternative ways for China to be governed and whom they would like to see running the country. Unknown to Hawke until two decades later, a popular choice for at least one group of Beijing activists was the Prime Minister of Australia, Houke Lober, the Mandarin Chinese pronunciation of Hawke's family and given names.

A young American, Josh Klenbort, who spoke Mandarin and was staying in the capital, recalled,

> There was a lot of idealism in the air in the months between April and June of 1989 ... It was a moment when people believed that almost anything could happen. It was a very positive feeling for a vast majority of people. My friends in the artistic community were all very pleased and excited and there were lots of ideas in the air that nobody had dared to think for many, many years. Everyone was very optimistic about what the outcome could be. They would have regular get-togethers at a restaurant or at somebody's apartment and during one of these informal forums the idea popped up that China should have a foreign prime minister, a foreigner as head of government. Of course, this sounds completely preposterous today, and it would be. It would've been even then – but it was a measure of the times that people had such an open mind. The idea was not that Chinese people are incompetent or that they are not capable of running their own country. Far from it. But they did feel that the cultural and historical pressures on China were too great for the period of change they were going through. That was the root of the thought. It makes a lot more sense than the idea itself ... They drew up a short list of foreign leaders, and Bob

Hawke was on it. He had visited China a couple of times in the '80s as Prime Minister and he had invited Chinese leaders down to Australia at least three times. It's hard to remember now, but this was not normal back then. The world had yet to start tramping to Beijing to meet the leadership of the Chinese Communist Party. China was still something of a footnote. In trade relations China's percentage of exports and imports in world trade was in very low single digits. Its foreign reserves would have been $10 to $20 billion. It was an important Cold War country, but it wasn't important politically in the world. It just wasn't. They were still very poor. So when a foreign leader did go to China it got a lot of press. It was a good opportunity for people who were more liberal to get on the front pages and talk about how China is opening up to the world: here we have these foreigners visiting us – that sort of thing.

Hawke's physical appearance seems to have been in his favour. In the late 1990s, a Chinese press photographer gushed to this author, 'Mr Hawke is very handsome. He is the most handsome man I have ever seen. I think he is the most handsome man in the world!' The photographer wanted a picture of himself with the Prime Minister, but his flattery would have been utterly ridiculous had it not contained an element of truth. Hawke's mane of silver hair and thick eyebrows made him easy to recognise for the Chinese, to whom into the 1980s and even the 1990s all Caucasian males looked more or less identical, the slang for 'foreigner' being 'big nose'.

In 1984 Zhao Ziyang had done Hawke the honour of inviting him to review troops of the People's Liberation Army drawn up in Tiananmen Square, which is bounded on one edge by the Great Hall of the People and on another by the Forbidden City. On 21 April students from Beijing, Shanghai, Xian and Nanjing began protesting in the square.

In Canberra, Hawke, already sad about the death of his friend Hu, began to feel anxious about the situation in Beijing. After his meeting with Gorbachev eighteen months earlier, he had predicted to his chief of staff, Sandy Hollway, that the Soviet Union was going to be a train wreck – such an unfashionable view at the time that Hollway kept quiet about it, as did Hawke. A collapse of one pillar of the Communist world would inevitably shake the other. Cables from the Australian ambassador to China, Ross Garnaut, advised Hawke that his friend Zhao was being blamed for the inflation in 1988, while Zhao was objecting that it was the policies of Deng Xiaoping that were the real issue. This was risky on Zhao's part, for in China there is a tradition that The Boss is never wrong: problems are the fault of underlings.

Referring to the students gathering in Tiananmen, Garnaut said,

> Normally there would have been a big police and army presence to control what was happening in the square. The Chinese sit on these things. But there were two very important visits in May of that year: China was hosting a board of governors meeting of the Asian Development Bank, and there were all these VIPs in town – the secretary of the US Treasury, and so on. They were meeting in the Great Hall of the People.

The Chinese leadership knew it could not be seen to be intimidating peaceful demonstrators under the very noses of the world's bankers. Immediately after the Asian Development Bank meeting, Gorbachev was due to arrive, the first Soviet leader to do so since Khrushchev's disastrous visit in 1959. For Deng Xiaoping a visit by the 'Pope of Communism', as Chinese leaders sardonically referred to the leader of the USSR, would be the crowning moment of his career. Gorbachev was no ordinary pope either, but the most charismatic political leader in the world (outside his own country, where he was cordially disliked).

Gorbachev's visit was a cause of excitement across China. The world media had arrived in Beijing for the bank meeting and stayed on for the Soviet leader's visit. So, once more, police and troops could not be sent to clear the square, lest China be seen in a negative light in the world in which it now sought acceptance. With so many foreigners in town and the weather getting hotter, more students were filling the square, many of them just curious. On 12 May, the first day of Gorbachev's visit, Zhao pleaded with the student leaders not to damage the Sino-Soviet summit. They ignored him and called their followers to go on hunger strike. In China fear of famine is bone-deep: the mere suggestion of skipping lunch to get a job finished is alarmingly impolite, while a hunger strike arouses such age-old fears it is of almost magical potency. The hunger strike brought tens of thousands of sympathisers to the square, and not just students, but people from government departments and urban residents. Weeping grandparents appeared on Chinese television, pleading with the young people to stop their madness. On 19 May, with Gorbachev's visit over, Zhao went to the square to try to calm the growing hysteria and persuade the hunger strikers to desist. He was too late. Li Peng believed the country was already riding a tiger and on his advice Deng Xiaoping decided to impose martial law. The announcement was made on 20 May. Zhao refused to endorse it. On 24 May, Hawke was horrified when he was informed that Zhao had been stripped of office. The students became more febrile and headstrong and erected a ten-metre tall Goddess of Democracy statue in the square, their version of New York's Statue of Liberty. Meanwhile, under the martial law order, soldiers from other provinces were being transported to the capital.

On the night of 3 June the guillotine was raised. On 4 June it fell.

Deng is reported to have said, 'We spill some blood now and we'll have twenty years to complete the reforms.' Zhao Ziyang, fifty-nine years old, was placed under house arrest. He would spend fifteen years, the rest of his life, a prisoner.

In Canberra, Hawke was distraught: the People's Liberation Army had shot dead an unknown number of their fellow citizens,

Three successive prime ministers – Gough Whitlam, Malcolm Fraser and Hawke – give their different perspectives on government in 1992.

With Kim Beazley at Parliament House in Canberra, October 2006.

Bob Hawke and Blanche d'Alpuget at their wedding, 23 July 1995, Ritz-Carlton Hotel, Double Bay, Sydney.

Bob and Blanche, 2008, photographed for an interview with the *Australian Women's Weekly*.

Venice, 2009.

Bob and Blanche, 1998, an image that appeared on the cover of *The Good Weekend*.

On honeymoon on Haggerstone Island with red emperors.

China, 1990s.

China, late 1990s.

Xian, with entourage, after visiting the famous Terracotta Warriors.

In Myanmar, with a Buddhist mystic, 1995.

Hawke at the Great Wall, October 1995.

Benxi Water Cave, China, Liaoning Province, China, 2002.

Hawke after receiving an honorary doctorate, 2003 at the 100th anniversary of the Rhodes Scholarship, Oxford University.

Attending the University of South Australia's Annual Hawke Lecture at the Adelaide Town Hall.

With Mikhail and Raisa Gorbachev, Sydney, 1999.

Hawke with his Archibald portrait by Paul Jackson, at left, 2007.

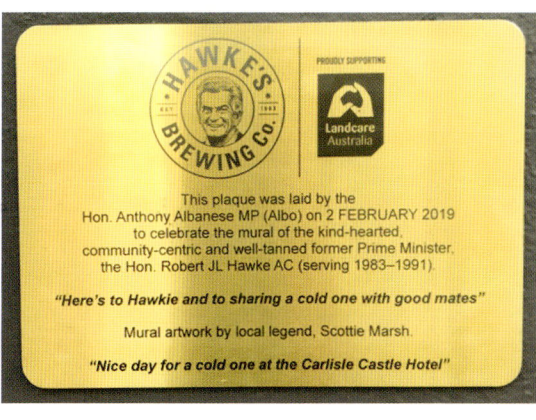

'Nice Day for a Cold One' mural in Newtown, Sydney, and the commemorative plaque celebrating the 'kind-hearted, community-centric and well-tanned former Prime Minister'.

Hawke at his
70th birthday
party at home
in Northbridge,
Sydney, 1999.

Sharing a laugh
with Blanche at the
birthday party.

Hawke at the Boao Forum for Asia press conference, Hainan, February 2001. The forum is a non-profit organisation that hosts leaders from government, business and academia in Asia and other continents to share their vision on regional issues.

Hawke at the Boao Forum for Asia with John Howard in 2005.

At the Australian Captains' Dinner to Tackle Youth Cancer, 2010.

At a charity function in November 2010.

Former PMs Hawke and Whitlam at the opening of the Hawke Building at the University of South Australia, Adelaide, 2007.

Former prime ministers Bob Hawke, Gough Whitlam, Malcolm Fraser and Paul Keating, and Prime Minister Kevin Rudd at the Apology to Australia's Indigenous Peoples, Parliament House, Canberra, February 2008.

Rudd, Hawke and Gillard at the 45th ALP national conference when Hawke was presented with life membership, Sydney, August 2009.

'Hawke, my mentor, was a nation builder and our greatest PM,' says Labor leader Anthony Albanese, pictured here with Hawke in 2016.

On board ship in Antarctica,
January 2004.

With Al Gore for a special
screening of the sequel to
An Inconvenient Truth, 2017.

China's international reputation was mud, his friend was branded a criminal – and, according to a raw intelligence report he had just read, the PLA had run down civilians with tanks, squashing them into the roadway as if they were worms. (The report, like much raw intelligence, turned out to be mostly false.) Hawke had spent seven years patiently building the Australia–China relationship, doing all he could to assist China emerge into the modern world, winning no domestic political kudos for his efforts but keeping at the task because he believed in it. In three days of violence he watched it all collapse.

Hawke cancelled his planned October visit and, with Beazley's approval, put defence co-operation on ice. Without asking for Cabinet approval, he decided to extend the visas of all Chinese students already in Australia, to the delight of more than 30 000 who would ultimately benefit – and to the disbelief of Immigration department officials who had to sort it out. On 9 June, just after reading the gruesome raw intelligence about tanks squashing unarmed citizens, Hawke was to speak at a service in Parliament House to memorialise those slain in the massacre. As he spoke of the killings, reading from the report he had just received, he began to weep profusely. It was a television moment authentic in a way rarely seen. Gleaming in the blue-black room, tears and translucent filaments of mucus flowing from his eyes and nose created an image people would not forget, especially the Chinese. In their 4600-year history, they had never imagined one day to see a white man, the leader of a foreign country, weeping for them.

In Australia the feeling was a guilty embarrassment about Hawke's tears, and fury with China.

At the official level in China, Hawke's tears caused anger. Li Peng, who had now been promoted to Zhao's job, told Garnaut he found Hawke 'a difficult man'. He did not need to mention that the seven years of exquisite friendship were over.

'The old intimacy was never restored,' Garnaut said.

Many Australian businesspeople (including Sir Peter Abeles, who had been extremely active in China) left. The Chinese economy went into recession. But Deng kept sending out the message: 'Come back. We want to open up to the world.'

Garnaut said,

> Despite what had happened, such a strong base had been laid that nothing was actually lost: it was built on. I think how Bob handled it was terrific: he did some symbolic things, but did nothing to damage the future. A really important thing historically is that Bush found it very helpful to follow Bob.

The United States Congress had worked itself into a paroxysm of righteousness over the Tiananmen massacre and was demanding that China's punishment must hurt. Hotheads thundered for trade and investment to be terminated. In a press conference journalists badgered the new President with questions about cutting off trade, and where he stood on human rights. *'Did he stand for human rights?'*

Bush, who had been ambassador to Beijing and knew the need for China to modernise, replied that the United States had to be careful to do nothing to set back Chinese market reforms. He cited as an example of a measured response the action of Australian Prime Minister Hawke. Garnaut said, 'The Europeans did more negative things, but the Japanese reaction was very similar to ours. So we and Japan set the tone for the USA, and that really was critical in allowing the reforms to keep going ahead.'

Within six months, a Chinese Trade minister was on an official visit to Australia, but Hawke would never return to China as Prime Minister.

The Australian economy had taken off when monetary policy was eased after the stock market crash of October 1987: jobs were increasing, investment spending was enormous, an asset bubble was expanding, executives were awarding themselves monster salaries, and home loan interest rates had risen to 17 per cent.

In the *Age* of 10 June 1989, Michelle Grattan asked, 'But when will the economy slow? When will rates fall? How certain is it that the landing will be "soft" rather than "hard"? Don't ask the Prime Minister. He doesn't know.' Hawke had been out testing the electoral waters in regional Victoria, where the crowds, as ever, loved him. The story's headline was 'PM still has that magic, but voters need answers'. Glenn Milne of the *Australian* made a sharper point when he wrote, 'a paradox that will dog [Hawke] until the next election [will be] how to explain to voters that an economy that is performing too well is somehow threatening the living standards of ordinary Australians'. In his 1988 Budget, Keating had promised tax cuts in 1989. These would further accelerate the economy but, ignoring advice to scrap his promise, Keating went ahead with the cuts in July 1989. The Treasurer's economic policy at this moment became oxymoronic, but it made political sense for Keating, for by now he and the ACTU were, in Paul Kelly's words, 'hostages to each other'.[1] The Treasurer's career had become dependent on the ability of Bill Kelty of the ACTU to deliver wage restraint. To achieve wage restraint, Kelty had to depend on Keating to deliver tax cuts and more money in the way of welfare. If 1988 was Keating's most difficult year in terms of thwarted ambition, 1989 was his most difficult for managing the economy.

A couple of months earlier Hawke's Labor Unity faction (the Right) strongly opposed the privatisation of Qantas and its domestic offshoot, Trans-Australian Airlines, which, after decades of being government cash cows, were running dry; the herd needed culling and revitalisation, which would be expensive. Privatisation of government-owned assets was an ongoing, constant struggle within the Labor Party, especially between Hawke and the Left. The objection was sentimental and often based on ignorance, as in the case of Qantas and TAA. Bob Hogg, by now the national secretary of the party, and a member of the Left, had studied the issue. 'I had to remind them,' he said,

that Chifley set up the domestic airlines to force competition on the railways, to make them lower their prices. That was the reason. There was no great socialist ideal. Governments in that period had to set up new industries, but once they had matured there was no role for government.

But Qantas was a cherished symbol; the party would not listen. A cartoon showed two trade unionists walking past a newspaper poster that read 'Hawke: on Qantas sale'. One asks the other, 'What's happened to his soul?' to which the reply is, 'Privatised'. The rejection of privatisation was a disappointing setback for Hawke. Within weeks it would fade to invisible as a new, much more vexatious airline drama began to unfold.

Australia had a lazy domestic airline policy going back to 1957: it was a duopoly of Ansett-ANA, privately owned, and TAA, owned by the government. The pair operated as carbon copies of each other, flying the same routes, charging the same inflated fares, leaving and arriving within five minutes of each other. But although they were happy to gang up against their passengers, neither would risk grounding their aircraft by ganging up against their pilots' pay demands. The result was that Australian domestic pilots were on astonishingly high salaries by international standards for the number of hours they flew: an average of 36.8 per *month*. At the beginning of 1989 they demanded a 30 per cent pay increase; in February they went on strike for a day to show they were serious. Hawke had disliked the Australian Federation of Air Pilots ever since his ACTU days when the pilots' union had refused to join the umbrella body, considering themselves a cut above. They were quite willing, however, to pocket the gains that other trade unions had fought to win. Community values are destroyed by free riders. Hawke decided he had to fight and defeat the pilots' union or risk a nation-wide wages breakout that would wreck the Accord and fuel inflation. In mid-August, Keating's 1989/90 Budget, with a $9.1 billion surplus, few spending promises and enforced superannuation savings of 6 per cent, was greeted as a sign of the government's responsible economic management. It was a clear sign that Keating now realised how badly he, his department and the Reserve Bank had blundered in 1988. Hawke and Keating sold the Budget around the country, performing side by side with such displays of bonhomie that the new shadow Treasurer, John Hewson, referred acerbically to a 'dog and pony show'. The temperature of their friendship was lower but their solidarity as brothers-in-arms was unshaken. The Opposition had been up to its internecine tricks again. Plotters, including the tempestuous troublemaker Wilson Tuckey, had secretly organised a coup against John Howard, replaced him with Andrew Peacock in May, then boasted on national television of what they had done and how they had done it. In a few minutes of public vanity, they shattered Peacock's moral authority. The effect on the electorate, and on the press gallery especially, was to increase cynicism about politics and politicians.

On 23 August, just after the government had successfully sold the 1989/90 Budget, all 1645 domestic pilots resigned from their jobs. This crippled air transport, undermined the burgeoning tourism industry, drove hundreds of travel-dependent small businesses towards the wall, and the flying public and the Prime Minister to fury.

But Hawke held a card the pilots had not bargained on.

Hawke had always believed in the importance of friendship for its own sake; he was about to test it for the sake of the economy. His close friend, Sir Peter Abeles, was the chairman of Ansett, close to Bill Kelty and fully in support of the Accord. When the pilots first began threatening to go on strike if they did not get their pay rise, Hawke asked Abeles to stand firm. His friend agreed without demur and without consulting his board or any of his staff. The government ordered TAA to do the same. Hawke met the AFAP leader, Captain Brian McCarthy, and told him the world had changed: this time there would be no backing down by either airline.

Used to getting his own way industrially, McCarthy did not believe the Prime Minister. His union had already advised members to put their financial affairs in order, pay off mortgages and other debts, be ready to take jobs overseas if they could, and be prepared for a long strike. Whatever it cost them, it would cost the companies $50 million a day and the pilots did not believe it possible that the airline managements could hold out longer than the union.

The day before the resignations, on 22 August, the *Age* ran a story, 'Pilots War: PM Backs Total Airline Shutdown'.

Then the pilots resigned en masse.

Their resignation, which followed Hawke's meeting with McCarthy, put the Prime Minister in a rage. During a press briefing he used inflammatory language, calling the pilots 'greedy' and 'glorified bus drivers', asserting they were waging 'war' against the wages system.

'Why the Wages Accord Is Tailspinning to a Crash' was the headline in the *Australian* in which Richard Blandy, professor at the National Institute of Labour Studies, Flinders University, argued, 'Bob Hawke's confrontationist approach has served only to weld the pilots firmly together.' Des Keegan wrote in the *Financial Australian*,

> Mr Hawke's contempt for the pilots' skills is a dangerous punt that could lose him and his party their collective shirts … Labor leaders are looking more and more like the generals who bled their armies to extinction through fog, mud, shot and shell in the trenches of Flanders …

On 27 August, the *Sunday Age* headline was 'MAYDAY! MAY-DAY! The Full Story on the Biggest Industrial Battle Since World War 2'.

The public was used to Hawke the industrial peacemaker and shocked to see him as a union warrior again after all these years. He quickly moderated his language, but threatened to take the pilots to court, a traumatic step for a Labor leader. He was supported in this by the Opposition. Under a cartoon of the Prime Minister as a kamikazi pilot, Paul Kelly wrote, 'Bob Hawke sees the pilots dispute as the single most critical threat to his economic policy and political position in nearly seven years as Prime Minister – an issue, quite literally, he cannot afford to lose.' On 29 August, the *Australian*, on its editorial page, had a cartoon of two Hawkes: the first was a gunslinger, saying, 'Okay, okay … So I made the wrong choice from the arsenal when shooting from the hip at the pilots!' The second Hawke was a bare-chested Rambo declaring, 'It won't happen again!' Rambo–Hawke toted a bazooka.

Headlines were 'Tourism Loss May Hit $600m'; 'Houdini Hawke Bound by Pilots' Tightening Chains'. The few pilots who had refused to join the strike received death threats; the wife of one had a coffin delivered to her; another man broke down in tears in Sir Peter Abeles' office. Abeles, although his company had benefited from the two-airline policy inherited from Menzies, believed it was bad for Australia. He privately argued to Hawke, 'You can have one airline or you can have many: you cannot have two.' One of Abeles' closest friends told him, 'It's your own fault: you and your predecessor, Reg Ansett, have treated the pilots like princes – letting them fly first class and be driven around in limousines. Of course they can't believe what's happening.'

The strike would run for thirty weeks and cost hundreds of millions of dollars in the short term. (But in the long term, the aviation industry was reformed under the surveillance of businessman and aviator Dick Smith, whom Hawke appointed chair of the Civil Aviation Authority. By 1991, the reforms were saving more than $100 million annually in aviation costs.) The strike was finally broken by English-speaking pilots from the United States, England, Canada, India, Malaysia and Singapore, who took the offer of Australian jobs. It ruined the careers of hundreds of Australian pilots and the businesses of thousands of people who depended on tourism. As it dragged on and the pilots became more desperate and paranoid, they adopted political guerrilla tactics and issued death threats to Abeles, whom some claimed had engineered the strike for nefarious purposes of his own. They ranted on talkback radio, wrote letters to newspapers, and arrived en masse at venues where Hawke was appearing to shout abuse and jostle him, disrupting his 1990 election campaign.

To no avail. By the time the pilots' federation accepted defeat, the airlines had engaged other staff, and few of its members would be rehired. Hawke took no personal satisfaction in the pilots' defeat, although he maintained a certain satisfied disgust for Captain McCarthy for being an arrogant shepherd who led his flock to disaster. The Accord remained intact.

For the country as a whole the seven-month strike was a time of inconvenience and irritation that tended to wash off on to the government. But even before the pilots had resigned, hard-heads in the party were working on a strategy for overcoming the government's weaknesses. Its design owed most to the ingenious, blunt-fingered Machiavelli, Graham Richardson, the Minister for the Environment, whose soul had experienced a Damascene moment and whose sharp political nose had picked up a scent. By the 1980s, the Baby Boomers had exchanged their idealism of the 1960s for rank consumerism, but in a corner of their souls they had left flickering a candle of the old ideals: it burned for the environment.

Richardson knew that the Australian Democrats, who since the late 1970s had been the pivot of the Senate, would be of increasing importance until they died off (which he saw as inevitable) and were replaced by green independents. Almost alone, he had spotted the coming political shift. In conversations with Hawke, he told the Prime Minister what he had observed and believed; Hawke agreed with him, and had already off his own bat, based on advice from his office, set out to court the green vote. But herein lay danger for him in Cabinet, and in the party.

Virtually all the ERC ministers were opposed to environmental protection, so if the government were successfully to attract the greens it would be up to Hawke to persuade or to hammer environmental protection policy past the objections of his economic ministers. His style as leader was to allow Cabinet debate to flourish without showing his own hand. His fiercest detractors allowed he was an outstanding chairman of the

Cabinet, guiding it with a light touch, summing up the arguments and only coming in to fight if he believed a wrong decision to be imminent. Once Hawke had declared, the debate was over: what the Prime Minister said, even if all others were opposed, became the government's decision and according to the rules of Cabinet solidarity, all had to adhere to it as their own. Hawke used his hammer sparingly to overcome his colleagues with his own unpopular views, but it was always at a cost to his goodwill among them, so his normal method was to steer the arguments towards the view he already held, or if he had not preformed an opinion, to develop one from the debate itself. On environmental issues the large, mild-mannered Minister for Primary Industry, John Kerin, was so furious with Richardson's political influence in the year before Richardson was promoted to the ministry, that after one debate Kerin kicked the sideboard in the Prime Minister's office, declaring of Richardson, 'Fucking *backbencher!*' The dour, tough Finance minister, Senator Peter Walsh from Western Australia, was another who was rabidly anti-green. His view, a close observer remarked, was that the government, by supporting environmental issues, 'was screwing the most vulnerable workers, who go out in the forests. And this isn't really a Labor government.' Richardson and Hawke shared a view that Walsh, brilliant as a logician and analyst, had the worst political judgment they had encountered in a senior politician. Walsh would later join a pressure group that resisted signing the Kyoto Protocol and rejected the whole notion of an anthropogenic element in climate change.

Environmentalism would also meet obstacles in the heart of the party, since trade unions by tradition were opposed to environmental issues, which they saw as hostile to industry, thereby robbing them of jobs. But the urban middle class and young people of all classes were increasingly sympathetic to environmental protection, and likely to vote for it. Unrecognised by virtually everyone, a headline on 12 June in the *Australian* announced what a large part of the government's election strategy for the following year would be. It read, 'Power Hangs On

Greens: Richardson'. He even explained its mechanics: 'What [the Greens] do with their preferences, particularly in the House of Representatives, may well determine our fate.' Neither commentators nor Opposition nor many in the ALP seemed to understand that Richardson was describing how the government could fight the 1990 election. To chase preferences rather than primary votes was a political idea of such originality it remained beyond comprehension – and from his own memoir, *Whatever It Takes*, it seems Richardson himself had not at that stage fully developed his thinking about it.

Hawke was a genuine green convert. He accepted the truth of the argument that Australia's environment was unique, fragile, damaged and of the highest value, and that the planet was an interconnected whole. After the economist Craig Emerson had joined his staff in 1986 and become his environmental adviser, Hawke had grown close to the young man and, enjoying his company, had tended to indulge him with listening to his ideas. Some staff were jealous of Emerson who, besides being something of a prime ministerial pet, was tall, dark and handsome, with beautiful brown eyes, a beautiful white smile and a boyish attraction for women that made other men want to thump him.

In the bitter, vehement and hysterical ALP uranium conference of 1984, Hawke and his supporters had won the adoption of a 'three mines' policy on uranium. This translated to the Left as 'pro-uranium'. In early 1986 Joh Bjelke-Petersen announced a new road would be built through one of the most beautiful wet tropical forests of North Queensland, the Daintree. The area was in the marginal Labor electorate of Leichhardt, where the local member, John Gaylor, pleaded with the government not to oppose Bjelke-Petersen, for the road was so popular with locals he could easily lose his seat. Emerson said,

> The public had in mind that Labor is pro-uranium mining. Labor will allow Bjelke-Petersen to drive a road through the Daintree. It was all going over like a shower of shit. The Left of the electorate had abandoned us.

By 1987 Hawke had begun to reverse perceptions of the government's commitment to the environment by halting logging in Tasmania. But as he had discovered by then, the environmental movement of the time, given a metre, demanded a kilometre. Richardson, after three years as minister, was driven to fury with green activists, losing his temper during a public meeting and shouting abuse at a woman. He shocked himself at how they had worn down his nerves. 'I was in a lift one day, and this woman said, "You dog! You shit!" And she spat on me,' he recalled. Hawke showed some environmentalists the door after a one-minute interview when, invited to put a case to him, they threw photographs of logging on his desk, saying, '*That's* our case!' Two exceptions were Philip Toyne and Peter Garrett of the Australian Conservation Foundation, who enjoyed the respect and trust of Hawke, Richardson and their staff. Both men were fighters who, when they came to an agreement, would not try to change it later or stab the government in the back with off-the-record press briefings.

Hawke told Emerson, 'I want a fixed agenda with them. I do not want this *elastic agenda* they are pushing. We need absolutely fixed, manageable targets that we can meet and that are good things to do.' The upshot was an environmental agenda of four major items: World Heritage listing and protection of the Tasmanian forests; of the wet tropical forests of North Queensland; of Kakadu National Park Stage II; and the rejection of silica sand mining by Japanese investors at Shelburne Bay in the Cape York Peninsula. The Shelburne Bay project would create long-term employment for only fifteen people and a section of the Great Barrier Reef would need blasting away to build a port. Oddly, of the four projects, the last was the most difficult for Hawke to negotiate through Cabinet. Emerson said,

> We were still going through the economic trauma [post-1986] and Paul was very worried about Japanese foreign investment. It had got to a stage where very senior people in Japan were saying, '*Shelburne Bay is a litmus test for Australia.*' Paul later

tried to say he drove a lot of it. Well, he didn't. But he was not sitting there as a conventional Treasurer would, saying, 'My brief is to oppose all of this because it will damage the economy.' He was quite good. But it was really driven by Bob, me and Richo, and in the end, and again to his credit, Paul finally agreed to include it.

After the Shelburne decision, Keating came to Hawke's office and announced, Emerson said, "'That's it! No more! We're not going to be jamming any more green bits down people's throats. Just the four! That's all!" But four was all we wanted.'

By July 1989 Hawke's office had developed Richardson's idea about green preferences, and created an image known as 'the holding paddock'. Labor's primary vote had been stuck for months at 39 per cent, which in a normal election would mean defeat. The party's polling revealed the electorate was thinking, 'We will not vote Labor, but we're not convinced the Liberals are better.' Emerson said,

> So there were all these people in a holding paddock, not knowing whether to go to the Liberals or to us. We had to get them to walk out of the holding paddock into the Labor paddock with their second-preference votes.

Hawke's office, working closely with Simon Balderstone in Richardson's, wrote a comprehensive environmental statement that Hawke took to Cabinet, explaining to his colleagues that besides the four areas to be protected, the government had brokered an alliance between the Australian Conservation Foundation and the National Farmers' Federation for an initiative called Landcare Australia. Peter Walsh, the Finance minister, was suffering from shingles and so depressed by illness and about the wrong direction in which he believed the government was headed that he wanted to resign, but Dawkins dissuaded him. When Hawke announced the statement Walsh, in a fit of

Celtic gloom, muttered, 'You know you've got a bad policy if the farmers and the greenies get together.' John Kerin's reaction was sarcastic pique. He immediately dubbed it 'The World's Greatest Environment Statement'.

Despite Kerin's cynicism, which news media parroters used to discredit it, the statement did, indeed, address the world: in it, for the first time, an Australian government spoke of the dangers of the greenhouse effect – but outside the Conservation Foundation and a few other green groups, it went unnoticed.

The Prime Minister delivered his statement in July 1989 in the town of Wentworth in New South Wales, at the confluence of the Murray and Darling rivers. It was a gorgeous landscape made ominous by the white death of salt creeping towards the river red gums. Red gums need regular spring floodwater but agricultural irrigation was already robbing them of this necessity for survival. The background made splendid television footage, but the commentary that accompanied the pictures that evening was jaundiced. Its tone was: 'In a blatant attempt to grab the environmental vote, Bob Hawke today announced ...' Emerson said,

> But the pictures were magnificent, and that's what people were taking in. Bob Hawke is going to save these areas: Kakadu, the forests. He's going to protect our fragile environment. And they loved it. Absolutely loved it. In a sense, the electorate didn't care whether he was doing it for political reasons, or cynical reasons, it was just something that needed to be done and this government was going to do it. He used a phrase I'd thought up while on holiday, which Stephen Mills [the press officer] decided to include in the speech. It was: *'We've taken too much from the earth and given back too little. It's time to say, "Enough is enough".'* So we pointed the TV cameras to that part of the speech and they just ran that grab. Bob delivered it with great weight and moment. And it was magical.

Richardson noted, 'By the banks of the Murray and Darling rivers, Hawke took a giant step towards re-election.'[2]

Quite unknown to the electorate, but of further irritation to his Cabinet colleagues, Hawke in 1989 had undertaken another environmental initiative that would be difficult to manage and would win the government not a single vote – but it would be of importance to the planet in decades to come.

One weekend Hawke and Emerson each took home a Cabinet submission for the Australian government to ratify the Antarctic Minerals Convention, an international agreement that would allow 'regulated' mining in the Antarctic. The regulations would protect the environment from damage, the Convention said. Enormous quantities of oil lay beneath the ice and, as no country clearly 'owned' the continent, it was booty to be snatched. Reading the regulations, both Hawke and Emerson individually realised the Convention was nonsense: how could the regulations be policed? And by whom? If there were an oil spill, how could it be cleaned up? Technologies for mining such an area without environmental damage did not exist. Instead of 'regulated mining' there would be a free for all led by giant oil companies that would foul the last virgin area of earth.

On Monday morning, after discussing the paper with Emerson, Hawke decided to take it to Cabinet and oppose it, although Australia was already well down the road towards ratification. Emerson recalled,

We were confronted with very strong advice from the departments of Foreign Affairs, PM&C [Prime Minister and Cabinet] and Treasury that we should hold our horses. Gareth [Evans, the Foreign minister] in particular objected. He pointed out Australia had been part of the process of drawing up the Convention for a very long time, and we could not just pull the plug. It would be disastrous for our relationships with the United Sates and Britain, in particular. They were passionate about it and were leading the charge. And lots of other countries had lined up. It was ready to roll.

There was no opposition in Australia to the Convention since the public was unaware of its existence. A lone voice had been raised on the other side of the world: that of the celebrated underwater explorer and inventor of scuba diving, Jacques Cousteau. Emerson said,

> We started our initial discussions with his son, and then we met Cousteau in Tasmania, then met him again, in Paris. Before that we met Rocard, the French Prime Minister. Bob sat in the garden with him at Matignon and talked it through and Rocard said, 'I'm on board.'

The French in 1989 were in bad odour in the Anglo-Saxon world and the South Pacific for bombing the Greenpeace ship *Rainbow Warrior* several years earlier. The explosion killed a man on board the ship. The French then lied about it, and tried to blame the British Secret Service. All of this added to a growing hatred of France for its nuclear testing on Mururoa Atoll. France paid Greenpeace compensation of some $8 million in 1987, but the stain of what the French secret service had code-named '*Operation Satanique*' still clung to the Republic. It was one thing to convince Rocard. It was another to convince the President, François Mitterand. Hawke said he 'loved' both Rocard and Cousteau from the moment he met them, but he found Mitterand 'a most disagreeable man, comprehensively up himself'. But Cousteau, a national treasure, was on good terms with the French President and laid the groundwork with him for Hawke's meeting.

Emerson said,

> Within a day of meeting Cousteau again in Paris we met Mitterand, who tried to wriggle out of supporting us. He was using weasel words. I remember giving Bob a note saying, 'He's trying to wriggle away. You've got to nail him.' And Bob said, 'Well, François, we need to know whether you are with us in opposing this.' And when it was put straight to him he said, 'Yes, I am.' So that got the French on board.

As an international meeting and vote was needed for the Convention to be overturned, the next step was to gather as much support as possible to fend off the might of the British and Americans. Hawke said, 'My Cabinet, and especially Graham Richardson, thought it was mission impossible. They took the view that if the old boy wanted to have a go, good luck to him.' By now the media was aware of what was afoot, but was not sufficiently interested to report it. The *Australian* ran an editorial on 28 June under the headline 'Hawke's Icy Reception'. It read,

> the futility of the Federal Government's political posturing on Antarctic has been underscored by the short shrift Mr Hawke received for his ideas in London and Washington, Mrs Thatcher and President Bush rebuffed him ... True, the convention does allow for mining in the Antarctic. But it seeks to regulate it. In its absence, controls are non-existent. Antarctica sits there, ripe for the plucking. Mr Hawke insists otherwise, but the reality is that the outright rejection by Mrs Thatcher and Mr Bush sounds the death knell for Australia's Antarctic proposals. This is just as well, for Mr Hawke's plan would see negotiation started all over again with the objective of establishing an international wilderness park in Antarctic. In the meantime, the continent would be vulnerable. This is why the Minister for the Environment, Senator Richardson, recently said the convention would at least have 'kept the bastards honest' in the event of any attempt to mine the Antarctic's rich mineral resources ... After London and Washington, Mr Hawke should realise just how isolated he is on the issue, and just how hopeless is his tilting at windmills. He should, for a moment, think beyond the ALP's wooing of the 'green vote' and sign the convention before the deadline.

Undeterred by this advice Hawke's office, now with the support of Foreign Affairs, began a campaign with countries for whom Antarctica was a place so far away and so foreign they did not mind one way or another what happened there. They just needed to be asked nicely. Emerson said, 'We started with countries like Greece, Malta and Italy. We were either writing to them or ringing them, and one by one we built up the opposition, to the point where we met Al Gore.' Gore, later Democratic Vice-President and in 2007 a Nobel laureate for his environmental work, was already passionately interested in green issues. By 1989 he had founded a large, well-funded environmental research institute. He and Hawke took to each other immediately when they met at Blair House, where Hawke was staying in Washington. But when Hawke put the proposal to oppose the Convention, Gore objected, 'I'm being advised to sign, because it would regulate mining and that's much better than unregulated mining.' Emerson recalled,

> Bob said to him, 'Look – you *can't* regulate mining in the Antarctic. The technology has not been invented.' Gore said, 'Well, I can't give you a commitment now, but I will certainly take on board what you've said.' And about three months later he announced, on behalf of the Democrats, that they did not support the Mineral Convention. And in the end the Bush administration, with whom we'd raised it, said, 'We'll just agree to disagree on this.' The Poms were the last ones hanging out, but it was all over by then. That was the result of just one Sunday and Monday morning, and setting out on a crusade: it can be done.

The parties to the Antarctic Treaty signed the Madrid Protocol on 4 October 1991 after two years of negotiation. The Antarctic was not to be mined for fifty years. Events since then have moved so far and so fast in environmental understanding it is still possible, despite Chinese probing, that Antarctica will remain in its state of sublime, measureless white beauty.

There was no political kudos in all this for Hawke: the Australian public remains largely unaware of his efforts. But there are two curious footnotes to the episode. Paul Keating told the author Paul Kelly that it was *he* who initiated opposition

to the Minerals Convention. Kelly duly recorded this claim in
The End of Certainty:

> In May 1989 the government, at Keating's instigation,
> decided to oppose the international treaty designed to permit
> but control mining ... In September 1988 when Keating met
> French prime minister Rocard in Paris they canvassed the idea
> of turning Antarctica into a protected international park – a
> proposal Keating pushed as his own, not necessarily that of
> the government ... and this became Hawke's own view.[3]

And in 2005, President Mitterand was posthumously revealed
to have personally ordered the bombing of the *Rainbow Warrior.*

TWENTY-EIGHT

OTH THE COALITION AND virtually all in the government
were sure the Opposition would win the 1990 election. Warwick Smith, Liberal member for the sensitive
Tasmanian seat of Bass, recalled that his party had been confident
in 1984 that Peacock 'would be the giant slayer of this former
union leader'. Tucked into their procrustean bed of dogma and
ideology about the working class, many Liberals still thought of
Hawke as a trade unionist. A union leader was a person so alien to
their idea of the right man to run a country some were still finding
it incredible that he actually was the Prime Minister. But Hawke
was also alien to many in his own party: he had not followed the
accepted method of becoming leader by spending years in the
grind of parliament; he was committed to being a winner. Many
of the rank and file of those days were so accustomed to what
Whitlam had described as 'the eunuch's virtue' they found disturbing Hawke's conviction that only through power could ideals
be implemented. At party conferences, he lectured delegates
about their sacred cows. 'Bob was pretty much a meat-grinder of
a politician,' Beazley said. 'He would hammer his argument into
the turf.' Hawke applied to the ALP the same fierce, demagogic
tone he had used as a young advocate before the Conciliation and
Arbitration Commission. As Whitlam before him was unloved
by much of the party until he was sacked by Kerr – whereupon
he transformed into a Labor saint – Hawke too was quietly
resented by many on his own side. Nor did the press gallery like
him much. 'New members of Parliament assiduously court the
press to establish their profiles,' Hawke said. 'When I arrived

in Parliament I was already a national figure. The press gallery was never very happy with me because I never sought out their favours.' Some, like Alan Ramsay of the *Sydney Morning Herald*, hated Hawke. Ramsay had been on Hayden's staff and waged a relentless, decade-long campaign against Hawke, who considered it payback for his defeat of Hayden – which entailed denial of the job of prime ministerial press officer to Ramsay.

Politicians and political journalists usually coexist in an atmosphere of tension – and of hypocrisy if the politician pretends to treat the journalist as an equal. This causes, as Max Weber noted, 'a relentless, albeit unacknowledged and denied inner turmoil for the political journalist: despised, he despises as a way of releasing his tension'. Unlike Keating, Hawke did not invite intimacy with the press gallery; unlike Keating his speech patterns were often contorted and made for bad copy; unlike Keating, he rarely provided the gallery with a witty quip; Keating, with his love of art, beauty, clothes and shopping was sexually unthreatening to female journalists, whom he wooed and wowed in long conversations, whereas Hawke had a sexual edge that made many women uncomfortable. With the exception of Alan Reid, Alan Barnes and Ian Fitchett, all of whom he had admired but who by his time in office were retired or had died, Hawke had only minor respect for members of the gallery. He admired Laurie Oakes for his scoops, Paul Kelly for his seriousness and Michelle Grattan for her industriousness. He made up for his somewhat aloof treatment of the gallery on overseas trips, when he took the news media with him. Trips on the prime ministerial plane were rollicking fun, thanks to the happiness of his office staff and his own high spirits. While he was teetotal, he vicariously enjoyed accounts of the adventures of his travelling companions and the all-night drinking and card games held on long-haul flights at the back of the plane. There were hilarious mishaps, especially in Asian cities, where members of the entourage, media and staff members got lost occasionally, returning with excuses along the lines of 'the dog ate my homework'. One serious senior man arrived late and exhausted for a morning press conference, his face covered in green glitter, a circumstance for which he had no coherent explanation. The staffers who sat in on lunches between presidents Reagan and Bush and Hawke often found themselves breathtaken at the raunchy banter amidst formal splendour, and the exquisite sense that history was standing, listening, at their elbow.

When Peacock lost in 1984, tensions in the Liberal Party had created seven years of internal chaos, but by 1990 Peacock had shoved aside John Howard and the leadership pretensions of Sir Joh Bjelke-Petersen and John Elliott and was back as Liberal leader. At his side he had a glossy young shadow Treasurer, John Hewson. Hewson was a professional economist, had been John Howard's economic adviser when he was Treasurer under Fraser, and was the only person in the parliament who could, with the authority of knowledge, attack Keating convincingly. He did so frequently, vigorously and aggressively, drawing sprays of rainbow venom from the Treasurer. When Hawke announced an election in February, the Liberal Party's internal polling was optimistic. Hawke had already agreed to debate Peacock, who looked forward to beating him once more, as he had in 1984.

For three men the 1990 election would spell political death or glory. For Hawke, victory would mean he had reached his highest goal: Labor would be the natural party of government domestically, a civilising force that aimed at the best and most intelligent version of the Labor tradition. Internationally, his government had gone far in establishing Australia in the eyes of the world as an independent, beneficent and innovative middle power, integrated into the newly dynamic Asian neighbourhood. Winning would crown a career built over more than forty years.

For Keating, whose political ambitions also went back to school days, Hawke's victory, ironically, would be his only chance of becoming prime minister. Keating knew that he could not call to himself the people's adoring gaze, that he could not win from Opposition. He would need the power of office behind him.

For Peacock, 1990 would be the final curtain on his years of waiting in the wings, eternal man of promise, heir to Sir Robert Menzies, whose seat, Kooyong, the crown jewel of Liberalism, he had held since 1966. If Peacock lost, his political career would be dead. If Hawke lost, both his own and Keating's careers in politics would be dead. This was grimly amusing for those who were aware that by now Keating's envy of the Prime Minister verged on hatred, while he desperately wanted him to win.

Hawke called the election for 23 March, March being the month that marked for him eight years in office.

While virtually all professional politicians believed the election would have to be Hawke's last hurrah, just how he would pass from centre stage, how he would part from the Australian people with whom he had enjoyed 'a love affair' for so long, was an enigma. The Opposition believed he *could not* win a fourth time. The current account deficit was a weekly scandal for those who understood its significance, and an increasing percentage of the Australian population, educated in economics by Hawke, Keating and a handful of financial journalists, now did. With financial deregulation in 1984, the banks had launched themselves into a frantic competition for customers in both business and housing. Cash poured into the economy, fuelling the spending spree of the 1980s. Throughout the Western world an ocean of money was flowing. By 1990 interest rates were 17 per cent. The government, naturally enough, was blamed. Hawke's popularity was also adversely affected by the pilots' strike that was dragging on into the new decade. After the excesses of the 1980s, the 1990s began to show an irritable fatigue. The hangover was setting in. And meanwhile, the world had changed. The Cold War was over and, unrecognised for what it was – not just a bubble economy bursting, but a historic decline – by 1990 Australia's biggest trading partner, Japan, was running out of puff. Within a few years it would be selling its golf courses, resorts, hotels and office towers in Australia at knock-down prices.

A salient but rarely mentioned fact was that the IT revolution was already underway. From the office, computers had invaded the home; personal mobile phones were becoming widespread and the noise and tempo of life were increasing. It was as if the dark, satanic mills of an earlier age had slyly transmogrified into fascinating toys, turning the houses people lived in, the parks where they walked and the cocooning interiors of their motor cars into places of work. Private time was beginning to vanish and a sense of peace and restfulness was going with it. For many, the new technology was thrilling, but there was an almost imperceptible sense of overload as householders moulded their lives to the challenges of their new gadgets. Married women and mothers now worked not to enrich their intellectual and social lives, as the women's movement had envisaged, but of necessity, to pay for the changes in lifestyle the 1980s had brought. The winners of the 1980s boom flaunted their wealth while the less well off discovered that luxuries in the 1970s – two cars, for example – were now necessities. AIDS scythed through the inner-city suburbs. After twenty years of liberty, sexual relations were once again fearful. Statistics on mental illness were rising. The Age of Anxiety had appeared.

Richardson commented, 'By 1990 the electorate had no faith in politicians or political parties. They would be choosing whomever they believed to be the lesser of two evils.'[1]

When the election campaign got underway in late February, the pilots developed a new tactic, holding banners for the television cameras that said: 'Vote 1 Abeles, Cut Out the Middleman'. Abeles – European, Jewish, highly remunerated, overweight, with a whale-sized head and heavy features – was an easy target for arousing hatred in anti-Semites, in Leftists who feared and distrusted power, and in ordinary people who, by and large, feared the very rich unless they were publicly known philanthropists. Abeles was philanthropic, but privately. There was a lugubrious streak to his personality, not unjustified in someone who at eighteen had been forced into a labour battalion in the Hungarian army, under Nazi control, and whose extended family had been murdered. His sweetheart in Budapest had vanished: also murdered, he assumed. As a very large man – he bought his

clothes in what he called 'the elephants' shop' in Bond Street –
he had a discomfiting intensity, holding one's gaze a few seconds
longer than normal. Among journalists there were wild stories
going back to the 1970s that he was importing cannabis concealed in secret compartments in shipping containers, a rumour
for which there was no evidence at all, according to Brian Toohey,
who read boxes of material and case studies from the Costigan
Royal Commission. 'There was nobody in the twenty-six case
studies we reported [in the *National Times*] who could remotely
be believed to be Abeles,' Toohey said in 2010. Hawke had
always regarded the stories with contempt. He never attempted
to downplay their friendship. But for those whose cosmologies
swarmed with class enemies the Hawke–Abeles relationship was
taken as a sign of evil afoot. In the ALP it damaged Hawke. As
far back as 1982, Peter Bowers of the *Sydney Morning Herald* had
written, 'Hawke's relationship with Abeles is seen by his Labor
opponents as unnatural, even sinister, and the Abeles connection
is frequently used to discredit him.'

Hawke yearned for intellectual companionship all his life
and, once he had abandoned academia, he often found it among
European Jews. Garnaut wrote of Hawke in 2009, 'his is one
of the few best informed, retentive and analytically clear minds
with which I have interacted intensively'. While discussions in
the Prime Minister's office and in Cabinet were often interesting, they were limited by pragmatism.

With Garnaut gone from his office, Hawke found in Abeles
intellectual companionship. Abeles' urbanity, wry wit and deep
affection for a man he treated as a beloved nephew – he had
no sons of his own – made him a fine sparring partner for the
Prime Minister. There was much over which they disagreed and
Hawke was often intemperate in his arguments with him, which
he never was with Garnaut. The industrialist stood his ground
with the solemnity of a gothic cathedral. One topic they rarely
discussed was Israel. Abeles admired Hawke's support for Israel
in the 1970s, and his rescue of Russian Jews while Prime Minister,
but as a secular Jew, his own interest in the country was 'passive',

according to Hawke. Abeles rarely visited Israel, and when he did found its inhabitants rude. By 1990 Abeles was showing irritation with Israel, remarking of its frequent fund-raising appeals, 'We [diaspora Jews] have paid for every tree in Israel twenty times already.' He spoke English slowly, sometimes puffing on a pipe or a cigar; he was an oasis of calm intelligence for Hawke, who teased out ideas with him and picked up international trends and gossip. As chief executive of TNT, a trucking company that employed 170 000 people worldwide, Abeles was in touch with business and national leaders from many countries. He was always in a jolly humour when he was with Hawke, and was himself given to bouts of cock-eyed optimism. But, from time to time, even he found Hawke's self-confidence unbearable. On one occasion he remarked, 'I tell you what, Bob: put on a false beard and moustache; I'll lend you a hat. Then sit in a coffee shop and listen to what they are saying about the government.' Abeles had learnt young a survival skill that he tried to impart to Hawke with little success: how to distinguish friend from foe. Hawke's political advisers were often appalled at how inept Hawke was in his discrimination about others' motives. Although agnostic, Hawke remained his parents' son, imbued with the Christian ethos of the brotherhood of man. He trusted people to a degree that would have been stupidity in others, and too often was also for himself. He found it not only too difficult, but almost imposible to see a rogue for what he was. Once he realised his mistake, however, his loathing set in concrete.

While the pilots were saying that a vote for Hawke was a vote for Abeles, the Opposition began chanting, 'A vote for Hawke is a vote for Keating'. Television advertisements showed a smiling Hawke who suddenly removed what was only a mask to reveal beneath it the face of Paul Keating. As the Treasurer was highly unpopular, Hawke needed quickly to silence this assertion. He did so by promising that were he to win, he would stay on and fight the 1993 election. In the circumstances he had little option, but it meant that if he kept his promise to the people, he would have to break his promise to Keating.

By 1990, Australian elections had become as staged as a Peking opera. Media commentators lamented constantly that the campaign was driven entirely by polling, by grabs for television's evening news programs, by defensive strategies. Labor, indeed, had much to be defensive about, for ALP state governments in Victoria, Western Australia and South Australia were in dire financial or political straits, or both. (The jewel, New South Wales, had been lost to the Liberals two years earlier, prompting, insiders believed, Keating's first attempt to unseat Hawke, as he feared his own time was running out.) In the same week that Hawke announced the federal election, the State Bank of Victoria announced its merchant banking arm, Tricontinental, had lost $1.3 billion. It was taxpayers' money. The premier, John Cain, unable to come to terms with the disaster, insisted that no one was to blame, thus adding to the electorate's disgust with him, his government and Labor. Richardson wrote 'the general public wore that stony look of insolence they get when they are about to hand out punishment'.[2] With state Labor beyond its reach for the time being, the Victorian electorate set out to punish Labor federally.

In Western Australia, the state government's association with the west's version of the white-shoe brigade, WA Inc., had turned from dream to nightmare as its cowboy capitalists went broke, dragging the government's reputation down with them. In South Australia, the State Bank was also due to collapse under its burden of debt. People there were edgy; the party worried it would lose more federal seats.

The Opposition only needed to make a case for Labor mismanagement. It did so, but not single-mindedly. It chose a slightly pompous slogan, *'The answer is Liberal'*. Keating punctured it instantly with the riposte, 'If the answer is Liberal, it must have been a helluva question.'

Because the government did not want the economy to be an issue, Keating was kept out of sight for most of the campaign, and the launch, in Brisbane, where Labor was popular, was low-key. It was to have no slip-ups like the 1987 'We set ourselves this goal: no child shall live in poverty'. The political world, as the Canadian writer and politician, Michael Ignatieff, noted, is a realm of 'sometimes lunatic literalism, where the slightest divergence between what you meant to say and what you actually said is a punishable offense'. One journalist, trying to be helpful, pointed out that Hawke's statement in 1987 could never have been misrepresented had it been possible to show a full colon on television. As Graham Freudenberg pointed out, the remark had been totally excised from its context. What Hawke had said in 1987 was, 'For our next term . . . we set ourself this first goal: by 1990 no Australian child will be living in poverty'. It was a statement of intent. It was not an election promise. To this day the statement, taken out of context, is used against Hawke; in July 2019 Stan Grant on the ABC's *The Drum* did so. The Opposition, through parliament and the media, had managed to establish in the public's mind that Hawke had lied or made an outrageous promise to Australia's children, then cruelly broken it. Once the public is convinced of something, argument will not prevail and Hawke simply had to put up with the taunt throughout the election, and even into the following century, until the day he died. It was doubly bitter for him since his government had spent more on child support than any other in Australian history. To the rage of the Finance minister, Peter Walsh, at the launch of the 1990 campaign Hawke made a further large commitment, $398 million, to child care. The drafting error of 1987, however, almost recurred. There had been an argument between the speechwriters, the young Stephen Mills and the venerable Freudenberg, who at one point declared, 'It doesn't matter what the Prime Minister wants to say. This is what he *has* to say. Because this is what the audience wants to hear.' Their struggle delayed delivery of the final speech. Sandy Hollway, the chief of staff, recalled being in a Brisbane hotel on the night before the launch, co-ordinating the production of 200 copies of the speech, with attached supporting documents, for distribution the next day. There were, he said, only antiquated photocopying machines in those days and we worked until 3 a.m. I remember taking a nap on the floor at one stage. Everybody was working their heart out. All the photocopies were finally lined up when Craig Emerson came up to me and said, 'Can I have a word with you?' We went into the bedroom and he told me, 'We've got a problem.' I said, *'What!'* He said, 'I think there's an inconsistency between the speech and the supporting documents.' We didn't say anything to the other staff, but waited until about 5 a.m., when we called the economist who would know the answer. Sure enough, there was an error in the speech. There was no time left to re-photocopy the whole thing. I had to say to the staff, 'Look, you have to go through every one of these and pull out page X and slot in a new one.' And I remember all those terrific admin people, who had slept only two hours, taking a deep breath and, as the sun came up, saying, 'Okay.'

Hawke's speech for the campaign launch acknowledged the pain of high interest rates, but presented them as an unpalatable fact of life in modernising the economy. He said 'anybody who tells the people of Australia that the future lies at the end of an easy road is not fit to be your prime minister'. He announced the government wanted to make Australia 'the clever country' (as distinct from 'the lucky country') and to that end would be establishing fifty world-class research centres. He declared, to wild applause, 'Medicare stays.'

Peacock had a disastrous start to his campaign when the deputy leader of the Liberals in the Senate, Austin Lewis, said on national television that the Liberals had been unable to convince Australians of their fitness to govern. Peacock sacked him immediately, but the damage was done. It gave Hawke an opening that stuck: 'If you can't govern your party, you can't govern Australia,' he said, turning it into a nostrum to be used at every opportunity. It was an observation that would return to haunt him.

Although many claimed after the event that they had believed Labor would win in 1990, aside from Hawke there was virtually nobody before the campaign got underway – Richardson and Keating included – who shared his optimism. The crunch moment would be the debate between Hawke and Peacock. Hawke's success in every endeavour was driven by three forces: optimism, will power and self-confidence, and the greatest of these was self-confidence. His team, aware of how highly strung he was, how a negative thought of his earlier failure in debate against Peacock could unnerve him and turn him shrill, were on tenterhooks. But Hawke was not now the nervous wreck with a glassed eye he had been in 1984. He was calm, focused and statesmanlike. He beat Peacock with ease. With their champion back on top, the campaign committee knew they had a fighting chance.

Journalists complained throughout the five weeks of electioneering that it was dull, lacking in sparkle and spontaneity. The most exciting event was when Hawke lost his temper while launching an environmental magazine. A staffer recalled, 'Some hairy ratbag wearing shorts and sandals started shouting at Bob, who made a gesture that knocked over a microphone, then got annoyed with all the microphones on the podium and swept them off with his arm.' The scene lasted only seconds, but was replayed so often on television that the rest of the week's campaign was a lost cause: the story for that week was Hawke's temper. His temper was, indeed, a constant source of anxiety to his minders during campaigns, when the pressure on a leader is most intense. Because he could not be glimpsed in public as a smoker, he gave up cigars leading up to the election, but nicotine withdrawal made him irritable and it was the staff who bore the brunt of his bad temper. He performed 139 election events, including ten visits to senior citizens clubs, hospitals, bowls days, child care centres; ten more to schools, TAFE colleges, Skillshare centres; and ten more to other community events, including the Derwent Hop Festival, the Family Fun Day at

Morphett Vale and the Ballarat Begonia Festival. He also visited war veterans, farewelled RAN ships sailing for the 75th anniversary of Gallipoli, and toured various factories.[3] The staff kept him out of shopping malls and away from street crowds because polling showed that he would be in danger of verbal abuse. And whatever else had been announced that day, on the evening news the abuse and how Hawke handled it would be the lead story. He was kept in the dark about negative focus-group polling, lest it damage his self-confidence.

The campaign committee used every weapon it had, including a new and very popular one, Hazel. Initially uncertain in public, she had long been a strong, forthright performer who had won respect over the years for causes, such as reforms in children's television, that she championed. She was the patron of 40 charities. She had also won the sympathy of women when, in 1989, Hawke had replied 'Yes' to a television question about whether he had ever had an affair. (He looked so contrite, even tearful, the interviewer did not ask the obvious follow-up, 'Just one?') Hazel made many appearances during the campaign and had a soft-focus personal column published under her name in some of the tabloid press.

Until the 1970s, campaigning had provided many moments of rambunctious fun, both for voters and for politicians. Menzies was famous, and celebrated, for his scintillating repartee with hecklers. Years after his death Liberals and even Labor politicians would repeat with admiration some of his wittiest put-downs. Everyone in Parliament House knew the possibly apocryphal story of the politician who introduced himself at an election rally by explaining, 'I'm the Country Member,' to which a voice from the back shouted, 'We remember!'

Television ruined all that.

Hawke's speechwriter, Stephen Mills, noted,

> The enduring image of the 1990 campaign was of Hawke, having delivered his policy speech ... standing on the stage with Hazel acknowledging the applause of the audience. As

they stood there, holding the pose for photographs, their gestures and expression fixed, they seemed transformed into figures of wax.[4]

This is the pathos of politics: the theatre of keeping up appearances, of repeating the same speech over and over, forcing smiles, waving to strangers when one is tired, or bored or just wanting a cup of tea. 'Saying the same thing twenty times, as if you were saying it for the first time – that was the hardest part of campaigning for me,' Hawke said. Political leaders must inspire confidence. They repeatedly improvise by reacting to events as they unfold, trying to stop them spinning out of control. British Prime Minister Harold Macmillan, when asked what was so difficult about political leadership, is reported to have replied, 'Events, dear boy. Events.'

The ALP campaign committee was determined to limit the possibility of events during the election. This, of course, frustrated journalists, whose livelihood depends upon events. They griped about the influence of market research, none realising that the politicians interpreted research in a more creative and practical way than they did. Under a headline that said, 'Drowning in the sunless sea of market research' Phillip Adams, an influential commentator, wrote in the *Weekend Australian*, 'Hawke [used to have] a genius for articulating the collective dream of a nation. Well, you won't plug into that through market research . . .' Actually, you will, if you're clever enough. Adams, like all his colleagues, had missed the genuinely interesting story that was under their noses: politics was being done differently in the 1990 election. As Richardson had first mentioned nine months earlier, the votes to win were the *green preferences*. This election would collect people's dreams and unconscious wishes, as elections always do, but quietly, in marginal electorates. Slowly and silently, the tens of thousands of people in 'the holding paddock' of the marginals were about to push the government back into office by voting Labor *second*. Warwick Smith recalled,

It was quite masterful. It was about enchanting the living rooms of Sydney, and to a lesser extent Melbourne, with the need to have a green agenda. While Peacock and others in the party had inclinations to be aware of the environment, they just had no marketing pizzazz whatsoever, and they were left flat-footed by Labor's capacity to swing the votes on the green issue. In the late 1980s and early '90s the environmental movement was seen to be more extreme than it was later, and what Richardson and Hawke did was try and popularise green issues and say, 'Extreme Green is not good, but Extreme Development is not good either – and in Tasmania you've got Extreme Development.'

Smith had a desperate fight, often against Richardson, who campaigned vigorously in Bass – 'picked my nose in public for me', Smith said – to retain his seat.

By 1990 Labor's marginal campaigning was so refined that in Western Australia, where there was an overall swing against the government of 4 per cent, it held marginal seats the Opposition could have won with merely a 2 per cent swing.

On a two-party preferred basis, the swing from Labor was only 0.9 per cent. In Victoria, furious with its state Labor government, nine seats fell. Had Victorians reacted like the rest of the country, Hawke would have won with the government's eighteen-seat majority unchanged. As it was, it came home eight seats ahead. But the number of people who had voted Labor was only 39.4 per cent, fewer than the 39.6 per cent who had voted Labor in the Whitlam disaster year of 1977. The message to the ALP was clear: its traditional supporters had deserted. It was a challenge for the party, but as Paddy McGuinness, having predicted a Peacock victory before election day, wrote immediately after it, 'If the Coalition has not managed to roll Bob Hawke this time, what makes it think that it will be able to do so next time?' He went on to write that Hawke, who was only sixty and very fit, could well stay on to fight the next election, then added the $64 000 comment, 'Of course, there is the problem of Paul Keating.'

But having achieved glory, Hawke blundered.

The exuberant maverick John Singleton, rabidly anti-Labor under Whitlam, had again run the party's advertising campaign and announced he was throwing the staff a celebration party. Singleton is a man who treats life as a cornucopia; he spends over his head. He seems to live by the injunction 'MORE!' More wine, women, song, wives, flowers for them, children, parties, fun, pranks, adventures, racehorses – and, in the twenty-first century, large South American parrots. For the dinner, Singleton hired Eliza's Restaurant in Double Bay, the shopping epicentre of Sydney's wealthiest individuals and just up the street from the electoral office of John Hewson, who would within days, everyone realised, become the new leader of the Liberal Party. Labor traditionally celebrated in hearty, sluttish, down-at-heel Chinatown. Eliza's could not have been a less appropriate venue for a Labor victory party. Hawke was uneasy about it. Singleton, archetypal larrikin, had become a close friend and the party owed much of its success to his agile brilliance in the last week of the campaign when the 'Vote Labor Second' strategy was finally unveiled. Seated with him in Eliza's, Hawke's uneasiness turned to ghastly embarrassment when a horseman wearing a spangled cowboy outfit rode up the steps of the restaurant onto its dance floor and began performing tricks. 'I hated it!' Hawke said later. Thrown off-key by the glitz, he made a speech of thanks to his staff in which he inadvertently insulted both his political officer, Geoff Walsh, and his environmental adviser, Craig Emerson. They had slaved throughout the campaign, getting hours less sleep each night than their boss, but while Hawke praised others he forgot to mention them. They were so annoyed they left the party, went out and got drunk and refused to return to Canberra with him.

This was trivial compared with Hawke's next blunder.

Graham Richardson wrote in his memoir that, after the election,

Hawke's reception of me was very different from any I had received from him over the previous twenty years. My great friend whom I had served so loyally for so long, who had repeatedly acknowledged all I had done for him, was cool towards me for the first time, treating me like just another minister waiting in a very long queue [to receive a portfolio]. This took a while to sink in because, not unnaturally, I had thought I would be king of the kids for at least a week or two.[5]

He seemed to have forgotten referring to his great friend as 'the cunt' two years earlier in a car phone conversation with Keating. He supported his case for being hard done by with a quote from Peter Smark of the *Age* and the *Sydney Morning Herald*, who wrote it was no longer a Hawke–Keating government, but a Hawke–Keating–Richardson government 'because of my contribution to the victory'. Richardson went on to suggest that the article and others like it may have been the reason for the Prime Minister's unusual treatment of him. He told Marian Wilkinson, journalist and author, that years earlier when he had been a nobody, Hawke, already a Somebody, had 'treated me really well, and he was a hero. He was a major, major, major hero and treated me well.'[6] Not expecting kindness from strangers let alone major, major heroes, Richardson had responded with adulation, in thrall to Hawke's charisma.

In his memoir, Richardson wrote,

Like all the other ministers though probably a little earlier than most I trooped into the Oval Office to stake my claim. I told Hawke that after the contribution I had made during the election campaign, I was entitled to a promotion, and the job I wanted was Transport and Communications.[7]

Hawke's old friend, Ralph Willis, had the portfolio but his management of it had been lacklustre; he needed a job more suited to his talent.

For months, Richardson had been telling colleagues and journalists that after the election he would be Minister for Transport and Communications. In Canberra this job had the sobriquet Minister for Mates – because its communications arm dealt with policy affecting the media moguls Kerry Packer and Rupert Murdoch, whose empires during the 1990s were about to undergo great changes. Pay television was to be introduced, while the third media empire, the once-great Fairfax, was on the brink of collapse. The other two were poised to loot it. The Minister for Communications would draft the policy to referee this competition between titans; a misstep could make deadly enemies for the government. Already Murdoch was shaking his fist at Labor by urging readers of his national paper, the *Australian*, to vote against the government in the 1990 election. Richardson's best friend was still Peter Barron, now on Kerry Packer's payroll as a political adviser. The government needed, somehow, to keep both Murdoch and Packer onside, especially Packer, because of the influence of his Channel Nine television network. (Although Packer had sold the network to Alan Bond, by March 1990 Bond had collapsed with the rest of the WA Inc. cowboys and Packer was ready to buy it back. The sale went through in July that year.) Richardson thought, not unreasonably, that he had the political skill to do the job, and had earned it. He had positioned himself to become the third most powerful man in government, so it was a shock when he sauntered into the Prime Minister's office, jaunty as a punter whose horse has come home at 30 to 1, to discover Hawke cold-eyed. More than a shock: it was a slap in the face.

Their former intimacy had cooled since Richardson had become a minister. Partly it was due to the pressure of work: Richardson, always industrious in whatever job he did, no longer had time to spend shooting the breeze with the Prime Minister at the end of the day. In the dynamic of their relationship there was also a deeper shift: as a minister, Richardson was officially a Somebody, no longer the star-struck fan. And there had been an incident over a bet on a putt during a golf game – they used to play together regularly at sunrise – that had left both men annoyed with each other. There was also Hawke's knowledge of Richardson's abuse of him behind his back. Before the election Richardson had been saying openly that it would soon be time for Hawke to step down in favour of Keating. The Prime Minister knew Richardson was now an undeclared enemy.

Richardson continued,

> [My] claim was summarily dismissed ... The only job left, I was told, was Social Security ... It wasn't the refusal that upset me, it was the manner of it. I was being put in my place, and I couldn't – and still don't – understand why.

It is difficult to know how much of this statement is disingenuous.

Richardson, from his earliest years as a New South Wales Right apparatchik, had revelled in the colourful side of inner-city life. He seemed fascinated by gangsta chic. In her deeply researched biography, *The Fixer: The Untold Story of Graham Richardson*, Marian Wilkinson provides a wealth of detail about his life in the 1970s. Richardson's parents had died when he was a young man; he matured, as Wilkinson portrays his life, in a sort of weed-filled prelapsarian Eden. As he rose up the political ladder, he became a fund-raiser for the party in New South Wales, and herein lay a source of his power. Richardson always sought to project it as something inexplicable, mysterious and glamorous. Actually, it was prosaic: he pulled the purse strings. He was the man who, controlling the slush funds, could provide money for a candidate fighting in a marginal seat, or for selection for a seat, or in a by-election. He had perfected an approach for soliciting donations to the party that exquisitely balanced the suggestion that, while the donor had better make a friendly gesture, no promises were being given in return.

But control of money was only part of Richardson's strength. The other part was his true virtue. There was a well of sympathy and kindness within him that he concealed behind his tough-guy image but which was known to the hundreds of people whom over the years he had gone out of his way to help – insignificant people, battlers, who would never be able to repay him with more than their thanks. When he had the funds to do so, Richardson gave generously and anonymously to charities.

Richardson had the sweet, uncommon gift of gratitude. It was his gratitude to Hawke that had made him such a fan for so long. John Bowan, who had once done Richardson a good turn, recalled that years later he and Sandy Hollway were working on the Sydney Olympic Games Committee when they fell foul of the Olympics Minister, Michael Knight. According to Bowan, Knight wanted to sack them both. Richardson intervened, using his weight in the New South Wales Labor Party and his authority as mayor of the Olympic Village to dissuade the minister. It was only later that Bowan learned who had saved his and Hollway's jobs.

Hawke said, 'There were a lot of negatives to Graham, but I have never doubted he is a true Labor man. He genuinely wants to help the poor and weak.' And he truly, madly, deeply wanted never again to be poor and weak himself. He wanted to live glamorously. A Tory dowager exclaimed with disgust (to this writer), 'In Paris that man stayed in the Georges V Hotel!'

By the early twenty-first century, after sixteen years in state government, the New South Wales Right had degenerated into a hybrid of Tammany Hall, ethnic gang and *opéra bouffe* and turned to a new premier to save it. Kim Beazley said,

> The New South Wales Right fought a lone battle for decency in the party for the best part of a century. They were basically always in the minority up until the 1980s. The Left always had the greater numbers. And the New South Wales Right was consistently trying to produce a Labor Party that had a halfway chance of winning an election decently. Basically they were totally connected to the thinking of the average middle-Australia Labor voter, and the Left wasn't. And then in the 1980s they solidified, and transformed, and emerged as the leaders.

Geoff Walsh recalled,

> When I worked in the national office, the New South Wales office was absolutely dismissive of us and talked about 'the way we do things in New South Wales', and that they had a higher level of political professionalism in the presentation and execution of events, research and advertising. The Victorian Right was equally organisationally effective, but it tolerated more diversity. Victorian institutions tend to be more thoughtful, more diverse in a range of views.

In the course of a century of struggle, the New South Wales Right found its cohesion in a tribal spirit and an unforgiving attitude to outsiders. It was held together by passionate anti-Communism with a rancour that today can be observed in Donald Trump's America. When the ALP split in the mid-1950s, ushering in almost two decades of power to the Liberal Coalition, New South Wales did not split, thanks to the decision of the Right to heed the advice of Sydney's wily and astute Catholic archbishop, Cardinal Gilroy, acting through his bishop, James Carroll. (His 'right hand blesses the victims of his left' the Catholic-convert poet, James McAuley, wrote, in fury, about Gilroy's political role.) Branch-stacking for preselections, frequently presented as a recent evil in Australian political life, is in fact an ancient and noble tradition in both the Labor and Liberal parties. Beazley said, 'There were stories in the 1950s of busloads of nuns in New South Wales being brought in to vote in preselection ballots.'

For the New South Wales Right – cynical, self-righteous, narrow-minded and now powerful – it was but a short step to a sense of entitlement. The title of Richardson's book, *Whatever It Takes*, sums up the Right's ideology by the 1990s: nothing was more important than winning. There were no principles to guard. There was only pragmatism.

*

Hawke, other than his suddenly cold demeanour, gave Richardson no reason then or later as to why he could not have the job he coveted. Instead he gave Transport and Communications to Kim Beazley.

In Hawke's next move, he made a blunder, according to Richardson.

Richardson had left Hawke's office in dudgeon. The Prime Minister, Richardson wrote, had been keeping open the post of High Commissioner to the Court of St James for Willis, whom the New South Wales and Victorian Right wanted dumped from the ministry. Hawke had refused, insisting that the Right in both states support Willis, whom he intended to promote to a portfolio suited to his considerable talent as an economist. If that did not work, Hawke had said that he would offer him London. Richardson had replied jocularly that if Willis didn't want to go to London, he would, 'in a flash'. The job's perquisites would be a mansion in the centre of a fascinating city, presentation to the Queen at Buckingham Palace, rubbing shoulders with the international big league, his lovely red-haired wife pampered with servants, gorgeous shops, lavish parties and easy travel to Europe. Richardson wrote that that night Hawke rang him to offer him the high commissioner's position. He was, he said, 'appalled, hurt, furious. Without taking any time to think about it, I just said, "No."'[8]

Hawke says he has no memory of offering London to Richardson. The Prime Minister's relationship with the Queen was warm – they shared a good sense of humour and love of racehorses and he was reputed to be Her Majesty's favourite Commonwealth prime minister. Hawke says he considered Richardson could have been an appropriate envoy since Her Majesty had clearly liked Doug McClelland, the rough diamond whom Hawke had previously sent her. It was simply that he did not consider Richardson for the job at all. Richardson's written account sounds odd, since he had so recently acknowledged that the job was a plum indeed. His account begs the question: why would he reject it out of hand, as an insult?

That night, Richardson wrote, soon after the disputed phone call from the Prime Minister he made two calls himself. The first was to his very close friend, Peter Barron, to tell him of the day's events. 'I said to him: "I'll get this bastard, I'll do whatever it takes, but I'll get him."' Richardson's next phone call was to Paul Keating.[9]

Hawke meanwhile mulled over what to do about Richardson's sense of grievance over the ministry he had offered him and by the following morning had come up with another idea.

Richardson was having breakfast in a Canberra restaurant when he was summoned to the telephone by a call from the Prime Minister. Hawke wanted to discuss with him the Ministry for Defence. Defence is a mammoth portfolio, with the largest staff, the biggest budget, the most formidable subordinates and insubordinates. Beazley had been brilliant in it, sensitive to the mentality of both the brass and the infantry. He recalled that just before the 1987 election he had asked the Prime Minister to inspect a brigade in the marginal seat of Townsville. The visit would be politically useful to the coming election. But to Beazley's horror, Hawke began talking to a corporal, who opened his pack to show the Prime Minister what was inside. Hawke said, 'Oh – you've got a lot of equipment there. What do you think of it?' The corporal replied, 'It's a heap of *shit*. Sir.' As they moved out of earshot Hawke said, 'What sort of Defence minister are you! Four years in the job and you have one of your soldiers describing his kit as shit!' Beazley explained,

'Bob, for thousands of years the whole purpose of warfare has been to kill infantrymen. They're naturally a morose group. Next week there's a battalion of US marines visiting for exercises. This bloke's unit will go to the marines, who think the same about their own kit, they will swap kits, and they will both be happy.'

At another of Hawke's brigade inspections in Townsville, a regimental sergeant major with the voice of a Jurassic bullfrog roared, 'GENTLEMEN! I want to introduce to you now the PRIME Minister of Australia, Mr Bob MENZIES!' Hawke also inspected a military barracks. Each time the man running it referred to another service – the navy, or the air force – he spat on the ground. 'Bob left thinking we were all lunatics,' Beazley said. He desperately wanted to stay in the portfolio but Hawke was determined to broaden his experience, for already at the back of his mind he wondered if Beazley, rather than Keating, might replace him, since Keating could yet 'take the Paris option'. Inevitably, anyone who followed Beazley in the Defence job would, for months at least, be overwhelmed by it.

Richardson wrote that the Prime Minister told him he had offered Defence to Robert Ray the day before, but on reflection he believed Ray's 'legendary temper' could make him unsuited to the delicate negotiations with foreign governments that a Defence minister conducts.[10] Hawke says,

> I never thought Robert Ray had a bad or a hot temper. He was sharp and direct and many people felt intimidated by him, but his temper was not an issue. I don't believe I would have discussed Robert with Richardson in these terms.

Richardson wrote, 'We talked it through and I accepted.' As he left Hawke's suite a new press officer saluted Richardson and called out, 'Good morning, Admiral.' Richardson was chuffed: the man he used to love did, after all, still value him.

But Hawke's handling of Richardson was sliding from poor to disastrous. When he rang Ray to tell him he wanted to switch Richardson to Defence and Ray to Social Security, Ray flatly refused. Hawke knew he was right to do so, and knew that he was temperamentally far better equipped for the job than Richardson. Hawke also knew that in a showdown with Keating he would inevitably lose the New South Wales Right, which would rally to the banner of its tribal brother. He depended on

Ray to hold Victoria for him. Hawke said later, 'My handling of the Richardson and Ray portfolios was dreadful.'

He summoned Richardson once more. He could not be Defence minister after all, the Prime Minister said. He was stuck with Social Security. The pain Hawke had inflicted on Richardson two days earlier seemed, in comparison, a mere tap on the wrist. Now Hawke whacked Richardson's face, and did so with the same steel-eyed chill of the earlier meeting. Richardson was devastated, but as he refused to be the victim of any man, his rage was directed outwards. 'Nothing in politics, or indeed in any facet of my life, has ever made me as angry as I was that morning,' he wrote later. 'All I could think of was revenge ... I was now completely won over to Keating's side ... From that moment the Hawke prime ministership was doomed.'[11]

It was doomed, but as Richardson knew, Hawke was a hero. No hero can be destroyed by others: from the age of myths into and throughout history, the hero's reward for heroism is the freedom to choose himself his path to destruction.

Richardson, meanwhile, was too proud and clever to reveal how deeply Hawke had wounded him, and how much he now hated the Prime Minister. Indeed, he gave the impression of having copped his demotion on the chin and although disappointed for himself, was still on Hawke's side.

Publicly, the government was united but the inner circle knew otherwise. Keating to his staff, to other ministers and to journalists, blamed every difficulty in his life, even strains in his domestic affairs, on Hawke. He denigrated the Prime Minister. Hawke in his own day had denigrated Hayden – but he had not Keating's fire-tipped tongue. And he was never as talkative as Keating, who was famous for telephone monologues, always the super-salesman selling, selling, selling his point of view.

The show went on. By the second quarter of 1990, the government could boast it had created 1.6 million jobs and while the booming economy was beginning to slow, Keating promised a soft landing. He publicly attacked all those who doubted his handling of the Treasury, including the Industry minister, John Button, and the former Finance minister, Peter Walsh, with such an edge of furious scorn that more observant journalists realised his feelings were almost desperate. David O'Reilly in a *Bulletin* cover story of 29 May wrote,

> Quite simply there is a real prospect that, after seven years as the driving force of economic policy for Australia, Keating has got it all wrong ... Keating produced in parliament a display of intellectual and oratorical brutality that was almost overwhelming for those sitting in the galleries. At times he leaves his opponents seemingly mesmerised by his capacity to translate complex government policies into plausibly defendable positions. From there he turns a machine gun of invective on to any contradictions or political problems in Opposition arguments. In an hour-long Question Time he made the pugnacious and ambitious Liberal Shadow Treasurer, Peter Reith, pale into retreat. In the next salvo he dismantled John Howard's latest foray into industrial relations policy. And he slapped contemptuously at Hewson.

Hewson's barrage of economic statistics inspired Keating to dub him 'feral abacus'.

Hawke had an ambitious fourth-term agenda for microeconomic reform, especially in Commonwealth–state relations. Ross Garnaut wrote, 'In that fourth term cooperation with Premiers from both sides of Australia's political divide was moving towards far-reaching and productive reform of [our] Federal arrangements ... [it] reached across the partisan political divide to generate what stands in history as a unique period of cooperative Federalism. The move towards centralised wage formation [began] in the fourth term.' But it was less publicised than it should have been for several reasons: one was that few journalists understood it; another was that

Keating was unenthusiastic about supporting an initiative that had come from the Prime Minister and that would be seen as a further great reform. Another was that the government, and particularly the Prime Minister's office, no longer had the sharp edge in self-publicising that it had enjoyed after the end of the Combe–Ivanov affair. Senior Canberra journalists were bored and cynical about the government. For a politician, years in public life entail years of being satirised, lampooned and criticised. In time, only her or his flaws seem evident. The virtues are overlooked.

Meanwhile, the new leader of the Opposition, John Hewson, was a shiny, sharp cobra of a man. He drove fabulous cars and was known as 'Fast Lane'. He was a political greenhorn, which of itself made him interesting for the gallery. He was far more exciting than the greying team that ground out government business day after day. While Keating was fourteen years Hawke's junior, Hewson was almost twenty.

In April, Hawke enjoyed his greatest pleasure and his final moment of peaceful reflection as Prime Minister when, at break of day on the 25th of the month, he stood with a handful of Australian and Turkish veterans and thousands of young backpackers above Anzac Cove to honour the dead of seventy-five years earlier. Former enemies embraced; the young embraced the aged. It was a moment of human brotherhood, as if an age of peace yet to dawn had cast its soft light backwards onto the turbulent present.

A few weeks later Hawke suffered a private setback that temporarily did his standing as much harm as his world record in beer drinking had served him well over decades. He needed a prostate operation. The fact was widely reported. Suddenly, the leader who embodied the Aussie larrikin ideal of boozing, playing sport and womanising transformed into the image of the male terror of impotence. The medical procedure was minor, but at the time prostate operations of any kind were relatively rare, and frightening. While the press gallery restrained themselves in what they wrote, what they said to each other was as vulgar as it was vicious. Three months earlier Hawke had been 'still young'. Now John Hewson referred to him as 'old' and 'losing his grip on the party'. Hawke and the government began falling in the polls soon after the election and by June Hewson outpolled Hawke as preferred prime minister 46 to 38 per cent. Glenn Milne wrote in the *Australian* on 7 June,

> Consider some of the headlines generated in recent weeks . . . 'Time may be right for Hawke to go'. 'Keating shows the troops who's boss.' 'Hawke opens up leadership issue in quelling row.' 'Hawke is on trial' and the doozy of them all, 'Crusher Keating: How desperate is he?'

Milne went on to argue that, while Keating was restive and Richardson had deserted the Hawke camp, Keating did not have the numbers in Caucus for a challenge and Hawke was safe in his job. Laurie Oakes, in the *Bulletin* of 12 June, wrote, 'Hawke appeared older and frailer than before his surgery. Hardly a PR triumph.' Walking past a motor mechanic's shop in Sydney around the same time this author heard young tradesmen refer to 'our senile Prime Minister'.

Had Hawke taken Abeles' advice then, sipping coffee through a false beard, he could have decided it was the moment to bow out. But giving up was no more in his character than it was in Mrs Thatcher's. And, by mid-1990, economic upheaval loomed. The worst recession in sixty years was emerging. Ralph Willis recalled Grand Final Day in Melbourne the year before, chatting to a man who sold cars. 'How's business?' Willis had asked. 'Going gangbusters,' his companion had said. 'Can't hire enough staff. But I don't know where we'll be in six months. I haven't got a single forward order.' Willis had felt his blood run cold.

In the *Weekend Australian* of 23–24 June, the publisher, poet, intellectual and columnist, Max Harris, wrote:

There is little but Band-Aiding that any Australian government can do to ameliorate the economic chaos and disorder that has become a world affliction. With hundreds of nations around the world in an economic mess, it is idiotic to blame the Government or to call for therapies for economic miseries over which it cannot have the slightest control.

Like summer lightning, the air flashed with signs of a boom busting. Perhaps economists and bankers resemble generals: they forever fight the last war. After the stock market crash of October 1987, there was a worldwide belief that monetary policy had to be loosened to prevent another Great Depression. The ocean of money that was let loose caused the boom. By January 1988 economists in Hawke's office were arguing that the October crash had not been the cataclysmic event it was supposed to be and the response had been overdone. They wanted interest rates tightened. But the Labor jewel, New South Wales, was due for an election in March that year and the government, especially the Treasurer, did not want to raise interest rates before then. The decision to wait was both foolhardy – the New South Wales Labor government was beyond salvation – and a blunder. Craig Emerson recalled,

> Ross Garnaut came over from Western Australia and said, 'It's going to hit the wall.' I don't think anyone fully accepted Ross' view. But he was right. And by 1990 the economy was a bloody runaway beast. It didn't seem to matter what interest rate increases were made, it just kept going. By then it was too late: we were too close to the wall.

Immediately after the 1990 election, the economy gave a shiver of contraction. Some professionals understood; most did not for several months. Hawke would say repeatedly, in Cabinet, in the ERC, in his office, to the electorate, 'We tightened too much, too late.' It was his greatest regret as Prime Minister.

His government's misjudgment of monetary policy was its greatest error. Keating meanwhile refused to apologise for his role.

The rumbling of decay in Eastern Europe that thundered in 1989 as the Berlin Wall collapsed kept rumbling through the early months of 1990. The world watched, fascinated, as country after country, collected over centuries by sabre, cannon, horses and tanks, broke away from the Soviet empire. Suddenly, like a sandcastle under a wave, the empire dissolved.

An eminent international policy analyst, Professor Francis Fukuyama of Johns Hopkins University, wrote an essay titled 'The End of History?' suggesting that the collapse of the Soviet Union marked the advent of Western liberal democracy as the end point of humanity's sociocultural evolution and the final form of human government. Fukuyama was a little too quick off the mark. Certainly the West had won the Cold War. But what exactly was the prize? It was not as obvious as he and jubilant US Republicans and a strange new intellectual breed called neo-conservatives, who had lived in the shadows for a decade or more, believed. But it was a time of great hope and great relief. The threat of 5000 nuclear weapons exploding in two and a half hours over the cities of Europe, America, Japan and possibly Australia vanished. But there began to emerge an uneasy feeling that the world was not shifting into a glory of liberal democracies. It seemed to be moving towards a hazy no man's land. The victory prize remained tantalisingly out of reach. History announced its puzzling reward nine months after the Wall came down. Early in the morning of 2 August 1990, President Saddam Hussein of Iraq invaded Kuwait, his army halting at the border of Saudi Arabia. If it crossed the border and prevailed against the Saudis' far smaller armed forces, Saddam would be a master of the universe. He would control the majority of the world's oil.

The prize for winning the Cold War, it seemed, would be more war. The booby prize: anarchy.

By this stage, the American economy was flagging and many spoke of 'imperial overreach' – that the United States had won the Cold War but had been weakened in the process and would now have to pull back from global leadership. Dr Hugh White, an international analyst and by now Hawke's Defence adviser, said, 'Nobody, including no Americans, assumed that with the end of the Cold War the United States would retain the global role it had played.'

Saddam Hussein and the Bush family would change all that.

A twisted seam of atavism ran through the vulgar tyrant who was President of Iraq. He believed himself to be, and represented himself to his people and to the wider Arab world, as a resurrected Saladin, the paragon of Arab chivalry. Even the Christian warriors of the Third Crusade – Richard the Lionheart among them – admired Saladin's strategic genius, his justice and his compassion for prisoners. Saddam's evocation of glories past conjured from the vast empty spaces of the desert what sounded like the distant thunder of hooves. People wondered: in which direction was the horse of history galloping? Some said this way, others said that. Hawke was quite certain what he thought: the horse should be pulled up hard and guided into a stall. Saddam had to leave Kuwait, by a face-saving negotiated settlement if possible, by force if not.

Hugh White said,

I remember sitting in my cubby hole in the Prime Minister's office when news of the invasion came in, and the first responses from America were very ambiguous. The first responses from [President] Bush Senior were very ambiguous. I said to someone, 'Well, this is what it's like after the Cold War: small countries get invaded by big neighbours and nobody gives a damn. This is a really bad model for the way the world works.'

That was Hawke's attitude too. On Keating's recommendation – he and Hawke were still spending time together, still discussing ideas, still a team – the Prime Minister had been reading William Manchester's biography of Winston Churchill. White believed the book influenced Hawke's thinking: that a strong international response mediated through the UN was essential to stop Saddam.

White had been a little too quickly pessimistic about the world's reaction, for on the day of invasion the Security Council, at last able to play the role envisaged for it in 1945, passed Resolution 660, demanding an immediate and unconditional withdrawal from Kuwait. A sigh of relief, even joy, ran through the international community. White said, 'You can't understand what happened in August through to December 1990 without understanding the *hope* that we could now build an international order in which the UN at last played the role envisaged for it.'

The Cold War had consigned the Security Council to the deep freeze. What the world's leaders and diplomats suddenly realised was that the Security Council had been, as it were, cryogenically preserved: it was still alive. It could be brought out, warmed up, and get back in business.

In speech after speech, Hawke stressed the importance of the reborn United Nations, telling parliament that now,

> with real hope in our hearts, [the UN can become] an effective international system against aggression; a system in which all countries, great and small, play a part. If we fail in this obligation, in this the first test of the new international order after the Cold War, the consequences for our medium- and long-term security and for that of many other countries are deeply disturbing.

Saddam ignored the UN and began looting Kuwait.

Bush rang Hawke to say he was having trouble persuading the Canadian Prime Minister, Brian Mulroney, to agree to support intervention because of Canada's huge wheat exports to Iraq. Hawke replied, 'We've got a bloody big wheat trade with Iraq too. Leave Brian to me. He's my mate.' He rang Mulroney and told him Australia was prepared to sacrifice its wheat trade and Mulroney agreed his country should also be willing to make the sacrifice. He told Hawke that Australia's action would be helpful in persuading his Cabinet to support the Bush initiative. On 6 August the Security Council ordered a global trade embargo against Iraq. White said, 'Bob was very careful to make sure the Canadians were taking the same view we were, so if we lost the market, they would too.' A few days later, on 9 August, Hawke discussed Australia's other options with Gareth Evans and Robert Ray, privately giving thanks that Ray had refused to forgo the Defence job. He was already across the issue and told Hawke three ships could leave for the Persian Gulf within three days to help enforce the trade embargo. Early next morning Hawke rang President Bush to confirm Australia's support.

On 11 September 1990, the American President announced that he would use force if necessary to remove the Iraqi army from Kuwait. Saddam responded by seizing all the foreigners in Iraq and Kuwait as hostages: he would use them, he said, as human shields in front of targets that might be attacked by a UN force. (Saladin would have done the same, but he lived in the twelfth century.) Hawke said, 'There were about 150 Australians in Iraq and Kuwait and their safety became a constant anxiety for me and the government.'

Hawke, passionately interested in the Middle East since the 1960s, eager to help edge Israelis and Palestinians towards peace, often seemed like a temperance worker patiently explaining to a drunk the logic of teetotalism. Devoted to logical argument himself, he had not been able to accept that these lands that gave birth to civilisation, to writing, to all the prophets from Abraham to Mohammed, to the mystery of Golgotha, are indeed unique and intoxicated with something more powerful than the humdrum of enlightened self-interest. At first he could not believe that Saddam, who had a case to argue for his claim on Kuwaiti territory, could not be persuaded it was in his best interests to withdraw. Hawke was on good terms with the Crown Prince of Jordan, whom he thought might be able to act as a go-between. He talked it over with Bush, who agreed it was worth trying, and on 24 August Hawke rang Prince Hassan. The Prince was sympathetic but categoric. Saddam, he said, would not even consider the idea Hawke suggested: withdrawal, with the guarantee of an international tribunal to hear his claim against Kuwait.

Saddam was highly intelligent and cunning, but he was primitive. He could not imagine the world outside himself; he did not understand what a superpower is, or what it can and will do.

For three months, feverish international diplomacy ruled the news media while in the party and the Caucus there were heated, sometimes tearful, debates. It was only fifteen years since the Vietnam War had ended – objection to that war being the very reason many people had joined the Labor Party. The horror and shame of it still carried a weight in the community and even more in the party. 'It was a hard sell in the party,' White recalled.

> We were the Vietnam generation. We were very suspicious about the use of armed force. We were very suspicious about the idea of going off and fighting other people's wars. In the debates in the office, for example, Stephen Mills, a very dear friend of mine, represented the 'Hang on! Let's not get carried away' argument. A sociological thing happens when people start discussing the use of armed force. It's not like putting on a new tax, or changing the qualifications for the single mothers' allowance. Deep emotions get involved; the back of the brain starts to take over. It gets pretty blokeish very fast. The capacity to stand back, to make a rational, structured, logical, contestable argument as to whether this is a good idea or not quickly goes out the window.

The Left in Australia and throughout the world was beside itself with distress: over renewed militarism and the possibility of another war, over the sanctions (causing Iraqi people starvation, the death of Iraqi babies), over the hostages, over the idea that the world's response was 'just about oil'. Australian's most famous historian, Emeritus Professor Manning Clark, deemed a living national treasure, an icon of the middle class and the soft Left, wrote an article in the *Sydney Morning Herald* saying that Saddam Hussein and George Bush were just two people with a difference of opinion. Clark's own opinion carried great clout. There was intense fear, especially in Israel and among diaspora Jews, that, if under attack, Saddam would use chemical weapons against Israel. He had used them against his own people and against Iranians and he was already having Kuwaitis raped, tortured and murdered. Prince Hassan had explained to Hawke the realities of Arabic politics, but Hawke and other western leaders were unable to educate their citizens. Tragic cultural ignorance ruled. A constant stream of well-meaning people travelled to Baghdad to beg for the hostages' release. Saddam would release a few but that, as Hawke said, 'only made the situation more unbearable for the ones left behind'. The Australian government refused to negotiate over hostages, which, within the party and Caucus was further cause for grief.

By mid-November Hawke realised war was inevitable. He believed that, for three reasons, Australia had to take part. First, it was unacceptable for a country, unprovoked, to invade another. Second, he, like many other leaders around the world, fervently wanted to support the UN in its renaissance as an international force for justice and stability. Third was his support for the Australia–United States alliance. But of the three, the UN was by far the most important, for it was the hope of the future for a civilised world.

On 29 November the Security Council passed Resolution 678, which gave Saddam until 15 January 1991 to withdraw from Kuwait. This was the War Resolution. After that, member states were authorised to use 'all necessary means' to reverse the invasion. The same day Hawke called together Robert Ray, Gareth Evans, Paul Keating – who since the election had been deputy Prime Minister as well as Treasurer – and John Button, leader of the government in the Senate. They were to agree on a position to be put to Cabinet. White said,

> It's hard now [in 2009] when we seem to send off troops at the drop of a hat, to remember what it was like for Australia to be a country that believed you didn't ever use armed force. But that was the country we were.

After Vietnam there had been a taboo on sending forces abroad. White added, 'A lot of people, including a lot of people in government, just didn't think it would happen: *we don't go to war any more.*'

Hawke was saying publicly that Saddam was a tyrant and as evil as Hitler – but it was difficult for Australians to believe in the evil of political tyranny since, refugees aside, relatively few had experienced it. Two generations had grown to adulthood convinced evil was a construct designed to enforce obedience to Christian theology. The Left, the Centre Left and many others thought Hawke was blustering about Saddam. White recalled,

> People hung on to the thought that maybe Saddam is not that bad. Because if you believed he was, it was very hard not to believe that going to war was the right thing. And people didn't want to believe that, so they looked for ways to avoid it, and when people are looking for ways to avoid the obvious they'll believe the most remarkable things.

Hawke was confident a war against Iraq would be easy to win because the United States and its NATO allies had been planning to fight the Soviet Union on the north German plain for about forty years: they had forces specifically designed for such a war. The Iraqi forces were poor versions of Soviet divisions, and they were deployed on the flat, treeless landscape of a desert, the optimum terrain for tanks. White recalled,

> A lot of people said, 'Oh this will be a disaster: it will be like Vietnam again.' And I said, 'No it won't! There are some battles the United States are very good at' – and this was one of them.

The ultimate strategic objective could be defined in very precise military terms; there was a direct connection between the military operation and the strategic goal. 'The big proviso,' White said, 'was: "*Don't cross the border, guys* – because then you'll end up governing Iraq, and Iraq is inherently ungovernable unless you're prepared to operate in the same way as Saddam Hussein."'

Despite the prospect for military success the government could not be confident of avoiding casualties. Its ships could be blown up by mines in the Persian Gulf (as one American ship was), or bombed by the Iraqi air force. When a ship is hit it burns furiously and casualties are high. Gareth Evans' Department of Foreign Affairs and Trade had written a position paper for him with the opening sentence, 'The worst possible outcome would be to find the international community drawn into a conflict in Kuwait.' White argued to him that this was the second-worst outcome: the worst would be for Saddam to end up owning Kuwait. Evans agreed, but remained ambivalent and anxious about the use of force. Being in the role of peacemaker in Cambodia, he was in an invidious position. Button was opposed, but agreed to keep his opposition to himself. Hawke, Ray and Keating – after an initial objection 'What has the United States done for us?' to which Hawke replied this was about the UN, not the United States – were in favour. White recalled,

The politics were *interesting* because the Keating challenge was already in the air – but once national security comes on the agenda, the prime minister becomes a king. That has to be noted. No matter how strong your Defence minister is, this is one issue that absolutely must be owned by the prime minister.

Ray wanted two more ships to be sent. Hawke overruled the idea. 'We had good reason to expect that Iraq's seemingly formidable air forces would pose a serious threat to our ships,' White said.

A tormenting period for Keating had begun. In June 1990, he had seemed to have a headlock on the Prime Minister. Now Hawke was the king and the undisputed centre of power in government. A whole new aspect of his leadership abilities emerged, and by early October he had reversed by 14 per cent Hewson's former lead over him and was once again pre-ferred prime minister. The Coalition, however, led Labor by 10 per cent.

Paul Kelly noted, 'Keating was burning with frustration, fear-ful that Hawke would repudiate his Kirribilli pact, yet resentful that if he became prime minister he might inherit only the ashes of an era.'[12]

In October 1990, Hawke had told Keating he wanted to stay in his job until the South African issue was settled, at the CHOGM to be held in one year's time. Keating had said *he* needed time to change his image in the electorate, and October 1991 would allow him very little leeway. Hawke had been unmoved. Keating had then approached both Kelty and Abeles to ask them to pressure Hawke. Pressure is the least effective way of influencing Hawke, as it stimulates his formidable will power. He had begun to harden further against Keating and a cat-and-mouse game of leak and counter-leak from their offices began.

Meanwhile, the economy was sliding into recession.

On 29 November 1990, the national statistics revealed a second quarter of negative growth and Keating, in a moment of lamentable political judgment, issued a press statement announcing, 'this is a recession that Australia had to have'. Keating and Hawke had repeatedly promised there would be no recession. In one phrase the Treasurer and deputy Prime Minister presented himself to the voters as a heartless deceiver, uncaring for those who were losing their jobs and businesses. Hawke publicly apologised for the recession, repeatedly expressing remorse. Keating refused to do so, further entrenching the findings of Labor and other polling that, while brilliant and exciting, he was considered arrogant and nasty. Hawke had been spending a lot of time in public and at Labor branches, where he was constantly hearing complaints against Keating. There was a strong 'Keating has to go' sentiment in both the electorate and the party. Much of Keating's problem as a politician was that he was introverted; while with intimates he was warm, affectionate and funny, with strangers he was shy and even nervous. A journalist recalled walking through a crowd with him, Keating muttering, 'Don't make eye contact! Don't look at them. Just keep going.' Hawke, by contrast, was forever eager to meet people, to stop, shake hands, tell a joke, ruffle the hair of a child. He loved 'the mob' and exuded the disarming conviction that every stranger would like him. Many people who liked neither him nor his government found themselves apologising for not voting Labor and asking for a photograph with him. If encountering outright hostility Hawke would react with a tomcat glare, and stalk off, tail lashing.

To preserve his claim on The Lodge, Keating needed to reserve his position on the war carefully in case it turned out disastrously. He needed to be able to claim that he had been against it all along. Although he and his staffer, Don Russell, denied it later, White says 'Keating expressed significant reservations'. White kept a daily diary of events; he was in the room when Keating spoke, as was Russell, and was 'paying careful attention, because this seemed pretty relevant to me', he said. Keating would later claim that Hawke was indecisive, and that he, Keating, had had to push Hawke into the war. White, who likes Keating, later spoke to him about these assertions, 'and what he had to say was quite profane'.

On 3 December 1990, Hawke consulted the Caucus leaders and 'received solid support', he wrote in his memoirs. He had spent hours, from night into the morning, reassuring them that this war would in no way be a rerun of Vietnam, explaining that 144 nations supported Resolution 678, that forty of them had agreed to provide, or to help sustain, military forces deployed in the Gulf, that these included NATO countries, former Soviet-bloc countries, Arab states, Muslim nations, Pacific nations – indeed people from every inhabited continent. He pointed out that the centrepiece of the United Nations Charter was the collective use of force in extreme cases where no other way was left to punish and defeat aggression. The Left, and more especially the Centre Left, Hayden stalwarts who had never really forgiven Hawke and were now solidly behind Keating's leadership ambitions, remained deeply troubled at the prospect of war.

That afternoon Cabinet agreed Australia must support Resolution 678 and the next day Hawke made a second statement to parliament on the Gulf crisis, noting:

For much of its one hundred years the ALP has struggled to ensure that Australia's armed forces are not used to fight other peoples' wars. In the 1930s that led Labor to turn its back on aggression ... But Labor learned the lessons of that mistake.

Parliamentary debate went on for days.

White said, 'I was struck that right from the beginning Hawke had a framework for thinking about these things that was very clear.' That framework was sophisticated, and included the possibility that the United States, having worked through the UN, might peel off and rush into Iraq. 'That was a huge concern for Bob,' White said. The United States was already on oil life support, and had been for more than a decade. Saddam's flashing of a blade near the superpower's carotid artery made the American response unpredictable.

By December enormous numbers of armed forces from all over the world were gathering on Kuwait's borders. The terrible days of waiting began.

For Keating, too, they were days of waiting that became unbearable. On 6 December his head of department, Chris Higgins, a man of whom he was very fond, and who was just a few months older than Keating, suddenly died. The following evening Keating was to address the annual Press Club dinner. He arrived in an emotional state, a Hamlet mood, and after a few jokes, launched into a rambling but fascinating *tour d'horizon* of how he saw the world, Australia, leadership and Australia's leaders. 'Leadership is not about being popular, it's about being right ... The trouble with Australia is that we've never had [a great leader]. We've never had one leader, not one, and it shows.' Curtin, he said, was a 'trier'; Chifley 'a plodder'. He ended with a lightly masked appeal to the 120 journalists, spellbound at what a great story they had, to support *him* against Hawke. He had raised to an art the management of economics and politics, he said. His economics was a pure, consummate form devoid of personal content, to be admired for its astounding intelligence and the beauty of its craftsmanship. He was, he said, the Placido Domingo of Australian politics. Everyone knew he considered the Spaniard far superior to Hawke's favourite tenor, the lovable fat Italian, Luciano Pavarotti.

Keating's speech was off the record. Next morning Hawke received a full report of it. He had believed for many years that Keating not only did not love the Australian people, as he,

Hawke, did, but actually rather despised them. The Treasurer's speech demonstrated that. It condescended to Australia as a second-rate country.

Keating's timing could scarcely have been worse. Hawke was himself nursing a private grief: his greatest love, his father Clem, who had suffered a minor stroke earlier in the year, was fading towards death, while Hawke was emotionally keyed up to shoulder the burden of sending scores of young Australians into harm's way with the distinct possibility of some returning in coffins. Curtin, who drove himself to death with worry over the men he sent to be slaughtered, was in Hawke's mind constantly. Keating had been dodging and weaving in his commitment to the war; his gratuitous scorn for Curtin (which he had absorbed from Jack Lang, who hated Curtin and had been expelled from the party by Curtin) drove Hawke to fury. By implication Keating also scorned the ALP. As Hawke interpreted it, not only did Keating lust for his job, he was also attempting to destroy Hawke's place in history by rewriting it, inserting his own name into reforms that had been Hawke's. There was plenty of evidence for Hawke to point to about Keating's rewriting of history. He had been busily doing so with the press gallery for years. *And he didn't even love and respect Australia.* He had virtually said so himself: if he could not become prime minister, he would decamp and live in Paris.

The Sunday newspapers carried versions of the speech. All the professionals – politicians and gallery journalists – recognised that the Hawke–Keating team was now a façade.

On Monday morning Keating publicly performed a mea culpa, saying he had intended no disrespect to past or present Labor leaders. Headlines read, 'Keating Speech Puts New Strain on Ties with Hawke', 'Can They Last?' and 'Labor's Love Lost'. On the afternoon of 10 December, Hawke called Keating in for a long discussion, during which he hammered Keating on Curtin's greatness. It was left unspoken, but Keating knew Hawke now had no intention of abiding by the still-secret Kirribilli agreement. The next day Hawke made this clear to Keating when, in a press conference, he said he would stay on until the next election, and were he to win, would lead the party through that term: that is, he would be staying for another five years if the party wanted him.

It was Richardson, now fully rehearsed to the role he had chosen – a wolf in sheep's clothing – who had advised Hawke to make this statement, hoping, as he was to write in his autobiography, that it would be regarded as ridiculous by the media and bring discredit on the Prime Minister. He was not disappointed. The gallery, having accepted Keating's invitation to become participants in the question of leadership of the Labor Party, greeted Hawke's statement with supercilious chuckles. By the end of the week the *Financial Review* carried a page-one story by Geoff Kitney that said,

> An important, unstated motivation for the Prime Minister's decision to commit himself to another five years as Labor leader appears to be a decision ... that he now does not want ... Mr Keating to be his successor. Senior Labor figures believe Mr Hawke has had a decisive change of mind ... and that he no longer believes Mr Keating has the qualities of leadership that would make him a successful inheritor of his job.

Other headlines spoke of 'Richardson bid to heal rift'.

On 21 December, Clem Hawke said, 'I can't go yet. Bobby needs me.' But two days later he died. 'He just ran out of breath,' Hawke said. He had flown as frequently as he could to Adelaide in the last weeks of Clem's life. On their final meeting, Clem had drawn from his old hand a gold signet ring and pressed it into his son's palm. Hawke slipped it on his little finger. He found the ring brought Clem's presence to him, and was a comfort in the harsh times that lay ahead.

The year 1990 had been a year of triumphs and setbacks: Labor had won an election against the odds and the ALP national conference had been a huge success, thanks largely to the efforts of Kim Beazley, who was as excellent in Transport and Communications as he had been in Defence. Against the gnashing teeth of his friend, Keating, for whom telecommunications had become a new passion, Beazley developed policies for opening the Australian telecommunications industry to competition – Keating wanted a much more dramatic scheme – and for the sale of Australian Airlines and 49 per cent of Qantas. In the Prime Minister's office, Beazley debated his telecommunications policy against the one Keating had designed, with Hawke adjudicating. Having won Hawke's endorsement, Beazley won Cabinet approval, then had both policies accepted by the national conference and steered them through the House and the Senate. The sale of a new telecommunications licence (and of the airlines) added $5 billion to the government's coffers and took place without a single day lost from industrial action by the telecommunications unions. But for each silver lining there was a cloud. There had been a dreadful brawl in Cabinet about telecommunications – Keating flung his pencil on the table, swore at his colleagues and stalked out, Robert Ray jeering after him, 'Spit the dummy' (Jack Lang had always said if you couldn't win a debate, then wreck it) – and the Treasurer's behaviour in Cabinet was so widely reported it overshadowed the reform itself. The Liberal Party was now united. And the government won scant plaudits for airline privatisation, although this had entailed the Herculean task of overturning a venerable plank in the party platform and would save taxpayers hundreds of millions of dollars.

Above all, the economic downturn now darkened everything: the vaunted 1.6 million new jobs of one year earlier had evaporated and unemployment was approaching 10 per cent. Businesses were going bankrupt; families were losing their houses. The doyen of the gallery, Laurie Oakes, had an article in the Christmas issue of the *Bulletin* with the double-entendre headline, 'Wanted: a new tenor'.

Meanwhile 100 000 armed men and women had already arrived in the Persian Gulf, ready to fight the first great conventional desert war since Rommel and El Alamein.

TWENTY-NINE

A S THE NEW YEAR BEGAN, Saddam released all his hostages. He was still plundering Kuwait.

Frantic international diplomacy in the first two weeks of January 1991 came to nothing and at 4 p.m. on 16 January, Australian eastern daylight-saving time, the UN deadline expired. War was expected at any moment. The government's popularity sank to 32 per cent, its lowest point ever. People were frightened of a war and about the economy. Melbourne, where the Left was strongest, held a huge 'Save Australia' rally, evocative of the rallies against the Vietnam War. Hawke called a Cabinet meeting to tell his colleagues that hostilities would begin within twenty-four hours. Early next morning the head of Australian forces in the Gulf rang to alert the Prime Minister that the attack would start that day. At 9.50 a.m. President Bush rang Hawke to say that within an hour action would be underway. Hawke then authorised the Australian chief of the defence force, General Gration, to signal to the Australian ships that they were to join operations against Iraq in accordance with Resolution 678. An hour later he called a press conference to remind the nation why, for the first time since 1972, Australian forces were fighting in a foreign land. He finished by saying, 'War is full of terrible uncertainty.' Having praised the serving men and women, he concluded, 'We know they will serve bravely and well, and we hope, above all, that they will return safely home.'

Within hours demonstrators were on the streets and by the weekend there were protest rallies in all the capital cities and many provincial centres. The Anglican and Catholic churches were moderate in their response, but Sir Ronald Wilson, President of the National Assembly of the Uniting Church, declared, 'This is a senseless war. History will condemn us for having allowed national pride and self-interest – although hidden behind fine words about right and wrong – to dictate the course of events.' The general secretary of the Australian Council of Churches, the Reverend Mr David Gill, said the war was 'pure madness with no moral justification ... the most monumental stupidity'.

Failure goes with the job of politics and all great politicians must be unafraid of it. They hold to their own judgment with intransigence, convinced that in the end history will vindicate them. The balance to this is humility, their regret for terrible actions. Hawke had no second thoughts about going to war. He was deeply distressed about the possible loss of young lives.

The CNN version of what was happening in the Gulf was full of hype about the destruction of Saddam's weaponry, but Hawke had intelligence that the television reports were incorrect and Iraq's Scud missiles were still intact. Saddam had let it be known they were equipped with chemical warheads. The next day Iraq launched eight scuds at Israel, none chemically armed. The world held its breath, awaiting the Israeli response – which might, Hawke wrote, 'rupture the coalition by alienating the Arab and Muslim members'. When it was clear that Israel had stalled – temporarily, at least, its policy of massive retaliation – and that the coalition would hold, Hawke recalled parliament in the third week of January.

In half a century of parliamentary debates, those of 21 and 22 January 1991 were among the finest. The parliamentarians spoke with sincerity, thoughtfulness and deep feeling about the violence and turmoil that again confronted a world so recently liberated from the tensions of the Cold War. For once Hawke did not detest the House as a game of charades. He gave his best parliamentary performance, speaking at length, his conviction untainted by point-scoring or rodomontade, unfazed by a group of demonstrators who screamed at him from the Visitors' Gallery. Hugh White recalled, 'The parliamentary atmospherics were remarkable. We in the office were watching the debate *to see how our side voted.*'

Despite Hawke's hours of reassurance to Caucus, there was still no certainty that the Left would support Resolution 678 for Australia to continue in the war. Left and Centre Left support almost collapsed when the Americans asked for twenty-five skin divers to clear mines. White said, 'The Americans were planning a massive amphibious assault by marines on the Kuwaiti coast and there were a lot of mines around. The US doesn't have very good mine countermeasure capacity, but we do.' A few years earlier Saddam had mined the Gulf, endangering ships carrying oil from Iran. Australian divers had cleared the mines with an expertise the American navy noted well.

White said,

> I remember getting a request from the Americans and talking to Robert [Ray], saying, 'Look – they are not just trying this on. This is a serious operational request. They really need our guys.' Robert was persuaded and he took it to Bob who said, 'Yep. OK. We'll send them.' They had to be based on American ships. Just twenty-five divers – but it almost undid the whole deal with the Caucus.

Throughout his speech to parliament, Hawke had stressed the importance of the UN members acting in unison. Hewson, the leader of the Opposition (whom Hawke had invited to accompany him to Gallipoli nine months earlier), strongly supported the Prime Minister's motion, saying,

> that Gallipoli pilgrimage was one of the most moving experiences of my life ... and taught me a lot about my country. Throughout our history we have been a genuinely peaceful people, but we have never been a pacifist people. We have been a proudly independent country, but never a neutral one.

Hewson's response was an enormous relief to the government, which had been concerned that, once again, the Opposition might seek a way to attack Labor as not tough enough on national security.

More than 100 parliamentarians spoke over two days. The most poignant moment came when Gerry Hand, leader of the Left, announced in a shaking voice, 'I support the resolution,' and began to weep.

No vote was needed and only one man, Ted Mack, the Independent member for North Sydney, demanded that Hansard record him as opposed.

The air war in the Gulf concluded quickly and by mid-February the land war was about to begin. There were no Australian casualties. White recalled,

A bizarre situation arose in which it appeared there might be a peace deal on the table, brokered by the Russians, which the Americans weren't prepared to accept. Now this was a fascinating and marvellous study of confusion in policy making: Brent Scowcroft, the President's national security adviser, rang Bob at The Lodge in the middle of the night. They had a conversation which, when Bob recounted it to us half an hour later – at 4 a.m. – just didn't make any sense. I phoned Michael Cook, head of the Office of National Assessment, and told him what Scowcroft had said to the PM. He said, 'What!' So he rang the [United States] National Security Council to say, 'Your boss has just said to my boss ...' and they said, 'What!' And this went round and round in international phone calls – there were no emails in those days – and we all spoke elliptically, because we didn't know who was listening in. It got very confusing. For a while it seemed that the US was putting to us the proposition that they were not going to pay any attention to the possibility of a peace deal, and that even if Saddam said he was now prepared to withdraw, the Americans would expel Iraq from Kuwait anyway. It seemed to us, on good grounds, they were saying, 'Bugger

Saddam: whatever he promises, we're going ahead with the land war.' And what was interesting to me was that Bob was *absolutely* prepared to walk up to these blokes and say: 'No. In that circumstance, you will lose our support.'

Another idea to which Hawke was opposed was 'going on to Baghdad'. First, such an attack would destroy the UN foundation for the war, which in turn would destroy the objective of strengthening the UN. Second, Hawke and his office had made the judgment that invading Iraq would be simply stupid.

'In the end,' White said,

> that was a view shared by Bush, Colin Powell [chairman of the American joint chiefs of staff] and, interestingly, Dick Cheney [American Secretary for Defense]. We discussed in the office the possibility of the US going off on a hay-making expedition to Baghdad and Bob was absolutely clear that we would say, 'We're not with you on that.' For us, the UN concern was more important than the alliance. It's hard to imagine now, because those hopes have been washed away into history.

In the *Bulletin* edition at the end of January, Laurie Oakes, who had been a leader of the press gallery's chorus for a change to Keating, wrote,

> Since hostilities began, Hawke has given some strong media performances. Particularly in his first news conference ... the Prime Minister struck exactly the right note – authoritative, determined, but suitably grave, and obviously affected by the decision ... Gone was the sense of drift which had fed the speculation about a leadership change.

Hawke's speech to parliament, Oakes said,

> was one of the most carefully crafted and persuasively argued of his career ... It was strong, uncompromising – the speech

of a leader ... Keating in contrast, did not bother to break his holiday to attend the final Cabinet briefing before Australians were officially committed to the war – strange, some Caucus members thought, for a man who is deputy Prime Minister and who has leadership ambitions.

The headline of Oakes' piece was 'Keating: our first Gulf casualty?'

On the last day of January, Hawke called Keating in for a further discussion of the leadership, during which they argued over which of them would be able to revive the party's chances at the next election. Hawke's popularity had shot up. He asserted he had a better chance than Keating, who was very unpopular. He pointed out that Hewson was a greenhorn, with little idea of how intense the heat of a national election campaign could be, while he, Hawke, bore the scars from campaigns going back to 1963. Keating asserted Hawke had no chance, whereas he, Keating, might have a chance. Hawke dismissed his argument as delusion. By this stage Hawke considered Keating's desperation for the leadership had made him slightly mad. Keating held a similar view of the protagonist.

The stalemate made one thing certain: Hawke believed his promise to the people to stay on and fight the next election was a matter of honour of a higher order than his promise to Keating made two years earlier in Kirribilli. He could not keep both promises, therefore he would keep the more important one.

Keating was furious. Believing himself to be the energy source that drove the government, the anodic electrode that is gradually devoured, Keating's sense of being used up by the dynamic of the relationship was revealed soon afterwards when he lamented his fate to Paul Kelly, who wrote:

Keating never recovered from the war. He complained later that his support had peaked before Christmas 1990 ... 'The war changed the thinking about my leadership from being an expectation to an act of sedition,' Keating bemoaned.

As 1991 advanced Keating drew his own deadline – a challenge before the winter recess ... [he] was hellbent upon a showdown in the current term.[1]

The trauma for the Labor Party was that it had two leaders in one government. Keating, like Hawke, was convinced in every cell of his body that he was meant to be prime minister, impregnated with the idea of something within himself that he must bring into the light. Like a woman in childbirth, he had no choice in the matter: the man had to give birth to The Man. Or die in the attempt.

Keating's political mentor, Jack Lang, had wired into his protégé the idea that he had to move fast. It seems Keating had developed an image of himself as prime minister by the age of forty-five; his emotions, his intellect, his physical stamina focused on that ideal. When it was denied him in 1988, as with an athlete denied the race for which he has trained for a lifetime, a sense of debilitation began to engulf him. But in 1991, as distinct from 1988, there was a significant difference. Keating had a skilled and eager new coach. He had Graham Richardson. It was Richardson who would tell Keating and his team when to rush forward, when to pause, when to strive again. Many months, perhaps years earlier, Keating had told Richardson about the Kirribilli agreement, one of a number of people Keating told. It was something Richardson was keeping in reserve, to be used at the right moment.

Keating had to act before winter 1991, otherwise he would have to frame and sell the next Budget, be Treasurer for another year with an economy in deep recession for which he was much to blame.

The war in the Gulf meanwhile was moving swiftly to a UN victory. By 28 February it was over, but not before Saddam had ordered all Kuwait's oil wells set on fire. Huge, pungent black clouds billowed for weeks from the well heads as millions of tonnes of oil burned. All of Kuwait and some neighbouring countries became covered in oily black dust, as if hell had opened its terrible mouth and roared from beneath the earth. With his air force vanished and his army in tatters, President Saddam Hussein announced a week of jubilation to celebrate his amazing and blessed victory over the United States and the rest of the world. Truly, he declared, Almighty God, The Beneficent, The Merciful, had shone His face upon him.

Hawke remarked that God must be very confused, since He was known to be fighting on the UN side as well.

With the war over, the Prime Minister refocused his attention on the economic reforms with which he hoped to crown his fourth term in office.

In July 1990, in a speech to the Press Club, Hawke had launched a concept titled 'New Federalism'. He wanted to establish in the public's mind how inefficient and conflicted Australia was in its duplication of services and regulations. He told the gathered journalists,

> Schools in different states have different minimum starting ages, and different patterns of [primary and secondary] schooling ... different curricula and different ways of assessing Year 12 students ... Lawyers and doctors and other professionals may have qualifications from the best universities ... skilled tradesmen may have the finest on-the-job experience – but to work outside their home state they need a licence from a state licensing board.

The rail system was not integrated, there were six different sizes of loading gauge, ten different engineering standards for basic rail trade, products in one state needed relabelling to be sold in another, daylight saving started on one date in one state and another elsewhere, and so on and on in knots of red tape. In some states, margarine could only be sold in round tubs; in others, only in rectangular. There was not even a national electricity grid. There was no national water plan, or even a plan for managing the waters of the Murray–Darling basin, which Hawke had proposed before the 1990 election. He described much of the economy as 'Balkanised', but because of the federal system there was little his government could change without the agreement of the states.

The idea for reform had been presented to him by Mike Codd, the head of the Prime Minister and Cabinet Department, who had mulled over Commonwealth–state relations for more than twenty years (as had Hawke who, in his 1979 Boyer Lectures, had proposed abolishing the states).

Codd had been unable to snag the interest of John Gorton, Bill McMahon, Gough Whitlam or Malcolm Fraser in a reform that to those outside politics appears both necessary and virtuous. But good public policy and good politics do not necessarily mate, especially when good public policy may cause the government to lose the next election. The kilometres of red tape created jobs and power, some in the Commonwealth, most in the states. The Commonwealth would have to give up a portion of its power to win the states' agreement to change. This meant that federal parliamentarians – backbenchers, mostly – would be deprived of the privilege of announcing new playgrounds or swimming pools in their electorates and having their photographs in the local newspapers. In this lay danger for Hawke: the government was unpopular, unemployment was rising, and the backbenchers were nervous. Any move that would weaken their local appeal and thus reduce their chances for re-election could panic them.

Codd first put the proposition of Commonwealth–state reform to Hawke in 1987, on the Sunday after the election.

> Bob was attracted to it, and so was the political side of his office [but] he got back to me a week or two later to say that having talked it through with his colleagues it was not a possibility in this term of government. There was too much else going on that would be difficult for the Labor Party to come to terms with – uranium mining was one of the problems – and I should bring it back to him at a more appropriate time.

Codd believed that Keating and Button had opposed the idea. His paper sat in a drawer for three more years, until the Sunday after the 1990 election. 'And this time Bob said, "Right. We're going to do this!" And away we went.'

A Commonwealth–state steering committee was set up to write proposals for an initial Special Premiers' Conference to be held at the end of October 1990 in Brisbane.

Nick Greiner, Premier of New South Wales, recalled his first Premiers' Conference, in 1988, as 'old nonsense'. He said,

> We – premiers and our Treasurers – all stayed at the Hyatt Hotel in Canberra and in the middle of the night someone from the Commonwealth would put a letter under your door, telling you what you were being offered. And I remember [Premier] Robin Gray from Tasmania, who was a stirrer, saying to me next morning, 'Why don't you threaten to walk out? That will get Hawkey going.' So I made the first statement and said, 'Well, if this is all we get, Prime Minister, we may as well go home now.' Bob had a look on his face that said, *'Who is this kid?* He's only just arrived and he's carrying on.' Anyway, we had the usual toing and froing – but the reality was that Commonwealth–state relations were a joke. There was no single direction, no notion of what was good for the nation. We'd argue over money and at the end we'd come out and say, 'Well, the Commonwealth won't give us enough, so we're going to have to put up taxes.' We could tax cigarettes and stuff. Whichever party you were in there was a standard state response: *blame Canberra*. It was completely dysfunctional, both financially, and in health and education. To this day [late 2009] the Commonwealth has 300 people in Canberra playing around with education, but they run no schools at all. There was duplication – even triplication, when local councils got involved.

Since World War II the Commonwealth had collected all major taxes – personal income tax and business tax – and had the money. It called the tune. But the conditions it imposed on the states in 'tied grants' made it difficult, even impossible, for the states to manage themselves financially.

By 1990 Greiner was the only non-Labor premier and unusual in that he was not a knee-jerk decentralist. 'I was actually interested in getting national outcomes,' he said. 'And Bob was not the normal, centralist Labor prime minister, but interested in getting a workable compromise. Most of the Labor premiers would go along with Bob, if I did. So there was a unique opportunity for reform.' The electoral cycle was also benevolent, for aside from some local councils, there was no election due anywhere in Australia for at least eighteen months. Greiner said, 'I thought, and I'm sure Bob thought, "The bloody Federation is going to be 100 years old in 2000 and the notion that you don't change the way we manage ourselves is bizarre."'

Hawke established a secretariat of federal public servants, each with a state counterpart, led by Helen Williams from his department. Slender and softly spoken, with an aura of gentle, civilised wisdom, Williams was one of Australia's most outstanding bureaucrats. An economist, she was the first woman, aside from typists, to be employed in Treasury and the first to break the glass ceiling and become a departmental head (Education, in 1985). Greiner recalled,

> There was a group of public servants that developed a very unusual camaraderie. They all felt, 'Gee – we're driving some real reform.' They thought it was fantastic that they were being given a chance to do something new and different, rather than just incrementally changing things, the way things normally change.

The group called themselves the Piglets, because they were the offspring of the HOGs, the heads of government: Prime Minister, premiers and Treasurers. Williams recalled that before the Brisbane conference, 'There was a buzz in the air, there was excitement. We really felt there was a different way of working together, a different partnership, a real window of opportunity that we all felt we could grab.'

Codd said,

> What was to be put at the conference was quite wide-ranging and the scope for the premiers to get bogged down in one issue or another was significant. How to manage the meeting was a huge challenge. Kevin Rudd was advising Wayne Goss [Queensland's Premier] and Gary Sturgess was Nick Greiner's adviser.

Sturgess was another outstandingly effective state-level public servant, known for his forceful personality, verve and drive. Some of the premiers disliked what they saw as his arrogance, condescending airs and self-appointed role as policy savant. Codd said,

> I knew Rudd and Sturgess, and I knew they would want to put their own views forward. They were keen and enthusiastic for something to be done, but they wanted their own model. I could see it would end up in turgid debate. So I actually drafted a press release before the meeting and suggested to Bob that he have a private dinner with just the premiers, at which he would give them each a copy of the press release and try to get their agreement to it before the meeting even started. And that's what happened. The advisers were furious.

Another person who was at least miffed was Paul Keating, who had not been included in the dinner the night before. His discomfit at the press conference when the joint communiqué was announced was not reported by the media. Codd said, 'But you could see it in his body language.'

The conference was a huge success. There was progress on a wide front, from uniform vehicle regulation to an intergovernmental agreement on the environment. At the press conference, Greiner said it was 'the most constructive thing that I've done in two and three-quarter years as premier'.

The Victorian premier, Joan Kirner, a Centre Left politician who did not much care for Hawke, said, 'May I ... Prime Minister, again thank you for having the vision and the leadership and the patience to enable this conference to happen.'

The states were delighted that, almost immediately, they would be getting a new income stream, thanks to a correction of 'vertical fiscal imbalance'. This is the gap between the money raised by the states and what they spend. In his initial announcement of his New Federalism in July 1990, Hawke had announced that the Commonwealth, as a gesture of good faith towards New Federalism, would forgo bank account debits tax to the states. The Brisbane conference confirmed it, adding \$385 million to state revenues. Keating had worked with Hawke on the vertical fiscal imbalance proposal, but by the time of the Brisbane conference, Codd noticed, especially at the press conference, 'Keating was a reluctant participant.'

Like all heads of the Prime Minister and Cabinet Department, Codd had a good political eye. He recognised then or soon afterwards that Keating could engineer from these proposals a battle favourable to himself in his struggle against Hawke.

In the same press conference, Nick Greiner warned, 'The Empire will strike back.' He was referring to the various state authorities that controlled utilities: water and electricity, for example. 'I was trying to make the point that all the people whose power was going to be affected if you moved to a national approach were not going to just roll over to have their tummies tickled,' he said.

Nevertheless the mood was almost euphoric and two further special conferences were scheduled for mid-1991 and late 1991 to consolidate progress. New Federalism had a new name and status: the Council of Australian Governments, COAG.

Besides his planned reforms of Commonwealth–state relations, which – as events were to show – became, mostly, casualties in the war of succession, Hawke had a second major reform for his fourth term. More than two years earlier, in October 1989, Ross Garnaut, by then a professor at the Australian National

University, had completed a report Hawke had commissioned from him. The full title was *A Report for the Prime Minister and the Minister for Foreign Affairs and Trade: Australia and the North-east Asian Ascendancy.* Garnaut had prepared it with the assistance of another very highly respected Australian National University economist, Dr Peter Drysdale. Their research was a prescient analysis of where the countries of north-east Asia, China in particular, would be in the future, and how their arousal after centuries of economic slumber would affect Australia. But because the economy was 'a bloody runaway beast' in 1989, because an election would be held in 1990 and because there was a war in 1991, Hawke kept the report, and policy recommendations based on it, under wraps until he had some clear air. He chaired the Structural Adjustment Committee (SAC) that, taking the report as its premise, worked out policy options for the nation. The report established Garnaut as the *éminence grise* of Australia's economic reform.

On 12 March 1991, as soon as Saddam was off the front pages, Hawke made an economic statement, based on Garnaut's and the SAC's work, that was, arguably, the most important of his term in office. Called 'Building a Competitive Australia', it recommended further dismantling of Australian protectionism to ready the country for the challenge of north-east Asia rising. Back in 1984, after conferring with Hawke and Treasury, John Button had put an end to protectionism in the motor vehicle industry and since then quotas on steel imports, white goods and some heavy engineering products had been removed. Hawke's March statement announced a brave new Australia of free trade. John Hyde, the Liberal intellectual, described it as 'an impeccable statement of economic principle'.[2]

Hawke, reaffirming his government's intention to open the Australian economy to the world, told parliament:

> The most powerful spur to greater competitiveness is further tariff reduction. Tariffs have been one of the abiding features of the Australian economy. Since Federation . . . the supposed

virtues of this protection became deeply embedded in the psyche of the nation. But what was the result? Inefficient industries that could not compete overseas. And higher prices for consumers, and higher costs.

Hawke believed the new policy would give body to his announcement a few months earlier, at the launch of the 1990 election campaign, that Australia should become 'the clever country', a phrase John Dawkins had coined.

Next day Ross Gittins, a respected economic commentator, wrote in the *Sydney Morning Herald*,

> In the depths of this recession, Bob Hawke has not only resisted the temptation to reverse the phased tariff reductions he began in 1988, he has extended and hastened them. Rightly or wrongly – I think rightly – the government is sticking to its guns.

Hewson, who agreed with the policy, tried to deflect interest in it and stir up trouble by asserting on 14 March that there was a 'leadership vacuum' in the federal government. It was known that Richardson had opposed Hawke in Cabinet over the statement.

On 15 March, Peter Hartcher, political commentator for the *Sydney Morning Herald*, wrote,

> the [decision] to cut industry protection in a single, breathtaking sweep ... was the most dramatic cut in protection that any Australian government has made ... Standard political theory would dictate that a government in the grips of a self-made recession, lagging in the opinion polls, and periodically unsettled by the prospect of a leadership challenge, should not take such profoundly controversial and potentially divisive decisions. But it is. Is this evidence of a wimpy government? Does it expose a weak-kneed Prime Minister? Does it demonstrate a leadership vacuum? No. It suggests a

government which, despite eight tiring years in office, is well able to make fundamental and hugely controversial decisions about the restructuring of the economy, even at the potential expense of a large loss of Labor's electoral support.

Paul Kelly, at this time a Keating supporter, later described the statement as 'an historic milestone ... [Hawke] demolished the edifice of Protection, the cornerstone of the post-federation Settlement. It is this decision, providing it sticks, which will guarantee that the direction of the 1990s maintains the course launched in the 1980s.' Kelly added, 'Hawke's announcement effectively terminated Australia's century of Protection ... [it] confirms the transformation in politics and economics which his government launched in the 1980s.'[3]

The March 1991 policy statement did stick. It is difficult to overstate its importance, for it transformed Australia's identity: as the country saw itself, as it was seen in the region, as it behaved in the world. Garnaut had recommended, and Hawke fore-shadowed, among other things: faster cuts in protection, more Asian investment, new foreign-financed ports, foreign competition on shipping routes, complete aviation deregulation, more emphasis on age, skill and education in the immigration program, and compulsory Asian languages and history courses in schools. Garnaut's thesis was that closer economic integration between Australia and the Asian region would pay huge export dividends in primary products, secondary processing, and in services. Time proved him correct. Hawke's acceptance of Garnaut's work and the 'Building a Competitive Australia' statement of March 1991 became granite in the foundation of a national prosperity that has stretched almost two decades into the twenty-first century. Garnaut had no part in drawing up the statement and by now was outside the policy-making loop; he remarked with pleasure that the changes were bigger than the end of the British Corn Laws that had earned Peel and Cobden a dozen pages in high school history books. Hawke said, 'The Keating camp and the press gallery were saying I'd run out of puff for a fourth term.

The March statement ['Building a Competitive Australia'] proves
that is crap.'

In 2010 John Bowan remarked,

> Hawke is really the unsung hero of Australia's strong economy
> today, of how well we've come through the global financial
> crisis. It was his idea to establish a China trade, and to dis-
> mantle protectionism so that trade with Asia could flourish.

By 2019 all sides of politics accepted that Australia's unique
prosperity came thanks to March 1991. Support by successive
Liberal leaders, especially John Howard, was critical to this
golden era.

Meanwhile, back in the 1990s Hawke had another idea for
increasing national wealth – but politically it was radioactive.
He took seriously the environmentalist argument that humanity
has only one home, which must be husbanded. He was aware
that the storage of nuclear waste from power plants, weapons
and medicinal manufacture, especially in Europe and the former
Soviet Union, potentially endangered the planet. At the 1990
election he had announced that as part of being 'the clever
country' Australia would establish a network of Co-operative
Research Centres. This idea had come from Professor Ralph
Slatyer, the chief scientist, a friend from Hawke's school days at
Perth Modern. Hawke knew he could trust Slatyer with a delicate undertaking: the Prime Minister believed that Australia had
the safest geological areas in the world for the long-term storage
of nuclear waste. He asked Slatyer to confirm their existence,
and that they were far from centres of population. Hawke's idea
was that Australia could become the world's guardian of nuclear
waste – for a price. Nations storing waste in Australia would have
to pay rent and this rent could be an abundant national income.
His estimate, confirmed by Slatyer's figures on the quantity of
waste in storage and its annual increase, was hundreds of millions of dollars annually. It would be hypothecated for education
and health in Indigenous communities, and for environmental

protection. Slatyer reported back in 1991 that large areas of northern Western Australia and the Northern Territory were indeed so geologically stable and far from human habitation they would be ideally suited. Thanks to geology, remoteness and the political stability of Australia, these areas offered the safest planetary option for storing nuclear waste. The problem was emotional: the very people who proclaimed the importance of 'one world', when discreetly sounded out, reverted noisily to 'my backyard'. Environmental movement leaders warned Hawke that activists would instantly respond to his suggestion as an immoral outrage. From then until his final years of life he quietly proposed it to ministers, shadow ministers and business groups, but no government, state or federal, has yet been willing to face the cannonade of hysteria that discussion of the idea will attract. Nuclear waste increases internationally year by year while the problem of long-term safe storage remains. But in February 2010, at a meeting of the American Association for the Advancement of Science in California, Finland announced that in 2020 it would open a deep geological repository for the disposal of spent nuclear fuel. Sweden announced it would do the same in 2023. European experts at the conference said, 'A growing consensus both in Europe and in other parts of the world is that deep geological disposal is the most appropriate solution for long-term management of spent fuel, high level waste, and other long-lived radioactive wastes.'

With the foreign war over and the sailors safely home, the civil war, which had been abandoned for the duration of hostilities in the Gulf, began heating up again.

Keating's generals, especially John Dawkins and Gary Punch from the New South Wales Right, had been working both the ministry and the backbench as hard as they could, but had been unable to gain enough numbers for a successful Keating challenge. Richardson was playing a duplicitous game. Anger and resentment had destroyed his affection for Hawke but he pretended to the Prime Minister to have recovered from his shock over the Communications and Defence jobs and was still Hawke's admirer. To others he presented himself as a man with only the welfare of the government at heart. Meanwhile, master tactician that he was, he bided his time on how to use the Kirribilli agreement against Hawke. Richardson had chosen for himself and would successfully fill the role of Judas.

In itself, he saw the political agreement reached at Kirribilli House in November 1988 as a piece of straw. But he recognised that in skilful hands it could be fashioned into a length of iron. It could become a bar with which to beat the Prime Minister over the head, and a lever to raise Keating to the moral high ground.

Having talked itself into the belief that the Prime Minister was lacking courage, the Keating camp still hoped to scare Hawke out of office. Peter Walsh, who had often found Hawke annoying for one reason or another, although he considered him the best prime minister of his political lifetime, had nicknamed him in a fit of pique, 'Old Jellyback'. This estimation of Hawke's strength of character was the one to which his enemies clung. Few understood that Hawke's emotional softness, his tendency to tears, his habit – maddening to staff and colleagues – of wanting to listen to the stories of ordinary Australians, was the saving balance in his character, a humility without which his alpha-male swagger would have made him unbearable. The electorate had come to admire him for being a leader unafraid of showing tender feelings. As Hazel said publicly several times, people respected a man who had the strength to cry.

While in Canberra internal Labor affairs were bad, in the west they were atrocious. A Royal Commission was underway to investigate the doings of WA Inc., the nexus between the state government and New Capitalists. Scandalous behaviour was being reported on a weekly, sometimes daily, basis. Respect for Labor in Western Australia plummeted, while the behaviour of its former leader, Brian Burke, once premier, now ambassador to Ireland and the Holy See, cast a garish light east, north and south onto the whole of the ALP and especially the Prime

Minister, who had given him the job and continued to stand by him. In the midst of the WA Inc. drama, Hawke blundered. On Thursday, 11 April 1991, he gave a woeful performance in parliament when questioned about allegations made by a corrupt businessman, Laurie Connell. Some years earlier Hawke had met and instantly disliked Connell, his sentiment confirmed when a racehorse trainer told him of Connell's cunning illegalities in the racing industry. Hawke was annoyed and embarrassed when Connell unexpectedly joined a West Australian fishing trip and was photographed in a dinghy with him. Hawke warned Premier Brian Burke to keep away from Connell.

While the Prime Minister had judged Connell accurately, he showed lamentable judgment about Burke, whose charm with his Labor colleagues and even non-Labor people had the potency of an opiate. There was something ineffably beguiling about Burke. Kim Beazley, a man incapable of dishonesty himself, maintained affection for him decades after he was proven crooked and sent to prison. In the early 1980s Hawke wanted Burke to transfer to federal politics, believing he would be a fine future minister. On Burke's advice, and against his own wishes and instinct, in 1984 Hawke ditched legislation that would benefit Indigenous people in Western Australia. This action caused a bitter rupture with his son, Stephen, who was devoting his life to improving the lives of Indigenous people. When in 1987 Burke asked for a grace and favour appointment as ambassador to Ireland and the Holy See, Hawke obliged him, asking Hayden, who was still Foreign minister, to arrange it.

Burke told Connell what the Prime Minister thought of him, confirming what Connell already guessed. In the Royal Commission, Connell found his moment for revenge: he claimed Hawke had promised to remove the gold tax in exchange for a $250000 donation to the Labor Party. It was a straight lie. Hawke had made no such promise. In fact, the government's decision on the tax was made weeks in advance of a lunch with Connell. Hawke's answer about the dates of meetings and decisions was based on misinformation provided by his new chief of staff, Dennis Richardson. Hawke had to return to the Chamber to correct himself. This was the most embarrassing moment of his parliamentary career. It became excruciating when Keating, fully versed in the issue, in which he had taken an interest for more than a decade, leapt to the Prime Minister's defence with dazzling acumen. 'Who taxed the gold industry?' Keating shouted.

> Who removed the exemption [from tax]? The Government! Who did not? The Opposition! The question is: why? Why did those opposite not remove the exemption? We know, but we are waiting for their answer. Who was contributing to them? Who was so successful in their contribution as to keep them loyal to their cause ... It is very interesting to get this question [from the leader of the National Party]. The most proven corrupt party in this country is the National Party of Australia ... The proven corrupt party. Half of the former Queensland Cabinet is in gaol. And we have the Leader of the National Party up asking questions about issues of propriety. Do not make us laugh![4]

On the same day the unemployment figures were announced: 9.2 per cent. Caucus was reported to be feeling helpless, hopeless and guilty.

Then things got worse.

A short time later that day Hawke had to enter the Chamber a second time to explain that he had again given incorrect information about the gold tax dates. He apologised and asked the House's indulgence. Dennis Richardson offered his resignation. Hawke refused to accept it. Hewson launched a censure motion against Hawke, referring to 'a stench' about the government and accusing him of lack of leadership. The government made barely a token of defence and allowed Hewson's motion to be defeated on party lines. That weekend in a state by-election in Western Australia Labor's primary vote dropped 30 per cent.

The incident – short, sharp and humiliating – dramatically raised Keating's stocks in the ministry and the Caucus. Laurie Oakes wrote in the *Bulletin*,

> the admiration for Keating's brilliance in single-handedly turning the issue back on the coalition is just about universal. Without Keating's parliamentary skills, his toughness, his aggression, his cold gunfighter's nerve, the government would have been routed and every MP ... knows it.

John Howard, rather conveniently for Hawke, riposted that Keating was so unpopular 'you can't give him away'. It was an autumn of miseries for the government. By mid-May, Australia's big banks were forced to admit they were reaping the whirlwind of their profligacy. Westpac and the National Australia Bank announced a combined total of $10 billion in bad debts.

On 24 May 1991, Bob Hogg, the ALP national secretary, advised Hawke to organise a transition to Keating. He told Paul Kelly,

> You can't win if the party's divided. [Keating's] challenge, obviously, wasn't going away and would only get worse ...
> I think Hawke was beyond the point of electability. In terms of getting energy, drive and unity in government, I just don't think it was possible under Hawke.[5]

During their face-to-face conversation Hawke told Hogg his analysis and judgment were wrong. Hogg said in 2009, 'The one regret that I ever had was that I succumbed to the view that on balance it was better to go with Keating. But by that time, the party was in a mess.'

Ground down by the pressure from Keating's camp and disheartened by the recession, Hogg and many others in the party and the Caucus had reached a point of solipsism: they had forgotten that their enemy was the Opposition, and that it was the Opposition's actions, and the skills of its leader John Hewson (who had replaced Andrew Peacock after the 1990 election loss), which would be a determining factor in the next election. The election was two years away, time in which the economy would come out of recession and return to growth. Hawke believed that Hewson had no chance of connecting with the Australian electorate: he was too fast, too impatient for change, too much the blue-eyed hitman. He had been talking since his election as leader of the Liberal Party about a consumption tax and lower income taxes. But he was too inexperienced, Hawke believed, in how difficult it is to straighten the bent timber of humanity to accept the shape of a new idea. The Prime Minister believed that if Hewson went to the electorate with his consumption tax package, he would cause lots of excitement and praise in the media and be slaughtered in the electorate. Keating bore scars from 1985 to show how dangerous it was to handle a consumption tax.

Within days of Hogg's visit to Hawke, Keating decided he could wait no longer: to do so would saddle him with formulating the 1991/92 Budget – and as he had warned Hawke earlier, the job and his frustrations were driving him 'ga-ga'.

Trying to scare Hawke out of his job had proved ineffective, so by agreement with Keating and the other leaders of his camp, on 29 May 1991 Graham Richardson visited the Prime Minister to lie to him that he was *shocked. Shocked!* He had just learned of the Kirribilli agreement. Therefore, Keating would challenge for the leadership.

Keating, as he had promised he would if it ever came to this, personally called on Hawke on the evening of 30 May to tell him he was about to challenge.

Keating's supporters had already briefed Laurie Oakes on the Kirribilli pact and on the six o'clock news of 30 May, Oakes broke the story on Channel Nine. It was presented as a scandal: the fate of the nation decided in secret by the Prime Minister behind closed doors. The scandal was confected, but the crisis was real.

The press gallery and the general news media turned on the Prime Minister with hectic glee. There was a frenzy of indignation in the press, on television and in talkback radio. In parliament Andrew Peacock, harking back to the ads 'a vote for Hawke is a vote for Keating', shouted at the Prime Minister, 'I was the victim of your lie!' Hawke, actually, had not lied to the electorate; having promised the people he would stay on and fight the 1993 election, that is what he was committed to do. The media chose not to point this out but instead went into uproar over Sir Peter Abeles being Hawke's witness.

This was poker for the highest stakes, and there were no options but to raise or fold. Keating had tried 'call' in his earlier moves against Hawke. In big poker, calling is for wimps.

Unknown to everyone except a few of their staff, both men were preparing to fold. Keating was negotiating to buy a piggery. For a man who described himself, and is, at heart an aesthete, a piggery was a curious choice. Life was not imitating art, but rather the old north England saying, 'Where there's muck there's brass.' Keating had studied the international pork and bacon markets with the intensity he brought to all his hobbies and was confident his investment would provide a lucrative retirement income. His love of art, architecture, music and his family would sustain his soul. Meanwhile Hawke, with the help of Sir Peter Abeles' secretary, Joy Annan, was hunting for a house to buy in Sydney. The Hawke family home in Melbourne had long since been sold, the income used to help the three children buy their own houses. Hawke had no more than a hazy idea about what he would do after politics, but having spent forty years as an interviewee, he fancied turning the tables and being an interviewer himself. He was as unsuited to this as Keating was to pig farming, an indication that both men, after a lifetime in politics, really did not know what to do next. The horrible anomie that overcomes old soldiers loomed at them. In politics, happiness comes from the knowledge that one has made the lives of others better than they were, but this is very difficult to achieve and to maintain. As the saying goes, most political careers end in tears.

From the end of the Gulf War to the end of the Hawke–Keating war, there were months of tears in the party.

In the Keating camp there was no political advantage or desire to resist the reforms of 'Building a Competitive Australia'. But Keating had much to gain in backbench support by rebuffing its close relative, Hawke's New Federalism (COAG) reforms.

By the beginning of June the government was 18 percentage points behind the Coalition in the polls and Keating's supporters were stressing to journalists 'the stability of Mr Keating's private life and his commitment to his family'. (There was a sad irony to this: whereas life in The Lodge had strengthened Hawke and Hazel's partnership, and brought Hazel the happiest years of her married life, the Keating marriage began to disintegrate from the time they moved in. A former staffer said, 'We knew there was something wrong at home, but we never knew what it was.')

Keating challenged Hawke on 3 June 1991. That morning Max Walsh predicted in the *Sydney Morning Herald* that Hawke would win, but the government's great problem would be in drawing up and selling a Budget without Keating. The Treasury bureaucracy was at its weakest in decades. Walsh wrote,

Tony Cole would not be heading up the department at this stage of his career had he not served as a personal economic adviser to Paul Keating. The combination of a massive brain drain out of Treasury to the private sector [many of the best and brightest had gone to merchant banks] ... and the premature death of Dr Chris Higgins ... saw Cole installed by Keating. The intellectual firepower of Treasury may still be high but this is, without doubt the most inexperienced team it has ever fielded for a Budget ... Keating has demonstrated quite remarkable marketing skills, especially in enlisting the support of the Canberra press gallery, in selling his economic policies. His successor will not exert the same seductive charm ... there is simply nobody, within Labor ranks, who has Keating's chutzpah, who can tell an audience black is white and have half of them believing it.

Walsh's pronouncement was both shrewd and prophetic.

Hawke defeated Keating 66 votes to 44. Keating resigned as Treasurer and went to the backbench, declaring he had 'only one shot in the locker'. Many, including Hawke, believed Keating had folded. But Richardson, when asked by journalists about Keating's vote, muttered it was 'enough'. This cryptic comment lay uninterpreted for what it was in the Hawke camp, certainly by Hawke, whose optimism bore him up to a cloud of belief that he had prevailed. But Keating had not folded. 'Enough' meant enough for a second challenge for which he would gamble his bottom dollar. It was: make the government unworkable.

As soon as the challenge was lost, the government and Hawke leapt in the polls. Hawke led Hewson by 9 percentage points, but the Opposition was still well ahead of Labor.

A fortnight later there was an excruciating Cabinet meeting over further mining at Coronation Hill in the Northern Territory. The Australian Mining Industry Council (AMIC) had been running a campaign of misinformation and intimidation about the value of mining at Coronation Hill and the worthlessness of the local Jawoyn people's beliefs about disturbing the earth spirit that ruled the area. John Hewson and the Opposition loudly embraced the AMIC's assertions. In Cabinet, Hawke, alone, opposed them, on the grounds it was discriminatory to Jawoyn beliefs about the spirit, Bula. To simply dismiss them was racist, he said. He accused his ministry of rank hypocrisy – able to accept, and some to believe, in Christian metaphysics (the virgin birth, the resurrection, the holy trinity) – but not to allow Indigenous people credence for their metaphysics. 'There's no doubt,' he said, 'that calling them hypocrites upset quite a few. But I believed so profoundly in the principle I didn't give a bugger if they were embarrassed.' For five and a half hours the Cabinet argued, Hawke vehement from the outset. Richardson and the economic ministers were equally vehement in their opposition. The meeting ended in acrimonious fatigue, a sullen Cabinet falling in behind the leader. This was the first time an Australian government had rejected a mining venture through respect for Indigenous belief.

Next day there was outrage in the mining community and news media. Richardson told anyone who would listen that he had talked to the Aboriginal elders at Coronation Hill and Bula was 'Bula-shit'. He intimated to selected journalists that Hawke's Cabinet performance was the 'worst'. Hawke was very proud of it. He had argued on principles he had held to throughout his life: tolerance for other beliefs and abhorrence for all forms of racism.

Richardson, Punch, Dawkins and others meanwhile kept themselves busy blackguarding the Prime Minister to the media, to the unconverted within the Caucus and party branches, and to business. The most favoured – Kerry Packer, for example – were quietly informed there would be a second Keating challenge.

By now the news media was fully engaged as a player in the leadership struggle. As Max Walsh had pointed out in the *Sydney Morning Herald* on the day of the challenge,

> Rupert [Murdoch] now controls, thanks to Paul Keating, most of the Australian newspaper market. So it was hardly surprising to see his paper enthusiastically endorsing Keating over the weekend. Should they continue to push the Keating cause over the next 18 months or so this will eat at the morale of the Government.

There was, perhaps, a personal element at play. Notwithstanding that Murdoch and Abeles were friends, Hawke had felt an aversion to Murdoch from their first meeting, in the 1960s. From time to time Abeles tried to form a bridge between them, without success. But Keating and Murdoch enjoyed each other's company.

On the morning of the challenge, the *Age* began its editorial, 'We will say it at once, and say it clearly. Today's climactic Caucus meeting in Canberra ought to elect Paul Keating to replace Bob Hawke as Prime Minister of Australia.' But the *Age* did not say it once. It said it three times, for it also ran two pro-Keating articles, one by Michelle Grattan, its Canberra bureau chief, and one by its business and finance commentator, Glenda Korporaal. The next morning it pontificated that Caucus had been guilty of a 'tragic mistake'.

The *Australian* of 5 June ran an article by Richard Farmer, one of the few Hawke supporters, who wrote that the press campaign was similar to that by the press barons Lords Rothermere and Beaverbrook against British Prime Minister Stanley Baldwin in 1928. Baldwin described their methods, Farmer recorded,

> [as] direct falsehood, misrepresentation, half-truths, the alteration of the speaker's meaning by publishing a sentence apart from its context ... this contest is not a contest as to whom is to lead the party, but as to who is to appoint the leader of the party.

He remarked, 'The journalists in the era of Hawke are trying just as hard to be kingmakers as the proprietors in the age of Baldwin.'

On 18 June, Sam Lipski wrote in the *Bulletin*,

> the Press displayed naked triumphalism about its perceived role as would-be kingmakers before [Keating's challenge] and a quantum leap in fury afterwards when the majority of the caucus ignored its 'advice'. The rush to judgment undoubtedly affected the fairness of reporting – against Hawke, for Keating ... [journalists] have made it clear they will continue to promote [Keating's] candidacy until they have their way or until their hero chooses the Paris option.

The ALP National Conference was scheduled for the very end of June, in Hobart. Keating's supporters hoped, and were whispering to all and sundry, that Hawke would take this chance to fold.

Instead, Hawke raised.

Always at his most determined when under pressure, his address to the conference was among the great fighting speeches of his career. He spoke of his forty-five years of membership of the party and how he had been nourished throughout by 'steadfast commitment to its fundamental goal – the welfare of the Australian people'. He argued that the Opposition's proposed consumption tax would be 'the most concerted attack in the history of this nation on the living standards of the poor, the underprivileged, the aged and low- and middle-income families'. It would, he said, 'pay the rich by slugging the poor'. He concluded: 'That is why I am determined, delegates, to work to the limit of my capacity for a fifth Labor victory in 1993.'

He was talking to a dispirited audience. Delegates from Western Australia, Victoria, South Australia and Tasmania knew their state governments were facing defeat at the polls. And privately, Hawke had to confront a deep sadness. Jean Sinclair had been his secretary and confidante/lover since 1973 – and was the one member of his staff whom Hazel had always disliked. The low pay at the ACTU had not been an issue, since Mrs Sinclair had private wealth. She and her husband, Professor Angus Sinclair, lived in a large house in East Melbourne, where Hawke would call in for a drink or dinner with them after work. She was an economics graduate, English-born, with English restraint and a merry sense of humour. By her late fifties she had changed little in appearance – still slim, with a pixie face and long, straight sherry-coloured hair that she wore up. She dressed in quietly expensive clothes. Earlier in the year she had told Hawke she had cancer and needed time off for treatment. She was back at work for the conference, attired for the cold in long dark skirts. Hawke asked how her treatment was progressing. For answer she drew her skirt aside to reveal a hugely swollen limb. 'It was an elephant's leg!' Hawke lamented. Her doctors had advised her, she said, that she had three months to live. Discreet to the end, she was not telling colleagues. Hawke was grief-stricken but respected her wish not to speak about her approaching death in the office. Nor could he release his grief at home. Hazel, by temperament spontaneously kind, compassionate and nurturing, drew the line at Mrs Sinclair, who had been a thorn in her side for twenty years. Jean was a taboo subject. Hawke's private world was beginning to unravel.

Graham Freudenberg, who was Sinclair's closest friend in the office, recalled, 'Jean didn't talk about herself, but I remember she was very worried about a second Keating challenge. She thought it would happen, although Bob did not.'

In Adelaide in July 1991 there was a second Special Premiers' Conference. Greiner recalled,

> I wanted a big bang deal. I said I thought you could justify the Commonwealth getting out of education up to the end of high school, and get the states out of post-school education. My point was that you ought to be able to allocate responsibility, rather than having everything shared, which is where we still are today. I said, 'Can't we cut through this bullshit and do an allocation of what goes to the Commonwealth and what goes to the states?' I said, 'If you try to do it in detail, it won't work, because every little vested interest will defend its turf.' But that didn't fly. And it still [in 2009] hasn't.

A decade later there has been no great progress.

Nevertheless, a further raft of reforms was agreed, involving devolution of power in some federal portfolios to the states. Hawke was immensely proud: here, in his fourth term, he had innovative reforms that could bring improvements for the next half-century, or more. He was not feeling worn out or politically disheartened. The prospect of new achievements invigorated him. The media, however, remained unimpressed. The Commonwealth–state reforms resisted snappy explanation; as their complexity was beyond the competence of many journalists, most of the media ignored them altogether. By this stage the press gallery was so sullen about Hawke that a majority was unwilling to report anything positive about him.

Hawke, meanwhile, continued his attack on Hewson's consumption tax proposal, which was yet to be fully revealed. He told a union conference in July that it would make 'every trip to the supermarket, every trip to McDonald's, a visit to the tax man'.

Hawke promoted John Kerin, his very successful Primary Industries minister, and a good economist, to the Treasury job.

On 20 August Kerin brought down his first Budget. It was, as Max Walsh had cannily predicted, a lemon: poorly expressed, poorly delivered and containing political poison in the form of Medicare co-payments. The new deputy Prime Minister, Brian Howe, leader of the Left, had proposed the Medicare payment, assuring Hawke and Kerin that the Left would accept it. But the Left promptly rebelled. Keating immediately promised Caucus to reverse the proposal were he prime minister. The timing of the Budget was also unfortunate for it coincided with the anti-Gorbachev coup in Moscow. Trying to sell the Budget, with a nervous new Treasurer, Hawke was distracted by questions about the violence in Russia. Kerin made numerous small mistakes, upon each of which the media seized, having had them pointed out by Keating. The Treasurer became more nervous. Dawkins was leaking from Cabinet so much that Brian Howe, who had been a Baptist minister before entering politics, felt moved to quote from the Book of Proverbs, declaring publicly, 'a house divided against itself simply cannot stand'. That may have worked with an unruly congregation; it was a faux pas for a divided government. The New South Wales Right was now in such a state of atavistic tribal anger that some were ready to cut off their noses to spite their faces, willing for their struggle against the Prime Minister to destroy the government. Gary Punch was warning, 'We will take this into Opposition if we need to.'[6]

The most vehement fights were between the staff of the competing camps, for many of whom personal careers were at stake. Once happy offices roiled with discontent and ill temper. A gloom settled over the government wing of Parliament House.

Graham Richardson, for all his determination to bring Hawke down, did not want to bring the government (and therefore himself) down in the process. In late August, after the Budget embarrassment, he called on Hawke at The Lodge to discuss the danger of destabilisation. He was friendly. He gave the Prime Minister a guarantee: provided Hawke made no mistakes, there would be no challenge. He was lying. Richardson was as ruthless and skilful for Keating as he had been for Hawke; he could still influence preselections in New South Wales, still tell people they would be political corpses if they did not vote for Keating. And Richardson was the one person in Keating's camp with the tactical nous to plan a successful second challenge. But he was treading very carefully, and not prepared, like the hotheaded Punch, to wreck the government by keeping up the pressure for Keating indefinitely. A sidelight to this was that Keating and Richardson did not consistently like each other; 'Keating's lack of discipline was and is his biggest problem,' Richardson wrote of him in a tone of irritation.[7] Their friendship ran hot and cold – inevitable between two such contrasting characters. But Keating had offered Richardson the reward he craved: Richardson would be Minister for Transport and Communications in a Keating government.

After his talk with Richardson at The Lodge, Hawke immediately made a mistake. Wreathed in smiles, he told journalists he believed Cabinet leaks would now cease. They ferreted around for the background to the Prime Minister's confidence and good humour, discovered his private meeting with Richardson, and thus had another story to write on the woes of the government.

In September, Jean Sinclair died. Hawke sat through the funeral as though thunderstruck, too distressed to deliver her eulogy. Her death was the end of an era for him: 'It is difficult,' he said later,

> to overstate Jeanie's importance in my life and career – as a supremely efficient assistant, friend and stabilising counsellor. The deepest respect and affection I had for her was only

enhanced by the courage with which she comported herself in those final months and days.

Graham Richardson meanwhile set out to cool press gallery expectations of a challenge. In the same month as Jean's death, in very matey tones, he interviewed Hawke on Sydney radio station 2KY, giving the Prime Minister another opportunity to attack the proposed consumption tax. Hawke did so, asserting dire social and economic consequences for ordinary people from such a tax, which would put up the price of their food, education and medical services at the same rate for the poor as for the rich, while income tax offsets for the rich would be far greater than for the poor. He added, 'That's why I want to lead us to victory in the '93 election, and that's what's driving me.' Still on air, Richardson again lied – as he later admitted[8] – saying he did not think there would be a second challenge. Hawke believed him, admitting later, 'I think my natural tendency to think the best of people has generally served me well though life – but I was a sucker not to make an exception for Richo.'

During October planning was underway for the third Special Premiers' Conference to be held in November. John Bannon of South Australia and Nick Greiner of New South Wales drafted a submission, with which all the other premiers agreed, asking the Commonwealth to surrender some taxing powers to the states. Greiner and Bannon called on Hawke at The Lodge to present it to him. But Keating heard of the plan's existence. According to Paul Kelly, 'he decided to destroy Hawke's New Federalism [COAG] initiative to the extent it undermined the revenue powers of the Commonwealth'. Keating had made 'the accurate assessment that the ALP caucus, forced to choose, would back [his] centralism against Hawke's devolution option'.[9]

Mike Codd recalled,

COAG was rolling along and it was known that I was the key driver of it in the bureaucracy. On Monday mornings we had a regular meeting of heads of all departments, which

I chaired. I was busy chairing when a message came in from my staff that Senator Richardson wanted to come and see me in the department, and was on his way, and would be there in ten minutes. It was the only time in my memory that any minister had ever come to a department to talk. So Richardson's visit was very unusual. We sat in my office and I offered him coffee, and he proceeded to tell me that I should find a way of slowing the COAG process down, and preferably of stopping it altogether, because he said, 'The PM is going to lose in the Caucus on this.' He said, 'I know the numbers' and he proceeded to rattle off names and numbers in Caucus. It was really quite extraordinary for a political leader to come in to a public servant's office and say, 'You don't do such-and-such. I know what the numbers are in the Caucus.' He basically gave me the message [to kill the reforms]. I listened politely and thanked him for coming over, and he left. But his visit made no difference. Bob would not back off.

Helen Williams recalled,

Gary Sturgess wanted principles of federation: we needed to sort out clearly exactly which area of government was doing what. And that area should take *the whole* of the functional area ... We were trying to progress all these streams and parallels. And certainly there was a feeling that a very careful look at the taxing powers was necessary. My memory is that the premiers' Adelaide meeting actually recommended that the Commonwealth would reduce personal income tax by a particular percentage to leave way for the states to introduce their own tax, and that was going to be revenue neutral, tax neutral. The Commonwealth was collecting and not spending, the states were spending and not collecting – or at least, spending far more than they were collecting.

On 22 October, Keating launched his offensive against COAG in a speech to the National Press Club in which he argued against surrendering any Commonwealth revenue powers to the states. He was reasserting Labor's tradition of centralism. Hawke and Kerin had assured Caucus no taxing powers would be surrendered, but Kerin then circulated a Cabinet submission that left this option open. The death blow came when the premiers' submission was leaked in its entirety to Keating. The premiers asked for 6 per cent of national revenue to be handed to the states. Keating used their submission to white-ant the proposal through a whispering campaign in Caucus. The whispering campaign sapped the collective will of the government and Hawke was now unable to deliver to the premiers the extra tax he had led them to believe he could. On hearing the rumblings from Canberra, the premiers conferred and, not realising how precarious the situation was inside the government, decided if they could not have the whole loaf, they would not settle for half. They pulled out of the November conference and the reform process collapsed.

The Prime Minister's COAG agenda for his fourth term was in ruins.

Keating's tactic had worked, but the correction of vertical fiscal imbalance had to be tackled somehow. And it was, when in 2000 John Howard introduced a goods and services tax with all the revenue going to the states.

Williams remarked in 2009,

In education, in welfare, in health, in disability services, there's still this pull between the Commonwealth and the states and we still haven't got much clarity as to who is doing what, everything complicated now [post-GST] by cost-shifting ... In essence, we're still fighting the same battles.

Greiner made a similar point when he commented,

Basically, since Bob's left, no one has been willing to take it on. Keating wasn't interested because he used COAG against Bob. I tried to persuade Howard and Costello but they were never remotely interested. I think they had the view that the states were hopeless and couldn't organise a chook raffle in a pub, therefore any attempt to separate and clarify responsibility would fail because it would involve the states. Since then Victoria has come up with a reform agenda, a national program for obesity, for Indigenous health, which is all useful, but they are motherhood issues on which everyone can agree. The hard questions are where the states disagree: like the allocation of water. We've lost eighteen years.

A decade later (2019) Australia has no effective agreement on managing the country's most important river system, the Murray-Darling, causing irreparable damage to the environment and agriculture.

Keating did implement a few ideas from COAG, but Greiner's statement is broadly accurate. In the November 2007 election COAG was a strong feature in Kevin Rudd's successful campaign. He promised to usher in a new era of co-operative federalism.

Hawke should have prepared the Caucus for an ideological shift on COAG, but by late 1991 his authority was fracturing through the fissures within the government. Only if he could end the Keating destabilisation would the ministry and Caucus reunite and focus on being a government. Like an army, a government needs *esprit de corps*. The military rule of thumb is that an army without bonding will break and run when 10 per cent of its soldiers are killed; an army well bonded will fight until only 10 per cent of its soldiers are still alive. The government's *esprit de corps* was steadily eroding.

In the first week of November there was some good economic news: interest rates were to be cut by 1 per cent. But Kerin was too rattled by the media to come out of his office to make the announcement. Instead, he put out a press release. At that moment Hawke realised that he would have to shift Kerin out of Treasury. He planned to do so over the Christmas break.

The *Age* editorial of 5 November was headlined 'Labor and the Pain of Decline'.

> The Labor Party is entering a state of advanced political decline as Mr Paul Keating continues his campaign to topple Mr Bob Hawke ... It is hard to see how Labor can now prevent decline becoming fall. Part of the problem is Mr Hawke's obdurate insistence that he is Labor's best hope for another election victory. The other part is Mr Keating's transparent opportunism and obvious unpopularity ... He wants to be prime minister, and will do and say what he judges will achieve that end. The painful dilemma for the Caucus, which makes and unmakes Labor leaders, is the choice between a diminished Bob Hawke and an opportunist Paul Keating. Given Labor's parlous electoral outlook, the party ought urgently to consider putting the leadership to another Caucus vote. The alternative is to allow this debilitating struggle to continue thereby ensuring that decline becomes fall.

Hawke by now was determined to ignore all negative comments. He knew Keating did not yet have the numbers for a challenge.

On 8 November Keating told the ABC radio program *PM*, 'I will not be challenging the Prime Minister.' He had made the statement under duress from Richardson. With Dr Hewson at last ready to launch his economic policy, Keating would be seen as a saboteur if he did not back down. Richardson intensified his media campaign to persuade the leaders of the press gallery that Keating had, indeed, folded. Michelle Grattan wrote, 'Hawke has won an important round.' Keating's popularity was stuck at 30 per cent, while Hawke's edged up 2 percentage points, to 54 per cent. Bruce Jones, reporting for the Sydney *Sun Herald* on 10 November remarked of Keating's statements of recent days, 'The current flurry of activity should be seen for what it is, a last desperate bid by Keating to crank up support for a final tilt at the leadership.'

By 14 November the economy was still stubbornly flat. That day Hawke unveiled a $300 million stimulus for education and training to help the unemployed, now numbering 800 000 people.

One week later Hewson detonated his tax bomb. It was called '*Fightback!*' and was a 600-page monster riddled with statistics. As expected, it proposed a 15 per cent goods and services tax on everything, with offsetting income-tax cuts. To the government's chagrin the media, especially economic journalists, embraced *Fightback!* with rapture. Not that they understood it. Neither did the government. Yet Hewson and some others in the Opposition did. Warwick Smith, a member of the shadow Cabinet, recalled the optimism and *esprit de corps* in Coalition ranks over Hewson and *Fightback!*.

> With Hewson we were looking at a fresh face, new ideas, modern man, an investment banker with a globalised feel of things, someone who could take Australia to the next level. People like me were saying, 'This breaks the nexus between the Hawke and Peacock thing. We've got a new horse.' We thought we might be able to run Hawke down ... I never thought [Keating] was going to take the gun out and try to shoot everyone. We thought we were going to be up against Hawke.

Cautious after his embarrassment over the gold tax, and lacking Keating's parliamentary power of demolition, Hawke was determined not to appear on the field of battle against Hewson's policy without full armour. He wanted a thorough analysis of *Fightback!* by Treasury before launching into its dismantlement. He knew that the public did not understand the ramifications of a consumption tax, although he had been railing against it all year. He was also certain that the financial journalists who were so joyfully embracing it did not really understand it either. He (and Keating) understood economics and politics too well to want to rush in, half-baked, against a document prepared after more than a year's work by an expert and experienced professional economist and a team of assistants. Hawke said he wanted time to respond. Keating remained silent. For the Prime Minister, it was good policy but poor politics, for he seemed scared of Hewson. For Keating, it was good politics: as a backbencher, he had no obligation to speak up.

By 26 November the government had found the first of many weaknesses it would uncover in *Fightback!*. Dr Hewson had failed to take account of the cost of new road-user charges that would reduce the value of his promise to lower petrol prices, and would add to inflation. Hawke waded in to attack during Question Time. The result was bedlam. The Opposition, recognising Kerin's shaky nerve, set out to stop the Prime Minister by demanding that the Treasurer debate the whole package, which Kerin was not yet equipped to do. Nor was Hawke. His only weapon was the one flaw so far revealed. He and the government repeatedly dodged Opposition demands to debate the whole of *Fightback!*. The Speaker of the House, Leo McLeay from the New South Wales Right, allowed the Opposition to turn parliament into a madhouse. Instead of naming then having members of the Opposition expelled from the Chamber, as was the Westminster practice in such circumstances, he actively undermined the Prime Minister. As Hawke attempted to drive home his attack on the flaw in *Fightback!*, McLeay interrupted him 53 times in thirty minutes. Each call to order from the Speaker pulled Hawke up in mid-sentence. The message was clear: the Keating camp had decided to make parliament unworkable for the government.

'Leo: how the lion became a squeaker' was the headline to a story by Mike Seccombe in the *Sydney Morning Herald* the next day:

It was virtually impossible for Ministers to make themselves heard. Hawke looked particularly bad, because he stopped innumerable times to glare at the Speaker in the vain hope Leo would do something. Hawke even pointed out at one stage that the opposition was not heeding Leo's call to order, but Leo steadfastly did nothing. Question time was a disaster from beginning to end for the government, as a result.

The following day the House was a rumpus of baboons. McLeay called for order or warned parliamentarians they would be named 89 times in sixty minutes. But he named no one, expelled no one.

That week the Morgan poll had Hewson as preferred prime minister, 45 to 43 per cent, over Hawke. It was joyous news for Keating since it destroyed Hawke's major claim to the leadership: that he could win.

But by the first week of December the Treasury officials who had been analysing *Fightback!* for the government had struck gold. There was a $2.6 billion hole in Hewson's policy – and that was just the beginning of its problems. Parliament was to sit on Monday, 9 December: Hawke's birthday, a day when he always felt cheerful, although he was not as cheerful as usual leading up to this birthday, since Hazel had fallen ill for the second time in a few months and needed surgery.

Hawke had arranged that on 9 December the government's own fight back would begin. Ministers were briefed during the preceding week so the attack on the Opposition could be launched across a broad front. On the morning of 5 December, John Kerin announced the economy had turned around – but he was in error, and by lunchtime he had to contradict himself: for the fifth consecutive quarter, the economy had contracted. The recession was still in force. Hawke was in Sydney to address a luncheon and listened to Kerin's press conference on his car radio. Kerin fell into a panic in front of the media, so flustered he could not remember what the initials GOS (Gross Operating Surplus) meant. Finally he turned to the assembled reporters to ask them. Hawke, who was travelling across the Harbour Bridge from Kirribilli House to the CBD, clasped his head in his hands and yelled, 'Fuck!'

Richardson, also listening to Kerin's press conference, recognised that the moment to attack once more had arrived. Within hours he had leaked a story to the *Sydney Morning Herald* that he, Robert Ray and Kim Beazley, the latter both known Hawke supporters, had already advised the Prime Minister to sack both Kerin and Button, and to make a major reshuffle of the ministry. Button, the Industry minister, always keen for attention and admiration as a free spirit, had in the past few years appointed himself devil's advocate, publicly criticising the government whenever he felt moved to do so. Privately he was inactive in his portfolio.

Saturday, 7 December, was an appalling day for the Prime Minister. That morning's press was almost universally opposed to him. Later that day he was due to address the New South Wales state ALP conference. The word had gone out to the Right 'to get Hawke'. Graham Freudenberg, who loves the party as if it were his child, recalled, 'I knew it would be very ugly. I refused to attend.' The delegates greeted their Prime Minister with cold silence at first, later with jeers and abuse. 'It was a disgrace,' Freudenberg lamented.

Next day, Hawke declared he would not be standing down.

He made the smallest reshuffle possible. He moved Willis to Treasury – the job he had promised him back in 1982 but had been unable to deliver – and put Kerin into Transport and Communications. He moved Beazley into Finance.

Years earlier Keating's adviser, Don Russell, had predicted, 'the caucus will only turn to Keating when it feels the government is completely demoralised'.[10] Now it was. Hawke's minor reshuffle was interpreted in the media as a condemnation of the government's handling of the recession. History's wheel was turning, and whatever Hawke did was destined, by this stage, for damnation.

Richardson, meanwhile, was working furiously to isolate the Prime Minister from the support of his inner-most circle of political allies: those in Cabinet, his backbench friends, even his friends in the business community. Peter Hartcher, who researched the final days of the Hawke government, wrote later, '[Richardson] wanted it to become utterly clear to Hawke that he was hopelessly, desperately, friendlessly finished.'[11]

Richardson was still trying to pressure Hawke into resignation. On the night of 11 December, Kim Beazley, Robert Ray, Gareth Evans, Michael Duffy, Nick Bolkus and Gerry Hand, all Hawke supporters, arrived in a body to ask the Prime Minister to give up. He listened to their arguments, promised to consider them, and said he would meet them later with his answer.

Richardson wrote, '"That's enough", I thought. He has no choice now. He will resign.'

But Hawke's answer was 'No'.

Richardson said in his memoir, 'All of them were aware that the fatally wounded leadership that was Hawke's could not recover.' To Richardson it was incredible that Hawke would fight on. But then an awful fear entered his mind: the Prime Minister could 'get in his car and drive out to Yarralumla to advise the Governor-General to dissolve the Parliament and call an election'. He and the Keating camp became panicky. As Hawke stood firm, they began to feel their numbers waning.[12]

But Richardson, for all his earlier hero worship of Hawke, did not understand what a hero is, nor what a hero does. Throughout history, and in every culture, the hero cannot surrender. He will fight and die for his beliefs. Hawke believed he was the only one at that stage who could successfully lead the party and the country. For this he would fight to his political death.

In droves, friends advised Hawke to stand down. Kim Beazley said,

I always accepted the view that Bob was not burnt out – as I had a practical example [of his energy] from what he was making me do in Communications. He was far and a long way our most successful leader and if everybody was loyally in behind him, then we would win the next election. I always accepted that Paul was the legitimate successor to Bob, and I accepted that Paul would bring a sharper attack on the other side. But whereas Paul thought he was the only one who could exploit the consumption tax issue, I thought many could. *Fightback!* was a long political suicide note that

Hewson had written. But before the second challenge I didn't think Bob had nearly enough supporters. I couldn't *bear* the idea of him being humiliated in Caucus. I tried very hard to get him to stand down.

Twelve out of sixteen Cabinet ministers tried to persuade the Prime Minister to resign. Gareth Evans told him, 'Pull out, digger. The dogs are pissing on your swag.' Hawke's reply to them was always the same: first, he was convinced Keating could not win against Hewson. Second, he had not devoted his life to the Labor Party to allow it to commit suicide.

By 18 December Ray and Beazley knew most of the Caucus numbers: Keating had about 60, Hawke about 50. By now Senator Evans had left Canberra for emergency talks in Jakarta about a massacre in Dili some weeks earlier. Everyone knew there would be no chivalrous offer from the Keating side of a 'pair' for Senator Evans. Hawke had to decide between the national interest – leaving the Foreign minister in Jakarta – and giving himself an extra vote by recalling Evans. He chose the national interest. Ray and Beazley came to The Lodge to tell Hawke he was beaten and to make one last plea to him to step down. They stayed with him until 3 a.m. Hawke had decided to call on the challenge for the evening of 19 December. At around 4 a.m. Hawke and his press secretary, Grant Nihil, woke Hazel to tell her the challenge was on. Warrior queen that she now was, she supported her husband in the determination to fight. Hawke had a few hours sleep, then set out, in the little time he had left, to gather his forces.

He was fighting virtually alone.

Hartcher wrote,

Most of Hawke's numbers men had resigned themselves to defeat and did not work to maximise his vote. For the first time in his Federal political career, Hawke did most of the numbers work himself... If his supporters had not despaired, if the Left had not freed its members to vote as they pleased, and if Hawke had decided to recall Gareth Evans ... the ballot would have been tied at 54 votes each.[13]

In Keating's camp the same nerve-racking process was in train, but Keating was not working on his own: he had his generals Richardson, Punch and Laurie Brereton working for him. Friendships of a lifetime broke during the struggle. Hearts broke. Richardson recalled,

> I prevailed on David Simmonds – without any threat of repercussions – but I said to him, 'You've got to vote for Keating, because New South Wales can't be left alone on this. We can't have anyone going outside the tent. We'd already had Roger Price [New South Wales Right] going outside the tent and we can't afford anyone else.' I said, 'We have to make sure the numbers are respectable – and I need you.' So I asked him as a favour to me. And he did it. And he cried. He was very upset because he loved Hawke. He loved him. But he did the right thing.

Kim Beazley, who loved both Hawke and Keating, said,

> I lost the joy of politics during that time. I [still] enjoyed it as a profession, but the sparkling joy that you got out of what you thought was the most important game in town receded as you confronted the misery. It was just appalling.

Richardson recorded,

> At 5.30, an hour before the ballot was due to begin, a very worried Gary Punch entered my office. Without even bothering to sit down, he said, solemnly: 'We can actually lose this challenge.' I stood up, took a deep breath and told him that, yes, we could lose because it was very close.[14]

At the appointed hour, Hawke presented himself for what he expected would be his execution.

The vote was 56 to 51. Many were in tears as the numbers were read out, among them John Dawkins, who had fought relentlessly to defeat Hawke. Richardson, seeing Dawkins' tears, described a feeling of numbed disgust. The destruction of Hawke was, he said,

> Very ugly. I was looking around at all these people crying and thinking, 'Jeeze! You know, if you're in it, you're in it.' I wasn't crying. I thought, 'I can't believe these people.' Everyone wants to salve their consciences all the time. But you can't do that. The truth is, if you're going to shaft someone, then you can't cry after you've shafted them. It's ridiculous. And Dawkins did a lot of the shafting. I've never forgotten him sobbing. There was no joy in any of it. No joy. It was just a job. Hayden had to go because Hayden wasn't going to win. And Hawke had to go because Hawke wasn't going to win.

Keating was almost trembling as he stood at the podium to accept victory. But the slightly nervous hand he laid upon the wheel of history was pleasing to it, and fifteen months later it rewarded the new Prime Minister with the 'sweetest victory of all': winning the 1993 election. Hawke would have won it too – *Fightback!* was indeed a long political suicide note – but history had judged it was time for Keating to have his turn at holding the reins of power.

THIRTY

BRIAN TOOHEY SAID LATER, 'Hawke would have won the
1993 election. *Fightback!* looked worse and worse the
longer it was examined.' Many political observers shared
this view. Hawke was certain it was true, and deeply angry that
his colleagues had rejected him too soon.

For months after he left parliament, in January 1992, there
were malicious stories about him in the media, some true, some
fabricated, to suit the mood of triumph that, finally, the man
journalists had once called 'The Messiah' had been crucified.

It was a time of purgatory and bitterness, both for him and
for some of his former staff who were also out in the cold, without jobs. Aged sixty-two, Hawke found himself beyond a comfort zone. His life had been spent within organisations: church,
university, trade union movement, parliament. Suddenly he had
no structure to shape and discipline his time. He was used to the
advice and information of an army of professionals when in private, in public to protection by armed men; to a chauffeur and his
own aeroplane. He had lost the small repertoire he once had of
normal urban skills and when, for the first time in years, he did
some shopping, did not recognise a fifty-cent piece. From two
houses staffed with servants, he and Hazel were living in a hotel
suite in Double Bay. The hotel was comfortable and sumptuous
enough for Lady Diana to stay there some years later but it was
cramped by the standards to which the Hawkes were accustomed.
The Sydney property they had bought needed demolition and
their new house would take almost two years to complete. Aside
from close political colleagues and old buddies from union days,

Hawke was relatively friendless after defeat. There were some notable exceptions: among the well known, Sir Peter Abeles, Richard Pratt and John Singleton stood by him, but many others in the business world who had been delighted to brag of their friendship with the prime minister swiftly moved their allegiance to Paul Keating (and in due course dropped him for John Howard).

Hawke did not seek power once he had lost it, but he had occasional fugues of hollow bombast, speaking as if he were still a national leader with an army at his command. Whereas he had adjusted to the role of prime minister 'instantly' as Graham Freudenberg observed, it took several years to adjust to being the ex. His cherished self-image needed time to decay.

But when it had mouldered away, Hawke began to flower again, and from the death of his old persona a new, more autonomous man started to take form.

Freed from the constraints of power, at liberty to act without political tensions pulling this way and that, away from relentless media scrutiny, Hawke arose, liberated, from the grave of his ambition. He brought with him a gift whose value he did not himself recognise at first but others did: his altruism. From childhood his ideal had been to work for the welfare of others, while his entire career had been lived beneath the shadow of, and had been shaped by, the Cold War. His career died as the Soviet empire collapsed. Now a new world order was struggling uncertainly to its feet. It was in this not-yet-brave new world that he would take a stand and set out to advance, once more, his vision of reconciliation, recovery and reconstruction.

On a trip to Europe in 1992, Hawke met the secretary general of the International Federation of Free Teachers' Unions, Fred van Leeuwen. van Leeuwen was a physically slight, politically astute Dutchman of profound humanity. He lived on a farm outside Amsterdam with his partner, an Amerindian veteran of the Vietnam War, and a family of dogs, horses, goats and other creatures. On first meeting it was as if Hawke and 'Freddie', as he always called him, had known each other forever. The Dutchman, young enough to be Hawke's son, proposed he join in a socio-political adventure that would reach across the globe: he wanted the former prime minister and former president of the ACTU to involve himself once more in the trade union movement.

For the forty-three years of the Cold War, there had been two separate industrial blocs: on one side, genuine trade unions; on the other, organisations that called themselves unions but that were in fact arms of government. In 1989 van Leeuwen, observing the approaching death of European Communism, proposed that the world's teachers' unions try to amalgamate. He and a working party envisaged that through such an organisation teachers in rich countries could help those in poor nations; the status of teachers, their terms and conditions could be improved by pressure on governments; their training upgraded and international agreements negotiated on basic curriculum development and issues like the right to education for girls. It would be not only a professional but also a human rights organisation. 'For us it was very important in creating this new organisation that it would consist of genuine teachers' unions,' van Leeuwen said.

> During the Cold War many unions claimed to have millions of members but really many of these simply did not exist and were yellow unions, mailbox organisations. So the question arose: how do we determine genuine from false? There is not a universal answer to what independence means for a union, and maybe also to what democratic means.

The planning group came up with the idea of an independent committee of experts, people with a trade union background and political nous, who could be called in to investigate and report on disputed unions. The idea was the final piece to the puzzle that empowered the new organisation to come into creation. 'Everybody thought Bob would be the best possible solution as the chairman of the committee of experts,' van Leeuwen said, 'because he would be acceptable across a broad political spectrum, but many of us thought he'd never accept. The organisation was still to be born.'

But Hawke did accept and in 1993 took up his role in chairing the committee of experts of Education International, which met annually in Brussels. By 2010 EI was one of the world's most important non-government organisations, internationally recognised as the voice of the world's teaching profession.

EI has helped and sometimes saved the lives of teachers in countries from Afghanistan to Zimbabwe. Teaching can be a dangerous job in the Third World: as the only literate people in illiterate communities, or in areas ruled by drug lords – Colombia, for example – teachers' influence riles the powerful. Thousands of teachers have been murdered in the past three decades. In the 1990s, Albanian teachers were under death threats from Serbs for teaching the Albanian language. EI managed to rescue some. In other countries EI provided funds to keep destitute teachers from starving. Hawke went to Mongolia, Moldova, Malaysia, Serbia and twice to Turkey (especially difficult because of the Kurdish issue) to investigate. In Belgrade and Ankara passions turned the meetings into shouting matches. In Ankara, a Turk with a walrus moustache and a wrestler's neck became so angry about Kurdish teachers he shouted at Hawke – and was stunned when Hawke roared back at him, louder, longer, stronger. Turks and Kurds were accusing each other of murder. In Belgrade, a two-metre-tall Montenegran kept interjecting. Hawke finally shouted at him too – whereupon the giant leapt to his feet, grinning, to shake the hand of a man more aggressive than himself.But in the collapsed economies of Soviet satellite states the meetings with teachers' unions were tragic affairs. Their members had been unpaid for months. In Mongolia, some female teachers had become prostitutes to stay alive. In Moldova, old women and children could be seen on their knees in the snow, begging. Other members of EI's committee of experts, all former leaders of their unions, have travelled to inhospitable, dangerous, impoverished and difficult countries in Africa, South America and the Middle East to find out what can be done to help teachers. Van Leeuwen, the

secretary general, said, 'No international organisation, not the
United Nations or UNESCO or the World Bank, would decide
on plans involving education without asking our opinion.' Hawke
said,

> I've always had a passionate commitment to the importance
> of education, so it's been not just a challenge, but a joy, to
> play a small but, I think, important role in the work of EI for
> improving the quality and the equity of global education.

Hawke resigned from the committee in June 2011. By then EI
had a membership of 396 national organisations in 171 countries
and territories, representing 29.6 million teachers and other
educational workers.

Hawke's most influential contribution to world development
is closer to home. In 1993 the new Chinese leadership invited
him to Beijing, his first contact with China since the rupture after
Tiananmen. Despite his apprehension, President Jiang Zemin
welcomed Hawke as 'an old friend'. On this trip he was waiting
in the hotel lobby one day when a slender man with a refined,
elfin face introduced himself, explaining he recognised Hawke
from media photographs. He was Jiang Xiaosong, an entrepreneur who had prospered in television production and real estate
development in Japan. Unknown to Hawke, Jiang was the son of
the 1930s and 1940s movie star, Bai Yang, who counted among
her fans Mao Zedong, Zhou En-lai and the new President of
China, Jiang Zemin. After the Communist takeover, Bai Yang
had had the unique honour, for an actress, of being appointed to
the People's Congress. Her son was friendly and modest in his
demeanour, giving no hint he was already a multimillionaire. (He
was also a member of the People's Congress.) He did not speak
English but, through an interpreter, pleasantries and cards were
exchanged in the lobby, and that was it.

Except it wasn't. Five years later, in mid-1997 when Hawke
was visiting Tokyo, Jiang Xiaosong again made contact. He
wanted Hawke and the liberal, reformist former Japanese prime

minister, Morihiro Hosokawa, to come as his guests to the island of Hainan to see the site on which he planned to build a resort. He thought it could include a conference centre for regional economic discussion. The Asian financial crisis of 1997, which began on 2 July when the Thai baht collapsed, was threatening to engulf not only the region but to become a worldwide economic meltdown. Jiang knew Hawke was 'an old friend of China's' and 'the father of APEC'. The need for more profound regional discussion was evident. Jiang's other guest, Hosokawa, had an impeccable humanitarian and social pedigree. He had been born a marquis, son of the lord of the Hosokawa samurai clan, and descendant of emperor Morihiro's grandfather, Prince Fumimaro Konoe, who had tried to limit the power of the military in the 1940s and keep Japan's war with China from spreading into a world conflagration. Hosokawa himself had resigned from his party, the Liberal Democrats, because of its corruption, but in his eight months as prime minister he did what no other Japanese leader would: he described Japan as having launched 'a war of aggression, a mistaken war' and expressed his country's responsibility and condolences. In 1994 Hosokawa had visited China and signed an environmental protection treaty between the two nations: a stride forward, given Chinese feelings about the Japanese.

On 28 July, after a long drive from Hainan's main airport, Jiang's guests arrived at a smaller island. It was contained within a pretty river that ran down to a yellow sandy beach and the South China Sea. Hainan is China's only tropical island and, apart from two cities, was still largely uninhabited. Next to Jiang's resort site there was a traditional walled village entered through a moon gate. Every house had small pictures of the ancestors outside its front door. The landscape around it was an emerald stretch of rice fields and hills covered in tropical forest – except for a half-finished golf course and a small concrete building from which lunch appeared, to be served alfresco beneath beach umbrellas. The area was called Boao, after a monster, Ao, whom the goddess of mercy had conquered, turning his lair into a place of tranquillity and beauty: thus Boao. Over this lunch in a rice field, the seed of the Boao Forum for Asia was sown. Jiang asked Hosokawa and Hawke to use their contacts to gather a board of former leaders that he asked Hawke to chair. (A Japanese chairman at the time would have been too much for the Chinese to countenance and, English being the lingua franca of business in Asia, someone fluent in English was desirable.) Hawke objected that the chair would have to be Asian and nominated his friend, Fidel Ramos, former president of the Philippines, a hero of the war in the Pacific and a charming, playful dynamo who chomps constantly on an unlit cigar and wears spectacles with empty frames, occasionally alarming audiences by wriggling his fingers through what they thought was glass. Ramos had helped revive his country's economy and democracy after the misrule of Marcos. After more than a year of meetings between the Chinese, the Japanese, Hawke and Ramos, on 5 September 1998 in Manila they laid out the vision for the Boao Forum for Asia. Twenty-eight countries were foundation members – Australia, Bangladesh, Brunei, Cambodia, China, India, Indonesia, Iran, Israel, Japan, Kazakhstan, Kyrgyzstan, Laos, Malaysia, Mongolia, Myanmar, Nepal, New Zealand, Pakistan, the Philippines, Republic of Korea, Singapore, Sri Lanka, Tajikistan, Thailand, Turkmenistan, Uzbekistan and Vietnam – and the first annual conference was in April 2002. By then rice fields had vanished beneath a five-star hotel, a conference centre and landscaped gardens. The golf course was manicured and a towering white statue of the goddess of mercy blessed the enterprise from another small island in the river.

While Jiang spent millions on infrastructure, Ramos as chairman and Hawke as deputy spent thousands of hours over eight years in nurturing BFA's life and growth. It was exceptionally difficult. They and their associates had to create a new culture in China, which at the time was familiar only with government-to-government meetings.China still had a long way to go in introducing herself to the world and to understanding other cultures. The inclusion of non-government participants was neither understood nor greatly appreciated, and the whole enterprise almost collapsed several times in its early days. Ramos and Hawke had to go to Beijing to make representations to the leadership, asking for continued support. But with the appointment of a new and very astute secretary general, Long Yongtu (the main negotiator for China's entry to the World Trade Organization), the forum's original intent of being the pre-eminent intellectual resource centre in Asia began to shape up.

Chinese leaders had been used to a command-and-obey system and, as Long said, were unused to speaking to foreign audiences: they read speeches to bored delegates. Unfortunately, this was taken to be correct form, and copied. But gradually the culture changed. Set-piece speeches were abandoned; in their place came lively panel discussions with media personalities from the BBC, CNN and the *Financial Times* as moderators. There were questions from the floor that, a few years earlier, would have been considered 'rude'. By April 2010, Boao was the foremost meeting place in the Asia–Pacific region for leaders in government, business, academia and the media. Only the World Economic Forum in Davos, which began in 1971, outdid it as a venue for the planet's movers and shakers. 'Chinese people felt uncomfortable at Davos,' Long said.

> But we learned from Davos. We have famous people, like Old Bush and Young Bush, Colin Powell and outstanding states-men from Asia, and these famous people have an impact. Others want to come. Boao has given Chinese businesses a world perspective, and for foreign business leaders it has great networking value: if they go to Beijing, it will taken them ten days to meet ten government or business people. In Boao in one day they can meet twenty people. Hawke is very sensitive and has a deep understanding. His greatest contribution has been to bring the West and the East together. He has been a bridge, because both sides have confidence in him.

In 2010 Ramos, Hawke and Long all stepped down from the leadership, the former national leaders being immediately appointed to a Boao advisory board. Hawke said,

> I find it difficult to describe the satisfaction – and the pride – I feel in the evolution of the BFA. The rise of world-class conference facilities from an expanse of paddy fields that we contemplated in 1997 is the physical manifestation of something much more important. My goal was the creation of a Davos, but better, in Asia, and I think we have – certainly by the comments of many European participants – already achieved that. At the annual April conference political, business and academic leaders meet formally and informally to discuss and co-operate on issues of significance to the welfare of the Asian region and beyond. In particular, the continuing strong support of the Chinese government means that attendees can hear and get a real sense of the thinking of the Chinese leadership in government, business and intellectual circles.

Australia's Fortesque Metals Group, founded by Andrew Forrest, has been a leading sponsor of BFA since 2008. Forrest said in 2019, 'Bob's strong leadership and his attendance every year drove strong Australian participation in the forum . . . his personal commitment has been second to none, helping to build long-term friendships at the highest levels . . . if Chinese leaders have a longlist of trusted foreign friends, Bob would certainly be highly placed on that list.'

Besides helping to build friendships Hawke injected an Australian sense of fun into Boao by singing a dramatic rendition of 'Waltzing Matilda' at each year's major dinner. This became so admired that at every Chinese party he attended, anywhere in China, host or guests demanded he sing it. By 2018 Hawke had visited China 106 times.

One of his most unusual Education International meetings was held in a herdsman's yurt on the Mongolian steppe, where the refreshment was fermented mare's milk. But Hawke's most dramatic experience in pursuing his ideal of reconciliation was a journey from Jerusalem to Ramallah to see Yasser Arafat in September 2003. The second intifada was raging and Hawke travelled in an armoured four-wheel drive. His self-appointed mission – to which Australian businessmen Dick Pratt, a Jew, Fred Shahin, an Arab Palestinian, and John Symond, 'Aussie John', whose family was Lebanese, gave financial support – was to present Arafat with a plan to bring peace and prosperity to Palestine. Hawke had developed it during 2002, alarmed at the warmongering that was beginning to engulf the West. He considered a war in Iraq would be a disaster, and wrote and gave speeches against Australian participation. He had long held the belief that there could be no peace in the Middle East until the Israel–Palestine issue was settled, and that the United States and the West would only continue to make themselves more hated the longer the fighting between Israel and the Palestinians continued. He also believed that Israel was destroying its own future through endless war. He thought that seeking a political solution as the first step on the so-called 'Roadmap to Peace' was putting the cart before the horse. He was convinced that the Palestinian economy had to be revived before Palestinians would have any good reason for wanting peace: with 55 per cent unemployment, shattered infrastructure and houses, why not fight the Israelis? There was nothing much else to do.

By December Hawke had developed an idea that he named after the American Secretary of State, Colin Powell, 'The Powell Plan for Palestine' (see Appendix). It envisaged that the world community, led by the United States, would rebuild the economy and social infrastructure of Palestine, in return for a guaranteed halt to attacks on Israel. He sent the plan to, or talked it through with, Powell himself; George Bush Senior; John Major, the former UK prime minister; President Musharaff of Pakistan; Prince Hassan of Jordan; Alexander Downer, the Australian Foreign minister; UK Prime Minister, Tony Blair; the *éminence grise* of Egyptian politics, Osama el Baz; the Egyptian Prime Minister, Dr Atef Ebeid; Shimon Peres and Ehud Barak, leaders of the Israeli Labor Party, both former prime ministers; Ehud Olmert, the Israeli deputy Prime Minister, of the Likud Party; Ahmed Qurei, the Palestinian Prime Minister ('the smartest man in the world' Peres called him); James Wolfensohn, head of the World Bank; and George Soros, the billionaire financier and philanthropist. Wolfensohn and all the politicians thought the plan was worth trying. Soros alone dismissed the idea as futile.

By the time Hawke had garnered the interest of world leaders, the second Iraq war had begun – and was, the American administration announced, in a fit of inane vanity, a triumph.

A pall of misery and despair hung over the towns and villages of the West Bank in the autumn of 2003. The few food shops that were open had scant supplies: limp carrots, tinned milk, some apples, bags of rice. Israel was already building the Separation Wall. It ran through the middle of the village of Abu Dis, where Qurei had his office, and was made of concrete. Hawke had to get down from the armoured vehicle and climb over a sort of stile to call on Qurei. The new Palestinian Prime Minister thought the plan was a good idea, but he was clearly distracted by a myriad of worries that he found more pressing.

Hawke was driven on to Ramallah, which seemed a ghost town. There was a high wall around Arafat's compound and Israeli soldiers on the top of all the buildings that overlooked it. Inside the compound a number of buildings had been bombed and lay in ruins, as did the entrance to Arafat's house. Hawke was ushered through khaki canvas flaps, which now served as a door, up a flight of stairs where a wardrobe and sandbags covered a bomb-hole in the wall. Hawke had detested Arafat for decades as the embodiment of violence. It was only his conviction that the international situation was increasingly dangerous that had brought him this far.

The chairman of the Palestinian Authority had been the world's foremost political trickster for more than thirty years, its Great Survivor, the Br'er Rabbit of international affairs: smart, cunning, funny, charming, lucky. And a killer. But when he entered dressed in military uniform, surrounded by aides, he was a pitiful figure, a warlord defeated, depressed and enervated. (To this day speculation continues that the Israelies were slowly, secretly, poisoning him.) The dream he had pursued for decades lay in rubble. Whatever his other illnesses, the visible one was vitiligo. It had bleached his face chalk white but left the skin on the backs of his small hands brown, with pale mottles. He immediately launched into a lament, reciting the horrors of what had occurred in the past forty-eight hours – a church bombed in Gaza, a statue of Mary destroyed, 'Our Mary! Our Mary!' he wailed, as if speaking of his own mother. But he had the strange, charismatic power of narcissism. Vanquished and half-dead – he would die fifteen months later – he was still mesmerising.

Arafat liked the plan when Hawke explained it to him. They talked at length, 'between four eyes'. Hawke stressed that the World Bank would be in charge of distributing funds, that the process would be transparent. Arafat knew the head of the bank, James Wolfensohn (Hawke's friend, who had helped break apartheid). 'I trust him,' the chairman said. He was genuinely enthusiastic. Hawke questioned him repeatedly about attacks on Israel. Arafat told Hawke he believed he could persuade the most extreme elements to stop attacks in exchange for the implementation of the proposal. Over lunch he cheered up, declaring, 'Why not? We'll be getting the money.'

Lunch was served on the conference table, and turned out to be a feast of grilled chicken, barbecued prawns, rice, lamb, sweet corn and vegetable dishes. As a host, Arafat could not have been more gracious. The conference room, with its noisy air conditioner and bricked-up windows, became an enchanted place far from bloodshed and violence. The defeated warlord turned into an indulgent father, choosing from the serving dishes delicacies that he placed on the plates of his guests, and passing to them sections of sweet corn delicately held in the tips of his fingers.

After lunch Hawke and the chairman withdrew for another serious talk. Hawke left believing at least one step forward had been taken.

Wherever and whenever he met senior members of the American government, at conferences around the world, in universities, in Washington itself, he continued to sound them out. But the Bush administration had psychologically shifted into a parallel universe, and from that curious unreality was dragging the nation and the world ever more deeply into the quicksands of Mesopotamia. There was no one in the White House who would listen. Years later, after he had left office, Powell told Hawke, 'Bob, I thought your plan was great, but I couldn't get it up on my watch because all they wanted to talk about was Iraq.'

Despite the relentless ethos of hatred between Israel and Palestine and the lack of interest in the United States in doing anything that could offend the Israeli or Christian lobbies, Hawke did not give up his ideal of fostering peace. But in a slow, relentless tide, hatred was spreading.

One avenue blocked, he sought another.

PART III
At Large

THIRTY-ONE

In 1998 the University of South Australia established the Bob Hawke Prime Ministerial Centre, an institution modelled on the presidential libraries of the United States. Hawke is the only prime minister to have been born in South Australia and the university wanted both to honour him and to extend its range of courses. Its vice-chancellor was Professor Denise Bradley, an ardent advocate for women's rights and engaged in education her whole career. She said,

> The establishment of the centre was a crucial decision for the university. It may look now as though it was a great coup, but at the time it was problematic. The university was flat broke, in very serious financial trouble, and Bob's image and legacy were controversial. Nevertheless, a 'courageous' decision was made and we approached Bob. He agreed to it, knowing we had few resources and he would need to assist us to get external funds for it. [He made a large personal contribution.] No matter where he was, he was well prepared, focused, charming and relentless. I saw that he was always across his brief, always on message. As we worked to gain funds for the centre to support its public and research program he became a great friend of UniSA and an advocate for South Australia. What we hadn't expected was that he would spend so much time at public functions in the university, giving papers and contributing to scholarly discussions. We all saw then what some others who worked closely with him have remarked upon. This was a brilliant man, hardworking and capable of

extremely sophisticated analysis . . . I have vivid memories of watching Bob as he prepared to go on stage to speak, nervous and tense and still going over a speech I knew he had drafted days ago and which had been the subject of his endless revisions. He never took an audience for granted and he always sought to be his best. One might think someone so famous and so long in the public eye would wing it, but I never saw him do this. Everything he did he did with passion, intelligence and intensity.'[1]

The Hawke Lecture, given annually in the Adelaide Town Hall by speakers from all over Australia and around the world became a fixture in the city's intellectual calendar, and a source of joy and pride for him. He revelled in immersing himself once more in the cut and thrust of university life, and apart from electioneering – which he continued to the week he died – would put all other engagements aside to attend discussions in Adelaide. He had realised the university could contribute positively to a social issue he recognised as ominous and increasing: the hostility around the world between Muslims and non-Muslims. He set out to establish a centre within the centre for 'Muslim–non Muslim Understanding' and raised $10 million to kickstart it. The school has been re-named the Centre for Islamic Thought and Education and has moved into the School of Education at UniSA. Its director is Professor Mohamad Abdalla, a scholar of international renown and a community leader. His students are winning awards for outstanding achievements, including one of the first PhD graduates carrying off the Chancellor's Medal for Exceptional Performance.

Meanwhile, the Hawke marriage was in trouble. From 1983 to the end of 1991, life in the Lodge and Kirribilli House had brought a seemingly endless spring and summer of affection, mutual support and admiration. Hazel became such an asset to the government that the ALP used her during the fourth election campaign when its polling showed how popular she was. The Lodge was the fulfilment of a dream, for the achievement

At large in the world. Vanuatu, 2009.

Two tourists on the trail in the Galapagos islands.

Another favourite destination, Easter Island.

With Rodney the 200-year-old tortoise, Galapagos.

Haggerstore Island, far north Queensland, 2012.

Hawke poses with his bust at the opening of the Tatiara Civic Centre in his hometown, Bordertown, SA, in 2011.

Bob and Blanche enjoy a relaxing moment on the island of Pulau while holidaying with Japanese friends.

Celebrating his 88th birthday with Hawke's Lager.

Hawke at the Woodford Folk Festival. He loved Woodford and the festival loved him straight back. Woodford festival, Queensland, 2016.

Meeting a fan (Elke Hauritz, granddaughter of festival director Bill Hauritz) at Woodford, 2018.

Hawke with stepson, Louis Pratt, at Woodford.

In top form at a cricket match, Woodford.

With Julia Gillard and Woodford Festival director Bill Hauritz.

Woodford, with Kerry O'Brien.

With Paul Hogan and publisher Kevin Weldon, 2019.

Hawke and Galarrwuy Yunupingu at the Garma 2014 Key Forum.

ALP campaign launch, 2016.

Former prime ministers Bob Hawke and Paul Keating reunite to endorse Bill Shorten's plan for the economy, 2019.

Craig Emerson joins the two friends he helped reconcile.

At home in Northbridge with crossword, 2019.

Louis and Brianna's wedding, Mount Wilson, May 2019.

A triumphant Hawke. He was determined to attend Louis's wedding.

Tony Pratt, father of Louis, Blanche and Bob, at Louis and Brianna's wedding, Mount Wilson, May 2019.

The newlyweds bow to their parents.

Hawke at the Woodford Folk Festival, 2018.

When asked how he would like to be remembered: 'As a bloke who loved his country, still does. And loves Australians and who wasn't essentially changed by high office.'

of which both had been willing to make sacrifices. Hawke and Hazel had known each other since they were teenagers and by the time they were in their early twenties had agreed to shoot for the stars together. Hazel's sacrifices were known to many of Hawke's male friends: he was a 'married bachelor'. In the years before 1970s feminism, 'married bachelors' were frowned upon but wives accepted them, sometimes amicably, more often with tears or gritted teeth. While a husband was a reliable provider for his family, his extramarital behaviour was a topic socially taboo. A man who provided material comfort for his wife and children and did not flaunt or spend his salary on other women – in those days no married man was conceivably homosexual – he could consider he was upholding his side of the relationship. That was Hawke's position. He had married, he said, 'With my fingers crossed behind my back'. He wished he had more time to spend with his children, but to reach the goal he had set out to achieve he could not. Or did not. He was as good a husband as he was able, given his hot temperament: he loved Hazel, and was perpetually unfaithful.

When he lost office in December 1991, winter struck the relationship.

Hazel had written an autobiography, *My Own Life*, announcing what her friends already knew, that she was no longer 'Bob's handbag'. It was published in May 1992. The manuscript, which he had read before publication, contained passages about the earlier years of their marriage, when Hawke's drinking and womanising were out of control. He insisted some be deleted, but old wounds had opened and were not rehealing. The situation became acute when a friend of Hazel, in launching her book, took the opportunity to attack Hawke publicly, in the presence of media, as a bad husband, even a bad man – despite Hazel declaring at the same function, 'When you're on a good thing, stick to it!' Hawke was furious with the friend, a woman of outstanding competence, whom he had promoted to a senior role in national life. Rightly or wrongly, he felt betrayed at a time when he was hypersensitive to betrayal.

Then Fate intervened.

Some months after the book launch, a woman (this author) whom he had loved for many years was in a seaplane crash in Far North Queensland. Told the news in bits and pieces, Hawke thought she was dead or terribly injured. 'I felt myself die,' he said. By the time he learned she was alive and unharmed his mindset about the future had changed. Although divorce laws had softened dramatically during the Whitlam era, after 1978, when he had wanted a divorce, he had never again entertained the idea. He and Hazel were now in their sixty-fourth year; the prospect of a future of unsettled domesticity filled him with gloom. He was already depressed by being thrown from office. He was worse than most men of his generation in his domestic incompetence. He could make a cup of tea (with a teabag) but could not boil an egg or change a lightbulb. Hazel remained buoyant, looking forward to the house they were building, close to grandchildren, without the grind of public life and constant intrusion by the news media.

When they moved into their new four-storey mansion at the end of 1993, life became difficult. At the end of 1994 Hawke returned to live in the Ritz-Carlton hotel in Double Bay, divorced in early 1995 and in July that year, remarried. On the day of his wedding Hazel threw a 'Liberation Party'. She set out to rebuild her life as a single, independent woman accustomed to leadership. In her generation, women had rarely been able – or permitted – to express their potential. Tens of thousands of Australian women identified with her.

The divorce and Hawke's remarriage were a national scandal – no previous prime minister had divorced, although at least since World War II many had enjoyed mistresses while in office. The hostility to Hawke during the war of succession with Keating now became of far greater interest to the general public; women in particular took his divorce personally. A wave of sympathy rose beneath Hazel and would stay with her for the rest of her life – as, in sections of the news media, opprobrium would dog Hawke until the end of his. One consequence was that he was never named a National Living Treasure by the NSW branch of the National Trust, although all other prime ministers, from both sides of politics, were. Hazel was among the Treasures. The slight to Hawke was seemingly malicious, since other NLTs were known divorcees and adulterers. The snub, however, rather paled beside honours that greater institutions heaped upon Hawke. The King of Thailand awarded his nation's highest award, Knight, Grand Cordon of the Most Exalted Order of the White Elephant (in Thailand white elephants are symbols of kings); Baron Levene of Portsoken, Lord Mayor of London, admitted Hawke 'into the freedom of the City of London' in a celebration in the magnificent medieval Guildhall, Prince Charles presiding over a banquet of celebration, complete with trumpeters; the Emperor of Japan conferred the Grand Cordon of the Order of the Rising Sun, his country's highest honour for anyone not of the Japanese imperial family. The University of Oxford made him a Fellow in a ceremony conducted entirely in Latin; universities throughout Australia and from around the world awarded him honorary doctorates, ten in all. But annually, when the Treasures were announced, Hawke was not among them, although he had done more for the nation, in terms of its people of all colours, its environment and its place in the world, than any of those honoured. One had to wonder who was so determined to blackball him. Unlike the man they were punishing, they were certainly A grade haters.

Remarried at the age of sixty-five, he became as deliriously happy as in his youth. He lived in a house he loved, with a woman he loved with an intensity he had never before experienced. If he had married with his 'fingers crossed behind my back' the first time, he was determined that his second marriage would be pure. The wedding vows were poetic and mystical, addressing a spiritual union rather than a fleshly one, with no mention of fidelity. Hawke insisted on having the traditional words 'to the exclusion of all others' inserted, a clunk of a phrase in the midst of the musical language of the liturgy. For this marriage he chose to wear a wedding ring, a gold band with a decorative knot, that he never allowed to leave his finger. As death approached, he vowed that in his second marriage he had honoured his oath of exclusive devotion. If his memory was at fault, his intention was not.

One of the first effects of being happily remarried was that he forgave Paul Keating. Hawke hated losing at anything, being so intensely competitive that while waiting for a lift he would bet with his driver or his secretary on which would arrive first. It took him many years to tell Keating to his face that he was indebted to him, although he often remarked privately, 'Paul is my best friend. If I'd stayed PM I couldn't have married Blanche.' This sounds a backhanded compliment, but it was sincere: somewhat shame-faced, he saw Keating as the agent of Providence, an essential goad into the next and happiest phase of his life. It was a tacit admission of his own hubris and irrationality in clinging to office longer than he should have. His tenacity could be almost superhuman: on holiday in Far North Queensland he fought a 300 pound bottom-dwelling shark known locally as a 'Lazy Mary' for four hours, on a handline, finally dragging it to the surface, where he set it free. He was seventy-two years old. In a principled political fight tenacity was one of his highest virtues, but misapplied it stagnated to pig-headed folly – as in the struggle against Keating.

Among Hawke's greatest joys as he entered old age was that he and Keating renewed their bond of camaraderie. One day Craig Emerson, who was a frequent visitor, asked, 'Would you like me to try to bring Paul around to see you?' Emerson recalled, 'Bob looked at me with childlike joy and anticipation on his face and said, "Could you?"' Their reconciliation was an unalloyed success. They spoke of how few were their disagreements until the leadership challenge, and afterwards Keating reiterated how close he and Bob were. They talked politics, at some point agreeing that Keating would draft a statement of support for the ALP and Bill Shorten that he and Hawke would sign for a forthcoming general election. Both were keen to have it known they had reunited, as they recognised it as a healing of the rift in the party their struggle had caused.

After leaving parliament, Hawke had thrown himself into business, social and academic relations with Asian countries, particularly China and America. He flew out every six weeks to travel for two to four weeks in the Asian region, America and Europe.

For several years he attended an annual seminar at Stanford, California, where in 1997 the university's scientists warned 'the bugs are winning'. At that time the word 'superbug' was unknown; the claim sounded preposterous. There were talks about what might be found in outer space, about geopolitics . . . He was especially excited by discussions with astrophysicists from SETI (Search for Extraterrestrial Life), founded by Carl Sagan and Jill Tarter in 1984. A SETI man told him he was confident that intelligent life would be found beyond earth before the end of the twenty-first century. 'If only! If only!' Hawke exclaimed. As in almost all situations, he saw the possibility as bringing people together, which life elsewhere in the universe would do, he thought. The atmosphere of high thinking and advanced research was nectar to him.

Back in Sydney he engaged in charity work, especially Engineering Aid, a national organisation that encourages Indigenous schoolchildren from Year Nine to continue to university, preferably as engineers. He was patron for twenty-two years, known to the 600 Indigenous children who graduated from its annual summer school, as 'Uncle Bob'.

Another favourite charity was Bestest, also a national organisation established to help children in need who would otherwise fall outside the boundaries of larger charities. As with Engineering Aid, 100 per cent of funds raised go directly to their specified purpose. By 2019, 4000 children had benefitted. Initially Hawke was chairman of the fundraising committee, spending hours on the telephone cajoling well-heeled friends and acquaintances to attend an annual black tie dinner. By 2018 this job had become too arduous for him and he moved to patron. At the gala dinner that year he announced, 'Despite turmoil in various parts of the world, human instinct for wanting to bring about a better world still triumphs . . . We need to extend the hand of kindness to those who for one reason or another are suffering hardship in their lives.'

Another small charity he helped was Inala, a Sydney organisation for people with intellectual disability. Annually, he allowed himself to be raffled for golf days, lunches or dinners. The older Hawke grew, the more he was able to return to the ethic of kindness and compassion in which he had been raised as son of the manse.

Having achieved his greatest goal in life, he now had time for play: attending the races, hosting dinner and lunch parties at home, fishing from the jetty at the bottom of his garden, sitting in the sun smoking cigars, and doing cryptic crossword puzzles. His holidays were adventurous rather than luxurious: Antarctica on a small Russian ship; game parks in Africa, the Galapagos Islands; Easter Island; Pulau Island; by boat from Broome to Darwin with land trips to view Indigenous art. Special favourites were Lord Howe and Haggerstone islands, the latter able to accommodate only six adults; there was a saltwater crocodile in its lagoon, and guests caught their own lunch and dinner from the sea. Meanwhile, he had acquired another child, a stepson, Louis Pratt, whom he had met on his wedding day. Louis became embedded in Hawke's family life when he requested a bed for two weeks between moving apartments. Hawke always craved male company and so took to having a man around that Louis ended up living seven years with his stepfather. Night after night they played snooker competitively (to Hawke's frustration, his stepson had longer arms and excellent vision), or watched sport on television, shouting and whooping. His own philandering days over, the stepfather found delight in the variety of girlfriends the stepson brought home.

Hazel, meanwhile, had achieved for herself a life of contentment one suburb away from the mansion in which she had lived briefly and rather unhappily. She never really loved the four-storey house, equipped with a lift and a plethora of high tech devices; its vast garden, invisible from the street, a rainforest so steep and deeply shaded no flower could bloom in it. She had bought a comfortable brick house, on flat land, where she could indulge her twin passions for nurturing the plants of the earth and her growing brood of grandchildren. And she could play the piano night and day. But in 2001 she was diagnosed with Alzheimer's disease. With classic grit, she announced it publicly, to help dispel the stigma of the most feared disease of the elderly. Her decision further enhanced her reputation for courage. Her daughter Sue and her granddaughter, Sophie, living next door, kept her at home as long as they could but eventually had to move her to a nursing home when her symptoms became too severe to support at the house.

By 2013 Hazel was fading, unable to recognise even her closest friends. She did recognise Hawke, however, when he visited her and sang a song of their youth, 'Danny Boy'. She died a few weeks later, surrounded by children and grandchildren. At the wake after her state memorial service, Hawke asked if he could say a few words. He praised Hazel, acknowledging all she had done for his career, adding he regretted any hurt he had caused her. His sincerity was patent. Sue said, 'Some there couldn't help but forgive him. It was very healing.'

When Hawke passed the age of eighty his own health began to deteriorate. He needed a pacemaker and hearing aids; he developed glaucoma. He was playing golf three days a week (and had shot three holes-in-one), but his back became increasingly problematic. Unknown and undiagnosed, he was developing peripheral neuropathy in his feet. Walking became precarious and he needed a stick. He reduced golf to once a week, but his game became painfully slow and erratic. None of his golfing buddies could bear to tell him he should throw in the towel; eventually the club wrote to him saying that, having broken the rules with a golf cart – he had parked somewhere he should not have because he could not walk – he was suspended for three months. He recognised he would never be able to play again but was too devastated to speak about it. Robi Roland, a golf partner for fifteen years, said, 'My heart was bleeding for him. He was so determined to play he would have crawled on all fours if he could have.'

In 2015, on a trip to Saudi Arabia, Hawke picked up a gut bug so severe that without the intervention of Professor Thomas Borody, a brilliant gastroenterologist, he would have died. Borody, a family friend, diagnosed the problem from a telephone conversation with me.

From then on, Hawke cut his travel, willing to fly to China only twice a year, unwilling to travel to Europe or the USA, and unable to walk the long distances in airports. He needed either a people mover or to be pushed in a wheelchair. By late 2017 he was, in effect, housebound.

The following year he had two transient ischaemic attacks (small strokes) that confined him in rehabilitation for weeks. When he emerged he was set on a mission to die. 'I can no longer make a contribution to society,' he said. In his mind was his mother Ellie's insistence that one lived, in the biblical parable, 'to use one's talents'. As he could no longer, he believed he should be dead.

For years he had supported the idea of euthanasia and began hunting for a doctor who would help him. He approached his cardiologist, asking for the pacemaker to be removed: the specialist pointed out that with a pacemaker he could still die from a heart attack, but without one he would merely feel wretched. Hawke was close to his GP, and asked her. She smiled enigmatically and made no commitment. Personally, I was convinced he was not ready to die – there was something, I had no idea what, that his soul needed before it would leave his body.

At the end of the year he flew to Queensland for the Woodford Folk Festival, an annual holiday ritual. The festival director, a former folk musician, is Bill Hauritz, a huge, gentle man of commanding presence, radiant bonhomie and acute intelligence (who often appeared to have slept in his clothes, or lost his comb). He became one of Hawke's closest friends in the final ten years of his life, on every trip to Sydney visiting the house to smoke a Cuban cigar from the box he always brought as a gift. Hawke's attendance at the festival, which had been ignored by the news media, had so raised its profile that it became a fixture for east coast media over the holiday period, and greatly extended the range of serious speakers – and government financial support – it attracted. Hawke described Woodford as 'bringing happiness to hundreds of thousands of people'. This was accurate: the festival is famous for its friendly inclusiveness, laidback vibe and advanced ideas.

Once his stepfather's walking had become a problem, annually Louis attended Woodford to help keep an eye on him. Driving up on Christmas Eve 2017, Louis proposed to his girlfriend, Brianna Roberts, a philosophy graduate and journalist. The age difference between them was the same as between Bob and me. They decided they needed to wait seventeen months, until May 2019, for the wedding.

'I'll be there,' Hawke announced with habitual bravado.

But in early 2019 he had a stroke. Immediately, family and friends united around him, three of the grandsons taking turns to live in the house to help him physically, as did Steve, Louis and Craig Emerson who, for many years had been, like Kim Beazley, an honorary son. Sue and Sophie cooked meals. Rosslyn rang every few days to send messages of love. The bond between Hawke and his biological son, Steve, became sweeter than ever, as they sat for hours doing crossword puzzles and sudokus.

The stroke had slurred Hawke's speech and weakened the right side of his body, but with physiotherapy he improved and was able to fill in the crosswords and sign his name. His speech returned to almost normal. Intellectually, the effect of the stroke had been minimal. Paul Keating remarked, 'He's sharp! Hasn't lost it at all!' Close friends visited but by now Hawke was awake for only seven or eight hours a day and tired quickly: oral morphine and fentanyl were necessary for the pain in his legs and feet.

Throughout the early months of the year he had visitors every couple of days, including John Howard, Bill Shorten, Kim Beazley, Jack and Jacqui Newton, Ross Garnaut, Craig Emerson and John Singleton who, after saying goodbye, sat on the front doorstep of the house and wept. Hawke had told him he wanted to die, and the sooner the better. He had already signed legal documents stating he was not to be revived if he had another stroke or a heart attack, was not to be treated with antibiotics for an infection, and would take only medication to relieve pain.

Unexpectedly, this period turned into one of the happiest of his life. As the flesh weakened, the gifts of the spirit increased, and the first of these was love. Hawke and Hazel had enjoyed young love; he and I had enjoyed mature love. Now we entered the delight that is held in the love of old age; feelings of inexpressible tenderness and unity. Totally vulnerable, he became more loving and lovable than he had ever been when he was The Man. He was not The Child. He was, when alone with me, a radiant spirit trapped inside a cage of thinning flesh and bone, saying, as I helped him into bed each night, how lucky we were to have this time together. In his early twenties he had intellectually accepted the idea from a Buddhist monk that the soul reincarnated. Occasionally we played with this concept, joking in what human form each of us might return. He wanted to be an orchestra conductor. That was fine with me: I wanted to come back as an opera singer.

Every morning I awoke wondering if he had died during the night. But clearly, there was still something on earth that his soul needed to experience.

Louis and Brianna's wedding was to take place in May 2019, the same month as the federal election – and despite the opinion of friends, on the morning of the eleventh Hawke was alive and determined to attend it. The ceremony took place on a fine, cold autumn day in a garden on Mount Wilson, a couple of hours drive from Sydney. He was not strong enough to stay on for the reception that evening. The newlyweds promised they would return after the weekend to perform their wedding waltz for him.

The election, which Labor was expected to win, was four days away.

'I won't postal vote. I'll go in my wheelchair,' Hawke announced. With the help of Keating and Emerson he had contributed to the campaign, with two articles and photographs of himself and Keating, laughing and sharing a pot of tea.

On Tuesday 14 May the bride and groom arrived with their wedding clothes and music. Maria Finlay, one of Hawke's oldest friends, a famous Hungarian-born beauty and fashion icon, model for the main character in the film *Ladies in Black*, had advised Brianna on her dress. She too was invited to watch the dance. The audience was Maria Finlay, Bob Hawke, Andrew Adams (Bob's driver), Vicky Ma, a carer, and me. Furniture was moved aside, the music, *True Love*, began to play, and suddenly there was magic. The bride in her glorious dress and the groom in a tuxedo transformed a suburban sitting room into a grotto of enchantment, a palace of dreams. 'I shall remember this for the rest of my life,' Maria murmured. Hawke smiled until his face was alight with bliss. Andrew, sitting opposite, said, 'I've never seen him so happy.' The thought grabbed me and would not leave: he is imagining us reborn as young lovers.

The next afternoon the couple left on honeymoon. A few hours later Hawke said he needed to lie down. I rang his doctor, Mark Haran, who was dining close by, and Craig Emerson, who with his partner, Tracey Winters, lived fifteen minutes away. Hawke began to have extreme pain in his torso, in the area where, seventy years earlier, his spleen had ruptured and was cut out to save his life. We both realised what the doctor had just told me: 'This is probably the beginning of the end'.

I knew that if one fought pain, it increased. 'Try to surrender to it,' I whispered.

My husband turned to look at me as if I were mad; the life force in him reared like a tiger hiding in the grass. He roared, 'I can't surrender!'

That was the last coherent sentence he spoke, for a few minutes later Craig, Tracey and Dr Haran arrived. In moments the doctor had injected a sedative and morphine.

Less than twenty-four hours later I was seated close to Hawke's head, holding his hand and squeezing droplets of water into his lips to assuage thirst. Craig was on the opposite side of the bed, keeping watch on the pulse in his neck. Tracey sat at the foot of the bed. Hawke was in a deep morphine sleep. Pneumonia laboured his breathing. He would take a breath, then pause: was it his last? We didn't know. We waited and watched. Another breath would come. Suddenly it seemed an invisible light filled the air around him and an inaudible whoosh issued with another ragged breath. Craig placed two fingers on his neck and shook his head. With astonishment, the three of us felt intense, uplifting joy.

It was 5.04 pm, Thursday, 16 May.

Across Australia the next day, Friday, flags flew at half-mast and a national outpouring of grief swept the nation. Hundreds of thousands of texts, tweets, emails and cards of condolence gushed out to family members and friends. People felt they had lost part of themselves. Labor lost the election on Saturday. On Sunday a minute's silence was observed at every football stadium by every code around Australia.

Hawke had been in public life for more than six decades, he had gladdened and made flourish the lives of millions of Australians and, in some instances, of tens of thousands around the world.

The golden bowl was broken.

AFTERWORD

The following are three of the eulogies to Bob Hawke
shared at the state memorial service for the former
prime minister by Kim Beazley, Bill Kelty
and Paul Keating.

'Bob never forgot who he was fighting for. He once said, "The essence of power is the knowledge that what you do is going to have an effect – not just immediate, but perhaps lifelong effect on the happiness and wellbeing of millions of people, so I think the essence of power is to be conscious of what it can mean for others".'

The Honourable Kim Beazley

I loved Bob. He was my mentor, he was my friend. He allowed me to be a member of a government that transformed this nation for the better.

I would love to speak about the personal aspects of the man for whom I had and have such affection. A man who, in the extremity of his last illness, would cross the country to my installation as Governor to sit outside in the cold to smoke his last cigar in WA.

What I need to do is talk about how he governed because that, with what he did, is what cements him in history.

Was he our greatest prime minister, or our greatest Labor prime minister? Bob told me he was neither. His aspiration was to be our greatest peacetime prime minister.

He deferred always to John Curtin. Bob believed Curtin faced a national existential crisis and responded correctly, with a national strategy of alliance building, wholehearted national mobilisation and planning for post-war reconstruction. He saw himself pursuing that necessary complexity in peacetime conditions that also presented existential national challenges.

Bob exemplified Bagehot's view of great prime ministers as men of commonplace opinions and uncommon administrative abilities. Perhaps with opinions not quite so common but he was certainly trusted by the public, whose values and characteristics

he shared and he loved. But as an administrator he was unsur-
passed. He had an encyclopaedic knowledge of how this nation
worked, how the system could be creatively deployed to achieve
the necessary reforms.

So, first he governed with his ministers. He had a superb
office, an engine of reform, but they were not there to dominate
his ministers and sideline them, so as not to dull the glow of the
sun king. He told each of his ministers, 'You know the policy,
you know your resources, you proceed. I will interfere when you
invite me. My reputation will rise or fall on the quality of my
ministers' performance.'

Second, and above all, he governed with the Cabinet. As I
sat weeping on my porch as I absorbed the news of his passing, the oddest memory came to mind. It was back at the time
of the navy's seventy-fifth birthday. I nagged Bob into taking
the Cabinet to sea for a meeting. The biggest ship, *HMAS
Stalwart*, had enough space but no Cabinet table. One was duly
put aboard. We all came aboard. The *Stalwart* passed through
the Sydney Heads and began to roll. The table started to move.

It pinned the prime minister to the bulkhead, then it retreated
and then it came back harder as momentum gathered. 'F— this'
he said repeatedly as he fought the beast and continued the meeting. Afterwards, pretty cross, he said to me, 'You know, Cabinet
is the heart of our government, we cannot have the Cabinet table
running away and killing a couple of us on the way through.'

The late Peter Walsh, no great supporter of Bob, said to
me, 'You know, only two ministers read every Cabinet submission, myself and Bob.' On Sunday afternoon his senior public
servants would come around to his home for a game of tennis.
Then they would settle down for detailed consideration of every
submission.

Third, there was the party and the Labor movement, the
focal point of support for a Labor government but also, frankly,
potentially a base for effective opposition. Bob accepted their
legitimacy as major participants in the Australian democratic
project, as had Curtin, of course, in seeking to overturn Labor

opposition to conscription during the war. He did not move, Curtin did not move, until he had secured a federal conference decision.

Bob didn't circumvent the machinery, he used it. He was particularly emphatic to me on that, when we focused on micro-economic reform. He had given me the key transport and communications portfolio at the beginning of his last term. He said this: 'Your first job is to get this through the caucus and the union movement, then to a successful outcome at the federal conference.'

Finally, he governed with peak organisations, unions of course, but also the employer groups, Indigenous, environmental and rural groups, multicultural, arts, sporting, social, religious groups. For him, they were the transmission belts of change to the community, feedback and adjustment. Not all or even most of them Labor supporters but all part of the Australian community. So he loved them and many, despite themselves, requited it.

In all this, Bob never forgot who he was fighting for. He once said, 'The essence of power is the knowledge that what you do is going to have an effect – not just immediate, but perhaps life-long effect on the happiness and wellbeing of millions of people, so I think the essence of power is to be conscious of what it can mean for others.'

He was massively persuasive from his experience as ACTU advocate and president. He was deeply effective publicly. But at the heart of his ability to persuade was trust. Most people believed, as that quote indicated, that whether you agreed or not, your happiness was his motive. He could afford risk-taking in leadership. He was confident in the effectiveness of argument to succeed.

Yet there were some who were hurt and some who mattered most to him. We owe a deep debt to Hazel and their children – Sue, Ros and Stephen – and to Blanche. We owe Blanche for the joy she provided him and the care in his decline. On behalf of all of us to the family, thank you.

Well, where is he now? Bob set great store by his pastor father Clem saying, 'If you believe in the fatherhood of God, you must believe in the brotherhood of man.' We talked of his destination in our last conversation. He still firmly held the second part of Clem's saying but no longer the first.

But for me, I am sustained by the belief he is in the arms of a loving God. He believed he would live in the hearts or at least the minds of those who knew him, then when we all pass, in the history books and stories of future generations. There he will reside while ever this nation abides.

The Honourable Kim Beazley
Governor of Western Australia
Eulogy at the State Memorial Service for R.J.L.Hawke
Sydney Opera House
13 June 2019

'Bob Hawke loved this country to the depths and breadths and height that his life could give, and he was loved in return.' Bill Kelty AC

I first met Bob Hawke in 1966. As a young student and ALP member, they told me that the best act in town was Bob Hawke and the Conciliation and Arbitration Commission. And there I went. And what did I see? Bob and his able assistant, Ralph Willis, against an army of QCs.

He was tenacious, tough, irreverent and persuasive. The only thing that I had a query about was the ad hoc nature of the adjournments. I asked Bob why it was so erratic. He said, 'Bill, we time the adjournments to coincide with the races. Richard Kirby and I are really interested in the races.'

What I noticed in this great class battle of capital and labour, everybody gathered in the middle to get the results.

I said to myself, 'It says something about Bob, it says something about Australia.'

Lenin was right. This is no place for revolution, no place for revolutionaries.

But when Bob became the president of the ACTU you had seen nothing like him ever before: a man of conciliation, the captain of consensus. But at the same time, he led the biggest industrial disputes in our history and the biggest political disputes. At the same time he was a friend of business, unashamedly the friend of many, many business people but he caused competitive mayhem by getting rid of a whole range of competitive vehicles, particularly retail and price maintenance, and leading competition in a lot of industries.

He was, to some people's chagrin, really, an opponent of the Russians' invasion of Afghanistan – as deep as his opposition to the American participation in the war in Vietnam. He was loving and kind and charismatic . . . but, boy, could he be frightening. He could be really frightening on occasions.

His undiluted belief in the power of education. His undiluted belief in the power of democracy. His belief in unions and the ALP and this thing he called Australia, not a geography but a belief. Hazel and the family, they provided him ballast and buoyancy in times of happiness and joy, but equally in times of doubt and uncertainty.

What Bob did for the ACTU was to change it forever, with the industrial campaigns that he led, with the future funds that he built up and the financial assets of the organisations and their amalgamation. He gave the ACTU a base from which it could negotiate with government effectively, for everybody in the union movement – not just for some but for all unions.

But it was not always easy. It was not always kind; there was not a woman on the ACTU executive the entire time. The fight with Bill Hayden, tough and hard, was just simply painful. There were tough times. Many tough times. And the reality was we never did as much as we could have with the Whitlam government.

But when Bob became prime minister, Jan Marsh, the ACTU advocate, and Simon Crean, we went to his place in Sandringham and there he spelt out his vision of what he would do for Australia.

He would, of course, fix the economy. The most important thing was fixing double-digit inflation and double-digit unemployment, investing in education and in social welfare, and making the country more confident and more co-operative to achieve these objectives. He would put Medicare in place, but this time it would be set in concrete so it could never be removed. He would open Australia to the rest of the world and he would do something for women, to make their place better in this country.

Was he inspirational? He was. The greatest legacy to me is a simple one. He raised the aspirations of this nation, got us to set bigger objectives but provided us with the inspiration to achieve them. On the eve of the Springbok tour, as we sat there contemplating the next step, waiting for Bob to appear in a crowded ACTU room, he did appear, shuffling his papers, and he told two stories.

One story was the dignity of Nelson Mandela. The other story, the indignity of apartheid. He took us to Soweto and he took us to the prison of Robben Island. He was truly inspirational. And we went to the streets and we went to the factories and we went to the ports and we went to the airports to stand up for this cause.

When confronted with the political pressure to make a step backwards following the implications of his decision to allow 40,000 Chinese students to stay in this country after Tiananmen Square, Bob didn't take a step back. He didn't take two steps back, but he took two steps forward. And it wasn't for a cheap political ploy, it wasn't for a political gain. As he said, it was to put the knife into a policy that had stained this country – the white Australia policy.

Bob was always – always – about those two things. When we went to see him in his last weeks of life, he was still thinking about the treaty with the first Australians. He was still thinking about climate change. He was still aspiring for this country to be better and do better, and providing the inspiration for us all.

Bob was no saint. Bob had his faults. But he did a power of good for this country, a power of good for all of us. He helped make the country what it is. And he made this country play a better part in the rest of the world.

Bob loved trade union songs. He was one of the few people who actually knew the words of the songs. Most of us just mumble and shuffle along, hoping we've got the right word at the right place, but not Bob. He knew the words.

And he loved the poets. But above all he loved Blanche d'Alpuget. And these words, from a poem by Elizabeth Barrett Browning, are for her:

How do I love thee,
Let me count the ways.
I love thee to the depth and breadth and height
My soul can reach.

If I had one line for Bob, if people asked me just to explain one line for Bob, I would say Bob Hawke loved this country to the depths and breadths and height that his life could give, and he was loved in return. Thank you for everything you ever did, Bob. Thank you.

Bill Kelty AC
Eulogy at the State Memorial Service for R.J.L. Hawke
Sydney Opera House
13 June 2019

'None of us can be on the stage for long. What matters is the value of the legacy – its quality and endurance. On both counts, Bob Hawke well earned five-star rank and twenty-four carat stars at that.'

The Honourable Paul Keating

When Bob invited me over to see him, the better part of a year ago, he and I were again joining the circle on the great friendship and partnership that drove the longest reform period in the country's history.

Eight and a half years we were together and with a great Cabinet we were able to give the country what it formerly never had – at least not since the war – policy creativity, coherence and continuity. And as it turned out, not just for eight and a half years but thirteen years.

At the core of it, Bob and I shared one primary idea – that Australia's creativity had been locked down by a stultifyingly paternal policy regime – the idea that the government knew best and that Australia was best protected and nurtured as a closed economy behind policy barbed wire – a framework that both the Labor party and the coalition then heavily subscribed to.

Bob and I had clear ideas as to how each of us had independently reached the same conclusion and as to why Australia had operated sub-optimally for so long, and broadly what had to happen to change it.

But we also knew that to change it required wholesale policy reform on a scale the country and the Labor Party had never experienced.

We knew we were in for it. And so did our senior Cabinet colleagues who shared our view – we knew that none of the factions of the Labor Party would embrace so great a philo-sophical shift without a lot of persuasion and heft.

It was this quest that was central to my eight-and-a-half-year partnership with Bob – the long and weary externalisation of the country – binding up sections of society as the changes bore their fruit and, inevitably, their cost.

Eight budgets and six major economic reform statements – the equivalent of more than fourteen normal budgets, along with singular standout reforms, put in place along the way, was a major undertaking.

Through this great body of work, Bob and our Cabinet colleagues remained focused on the target – the nirvana of an open, creative and free society – with enhanced opportunities for all.

It was a big agenda and one moving on a broad front.

Bob was a great chair of a very creative and independent Cabinet. Contestability was its hallmark; loyalty and commit-ment was its binding strength.

The quality Bob brought to the prime ministership was of an open mind – regard for policy creativity and a commitment to reform in areas central to Australia's economy and society and place in the world.

Areas long neglected and passed over by a succession of gov-ernments, broadly since World War II.

The shape and direction of the government came about with Bob setting the overall direction – balancing off the competing policy demands – giving the whole a recognisable and compel-ling coherence.

He presided over the Cabinet in a manner where all matters were generally contested – but where, importantly, he allowed ministers to prioritise their issues and proselytise for them in public. He led a very 'can do' collegiate group.

In a perpetual contest of ideas, inevitably egos clash. Bob and I would have private skirmishes over this policy or that, even criticise one another to immediate staff, but by instinct and a large dollop of friendship, we always remained welded to the same objective – a point even the closest of our staff sometimes failed to comprehend.

Through ups and downs, each of us knew the other would remain faithful to the obsession.

In the end, it was trust that held Bob and me together.

He knew I would never leave a landmine in some budget or economic statement to explode in his face, as I knew, when push came to shove, he would not rat on the big ones – on the big changes.

And we both loved the game of political dodgems – off with a spurt, banging our way round the course – often trying to sell the near impossible. We were sometimes wary of particular dodgems, but always exhilarated by the wild ride that generally followed.

The thing about truly big confidence plays is that there is no substitute for the psychological reward – the bounty of major policy achievement.

We truly relished those achievements, often celebrating them with family dinners at The Lodge.

Much of the very late focus on my relationship with Bob was, of course, on the termination of cooperation between us and his displacement by me as leader.

But any cursory observation of these events generally fails to comprehend the very high level of friendship and cooperation between us for those eight and a half years – a long time in so hot a policy hothouse. And, in policy terms, it lasted right to the end.

In the event, between us, Bob and I won five elections successively – not far short of four American presidential terms in a row.

Underlying the fact that Bob asked me to speak at this Memorial was his recognition that our control over the 1993–1996 parliament broadened Labor's policy frontier, well annealing the policy achievements he believed the country sorely needed and which bookended the policy framework begun during his own period of office.

And I think I can say, the template which we and our remarkable Cabinet colleagues set into place in those thirteen years, has provided the foundations for Australia's burgeoning growth and wealth – in a fundamental sense – really ever since.

People seek leadership in political life for all manner of reasons. We will never know what particular mix of influences propelled Bob Hawke or whether, what Immanuel Kant called 'the inner command' – the commitment to more exalted objectives – drove him. Certainly that higher calling rang loudly in his head.

None of us can be on the stage for long. What matters is the value of the legacy – its quality and endurance. On both counts, Bob Hawke well earned five-star rank and twenty-four carat stars at that.

The Honourable Paul Keating
Former Prime Minister of Australia
Eulogy at the State Memorial Service for R.J.L. Hawke
Sydney Opera House
13 June 2019

APPENDICES

Appendix 1

1982 PREFACE TO HAWKE: THE EARLY YEARS
(Part I in this edition)

There is a school that holds that biographies of the living should not be written, because they cannot be honest. Indeed, the problems confronting the biographer of a living subject are daunting, especially if – as in the case of R. J. Hawke – the writer knows that much of what she reveals about her subject may be used and misused against him, in his lifetime, perhaps to the detriment of a career that is in mid-term. Such considerations have also concerned Hawke. It is a mark of his candour and integrity that he has permitted me, as an authorised biographer, to write about him critically and often unflatteringly and that, in the tradition of his spiritual ancestor, Cromwell, he is willing to be presented 'warts and all'. The only area I have avoided is a discussion of the Hawke children, whose privacy has already been invaded over many years. I have omitted information about the children at the request of Hazel Hawke. Her desire to protect them, and not to have republished matters that have already appeared in the press, has been a price worth paying for her help and unflinching frankness, both in giving information and in reading the manuscript for accuracy of detail. I have been guided by her perceptions a great deal, while exercising the responsibility to reach my own conclusions.

It is, surely, one of the most unnerving experiences in any life to have the past loom up, made solid in words. When Sir Richard Kirby first read the manuscript of the biography I had written about him, he exclaimed, 'Oh, God. I feel like a full frontal nude!' Hawke made a similar remark in the same situation: 'This is traumatic – like seeing your face in a mirror with a thousand facets. Some of the images seem to me grotesque.'

I have taken the view that there is no single truth to be told about something as complex and shifting as a fifty-year life span, but rather many truths, from various perspectives that, when viewed together, reveal the dimensions of personality. To do this I have had to rely on people who have known Hawke at different stages of his life. Throughout the book I have allowed them to speak for themselves about him, offering opinions that, sometimes, are contradictory but out of which, I think, a coherent pattern emerges.

While the great drawback to biographies of the living or recently dead is the problem of candour – and, under Australian law, libel – an advantage lies in the wealth of information that may be collected, either from the subject or from those people who have known him or her. Importantly, too, friends, enemies and relations can provide a heavy counterweight to the subject's self-view. In Hawke's case their assistance to me has been crucial, for he is a man of dominating personality and persuasiveness and one, moreover, whose legal training has enabled him to confound critics with dextrous, logical argument. I make no claim to have been able, at all times, to withstand the force of Hawke's self-perceptions, but I have tried to present them as his own, by giving them as transcripts of his descriptions of situations, and where possible, presenting different views. The book is full of voices, for it is largely an oral history.

The use of oral history – in plain language, interviews – overcomes to some extent a major difficulty in writing about twentieth-century lives: lack of documentation. Telephones, radio, television, the whole world of audiovisual technology, has altered us so much: people have abandoned, for example, the custom of committing their intimate thoughts to letters and diaries, the documents that were once the primary source of a biographer. But oral history is only a partial solution – for what the middle-aged man recalls, let us say, about his parents is, generally, different from what the child, writing a diary, may have thought of them and may have later, unconsciously, built in to his behaviour in reaction to those thoughts. Again, the recollections of people who knew the subject in childhood are an important counterweight.

A particular problem created by the telephone is that much historically relevant communication is given over to it in the adult's career, where once the same transactions would have been made in writing. Oral history helps bridge the gaps – sometimes inadequately, sometimes much better than any written record: the Nixon White House tapes are, so far, the most celebrated example of the superiority of an oral record to a formal, written one. Wherever possible I have tape-recorded interviews.

I did some early work on this book in mid-1979 but did not turn my full attention to it until the beginning of 1980. At the time Hawke was still, as he described it later, 'climbing the mountain' – that is, struggling with his drinking problem. By the time I began writing, in mid-1981, he seemed to have conquered the mountain. By now he has been a teetotaller for two years. Much of this book is the story of Hawke's battle with alcohol. Much of it also is the story of a life contending with what I have called 'a dream' – that is, Hawke's ambition to be the political leader of his country. I have labelled it a dream not to suggest unreality but because it is an aspect of something that is larger and vaguer than the specific goal of political leadership, and is, rather, a yearning towards unity. The vision has come and gone throughout his life, like a recurrent dream that is part of a broader field of emotion. Interwined with it are other 'dreams' – International House, the ACTU enterprises, peace in the Middle East – whatever their focus, all of them flowing out from the same powerful source.

One of the Hawke family dreams was so like gossamer that I felt I could not include it in the text, but record it now: Hawke's father told me that his favourite chapter of the Bible concerned the Building of the Temple, explaining, 'David planned it, but it was his son, Solomon, who executed it'. It was only when this biography was almost complete that Hawke learned that his father had been an office holder of the ALP and in youth had wanted a political career himself.

At the time I began research Hawke had decided to try to live out his ambitious vision of political leadership. That, and his recent struggle with drink, have given a shape and motifs to the book that may well, from the longer view, seem artificial. A life of Hawke written posthumously would perhaps give a very different emphasis to the themes of alcohol and ambition – or what may be termed hedonism and social integration. This is, therefore, a partial life and will be to some people an example of the wrong-headedness of not only attempting the biography of a living subject but of one in mid-career.

I think it has been worth writing, for a number of reasons: one, obviously, is the intrinsic interest of the subject. Another is that it has provided an opportunity to trap information that otherwise will vanish as its living sources die, information about a social institution for which I feel profound respect (and often irritation): the Australian trade union movement. Frustrating and foolish as it sometimes is, I believe the freedoms of our society are carried on its shoulders.

Blanche d'Alpuget
May 1982, Canberra

Postscript: In less than a year our political landscape has been transformed: in May 1982 the Australian mainland had only one Labor government and Malcolm Fraser bestrode the continent with such authority that it seemed the Faustian pact his party had made to gain power in 1975 could stretch forward, without horizon. Today there are five Labor governments in Australia, and Hawke is prime minister. His personality, as delineated in the following pages, has changed in emphasis in the past three years: the process of struggle and suffering that leads to wisdom and that began in Hawke in the late 1970s has produced a man at peace with himself, prepared, finally, for the task to which he was trained. Or, as it may appear now, was destined.

I finished writing this book in May 1982. It first appeared in print in October that year, when Bob Hawke was the shadow Minister for Industrial Relations. At the time members of the Canberra press gallery considered his ambition to become prime minister derisory. Four months later, however, he was master of The Lodge. This updated edition was published and republished in the 1980s.

Appendix 2

2010 PREFACE TO HAWKE: THE PRIME MINISTER
(Part II of this edition, revised and updated)
Bob Hawke's political career began in 1929 when his pregnant mother, Ellie, a woman who was both religious and spiritual, found her Bible opening as if of its own volition at the verse in Isaiah that says, 'and the government shall be upon his shoulder'. Ellie Hawke took this as a sign that, disappointingly, the baby she was carrying would be a son and not the daughter she longed for, but that God had destined this son for leadership.

By the early 1980s Hawke was an Australian political phenomenon.

Before he had achieved the destiny foreseen for him more than thirty years earlier, I wrote a biography that explored the tensions in his life, attempting to answer the question people were constantly asking, 'What's he really like?' That is Part I of this volume. The second part appeared at a time when Hawke's political career was over but the long tail of its comet still shone.

Many books have been written about his period in office, including by Hawke himself. Members of his government have been the subjects of biographies; they have written autobiographies and memoirs; there are academic and other assessments of Hawke's prime ministership; there are books devoted to single issues, like the Combe–Ivanov affair. I have drawn information from all these works, but am most indebted to Paul Kelly's *The End of Certainty*, a magnum opus on the economics and politics of the 1980s.

In this second part of my description of his life, I have not attempted a full account of Hawke's prime ministership and have not even touched some important areas – the creation of the Aboriginal and Torres Strait Islander Commission (ATSIC), for example. Instead I have tried to answer the question, 'What sort of leader was he?'

For answers I turned to the prime minister's personal staff and senior public servants. They are people whom other writers have ignored, often from necessity, since an unofficial – and, in some cases, an official – vow of silence was cast upon them while Hawke was in office. I was fortunate that Hawke's office family were now at liberty to speak and that their memories of those days are clear and sharp. Only one professed scant recall. But constrained by time and distance – some, including Gareth Evans, were living abroad – I was unable to interview all. I did speak to at least two from each period of Hawke's four terms as prime minister. Unless otherwise indicated, all quoted statements, direct and indirect, are from interviews or remarks made to me. Except with the famously anonymous and invisible Peter Barron, with two journalists and two Chinese speakers, whom I had to interview by telephone (one with the help of an interpreter), I tape recorded all interviews. These tapes are archived in the Bob Hawke Prime Ministerial Centre in Adelaide as a resource for future researchers. Many of the interviews happened in noisy venues – in hotel lobbies and bars, with the sound of ice makers, espresso machines and exuberant patrons creating colour and inaudibility. My badly spelt and typed transcriptions are also archived and, in most cases, fill in the audio gaps. There are also properly spelt and typed transcriptions of some later interviews by Elizabeth Dale, who came to my assistance when I was very pressed for time.

Since he had already published his memoirs, the person I avoided as an interviewee was the subject himself. Only when I had the manuscript almost finished did I ask him to give comments. There are no taped interviews with Hawke.

The account of his 2003 trip to Ramallah to see Yasser Arafat is drawn from notes that I, being present, made at the time. The descriptions of meetings of Education International and the lunch at which the Boao Forum for Asia was planned are also from my own memory. I hope readers will enjoy discovering these and other aspects of Hawke's life that were unrecorded or unknown in Australia.

Blanche d'Alpuget
Sydney, April 2010

Appendix 3

A POWELL PLAN FOR PALESTINE

The fall of the Berlin Wall and the collapse of the Soviet Union gave birth to heroic assumptions about a New World Order. Those assumptions were strengthened with the emergence of the Oslo process and what seemed to be substantive developments based on that apparent accord. But now, a decade on the elements of instability have changed dramatically. In the Cold War the threat was constituted by a hegemonistic, atheistic nation-state – the Soviet Union. States and forces of differing political persuasions were united against a threat which was equally offensive to the Judaeo-Christian and Islamic religious traditions. The menace of Soviet Communism made allies of Bin Ladens and Bushes.

But with the dissolution of the cement of anti-Sovietism, restrained hatreds have been released and violently manifested, from September 11 2001 in New York to 12 October 2002 in Bali. This is not the occasion to attempt to analyse all the strands that go to make up the totality of the threat of international terrorism from fundamental Islamic extremists and their supporters. But, for present purposes, two points are relevant.

First, America, the world superpower, and those deemed to be its supporters, are designated as the 'enemy' for having no respect, understanding or sympathy for Islamic people and their aspirations, and indeed for contemptuously acting against those interests.

Second, whatever may be said or done to attempt to correct this extremist representation, which resonates in many quarters of the globe, nothing effective can be done in this direction while the festering sore of the Palestinian problem continues. This issue is used to encapsulate and dramatise the 'enemy' syndrome, with America and its deemed supporters cast as the villains.

It is imperative, therefore, that an entirely new approach be formulated to the Palestinian question, an issue which, in any case, cries out for resolution in terms of the aspirations of the Palestinians themselves, and the security of Israel and the region. It is not argued that resolving this issue resolves the challenge of international terrorism but that it is a sine qua non for meeting that challenge.

The only proposition concerning the Israeli–Palestinian crisis that can be advanced with any certainty is that everything that has been tried to this point has not worked and that, if anything, the situation is now, in many respects, worse than it has ever been. The hurdy-gurdy of hatred has ground on remorselessly with increasing casualties and diminishing hope. The cycle of hatred and violence, I repeat, can only be broken and a positive outcome achieved by radically new thinking.

In looking for historical support for such an approach we can do no better than look to immediate postwar Europe and the Marshall Plan, named after the then Secretary of State, George Marshall. In an act displaying a generosity of spirit and enlightened self-interest unequalled in the twentieth century, the Truman administration poured billions of dollars into creating viable economic entities in the war-torn countries of Western Europe. In addressing, practically, the needs and aspirations of the peoples of those countries it did as much to meet the threat of Soviet hegemony as any military outlays.

There is a general recognition, including among the majority of Israelis, that the Palestinians are entitled to their own independent state, an outcome that was envisioned by the 1947 United Nations Resolution enabling the creation of the state of Israel. But the political shell of a state lacking a viable and vibrant economy is a recipe for even greater disaster.

Palestinians, particularly young Palestinians, exist in a dysfunctional economic environment with virtually no hope of employment or maintenance, let alone improvement, of their living standards. This is a breeding ground for despair and worse – while there is no hope among the young for jobs and the constructive development of their talents there will be no shortage of recruits for the martyrdom of the suicide bomber.

What is required now is the 'Powell Plan'. The United States should take the lead, with the support of Europe, the moderate Arab states and Israel in making an unequivocal commitment to a massive supply of capital, technical and educational expertise and equipment dedicated to the creation of an education system and an economic structure that will give the reality of hope to the Palestinian people.

The World Bank should provide the delivery mechanism and technical assistance for the implementation of this program and there should be co-operation through the World Trade Organization to provide a period of most favoured access to export markets for the products from the new economy. The genuine commitment of the United States and other donors should be communicated and detailed to the Palestinian Authority, the leaders of the militant groups and, through television and other media, to the people of Palestine and the region.

The financial and technical capacity of the donor states to meet the requirements of this initiative is not in question. What is required is the will and the imagination. It is easy enough to list the difficulties that may lie in the path of carrying through with the initiative, but that is the counsel of despair and hopelessness. If genuinely embraced, I believe this concept can mark the beginning of a sea change in the poisonous atmosphere of hatreds and misconceptions that threaten the very stability and existence of the world as we know it.

R.J.L. Hawke
17 December 2002

ACKNOWLEDGEMENTS

THE EARLY YEARS (Part I of this edition)
I am deeply indebted to many people for providing me with material for this book. I wish to thank Sir Peter Abeles, Jose Aguiriano, Reo Allen, Gil Appleton, Lila Baillie, Kate Baillieu, Jim Baird, Lily Ballard, Ephraim Bar-Schmuel, Rhonda and Ron Blake, Francis Blanchard, Elizabeth Brenchley, Maggie Broadbent, Geoff Brown, Senator John Button, Helga Cammell, Sir Roderick Carnegie, Bernard Cherrick, Dr Colin Clark (for a letter), Professor Manning Clark, Dr Harry Cohen and June Cohen, Justice Judith Cohen, Peter Coleman, David Combe, Sir John Crawford, Chris Crellin, Col Cunningham, Sir George and Lady Currie, Cliff Dolan, Barry Donovan, John Ducker, G. L. Duffield, Don Dunstan, Sir John Egerton, H. E. Michael Elitzur, Senator Gareth Evans, Coral and George Fisher, Charlie Fitzgibbon, Bernard Fortin, Gwen Geater, Ray Geitzelt, Saadia Gelb, Rev. Allan George, Professor Jim Hagan (for books), Professor Keith Hancock, Albert Hawke, Rev. Clem Hawke, Dr Ron Hieser (deceased), Bob Hogg, Clyde Holding, Beatrice Holt, Rev. Clarence Hore, Jock Innes (for a letter), Bill Kelty, Pat Kennelly (deceased), H. E. Abraham Kidron and Shoshana Kidron, Sir Richard and Lady Kirby, Jack Knight, Eddie Kornhauser, I. L. Lagergren, Bill Landeryou, Harry Leece, Isi Leibler, Bill Leslie, Sam Lipski, David McBride, Mr Justice McClelland, Jennie McLellan, Gail and Rod Madgwick, Isadore Magid, Heribert Maier, Bruce Masters, Gwen May, Sir John Moore, Robin Morison, Joe Morris, Amal Mukherjee, Paul Munro, Zvi Netzer, Peter Nolan, David Pearce, Shimon Peres, George Polites, Oliver Popplewell, Professor John Poynter, George Poyser, Ben Rabinovitch, Dr Don Rawson, Peter Redlich, Oscar de Vries Reilingh, Doris Rhodes, Joe Riordan, Mr Justice Robinson, George Rockey (deceased),

Bob Rogers (for letters), Ben Same, Saul Same, Prof. Geoffrey Sawer, Mike Schildberger, George Seelaf, Dr N. Shavit, Jim Shea, Michael Siew (for letters), John Simonds, Jean Sinclair, E. F. Sivyer (for letters), Dr Bob Smith, The Rt Hon. Michael Somare (for letters), Harold Souter, Don Stewart, Prof. Sam Stoljar, The Hon. Tony Street, Ari Tel-Shahar, Mr Justice Toohey, Uniting Church parishioners in Bordertown and Maitland, Barry Watchorn, Senator John Wheeldon, Sir Frederick Wheeler (for books), David White, Professor David and Marjorie White, The Hon. Gough Whitlam, Kelvin Widdows, Edgar Williams, Ian Willis (for books), Ralph Willis, Terry Winter (deceased) and Beryl Winter, Francis Wolf, Meg and Jules Zanetti, Patsy Zeppel.

I thank, too, the staff of the current information section of the Parliamentary Library, especially Bobbie Sluyters and Margaret Healy; the staff of the National Library, especially Leoni Warne and Mark Cranfield; and the librarian of the ACTU, Anne Wilson.

A group of four friends, whose expertise is in psychology and political science, were unfailingly generous with their time and their libraries. Many of the insights and ideas in this book are thanks to them. I am especially grateful to Dr Michael Epstein, a child psychiatrist; Professor Ross Martin and Dr Angus McIntyre of La Trobe University; and Dr Graham Little, of Melbourne University. Dr Epstein and Dr McIntyre also had the dubious pleasure of putting up with me as a houseguest for weeks at a time, in Melbourne. Carol Treloar and Ruth Dewar were similarly generous with accommodation in Melbourne and Adelaide, as were Harry and June Cohen and George and Glen Browne in Perth, Sandra Alexander and Nick Herd in Sydney, and Mark Pierce in Tel Aviv. I thank also Margaret and Harry Leece for accommodation in Paris, and Kelvin Widdows for accommodation in Geneva. Travelling costs for this book were large: the hospitality of these people, most of whom had never met me before I arrived on their doorsteps, was of great help in keeping my expenses down. H. E. David Goss and Ann Goss from the Australian embassy, Tel Aviv, and Jim Shea, from the US embassy, Tel Aviv, were kind to me beyond the bounds of diplomacy. I wish to thank also staff of the ILO, especially John Simonds, who arranged my program there, and staff of Histadrut, especially Ephraim Bar-Schmuel, for arranging my program and taking me on a tour of Israel.

I could not have begun this book had it not been for the Literature Board of the Australia Council: it provided me with a two-year senior writer's grant to live on while I was researching. My publisher, Morry Schwartz, gave me a handsome advance to meet travelling costs.

The book could not have been brought to conclusion without the help of three women: Tess van Sommers, my psychological companion, who, as ever, advised and encouraged me; Elizabeth Douglas, who edited the manuscript with great care; and Jan Bourke, who typed it beautifully. I thank them all. I am grateful, too, to Jean Sinclair, the personal assistant of R. J. Hawke, for spending so much time in passing messages to him from me, and in finding research material; and to John Ducker for reading the manuscript.

My mentor and friend, Peter Ryan, of Melbourne University Press, also read the manuscript for me when he was very busy, and when I had reached a stage of exhaustion and despondency. There was great pressure of time in producing the book: chapter by chapter, in the later stages, it was edited and marked up as it was written. This speedy delivery caused in me a sort of post-natal depression during the fortnight's break between finishing writing and waiting for typesetting to begin, and I was overcome with doubts. Peter Ryan's encouragement arrived like a basket of flowers in winter.

Finally, I thank my husband, Tony Pratt, for his patience, and my son, Louis Pratt, who, for a nine-year-old, takes great care of his mother.

May 1982, Canberra

PART II: THE PRIME MINISTER (Revised and updated for this edition)

This book owes its initial existence to Louise Adler, then at the helm of Melbourne University Publishing. We agreed on an addition to the original book – perhaps 20 000 words, perhaps more – to be launched just before Hawke's eightieth birthday on 9 December 2009. It was this milestone birthday that persuaded me to undertake the effort I knew would be in store. But, despite setting aside nearly all my other commitments, a civilised life and the company of my friends, I missed the deadline.

The original concept of an add-on turned out to be lucky, however, because it forced me to bring into focus what I thought would be the most important thing I could say about Hawke as prime minister. I would leave to others a full account of his prime ministership, which will perhaps have to wait until Cabinet and other classified documents are released. I decided to address the question of his leadership.

By the time I had the manuscript finished, Ms Adler and I decided to publish my new work as a separate volume.

Many people have helped me. I would like to thank first Hawke's current office staff, Jill Saunders and Francie Grew, who assisted with digging out speeches and providing me with space in his office to read Hansards from the period 1983 to 1991. Hawke's personal advisers and public service staff from his prime ministership have been extraordinarily helpful in finding time for interviews, some of them several times. I thank Peter Barron, John Bowan, Craig Emerson, Graham Freudenberg, Ross Garnaut, Bob Hogg, Sandy Hollway and Hugh White. Former politicians Kim Beazley, John Dawkins, Michael Duffy, Nick Greiner, the Hon. John Howard, Graham Richardson, Warwick Smith and Ralph Willis were also gracious, as were public servants Mike Codd, Michael Costello, Helen Williams and Richard Woolcott. David Combe, Michael McHugh and Neil Young were very helpful in explaining aspects of the Combe–Ivanov affair. I sought to interview the Hon. Paul Keating, through direct and indirect approaches, but he declined. He was, however, gracious in refusal and spent almost an hour on the telephone explaining his reasons.

MUP provided press cuttings for me, but in addition I sought interviews with three political journalists: Paul Kelly, Brian Toohey and Marian Wilkinson. All three were generous in sharing their insights. Josh Klenbort, a colleague from Shanghai, provided fascinating insights into the early years of Hawke's association with China.

Chapter 30 deals with Hawke's time after leaving parliament, and for this period I want to thank the contributions of President Fidel Ramos of the Philippines, Jiang Xiaosong and Long Yongtu, respectively founder and former secretary general of the Boao Forum for Asia. Liz Ho, director of the Bob Hawke Prime Ministerial Centre, gave me a long and fascinating interview of which, alas, I have been able to use very little. I am confident it will be of use and interest to future researchers. Fred van Leeuwen, secretary general of Education International, found time for an interview in Brussels in the midst of a schedule of international meetings.

My close friend and confidant, John Lonie, read early drafts and discussed the structure of the narrative with me, sometimes over my kitchen table in Sydney, sometimes on long walks beside the Brisbane River. The finished work owes much of its dramatic pace to him.

At MUP, executive publisher Foong Ling Kong gave calm, lucid support. Susan Keogh, whom MUP assigned to edit the book, was a pleasure to work with and an excellent editor.

Finally, I would like to acknowledge the help of Bob Hawke himself, who provided quotes on request, corrected errors, read the page proofs and made many useful suggestions. I also thank his daughters, Sue and Rosslyn, for their quoted comments, and my son, Louis, for bringing my computer skills up to date.

PART III: AT LARGE

In 2019, when Hawke was in the last stage of his life Simon & Schuster asked me to update the missing nine years. Craig Emerson, Chris Conybeare, Sandy Hollway and Paul Keating all have my gratitude for their help.

I thank Fiona Henderson, Dan Ruffino and the team at Simon & Schuster for their hard work in making this such a handsome book.

Finally, I thank my literary agent, Jeanne Ryckmans of Cameron's Management for negotiating the publication of this volume with Simon & Schuster and for her tender support while I was deeply grieving my husband's death.

Sydney, August 2019

PHOTO CREDITS

Newspix; *below*: Private collection of Bob Hawke and Blanche D'Alpuget. Page 13 *Above*: Getty Images; *below*: Courtesy of National Archives of Australia. NAA: KN28/7/89/198. Page 14 *Above*: News Ltd/Newspix; *below*: Private collection of Bob Hawke and Blanche D'Alpuget. Page 15 *Above*: Private collection of Bob Hawke and Blanche D'Alpuget; *below*: Bruce Postle/*Sydney Morning Herald*. Page 16 *Above*: Private collection of Bob Hawke and Blanche D'Alpuget; *below*: News Ltd/Newspix.

SECTION 3

Page 1 David Bartho/ *Sydney Morning Herald*. Page 2 Image courtesy of the National Archives of Australia. NAA: A6180, 23/3/84/10. Page 3 *Above*: David Bartho/*Sydney Morning Herald*; *below*: Image courtesy of the National Archives of Australia. NAA: A6180, 20/7/84/15. Page 4 *Above*: Courtesy of Craig Emerson; *below*: Andrew Taylor/*Sydney Morning Herald*. Page 5 *Above*: News Ltd/Newspix; *below*: Joe Sabljak/ *Sydney Morning Herald*. Page 6 *Above*: News Ltd/Newspix; *below*: Bryan Charlton/*The Age*. Page 7 *Above*: Neil Newitt/*The Age*; *centre*: Geoff Henderson/Newspix; *below*: Sebastian Constanzo/*The Age*. Page 8 *Above and below*: News Ltd/Newspix. Page 9 *Above*: Courtesy of Channel 9; *below*: Courtesy of the office of The Hon R.J.L. Hawke. Page 10 *Above*: Graeme Thomson/ *Canberra Times*; *below*: *Canberra Times*. Page 11 *Above*: Fairfax Media Archives; *below*: David Bartho/*Sydney Morning Herald*. Page 12 News Ltd/Newspix. Page 13 *Above*: News Ltd/Newspix; *below*: Michael Perini/Newspix. Page 14 *Above*: Neil Newitt/*The Age*. Page 15 *Above and below*: Courtesy of Peter Nicholson. Page 16 Graham Tidy/*Sydney Morning Herald*.

SECTION 4

Page 1 *Above and below*: Courtesy of the office of The Hon R.J.L. Hawke. Page 2 Courtesy of National Archives of Australia. *Above*: KN2/6/88/666; *below*: KN2/6/88/680. Page 3 *Above*: Rolls Press/Popperfoto; *below*: Courtesy of the office of The Hon R.J.L. Hawke. Page 4 *Above*: Private collection of Bob Hawke and Blanche D'Alpuget; *below*: Sahm Doherty/Getty Images. Page 5 *Above*: Courtesy of the office of The Hon R.J.L. Hawke; *below*: Courtesy of the National Archives of Australia. NAA: A8746, KN25/11/87/180. Page 6 *Above* and *below*: Courtesy of the office of The Hon R.J.L. Hawke. Page 7 *Above*: Courtesy of the office of The Hon R.J.L. Hawke; *below*: Barry McKinnon/Newspix. Page 8 *Above* and *below*: Courtesy of the office of The Hon R.J.L. Hawke. Page 9 *Above*: Courtesy of the National Archives of Australia. NAA: A8746, KN23/4/85/21; *below*: Courtesy of the office of The Hon R.J.L. Hawke. Page 10 *Above*: Courtesy of the National Archives of Australia. NAA: A8746, KN7/3/84/107; *below*: Courtesy of the office of The Hon R.J.L. Hawke. Page 11 *Above*: Courtesy of the National Archives of Australia. NAA: A8748, KN23/4/85/21; *below*: Private collection of Bob Hawke and Blanche D'Alpuget. Page 12 *Above*: Courtesy of the office of The Hon R.J.L. Hawke; *below*: David Rubinger/*LIFE* Images. Page 13 Courtesy of the office of The Hon R.J.L. Hawke. Page 14 *Above*: Courtesy of the National Archives of Australia. NAA: A6180, 26/11/86/3; *below*: Courtesy of the National Archives of Australia. NAA: A6180, 18/7/83/4. Page 15 *Above*: NAA/AAP; *below*: Courtesy of the National Archives of Australia. NAA: A6-8746, KN4/1/88/33. Page 16 Chris Pavlich/Newspix.

SECTION 5

Page 1 *Above*: Stevens/*Sydney Morning Herald*; *below*: John Feder/Newspix. Page 2 Private collection of Bob Hawke and Blanche D'Alpuget. Page 3 *Above*: Peter Brew-Bevan/bauersyndication.com.au; *below*: Private collection of Bob Hawke and Blanche D'Alpuget. Page 4 Peter Brew-Bevan/*Good Weekend*. Page 5 *Above and below*: Private collection of Bob Hawke and Blanche D'Alpuget. Pages 6–8 Private collection of Bob Hawke and Blanche D'Alpuget. Page 9 *Above*: Toby Zerna/Newspix; *centre and below*: Nelson Mercadal/*Broadsheet*. Page 10 Private collection of Bob Hawke and Blanche D'Alpuget. Page 11 *Above*: Private collection of Bob Hawke and Blanche D'Alpuget; *below*: China Photos/Getty Images News. Page 12 *Above*: Don Arnold/WireImage; *below*: Private collection of Bob Hawke and Blanche D'Alpuget. Page 13 Kelly Barnes/Newspix. Page 14 Courtesy of AUSPIC. Page 15 *Above*: Kelly Rohan/Newspix; *below*: Alex Ellinghausen/*Sydney Morning Herald*. Page 16 *Above*: Private collection of Bob Hawke and Blanche D'Alpuget; *below*: Brendon Thorne/Getty Images Entertainment.

SECTION 6

Pages 1–3 Private collection of Bob Hawke and Blanche D'Alpuget. Page 4 *Above*: Courtesy of *Border Chronicle*; *below*: Private collection of Bob Hawke and Blanche D'Alpuget. Page 5 Mark Metcalfe/Getty Images Entertainment. Pages 6–8 Courtesy of Woodford Folk Festival. Page 9 Private collection of Bob Hawke and Blanche D'Alpuget. Page 10 *Above*: Yothu Yindi Foundation/AAP; *below*: Kym Smith/Newspix. Page 11 *Above and below*: Courtesy Craig Emerson. Pages 12–14 Private collection of Bob Hawke and Blanche D'Alpuget. Page 15 Megan Slade Photography/Newspix. Page 16 Sean Davey/*Sydney Morning Herald*.

Every effort has been made to contact the copyright holders of material reproduced in this book. In cases where these efforts were unsuccessful, the copyright holders are asked to contact the publisher directly.

NOTES

The primary source of information in this book is R. J. Hawke. I made many hours of tape-recordings with him, which are stored in the Australian National Library. Copyright is jointly held by Hawke, d'Alpuget and the Library. The majority of quotes from Hawke are taken from these tapes; however, there are many other, briefer quotes from him drawn from notes of conversations I had with him. A major secondary source has been interviews with the people listed under Acknowledgements. My notes and transcripts of taped interviews with them are stored in the Library, but access cannot be granted for some years. The written page would be a thicket of numbers if a reference note were given for every oral source: I have decided to avoid that. Unless otherwise indicated in the text, all quotes in the book have been made during interviews with me. I list other references below.

CHAPTER 1
1 O. Pryor, *Australia's Little Cornwall*, Rigby, Adelaide, 1962, pp. 106–7.

CHAPTER 2
1 Jules Zanetti, to B. d'A.

CHAPTER 5
1 R. Pullan, *Bob Hawke: A Portrait*, Methuen, Sydney, 1980, gives a different emphasis to Hawke's role. See pp. 38–9.

CHAPTER 6
1 *Pelican*, 4 April 1952.
2 Ibid., 1 August 1952.
3 Letter to author.

CHAPTER 7

1 Letter to author.
2 Ibid.

CHAPTER 8

1 Hazel had an abortion not long before Hawke left for Oxford, an event she publicly exposed first in a newspaper and in 1992 in her autobiography, *My Own Life*. The abortion, which she believed was of twins, caused guilt and deep grief to both partners. Hazel referred to it often as a matter of regret that it had been necessary for Hawke's Rhodes scholarship. In those days Rhodes scholars had to be single men. The author omitted this episode in earlier editions because it had not then been made public by Hazel herself. The omission explains this somewhat enigmatic paragraph.
2 Letter to author.
3 G. Freudenberg, *A Certain Grandeur: Gough Whitlam in Politics*, Sun Books, Melbourne, 1978, p. 176.
4 Letter from R. J. Hawke to Geoff Brown, Maitland.
5 Ibid.
6 Letter from Dr Clark to author.
7 Letter from R. J. Hawke to Geoff Brown.
8 Ibid.
9 Interview with Terry Winter, former member of the ACTU executive, former commissioner of the Conciliation and Arbitration Commission. This interview was given when Winter was literally on his deathbed and too weak to talk for more than a few minutes at a time. I wish to thank his widow, Beryl, for allowing me to see her husband.
10 Hawke, B.Litt. thesis, p. 283.

CHAPTER 9

1 J. Hurst, *Hawke: The Definitive Biography*, Angus & Robertson, Sydney, 1979, p. 26.
2 In the late 1970s people were astonished when Hawke, as president of the ALP, insisted that a Labor research fund be named the Evatt Foundation. Fundraisers objected, 'We won't get a cent out of business for Evatt's memory'. Hawke replied, 'He deserves the honour. You'll have to work harder.'
3 In 1947 Foster had noted that the Arbitration Court judges were 'the economic dictators of Australia'.

4 It is generally thought that the Boilermakers' Case was the reason for splitting the jurisdiction, but see B. d'Alpuget, *Mediator, a Biography of Sir Richard Kirby*, Melbourne University Press, 1977, p. 143.

5 Kirby kept the title of 'chief judge'; it lapsed when he retired from the Commission, see d'Alpuget, *Mediator*, pp. 147–8.

6 Hawke maintained at the time, and later, that Coleman had hyperbolised, 'to give substance to what he wanted to say – that I did not know where I was going. He grossly exaggerated.'

7 *Observer*, 30 April 1960.

CHAPTER 10

1 Technological change made collective bargaining much easier; by the 1970s a few hundred workers, in the oil industry, for example, could bring the nation to a halt. This trend continued.

2 J. Hagan, *The History of the ACTU*, Longman Cheshire, Melbourne, 1981, p. 319.

3 My thanks to Mrs Jennie McLellan for allowing me to copy this poem.

4 In 1973 'Susie' was running down the street to help a neighbour who has having a domestic crisis, when 'everything went haywire'. She has been partially crippled since.

5 Transcript, p. 180.

CHAPTER 11

1 Hawke's personal papers, ACTU files.

2 Ibid.

3 Ibid.

4 In practice, supply and demand dictate wages and salaries. Employees in fast-growing industries or shops, and militants, get 'over-award' pay and, in the professions, increased fees.

5 Transcript, p. 1135.

CHAPTER 12

1 Hagan, *History of the ACTU*, p. 135.

2 Transcript, p. 343.

3 Ibid., p. 453.

4 Ibid., p. 454.

5 Ibid., pp. 558–9.

6 See Chapter 13, page 246.

7 A. M. Kiki, *Kiki, Ten Thousand Years in a Lifetime*, Cheshire, Melbourne, 1968, p. 94.

Chapter 13

1 Hawke's personal papers, ACTU files.

2 Ibid.

3 Geitzelt laid charges against Harradine that resulted in his expulsion from the ALP in 1975. The trauma in Tasmanian Labor politics, which came to public attention in late 1981, was directly linked to the split that occurred in the state's Labor machine when Harradine was expelled and his supporters in the Trades Hall joined him in exile.

4 Hawke's personal papers, ACTU files.

5 Ibid.

6 Ibid.

7 Interview with Jim Shea, former official of AFL-CIO and colleague of Meany.

8 Hurst, *Hawke*, p. 81.

Chapter 14

1 Of the thousands of cartoons of Hawke there has been only one, in a fly-by-night magazine called *Cocaine*, devoted to blasphemy, that has shown him as other than an honest and/or tough man. Leading up to the 1972 elections many large newspapers projected Hawke's toughness as that of a gangster, but this phase did not last long. The *Cocaine* drawing was of violent homosexual acts between a Hasidic Jew (drawn exactly as Jews were portrayed under Nazism), a CIA man and Hawke. In very small print it carried a disclaimer: 'With apologies to homosexuals and non-Zionist Jews', and was published in 1980, before Hawke entered parliament, accompanying an article that expressed views in sympathy with some of the Socialist Left in Victoria. Hawke wished to sue for libel by the cartoon, but the magazine disappeared underground.

2 On 25 June 1980 a Federal Court judge fined Dunlop Australia $25 000 for threatening a sports store owner because he discounted a product made by a Dunlop subsidiary. The judge also fined Dunlop's national sales manager $4000 for trying to enforce retail price maintenance, contrary to the *Trade Practices Act*.

3 Hawke's personal papers, ACTU files.

4 ACTU press release, ACTU library.

5 Hawke's personal papers, ACTU files.

Chapter 15

1 ALAC was known as CLAC, the Commonwealth Labor Advisory Council, before the election of the Whitlam government.

2   ALAC was reincarnated on 11 November 1975.

3   Cameron's lack of awareness was astonishing. An amalgamation of blue- and white-collar unions had been a major part of Hawke's campaign for the ACTU presidency; it became one of the most debated issues in the trade union movement for years.

4   Cameron in G. Evans and J. Malbon (eds), *Labor Essays 1981*, Drummond, Melbourne, 1981, pp. 13–25, *passim*.

5   Hawke's personal papers, ACTU files.

6   *Bulletin*, 28 July 1973.

7   Ross Martin, 'The ACTU Congress of 1973' in *Journal of Industrial Relations*, December 1973, p. 414.

8   Hawke's personal papers, ACTU files.

9   Ross Martin, 'The ACTU Congress of 1973' in *Journal of Industrial Relations*, December 1973, p. 415.

10 The obvious solution is amalgamation of Australia's several hundred unions into a half-dozen but not many officials are willing to give up their jobs for the greater good of the movement. Although until 1972 there was nothing in the *Arbitration Act* to inhibit amalgamations, few had occurred. Since then government fiddling with the Act has made amalgamations difficult. The McMahon government started the process; cruelly, Clyde Cameron's amendments, while passing through the mincing machine of the Senate, made matters worse.

CHAPTER 16

1   Briefing to author in Tel Aviv by staff of Australian embassy.

2   Hawke's personal papers, ACTU files.

3   Resolution 242 was promulgated on 22 November 1967, following the Six Day War. It includes these elements: inadmissibility of conquests; need to establish a just and lasting peace; withdrawal of Israeli troops from territories (according to the English text not from 'the territories': i.e., not necessarily all of them) occupied in 1967; termination of belligerency; acknowledgement of sovereignty; territorial integrity and political independence of all states in the area and their right to live in peace within secure and recognised boundaries; just settlement of the refugee problem and the establishment of demilitarised zones.

4   Transcript, current information section, Parliamentary Library, 'Hawke' files.

5   Hawke's personal papers, ACTU files.

6   Ibid.

7   R. J. L. Hawke, *Hawke on Israel*, Australian Friends of Labour Israel, Melbourne, 1977, pp. 53–4.

8   Shown to author by E. Kornhauser.

9   The voting for the Egerton–Combe motion was: in favour – Innes, Hartley, O'Byrne, Wriedt, Lourigan, Egerton, Ducker, McMullan; against – Whitlam, Barnard, Murphy, Enderby, O'Neill, Young, Geitzelt, Bryce. Neither Combe nor Hawke had voting rights.

10 Without going into the history of the 'Europa Plan' and the Nazi attempt to ransom European Jews for gold from their kinsmen in Palestine, this statement is disingenuous nonsense.

11 Pullan, *Bob Hawke*, p. 135.

CHAPTER 17

1   Report of International Labour Conference, 1975, pp. 236–7.

2   In fact, the Australian government voted for the Hawke amendment. When the motion was lost (74 in favour; none against; 305 abstentions), Australia voted for admission of the PLO. Watchorn said, 'Bob lobbied until the last minute: he asked me to reinterpret my instructions. I told him, "I can't. And it's your government, mate."'

3   The Loans Affair was the public excuse used by the Opposition to bring down the Whitlam government. It was an attempt on the part of a group of ministers – including the Prime Minister and led by Rex Connor, the Minister for Minerals and Energy – to borrow billions of dollars from Arab nations to spend on development in Australia. The Loans Affair was inspired by the purest and most benevolent motives but was executed secretly, deviously and with astonishing incompetence. The Opposition managed to drag out details about it over a period of months, presenting each new morsel of information as a fresh scandal. The impression of a huge and sinister conspiracy was created. Once, wary electors had been led to expect Reds under ALP beds; astute politicians that they are, the Liberal–National Country Party leaders had updated the bogeyman model into an Arab banker.

4   Patrick Tennison (ed.), Hill of Content, Melbourne, 1977.

5   Hawke's personal papers, ACTU files.

6   Conversation with author.

7   Hawke's personal papers, ACTU files.

CHAPTER 18

1   1974: 6 292 500 days lost; 1975: 3 509 900; 1976: 3 799 200, of which 55 per cent of days lost were due to the Medibank strike; 1977: 1 654 800

2 Mick Young had been a shearer and AWU organiser, secretary of the South Australian branch of the ALP, then federal secretary during the traumatic period of intervention into the Victorian branch, in which he had played a leading role. He entered parliament as member for Port Adelaide in 1974 and in 1977 became president of the South Australian branch of the party and shadow Minister for Industry and Commerce. He is an avid punter and he and Hawke had a regular Saturday morning telephone conference about which horses they would back.

3 *Labor Star*, 16 August 1977.

4 *National Times*, 24 September 1977.

5 Ross Martin, 'The ACTU Congress of 1977', in *Journal of Industrial Relations*, December 1977, pp. 427–30 *passim*.

6 Hawke's diary, 1977.

7 The Camp David talks were complicated peace negotiations between Israel and Egypt, mediated by the USA. They succeeded in achieving agreement for Israeli withdrawal from all occupied Egyptian territory, an act completed by April 1982. But because Jordan could not join the talks, the problem of Israeli occupation of the West Bank remained without solution. Egypt's willingness to seek peace with Israel infuriated other states in the region. In October 1981 President Sadat was assassinated.

8 Fifty-six per cent of the population of Jordan is Palestinian. For many years one of the proposed 'solutions' to the Middle East problem has been that the Israeli army should overthrow the monarchy in Jordan and 'give' the country to the Palestinians. The Jordanian royal family, a creation of the British empire, is understandably unenthusiastic about this idea. Kings tend to stick together: the Saudi royal family also finds such a proposal objectionable. Importantly, so too does the PLO.

9 As a direct result of a speech Hawke gave at Sydney University on occupational health in Australia, a leading Sydney hospital decided in 1982 to establish an occupational health unit.

10 Report of International Labour Conference, 1978, p. 28/7.

11 The NLCC is a tripartite body, the meeting ground of government, labour and employers. At times of particular tension between the government and the ACTU, the ACTU has refused to attend NLCC meetings.

12 Street said, 'My aim in calling NLCC together was to break the industrial impasse. Hawke's question appeared to provide the opportunity to do so.'

13 *Nation Review*, 12 April 1979.

14 Ibid.

15 Ibid.

16 Hawke's personal papers, ACTU files.

17 Ibid.

18 Report by Isi Leibler.

19 Copy of Department of Foreign Affairs record of conversation; Hawke's personal papers, ACTU files.

20 Hawke's personal papers, ACTU files.

CHAPTER 19

1 There is no satisfactory explanation for the communications confusion between Hawke and Lerner. It may have been due to overexcitement.

2 *Jewish News*, Melbourne, 8 June 1979. Resolution was passed on 4 June.

3 Hawke's report to Isi Leibler; copy in Hawke's personal papers, ACTU files.

4 Senior ILO officials later told Hawke they believed that Arapov was, indeed, a KGB officer.

5 Hawke's report to Isi Leibler; copy in Hawke's personal papers, ACTU files.

6 *Jewish News*, Melbourne, 15 June 1979.

7 If Arapov were having his meetings with Hawke monitored by more senior KGB officers, someone in a car parked near the restaurant or in a building across the road would have been able to listen to and record their conversation. Or it may be that a familiar place was chosen simply for its soothing effect.

8 Hawke's report to Leibler; copy in Hawke's personal papers, ACTU files.

9 Letter in Hawke's personal papers, ACTU files; anonymity requested.

10 *Sun-Herald*, 22 July 1979.

11 Hurst, *Hawke*, p. 240.

12 Either at this point or a while later, in the Rotunda Bar, a journalist taunted Hawke, 'What about those Jews you were going to get released from Moscow, eh?' Neither he nor anyone else present realised what anguish such questions caused, because Hawke had refused to reveal what had actually happened in Geneva.

13 *National Times*, 28 July 1979.

14 Hawke's actual words were reported to have been: 'a lying cunt with a limited future'.

15 *National Times*, 28 July 1979.

16 King David wanted to marry Bethsheba, wife of Uriah. He sent Uriah into the front line of battle against the Ammonites, with secret orders that the rest of the unit suddenly withdraw, leaving Uriah surrounded and defenceless. Joab, David's commander of the army, had to lose a battle in order to get Uriah killed, but even at this expense the king was satisfied.

17 March 1981 interview.

18 The Right–Centre ticket nominated P. McMahon as junior vice-president. A total of 892 formal votes were cast, yielding a quota of 447. Dolan won the senior vice-presidency with a primary vote of 556; Fitzgibbon got 42 primaries, McMahon 275 and Roulston 19. Dolan's second preferences went 208 to Fitzgibbon, giving him a total of 250; 72 to McMahon, giving him a total of 347; and 276 to Roulston, giving him a total of 295. Fitzgibbon was therefore out of the race. The second preference of his 42 first-preference votes split evenly, 21–21 to McMahon and Roulston. Fitzgibbon's third preferences (that is, the third preferences of the 208 voters who gave their first preferences to Dolan and their second to Fitzgibbon) were distributed. The Hawke ticket had Roulston as third choice. Of the 208, 75 went to McMahon and 133 to Roulston. Roulston won the junior vice-presidency by 449 to 443, on Hawke ticket preferences. (I am indebted to Professor Ross Martin of La Trobe University for these figures – B.d'A.)

19 *Tribune*, 19 September 1979.

20 Ross Martin, 'The ACTU Congress of 1979' in *Journal of Industrial Relations*, December 1979, pp. 485–96 *passim*.

21 *Quadrant*, May 1980.

22 Ibid.

23 *Financial Review*, 21 August 1980.

24 It may also be that Hawke's emotionalism, most apparent when he was boozing, is in part caused by physiology: his lack of a spleen. A Sydney naturopath, Dorothy Hall, who claims expertise in the functions of the spleen and liver, said that to be without a spleen is to be without a barrier to the expression of anger; that while other people naturally coop up anger, Hawke naturally releases it. She also held the opinion that he was born with a large, active liver that had grown bigger and more active when his spleen was removed, and that this allowed him to drink heavily for years with much less effect than such drinking would have on a person with an ordinary liver. I could not find a physician who was willing to give a medical opinion on these matters – B.d'A.

25 *Hansard*, 26 November 1980, pp. 97–101 *passim*.

CHAPTER 20

1 Eulogy by Kim Beazley.

2 Edna Carew and Patrick Cook, *Keating: Shut Up and Listen and You Might Learn Something!* New Endeavour Press, Sydney, 1990.

3 Bob Hawke, *The Hawke Memoirs*, William Heinemann Australia, Melbourne, 1994, pp. 178–86.

4 Hansard, 3 March 1983, p. 94.

5 *The Strategist*, 31 May 2019.

6 John le Carré, *A Small Town in Germany*, Heinemann, London, 1968, p. 303.

7 Meena Blesing, *'Was Your Dad a Russian Spy?': The Personal Story of the Combe/Ivanov Affair by David Combe's Wife*, Meena Blesing, Sun Books, South Melbourne, 1986, pp. 48–9.

8 Ibid., p. 49.

9 David Marr, *The Ivanov Trail*, Nelson, Melbourne, 1984, p. 285.

10 Blesing, *'Was Your Dad a Russian Spy?'*, p. 103.

11 Marr, *The Ivanov Trail*, pp. 295, 301.

CHAPTER 21

1 Max Weber, *Politik als Beruf* (Politics as Vocation), delivered in January 1919 to the Free Students Society, Munich University, and published in October 1919.

CHAPTER 22

1 Paul Kelly, *The End of Certainty: The Story of the 1980s*, Allen & Unwin, Sydney, 1992, p. 157.

2 Ibid., p. 160.

3 Ibid., p. 156.

4 Ibid., p. 157.

5 Ibid., p. 158.

6 Ibid., p. 161.

7 John Hyde, *Dry: In Defence of Economic Freedom: The Saga of How the Dries Changed the Australian Economy for the Better*, Institute of Public Affairs, Melbourne, 2002, p. 226.

8 Kelly, *The End of Certainty*, p. 170.

9 Ibid.

10 Ibid., p. 173.

CHAPTER 23

1 Foreign Affairs cable, 19 May 1986.

2 Letter to author.

Chapter 24

1 John Edwards, *Keating: The Inside Story*, Viking, Melbourne, 1996; Don Watson, *Recollections of a Bleeding Heart: A Portrait of Paul Keating PM*, Knopf, Sydney, 2002.

2 Stephen Mills, *The Hawke Years: The Story from the Inside*, Viking, Melbourne, 1993, pp. 91–2.

3 Graham Richardson, *Whatever It Takes*, Bantam Books, Sydney, 1994, p. 189.

4 Mills, *The Hawke Years*, p. 93.

5 Richardson, *Whatever It Takes*, p. 214.

6 Ibid., p. 205.

7 Hansard, 3 June 1987, p. 3880–1.

8 Ibid., 3 June 1987, p. 3890.

9 Richardson, *Whatever It Takes*, p. 249.

10 Ibid., p. 247.

Chapter 25

1 Bill Hayden, *Hayden: An Autobiography*, Angus & Robertson, Sydney, 1996, p. 380.

2 Ibid., p. 381.

3 Secret cable, Department of Foreign Affairs, 21 May 1986.

4 Quoted in an address by Prof. Kader Ismal, Minister for Education for South Africa, at the symposium organised by the Anti-apartheid Movement Archives Committee to mark the 40th anniversary of the establishment of the anti-apartheid movement, South Africa House, London, 26 June 1999.

Chapter 26

1 Mills, *The Hawke Years*, p. 168.

2 Ibid., pp. 168–9.

3 Kelly, *The End of Certainty*, pp. 440–1.

Chapter 27

1 Kelly, *The End of Certainty*, p. 492.

2 Richardson, *Whatever It Takes*, p. 257.

3 Kelly, *The End of Certainty*, p. 533.

Chapter 28

1 Richardson, *Whatever It Takes*, p. 264.

2 Ibid., p. 271.

3   Mills, *The Hawke Years*, p. 129.

4   Ibid., p. 130.

5   Richardson, *Whatever It Takes*, p. 278.

6   Marian Wilkinson, *The Fixer: The Untold Story of Graham Richardson*, William Heinemann Australia, Melbourne, p. 51.

7   Richardson, *Whatever It Takes*, p. 281.

8   Ibid., pp. 279–82.

9   Ibid., p. 282.

10   Ibid.

11   Ibid., pp. 283–4.

12   Kelly, *The End of Certainty*, p. 618.

CHAPTER 29

1   Kelly, *The End of Certainty*, p. 627.

2   Hyde, *Dry*, p. 234.

3   Kelly, *The End of Certainty*, pp. 665–7.

4   Hansard, 11 April 1991, p. 2447.

5   Kelly, *The End of Certainty*, p. 629.

6   Mills, *The Hawke Years*, pp. 255–6.

7   Richardson, *Whatever It Takes*, p. 302.

8   Ibid., p. 328.

9   Kelly, *The End of Certainty*, p. 641.

10   Ibid., p. 639.

11   Peter Hartcher, 'The Execution of Brother Bob: The Inside Story', *Good Weekend*, supplement to the *Sydney Morning Herald* and the *Age*, 2 May 1992.

12   Richardson, *Whatever It Takes*, pp. 335–6.

13   Hartcher, 'The Execution of Brother Bob'.

14   Richardson, *Whatever It Takes*, p. 337.

CHAPTER 31

1   Letter to author.

BIBLIOGRAPHY

Alexander, Fred. *Campus at Crawley*. Cheshire, 1963.

Australian Labor Party. 'National Committee of Inquiry Report and Recommendations to the National Executive', March 1979.

Barber, J. D. 'Strategies for Understanding Politicians', *American Journal of Political Science*, 18, No. 2.

— *Power to the Citizen*. Markham Publishing Company, Chicago, 1972.

— *The Presidential Character: Predicting Performance in the White House*. Prentice-Hall, New Jersey, 1972.

Brasher, Rev. F. W. *Methodism in the Maitland District*. South Australian Historical Society, 1958.

Clark, Claire. 'The Middle East since 1973: The Difficult Path to Peace', *World Review*, Vol. 17, No. 3.

Comay, Michael. *Zionism, Israel and the Palestinian Arabs*. Keter Books, Jerusalem, 1981.

d'Alpuget, Blanche. *Mediator, a Biography of Sir Richard Kirby*. Melbourne University Press, 1977.

Davies, A. F. *Skills, Outlooks and Passions, a Psychoanalytic Contribution to the Study of Politics*. Cambridge University Press, 1980.

Evans, G. and Reeves, J., eds. *Labor Essays 1980*. Drummond, Melbourne, 1980.

— and Malbon, J., eds. *Labor Essays 1981*. Drummond, Melbourne, 1981.

Evatt, H. V. *William Holman, Australian Labour Leader*. Angus & Robertson, Sydney, 1979.

Freudenberg, Graham. *A Certain Grandeur: Gough Whitlam in Politics*. Sun Books, Melbourne, 1978.

Gabbay, Dr Rony. 'Israeli Interests in the Middle East', paper given to the Australian Institute of International Affairs, March 1980.

Giblin, L. F. *The Growth of the Central Bank*. Melbourne University Press, 1951.

Hagan, Jim. *The History of the ACTU*. Longman Cheshire, Melbourne, 1981.

Hawke, R. J. L. 'An Appraisal of the Role of the Australian Commonwealth Court of Conciliation and Arbitration with special reference to the development of the concept of the Basic Wage', Bachelor of Letters thesis, University of Oxford, December 1955.

— *Hawke on Israel.* Australian Friends of Labour Israel, Melbourne, 1977.

— *The Resolution of Conflict, 1979 Boyer Lectures.* Australian Broadcasting Commission, Sydney, 1979.

Hevrat Ha'Ovdim. *The Labour Cooperative Sector in Israel.* Logos Ltd, Tel Aviv.

Histadrut. *The General Federation of Labour in Israel.* Histadrut, Tel Aviv, 1976.

Hurst, John. *Hawke, The Definitive Biography.* Angus & Robertson, Sydney, 1979.

Hyslop, Anthea. 'Christian Temperance and Social Reform: The Women's Christian Temperance Union of Victoria, 1887–1912' in *Women, Faith and Fetes,* edited by Sabine Willis. Dove Communications, Melbourne, 1977.

Industries Assistance Commission. *Structural Change in Australia.* Canberra, June 1977.

Innes, J. *Jock Innes: The Man – His Message.* Electrical Trades Union, 1965.

Israel, History from 1880. Israel Pocket Library, Keter Books, Jerusalem, 1973.

Jupp, J. 'The Victorian ALP', draft chapter for *Machine Politics in the Australian Labor Party.* In press for Allen & Unwin, Sydney, 1982.

Kiki, Albert Maori. *Kiki, Ten Thousand Years in a Lifetime.* Cheshire, Melbourne, 1968.

Killek, Teddy and Pearlman, Moshe. *Jerusalem.* Steimatsky's Agency Ltd, Jerusalem, 1975.

King's College, 1924–1944, The Friendly Years. King's College, Adelaide, 1944.

Kohut, Heinz. 'Forms and Transformations of Narcissism', *Journal of the American Psychoanalytic Association,* No. 2, 1966.

— 'Thoughts on Narcissism and Narcissistic Rage', *The Psychoanalytic Study of the Child,* 27, 1972.

— 'Creativeness, Charisma, Group Psychology: Reflections of the Self-analysis of Freud', *Psychological Issues,* 9, Nos 2–3, 1976.

Lasswell, H. D. *Psychopathology and Politics.* University of Chicago Press, 1930.

— 'The Selective Effect of Personality on Political Participation' in *The Authoritarian Personality,* edited by R. Christie and M. Jahoda. The Free Press, Illinois, 1954.

Latourette, Kenneth Scott. *A History of Christianity.* Eyre and Spottiswoode Ltd, London, 1955.

Levinson, Daniel J. *The Seasons of a Man's Life.* Ballantine Books, New York, 1979.

Little, Graham. 'Leaders and Followers: A Psychosocial Prospectus', *Melbourne Journal of Politics*, No. 12, 1980.

— 'The Liminal Character', paper given to an informal seminar on philosophy and psychoanalysis. University of Melbourne, June 1981.

Lloyd, Clem. 'The Federal ALP', draft chapter for *Machine Politics in the Australian Labor Party*. In press for Allen & Unwin, Sydney, 1982.

McCorkindale, Mrs, ed. *Torch-Bearers, The Women's Christian Temperance Union of South Australia, 1886–1948*. WCTU of South Australia, 1949.

McKinlay, Brian. *The ALP, A Short History*. Drummond, Melbourne, 1981.

McLeod, Jeanette and Carmichael, Ern. *Yorke Peninsula Sketchbook*. Rigby, Adelaide, 1974.

McVey, Margaret E. 'Australia's Middle East Foreign Policy', *World Review*, Vol. 17, No. 3.

Mann, Peggy. *Golda: The Life of Israel's Prime Minister*. Coward McCann, New York, 1971.

Martin, R. M. *Trade Unions in Australia*. Penguin, Melbourne, 1980.

— 'The ACTU Congress of 1961'
— 'The ACTU Congress of 1963'
— 'The ACTU Congress of 1965'
— 'The ACTU Congress of 1967'
— 'The ACTU Congress of 1969'
— 'The ACTU Congress of 1971'
— 'The ACTU Congress of 1973'
— 'The ACTU Congress of 1975'
— 'The ACTU Congress of 1977'
— 'The ACTU Congress of 1979'

All in *Journal of Industrial Relations*, December issue of relevant year.

Murphy, D. J. *Hayden, A Political Biography*. Angus & Robertson, Sydney, 1980.

—, ed. *Labor in Politics*. University of Queensland Press, Brisbane, 1975.

Murray, Robert. *The Split, Australian Labor in the Fifties*. Cheshire, Melbourne, 1970.

Nelson, Hank. *Papua New Guinea*. Pelican, Melbourne, 1972.

O'Farrell, P. J. 'The History of the New South Wales Labour Movement, 1880–1910: A Religious Interpretation', *Journal of Religious History*, Vol. 2, No. 2, 1962.

Olden, Christie. 'About the Fascinating Effect of the Narcissistic Personality', *Imago*, Vol. 2, No. 4, 1941.

Ormonde, Paul. *A Foolish, Passionate Man, A Biography of Jim Cairns*. Penguin, Melbourne, 1981.

Oxford University Handbook. Clarendon Press, 1950.

Parkin, Andrew. 'Party Organisation and Machine Politics: The ALP in Perspective', draft chapter for *Machine Politics in the Australian Labor Party*. In press for Allen & Unwin, Sydney, 1982.

Plowman, David. 'Unions in Conflict: The Victorian Trades Hall Split 1967–1973', paper given to the ANZAAS Conference, 1977.

Pryor, Oswald. *Australia's Little Cornwall*. Rigby, Adelaide, 1962.

Pullan, Robert. *Bob Hawke, A Portrait*. Methuen, Sydney, 1980.

Rawson, D. W. *The Impact of the Trade Unions*. AIPS Monograph: 3.

— 'Victoria 1910–1966', *Historical Studies*, Vol. 13, No. 49.

Renwick, A. M. *The Story of the Church*. Inter-Varsity Fellowship, London, 1958.

Reserve Bank of Australia, Functions and Operations. Reserve Bank, Sydney, 1975.

Ross, Lloyd. *John Curtin, A Biography*. Macmillan, Melbourne, 1977.

Rydon, Joan. 'Victoria 1910–1966', *Historical Studies*, Vol. 13, No. 50.

Sammi, Michael. *Refuge*. Am Oved Publishing House, Israel, 1981.

Santamaria, B. A. *Against the Tide*. Oxford University Press, London, 1981.

Sexton, Michael. *Illusions of Power, The Fate of a Reform Government*. Allen & Unwin, Sydney, 1979.

Sheehan, Peter. *Crisis in Abundance*. Penguin, Melbourne, 1980.

Shoeck, Helmut. *Envy*, translated by Michael Glenny and Betty Ross. Harcourt Brace & World, New York, 1970.

Smith, Rev. L. P. G. *Centennial of Christ Church, Kapunda 1856–1958*. Kapunda, 1958.

Somare, Michael. *Sana, an Autobiography*. Niugini Press, Port Moresby, 1975.

Stevens, Bron and Weller, Pat, eds. *The Australian Labor Party and Federal Politics*. Melbourne University Press, 1976.

Study Group on Structural Adjustment Report. The Crawford Committee, Canberra, 1979.

Tatiara, the Good Country. Tatiara Pastoral, Agricultural and Industrial Society, 1976.

Tennison, Patrick, ed. *Heyday or Doomsday: Australia 2000*. Hill of Content, Melbourne, 1977.

Thurow, Lester C. *The Zero–Sum Society, Distribution and the Possibilities for Economic Change*. Basic Books Inc., New York, 1980.

van Sommers, Tess. *Religions in Australia*. Rigby, Adelaide, 1966.

Walker, Judith. 'Restructuring the ALP – NSW and Victoria', *Australian Quarterly*, Vol. 43, No. 4.

Walker, Robin. *Congregationalism in South Australia, 1837–1900*. Royal Geographical Society of Australasia, South Australian Branch 1967–68, Vol. 69.

The Wallaroo and Moonta Mines. Hussey and Gillingham Ltd, 1914.

Walsh, Eric. 'Broken Hill and After, an Exercise in Self-Destruction', *Australian Quarterly*, Vol. 42, No. 4.

Walter, James. *The Leader: A Political Biography of Gough Whitlam.* University of Queensland Press, Brisbane, 1980.

Waters, Frank. *Postal Unions and Politics.* University of Queensland Press, Brisbane, 1978.

Wheelwright, Tom. 'The NSW Labor Party Machine', draft chapter for *Machine Politics in the Australian Labor Party.* In press for Allen & Unwin, Sydney, 1982.

Wilner, Ann Ruth. *Charismatic Political Leadership, a Theory.* Centre for International Studies, Princeton University, 1968.

Yehoshua, A. B. *Between Right and Right – Israel: Problem or Solution.* Doubleday, New York, 1981.

Zionism. Israel Pocket Library, Keter Books, Jerusalem, 1973.

OTHER PRINTED SOURCES

All Australian newspapers, as clipped by the current information section of the Parliamentary Library, Canberra.

Transcripts of Australian radio and television broadcasts, as held by the current information section of the Parliamentary Library, Canberra.

ACTU Executive Minutes, 1970–80.

Hawke's personal papers, ACTU files, 1959–80.

Hawke's diaries, 1967–81.

Hawke's speeches, ACTU files.

Commonwealth Arbitration transcripts of wage cases of 1959, 1961, 1965, 1966.

Transcript of the Local Officers' Case, Territory of Papua New Guinea.

Commonwealth Arbitration Reports.

Barnett, Harvey. *Tale of the Scorpion.* Allen & Unwin, Sydney, 1988.

Barry, Paul. *The Rise and Rise of Kerry Packer.* Bantam, Sydney, 1993.

Beazley, Kim. *National Security: A Report to the Constituents of Brand: A Collection of Speeches by Kim Beazley.* Glide, Perth, 2007.

Blesing, Meena. '*Was Your Dad a Russian Spy?*': *The Personal Story of the Combe/Ivanov Affair by David Combe's Wife, Meena Blesing.* Sun Books, Melbourne, 1986.

Carew, Edna. *Keating: A Biography.* Allen & Unwin, Sydney, 1988.

—— and Patrick Cook. *Keating: Shut Up and Listen and You Might Learn Something!* New Endeavour Press, Sydney, 1990.

Edwards, John. *Keating: The Inside Story*. Viking, Melbourne, 1996.

FitzSimons, Peter. *Beazley: A Biography*. HarperCollins, Sydney, 1998.

Freudenberg, Graham. *A Figure of Speech: A Political Memoir*. John Wiley & Sons, Brisbane, 2005.

Grattan, Michelle (ed.). *Australian Prime Ministers*. New Holland, Sydney, 2000.

Hartcher, Peter. 'The Execution of Brother Bob: The Inside Story', *Good Weekend*, supplement to the *Sydney Morning Herald* and the *Age*, 2 May 1992.

Hawke, Bob. *The Hawke Memoirs*. William Heinemann Australia, Melbourne, 1994.

Hayden, Bill. *Hayden: An Autobiography*. Angus & Robertson, Sydney, 1996.

Hyde, John. *Dry: In Defence of Economic Freedom: The Saga of How the Dries Changed the Australian Economy for the Better*. Institute of Public Affairs, Melbourne, 2002.

Kelly, Paul. *The End of Certainty: The Story of the 1980s*. Allen & Unwin, Sydney, 1992.

le Carré, John. *A Small Town in Germany*. Heinemann, London, 1968.

Lloyd, C. J. *Parliament and the Press*. Melbourne University Press, Melbourne, 1988.

Marr, David. *The Ivanov Trail*. Nelson, Melbourne, 1984.

Mills, Stephen. *The Hawke Years: The Story from the Inside*. Viking, Melbourne, 1993.

Oxley, Alan. *The Challenge of Free Trade*. St Martin's Press, New York, 1990.

Richardson, Graham. *Whatever It Takes*. Bantam Books, Sydney, 1994.

Ryan, Susan and Troy Bramston (eds). *The Hawke Government: A Critical Retrospective*. Pluto Press, Melbourne, 2003.

Thatcher, Margaret. *The Downing Street Years*. HarperCollins, London, 1993.

Watson, Don. *Recollections of a Bleeding Heart: A Portrait of Paul Keating PM*. Knopf, Sydney, 2002.

Weber, Max. *Politik als Beruf* (Politics as Vocation), delivered in January 1919 to the Free Students Society, Munich University, and published in October 1919.

Wilkinson, Marian. *The Fixer: The Untold Story of Graham Richardson*. William Heinemann Australia, Melbourne, 1996.

Zhao Ziyang (trs. Bao Pu, Renee Chiang and Adi Ignatius). *Prisoner of the State: The Secret Journal of Premier Zhao Ziyang*. Simon & Schuster, New York, 2009.

INDEX